A Guidebook to
South Carolina
Historical Markers

A
Guidebook to
South Carolina
Historical Markers

COMPILED BY EDWIN BREEDEN

THE UNIVERSITY OF
SOUTH CAROLINA PRESS

© 2021 University of South Carolina

Published by the University of South Carolina Press
Columbia, South Carolina 29208

www.uscpress.com

Manufactured in the United States of America

30 29 28 27 26 25 24 23 22 21
10 9 8 7 6 5 4 3 2 1

Library of Congress Cataloging-in-Publication Data can be
found at http://catalog.loc.gov/.

Publication of this book is made possible in part by support
from the Historic Preservation Fund, provided by the U.S.
Department of the Interior, National Park Service, and administered by the South Carolina Department of Archives and
History.

ISBN: 978–1-64336-155-0 (hardcover)
ISBN: 978–1-64336-156-7 (paperback)
ISBN: 978–1-64336-157-4 (ebook)

Contents

Illustrations

Acknowledgments

More than anything else, timing and conventions of attribution are why just one specific name appears on this book's cover. In fact, this guidebook was created by several individuals working on behalf of the South Carolina Department of Archives and History (SCDAH) over the course of more than twenty years.

Tracy Power, who served as coordinator for the marker program when the previous guidebook was published in 1998, started and for more than a decade maintained the draft marker guide that comprises most of this book. His successor, Ehren Foley, logged several years-worth of entries into the guidebook during his tenure as marker coordinator in the 2010s, during which time SCDAH entered into agreement with The University of South Carolina Press for the publication of this most recent edition. In early 2019, Edwin Breeden took over as the program's coordinator and made final edits to what was by then a more-or-less complete draft. In addition to the three program coordinators who maintained this book as part of their normal job duties, other individuals added entries or revised older ones, including Ben Hornsby, Mary Edmonds, Brad Sauls, Stephanie Gray, and Orin O'Connell, among others. Finally, the individuals who compiled the entries in this book are themselves indebted to staff working in the SCDAH research room, who regularly assist with the research done for every new marker proposal and that ultimately informs the inscriptions found in the pages that follow.

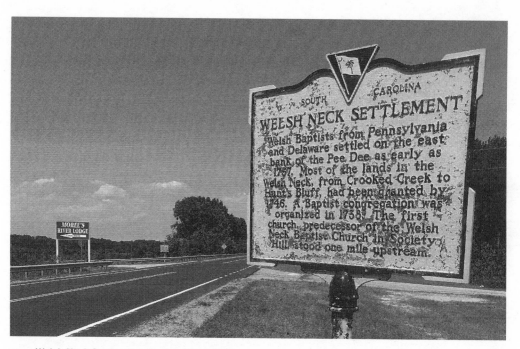

35–5 Welsh Neck Settlement, Society Hill vicinity.

Introduction

"Know Your State and Make It Known to Others":
The South Carolina Historical Marker Program

L ike many places throughout South Carolina, the intersection of state highway 15–401 and county road 167 in Marlboro County is surrounded by silent relics of the Palmetto State's past. Just to the west in neighboring Darlington County sits an idle textile plant, hailed when it opened in the 1960s as an economic godsend, now steadily being reclaimed by creeping vines and overgrowing shrubs just a few years after being shuttered. Between the plant and the intersection flows the Great Pee Dee River, historically part of the lifeblood of northeastern South Carolina and named for the Native people who for centuries inhabited what eventually came to be known as "the Pee Dee" region. Here, as the river courses between the two counties, to the east it carves out a jut of land roughly eight miles wide that in the 1730s was part of the area's first white settlement and from which it later derived the name, "Welsh Neck." Unlike the river or the plant, Welsh Neck is largely undetectable by travelers passing through the intersection—except for a pair of faded, cast aluminum plaques that stand on opposite sides of the highway and call attention to the settlement, a related cemetery, and the Revolutionary-era death of one its later residents. Rust bleeds down the base of each towards the ground, a sign of the plaques' decades of work, performed on behalf of the South Carolina (S.C.) Historical Marker Program, revealing an otherwise invisible segment of the intersection's past.[1]

Throughout its more than eighty years of operation, the S.C. Historical Marker Program has been managed by those state agencies tasked with preserving South Carolina's documentary and physical record. The S.C. General Assembly first created a permanent agency devoted to that cause in 1905 with the establishment of the S.C. Historical Commission, predecessor to today's S.C. Department of Archives and History (SCDAH). Among the powers originally granted to the Commission were "the direction and control of the marking of historical sites, or houses and localities," a somewhat vague mandate accompanied by neither regular funding nor any specific instructions on how such marking was to be done. Consequently, for several decades, new markers were erected sporadically, only as Commission secretary Alexander S. Salley could acquire resources from outside organizations or through occasional legislative appropriations. Unlike in later years, early markers erected by the agency included several different types with

Several markers erected before the program's formal establishment featured this design, part of an effort begun in the late 1920s to publicize the high iodine content of South Carolina–grown fruits and vegetables. Preceding the creation of iodized salt, the campaign touted Palmetto State produce as a safeguard against iodine deficiency symptoms like goiter. IMAGE COURTESY OF SCDAH

varied designs and media, including bronze tablets, granite boulders, and aluminum signs, the last of which are the closest antecedent to today's S.C. Historical Markers.[2] The most unique of these was the short-lived design motif that included colorful depictions of fruits and vegetables with the text "All Rich in Iodine." It was meant to promote the high iodine content of South Carolina-grown produce."[3]

This relatively ad hoc approach continued until the mid-1930s, when the Historical Commission created the Historical Markers Survey, the first systematic state effort to mark South Carolina's historically significant places and the forebear to today's S.C. Historical Marker Program. The survey's creation came amid a wider movement to mark places of historical significance, spurred partly by the rise of the automobile and desires to boost local commerce and tourism. Beginning in the 1920s and continuing after World War II, states across the country began erecting historical markers along well-traveled highways, hoping to entice drivers to stray from their planned route, educating themselves on the area's past and contributing economically to its present. As elsewhere, South Carolina's markers were often placed in the right-of-way and erected in coordination with the State Highway Department, now the S.C. Department of Transportation (SCDOT).[4] Many aspects of this early program—some of them later abandoned—were modeled on Virginia's successful marker program, established in 1927 as one of the first in the country.[5]

The Historical Markers Survey officially began work in 1936, the year after the Commission first directed member Oscar H. Doyle to initiate such a program. The Survey was initially a joint effort overseen by the State and funded by a grant from the Works Progress Administration (WPA). As has been true throughout the program's history, the markers themselves were paid for by local sponsors. With the WPA grant, Doyle hired Nora Marshall Davis to oversee the program's day-to-day activities. A native of Troy, South Carolina, Davis held an M.A. in literature and received a doctorate from Erskine

College in 1939. She served as the program's first director and continued in that role until 1945. During that time, Davis worked with local committees to identify eligible marker sites across the state; solicited groups to sponsor markers; conducted research on marker subjects and crafted most inscriptions; coordinated marker orders with the manufacturer; and publicized the program through newspaper articles and public appearances. In a draft article that later accompanied coverage of fifty new state markers erected as part of Columbia's 1936 sesquicentennial celebration, Davis summarized the mission of the program thusly, "Know your state and make it known to others."[6] By 1939, fifty-nine markers had been erected (including Columbia's fifty), the first of which was placed in Davis's hometown of Troy in 1937, near the site of the so-called Long Canes Massacre, an event during the Anglo-Cherokee War during which twenty-three white settlers were killed.[7] Since then, more than 1,700 markers have been approved by the S.C. Department of Archives and History, the agency's official name since 1967.[8]

Expectedly, the marker program has undergone a number of changes in its more than eighty years of operation—some small and technical, some broad and fundamental. For one, most new markers are now erected at the actual historic site, regardless of how well-trafficked it may be, a major shift from the program's initial concern for attracting travelers off of major highways. Among the most apparent changes has been the design of the markers, the earliest of which were roughly 42" × 42", employed black text on a silver background, and featured a naturally colored palmetto tree at their top, encircled with the initials "S.C." The current marker design, which includes vertical "city" and horizontal "country" variations, was first used in 1955. For several decades these markers employed a white-on-dark-blue color scheme that evoked the state flag, a representation of which replaced the palmetto tree as the marker's crowning element. The more durable black-on-silver motif was re-adopted in the 1990s, but markers otherwise retained the same basic design used since the 1950s.[9] Markers are still funded by local sponsoring organizations, but the general activities of the program have been supported by several different sources over the years. When the original WPA grant expired in late 1937, the state legislature agreed to fund the program coordinator position, which until 1948 technically came through annual appropriations to the American Legion, the program's official sponsor.[10] Funds for the position came solely from the state until the mid-1990s, when South Carolina's co-coordinator and historian for the National Register of Historic Places—a position in the State Historic Preservation Office (SHPO) funded through both federal and state appropriations—took on the responsibilities of the state marker coordinator.

Undoubtedly, the most positive change to the program has been the increasing diversity of people, events, and places represented on markers across the state. Older markers, though hardly homogenous, nonetheless disproportionately reflected those facets and interpretations of the past that most appealed to white South Carolinians.[11] Indeed, some older markers found in this guidebook feature texts that would be very quickly rejected by SCDAH today. Decades passed before markers began to acknowledge places for their important associations with African Americans, who collectively represented a majority of the state's population until the 1920s and who continue to represent a significant portion of South Carolina's citizenry. That gap, while by no means closed, has greatly narrowed in recent years, to the point that roughly half of the new markers approved annually focus on African American history. Most of that progress can be attributed to developments at the local level, where organizations have either shown greater interest in acknowledging African Americans' historical importance or long had such an interest but have become better able to secure the resources to pursue it in the form of a marker. Some of those groups have received assistance from the S.C. African American Heritage Commission, created in 1993 as the first state-level effort to preserve and publicize historic resources associated with the state's African American history.[12]

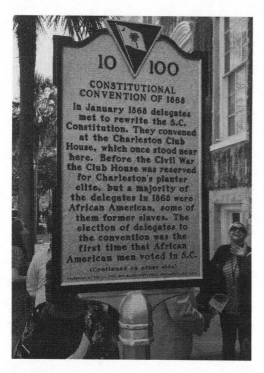

Dedication of 1868 Constitutional Convention marker, February 2018, Charleston, South Carolina.
IMAGE COURTESY OF SCDAH

In many cases, the increasing acknowledgment of African Americans' importance has overlapped with similarly overdue attention being paid to neglected topics such as the civil rights movement, segregation, Reconstruction, and slavery.

Recent years have also brought several new markers at places important for their associations with influential South Carolina women. Yet despite the vital support women have long offered the program through various heritage groups and civic associations, their importance in the state's history remains relatively underrepresented in the marker program. Even fewer are markers that highlight sites for important associations with South Carolina's Native American history, especially ones that frame Native Americans as the primary subjects and actors, rather than side characters in a Eurocentric story.

Still, a broad view of the markers approved through the program finds an eclectic mixture of subjects that testify to the diversity of the state's history and its connections to individual places, grand and unassuming alike. As you flip through the pages of this guidebook, you can find evidence of some of the changes described here and get a feel for the rich texture of the state's past. The compiled text, which offers an inventory of the individual stories recorded on more than 1,700 roadside markers, tells a collective story, not only of South Carolina's history but also of the history that South Carolinians have told about themselves and the ways that story has and has not changed over time. These stories may have been originally intended for passersby on newly constructed roads and state highways, but they have also been meant for internal consumption: a way to "know your state and make it known to others," just as Nora Davis said at the program's outset. That aspect of the program, at least, has changed little over the course of more than eighty years.

Yet, for all the markers erected and stories told, surely countless are the sites that remain unmarked; not for wont of importance but only because someone has not yet taken up the cause of making their stories available for those who would travel past. And so, there are at least two ways to read the material provided herein. One is as a record of the people and events that have come before. But another is as a challenge and opportunity to shape what will be in the future. When the next marker guidebook is printed, what stories, missing here, will have been recorded on the landscape? How will our understanding of the past, and the stories we tell about it, have changed? To the extent that South Carolina's historical marker program plays some role in the process of recording the state's collective memory, it will be the people of the state—through their sponsorship of individual markers—who will shape that narrative. Perhaps some who pick up this book will read its silences and do the work necessary to fill them, giving voice to the voiceless and helping to tell a fuller story of the state's past. One that will resonate in both the present and the future.

Applying for S.C. Historical Markers

South Carolina Historical Markers mark and interpret places important to an understanding of South Carolina's past, including locations of local, state, and national significance. The program's purpose is not to memorialize, honor, or glorify past figures or events but to educate the public about the state's history and its connections to local communities. Proposals for new markers are reviewed and approved through an application process that is state-managed but locally driven. New marker topics and locations are submitted for SCDAH review by local organizations, typically historical societies, heritage groups, civic organizations, or city or county governments (alumni groups and religious congregations also frequently sponsor markers for schools and places of worship). Applicants are expected to provide a 1–2 paragraph summary of the marker subject's history as well as corroborating primary and secondary sources. These materials are reviewed by SCDAH's marker program coordinator, who makes an initial determination of the proposal's eligibility. If the subject is deemed eligible, the coordinator conducts additional research as needed to verify information provided by the sponsor and then drafts an initial inscription. The text is then revised in conversation with the sponsor until they and the coordinator agree to the marker's exact wording. Some texts are accepted on the first pass, and others require as many as a dozen drafts and weeks if not months of dialogue between the sponsor and coordinator; most fall somewhere in between. When both parties are satisfied with a text, it is then submitted to the director of SCDAH for final approval.

Once SCDAH officially approves a new marker, sponsors are responsible for ensuring the approved marker is ordered, manufactured, and, ultimately, erected. Sponsoring organizations pay for the markers, placing their order directly with the manufacturer, which since the 1950s has been Ohio-based Sewah Studios.[13] The finished cast aluminum product is then shipped to the sponsor, who arranges for its installation and ensures the marker's location complies with any state or local regulations. Usually, SCDAH's only involvement after approving a marker is confirming the final wording with Sewah Studios just before production begins. Once a marker is in the ground, sponsors are expected to maintain it in perpetuity, including any needed repairs or, in some cases, total replacement.

For more information on the program, including additional details on the application process, please contact:

South Carolina Historical Marker Program
S.C. Department of Archives & History
8301 Parklane Road
Columbia, S.C. 29223
803-896-6182

Notes

1. Alexander Gregg, *History of the Old Cheraws* (New York: Richardson & Company, 1867), 77–79. Eldred E. Prince, Jr., "Pee Dee River," *South Carolina Encyclopedia,* last updated January 6, 2017, http://www.scencyclopedia .org/sce/entries/pee-dee-river/. Thom Anderson, "Klopman Mills Begins to Make Impact," Florence *Morning News,* December 31, 1967, p. 5. Jana E. Pye, "Galey & Lord Closing," Darlington *News & Press,* April 12, 2016. The two markers are "Welsh Neck Settlement" (35–5) and "Abel Kolb's Murder/ Welsh Neck Cemetery" (35–17), erected in 1970 and 1973 respectively.

2. *Acts and Joint Resolutions of the General Assembly of the State of South Carolina, Passed at the Regular Session of 1905* (Columbia, S.C.: Gonzales and Bryan, State Printers, 1905), 906–10. ("marking of historical sites" quotation on 908). A temporary historical commission had been appointed in 1891. *Annual Report of the South Carolina Archives Department, 1954–1955* (Columbia, S.C.: State Budget and Control Board, 1956), 3–4. *Report of the Historical Commission of South Carolina to the General Assembly of South Carolina at the Regular Session of 1931*

(Columbia: Joint Committee on Printing, General Assembly of South Carolina, n.d.), p. 5 (bronze tablets, directional signs, aluminum signs, "All Rich in Iodine"). A. S. Salley, letter to the editor ("More Information on Site from Which Sherman's Guns Took Pot Shots at Columbia"), Columbia *State,* August 6, 1955, p. 3B (granite boulders). Anne M. Gregorie to Mabel Montgomery, February 3, 1936, folder: Historical Markers Survey Correspondence About [. . .], box 3, WPA Marker Survey of Historic Places (hereinafter WPA Marker Survey files), South Carolina Department of Archives and History, Columbia, S.C. (hereinafter SCDAH). On Alexander Salley's significance to the early twentieth century archives movement, see Roberta V. H. Copp, "Alexander Samuel Salley," *South Carolina Encyclopedia,* last updated October 25, 2016, http://www .scencyclopedia.org/sce/entries/salley -alexander-samuel/.

3. Robert T. Oliver, "Iodine," *South Carolina Encyclopedia,* last updated March 14, 2019, http://www.scencyclopedia.org/sce/entries /iodine/. See also "All Rich in Iodine," *South Carolina Historical Markers* blog, May 6,

2014, https://schistoricalmarkers.wordpress
.com/2014/05/06/all-rich-in-iodine/.

4. "Would Mark Historic Spots Throughout
South Carolina," Columbia *State*, July 11,
1935, p. 11 (program motivations). "Brief
Sketch of the Marking of Historic Sites in
South Carolina," undated manuscript, box 1,
Historical Markers Survey—Papers of Nora
Davis (hereinafter Davis Papers), SCDAH.
"Marker Arrives in Capital City," Columbia
State, March 13, 1937, p. 2 (other marker pro-
grams). Kevin M. Levin, "When It Comes
to Historical Markers, Every Word Matters,"
Smithsonian Magazine, July 6, 2017, https://
www.smithsonianmag.com/history/when
-it-comes-historical-markers-every-word
-matters-180963973/. For references to
markers in other states, see also Clifford L.
Walker to J. M. Anderson, November 8,
1937, box 2, Davis Papers.

5. The early S.C. Historical Markers took some
design cues from Virginia's, and the program
also initially adopted, but later dropped, a
roadway coding system similar to one used
in Virginia. "Historic Sites to be Marked,"
Greenville *News,* January 28, 1936, p. 12.
Walker to Anderson, November 8, 1937, box
2, Davis Papers. Scott David Arnold, comp.,
A Guidebook to Virginia's Historical Markers
(Charlottesville and London: University of
Virginia Press, 2007), xi–xiv. For more information on S.C.'s early coding system, see
documents folder Code System for Markers,
box Abbeville-Chester Co., WPA Marker
Survey files.

6. "Would Mark Historic Spots Throughout
South Carolina," Columbia *State*, July 11,
1935, p. 11. "Erskine College Gives Degrees
to 73 Seniors," Charlotte *Observer,* June 8,
1939, p. 13. "Dr. Nora Davis Dies," Greenwood *Index Journal,* March 10, 1969, p. 11.
Curiously, the "know your state" appeal
appears in multiple documents drafted by
Davis, yet it is unclear if she ever used it
publicly. See June 15, 1939 draft of "Article
requested by Mrs. Simons for publication,"
("know your state and make it known to
others" quotation on page 3), box 1, Davis
Papers, SCDAH; Nora M. Davis, untitled
summary of program history ("Know your
State and help us to make it known to

others" on page 4, box 1, Davis Papers. See
additional files in the same box for more
examples of Davis's work on behalf of the
program. Nora M. Davis, "Standard Set for
Markers in This State," Columbia *State,* July
13, 1939, p. 14. See the same page for several
articles on the sesquicentennial commem-
oration, which began in 1938 but continued
until the following year.

7. Stemming from the early program's concern
for placing markers in well-trafficked areas,
the decision to install the Long Canes Massacre marker in Troy (Greenwood County)
ironically put it in an entirely separate county
from the actual event site, located nearby in
neighboring McCormick County.

8. Charles H. Lesser, *The Palmetto State's
Memory: A History of the South Carolina
Department of Archives & History, 1905–1960*
(Columbia: South Carolina Department of
Archives & History, 2009), 102.

9. Nora M. Davis, untitled manuscript ("A
forward step in the progress . . ."), ca. 1938,
p. 2–3, box 1, Davis Papers. A description of
the markers introduced in 1955 is available
at "Markers Will Be Placed Along Line of
First Successful Steam Railroad, Augusta to
Charleston," Greenwood *Index-Journal,* May
10, 1955, p. 12. "Cleaning, Repairing, and Re-
painting South Carolina Historical Markers,"
SCDAH pamphlet, revised December 2019,
available at SCDAH website.

10. Lesser, *The Palmetto State's Memory,* 48.

11. The two aforementioned markers in Marlboro County, "Welsh Neck Settlement"
(35–5) and "Abel Kolb's Murder/Welsh Neck
Cemetery" (35–17), erected in the 1970s,
illustrate some of the themes and topics that
predominated for much of the program's
history, including white colonial-era settlement, military history, and acts of patriotism.

12. "Council Will Help Preserve African-
American Heritage," Columbia *State,* October 16, 1993, p. 3B.

13. Sewah likely became the state's marker ven-
dor when SCDAH switched to a new design
in 1955. See "New S.C. Historical Marker,"
Greenwood *Index-Journal,* May 17, 1955,
p. 12.

South Carolina Historical Markers

T he following list includes all markers that SCDAH has approved since the program's establishment in 1936, as well as markers previously erected by the S.C. Historical Commission. Markers known to have been removed or relocated are noted accordingly. Recently approved markers may not yet have been installed. Marker inscriptions have been transcribed as faithfully as possible, including any typographical errors and inconsistencies in style. Relevant information (for example, sponsor, year of approval) not inscribed on the marker has been included in brackets. The numbers by each entry correspond to a marker's county code and the order in which it was approved. For example, Charleston County's county code is 10 (Charleston falls tenth on an alphabetical list of South Carolina's forty-six counties), so marker 10–10 indicates that it was the tenth marker approved in Charleston County. These numbers do not appear on many earlier markers, but they are included in the following list even in those cases where the numbers do not appear on the markers themselves.

Abbeville County

1–1 Patrick Calhoun Family Burial

Intersection of S.C. Hwy. 72 & S.C. Hwy. 823, Southeast of Abbeville

5.5 miles south of Abbeville is the burial ground of Patrick and Martha Calhoun, parents of John C. Calhoun. Patrick was made deputy surveyor, 1756; first representative from Up-Country to Commons House of Assembly, 1769–1772; member of First Provincial Congress, 1775; of the Second, 1775–1776; of the General Assembly, 1776, and frequently thereafter until his death, 1796. His greatest service to his state was his successful fight for the Circuit Court Act of 1769. Across the road opposite the burial ground is his home site.

[Erected 1950]
GPS Coordinates: 34° 8.102' N, 82° 24.856' W

1–2 Millwood Home of James Edward Calhoun

S.C. Hwy. 72 at the Savannah River bridge, 3.1 miles West of Calhoun Falls

Half mile southeast is Millwood, home of James Edward Calhoun, 1796–1898, son of John Ewing and Floride Bonneau Calhoun and brother-in-law of John C. Calhoun. After serving as lieutenant in the U. S. Navy, he developed Millwood, which ultimately included 25,000 acres. Seeing the value of Trotter's Shoals, a part of this estate, he was among

the first to encourage the use of Southern water power. [Erected in 1953]
GPS Coordinates: 34° 4.285' N, 82° 38.182' W

1–3 Bowie Family Memorial

Intersection of S.C. Hwy. 20 & S.C. Sec. Rd. 1-100, 6 miles North of Abbeville

Erected by the descendants of Abraham Bowie, who was born in Scotland and settled in Durham Parish, Charles County, Maryland, about 1700 A.D. The family of his grandson, Rhody Bowie, moved to Abbeville County, South Carolina, about 1800. Eli Bowie, son of Rhody Bowie, established Gilgal Church in 1817. This church is located 2 miles east of this memorial and is the site of the Bowie Reunion each year. [No longer extant. Originally erected in 1954 but later replaced by a stone marker with the same inscription.]
GPS Coordinates: 34° 16.436' N, 82° 22.589' W

1–4 Abbeville's Confederate Colonels

Intersection of N. Main St. and Wardlaw St., Abbeville, 2.5 blocks from Abbeville Town Square

AUGUSTUS J. LYTHGOE, 19 S.C. Inf./Killed Murfreesboro, 1862/J. FOSTER MARSHALL, Orr's Rifles/Killed Second Manassas, 1862/ GEORGE M. MILLER, Orr's Rifles/Wounded Spotsylvania, 1864/JAMES M. PERRIN, Orr's Rifles/Killed Chancellorsville, 1863/THOMAS THOMSON, Moore's Rifles/Served Oct. 22, 1861–Dec. 10, 1863. *Erected by Secession Chapter, U.D.C., 1956*
GPS Coordinates: 34° 10.86' N, 82° 23.012' W

1–5 Birthplace of Calhoun

S.C. Hwy. 823, 7 miles South of Abbeville

On this land settled by his father Patrick Calhoun in the 1750s, defended against the Indians in the Cherokee War and the enemies of liberty in the American Revolution, John Caldwell Calhoun, American statesman and champion of the old South, was born, March 18, 1782, and nurtured to young manhood. *Sponsored by Abbeville County Historical Society, 1962*
GPS Coordinates: 34° 3.598' N, 82° 26.986' W

1–6 Due West

Intersection of Main & Church Sts., Due West

As early as 1765, the site 6 miles NW—known to the Indians as Yellow Water and where the Keowee Path crossed the Cherokee line— was called DeWitt's Corner. In 1777, a treaty between S.C. and the Cherokee Indians was signed there. The present town was first called Due West Corner. Here in 1839, Erskine College, the state's first four-year church college, was founded by the Associated Reformed Presbyterian Church. *Erected by Erskine College, 1963*
GPS Coordinates: 34° 20.083' N, 82° 23.223' W

1–7 Burt-Stark House /Jefferson Davis's Flight

306 North Main St., Abbeville

Burt-Stark House (FRONT)
When Jefferson Davis, President of the Confederacy, left Richmond after its fall in April 1865, he traveled south, trying to reach and rally the remnants of his army. On May 2, he spent the night at the home of Col. Armistead Burt. In 1971, Burt's great-niece Mary Stark Davis gave this historic house and all its furnishings to Abbeville's Historic Preservation Commission.
Jefferson Davis's Flight (REVERSE)
Here, at the home of Colonel Burt, President Jefferson Davis held the last Confederate Council of War on May 2, 1865. He met with Secretary of War Breckenridge, Gen. Braxton Bragg, and 5 brigade generals; all agreed the only hope was for Davis to elude nearby U.S. cavalry and escape west. Though Davis passed safely through South Carolina, he was seized in Georgia on May 10th. *Erected by Abbeville County Historic Preservation Commission, 1979*
GPS Coordinates: 34° 10.833' N, 82° 22.898' W

1–8 Maj. Thomas D. Howie the Major of St. Lô

118 Pinckney St., Abbeville

(FRONT) Birthplace of Thomas Dry Howie (1908–1944), World War II hero famous as "The Major of St. Lô." Abbeville High School, Class of 1925. The Citadel, Class of 1929,

where he was an all-state football player and was president of his class. Coach and teacher, Staunton Military Academy, Staunton, Va., 1929–1941. Lt., 116th Inf., Va. National Guard (29th Division), 1941. Promoted to major; served at regimental H.Q. until […] (REVERSE) […] July 1944, when he took command of the 3rd Btn. Howie told his men, "I'll see you in St. Lô"—a major Allied objective in the weeks after D-Day. He was killed July 17, 1944, the day before American troops captured the town. In a tribute from his comrades, Howie's flag-draped body was carried into St. Lô on the lead jeep and lay in state on the rubble of St. Croix Church. "Dead in France, Deathless in Fame." *Erected by the Abbeville County Historical Society, 1995*
GPS Coordinates: 34° 10.703' N, 82° 22.9' W

1–9 Boonesborough Township (1763)

Intersection of S.C. Hwy. 184 and S.C. Sec. Rd. 1-248, near Donalds

Surveyed in 1762 by Patrick Calhoun and named for Gov. Thomas Boone, this 20,500-acre township was one of four townships laid out west of Ninety-Six as a buffer between white and Cherokee lands. In 1763 Scots-Irish families began to settle in the area near Long Cane, Park's and Chickasaw Creeks. The headwaters of Long Cane Creek are 500 feet south; the Cherokee Path crossed the township boundary one mile south. *Erected by the Donalds Historical Society, 1996*
GPS Coordinates: 34° 22.317' N, 82° 21.014' W

1–10 Thomas Chiles Perrin House

Corner of N. Main St. (S.C. Hwy. 28) and Wardlaw St., Abbeville

(FRONT) The Greek Revival residence of Thomas Chiles Perrin (1805–1878), prominent Abbeville District lawyer, planter, businessman, and politician, stood here from 1858 until it burned in 1877. When completed the house was described as "one of the finest and most commodious mansions in the State." Perrin served as mayor, state representative and senator, and for many years as president

of the Greenville and Columbia RR. (REVERSE) In December 1860, as chair of the Abbeville District delegation to the Secession Convention, Perrin was the first signer of the Ordinance of Secession. As the Confederacy collapsed in May 1865 President Jefferson Davis and his Cabinet held their last council of war across the street at the BurtStark Mansion. Thomas and Jane Eliza Perrin hosted most of the Cabinet here during its brief stay in Abbeville. *Erected by the Abbeville Co. Historic Preservation Commission, 1997*
GPS Coordinates: 34° 10.861' N, 82° 23.015' W

1–11 McGowan-Barksdale-Bundy House

305 N. Main St. (S.C. Hwy. 28), Abbeville

(FRONT) This 1888 Queen Anne house was the home of Gen. Samuel McGowan (1819–1897) until his death. McGowan, a lawyer, Confederate general, and jurist born in Laurens Co., had moved to Abbeville in 1841. He was an officer during the Mexican War and in the S.C. militia after it. During the Civil War he commanded the 14th S.C. Infantry 1862–63 and commanded a S.C. brigade in the Army of Northern Virginia 1863–65.
(REVERSE) After 1865 McGowan bought a house on this lot. Built by Col. James Perrin in 1860, it burned in 1887; this house was built on the old foundation. McGowan served as a justice on the S.C. Supreme Court 1879–93. The Barksdale family bought the house in 1905, and WWII Gen. W. E. Barksdale was the last to live here. In 1989 his nephew J. D. Bundy gave it to the Abbeville County Historical Society as its headquarters. *Erected by the Abbeville County Historical Society, 2006*
GPS Coordinates: 34° 10.792' N, 82° 22.871' W

1–12 Lowndesville

Main St., Lowndesville

(FRONT) This town, established in 1823, grew up around a store owned by Matthew Young (1803–1878), who was also postmaster 1831–43. It was first called Pressly's Station, for the post office opened in 1823 with David Pressly (1764–1834) as postmaster. The town

was renamed Rocky River in 1831 and then Lowndesville in 1836 for William Lowndes (1782–1822), U.S. Congressman 1811–22. (REVERSE) Lowndesville, incorporated in 1839, had about 150 inhabitants then and 150–350 inhabitants for most of its history. Cotton was the major crop in the area, with bales ginned here and shipped by the Charleston & Western Carolina Railway. In 1890 Lowndesville included a hotel, nine general stores, a grocery, a dry goods store, a drugstore, a stable, and three saw mills. *Erected in Memory of Capt. Herman Arnette Carlisle by the Town of Lowndesville, 2006*
GPS Coordinates: 34° 12.627' N, 82° 38.71' W

1–13 Action at Pratt's Mill /Pratt's Mill

S.C. Hwy. 184 at the Little River, just Northeast of its intersection with S.C. Sec. Rd. 1-59, Due West vicinity

Action at Pratt's Mill (FRONT)
The last action of the Revolution in this part of S.C. was at Pratt's Mill, a grist mill on the Little River owned by Joseph Pratt. On October 30, 1781, an outpost of 30 Patriots at the mill, under Capt. John Norwood, was surprised by 30 Loyalists and Cherokees under Col. William "Bloody Bill" Cunningham. Norwood, who was wounded, was the only casualty on either side.
Pratt's Mill (REVERSE)
The Patriots fled, leaving behind 30 horses and most of their weapons; the Loyalists burned the mill. The Pratt family later rebuilt the mill, which appears in Robert Mills's *Atlas of S.C.* (1825). They later built another mill on Hogskin Creek, about 500 yds. N of the first mill. That mill, which operated throughout the 19th century, was destroyed by a flood in 1908. *Erected by the Abbeville County Historical Society, 2007*
GPS Coordinates: 34° 18.383' N, 82° 26.45' W

1–14 Secession Hill

Secession Ave., near its junction with Branch St., Abbeville

(FRONT) On November 22, 1860, a mass meeting on this site was one of the first held in the South after Abraham Lincoln's election as president on November 6. A procession from the town square, numbering 2,000 to 3,000, made its way to a grove here, near the Greenville & Columbia RR depot. Many in the crowd wore palmetto cockades as bands played, militia and volunteer companies marched with flags and banners, and some units even fired cannon salutes.
(REVERSE) Andrew G. Magrath, arguing "the time for action has arrived," was typical of most speakers, who called for South Carolina's immediate secession from the Union. The meeting passed resolutions urging secession and recommended delegates to represent Abbeville District at the Secession Convention in December. This hill, then known as "Magazine Hill" for a powder magazine here, was soon renamed "Secession Hill" and has been known by that name since 1860. *Erected by the Abbeville County Historical Society, 2010*
GPS Coordinates: 34° 10.717' N, 82° 22.5' W

1–15 Broadmouth Baptist Church

543 Broadmouth Church Rd., Honea Path

(FRONT) This church, named for nearby Broadmouth Creek, was organized in 1837 with nine charter members. Rev. William P. Martin was its first minister, and William Long and Noah Riddle Reeve were its first deacons. This tract was purchased from Jesse Gent in 1838. By 1850 the church had 213 members, both white and black. The present sanctuary, the second on this site, was built in 1954.
(REVERSE) After the Civil War, former slaves left to organize New Broadmouth Baptist Church. Rev. William P. Martin, pastor here 39 years (1837–1877), was succeeded by Rev. Richard W. Burts, pastor here 33 years (1877–1910). William Pleasant Kay donated the land where the cemetery was first laid out. It contains the graves of early pioneer families, including veterans of several wars. *Erected by the Congregation and the Kay Family Association, 2010*
GPS Coordinates: 34° 27.533' N, 82° 21.067' W

1–16 Long Cane Cemetery

Greenville St. at its junction with Beltline Rd., Abbeville vicinity

(FRONT) This cemetery, sometimes called Upper Long Cane Cemetery, dates from 1760. It includes the graves of some of the most prominent families of this area from the Colonial era to the present. The first marked grave is the field stone of John Lesly, inscribed "A.D. 1776." The granite entrance pillars and stone wall were built in 1935 as a memorial to veterans of eight wars who are buried here. The cemetery was listed in the National Register of Historic Places in 2010.
(REVERSE) Among the notables buried here are a U.S. Senator, a U.S. Congressman, a lieutenant governor, a Confederate general, several state senators and representatives, judges, ministers, doctors, and soldiers of wars from the American Revolution to the present. Long Cane Cemetery also features many fine gravestones and monuments by noted 19th-century stonecutters such as J. Hall, Thomas Walker, and John, William T., Robert D., and Edwin R. White. *Erected by the Long Cane Cemetery Association, 2011*
GPS Coordinates: 34° 12.217' N, 82° 23.417' W

1–17 Quay-Wardlaw House

104 S. Church St., Abbeville

(FRONT) This house, built ca. 1786, is thought to be the oldest house in Abbeville. It was built as a two-story log building by John Quay, who also ran a tavern here. He sold it ca. 1798 to James Wardlaw (1767–1842) and his wife, Quay's stepdaughter Hannah Clarke (1778–1825). James Wardlaw was the Abbeville postmaster and Abbeville District deputy clerk of court 1796–1800, then clerk of court 1800–1838. Ten of the Wardlaws' eleven children were born in this house.
(REVERSE) Two sons were delegates to the Secession Convention: David L. Wardlaw (1799–1873), state representative and Speaker of the S.C. House, and later a judge; and Francis H. Wardlaw (1800–1861), newspaper editor, state chancellor, and state representative, from Edgefield. This house was later owned by Col. Thomas Thomson (1813–1881), state

representative, delegate to the Secession Convention, Confederate officer, state senator, and judge. *Sponsored by Clan Wardlaw and the Abbeville County Historical Society, 2013*
GPS Coordinates: 34° 10.5659' N, 82° 22.798' W

1–18 Colonial Block House/Fort Pickens

Washington St., just South of Hemphill Rd., Abbeville

Colonial Block House (FRONT)
A "block house," a log building with a stone foundation, stood SE on Parker Creek from ca. 1767 to the 1850s. It was built by Andrew Pickens (1739–1817), later a militia general in the American Revolution, a state representative and senator, and a U.S. Congressman. Pickens married Rebecca Calhoun in 1765, moved to the Long Canes settlement, and built his home nearby.
Fort Pickens (REVERSE)
The block house was an outpost near the boundary between Indian lands and white settlements and was later a refuge for area families during the American Revolution. Tradition holds that in 1785 Pickens held the first court in the new Abbeville District there. After his death the old block house was popularly called "Fort Pickens" and this part of Abbeville was long known by the same name. *Sponsored by the Little River Electric Cooperative and the Abbeville County Historical Society, 2014*
GPS Coordinates: 34° 10.95' N, 82° 22.45' W

1–19 Treaty of Lochaber

S.C. Hwy 71, Abbeville vicinity

(FRONT) In October 1770, the Congress of Lochaber assembled near here at the plantation of Alexander Cameron, who was deputy superintendant of Indian affairs for the southern colonies. Over one thousand members of the Cherokee nation gathered for the treaty negotiations. The resulting agreement revised the boundary line between the Cherokee and the colony of Virginia further to the north.
(REVERSE) The new boundary, which became known as the Lochaber Line, extended

colonial land claims west of the Appalachian Mountains. These claims had generated tension between colonists and the crown since the Proclamation of 1763, which limited western settlement and angered land speculators. The Treaty of Lochaber was part of the long negotiation to extend the southern segment of the boundary further to the west. *Sponsored by the Abbeville County Visitor's Council, 2014*
GPS Coordinates: 34° 11.267' N, 82° 24.670' W

1–20 Treaty of DeWitt's Corner

S.C. Hwy. 20 N at intersection of Corner Creek/ Barkers Creek, Due West vicinity

(FRONT) In May 1777 a delegation of roughly 600 Cherokees and representatives from South Carolina and Georgia met near this spot to engage in negotiations that would end fighting in the Second Cherokee War, 1776–77. On May 20, 1777 the parties signed The Treaty of DeWitt's Corner, which provided for an end to hostilities, prisoner returns, and large land concessions by the Lower Cherokee.
(REVERSE) The territory ceded included present day Anderson, Greenville, Oconee and Pickens Counties. The warfare ended by the Treaty of DeWitt's Corner was part of the revolutionary struggle between American patriots and their British and loyalist opponents. The

powerful southeastern Indian nations played an important role in the war and most sided with the British. *Sponsored by the Abbeville County Visitor's Council, 2014*
GPS Coordinates: 34° 23.953' N, 82° 26.697' W

1–21 Mulberry A.M.E. Church

2758 Mount Carmel Rd., Abbeville

(FRONT) The formal organization of Mulberry A.M.E. Church dates to ca. 1871, but many of the founding members were formerly enslaved people who had a tradition of religious organization that stretched back into slavery. Early meetings were held under a brush arbor. By 1872 members had built a log building. A second frame church was built in 1878 and remained until it burned in 1918.
(REVERSE) The current Carpenter Gothic church, with offset steeple and church bell, dates to 1919. A cemetery, located across the road from the church, was established ca. 1904. The one-teacher Mulberry School was once located here and served African American students until it closed in the early 1950s. Mulberry is mother church to St. Peter, Shady Grove and St. Paul A.M.E. churches in Abbeville. *Sponsored by the Essie Strother Patterson Legacy Foundation, 2017*
GPS Coordinates: 34° 3.771' N, 82° 26.847' W

Aiken County

2–1 The S.C. Railroad

Park Ave. & Laurens St., Aiken

(FRONT) The tracks of the S.C. Railroad, operated by the S.C. Canal & Railroad Company, ran here from 1833 to the 1850s. The company, chartered in 1827, began constructing a 136-mile long line from Charleston to Hamburg (near North Augusta) in 1830. Completed in 1833, the railroad was the longest in America at the time and the first to carry the United States mails. Aiken, chartered in 1835, was named for William Aiken (1779–1831), the railroad's first president.

(REVERSE) The original tracks through Aiken, one of the first "railroad towns" in the United States, ran along this street, then known as Railroad Avenue. Railroad Avenue was renamed Park Avenue in the 1850s after the tracks were moved one block south into the "Railroad Cut." Though the S.C. Railroad flourished before the Civil War, it struggled during Reconstruction and afterwards. It was eventually absorbed into the Southern Railway in 1902. *Erected by the Aiken County Historical Society, 2010* [Replaced a marker erected in 1962]
GPS Coordinates: 33° 33.587' N, 81° 43.416' W

2–2 Western Terminus South Carolina Railroad

U.S. Hwy. 1 & U.S. Hwy. 25 at the Savannah River, SW of Clearwater

Near the foot of this bluff in the old town of Hamburg stood the western terminus of the S.C. Canal and Rail Road Co. Begun in 1830, it was the first steam operated railroad to offer regular passenger service and to carry U. S. mail. Completed in 1833 to this point 136 miles from Charleston, it was the world's longest railroad. *Erected by Aiken County Historical Commission, 1962*
GPS Coordinates: 33° 28.947' N, 81° 56.991' W

2–3 Hamburg

U.S. Hwy. 1 at the Savannah River, Southwest of Clearwater

Situated between this point and the Savannah River, Hamburg was a thriving river port and trading center for cotton and tobacco. Founded in 1821 by Henry Schultz, incorporated December 19, 1827, Hamburg became the most important interior port in South Carolina. With changing times and fortunes, prosperous Hamburg declined. Only ruins remain. *Erected by Aiken County Historical Commission, 1963* [Replaced by marker 2–62 in 2018]
GPS Coordinates: 33° 28.947' N, 81° 56.991' W

2–4 Historic Church

U.S. Hwy. 278, at entrance to Redcliffe Plantation State Park, about 2 miles below Beech Island

This church was built in 1836 by Beech Island Presbyterian Church, organized in 1827 with the Rev. Nathan H. Hoyt of Vermont as first pastor. His son-in-law, the Rev. Edward Axson, was ordained and served here. His daughter, Ellen, wife of Woodrow Wilson, was baptized here. In 1950 the building was consecrated as All Saints Episcopal Church. *Erected by All Saints Episcopal Church, 1967*
GPS Coordinates: 33° 25.398' N, 81° 51.714' W

2–5 James U. Jackson Memorial Bridge/James U. Jackson (1856–1925)

U.S. Hwy. 25 Business, North Augusta, near the Savannah River

James U. Jackson Memorial Bridge (FRONT) The first North Augusta bridge was built in 1891 by James U. Jackson. The present bridge, built in 1939, was formally dedicated as "The James U. Jackson Memorial Bridge." The building of the 1891 bridge, the Augusta-Aiken street car line, and the magnificent Hampton Terrace Hotel earned him the title "Founder of North Augusta."
James U. Jackson (1856–1925) (REVERSE) A native of Augusta, Georgia, he graduated from Richmond Academy and the University of Georgia. In 1889, he founded the North Augusta Land Company, which built the old 13th Street Bridge. He was the prime mover in the development of North Augusta, S.C. A prominent railroad executive, he secured the Union Railway Station for Augusta. *Erected by North Augusta Historical Society, 1972*
GPS Coordinates: 33° 29.123' N, 81° 58.353' W

2–6 The Martintown Road

908 W. Martintown Rd., near adjacent cemetery, North Augusta (moved here May 2019)

In the 1730s, an Indian path from Fort Moore to the Saluda ridge was used by traders going to the Cherokee Nation. Later, a wagon road from Ninety Six to Augusta followed the same route. Named for the Martin family who lived beside it and served well the cause of the Revolution, it was widely used during that conflict by Patriots, Tories, and British. *Erected by Martintown Road Chapter Daughters of the American Revolution, 1972*
GPS Coordinates: 33° 31.607' N, 81° 58.783' W

2–7 Beech Island Agricultural Club

U.S. Hwy. 278 at its intersection with S.C. Sec. Rd. 2-1139, Beech Island vicinity

(FRONT) On January 5, 1856, Governor James H. Hammond and eleven other farmers of this area organized the Beech Island Agricultural Club for the diffusion of agricultural knowledge and the regulation of illegal slave traffic. Monthly meetings and barbecues have been held almost without interruption since the club's founding.

(REVERSE) In 1883 E. Spann Hammond donated to the Beech Island Agricultural Club a four-acre circular tract of land located less than a mile north of this site. The original club house was destroyed by fire on August 7, 1967. The site of the building is marked by a dedicatory plaque. The new club house was dedicated in June 1968. *Erected by the Beech Island Agricultural Club, 1973*

GPS Coordinates: 33° 25.472' N, 81° 51.982' W

2–8 Aiken County

Aiken County Courthouse, corner of Park Ave. & Chesterfield St., Aiken

Aiken County, created in 1871 from parts of Barnwell, Edgefield, Lexington, and Orangeburg counties, was named for William Aiken, first president of the South Carolina Canal and Railroad Company. Older industries in the county today are textiles, and the mining and processing of kaolin. In 1952, the Atomic Energy Commission's Savannah River Plant began operations. *Erected by Aiken County Historical Commission, 1979*

GPS Coordinates: 33° 33.483' N, 81° 43.2' W

2–9 Savannah Town/Fort Moore

S.C. Hwy. 28 at the Savannah River, Southwest of Clearwater

Savannah Town (FRONT)

Forerunner of modern towns and highways and known to the English as early as 1685, this Indian town stood at a major northwestern entrance into S.C. on the trading routes to the Creeks, Choctaws, Chickasaws, and Lower Cherokees. Both town and river were named for the Savannah Indians that lived in the area.

Fort Moore (REVERSE)

Following the disastrous Yamasee War, Fort Moore, "the most important of South Carolina's early forts," was constructed here in 1716 to protect the province from future attack and to guard the vital trading routes to the major

Southern Indians. It was garrisoned until 1766, when the growing settlement of Georgia made it no longer needed. *Erected by Andrews Masonic Lodge, Beech Island, 1985*

GPS Coordinates: 33° 26.359' N, 81° 54.607' W

2–10 Pascalis Plantation/Pascalina

U.S. Hwy. 78, .5 mi. Southeast of Montmorenci

Pascalis Plantation (FRONT)

Elizabeth Pascalis purchased these 790 acres in 1835, settled here with her son Cyril Ouviere, and brought the orphaned children of her daughter, here, to live. Cyril, a civil engineer, was a resident engineer constructing the Charleston-Hamburg railroad (world's longest when completed in 1833). In 1834 he helped lay out and survey streets in nearby Aiken.

Pascalina (REVERSE)

Elizabeth Pascalis willed this house, once know as Pascalina, to her granddaughter, Theodosia Wade, and husband John C. Wade, in 1863. The Wades were living here in February of 1865 when Union general Hugh Judson Kilpatrick used the house as headquarters during the Battle of Aiken. The house remained in the family until 1944. *Erected by Aiken County Historical Society, 1987*

GPS Coordinates: 33° 31.344' N, 81° 36.743' W

2–11 Samuel Hammond

101 Riverview Park Dr., Riverview Park Activity Center, North Augusta

(FRONT) Born 1757 in Virginia, this Indian fighter, who later moved to Edgefield District, attained the rank of Lieutenant Colonel of state troops during the American Revolution. Among the engagements he participated in were: Hanging Rock, Musgrove's Mill, King's Mountain, Blackstock's, Cowpens, Guilford Courthouse, Siege of Augusta, and Eutaw Springs. Hammond served in the U.S. Congress and after the Louisiana Purchase in [. . .]

(REVERSE) [. . .] 1803, President Thomas Jefferson appointed him Colonel-Commandant of the St. Louis District. He subsequently was elected to the Missouri Territory Council and became its first president in 1813. Returning to S.C. in the 1820s, he was elected Surveyor General (1826) and Secretary of State in 1830. Hammond died in 1842 and was buried nearby; the grave was moved about 1.6 miles north in 1991. *Erected by Olde Towne Preservation Association of North Augusta, 1992* GPS Coordinates: 33° 29.979' N, 81° 59.265' W

2–12   St. Thaddeus Church

Pendleton St., between Richland Ave. & Hayne Ave., Aiken

(FRONT) This Episcopal Church (cornerstone laid Sept. 5, 1842) was consecrated Aug. 9, 1843. It is the city's oldest church structure, having retained its Greek revival style through subsequent remodeling. Church purchased bell in 1853, Cornish Memorial Chapel completed in 1888, and Mead Hall School opened 1955. William Gregg (1800–1867), an important figure in the textile industry in S.C., was one of the church founders.
(REVERSE) Buried in the churchyard are John H. Cornish, rector of this church 1846–1869; George W. Croft (1846–1904), S.C. Senator and U.S. Congressman; William P. Finley, Ordinance of Secession signer; James M. Legaré (1823–1859), poet, artist, inventor who held several U.S. patents; Henry W. Ravenel (1814–1887), S.C. botanist whose name is perpetuated in many plants; and John F. Schmidt, a church warden in 1843. *Erected by The Congregation, 1992* GPS Coordinates: 33° 33.689' N, 81° 43.463' W

2–13   Site of Ellenton

Northeast side of S.C. Hwy. 125 at the Aiken County-Barnwell County line

Post office est. here 1873. Town chartered 1880. Ellenton and surrounding area purchased by U.S. Govt in early 1950s for establishment of Savannah River Plant. *Erected by Ellenton Reunion Organization, 1993* GPS Coordinates: 33° 13.507' N, 81° 43.834' W

2–14   Beech Island Baptist Church

170 Church Rd., Beech Island

(FRONT) This church was organized in the Beech Island Academy on January 21, 1832,

with Rev. Iverson Brooks as its first minister and Mathias Ardis and Randolph Bradford as its first deacons. This sanctuary, built on land donated by James T. Gardner and Abner Whatley, with lumber, other materials, and carpenters donated by Dawson Atkinson, was dedicated in September 1832; the Sunday School was organized in 1839.
(REVERSE) Charter members of Beech Island Baptist Church were Mathias and Louisa Ardis, Dawson and Marie Atkinson, Randolph Bradford, John and Ann Everett, James T. Gardner, Samuel and Rebecca Gardner, Eliza Gray, James Hankinson, Lida Lamar, Jonathan Miller, Pranmore Owens, John and Harriet Swain, Briton and Adeline Ware, Abner and Elizabeth Whatley, and Edmond Whatley. *Erected by the Congregation, 1996* GPS Coordinates: 33° 25.779' N, 81° 52.151' W

2–15   Storm Branch Baptist Church

153 Storm Branch Rd., Clearwater vicinity

This church had its origins at or near this site in 1772 as a plantation chapel, in what was Edgefield District until after the Civil War. Revs. Iverson L. Brookes and John Trapp, prominent ministers in the Savannah River region, preached here from the 1830s into the 1860s; Brookes died in 1865. Storm Branch Baptist Church became a wholly black church in August 1866 when Mrs. Sara Lamar, widow of planter Thomas G. Lamar, deeded this land to trustee Aleck Davis. About that same time the first permanent sanctuary was built. Rev. Robert L. Mabry, the longestserving minister, preached here from 1898 to 1943. *Erected by the Congregation, 1997* GPS Coordinates: 33° 29.371' N, 81° 54.443' W

2–16   Aiken Institute

In the block bounded by Chesterfield St., Whiskey Rd., Colleton Ave., S. Boundary Ave., and York St., Aiken

The Aiken Institute, which gave this area the name of "Institute Hill," was chartered in 1888. The main building, designed by I. F. Goodrich in 1891, includes a wing added in 1913. All grades attended the Institute until

1937, when a new high school was built and this became Aiken Elementary School. It was the second oldest school in use in the state when it closed in 1986. The 1913 wing became the Aiken County Public Library in 1990. *Erected by the Aiken County Historical Society, 1999*
GPS Coordinates: 33° 33.375' N, 81° 43.26' W

2–17 Hampton Terrace Hotel

1000 block of Carolina Ave., North Augusta

(FRONT) The Hampton Terrace Hotel, an exclusive winter resort, stood atop this hill from 1903 to 1916. The $536,000, 5-story hotel boasted more than 300 rooms and was the dream of James U. Jackson (1856–1925), founder of North Augusta. A private railway connected the hotel to major railroads. This, and its reputation as one of the finest hotels in the South, made the Hampton Terrace a leading destination for winter visitors.
(REVERSE) Guests enjoyed orchestra concerts in the music room and dancing in the hotel's magnificent ballroom. Other amusements included riding, hunting, tennis, an 18-hole golf course, billiards, and shuffleboard. Notable visitors included Marshall Field, Harvey Firestone, and John D. Rockefeller. President-elect William Howard Taft was the guest of honor at a banquet here in 1909. The hotel burned on New Year's Eve 1916. *Erected by the Heritage Council of North Augusta, 2000*
GPS Coordinates: 33° 30.124' N, 81° 58.166' W

2–18 Downer Institute & School/ Downer School, 1924–1986

Intersection of Hammond Rd. and U.S. Hwy. 278, Beech Island

Downer Institute & School (FRONT)
Downer Institute, founded in 1843, was originally located 1.5 mi. NE of this site and operated until 1865. It was named for benefactor Alexander Downer (1752–1820), whose will established an orphanage and school at Beech Island. By 1898 the General Assembly, at the request of Aiken County citizens, reestablished Downer School for the community at large; the school reopened in 1899.

Downer School, 1924–1986 (REVERSE)
Downer Elementary School, successor to the Downer Institute, stood here 1924–1950 and 1952–1986. A one-story school built here in 1924 replaced a two-story school constructed ¼ mi. SW in 1899, which burned in 1923–24. It burned in 1950 and was replaced by a second one-story school built in 1952, which served the Beech Island community until Downer Elementary School closed in 1986. *Erected by the Downer Fund Trustees, 2000*
GPS Coordinates: 33° 25.373' N, 81° 51.643' W

2–19 Schofield School

220 Sumter St., Aiken

(FRONT) This school was founded by the Freedmen's Bureau shortly after the Civil War to educate freedmen, women, and children. In 1868 Martha Schofield, a Quaker from Pennsylvania, came to Aiken and began her long career as superintendent. The school soon expanded to this two-block site and combined academics with instruction in industrial, farming, and homemaking skills. The 1897 Schofield School bulletin declared, "Character building is our most important work."
(REVERSE) Schofield School educated more than 6000 students by 1898. Many graduates became teachers and department heads here; others became successful business owners, professionals, farmers, and community leaders. In 1940 alumnus Sanford P. Bradby became its first African-American superintendent. As first a private and later a public school, Schofield has taught children of all races and creeds since 1866. The bell tower nearby once stood atop Carter Hall, built in 1882. *Erected by the Aiken County Historical Society and the Martha Schofield Historic Preservation Committee, 2001*
GPS Coordinates: 33° 33.695' N, 81° 42.73' W

2–20 Marie Cromer Seigler House

S.C. Hwy. 191, Eureka community, 8 miles north of Aiken

(FRONT) This house was for many years the home of Marie Cromer Seigler (1882–1964), educator and national pioneer in agricultural

instruction. In 1910, as teacher and principal of Talatha School, she founded a Girls' Tomato Club, the first of many such clubs nationwide and a forerunner, along with the Boys' Corn Clubs, of the national 4-H Clubs, supported by the U.S. Dept. of Agriculture. (REVERSE) Marie Cromer said of her efforts to encourage girls and young women interested in agriculture, "I made up my mind I was going to do something for country girls." With the support of Aiken Co. Superintendent of Education Cecil H. Seigler, whom she married in 1912, she established Home Demonstration clubs and created Home Economics courses in Aiken Co. schools. She died here in 1964. *Erected by the Aiken County Historical Society, 2000*
GPS Coordinates: 33° 41.826' N, 81° 45.971' W

2–21 Silver Bluff Baptist Church

360 Old Jackson Hwy., Beech Island

(FRONT) This church, one of the first black Baptist churches in America, grew out of regular worship services held as early as the 1750s at "Silver Bluff," the plantation of Indian trader George Galphin. At first a non-denominational congregation with both white and black members, it was formally organized as Silver Bluff Baptist Church in 1773 with Rev. Walt Palmer as its first preacher. (REVERSE) The church, dormant for a few years during the American Revolution, was revived in the 1780s by Rev. Jesse Peter. The congregation moved from its original site in 1815, again in the 1840s, and for the last time to the present site in 1866. A large frame sanctuary built in 1873 was covered in brick veneer in 1920; it was demolished and the present brick church was built in 1948. *Erected by the Congregation, 2001*
GPS Coordinates: 33° 24.606' N, 81° 53.51' W

2–22 Graniteville Mill

Corner of Canal St. (S.C. Hwy. 191) and Marshall St., Graniteville

(FRONT) This mill, the largest textile mill in antebellum S.C., was chartered in 1845 and

opened in 1847. It was founded by William Gregg (1800–1867), a Virginia native and advocate of industrial development who chose this site for its proximity to waterpower, granite deposits, and the S.C. Railroad. The company provided housing, a school, a store, and land for churches, creating a model mill village. Unlike most early textile mills, it was adequately funded. (REVERSE) Under Gregg's management early Graniteville families lived under strict rules and a rigid schedule, and became a close-knit community. During the Civil War the mill made fabrics for the Confederacy. After Gregg died in 1867 while fighting a flood on Horse Creek the company was run by its board, which expanded its operations. After several changes in ownership Graniteville remains one of the oldest textile manufacturing concerns in the South. *Erected by the Aiken County Historical Society, 2001*
GPS Coordinates: 33° 33.96' N, 81° 48.495' W

2–23 Aiken

Corner of Laurens St. and The Alley, Aiken

(FRONT) Aiken, chartered in 1835 and the county seat of Aiken County since its creation in 1871, was an early stop on the railroad line from Charleston to Hamburg. It was named for William Aiken (1779–1831), the first president of the S.C. Canal and Railroad Co. Aiken's mild climate and accessibility by rail soon made it a health resort for visitors hoping to escape the summer heat or seeking relief from tuberculosis and other lung ailments. (REVERSE) On Feb. 11, 1865, Federal and Confederate cavalry clashed here in the Battle of Aiken. The city's resort status was enhanced in the 19th and 20th centuries with its fame as a "Winter Colony," created by wealthy Northerners who built houses and sports facilities such as golf courses, polo fields, racetracks, and stables. Aiken later experienced a significant population boom in the 1950s after the construction and opening of the Savannah River Plant. *Erected by the Aiken County Historical Society, 2003*
GPS Coordinates: 33° 33.625' N, 81° 43.375' W

2–24 Pickens-Salley House

University of South Carolina Aiken Campus, Aiken

(FRONT) This plantation house, first known as "Edgewood," is an excellent example of Federal-era architecture. Originally near Edgefield, it was built in 1828 for Francis W. Pickens (1807–1869), state representative and senator, congressman, U.S. Minister to Russia, and governor 1860–62 during the secession crisis and the first two years of the Civil War. Lucy Holcombe Pickens was an ardent Confederate and novelist.

(REVERSE) In 1929 Eulalie Chafee Salley (1883–1975), pioneer woman suffragist, real estate broker, and developer, saved the house. Salley, architect Willis Irvin (1891–1950), and contractor Byron E. Hair supervised its dismantling, relocation to the Kalmia Hill area of Aiken, and restoration. It was moved here in 1989 when developer Ronny Bolton donated it to the University of South Carolina Aiken. *Erected by the Aiken County Historical Society, 2003*
GPS Coordinates: 33° 34.395' N, 81° 46.253' W

2–25 Millbrook Baptist Church

176 East Pine Log Rd., Aiken

(FRONT) This church, formally organized in 1884, had its origins in a Sunday school class organized in 1874. With 16 charter members and Rev. Arthur Buist as its first minister, Millbrook built its first sanctuary here in 1886. The frame church, built by J. V. George, was described as "one of the prettiest and best arranged" churches in this part of the state when it was dedicated.

(REVERSE) The original 1886 church was enlarged in 1909 and again in 1952. With the growth in Aiken County's population during the 1950s the congregation grew dramatically, building the present brick sanctuary in 1962. Dr. W. James Rivers is Millbrook's longest-serving minister, preaching here 1967–1996. The original sanctuary, renovated in 1979 and 1984, has served as a chapel since 1962. *Erected by the Congregation, 2003*
GPS Coordinates: 33° 31.448' N, 81° 43.059' W

2–26 Original Survey of Aiken

Corner of Laurens St. and Park Ave., Aiken

The town of Aiken, on land donated by Mr. Beverly M. Rodgers to the S.C. Rail Road in 1834, was laid out around a core of 27 city blocks bounded by Edgefield and Park Aves. and Newberry and Williamsburg Sts. This area was surveyed by civil engineers Cyril Ouviere Pascalis (1810–1836?) and Andrew Alfred Dexter (1809–1854), who had also helped survey the route of the new railroad between Hamburg and Charleston in 1832–33. *Erected by the Henry Tyler Chapter, Colonial Dames of the XVII Century, Jefferson Davis Chapter #2465, United Daughters of the Confederacy, and the Gen. David Williams Chapter, National Society of the Daughters of the War of 1812, 2004*
GPS Coordinates: 33° 33.65' N, 81° 43.244' W

2–27 Savannah River Plant

Intersection of S.C. Hwy. 19 and U.S. Hwy. 278 at the entrance to the plant, south of New Ellenton

(FRONT) The Savannah River Plant (SRP) was built 1950–56 by Du Pont for the Atomic Energy Commission. SRP, a nuclear production plant, produced tritium and plutonium for national defense during the Cold War. Creating a 310-sq.-mi. site in three counties meant moving all residents from their homes in Ellenton, Dunbarton, Meyers Mill, Leigh, and other area communities.

(REVERSE) The first reactor at SRP went online in 1953 and the free "neutrino," a subatomic particle, was first detected at P reactor in 1956. SRP also produced medical and research isotopes and energy sources for NASA. In 1972 it became the first National Environmental Research Park. Renamed Savannah River Site (SRS) in 1989, it is owned by the U.S. Department of Energy. *Erected by the Aiken County Historical Society, 2004*
GPS Coordinates: 33° 23.497' N, 81° 41.077' W

2–28   Jacksonville School/ Jacksonville Lodge

351 Huber Clay Rd., Langley

Jacksonville School (FRONT) Jacksonville School, built by the Jacksonville Lodge in 1895, taught the black children of this community until 1936. Grades 1–7, with two teachers, met in two classrooms on the first floor, without electricity or running water. The Jacksonville Community Commission acquired and renovated the building in 1991–92.
Jacksonville Lodge (REVERSE)
This building was constructed in 1895 by the Jacksonville Lodge, Grand United Order of Odd Fellows, a black fraternal organization. The lodge was led by Rev. Robert L. Mabry (1867–1943), also pastor of nearby Storm Branch Baptist Churches 1898–1943. The Odd Fellows met here on the second floor for many years. *Erected by the Jacksonville Community Commission, Inc., in Memory of Founding President Erwin M. Robinson, 2005*
GPS Coordinates: 33° 29.992' N, 81° 50.542' W

2–29   Aiken First Baptist Church

York St. NE (U.S. Hwy. 1) near its intersection with Richland Ave. (U.S. Hwy. 78), Aiken

(FRONT) This church, founded in 1805, predates the city of Aiken and was first called Levels Baptist Church. Its first location was a mile south of present-day Aiken. In 1836 the congregation joined with the members of the Wise Creek congregation to build a sanctuary here, on land deeded by the S.C. Railroad and Canal Co. They renamed their congregation Aiken Baptist Church. The frame church burned in 1876 and was replaced in 1878.
(REVERSE) The third church, a Gothic Revival sanctuary, was built in 1919. The kindergarten, founded in 1946, was one of the first church kindergartens in S.C. The present Classical Revival sanctuary was built and dedicated in 1958. Aiken First Baptist is the mother of four churches: Hispanic, Marion St., Memorial, and North Aiken. Its cemetery, dating from 1838, includes the graves of both Union and Confederate soldiers. *Erected by the Congregation, 2005*
GPS Coordinates: 33° 33.66' N, 81° 43.057' W

2–30   Graniteville Cemetery

Gregg Hwy. (S.C. Hwy. 895), Graniteville

(FRONT) This cemetery, established about 1850, is closely associated with the Graniteville Mill, the largest and most successful textile mill in antebellum S.C. William Gregg (1800–1867), founder of the mill, laid out the mill village and also helped plan this cemetery. Most of the early wooden grave markers do not survive, and burial records were not kept until 1892, when the Graniteville Cemetery Assn. was founded.
(REVERSE) William Gregg was buried here in 1867 and an obelisk erected over his grave. His widow moved his grave and monument to Charleston in 1876. In 1926 a daughter returned the original monument to this cemetery. Notable persons buried here include 83 Confederate soldiers and veterans, as well as many employees of Graniteville Mill. James Wesley Rearden (1861–1959) worked at the mill for 87 years, from 1872 to 1959. *Erected by the Horse Creek Historical Society and the Aiken County Historical Society, 2005*
GPS Coordinates: 33° 34.174' N, 81° 47.754' W

2–31   Hitchcock Woods

Near the entrance to Hitchcock Woods, S Boundary Ave. SW, Aiken

(FRONT) Hitchcock Woods, one of the largest urban forests in the United States, is an area consolidated between 1891 and 1898 by Celestine Eustis (d. 1921), Thomas Hitchcock (1860–1941), and William C. Whitney (1841–1904). Described as "the greatest equine playground in America," this tract of more than 8,000 acres was used for steeplechases, fox hunts, and other equestrian recreation by the wealthy Northerners who belonged to the "Aiken Winter Colony."
(REVERSE) The tract, now comprising almost 2,000 acres, has been owned and managed by the Hitchcock Foundation since 1939, when Thomas Hitchcock and his daughter Helen Clark established the foundation. Landmarks include Memorial Gate; Cathedral Aisle, a portion of the railroad bed built by the S.C. Rail Road in 1833–34; and Sand River, an unusual natural formation. Annual events

include the Aiken Horse Show each April and the "Blessing of the Hounds" each November. *Erected by the Aiken County Historical Society, 2005*
GPS Coordinates: 33° 33.34' N, 81° 43.525' W

and spurred major growth and development. *Erected by the North Augusta Centennial Committee and the Aiken County Historical Society, 2006*
GPS Coordinates: 33° 29.875' N, 81° 58.164' W

2–32 Aiken County Farmers' Market

Williamsburg St. SE at Richland St. SE (U.S. Hwy. 78), Aiken

The Aiken County Farmers' Market, founded in 1951, was originally an open air market sponsored by the Edisto Grange. This building, which opened on May 21, 1954, was designed by Woodrow Jackson and built by the Aiken County chain gang. Farmers and their families built 45 tables, still used today. This is the oldest county farmers' market in continuous service in the same location in S.C. *Erected by the Friends of the Aiken County Farmers' Market, the Aiken County Historical Society, and the Historic Aiken Foundation, 2006*
GPS Coordinates: 33° 33.394' N, 81° 42.506' W

2–33 North Augusta

John C. Calhoun Park, intersection of Carolina and Georgia Aves., North Augusta

(FRONT) North Augusta, chartered in 1906, includes the site of two early towns. Campbell Town was a trading post on the Savannah River before the American Revolution. Hamburg, founded in 1821 as a port on the river, was an early western terminus of the S.C. Rail Road. When the line was completed from Charleston to Hamburg in 1833, it was the longest railroad in the world. In 1890 James U. Jackson (1856–1925) founded the North Augusta Land Co. and bought 5,600 acres here. (REVERSE) James U. Jackson built a bridge over the river in 1891, and a trolley line in 1897. By 1902 the trolley ran from Augusta, Ga., to North Augusta, and on to Aiken. The Hampton Terrace Hotel, which stood here from 1902 until it burned in 1916, soon attracted visitors seeking a winter resort, and the population grew to 1,500 by 1913. The opening of the Savannah River Plant in 1950 swelled the population to more than 10,000

2–34 Jefferson High School/Rev. Austin Jefferson, Sr.

170 Flint St., Bath

Jefferson High School (FRONT)
Jefferson High School opened in 1956 as a junior high and high school for African-American students of Beech Island, Belvedere, Graniteville, Jackson, Langley-Bath-Clearwater, and North Augusta, with Herman W. W. Fennell (1910–1996) as principal. After county schools desegregated in 1970 it became Jefferson Junior High School, and in 1980 it became Jefferson Elementary School.
Rev. Austin Jefferson, Sr. (REVERSE)
This was one of three African-American schools in Aiken County named for Rev. Austin Jefferson, Sr. (1881–1966), longtime advocate for education. In 1944 the Langley-Bath Colored School was renamed Jefferson Grammar School in his honor. The original portion of this school was built in 1953 as the Jefferson Elementary School, with Augustus T. Stephens (1903–1992) as principal. *Erected by the Jefferson Alumni Association, 2007*
GPS Coordinates: 33° 29.828' N, 81° 51.859' W

2–35 St. John's Methodist Church

Richland Ave. SE (U.S. Hwy. 78), between Newberry & Chesterfield Sts., Aiken

(FRONT) This church has its origin in 1825 as a Methodist congregation on the Hollow Creek Circuit that predates the city of Aiken. Rev. John Reynolds was the first circuit rider serving St. John's, which shared a minister with St. John in Graniteville until becoming a separate congregation in 1856. The first sanctuary here, a frame Greek Revival church designed by Dr. E. J. C. Wood, was built in 1857–58.
(REVERSE) The 1858 Greek Revival church was demolished in 1961–64 and replaced by the present sanctuary, a brick church designed by local architect John Weems. This church,

consecrated in 1964, was built on the site of the old church cemetery. With the consent of their descendants, the persons buried there were exhumed and reburied south of the sanctuary. Their names are engraved on a marble plaque near the chapel entrance. *Erected by the Congregation, 2007*
GPS Coordinates: 33° 33.675' N, 81° 43.224' W

2–36 P Reactor

Road F, Savannah River Site (Not Open to the Public)

(FRONT) One of five production reactors at Savannah River Plant, now Savannah River Site, P Reactor was the site of cutting-edge neutrino research. In 1956, Drs. Clyde Cowan, Jr., and Frederick Reines used P Reactor to confirm for the first time the existence of the free neutrino, a sub-atomic particle of extremely small mass. As a result, Reines won the 1995 Nobel Prize in Physics.
(REVERSE) P Reactor not only generated prize-winning research but also produced plutonium and tritium for national defense. Built from 1951–1954, it was the second of five reactors here to go on line, running from initial start-up, Feb. 20, 1954, until final shutdown in 1988. During that period, it had the best safety record of any nuclear reactor at the Savannah River Plant. *Erected by the U.S. Department of Energy, 2008*
GPS Coordinates: 33° 20.719' N, 81° 44.523' W

2–37 R Reactor

Near the intersection of Roads E & G, Savannah River Site (Not Open to the Public)

(FRONT) One of five production reactors at the Savannah River Plant, now Savannah River Site, R Reactor produced plutonium and tritium for national defense. Built 1951–53, it was the first of the five reactors to go on-line, with initial start-up on Dec. 28, 1953. The first irradiated fuel left the reactor in June 1954. The reactor continued operation until final shut-down in 1964.
(REVERSE) This was the first production reactor to use heavy water as the neutron moderator and coolant. It was also the first to have

vertical fuel and control rod assemblies, with more than 600 positions in the reactor tank. Originally rated at 378 MW, R Reactor achieved power levels many times that. It was the largest of the SRP reactors and was a prototype for the other four. *Erected by the U.S. Department of Energy, 2008*
GPS Coordinates: 33° 20.719' N, 81° 44.523' W

2–38 The Augusta and Aiken Railway

Intersection of Barnwell Ave. NW & Laurens St. NW (S.C. Hwy. 19), Aiken

(FRONT) The Augusta and Aiken Railway, a 26-mile interurban electric trolley line between Augusta, Ga., and Aiken, operated from 1902 to 1929. In Aiken the line began at the corner of Park Ave. & Union St., proceeded west on Park, then north on Laurens St., then west on Hampton Ave., and toward Augusta on what is now Trolley Line Rd. The first passengers paid 24 cents to ride 2 hours one way or 4 hours for a round trip.
(REVERSE) In 1906 the railway bought 4 new passenger cars with 52 seats each. Built by the J. G. Brill Car Co. of Philadelphia, they were nicknamed "Big Reds." Stops between Aiken and Augusta were at Graniteville, Madison, Warrenville, Gloverville, Langley, Bath, Clearwater, Summerhill, and North Augusta. The trolley line struggled with the advent of the automobile and made its last run from Aiken on July 8, 1929. *Erected by the Aiken County Historical Society, 2007*
GPS Coordinates: 33° 33.938' N, 81° 43.235' W

2–39 Whitney Park

Corner of S. Boundary Ave. SW and Chesterfield St. S, Aiken

(FRONT) This park, laid out in 1904–05, was named for William Collins Whitney (1841–1904). Whitney, a lawyer, Secretary of the Navy 1885–89 under Grover Cleveland, and financier, was also an avid sportsman and a leading member of the "Aiken Winter Colony." He established the Whitney Trust in 1901 "for the institution and promotion of all kinds of sports and pastimes in the City of Aiken, S.C." Private and public donations alike paid for Whitney Park.

(REVERSE) William C. Whitney, called "Aiken's most distinguished citizen" at his death in 1904, expanded a small cottage into a rambling vacation house of more than 50 rooms. Joye Cottage, its stables, and squash court are Aiken landmarks. He also helped establish Hitchcock Woods, and the Whitney Trust owns Whitney Polo Field, the Court Tennis Building, Palmetto Golf Club, and the Powder House Road Polo Fields, all associated with the "Aiken Winter Colony." *Erected by the Aiken County Historical Society and the Historic Aiken Foundation, 2007*
GPS Coordinates: 33° 33.282' N, 81° 43.325' W

2–40 First Presbyterian Church of Aiken

224 Barnwell Ave. NW, Aiken

(FRONT) This church, founded in 1858 with 14 charter members and W. Peronneau Finley and John D. Legare as elders, first met in the Aiken Town Hall on Laurens St. Its first permanent sanctuary, a frame building designed by Charleston architect Edward Brickell White, was completed and dedicated in 1859. It stood at the corner of Laurens Street and Railroad (now Park) Avenue until it was demolished in 1924.
(REVERSE) The second sanctuary, a Classical Revival brick building, was designed by Aiken architect Willis Irvin and served the congregation until 1969. The church membership tripled during the Aiken population boom of the the 1950s and was renamed First Presbyterian Church of Aiken in 1959. The present sanctuary, designed by the firm of Hallman and Weems, was built here in 1968–69 and dedicated in 1969. *Erected by the Congregation, 2008*
GPS Coordinates: 33° 33.819' N, 81° 43.272' W

2–41 World War II POW Camp

Mattie C. Hall Health Care Center, 830 Laurens St., Aiken

(FRONT) German prisoners of war were held in a camp on this site from November 1943 to May 1946. This camp, one of 21 in S.C., was at first a sub-camp of the POW camp at Camp Gordon (now Fort Gordon), in Augusta, Ga. It was later a sub-camp of Fort Jackson, in Columbia. 250 prisoners captured in North Africa were the first held here. Men captured in Italy and France in 1943–44 increased the total to 620 prisoners by January 1945.
(REVERSE) German POWS lived in tents with wooden floors, up to five men in each. Their mess hall was a large frame barracks. They worked 8–10 hours a day, harvesting peanuts or peaches, cutting pulpwood or lumber, planting trees, or working in a fertilizer factory. POWs were paid 80 cents a day in credit at the camp store. When not working prisoners often played soccer, put on plays and concerts, and took night classes. *Erected by the Aiken County Historical Society, 2008*
GPS Coordinates: 33° 34.581' N, 81° 43.222' W

2–42 Highland Park Hotel

Corner of Highland Park Terrace SW and Highland Park Dr. SW, Aiken

(FRONT) The Highland Park Hotel, Aiken's first grand tourist hotel, stood atop this plateau. It was built in 1869–70 and opened in 1870. A four-story Second Empire wing built in 1874 doubled its capacity to 350 guests. Open from November to June, it was at first favored by visitors coming to Aiken for their health and later by wealthy Northerners who wintered here and formed the "Aiken Winter Colony" in the 1890s.
(REVERSE) Interior features included men's and ladies' billiard rooms and a bowling alley. The grounds included tennis and croquet courts, stables and riding trails, walking trails, and a pavilion. The hotel burned in 1898, and this site became a park. A new Highland Park Hotel, a Spanish Colonial Revival building, opened here in 1915. Originally 80 rooms, it was later enlarged to 125 rooms. That hotel was demolished in 1940. *Erected by the Aiken County Historical Society, 2008*
GPS Coordinates: 33° 33.539' N, 81° 43.57' W

2–43 Wagener

Gunter St. and Park St., Wagener

(FRONT) Wagener, established after the Blackville, Alston, & Newberry RR built its line from Blackville to Seivern in 1887–88, was originally known as Guntersville or Gunter's Crossroads. When incorporated in 1888 it was renamed for George A. Wagener (1846–1908), a Charleston merchant and president of the B. A. & N. RR. In 1891 the B. A. & N. merged with the Barnwell Railway to form Carolina Midland Railway, which would be absorbed by the Southern Railway in 1900.

(REVERSE) George A. Wagener was also president of the Standard Kaolin Company, shipping kaolin clay on the B. A. & N. from mines in Aiken Co. to railroads connected to Charleston and its markets. From 1898 to 1933 a freight and passenger train known as "The Swamp Rabbit" ran from Perry to Batesburg, at first on the Carolina Midland and the Sievern & Knoxville lines but for many years on the Southern Railway. It linked Wagener to several Aiken County and Lexington County towns. *Erected by the Wagener Museum, 2010*

GPS Coordinates: 33° 38.931' N, 81° 21.386' W

2–44 The Detection of the Neutrino, 1956/The Nobel Prize in Physics, 1995

Savannah River Site, Aiken vicinity

The Detection of the Neutrino, 1956 (FRONT) On August 27, 1956, at the Savannah River Plant (now Savannah River Site), Drs. Clyde L. Cowan, Jr. (1919–1974) and Frederick Reines (1918–1999) used P Reactor to detect the neutrino, a sub-atomic particle hypothesized in 1930 but unconfirmed until their experiment, one of the most significant in modern physics.

The Nobel Prize in Physics, 1995 (REVERSE) In 1995 Dr. Frederick Reines was awarded the Nobel Prize in Physics for his and Dr. Clyde L. Cowan's detection of the neutrino at the Savannah River Plant. The Nobel citation called their experiment "a pioneering contribution that opened the doors to the region of 'impossible' Neutrino experiments." *Erected by the Savannah River Site Heritage Foundation, 2010*

GPS Coordinates: 33° 33.613' N, 81° 43.122' W

2–45 The Hamburg Massacre

U.S. Hwy. 1 / 78 / 25, under the 5th St. Bridge on the North Augusta side, North Augusta

(FRONT) The Hamburg Massacre, which occurred nearby on July 8, 1876, was one of the most notable incidents of racial and political violence in S.C. during Reconstruction. White Democrats across the state organized "rifle clubs" to intimidate black and white Republicans during the gubernatorial election of 1876. Clashes between groups of armed men were frequent, in some cases even including the militia.

(REVERSE) After a dispute between whites and a black militia company, about 200 men from local rifle clubs tried to disarm 38 black militiamen and others barricaded in a warehouse. One white was killed and men on each side were wounded before the blacks fled. Two blacks were killed trying to escape. Whites captured 25–30 blacks and executed four of them. 87 whites were charged in the massacre but were never tried for it. *Erected by the Heritage Council of North Augusta, 2010*

GPS Coordinates: 33° 29.169' N, 81° 58.992' W

2–46 Coker Spring

Whiskey Rd. & Coker Springs Rd. SW, Aiken

(FRONT) The freshwater spring less than ¼ mi. SW was used by prehistoric Indians. It was deeded to the town of Aiken in 1844 by William Perroneau Finley (1803–1876) and furnished Aiken's drinking water throughout the 19th century. A regular stop on the stagecoach route from Abbeville to Charleston, it helped make Aiken a popular health resort. William Gilmore Simms described it in 1843 as "a fountain of delicious water, which is equally cold and unfailing."

(REVERSE) The brick springhouse, covered in stucco, dates from the early 19th century and features Greek Revival architectural elements. During the Civil War Confederate soldiers camped nearby, in what is now Hitchcock

Woods, were frequent visitors. The spring-house and retaining walls, neglected by the turn of the 20th century, were restored in 1972 after archaeological excavations. Coker Spring was listed in the National Register of Historic Places in 1978. *Erected by the Brig. Gen. Barnard E. Bee Camp #1575, Sons of Confederate Veterans, 2011*

GPS Coordinates: 33° 33.321' N, 81° 43.432' W

2–47 Aiken Hospital/Aiken County Hospital

828 Richland Ave. West, Aiken

Aiken Hospital (FRONT)
The first public hospital in Aiken, at the corner of Richland Ave. and Vaucluse Rd., was built in 1917 for the Aiken Hospital and Relief Society, with donations from members of the "Aiken Winter Colony." The City of Aiken donated 3 acres of Eustis Park for the hospital and grounds. The hospital, built by local African-American contractor McGhee & McGhee, featured a hexagonal cupola. It closed in 1924 but reopened in 1927 with additional funding.
Aiken County Hospital (REVERSE)
The Aiken County Hospital, funded by the Public Works Administration (PWA) and the Duke Foundation, opened in 1936. A four-story brick Colonial Revival building, designed by noted Augusta architect Willis Irvin (1890–1950), it was called "the last word in a modern hospital." After a new private hospital opened on University Parkway in 1976 the building here housed Aiken County offices for many years. *Sponsored by the Aiken County Historical Society, 2011*

GPS Coordinates: 33° 33.862' N, 81° 43.8' W

2–48 Camp Butler

Near intersection of Wagener Rd. (S.C. Hwy. 302) & New Holland Rd. (S.C. Sec. Rd. 2-21), Aiken vicinity

(FRONT) This is the site of Camp Butler, a Confederate "camp of instruction" that operated from the spring to the fall of 1861, in what was then Barnwell District. New companies, organized as independent companies or in state regiments, were sent here for training

and organization into Confederate regiments before being transferred wherever they were needed.
(REVERSE) This camp was described in a letter to The Edgefield Advertiser as "the admiration of every visitor . . . . every thing in every direction is kept in the nicest order." Companies of the 2nd S.C. Artillery, 7th S.C. Infantry, and 14th S.C. Infantry, as well as the Chesterfield Light Artillery, trained and camped here from April to October 1861 before service in S.C., Va., and N.C. *Erected by the General Joseph Wheeler Camp #1245, Sons of Confederate Veterans, 2012*

GPS Coordinates: 33° 34.575' N, 81° 36.25' W

2–49 Leavelle McCampbell School

82 Canal St., Graniteville

(FRONT) This Classical Revival school, built by the Graniteville Mill in 1921–22, was designed by noted Augusta architect Willis Irvin (1890–1950) and was called "the finest school in the state" when it was dedicated. An elementary and high school serving Graniteville, Vaucluse, and Warrenville, it was named for Leavelle McCampbell (1879–1946), who was later president of the mill for a brief period in 1924.
(REVERSE) In 1954 the elementary students were transferred to the new Byrd Elementary School, and this became a high school, unofficially called Graniteville High School. The Graniteville Mill sold this school and grounds to Aiken County for $124,000 in 1960. It remained a high school until a new Midland Valley High School was built in 1980, and has been Leavelle McCampbell Middle School since. *Sponsored by the Leavelle McCampbell School Alumni Association, 2012*

GPS Coordinates: 33° 34.011' N, 81 48.416' W

2–50 Aiken Graded School

Corner of Hampton Ave. & Kershaw St., Aiken

(FRONT) This park is the site of Aiken Graded School, a two-story brick school built 1924–25. It was built for black pupils in grades 1–7 and was one of almost 500 S.C. schools funded in part by the Julius Rosenwald Foundation

1917–1932. Black Aiken physician Dr. C. C. Johnson raised $3,500 in the black community toward the total cost of $33,500. Black brick mason Elliott Ball supervised the school's construction.

(REVERSE) The school, described as "one of the best in the state" when it was being built, had ten classrooms, a library, and an auditorium seating 600. It opened in the fall of 1925, with principal W. D. Drake, nine teachers, and almost 300 students. The school, the only black elementary school in Aiken until new schools began to be built in 1954, closed in 1969. It was demolished in 1973. *Sponsored by the Aiken County Historical Society, 2013*

GPS Coordinates: 33° 33.973' N, 81° 42.590' W

2–51 Aiken Preparatory School

619 Barnwell Ave., N.W., Aiken

(FRONT) Aiken Preparatory School (APS), founded in 1916 as a boarding school for "junior gentlemen" in grades 4–8, was a fixture in the city of Aiken for almost 100 years. Louise "Lulie" Hitchcock (1867–1934), a leader among the wealthy Northerners in the Aiken Winter Colony, founded it to prepare boys for boarding schools in the Northeast. APS emphasized a classical education and physical education.

(REVERSE) The original home for APS was a house built for U.S. Sen. George Edmunds of Vt. First headmaster Frederick A. M. Tabor was succeeded in 1938 by Harold A. Fletcher, headmaster until 1971. The school added grade 9 in 1960. It merged with Aiken Day School in 1989, added grades 4K-3, and became coeducational, then added a high school in 2000. Aiken Preparatory School was merged with Mead Hall Episcopal School in 2012. *Sponsored by the Aiken County Historical Society, 2013*

GPS Coordinates: 33° 33.898' N, 81° 43.576' W

2–52 Kalmia

Corner of Gregg Ave. & Richland Ave., Aiken

(FRONT) This is the site of Kalmia, the home and plantation of William Gregg (1800–1867), pioneer industrialist of the antebellum South.

A native of Va., Gregg moved to S.C. in the 1820s, becoming a craftsman and merchant in Columbia and Charleston. In 1837 he invested in the textile mill at Vaucluse, 4 mi. NW. In 1845 he founded the Graniteville Manufacturing Co. Gregg moved here from Charleston to supervise construction of the mill and mill village 3 mi. W.

(REVERSE) In 1847 or 1848 Gregg built a Greek Revival house overlooking the Horse Creek Valley and named it Kalmia for the mountain laurel growing here. A summer home at first, it was his year-round home by 1854 and he died here in 1867. It was built of black cypress, contained 17 rooms, and was lit by gaslights. An ornamental garden featured roses, and a vast peach orchard was among the first in S.C. to ship peaches to Northern markets. Kalmia burned in 1921. *Sponsored by the Aiken County Historical Society, 2014*

GPS Coordinates: 33° 33.844' N, 81° 45.613' W

2–53 Aiken Colored Cemetery /Pine Lawn Memorial Gardens

Florence St. & Hampton Ave., Aiken

Aiken Colored Cemetery (FRONT)
This cemetery, established in 1852 as a city cemetery, became Pine Lawn Memorial Gardens in 1988. The only burial ground for African Americans in Aiken until the mid-20th century, it was laid out by the City of Aiken on 4 acres, and later expanded to its present 9.5 acres. In 1892 the city deeded it to the Aiken Cemetery and Burial Association, helping that association maintain the cemetery.

Pine Lawn Memorial Gardens (REVERSE)
The earliest graves here are of slaves, free blacks, and freedmen from the mid-to-late 19th century. Many African Americans prominent in politics, the law, medicine, religion and education throughout the 20th century are buried. The cemetery also includes the graves of veterans of American wars from the Civil War to the present. It was listed in the National Register of Historic Places in 2007. *Sponsored by the Aiken County Historical Society, 2014*

GPS Coordinates: 33° 34.260' N, 81° 43.380' W

2–54 Graniteville Academy

Canal St. and the Gregg Hwy., Graniteville

(FRONT) This Carpenter Gothic school was built in 1848 by the Graniteville Mill, then the largest textile mill in S.C. William Gregg (1800–1867), who opened the mill in 1847, created a model mill village here. This academy, with five classrooms and a bell tower, opened with local ministers as teachers for students in grades 1–6. Gregg made attendance compulsory for all mill village children between ages 6 and 12.

(REVERSE) Wings were added to this building in 1853; a second building was added to the campus later. The academy added grades 7–11 in 1898, with its first high school graduating class in 1899. Leavelle McCampbell School, 4/10 mi. S on Canal St., opened in 1922 and replaced Graniteville Academy. The old academy was converted into houses, with the wings detached and moved. The original 1848 academy here was a residence 1922–1969. *Sponsored by the Horse Creek Historical Society, 2014*

GPS Coordinates: 33° 34.274' N, 81° 48.367' W

2–55 Adath Yeshurun Synagogue

154 Greenville St. NW, Aiken

(FRONT) Aiken's permanent Jewish community dates to 1890, when immigrants from Eastern Europe, many of them from Knyszyn, Poland, began to settle here. Adath Yeshurun Congregation (Congregation of Israel) held its first services in private homes or in the Masonic Hall. Several community leaders founded the Sons of Israel Cemetery, NW on Hampton Avenue, in 1913.

(REVERSE) The "Congregation Adas Yeshurun" was chartered in 1921 with Meyer Harris, J. S. Poliakoff, M. Poliakoff, B. M. Surasky, and Jacob Wolf representing its members. This Classical Revival synagogue was built in 1925 and has been in continuous use since as both a place of worship and a Jewish community center. Members have been leaders in Aiken business, politics, and civic affairs for many years. *Sponsored by the Jewish Historical Society of South Carolina, 2014*

GPS Coordinates: 33° 33.866' N, 81° 43.459' W

2–56 Carrsville

Barton Rd. & Boylan St., North Augusta

(FRONT) This African-American community was established in 1930 after two floods on the Savannah River washed away most of the town of Hamburg. That town had become a predominantly African-American community after the Civil War. Carrsville was most likely named for Charles W. Carr of the American Red Cross or for William Carpenter, an African-American businessman, both of whom gave lots for new homes here to families displaced by the flooding.

(REVERSE) Boylan Street here was originally named Red Cross Street in recognition of that organization's aid to the black families who had lost their homes on the banks of the Savannah River. This building, long called "the Society Building," was built in 1930 for the Young Men's Union Society, which later bought the lot from William Carpenter. The building has hosted many events for organizations such as Simmons Lodge No. 571, which acquired it in 1988. *Sponsored by the Heritage Council of North Augusta, 2014*

GPS Coordinates: 33° 29.180' N, 81° 57.462' W

2–57 Banksia

433 Newberry St., SW, Aiken

(FRONT) Banksia, named for the yellow roses of the same name that grow here, was commissioned in 1931 by Richard Howe—Aiken Winter Colonist. The 14,000 sq. ft. Colonial Revival mansion, with 35 rooms, 15 bathrooms, and a ballroom, was designed by noted Augusta architect Willis Irvin. His plans used a 3,500 sq. ft. house known as the Harrington House that had stood on the property since the 1850s. It was incorporated as the right wing of Banksia.

(REVERSE) After Howe's death in 1943, Banksia was eventually sold and was first used in the early 1950s as a boarding house used by construction workers building the Savannah River Nuclear Plant. In 1957 it was bought by the Southern Methodist Church and used as a college. Later, it served as the first home of USC-Aiken from 1961 to 1972. From 1973 to 1983 it was used as the Aiken County Public

Library. Since 1984 it has been home to the Aiken County Historical Museum. *Sponsored by the Aiken County Historical Society, 2016* GPS Coordinates: 33° 33.272' N, 81° 43.546' W

2–58 "The Middle Road"/Indian Head

S.C. Hwy. 389, east of Perry

"The Middle Road" (FRONT)

This road began as a Native American trading path that ran from the fall line of the Savannah River to Charleston. By the colonial era it was known as the Middle Road, Ninety Six Road, and the Road from Long Canes to Charleston. A statute of 1770 established it as a public road. It ran between the forks of the Edisto from Orangeburgh Bridge to the Indian Head, before continuing to the Ridge.

Indian Head (REVERSE)

The Indian Head, a series of springs at the head of Goodland Swamp, long served as a landmark and watering place. Travelers along the Middle Road referenced it and it appears on colonial plats. In 1781 Loyalists under command of Lt. Col. John H. Cruger passed near here after their withdrawal from Ninety Six. They were pursued by Whigs, including militia commanded by Col. Andrew Pickens. *Sponsored by the Aiken County Historical Society, 2016* GPS Coordinates: 33° 37.682' N, 81° 18.066' W

2–59 Providence Baptist Church

315 Barton Rd., North Augusta

(FRONT) Providence Baptist Church was established by enslaved and free people of African descent in the town of Hamburg. After the Civil War Hamburg became a center of African American political power in Aiken County. In 1868 three members of the Providence Congregation, John Gardner, Prince Rivers, and Samuel Lee, won election to the S.C. legislature. All three would rise to greater political prominence during the era of Reconstruction.

(REVERSE) In 1929 a massive flood inundated Hamburg and forced residents to move to higher ground. The town never recovered.

Many residents salvaged material to rebuild their homes. Providence Baptist Church was similarly dismantled and rebuilt atop the 75 foot bluff behind the old town. The new settlement was officially named Carrsville, but sometimes referred to locally as "New Hamburg." *Sponsored by First Providence Baptist Church and the Heritage Council of North Augusta, 2016* GPS Coordinates: 33° 29.197' N, 81° 57.440' W

2–60 Aiken Railroad Depot

406 Park Ave. SE, Aiken

(FRONT) The Aiken Railroad Depot was constructed in 1899 by the Southern Railway. Builtlargely to service the wealthy travelers who comprised the Aiken Winter Colony, including members of the Vanderbilt, Mellon, and Astor families, the depot was designed as a showpiece. It helped to facilitate Aiken's position as a popular sporting destination, especially among wealthy northerners, in the early 20th century.

(REVERSE) Paul Welles, Division Superintendent of Southern Railway, hailed the Aiken depot as "second to none in the state," when it opened. It served the community for over 50 years, but by 1954 had fallen out of use and was demolished. The depot that stands today is a reconstruction of the 1899 building. The reconstructed depot was completed in 2010 and now serves as the Aiken Visitors Center and Train Museum. *Sponsored by Friends of the Aiken Railroad Depot, 2016* GPS Coordinates: 33° 33.487' N, 81° 42.938' W

2–61 Aiken Training Track

538 Two Notch Rd. SE, Aiken

(FRONT) In 1941 a group including Pete Bostwick, Mrs. Ambrose Clark, and Skiddy von Stade Sr. organized to build the Aiken Training Track (ATT) on 75 acres that included parts of the Post and Mead polo fields. Frank Phelps designed the one mile oval track, which was modeled after Keeneland Race Track in Lexington, KY. The purpose of constructing the ATT was to have a facility for the training of Thoroughbred race horses.

(REVERSE) A unique feature of the ATT is its "Horine" turns (flattened curves). The new design gave a longer straightaway and allowed for easier turns at high speed. The Aiken Trials, which are still held here, began in 1943 as an impromptu event to benefit the American Red Cross War Fund. Six Kentucky Derby, three Belmont Stakes, and nine Preakness winners have trained here. *Sponsored by the Aiken County Historical Society, 2016*
GPS Coordinates: 33° 32.805' N, 81° 42.626' W

2–62 Hamburg

River North Dr. near the Hwy. 1 interchange, North Augusta

Hamburg, located in the surrounding area, was a thriving river port and trading center for cotton and tobacco. Founded in 1821 by Henry Shultz and incorporated on Dec. 19, 1827, Hamburg became the most important interior port in S.C. With changing times and fortunes, prosperous Hamburg declined. The flood of 1929 destroyed what had been left of the town—ruins remain. *Sponsored by Aiken County Historical Society, 2018*
GPS Coordinates: 33° 28.712' N, 81° 57.183' W

2–63 Zion Hill Missionary Baptist Church

5415 Wagener Rd., Salley

(FRONT) The congregation of Zion Hill Missionary Baptist Church originated ca. 1894, when tradition holds that members began worshipping at a brush arbor across the road. Rev. James Turner was the first pastor. Early church leadership included men and women born

enslaved as well as free. Many were farmers. (REVERSE) To accommodate the church's growing membership, congregants acquired the present site in 1897 and soon after built the first chapel. The first chapel was a one-story wood frame clapboard building with a three-story tiered bell tower projecting from the FRONT façade. It was razed after the current church was built in 1986. *Sponsored by Zion Hill Missionary Baptist Church, 2019*
GPS Coordinates: 33° 35.694' N, 81° 27.594' W

2–64 Legare-Morgan House

241 Laurens St. SW, Aiken

(FRONT) One of the oldest houses in Aiken, this was home to the Legare family, including writer James Mathewes Legare (1823–1859), who lived here beginning in 1846. Portions of the house date to as early as 1837. The south wing was built ca. 1852 as a detached workshop for James Legare, who was also an inventor and painter. The north wing was added ca. 1900, after the workshop was moved and attached to the house.
(REVERSE) While living here, James Legare published his best-known work, Orta-Undis, and other Poems (1848). He also produced several inventions, including a cotton-based plastic he called "lignine." In 1870, the Legare family sold the property to Thomas Charles Morgan (1824–1905), an English naval officer. His son, attorney Thomas Redman Morgan (1863–1931), was Aiken mayor from 1899 to 1900 and lived in the house for a number of years. *Sponsored by Aiken County Historical Society, 2019*
GPS Coordinates: 33° 33.490' N, 81° 43.459' W

Allendale County

3–1 Smyrna Baptist Church

S.C. Hwy. 22, SW of Allendale

Organized in 1827 as Kirkland Church, the name was changed in 1836 to Smyrna Baptist Church. Title to the site was conveyed in 1849 by William I. Mixon. Additional land was

given by Thomas H. Willingham in 1882 to extend the church property to the Matthew's Bluff Road. *Erected by descendants of organizers and early leaders, 1962*
GPS Coordinates: 32° 56.197' N, 81° 21.174' W

3–2 Beech Branch Baptist Church

S.C. Sec. Rd. 3-104, 1.2 miles North of its Intersection with S.C. Sec. Rd. 3-41, Barton vicinity

Constituted September 12, 1759 as Coosawhatchie Church, this church became in 1822 Beech Branch Baptist Church. The present lot was granted 1796 and occupied by 1815. The building was remodeled in 1908 and 1960, electricity having been installed and the porch added in 1959, when weekly morning services began. The annex was built in 1962. *Erected by Beech Branch Baptist Church, Luray, S.C., 1963* GPS Coordinates: 32° 51.434' N, 81° 16.626' W

3–3 Antioch Christian Church

S.C. Hwy. 3, 2 miles South of U.S. Hwy. 301, Allendale vicinity

Organized in 1833 by Dr. and Mrs. W. R. Erwin and Mrs. U. M. Robert, this was the second Christian Church (Disciples of Christ) founded in South Carolina. Dr. J. D. Erwin, II, served as minister for forty years. The present building was used as a court house in 1865. *Erected by The Antioch Association, 1960* GPS Coordinates: 32° 56.899' N, 81° 24.99' W

3–4 Bethlehem Church

Boundary St. at entrance of Fairfax Town Cemetery, Fairfax

This Baptist Church, organized by 1854, built its first house of worship near here on land purchased in 1859 from A. R. Stokes. The congregation obtained the land for its present location in 1910 from G. D. Sanders and had completed a building by 1914. In 1944 the name was changed to the First Baptist Church. *Erected by First Baptist Church of Fairfax, 1976* GPS Coordinates: 32° 57.959' N, 81° 14.289' W

3–5 Town of Allendale

In front of Allendale County Administration Building, U.S. Hwy. 301, Allendale

(FRONT) In 1810, pursuant to an Act of the South Carolina General Assembly, the state conveyed a 1000-acre landgrant signed by Governor John Drayton to Benjamin and G. Washington Allen. The acreage included the present town of Allendale, which is presumed to have derived its name from the Allen family.

(REVERSE) Allendale Post Office was established here July 11, 1849, and Paul H. Allen was the first postmaster. By 1873 the Port Royal Railroad had completed a line through Allendale, and that same year the town was incorporated by the South Carolina General Assembly. The town limits extended in a three-quarter-mile radius from the depot. *Erected by Allendale Civic League, 1980* GPS Coordinates: 33° 0.289' N, 81° 18.963' W

3–6 St. Nicholas Church

East Corner of th e intersection of S.C. Hwy. 641 and S.C. Sec. Rd. 3-40, .7 miles West of the Salkehatchie River, East of Sycamore

Lutheran church, org. by 1804, has occupied several sites. Today's structure, built in 1910, incorporates material from the 1884 church and stands about 2 mi. south. *Erected by The Congregation, 1994* GPS Coordinates: 33° 2.621' N, 81° 6.622' W

3–7 Old Allendale

Intersection of S.C. Sec. Rds. 3-107 and 3-47, Southwest of Allendale

Original site of Allendale, named for its first postmaster, Paul Allen, in 1849. Sherman's troops under Gen. Kilpatrick camped here. Town moved to present site by 1873. *Erected by Allendale County Museum, 1994* GPS Coordinates: 32° 59.086' N, 81° 20.834' W

3–8 Harmony Baptist Church

Harmony Church Rd. (S.C. Sec. Rd. 3-40), just East of its intersection with S.C. Sec. Rd. 3-134, Sycamore vicinity

This church had its origins in a brush arbor as early as 1830 but was formally organized in 1878 with Rev. H. C. Smart as its first pastor and W. H. Cone and R. H. Mixon as its first deacons. Named Harmony Baptist Church by charter member Sarah Gooding, it affiliated with the Savannah River Association. This sanctuary, on land donated by Josiah

Loadholt, was built in 1880. *Erected by the Congregation, 1999*
GPS Coordinates: 33° 0.464' N, 81° 10.134' W

3–9 Old St. Nicholas Cemetery

On South side of Confederate Hwy. (S.C. Hwy. 641), .25 miles East of Ulmer Rd. (S.C. Sec. Rd. 3-48)

The original cemetery associated with St. Nicholas Lutheran Church is ⅓ mi. S off S.C. Hwy. 641. The church, originally located nearby, was founded about 1804 in what was then Barnwell District, and the cemetery includes plots of the Platts, Harter, and other area families. The present St. Nicholas Lutheran Church, 2 mi. S, was built in 1910. *Erected by St. Nicholas Lutheran Church, 2001*
GPS Coordinates: 33° 2.372' N, 81° 7.966' W

3–10 Bethel Baptist Church

6486 Confederate Hwy. (S.C. Hwy. 641), Fairfax

(FRONT) This church was organized in 1851 by Revs. Lewis Parker and John Hoover, with twelve charter members and Rev. Hoover as its first minister. The congregation has worshipped on this site, on land donated by Mathias Mathis, since it was organized. It first met under a brush arbor, then in a log church built in 1852. The second sanctuary here, a frame church, was built in 1887.
(REVERSE) The present sanctuary here, built in 1949, is attached to the 1887 church; it was remodeled in 1984 and again in 1991. Four members later became Southern Baptist ministers: Revs. W. E. Weekley, W. H. Dowling, G. D. Kinard, and W. E. Brant. Pastors with the longest tenures at Bethel were Revs. John Hoover (1851–68) and L. S. Shealy (1917–20 and 1934–47). *Erected by the Congregation, 2001*
GPS Coordinates: 33° 2.417' N, 81° 9.613' W

3–11 Fairfax

Gazebo Park, at the intersection of 7th St. (S.C. Sec. Rd. 3-18) and Sumter Ave. S, Fairfax

(FRONT) Fairfax, chartered in 1893 and incorporated in 1896, grew out of an early community centered around Owens' Crossroads, where a store was established in 1814, and later including Bethlehem Baptist Church (now First Baptist Church), founded in 1852. When the Port Royal RR was completed through this area in 1873 a depot and post office were built 1½ mi. E and named Campbellton.
(REVERSE) By 1881 W. J. and J. F. Sanders ran a store and post office ½ mi. from the original Owens' Crossroads, and the area was soon called Sanders. After the South Bound RR completed its line through this area in 1891, it crossed the previous railroad line. The crossing became the center of Fairfax, named when a local child drew that name from a hat belonging to a railroad official. *Erected by the Citizens of Fairfax, 2004*
GPS Coordinates: 32° 57.517' N, 81° 14.23' W

3–12 Barker's Mill/Skirmish at Barker's Mill

Buford's Bridge Hwy. (U.S. Hwy. 321 at Tuten's Mill Pond), 1.5 miles South of Sycamore

Barker's Mill (FRONT)
Barker's Mill, which stood here on Jackson Branch, was a grist mill owned by William Ransome Barker (1816–1869), a planter in what was then Barnwell District. Barker moved to this area in the 1850s, built a house about 2 mi. N, and established a cotton plantation of 2,000–3,000 acres which he named "Sycamore." The town of Sycamore, chartered in 1891, was named for the plantation.
Skirmish at Barker's Mill (REVERSE)
On February 2, 1865, at Gen. W. T. Sherman's Federals advanced toward Columbia, units of Gen. F. P. Blair's XVII Corps clashed with Confederate cavalry at the bridge over Jackson Branch. The Confederates retreated across the bridge, but the Federals did not cross until reinforced after dark. A Confederate withdrawal then opened the way for a Federal advance to Buford's and Rivers Bridges. *Erected by the Rivers Bridge Camp # 842, Sons of Confederate Veterans, 2005*
GPS Coordinates: 33° 0.897' N, 81° 12.904' W

3–13 Speedwell Methodist Church

Speedwell Church Rd., Millett

(FRONT) This church, founded in 1885, was named Speedwell for a stagecoach stop and the first post office in the vicinity, now Millett. In 1884–85 Ogreta Brabham Dunbar and Savannah Barker Bates raised funds for a new congregation, in what was then Barnwell County. In 1885 Mary Dunbar Lafitte and her husband John H. Lafitte donated a five-acre tract here for the church.
(REVERSE) The first church on this site, built about 1885, was replaced by the present church, begun in 1922 during the pastorate of Rev. W. R. Jones. It remained unfinished during the Depression but was dedicated in 1941 during the pastorate of Rev. J. A. Graham. Attendance declined in the 1960s, and regular services ended by 1970. Homecomings are still occasionally held here. *Erected by the Friends of Speedwell Methodist Church, 2010*
GPS Coordinates: 33° 5.03' N, 81° 32.5' W

3–14 Happy Home Baptist Church

Memorial Ave., near Railroad Ave. W, Allendale

(FRONT) This church, founded soon after the Civil War, held its first services in a brush arbor in the Woods community of what was then Barnwell County. It built its first permanent church, a frame building, in the Zion Branch community near Old Allendale, and adopted the name Zion Branch Baptist Church. The church bought this site in 1875, built a new frame sanctuary here, and was renamed Happy Home Baptist Church.
(REVERSE) Rev. Jacob S. Daniels served the church for almost thirty years, and the congregation grew from 86 members in 1877 to 258 members in 1890. By 1902, his son, Rev. George C. Daniels, succeeded him as pastor, and the church had 379 members. In 1911, during the pastorate of Rev. S. J. Rice, the church received a state charter and built its present church, a brick Gothic Revival building. *Erected by the Congregation, 2011*
GPS Coordinates: 33° 0.579' N, 81° 18.578' W

3–15 Chain Gangs/Allendale Co. Jail

600 Hickory St. N., Allendale

Chain Gangs (FRONT)
In 1894 the S.C. legislature passed an act requiring all male prisoners sentenced to less than two years to serve their term performing hard labor on public roads. The law promised to improve rural S.C. roads, but many of those sentenced to hard labor had committed petty crimes and most were African American. A 1920 report found that the Allendale chain gang suffered poor and unsanitary conditions. Some inmates at the Allendale Jail served on road gangs well into the 20th century.
Allendale Co. Jail (REVERSE)
In 1919 the S.C. General Assembly issued $100,000 in bonds to fund construction of a jail and courthouse in the newly established Allendale County. Both were designed by Atlanta-based architect G. Lloyd Preacher, a Fairfax, S.C. native and graduate of Clemson College. The courthouse and jail were completed in 1922. The jail, which once stood here, housed not only prisoners, but also the jailer and jail administrator. The Allendale Co. Jail remained in use until 1971. *Sponsored by Allendale County, 2016*
GPS Coordinates: 33° 0.661' N, 81° 18.196' W

3–16 Gillette Methodist Church

Intersection of Alleluia Rd. (State Rd. S-3-492) and State Rd. S-3-47, Martin

(FRONT) Gillette Methodist Church dates to the early 19th C., possibly around the time that Rev. James Capers settled on land owned by Dr. Elijah Gillett in early 1813. Capers was born in Charleston in 1788 and became a minister with the Methodist Episcopal Church in 1809. He likely stayed on the Gillett's land for only a brief time, but may have helped to spread the seed of Methodism here.
(REVERSE) Early meetings were held under a brush arbor. Elijah Gillett, at the urging of his wife Elizabeth Scarbrough Gillett, donated land and lumber to erect a permanent meeting house, which they deeded to the Methodist Church. The Gilletts are buried 3 ½ miles N. of the church. The meeting house was remodeled in 1910, but retains original floors,

wainscoting, and pulpit. *Sponsored by the Gillette Church Family, 2018*
GPS Coordinates: 33° 1.724' N, 81° 25.464' W

3–17 Swallow Savannah Methodist Church

412 Walnut St. W., Allendale

(FRONT) This church first organized ca. 1815, when members met in a log house 2 mi. S that was adjacent to a sheet of water known as "Swallow Savannah," the church's namesake. Local preacher John McFail was likely instrumental in the church's organization. Through the 1800s, members used several sites along Old Augusta Road including a church built on land given by Dr. Cornelius Ayer and dedicated in 1848. The church cemetery remains there.
(REVERSE) The church was part of the Black Swamp Circuit until 1855, when the Allendale Circuit was formed. In 1880, members made plans to move to Allendale, then a growing railroad depot town. A white clapboard church was built at this site after Lawrence Williams donated the land in 1890. That building burned in 1942 and was replaced by the current church, which was dedicated in 1946. The Fellowship Hall was built in 1961.

Sponsored by Swallow Savannah United Methodist Church, 2019
GPS Coordinates: 33° 0.513' N, 81° 18.701' W

3–18 Swallow Savannah Cemetery

E. side of Bluff Rd., just S. of Coosawhatchie River, Allendale

(FRONT) This cemetery was est. by Swallow Savannah Methodist Church, which formed ca. 1815 at a log house 1 mi. S. The church was adjacent to a sheet of water known by the late 1700s as "Swallow Savannah," supposedly for the many swallows that gathered there. Members began worshipping at this site by 1848, when a church was dedicated on land donated by Dr. Cornelius Ayer.
(REVERSE) The church moved to the town of Allendale ca. 1890 but continued to use this cemetery for burials. Upon the election of a cemetery committee in 1894, a survey was completed that formalized burial plots. In 1898, a chapel was built at the cemetery using materials from the old church building. The cemetery has been expanded over the years and includes church members and non-members alike. *Sponsored by Swallow Savannah Cemetery Committee, 2019*
GPS Coordinates: 32° 59.583' N, 81° 19.497' W

Anderson County

4–1 Portman Shoals [first marker]

N. McDuffie St. and Whitner St., Anderson

Half mile West on Seneca River the Portman Shoals Power Plant, built by William C. Whitner, began in 1897 the transmission of high-voltage electricity over the longest lines then in use for that purpose in the United States. The success of this plant, now owned by Duke Power Company, caused Anderson to be called "The Electric City." *Erected by Anderson County Historical Association, 1956*
GPS Coordinates: 34° 30.224' N, 82° 38.915' W

4–1 Portman Shoals [second marker]

S.C. Hwy. 24 at the Seneca River, 1 mile South of I-85, East of Anderson

1,000 feet due north on a site now covered by Hartwell Reservoir, the Portman Shoals Power Plant, built by William C. Whitner, began in 1897 the transmission of high-voltage electricity over the longest lines then in use for that purpose in the United States. The success of this plant caused Anderson to be called "The Electric City." *Erected by Anderson County Historical Association, 1960*
GPS Coordinates: 34° 31.451' N, 82° 49.33' W

4–2 High Shoals

E. River St. at Broadway Lake Rd., 2 miles East of Anderson

2.9 miles south on Rocky River. Anderson Water, Light & Power Co., organized in 1894 by William C. Whitner, was successful the next year in transmitting electricity over the distance of six miles to Anderson. This achievement was a herald of the industrial revolution in the South. *Erected by Anderson County Historical Association, 1956*
GPS Coordinates: 34° 28.999' N, 82° 36.252' W

4–3 Big Creek Baptist Church

Greenville Rd. (S.C. Hwy. 20) South of Intersection with E. Main St., Williamston

One of the oldest congregations and the mother of several others in Anderson County, it was organized in 1788 by Elder Moses Holland who served as pastor for 41 years. Dr. James Bruton Gambrell's mother was a member here. Soldiers of five wars lie buried in the cemetery. *Erected by Anderson County Historical Association, 1958* [replaced by new marker with identical text in 2017]
GPS Coordinates: 34° 37.346' N, 82° 28.253' W

4–4 Farmers Hall

Town Green, W. Main St. (S.C. Sec. Rd. 4–29) at N. Mechanic St. (S.C. Hwy. 28), Pendleton

Built 1826–1828/Home of Pendleton Farmers Society./Organized 1815./Within this hall/ THOMAS GREEN CLEMSON,/one of the Society's presidents,/first discussed with its members/the plans for the founding of/CLEMSON COLLEGE. *Erected by Anderson County Historical Association and Pendleton Farmers Society, 1958*
GPS Coordinates: 34° 39.042' N, 82° 47.031' W

4–5 Good Hope Church

Near Intersection of S.C. Hwy. 184 and S.C. Hwy. 81, Iva Vincinity

Oldest Presbyterian church in continuous existence in Anderson County. Organized in 1789. First pastor, Rev. John Simpson. Congregation worshipped at three sites near

Generostee Creek, three miles west of Iva. Old cemetery at third site. Sanctuary built in Iva in 1909, 200 yards west of marker. *Erected by Anderson County Historical Association, 1958*
GPS Coordinates: 34° 18.206' N, 82° 39.953' W

4–6 Printer John Miller

Corner of N. Broad St. and E. Queen St., Pendleton

This London newspaper publisher and defender of a free press emigrated to Charleston in 1783 where he served as state printer and publisher of the first daily newspaper in South Carolina. Later in Pendleton, he founded Miller's Weekly Messenger the first Up Country newspaper. His body lies buried in the Old Stone Church Cemetery. *Erected by Anderson County Historical Association and New Era Pendleton Club, 1960*
GPS Coordinates: 34° 39.086' N, 82° 46.878' W

4–7 St. John's Methodist Church

Corner of S. McDuffie St. and E. River St. (U.S. Hwy. 76), Anderson

Organized in 1828, this was the first church in Anderson. A log meeting house built in 1830 on West Benson Street served the church until 1858 when a frame building was erected on this site. A brick church replaced it in 1888. The present sanctuary was completed in 1912, the Education Building in 1928, and the activities building in 1956. The church was named St. John's in 1897. *Erected by the Congregation, 1962*
GPS Coordinates: 34° 30.024' N, 82° 38.847' W

4–8 Confederate Skirmish

Corner of Main St. (S.C. Hwy. 20) and Park Dr., Williamston

On May 1, 1865, cadets from the Arsenal Academy at Columbia, under Capt. John Peyre Thomas, who were enroute from Greenville to Newberry to be disbanded, met a band of Stoneman's raiders near here in one of the last engagements of the war, which had begun in Charleston harbor with shots fired from a post manned by cadets from the Citadel

Academy. *Erected by Anderson County Historical Society, 1964*
GPS Coordinates: 34° 37.115' N, 82° 28.675' W

4-9 Barkers Creek Church

3207 S.C. Hwy. 252, 3 miles West of Honea Path

Founded in 1821, this is the boyhood church and burial place of Olin D. Johnston. He was decorated for bravery in World War I, served in the S.C. House of Representatives, was twice governor of S.C., in 1935–1939 and 1943–1945, and U.S. senator from 1945 until his death April 18, 1965. *Erected by Friends of the Johnston Family, 1967*
GPS Coordinates: 34° 26.154' N, 82° 26.704' W

4-10 Barnard Elliott Bee

St. Paul's Episcopal Church, E. Queen St. (S.C. Hwy. 300) between N. Depot St. and S. Elm St., Pendleton

Born Charleston, S.C. 1824. Graduated West Point 1845. Brigadier General, C.S.A., 1861. Commanded 3rd Brigade, Army of the Shenandoah, July 21, 1861, at Manassas, Va. where he gave Gen. T. J. Jackson the name "Stonewall." Mortally wounded, he died July 22, 1861, and is buried in his family plot in St. Paul's churchyard. *Erected by Piedmont District, South Carolina United Daughters of the Confederacy, 1968*
GPS Coordinates: 34° 39.098' N, 82° 46.609' W

4-11 University Hill

S. Main St. at its Intersection with W. Johnson St., Anderson

Three educational institutions have been in this immediate area: Johnson Female University (1856–63) named for William Bullein Johnson; the Carolina Collegiate Institute (about 1866–90) under W. J. Ligon; and Patrick Military Institute (1887–1900), J. B. Patrick, founder. A Confederate Treasury branch was located here in 1865, and University Hospital in the 1920s. *Erected by Anderson Historical Society, 1970*
GPS Coordinates: 34° 29.743' N, 82° 38.912' W

4-12 William Bullein Johnson (1782–1862)

307 Manning St. at First Baptist Church, Anderson

President of Triennial, Southern, South Carolina Baptist Conventions. Johnson Female University, founded here in 1848 as Johnson Female Seminary, was named for him because of his support for female education. From 1853 to 1858, while Chancellor of the institution, he lived in the house at the south end of this street. His grave is in First Baptist churchyard. *Erected by First Baptist Church, 1970*
GPS Coordinates: 34° 30.14' N, 82° 38.803' W

4-13 Hopewell Church

3530 Hopewell Rd. (S.C. Sec. Rd. 4-29), off S.C. Hwy. 81, North of Anderson

This Baptist church, which was first located about 1.5 miles northwest, was constituted in 1803. The congregation moved to the present 4.4 acre site after it was surveyed December 14, 1822. Two houses of worship were built here prior to 1891, when a third was erected. It was replaced by the present 1949 structure. *Erected by The Congregation, 1975*
GPS Coordinates: 34° 35.492' N, 82° 36.617' W

4-14 Old Hopewell Cemetery

Southeast Corner of Intersection of Williamston Rd. (S.C. Hwy. 81 N) and Hopewell Rd. (S.C. Sec. Rd. 4-29), North of Anderson

Located 1.09 miles northwest, this cemetery marks the original site of Hopewell Baptist Church which was constituted in 1803. The cemetery contains graves of Revolutionary and Confederate veterans. Some graves are marked by field stones with hand-chiseled initials. *Erected by The Congregation, 1975*
GPS Coordinates: 34° 35.811' N, 82° 36.994' W

4-15 Ashtabula

S.C. Hwy. 88 (Old Greenville Hwy.), 1.2 miles Northeast of Pendleton

This plantation on the old road to Pickensville has been the home of several prominent S.C. families. Many of its owners were members of the Pendleton Farmers Society, and during

the nineteenth century, studies, experiments, and advances in agriculture took place here. The house was built by 1828, enlarged about 1855. Ashtabula was raided by Union Troops in 1865. *Erected by Foundation for Historic Restoration in the Pendleton Area, 1974*
GPS Coordinates: 34° 40.66' N, 82° 45.289' W

4-16 Williamston Female College

Main St. (S.C. Hwy. 20) across from Williamston Springs Park, Williamston

This college was founded Feb. 12, 1872, by the Reverend Samuel Lander, DD, Methodist minister. The college building stood on this site until 1939. The school was removed to Greenwood, S.C., Sept. 27, 1904, becoming Lander College in honor of the founder, who died July 14, 1904. From an humble beginning there arose here a Christian institution of expanding influence, keeping faith with its motto: Puritas et scientia. *Erected by Alumnae Association of Lander College, 1942*
GPS Coordinates: 34° 37.107' N, 82° 28.713' W

4-17 Thomas Green Clemson, 1807–1888

St. Paul's Episcopal Church, E. Queen St., Pendleton

A native Philadelphian and leading agriculturist, Mr. Clemson was U.S. chargé d'affaires to Belgium, U.S. Superintendent of Agriculture, and the 1868 president of Pendleton Farmers Society. He married the daughter of John C. Calhoun, Anna, and later bought the Calhoun home, Fort Hill. An advocate of the national land grant movement, he left his estate to establish Clemson University. He is buried 50 yards south. *Erected by Student Alumni Council of the Clemson Alumni Association, 1977*
GPS Coordinates: 34° 39.097' N, 82° 46.618' W

4-18 Anderson Mills

Glenn St. at Anderson Mills, Anderson

Founded in 1888, Anderson Cotton Mills, later a division of Abney Mills, was the first textile plant established in the town of Anderson. It is said to be the first textile mill in the United States powered by electricity transmitted over long distance power lines. Electricity for the plant was generated at Portman Shoals, located on the Seneca River. *Erected by Pendleton District Historical and Recreational Commission, 1978*
GPS Coordinates: 34° 30.45' N, 82° 39.45' W

4-19 Moffettsville/Moffettsville Postmaster Appointments

Intersection of Elberton Rd. and Parker Bowie Rd., about 2.5 miles West of Iva

Moffettsville (FRONT)
At this site once stood the town of Moffettsville, originating with the establishment of Moffett's Mill Post Office on February 16, 1818. By 1883, the town had a population of twenty-five with a physician and general store. Mail service here was discontinued in 1901.
Moffettsville Postmaster Appointments (REVERSE)
James H. Davison Feb. 16, 1818/John Simpson July 15, 1822/Andrew Milligan May 16, 1826/Archibald Simpson Dec. 7, 1826/Joel H. Berry May 17, 1838/William Sherard April 23, 1842/Robert A. Reid May 21, 1866/Thomas A. Sherard June 5, 1890/William T. A. Sherard Oct. 8, 1895/Discontinued Sept. 30, 1901. *Erected by Anderson County Historical Society, 1980*
GPS Coordinates: 34° 17.388' N, 82° 42.644' W

4-20 Woodburn Plantation

U.S. Hwy. 76 and S.C. Hwy. 28 across from Tri-County Technical College, West of Pendleton

Some 200 yards west of here stands Woodburn, built by S.C. Lieutenant Governor Charles Cotesworth Pinckney by 1832. Dr. John B. Adger, Presbyterian missionary to Armenia, bought Woodburn in 1852; in 1881, Augustine T. Smythe began a model stock farm here. Jane Hunter, founder of the Phillis Wheatley centers for working girls, was born in a tenant house here in 1882. *Erected by the Foundation for Historic Preservation in the Pendleton Area, Inc., and Anderson County Historical Society, 1987*
GPS Coordinates: 34° 38.415' N, 82° 47.467' W

4–21 Richard W. Simpson

Cherry St. (S.C. Sec. Rd. 4-115), about 4 miles East of Pendleton

Born in 1840, Colonel Simpson, lawyer, farmer, and legislator, drafted and executed Thomas Green Clemson's will, establishing Clemson Agricultural College in 1889. Simpson was first president of the college's board of trustees and once owned land which became part of the Simpson Experiment Station. He died in 1912 and is buried in the Simpson family cemetery here. *Erected by Clemson University, 1988*
GPS Coordinates: 34° 38.936' N, 82° 43.698' W

4–22 Pendleton

Village Green, E. Queen St., Pendleton

On April 8, 1790, the Justices of the Peace for Pendleton County purchased this land to establish the courthouse town of Pendleton. Once Cherokee Indian land, the town became the judicial, social, and commercial center for what now are Anderson, Oconee, and Pickens Counties. Early Scotch-Irish settlers were followed by S.C. low country aristocratic families, who built summer homes nearby. *Erected by the Pendleton Bicentennial Committee and the Anderson County Historical Society, 1990*
GPS Coordinates: 34° 39.103' N, 82° 46.999'

4–23 Roberts Church

2716 S.C. Hwy. 187 S., 9 miles West of Anderson and 4 miles South of S.C. Hwy. 24

Organized by 1789 and sometimes called Simpson's Meetinghouse, this church is one of Anderson County's oldest Presbyterian churches. The Reverend John Simpson was the first minister, and the Reverend David Humphreys served here for 39 years until his death in 1869. Both men are buried in the church cemetery. The present sanctuary was built in 1937. *Erected by the Congregation, 1987*
GPS Coordinates: 34° 27.463' N, 82° 47.288' W

4–24 Pickens Cemetery

Three and Twenty Rd. (S.C. Sec. Rd. 4-485), off S.C. Hwy. 88 near Anderson County-Pickens County Line, Pendleton Vincinity

This land, Cherokee territory until 1777, became the final resting place after the American Revolution for early pioneers who settled the area. A number of soldiers of the Revolution are buried here, including Robert Pickens, who served in the state militia and was related to General Andrew Pickens. *Erected by the Colonel John Robins Chapter, Colonial Dames of the XVII Century, 1980*
GPS Coordinates: 34° 44.35' N, 82° 35.467' W

4–24 African American School Site

[This marker was mistakenly double-numbered. It should have been marker 4-25.]

131 Vance St., one block from the Village Green, Pendleton

The one-room frame public school, organized shortly after the Civil War, housed 76 students and 1 teacher by 1870. The school term lasted 1 month and 10 days. Jane Harris Hunter, founder of the Phillis Wheatley centers for working girls, attended the school for 3 years. She wrote the book, *A Nickel and a Prayer.* Vance Street is named after the family of Rev. Augustus Thomas Vance, who served as the school trustee. *Erected by the National Alumni Association, Anderson County Training School and Riverside School, 1995*
GPS Coordinates: 34° 39.154' N, 82° 46.917' W

4–25 Anderson "The Electric City"

Grounds of the old Anderson County Courthouse, Courthouse Square, Main St., Anderson

(FRONT) Anderson was dubbed "The Electric City" in 1895 when William C. Whitner, an engineer and native of Anderson, built a hydroelectric power plant which was the first in the South to transmit electricity over long distance lines. The plant, in McFall's Mill at High Shoals on the Rocky River 6 mi. E, supplied power to light the city and also operated several small industries in Anderson. In 1897 Whitner replaced the [. . .]

(REVERSE) [...] experimental plant with a larger generating station at Portman Shoals 11 mi. W on the Seneca River. The extra power from this plant powered Anderson Cotton Mills and a streetcar line which was the forerunner of the Piedmont & Northern RR. Both plants pioneered in transmitting high voltage electricity direct from the station switchboard. This innovation helped spur the modern industrialization of the Southeast. *Erected by the Anderson County Historical Society, 1997*
GPS Coordinates: 34° 30.2' N, 82° 39.017' W

4–26 Oliver Bolt's Cotton Gin

3200 Block of W. Whitner St. (S.C. Hwy. 24), 3 miles West of Anderson and 1.3 miles West of its intersection with S.C. Hwy. 128

The first cotton gin to be powered by electricity transmitted over a long distance stood near this site on the farm of Oliver "Duck" Bolt (1847–1922). In 1897 Bolt, whose gin had previously been powered by a steam engine, contracted with the Anderson Water, Light, and Power Company to furnish electricity for a 20-horsepower electric motor from its new plant at Portman Shoals, 7 mi. W on the Seneca River. *Erected by the Anderson County Historical Society, 1997*
GPS Coordinates: 34° 30.25' N, 82° 42.6' W

4–27 Carnegie Library

318 Shirley Ave., Honea Path

Honea Path is the smallest town of the fourteen South Carolina communities with libraries funded by the Andrew Carnegie Foundation. Dr. John Wright, Mayor John, and Miss Jennie Erwin were leaders in obtaining the $5000 grant. The Honea Path Library Association was established in 1907 and the library was opened in 1908. It was renamed the Jennie Erwin Library in 1958, when it became part of the Anderson County Library System. *Erected by the Honea Path Merchants Association, Honea Path Civitans Club, and Honea Path Lions Club, 1999*
GPS Coordinates: 34° 26.847' N, 82° 23.542' W

4–28 Sandy Springs Camp Ground/ Confederate Muster Ground

Milwee Creek Rd. (S.C. Sec. Rd. 4–58), near Sandy Springs United Methodist Church, just East of Sandy Springs

Sandy Springs Camp Ground (FRONT)
This Methodist camp ground, named for the large spring nearby, dates to 1828, when a fifteen-acre site was purchased from Sampson Pope for $45. Early meetings were under a brush arbor until a central wooden shelter and cabins were built about 1838. Entire families participated in revival meetings, held here for two weeks every September until the last camp meeting in 1897.
Confederate Muster Ground (REVERSE)
Col. James L. Orr's 1st Regt. S.C. Rifles (Orr's Rifles) was organized here on July 20, 1861, in a field adjoining the Sandy Springs camp ground. Ten companies—four from Pickens, three from Abbeville, two from Anderson, and one from Marion District—trained at Camp Pickens before serving first on the S.C. coast and then in Va. Veterans held annual reunions here for many years. *Erected by Anderson County Historical Society and Palmetto Sharpshooters Camp #1428, Sons of Confederate Veterans, 1999*
GPS Coordinates: 34° 35.846' N, 82° 44.759' W

4–29 Clement Hoffman Stevens

St. Paul's Episcopal Church, E. Queen St. (S.C. Hwy. 300) between N. Depot St. and S. Elm St., Pendleton

(FRONT) Confederate Brig. Gen. Clement H. Stevens (1821–1864) is buried nearby in the Bee family plot. Born in Connecticut, Stevens moved to S.C. after his father's death in 1836. In 1861 he invented the first ironclad battery, which was built on Cummings Pt. near Charleston and helped bombard Ft. Sumter. As an aide to his brother-in-law Brig. Gen. Barnard E. Bee, he was wounded on 21 July 1861 at First Manassas.
(REVERSE) In 1862 Stevens and Ellison Capers formed the 24th S.C. Infantry, with Stevens as col. After commanding the 24th in battles from S.C. to Ga. such as Secessionville, Vicksburg, and Chickamauga, he was given a S.C.

brigade and promoted to brig. gen. in early 1864. Stevens was mortally wounded on 20 July 1864 at Peachtree Creek, near Atlanta, and died 25 July. First buried in Charleston, he was reinterred here. *Erected by Dixie Chapter #395, United Daughters of the Confederacy, 2000*
GPS Coordinates: 34° 39.097' N, 82° 46.618' W

4-30 Grace Episcopal Church

711 S. McDuffie St., Anderson

(FRONT) This parish, organized in 1851 with the Rev. Benjamin Webb as its first vicar, grew out of occasional Episcopal services held in Anderson as early as 1844. The first church here, a frame Carpenter Gothic building, was completed in 1860 on land donated by Daniel Brown. Housing Anderson's first pipe organ, a tower was added in 1883, and stained glass windows in 1888. An 1890 fire did moderate damage.
(REVERSE) The second church, a brick Gothic Revival building first used on Easter Sunday 1904, incorporated windows from the original church and a fine collection of Art Glass nave windows. Several bishops have served here, including Ellison Capers, Theodotus Capers, and Rogers Harris. In recent years, the parish sponsored outreach efforts such as the Sunshine House, Interfaith Ministries (AIM), and Meals-on-Wheels. *Erected by the Parish, 2001*
GPS Coordinates: 34° 29.968' N, 82° 38.856' W

4-31 Generostee A.R.P. Church

Parker Bowie Rd., Northwest of Iva

(FRONT) This church, the first Associate Reformed Presbyterian congregation in what is now Anderson County, was organized about 1790 about 1 ½ mi. SW of this site. Rev. Robert Irwin, its first regular minister, served from 1803 until his death in 1823. The first sanctuary on this site was a log building, replaced in 1828 by a frame sanctuary which served the congregation until 1897.
(REVERSE) The 1897 sanctuary burned in 1985 and was replaced by the present building, the fourth on this site and the fifth in church history, in 1986. Generostee was the mother church of three congregations: Midway, later

called Concord, active 1796-1844; Grove, active 1877-1947; and Iva, founded in 1895. The cemetery here includes the graves of many early church families. *Erected by the Anderson County Historical Society, 2001*
GPS Coordinates: 34° 18.417' N, 82° 42.7' W

4-32 Good Hope Presbyterian Church Cemetery

Just off Parker Bowie Rd., in the triangle formed by its junction with Warren Watt Rd. and Old Bell Rd., 3 miles North of Iva

(FRONT) This cemetery, dating from the early 19th century, is at the third site of Good Hope Presbyterian Church, founded in 1789. A frame sanctuary was built here in 1856 during the tenure of Rev. David Humphreys (d. 1869), who preached here 1821-1869 and was Good Hope's longest-serving pastor. In 1909 the congregation moved to Iva, three miles east, and built a new brick sanctuary there.
(REVERSE) The sanctuary built here in 1856, the third to serve Good Hope, was demolished in 1924, years after the congregation moved to Iva. Rev. Richard Cater Ligon (1845-1906), buried here, was pastor of Good Hope 1876-1902; his son Rev. J. Frank Ligon was pastor 1947-49. The church cemetery also includes plots of the Beaty, McAlister, McMahan, McKee, and other early families. *Erected by Good Hope Presbyterian Church, 2001*
GPS Coordinates: 34° 19.15' N, 82° 41.65' W

4-33 Dean/Dean's Station

S.C. Hwy. 81, 1 mile North of Starr

Dean (FRONT)
Dean is named for the Dean family, whose cemetery is located about a mile west. Samuel Dean came to South Carolina from Maryland in 1786 and settled here in the Mountain Creek area along with the Cummins and James families. Dean and his wife Gwendolyn James raised a large family and his descendants have lived here for more than two hundred years.
Dean's Station (REVERSE)
A depot was built at Dean in 1886 by the Savannah Valley Railroad (later the Charleston

and Western Carolina Railroad). Described by the *Anderson Intelligencer* in 1896 as "a very pretty little town," this rural community included the depot, a post office, several stores, a gristmill and sawmill, a blacksmith shop, a school, churches, and several residences. *Erected by the Anderson County Historical Society, 2002*
GPS Coordinates: 34° 24.017' N, 82° 41.267' W

4-34 Nazareth on the Beaverdam Presbyterian Church/Townville Presbyterian Church

Fairplay Rd., just South of its Junction with Jolly Rd., 2.5 miles West of Townville

Nazareth on the Beaverdam Presbyterian Church (FRONT)
This is the first known site of Townville Presbyterian Church, founded in this area in 1803 as Nazareth on the Beaverdam Presbyterian Church. The church held its services at members' homes until 1849, when the congregation purchased a frame building and half-acre site here for $1.50.
Townville Presbyterian Church (REVERSE)
In 1877 the congregation built a new sanctuary in Townville, 2.5 mi. W. The church was renamed Townville Presbyterian Church in 1885. The cemetery includes the graves of many early church families. In 2002 the Stevenson family donated this site to the Old Nazareth Cemetery Preservation Organization. *Erected by the Old Nazareth Cemetery Preservation Organization, 2002*
GPS Coordinates: 34° 32.144' N, 82° 55.573' W

4-35 St. Paul Methodist Church

2513 Brushy Creek Rd., Easley Vicinity

(FRONT) This church, founded in 1803, held its first services in the home of John Wilson and was first known as Wilson's Chapel. That year the congregation bought two acres here from George Head; the first church on this site was built in 1810. St. Paul's early ministers were circuit riders, as it was part of the Saluda District until it joined the Pendleton District in 1871.
(REVERSE) The second church, a frame cruciform building, was built here in 1897; it served

St. Paul's until it was torn down in 1982. The present brick sanctuary, built in 1984, includes several architectural elements from the 1897 church. The cemetery, with graves as early as 1842, includes the plots of many early families as well as graves of veterans of seven American wars and conflicts. *Erected by the Congregation and Friends of St. Paul United Methodist Church, 2008*
GPS Coordinates: 34° 46.717' N, 82° 32.333' W

4-36 Greenville & Columbia RR /Belton

Belton Area Museum, at the Belton Depot, 100 N. Main St., Belton

Greenville & Columbia RR (FRONT)
The Greenville & Columbia Railroad, founded in 1845, began construction in 1849. It reached Greenville in 1852, with a branch at this point to Anderson—the Blue Ridge Railroad. The town of Belton grew up around the junction of the two railroads, which later merged after the Civil War. The two rail lines made Belton the hub of passenger and freight service for Anderson District.
Belton (REVERSE)
Belton, incorporated in 1855, was named for Judge John Belton O'Neall, president of the G&C RR. Its square was laid out around the first depot. The Blue Ridge RR was acquired by the Southern Railway in the 1890s, and this depot was built in 1908–09. With an electric rail line added in 1902 and the arrival of the Piedmont & Northern RR in 1912, as many as 85 trains passed through Belton daily. *Erected by the Belton Area Museum Association, 2009*
GPS Coordinates: 34° 31.317' N, 82° 29.617' W

4-37 Townville Presbyterian Church

9001 S.C. Hwy. 24, Townville

(FRONT) This church, founded as Nazareth on the Beaverdam Presbyterian Church, was established in 1803. It met in members' homes until they paid $1.50 for a half-acre tract and built a small frame church 2.5 mi. E. The founders' cemetery there includes graves of early church families. The congregation moved here in 1877.

(REVERSE) The church was renamed Townville Presbyterian Church in 1885. This sanctuary was called "a handsome wooden edifice" at its dedication in 1877. In 1954 it was covered in brick veneer, with a new narthex and rear addition. Townville Academy, which stood behind the church, became a public school in 1902. *Erected by the Congregation and Friends of Townville Presbyterian Church in Memory of Mel Woody, 2010*
GPS Coordinates: 34° 33.856' N, 82° 54.165' W

4–38 "The Hundreds"

305 West Queen St., Pendleton

(FRONT) This area was a hub of African-American life from the late-19th to mid-20th centuries. Anderson County Training School, built ca. 1922 as a Rosenwald school, closed in 1954 under the equalization program for black and white schools. It burned in the 1960s. The agricultural building is now a community center. The Faith Cabin Library, built ca. 1935 by a program to give black schools their own libraries, is one of only two such libraries still standing in S.C.
(REVERSE) A frame store built nearby by Benjamin Horace Keese (1881–1975) and long known as the "Keese Barn" was a favorite gathering place for many years. Built ca. 1900 as a grocery store, it was later expanded and served as a cafe and antiques store/auction house. In 2003 Clemson University architecture students dismantled the Keese Barn and reused its historic materials to build the Memorial Block, to honor the store and its significance in Pendleton. *Erected by Pendleton Pride in Motion, 2011*
GPS Coordinates: 34° 39.15' N, 82° 47.217' W

4–39 Ebenezer Methodist Church

Due West Hwy. (S.C. Hwy. 185) and S.C. Hwy. 413, Ebenezer Community

(FRONT) This church, formally organized by about 1800, is thought to be the oldest Methodist congregation in Anderson County. Circuit riders and other itinerant ministers held early services in a nearby brush arbor. Its first and second churches were small log buildings.

A frame sanctuary, built by church member Samuel Emerson before the Civil War, was the first built on this site.
(REVERSE) Church trustees acquired this site in 1839, purchasing 3 acres from Amaziah Rice and George Manning for "a House or Place of Worship." The present frame church, built in 1909 by church members according to plans by Joe Hembree, features a double entrance with gabled porticos. The historic cemetery here includes graves of veterans from the American Revolution to the present. *Sponsored by the Congregation and the Kay Family Association, 2012*
GPS Coordinates: 34° 23.95' N, 82° 33.45' W

4–40 Belton Academy/Central School

306 Anderson St., Belton

Belton Academy (FRONT)
This site, on a lot donated by Dr. George Brown, was the location of a school for more than a century. Belton Academy, a private school with a classical curriculum, opened ca. 1851 as the town grew up around the new railroad junction. Brown's nephew, Dr. William Carroll Brown, was the academy's first professor. The academy stayed open during the Civil War but became a public school after it. A new frame two-story school for grades 1–10 was built here in 1893.
Central School (REVERSE)
The enrollment in Belton's schools grew rapidly after Belton Mill opened in 1899, and trustees approved this two-story brick school, called Central School, for grades 1–10. Built in 1908, it was designed by Anderson architect Joseph H. Casey. In 1922, when a new Belton High School was built, this school became Central Grammar School, for grades 1–6. It closed in 1973, was sold to the town of Belton, and was renovated and rededicated as Belton City Hall in 1976. *Sponsored by the Belton Area Museum Association, 2012*
GPS Coordinates: 34° 31.303' N, 82° 29.804' W

4-41 Temple B'nai Israel

1302 Oakland Ave., Anderson

(FRONT) Anderson's Jewish community dates to the antebellum era but grew significantly after 1900 with the arrival of several families from Eastern Europe. This congregation was founded as Temple B'nai Israel (Sons of Israel) as early as 1911. It held services in the Masonic Temple on the square and a number of other buildings in downtown Anderson before the construction of this synagogue in 1948. (REVERSE) After World War II, with the Jewish population of Anderson almost doubling in number since 1937, the congregation needed a permanent home. This 150-seat sanctuary, with classrooms, a social hall, and a kitchen, was completed in 1948, when the congregation numbered 20 to 25 families. B'nai Israel's first Torah, from Russia, had belonged to Sam Poliakoff's maternal grandparents. *Sponsored by the Jewish Historical Society of South Carolina, 2013*
GPS Coordinates: 34° 30.95' N, 82° 39.067' W

4-42 Chamberlain-Kay House

205 River St., Belton

(FRONT) This house, built ca. 1854 for railroad supervisor Charles C. Chamberlain, was among the first homes constructed in Belton. When the town incorporated in 1855, Chamberlain was chosen as the first intendant. Ira Williams, who was active in Democratic politics, bought the home in 1860 and it was the site of political rallies. In 1946 Judge William P. Kay purchased the house and his wife, Alice, operated the town kindergarten from here. (REVERSE) The Piedmont-style farmhouse originally fronted the town square and featured a long carriage drive lined by cedar trees. In the early 20th century the home was reoriented to face River St. Stylistically, the house exemplifies evolving architectural tastes, combining original Greek Revival elements with later Folk Victorian embellishments. It was listed in the National Register of Historic Places in 1980. *Sponsored by the Kay Family Association and the Belton Area Museum Association, 2014*
GPS Coordinates: 34° 31.456' N, 82° 29.451' W

4-43 Pelzer Schools

214 Lebby St., Pelzer

(FRONT) The first Pelzer Mills School, built in 1881, was a two-story frame building. The school was described as having "the air of a city school" and the mill funded a ten-month term at a time when three-months was common. The school was free and open to local children whether or not their families worked in the mill. The standard family contract at Pelzer Mills, however, required attendance for children aged 5–12. Children older than 12 were required to take a job in the mill. (REVERSE) By 1890 there were 175 students and 3 teachers. In 1900 a new graded school was built at the corner of Hale and Lebby Sts. It was destroyed by fire in 1902 and a new building was constructed. Smythe School and auditorium, both designed by Joseph Sirrine, were completed in 1922. The upper floors of Smythe School burned in 1949, but the lower stories were salvaged and remodeled. It continued as Pelzer Elementary School until 2009. *Sponsored by the Pelzer Heritage Commission, 2016*
GPS Coordinates: 34° 38.555' N, 82° 27.683' W

4-44 Mt. Pisgah Baptist Church

101 Pisgah Rd, Easley

(FRONT) Mt. Pisgah Baptist Church was founded in 1791 as Brush Creek Church with 10 members. In 1809, the church name was changed to Mt. Pisgah Baptist Church. The early church included white and African American members. In 1824, the 2nd church building was constructed of hewn and hand sawed timbers. Subsequent buildings, constructed in 1876 and 1926, still served the congregation in 2017. (REVERSE) Mt. Pisgah Church Cemetery began in 1814 on land donated by Fredrick Owen. Owen was a Revolutionary War veteran and is interred here. Veterans from the Revolutionary War forward are also interred here. Agnes Wimpey was the first known burial in 1814. The cemetery has remained in use for over 200 years. *Sponsored by Mt. Pisgah Baptist Church Cemetery Committee, 2017*
GPS Coordinates: 34° 43.118' N, 82° 34.534' W

4-45 Craytonville

Intersection of Clinkscales Rd., Bethany Church Rd., and Trail Rd., Honea Path vic.

(FRONT) Once Cherokee hunting grounds, the area was opened in 1784 by settlers obtaining grants for Revolutionary War service. Listed on early maps as Craytons, this crossroad became a thriving community in the early 1800s, featuring a store, tavern, public well and stagecoach stop. Said to be a favorite stopover of John C. Calhoun, the tavern was run by the Hanks, Crayton, and Orr families.

(REVERSE) A post office was established here in 1828 with Christopher Orr as postmaster. His son, James L. Orr, born here in 1822, would later serve as Speaker of the U.S. House of Reps. and S.C. Governor. Craytonville was a polling station and center of political activities through the 19th and early-20th centuries. The well, located across the road, has served the community since its beginning. *Sponsored by the Belton Area Museum Association, 2018*
GPS Coordinates: 34° 26.186' N, 82° 28.983' W

Bamberg County

5-1 Battle of Rivers' Bridge

Rivers Bridge State Park, off S.C. Hwy. 641, 7 miles Southwest of Ehrhardt

Here on February 3, 1865, the 17th U.S. Army Corps led by Major General Joseph A. Mower and Lieut. Gen. Giles A. Smith attacked the Confederate division of Major General Lafayette McLaws and forced the crossing of Salkehatchie River, after a gallant defense by outnumbered forces which held up for two days Sherman's march through Carolina. *Erected by the Edisto District, United Daughters of the Confederacy, 1967*
GPS Coordinates: 33° 3.88' N, 81° 5.57' W

5-2 Mt. Pleasant Church

S.C. Sec. Rd. 5-25, about 1 mile West of Ehrhardt

In 1835 St. Bartholomew Lutheran Church moved here from about 1 mile south and changed its name to Mt. Pleasant. It is generally accepted that this congregation was organized ca. 1750 and that John George Bamberg preached there shortly after 1798. In 1873 the S.C. Lutheran Synod met at Mt. Pleasant in a new building since incorporated into the present structure. *Erected by the Congregation, 1988*
GPS Coordinates: 33° 5.524' N, 81° 2.388' W

5-3 Mizpah Church

U.S. Hwy. 301 about 1 mile North of Salkehatchie River, Southwest of Bamberg

Methodist Church established by 1832. Present 1856 house of worship is all that remains of pre-Civil War settlement of Buford's Bridge. *Erected by Mizpah Methodist Church, 1992*
GPS Coordinates: 33° 7.191' N, 81° 10.801' W

5-4 Carlisle Military School

East Side of S. Carlisle St., between Elm and Green Sts., Bamberg

S.C. Methodists began an institution on this site in 1892 naming it Carlisle Fitting School, for James H. Carlisle, president of Wofford College 1875–1902. It served as a coeducational preparatory institution for Wofford. Col. James F. Risher (1889–1973) leased Carlisle in 1932 and purchased it 1938, renaming it Carlisle Military School by 1943. It educated young men from the U.S. and many countries until closing in 1977. *Erected by City of Bamberg Board of Public Works, 1994*
GPS Coordinates: 33° 17.687' N, 81° 1.928' W

5-5 St. Johns Baptist Church

S.C. Sec. Rd. 5-93, between Ehrhardt and Rivers Bridge State Park, Southwest of Ehrhardt

(FRONT) This church, established 1829–30, was first named Three Mile Creek Church and held early services in a brush arbor 4 mi. W on the Salkehatchie River. In 1839 it moved to this site donated by George Kinard and was renamed St. Johns Baptist Church. A permanent sanctuary was soon built, some of which is still extant within the present sanctuary, renovated in 1865, 1938, and 1961.

(REVERSE) In February 1865, near the end of the Civil War, Federal troops took up the floorboards for a bridge over the Salkehatchie River and stabled their horses in the church; the U.S. government reimbursed the church for damages in 1912. Two of St. Johns' most prominent ministers were Rev. E. W. Peeples, who served 18771908, and Rev. E. W. Hollis, who served 1933–1961. *Erected by the Congregation, 1997*
GPS Coordinates: 33° 4.104' N, 81° 3.953' W

5–6 Voorhees College

Entrance to the Voorhees College Campus, E. Voorhees Rd. (S.C. Sec. Rd. 5-12), Denmark

(FRONT) Voorhees College, founded by Elizabeth Evelyn Wright in 1897 as the Denmark Industrial School, was an effort to emphasize a vocational curriculum for rural African American students on the model of the Tuskegee Institute. The school, with funding from philanthropist Ralph Voorhees, was renamed Voorhees Industrial School for Colored Youth in 1904, Voorhees Normal and Industrial School in 1916, and Voorhees School and Junior College in 1947.

(REVERSE) Voorhees, supported by the Episcopal Church since 1924, changed its mission during the first half of the twentieth century and in 1962 became Voorhees College. In 1967 it became a senior liberal arts college. The historic portion of the campus was listed in the National Register of Historic Places in 1982 as the Voorhees College Historic District. *Erected by Voorhees College, 1998*
GPS Coordinates: 33° 18.53' N, 81° 7.858' W

5–7 AT&T Building

124 North Palmetto Ave., Denmark

This Georgian Revival building, completed in 1923 at a cost of $300,000, was the third

Denmark office of the American Telephone and Telegraph Company. In 1898 long-distance lines from Va. to Ga. and from Ala. to Charleston crossed here, making Denmark an excellent choice for a switching station. This building, described as "the most modern telephone plant in the south" when it opened, carried calls from N.Y. to Fla. and from Ala. to the East Coast for many years. *Erected by the City of Denmark, 1999*
GPS Coordinates: 33° 19.27' N, 81° 8.537' W

5–8 Buford's Bridge

Burton's Ferry Hwy. (U.S. Hwy. 321) and Buford's Bridge Hwy. (U.S. Hwy. 301) at Salkehatchie River, Ulmer

(FRONT) Buford's Bridge, the earliest settlement in what is now Bamberg County, was established as early as 1792, when William Buford maintained a bridge and operated a ferry over the Salkehatchie River. It grew throughout the nineteenth century, with several residences, four stores, two taverns, a boarding house, a Masonic lodge, and Mizpah Methodist Church here by the 1850s.

(REVERSE) On February 3–5, 1865, as Gen. W. T. Sherman's Federals advanced toward Columbia, units of Gen. J. A. Logan's XV Corps approached Buford's Bridge. Gen. Joseph Wheeler's Confederate cavalry burned the bridge, then evacuated the earthworks here before Logan arrived on Feb. 4th. Federals destroyed most of the buildings in the area to build bridges and left only Mizpah Methodist Church intact. *Erected by the Rivers Bridge Camp # 842, Sons of Confederate Veterans, 2002*
GPS Coordinates: 33° 7.034' N, 81° 10.952' W

5–9 Battle of Rivers Bridge/ Memorials at Rivers Bridge

Confederate Hwy. (S.C. Hwy. 641) at the entrance to Rivers Bridge State Historic Site, Ehrhardt Vicinity

Battle of Rivers Bridge (FRONT)
On February 2–3, 1865, as Gen. W. T. Sherman's Federals advanced toward Columbia, units of Gen. F. P. Blair's XVII Corps attempted to

cross the Salkehatchie River at Rivers Bridge. The Confederate defenders there, in Gen. Lafayette McLaws's division of the Dept. of S.C., Ga., and Fla., delayed the Federals for almost two days. Each side lost about 100 men killed, wounded, or captured.

Rivers Bridge Memorials (REVERSE)
In 1876 local men reburied the Confederate dead in a mass grave a mile from the earthworks and formed the Rivers Bridge Confederate Memorial Association. Their annual services commemorated the battle and the Southern dead. The Association also preserved the battlefield, deeding it to the state in 1945 as Rivers Bridge State Park, now Rivers Bridge State Historic Site. *Erected by the Rivers Bridge Camp # 842, Sons of Confederate Veterans, 2004* GPS Coordinates: 33° 2.763' N, 81° 5.671' W

5-10 Woodlands

Heritage Hwy. (U.S. Hwy. 78), near its junction with Gilmore Rd., Midway Vicinity, about 3 miles South of Bamberg

(FRONT) Woodlands was the country home of William Gilmore Simms (1806–1870), the most prominent and prolific writer of the antebellum South, from 1836 to his death. A novelist, poet, historian, critic, and essayist best known for his novels about colonial and Revolutionary S.C., Simms was described as "the ornament and the pride of the State he loved so well" at his death in 1870.
(REVERSE) In 1836 Simms, a widower, married Chevillette Roach (1817–1863) of Barnwell District. He and his wife moved to this 4,000-acre plantation owned by her father, Nash Roach. The house burned in 1862, was rebuilt, burned again in 1865, and rebuilt on a smaller scale in 1867. Woodlands, described in a Simms poem as "these grand old woods," was designated a National Historic Landmark in 1975. *Erected by the Historical Society of Bamberg County, 2005* GPS Coordinates: 33° 16.349' N, 80° 57.625' W

5-11 South Carolina Canal & Rail Road Company

At the Intersection of Main Hwy. (U.S. Hwy. 301) and Heritage Hwy. (U.S. Hwy. 78), Bamberg

ORIGINAL TRACK LOCATION
Began first successful scheduled steam railroad service in America on December 25, 1830, and by 1833 its 136 miles from Charleston to Hamburg made it the world's longest railroad. It was later part of the Southern Railway 1894–1982, and then Norfolk Southern Railway 1982–1996. The tracks were removed in 1996. *Erected by the City of Bamberg, 2006, replacing a marker erected by the American Society of Civil Engineers in 1970* GPS Coordinates: 33° 15.067' N, 80° 48.95' W

5-12 Mountain Home Plantation

George's Creek Rd. and Ehrhardt Rd. (S.C. Sec. Rd. 5-22), Govan Vicinity

(FRONT) Mountain Home Plantation, named for the hill on which it is located, was established before the Civil War. In 1859 Samuel J. Hartzog (1823–1890) bought the plantation from his brother Joseph (1826–1862), and built this two-story brick house that same year, at a cost of $2,993.08. It was originally a Greek Revival house with a full-width two-story portico and turned posts.
(REVERSE) Cotton grown and processed here was hauled by wagon to the railroad at Graham's Turn Out (now Denmark). Samuel and Mary Hartzog's sons Henry Simms Hartzog (1866–1953), born here, was the third president of Clemson College (now Clemson University), 1897–1902. In the 1940s the house was remodeled in the Classical Revival style, with a second-story balcony and columns. *Erected by the Historical Society of Bamberg County and the Frank J. and Lucy C. Hartzog Memorial Foundation, Inc., 2006* GPS Coordinates: 33° 13.124' N, 81° 12.613' W

5-13 Salem Methodist Church

Old Salem Rd., at its junction with Juniper Creek Rd. (S.C. Sec. Rd. 5-366), about 3 miles Northwest of Govan

(FRONT) This church, founded by 1818, held its early services in a brush arbor; the first permanent sanctuary was built nearby. In 1848 Capt. J. D. Allen sold this 4-acre site to the trustees for $1.00. The present church, built soon afterwards, has been renovated several times since. The cemetery dates from 1856; its first burials were young children of Henry and Mary Ann Hartzog.

(REVERSE) Four members later became ministers: Revs. Charles Wilson (1802–1873), Jeremiah W. Collins (1824–1880), Holland Nimmons McTyeire (1824–1889), and B. T. Huggins (1922–2008). McTyeire, born on a farm nearby, was a Methodist bishop from 1866 until his death but is best known as the father of Vanderbilt University in Nashville, Tennessee, which he founded in 1873. *Erected by the Historical Society of Bamberg County and the Frank J. and Lucy C. Hartzog Memorial Foundation, Inc., 2009*
GPS Coordinates: 33° 15.465' N, 81° 12.758' W

5–14　Pinewood Plantation

3141 Capernaum Rd., Bamberg

(FRONT) This plantation was the home of Maj. William Seaborn Bamberg (1820–1858), planter, merchant, and the founder of Bamberg. Maj. Bamberg, a native of what was then Barnwell District, returned to this area from Georgia in the late 1840s. The town of Bamberg, called "Lawrey's Turnout" or Lawreys, was little more than a stop on the S.C. Railroad before a post office opened there in 1850.

(REVERSE) William Seaborn Bamberg, who built a store and depot at Lawreys by 1850 and built a hotel there in 1853, was the town's first mayor. Lawreys was renamed Bamberg for him in 1854, and chartered in 1855. W. S. Bamberg died before the present house at Pinewood was completed in 1859; his widow Philippine Piquette Bamberg (1820–1895), a native of France, lived here until her death. *Erected by The Historic Society of Bamberg County, Inc., 2010*
GPS Coordinates: 33° 17.12' N, 81° 5.652' W

5–15　Holman's Bridge

Holman's Bridge Rd. (State Rd. 34), approximately ½ mi. s. of South Edisto River, Denmark vicinity

(FRONT) In 1801 John Holman constructed a bridge spanning the South Fork of the Edisto River at a site previously known as Tyler's Ferry, about ½ mi. N. of here. Two acts of the General Assembly granted Holman the right to charge a toll for people, wagons, and livestock for a period of 28 years. In 1829 the crossing transferred to public ownership, with Barnwell and Orangeburg Districts sharing control.

(REVERSE) In Feb. 1865 retreating Confederate troops burned Holman's Bridge in an effort to slow the advance of the Union XV Corps during the Carolinas Campaign. Rebuilt after the Civil War, the crossing remained in use into the 20th century. By that time the land around the bridge on the south bank had become an established campground and recreation area known as "Holman's Beach." *Sponsored by Decendants of John Holman Sr. and Historic Society of Bamberg County, 2015*
GPS Coordinates: 33° 23.837' N, 81° 9.558' W

5–16　Denmark High School

4599 Carolina Hwy. (U.S. Rt. 321), Denmark

(FRONT) Denmark High School is the second school located at this spot. The first Denmark School, designed by Charles Coker Wilson, was completed in 1908 and once stood adjacent to the current building. The core of the current school was constructed in 1920. A gym addition was built in 1932 and a substantial classroom wing was added in 1948. In 1934 the school became one of the first in the state to have a lighted football field and play games at night.

(REVERSE) The building remained in use as a high school until 1957 when Denmark and Olar Schools consolidated. After the high school moved, the building was used as an elementary school until 1987. Among the prominent architectural features of the school are the gable-roof entrances. The 1920 entrance has a two-tiered glass transom and the 1948 entrance is framed by a segmental limestone arch. Denmark H.S. was listed in the National Register of Historic Places in 2001. *Sponsored by the Historic Society of Bamberg, Inc. and the Frank J. and Lucy C. Hartzog Memorial Foundation, Inc., 2016*
GPS Coordinates: 33° 19.672' N, 81° 8.503' W

5–17 Denmark Industrial School

1930 Church St., Denmark

(FRONT) The Denmark Industrial School was started by Elizabeth Evelyn Wright after she made attempts to start a school for black children in McNeill, Early Branch, Ruffin, Hampton, Brunson, Fairfax, Ulmer, Ehrhardt, and Govan. Wright faced suspicion, racism, and multiple arson attacks in her efforts to found the school. On April 14, 1897, Miss Wright opened this school with 14 students.
(REVERSE) Wright, a graduate of Booker T. Washington's Tuskegee Normal and Industrial School, sought to extend Washington's support for vocational training and teacher education. This building, owned by Teresa Sontag, was also a general store. In October Wright moved to a second location before moving to a 280-acre campus in 1902. In that year the school was renamed Voorhees Industrial School. *Sponsored by The Joseph C. Sanders Foundation, 2017*
GPS Coordinates: 33° 19.395' N, 81° 7.630' W

5–18 Bamberg County Courthouse

2959 Main Hwy. (U.S. Hwy. 301), Bamberg

(FRONT) Bamberg County, named for Gen. Francis Marion Bamberg, was formed in 1897. One of the first projects undertaken was the construction of a new courthouse and jail. The construction was financed by the City of Bamberg in return for the county seat being located here. Designed by architect L. F. Goodrich, the courthouse is built of red brick with solid masonry walls that measure two feet thick.
(REVERSE) The original location of the courthouse was on the western side of North Main St. When Hwy. 301 was relocated, however, it ran directly through the courthouse grounds. It was ultimately decided to move the massive building across the highway. Work began in 1950 and the total cost of moving the building 300 feet was $25,000. At that time the building was also remodeled, giving it a more modern appearance. *Sponsored by Bamberg County & Historic Society of Bamberg County, Inc., 2019*
GPS Coordinates: 33° 17.894' N, 81° 2.064' W

Barnwell County

6–1 Winton County Court House Site

S.C. Hwy. 3, about 5 miles South of Barnwell

Originally Barnwell County was part of Granville County, later a part of Orangeburg District. Winton County was created by act of the legislature on Mar. 12, 1785. Justices William Robertson, John Parkinson, Thomas Knight, Richard Treadway, Daniel Green, William Buford and James Fair were directed to erect a court house, gaol, pillory, whipping post, and stocks. These were built of pine logs. Winton County became Barnwell District in 1798 and Barnwell County in 1868. *Erected by the General John Barnwell Chapter, D. A. R.* [Erected 1951]
GPS Coordinates: 33° 9.867' N, 81° 23.43' W

6–2 Ellenton Agricultural Club/ Town of Ellenton

S.C. Hwy. 64, West City Limits of Barnwell

Ellenton Agricultural Club (FRONT)
Established March 24, 1894, this agricultural club was organized to promote the welfare and interests of the Ellenton farmers and to improve conditions generally. The first clubhouse, built in 1904, was moved here in 1953 after the town of Ellenton was abandoned to make way for the Savannah River Plant.
Town of Ellenton (REVERSE)
By 1873, a post office named Ellentown was located on the Port Royal Railroad, about 20 miles west of here. In 1880 the town of Ellenton was incorporated. According to local tradition, the town was named for Ellen Dunbar, a local resident. Ellenton was abandoned in the early 1950s to make way for the Savannah

River Plant. *Erected by the Ellenton Agricultural Club 1980*
GPS Coordinates: 33° 14.484' N, 81° 25.428' W

6–5 Blackville: Town of the Phoenix /Battle of Blackville, 1865

Instruction of S.C. Hwy. 3 and Main St., Blackville

Blackville: Town of the Phoenix (FRONT)
Blackville was founded in 1833 as the first overnight stop on the new railroad operated by the S.C. Canal & Railroad Co. It was also the scene of 4 major fires in the late 19th century (in 1865, 1876, 1887, and 1888), each of which almost destroyed the town. Editor A. E. Gonzales nicknamed Blackville "The Town of the Phoenix" in 1889 in honor of its ability to rise again and again from the ashes and rebuild.
Battle of Blackville, 1865 (REVERSE)
Early on February 7, 1865, Federal cavalry under Brig. Gen. Judson Kilpatrick advanced to Blackville from Barnwell. Col. Thomas J. Jordan's brigade attacked a Confederate cavalry brigade under Col. James Hagan, drove it through the town and three miles beyond, and captured many prisoners, scattering the rest. Kilpatrick destroyed the railroad at Blackville and advanced west to Reynolds Station, between Blackville and Williston, that night. *Erected by the Town of Blackville and the Blackville Historical Society, 1996*
GPS Coordinates: 33° 21.307' N, 81° 16.277' W

6–5 Morris Ford Earthworks, 1780 & 1865

[This marker was mistakenly double-numbered. It should have been marker 6–6.]

Old Allendale Hwy. (S.C. Sec. Rd. 6-70) just North of the Salkehatchie River, Blackville Vicinity

(FRONT) Nearby earthworks at Morris Ford, on the Salkehatchie River, built in the spring of 1780 by Loyalists under Ben John. In May, soon after Charleston fell to the British, Capt. John Mumford of the South Carolina militia was killed in action in a clash with John's Loyalists; he is buried at the site. In early 1865 Confederate cavalry under Maj. Gen. Joseph Wheeler rebuilt the old earthworks.

(REVERSE) Wheeler delayed the advancing Federal cavalry under Brig. Gen. Judson Kilpatrick. On February 6th a sharp skirmish occurred at the works. Elements of Kilpatrick's force crossed downstream, outflanked the Confederate cavalry and forced it to withdraw, then advanced to Barnwell while Wheeler's cavalry withdrew toward Aiken. Kilpatrick's Federals burned most of Barnwell later that night. *Erected by the Barnwell County Museum and Historical Board, 1997*
GPS Coordinates: 33° 12.568' N, 81° 21.165' W

6–7 Tarlton Brown (1757–1845)

Boiling Springs Rd. (S.C. Sec. Rd. 6-39), between Lyndhurst Rd. (S.C. Sec. Rd. 6-121) and June Ln., Boiling Springs

(FRONT) The grave of Tarlton Brown (1757–1845), militia officer, state representative, and state senator, is located here. Brown, a native of Virginia, moved to S.C. at an early age and settled in what was then Orangeburg District, near Briar Creek and Savannah River. He enlisted as a pvt. in the S.C. militia in 1776, was commissioned a lt. in 1778, and promoted to capt. in 1780.
(REVERSE) Brown, who served in the Revolution under Gens. Francis Marion and Andrew Pickens, wrote his memoirs in 1843, first published in 1862. After the war Brown served as coroner and sheriff of what was then Winton Co., then in the S.C. House 1792–97 and in the Senate 1797–99, resigning to become sheriff of the new Barnwell District, a position he held 1799–1804; he died in 1845 at age 88. *Erected by Barnwell Co. Museum and Historical Board, 1998*
GPS Coordinates: 33° 8.157' N, 81° 26.126' W

6–8 Boiling Springs Academy

Boiling Springs Rd. (S.C. Sec. Rd. 6-39), near its intersection with Lyndhurst Rd. (S.C. Sec. Rd. 6-121), Boiling Springs

(FRONT) Boiling Springs Academy was founded by the Boiling Springs Academical Society in 1823, with trustees Hansford Duncan, John Fowke, James Furse, William Gillette, Gideon Hagood, Fredrick Hay, Lawrence Hext, James

Higginbotham, Jennings O'Bannon, and Angus Patterson. The academy building, along with its records, was burned by Federal troops in February 1865.

(REVERSE) The academy was reopened, and the present one-room school building constructed, in 1908, largely through the efforts of Boiling Springs teacher Olive Hay. Students from grades one through seven attended the academy until it closed in 1947. The academy, which was purchased by Boiling Springs Presbyterian Church in 1969, now serves as a community center. *Erected by Barnwell Co. Museum and Historical Board, 1998*

GPS Coordinates: 33° 8.122' N, 81° 25.906' W

6–9 Boiling Springs Presbyterian Church

Boiling Springs Rd. (S.C. Sec. Rd. 6-39), 1 mile West of S.C. Hwy. 3, Boiling Springs

(FRONT) This church was organized in 1842 by Rev. James H. Thornwell on authority from the Charleston Presbytery; F. J. and W. A. Hay were its first elders. By 1846 Rev. Samuel H. Hay preached on alternate Sundays here and at a new church in Barnwell; this congregation soon merged with the new one as Barnwell Presbyterian Church.

(REVERSE) In 1896 Rev. F. L. Leeper and Dr. W. S. Hay, appointed by the Presbytery, reorganized Boiling Springs as a separate congregation with O. B. Hay and J. M. Gantt as elders and J. C. Fowke as deacon. The present sanctuary was built in 1897 by Hay Gantt and other members; the Sunday School building was built in 1955. *Erected by Barnwell Co. Museum and Historical Board, 1998*

GPS Coordinates: 33° 8.099' N, 81° 25.762' W

6–10 Bethlehem Baptist Church

177 Wall St., Barnwell

(FRONT) This church, officially organized in 1868, had its origins in the antebellum Barnwell Baptist Church, which was located on this site until about 1854, when it built a new church on another lot. At that time several free blacks and slaves who were members of Barnwell Baptist Church asked to use the old

1829 sanctuary for worship and meetings. The congregation agreed, and the group met here informally until 1868.

(REVERSE) In 1868 seven black members of Barnwell Baptist Church asked the congregation for letters of dismissal, which were granted so that they could formally organize Bethlehem Baptist Church. The old Barnwell Baptist Church sanctuary served Bethlehem Baptist Church until it was demolished in 1898. Some material was salvaged to build the present sanctuary, which was renovated in 1981. *Erected by Barnwell Co. Museum and Historical Board, 1999*

GPS Coordinates: 33° 14.763' N, 81° 21.918' W

6–11 Lower Three Runs Baptist Church

Patterson Mill Rd. (S.C. Sec. Rd. 6-20), between Snelling and Martin

(FRONT) This church, originally located 8/10 mi. W on the old Augusta-to-Charleston road, was founded in 1789 by twelve charter members, with Rev. Nathaniel Walker as its first pastor. Lower Three Runs was a mother church to at least five congregations organized in present-day Barnwell or Allendale Counties between 1802 and 1849.

(REVERSE) The second sanctuary here, built in 1833, was demolished in 1865 by Federal troops who used the timbers to bridge Lower Three Runs; it was never rebuilt. In 1868 Rev. C. A. Baynard and 213 members joined Tom's Branch Baptist Church, renamed Lower Three Runs to preserve the history and traditions of the mother church. *Erected by the Congregation, 2001*

GPS Coordinates: 33° 11.538' N, 81° 28.003' W

6–12 Barnwell County Courthouse

East Side of Solomon Blatt Ave. (S.C. Hwy. 3) between Pascallas and Reynolds Sts., Blackville

The county courthouse was on this site from 1871 to 1874. In 1869 Republican state senator Charles P. Leslie, a native of New York, sponsored an act to move the county seat from Barnwell to Blackville. Court was first held in a church until a two-story brick courthouse

was built at a cost of $8000. After the county seat returned to Barnwell the courthouse housed Blackville Academy, later a public school. *Erected by the Barnwell County Council, 2001*
GPS Coordinates: 33° 21.406' N, 81° 16.242' W

6–13 Barnwell County Courthouse

Intersection of Main St. (S.C. Sec. Rd. 6-70) and Wall St., Barnwell

(FRONT) Barnwell County, originally Winton County, was created out of Orangeburg District in 1785. Renamed Barnwell District in 1798 for John Barnwell (1748–1800), a S.C. militia officer in the Revolution and afterwards, it became Barnwell County in 1868. The first courthouse was built at Boiling Springs in 1789 and was replaced by a courthouse built here in 1800. Later courthouses here were built in 1819 and 1848.
(REVERSE) The 1848 courthouse was burned by Federal troops in 1865. Court was held at Barnwell Presbyterian Church 1865–69 and again 1874–78. The county seat moved to Blackville 1869–73 but returned to Barnwell permanently in 1874. This courthouse, the fourth on this site, was built in 1878–79 and enlarged in 1901 and 1921. The nearby sundial, donated by state senator J. D. Allen (1812–1880), was erected in 1858. *Erected by the Barnwell County Museum and Historical Board, and the Barnwell County Council, 2001*
GPS Coordinates: 33° 14.63' N, 81° 21.904' W

6–14 Hilda

E. Main St. (S.C. Sec. Rd. 6-59), near Collins Ave. (S.C. Sec. Rd. 6-14), Hilda

Hilda, in the "Sleytown" section of Barnwell County, was chartered in 1910. It grew up around a depot built here in 1903, soon after the Atlantic Coast Line R.R. extended its line through the area in 1897. H.C. Hutto was its first intendant, or mayor, and G. W. Delk, J. H. Delk, D. A. Dyches, and W. M. Dyches were its first wardens. According to tradition, Hilda was named for the friend or daughter of someone associated with the railroad. *Erected*

by the Frank J. and Lucy Cook Hartzog Foundation, 2002
GPS Coordinates: 33° 16.42' N, 81° 14.769' W

6–15 Barnwell

Collins Park, Corner of Main St. (S.C. Hwy. 70) and Marlboro Ave. (S.C. Hwy. 3), Barnwell

(FRONT) Barnwell, originally called "Red Hill" and later "the Village," was founded in 1800 when a courthouse was built on land donated by Benjamin Odom. Both Winton County and its new county seat were renamed for John Barnwell (1748–1800), a S.C. militia officer in the Revolution and afterwards. Barnwell was incorporated in 1829 with the town limits extending ¾ mi. from the courthouse. The heart of the city is the Circle, with its unique 1858 vertical sundial.
(REVERSE) Barnwell is perhaps best known for the dedicated public service of its citizens as governors, legislators, and jurists. The city is also known as the home of the "Barnwell Ring," a powerful group of twentieth-century Barnwell politicians who included Joseph Emile Harley, lt. governor 1934–41 and governor 1941–42; Edgar A. Brown, president pro tem of the S.C. Senate 1942–72, and Solomon Blatt, speaker of the S.C. House 1937–46 and 1951–73. *Erected by the City of Barnwell and the Collins Park Committee, 2002*
GPS Coordinates: 33° 14.675' N, 81° 21.557' W

6–16 Macedonia Baptist Church

3572 Dexter St. (U.S. Hwy. 78), Blackville

(FRONT) This church, the first African-American Baptist church in Barnwell County, was founded in 1866 when Rev. James T. Tolbert preached in Blackville under a brush arbor; the first sanctuary was built in 1868. The church hosted the first state convention of black Baptists, held here in 1875, and built its second sanctuary by 1887. The present sanctuary was built here in 1976.
(REVERSE) This is the mother church of eight churches founded 1867–1922: Ebenezer, Frost Branch, Pilgrim Rest, St. Peter, Sunshine, Tabernacle, Shrub Branch, and Central. Macedonia Baptist Association, which promoted the

education of area blacks, opened Macedonia School nearby in 1890. Macedonia High School was built here in 1954 and taught grades 1–12 until 1970, when it became Macedonia Middle School. *Erected by the Barnwell County Museum and Historical Board, 2002* GPS Coordinates: 33° 21.222' N, 81° 16.44' W

6–17 Ashley-Willis House

Corner of W. Main St. (S.C. Sec. Rd. 6-33) and David St., Williston

(FRONT) This Greek Revival house was built between 1833 and 1850 and features a wide gable-front form unusual for the period. John Ashley and then Elijah Willis owned this land before 1850; the house was likely built by the Ashley family. Williston, chartered in 1858, was named for the Willis family, which gave land for a depot on the S.C. Rail Road, for a church (now First Baptist Church), and for a school.
(REVERSE) The town's oldest house occupies a prominent location between the S.C. Rail Road and the Augusta-Charleston Road. As Gen. W. T. Sherman's Federal army advanced through the area on February 8–9, 1865, Gen. Judson Kilpatrick used this house as his headquarters before burning most of the town and proceeding to Aiken and Columbia. The house was listed in the National Register of Historic Places in 2004. *Erected by the Barnwell County Historical and Museum Board, 2007* GPS Coordinates: 33° 24.285' N, 81° 25.703' W

6–18 Bank of Barnwell/Edgar A. Brown Law Office

Corner of Main and Jefferson Sts., Barnwell

Bank of Barnwell (FRONT)
This building, constructed in 1887 as the Bank of Barnwell, was home to a succession of banks for 116 years. The bank occupied the first floor, and the law offices occupied the second floor, with additions in 1950 and 1961. This was the Bank of Barnwell 1887–1909, Western Carolina Bank 1909–1932, the Bank of Barnwell 1932–1963, State Bank and Trust from 1963 to the late 1970s, then housed several bank branches until First Citizens Bank

of S.C. was the last, 1995–2003.
Edgar A. Brown Law Office (REVERSE)
The law firm of Edgar A. Brown (1888–1975) occupied the second floor for more than sixty years, with later partners since. One partner, Herman Mazursky, was Barnwell's longest-serving mayor. Brown, one of the powerful politicians in "the Barnwell Ring," is best known as president pro tem of the S.C. Senate 1942–1972. The City of Barnwell renovated this building in 2008, with city hall on the first floor. *Sponsored by the City of Barnwell, 2012* GPS Coordinates: 33° 14.614' N, 81° 21.902' W

6–19 Fuller Park

Dunbarton Blvd., between Cemetery Rd. and Turkey Creek, Barnwell

(FRONT) This park, built and opened in 1933 with funding from the Reconstruction Finance Corporation (RFC), was named for Cornell G. Fuller (1895–1972), mayor of Barnwell 1932–38 and chair of this and other New Deal-era public projects in Barnwell. The park included a swimming pool and bathhouse, dance pavilion, tennis courts, and baseball stadium. The minor league Albany (N.Y.) Senators held spring training at Fuller Park for several years in the 1930s and 1940s.
(REVERSE) Fuller, an Ohio native, was a contractor and early innovator in building roads of asphalt instead of concrete. He moved his company to Barnwell in 1928 and paved 50 miles of the state's earliest asphalt roads, in Barnwell County. In 1932 Fuller, with S.C. Senator Edgar A. Brown and Perry A. Price, founded the Bank of Barnwell. When the Barnwell County Public Library was founded in 1953 Fuller and his wife Effie Barber Fuller donated their house as the new library. *Sponsored by the City of Barnwell, 2012* GPS Coordinates: 33° 14.715' N, 81° 22.111' W

6–20 Red Hill at Turkey Creek

Intersection of Dunbarton Blvd. and Jackson St., Barnwell

(FRONT) This high bluff was called Red Hill in the colonial era. It overlooks Turkey Creek,

which flows into the Great Salkehatchie River. The Charleston-to-Augusta road, along an old Indian trail, crossed the creek nearby. The waters of Turkey Creek and White Oak Springs, just north of this site, were incentives for the early settlement and development of what would later become Barnwell.
(REVERSE) McHeath's Tavern, the first business in what became Barnwell, was built nearby before the Revolution. The town, a county seat since 1785 when Winton District (later Barnwell District, and then Barnwell County) was created, was long called Barnwell Court House. Two cemeteries a short distance east, both established about 1800, include the graves of some of Barnwell's earliest families.
Sponsored by the City of Barnwell, 2012
GPS Coordinates: 33° 14.719' N, 81° 22.14' W

Beaufort County

7–1 Beaufort

U.S. Hwy. 21, ½ mile South of S.C. Hwy. 170, Beaufort

Second Oldest Town In South Carolina/Authorized by the Lords Proprietors, December 20, 1710,/ Chartered January 17, 1711./ Laid Out Prior to February 16, 1717,/ Incorporated by the State, December 17, 1803. *The Beaufort County Historical Society [1950]*
GPS Coordinates: 32° 26.416' N, 80° 41.152' W

7–2 Bluffton, S.C.

May River Rd. (S.C. Hwy. 46), Bluffton

Settled in 1825 as a summer resort of rice and cotton planters, this town was incorporated in 1852. Here in 1844 was launched the protest against the federal tariff known as the "Bluffton Movement." *The Beaufort County Historical Society* [Erected 1950] [Replaced by marker 7-51 in 2014]
GPS Coordinates: 32° 14.246' N, 80° 52.448' W

7–3 Chapel of Ease

Lands End Rd. (S.C. Sec. Rd. 7-45), St. Helena Island

To St. Helena's Church, Beaufort, S.C./Built about 1740/Made a separate Church/after the Revolution/Burned by Forest Fire/Feb. 22, 1886. *Beaufort County Historical Society*
GPS Coordinates: 32° 22.551' N, 80° 34.603' W

7–4 Prince William's Parish Church (Sheldon Church)

Old Sheldon Church Rd. (S.C. Sec. Rd. 7-21), just North of Bailey Rd., Gardens Corner vicinity

(FRONT) These ruins are of Prince William's Parish Church, built ca. 1751–57 and partially burned during the American Revolution, with its interior and roof rebuilt 1825–26. This Anglican church was primarily paid for by Lt. Gov. William Bull I (1683–1755), who is buried here. It is often called Sheldon, after Bull's plantation.
(REVERSE) Local Loyalists burned the church in 1779 during a raid by Gen. Augustine Prevost. It was assumed by many area residents in 1865 and has been widely believed since that Federal troops burned Sheldon Church during the last months of the Civil War. It was actually dismantled by local freedmen ca. 1865–67. *Sponsored by the Beaufort County Historical Society, 2013, replacing a marker erected by the society in 1955*
GPS Coordinates: 32° 37.091' N, 80° 46.866' W

7–5 Battle of Port Royal Island

Trask Parkway (U.S. Hwy. 21), near its intersection with Parker dr., N of Naval Air Station Beaufort, Grays Hill

Near the old halfway house, in the vicinity of Grays Hill, on February 3, 1779, a force of South Carolina militia, continentals, and volunteers, including men from Beaufort, under General William Moultrie, defeated the British in their attempt to capture Port Royal

Island. *Erected by Beaufort County Historical Society*
GPS Coordinates: 32° 28.849' N, 80° 44.387' W

7–6 "Robbers Row"

Ft. Walker Dr., near its Intersection with North Port Royal Dr., Port Royal Plantation, Hilton Head Island

After the occupation of Hilton Head in 1861, a civilian town grew up to serve the needs of the large Union base and its garrison here. The town boasted a hotel, a theater, 2 newspapers, and numerous stores, restaurants and saloons, centering along a street officially Suttlers Row but usually called Robbers Row, which ran east from this point about ½ mile to the army tent encampment. *Erected by Hilton Head Island Historical Society, 1961*
GPS Coordinates: 32° 13.952' N, 80° 40.632' W

7–7 Battle of Port Royal

Ft. Walker Dr., Port Royal Plantation, Hilton Head Island

A decisive battle in the Civil War took place here on Nov. 7, 1861, when 18 Union warships with about 55 supporting craft led by Adm. S. F. DuPont bombarded for 4 ½ hours the Confederate forces in Fort Walker on this shore and Fort Beauregard on the opposite point. About 13,000 troops under Gen. Thomas W. Sherman then landed on this beach to establish the main Union blockade base on the South Atlantic coast. *Erected by Hilton Head Island Historical Society, 1961*
GPS Coordinates: 32° 14.103' N, 80° 40.696' W

7–8 Fort Sherman

Ft. Sherman Dr., left side of Road at Bike Path, Port Royal Plantation, Hilton Head Island

Completed in 1862, this large earth fort was designed to defend the great Union blockade base on Hilton Head against Confederate land attack. Named after the first Union commander here, Gen. Thomas W. Sherman, the fort consists of two miles of earthworks enclosing a 14-acre area. With other fortifications Fort Sherman formed part of a defensive line 5 miles long across the north end of the island.

Erected by Hilton Head Island Historical Society, 1961
GPS Coordinates: 32° 13.336' N, 80° 40.743' W

7–9 Fort Walker

Ft. Walker Dr., on right just beyond its intersection with North Port Royal Dr., overlooking Port Royal Sound, Port Royal Plantation, Hilton Head Island

Hastily built in 1861 to protect the S.C. coast against Union attack, Fort Walker, commanded by Col. William C. Heyward, bore the brunt of the Union attack on November 7, 1861, when after 4 ½ hours, with only 3 guns left serviceable and ammunition almost gone, the troops under Gen. Thomas F. Drayton were forced to withdraw from the island. Rebuilt by the Union forces, it was renamed Fort Welles. *Erected by Hilton Head Island Historical Society, 1961*
GPS Coordinates: 32° 13.965' N, 80° 40.629' W

7–10 Beaufort Arsenal

713 Craven St., Beaufort

Erected in 1798 and rebuilt in 1852, the Beaufort Arsenal was the home of the Beaufort Volunteer Artillery, commissioned in 1802, which had its roots in an earlier company organized in 1776 and served valiantly in the Revolutionary War. The BVA was stationed at Fort Beauregard during the Battle of Port Royal on November 7, 1861. *Erected by Beaufort County Historical Society, 1961*
GPS Coordinates: 32° 25.961' N, 80° 40.226' W

7–11 Hilton Head

Ft. Walker Dr., Port Royal Plantation, Hilton Head Island

A prominent landmark for mariners since the voyages of the early Spanish explorers, this headland was known to the English as Hilton Head after the voyage in 1663 of Captain William Hilton which led to their first permanent settlement in Carolina. By the late eighteenth century the island had become known as Hilton Head Island. *Erected by Hilton Head Island Historical Society, 1963*
GPS Coordinates: 32° 14.095' N, 80° 40.689' W

7–12 Zion Chapel of Ease and Cemetery

William Hilton Parkway (U.S. Hwy. 278) at Matthews Dr., Hilton Head Island

A chapel of St. Luke's Parish, established May 23, 1767, built of wood shortly after 1786 under the direction of Captain John Stoney and Isaac Fripp, was consecrated in 1833. Members of the Barksdale, Baynard, Chaplin, Davant, Fripp, Kirk, Mathews, Pope, Stoney and Webb families worshipped here. By 1868 the chapel was destroyed. *Erected by Hilton Head Island Historical Society, 1973*
GPS Coordinates: 32° 12.118' N, 80° 41.961' W

7–13 Revolutionary War Ambush

William Hilton Parkway (U.S. Hwy. 278) at Matthews Dr., 100 ft. West of Zion Chapel of Ease marker, Hilton Head Island

In December 1781, returning from a patrol with the Patriot militia, Charles Davant was mortally wounded from ambush near here by Captain Martinangel's Royal Militia from Daufuskie Island. He managed to ride his horse to his nearby plantation, Two Oaks, where he died. Captain John Leacraft's Bloody Legion avenged his death. *Erected by Hilton Head Island Historical Society, 1973*
GPS Coordinates: 32° 12.154' N, 80° 41.969' W

7–14 Tabernacle Baptist Church /Robert Smalls

907 Craven St., Beaufort

Tabernacle Baptist Church (FRONT)
Tabernacle Church was formed by black members of Beaufort Baptist Church after other members evacuated the area due to Federal occupation in 1861. The Beaufort church's lecture room was used for services during the war. In 1867 the black congregation bought this property from the Beaufort Baptist Church. Its present building was dedicated in 1894. Many new churches have grown from Tabernacle.
Robert Smalls (REVERSE)
Born a slave in Beaufort in 1839, Robert Smalls lived to serve as a Congressman of the United States. In 1862 he commandeered and delivered to Union forces the Confederate gunboat "Planter," on which he was a crewman. His career as a freedman included service as a delegate to the 1868 and 1895 State Constitutional Conventions, election to the S.C. House and Senate, and 9 years in Congress. He died in 1915 and is buried here. *Erected by Beaufort County Council, 1980*
GPS Coordinates: 32° 25.959' N, 80° 40.34' W

7–15 Penn School

In front of Cope Administration Building at Penn Center, Land's End Rd./Martin Luther King, Jr., Dr. (S.C. Sec. Rd. 7–45), St. Helena Island

(FRONT) After Union occupation of the sea islands in 1861, two northerners, Laura Towne and Ellen Murray, came to help the freed blacks of this area, establishing Penn School here in 1862. The earliest known black teacher was Charlotte Forten, who traveled all the way from Massachusetts to help her people.
(REVERSE) One of the first schools for blacks in the South, Penn School, opened in 1862, was reorganized as Penn Normal, Industrial and Agricultural School in 1901. As a result of this change, incorporating principles of education found at both Tuskegee and Hampton Institutes, Penn became an international model. Its program was removed to the Beaufort County school system in 1948. *Erected by Penn Club and S.C. Department of Parks, Recreation, and Tourism, 1981*
GPS Coordinates: 32° 23.266' N, 80° 34.588' W

7–16 Mather School

Ribaut Rd. (S.C. Hwy. 281), 150 ft. South of its intersection with Reynolds St., Beaufort

Shortly after the Civil War, Mather School was founded here by Rachel Crane Mather of Boston. In 1882 the Woman's American Baptist Home Mission Society assumed support of the venture, operating it as a normal school for black girls. With some changes, the school continued until 1968, when it was closed and sold to the state for the educational benefit of all races. *Erected by Mather School Alumnae Association, 1982*
GPS Coordinates: 32° 25.203' N, 80° 41.305' W

7–17 The Martinangeles

Mary Dunn Cemetery, Daufuskie Island

Phillip Martinangele, born in Italy, immigrated to this country and settled in St. Helena's Parish. He married Mary Foster in 1743 but had died by 1762 when his widow bought 500 acres on Daufuskie Island. Their son Phillip, a captain in the British Royal Militia, in December 1781 during the closing days of the American Revolution, was killed by the Bloody Legion, a partisan band of Hilton Head Island. He is probably buried here with others of his family. *Erected by the Hilton Head Island Historical Society, 1982*
GPS Coordinates: 32° 5.509' N, 80° 53.251' W

7–18 Fish Hall Plantation /Thomas Fenwick Drayton

Roy Gall Rd., adjacent to Barker Field, Hilton Head Island

Fish Hall Plantation (FRONT)
This plantation was part of a 1717 Proprietary landgrant of 500 acres to Col. John Barnwell. Later owners included members of the Green, Ellis, and Pope families. Nearby tabby ruins are remains of fire places of slave cabins. Graves of blacks, who made up most of the island's population until after the 1950s, are in nearby Drayton Cemetery.
Thomas Fenwick Drayton (REVERSE)
Confederate Brig. Gen. Thomas F. Drayton was in command of this area at the time of the nearby battle of Port Royal, November 7, 1861. A brother, Capt. Percival Drayton, commanded the Union warship *Pocahontas* at the same battle. Earlier, General Drayton had married Emma Catherine Pope, whose parents owned Fish Hall Plantation. *Erected by Beaufort County Council, 1985*
GPS Coordinates: 32° 14.732' N, 80° 41.793' W

7–19 Charles Cotesworth Pinckney (1746–1825)

U.S. Hwy. 278, Pinckney Island, about 1 mile Northwest of Hilton Head Island

(FRONT) Born in South Carolina, Pinckney was educated in England and served in the First and Second Provincial Congresses. A commander in the Revolution, he later served in the S.C. General Assembly, signed the U.S. Constitution, and was a delegate to the S.C. Constitutional Convention of 1790 in Columbia. He spent part of his life on this island.
(REVERSE) Pinckney, a leader in S.C.'s educational, political, cultural and religious affairs, inherited this island in 1769. He was made ambassador to France in 1796. Appointed by President Adams in 1797 to a committee negotiating maritime problems with France, Pinckney became known for his refusal of bribery in the "XYZ" affair. *Erected by Beaufort County Historical Society, 1987*
GPS Coordinates: 32° 13.821' N, 80° 47.062' W

7–20 Pinckney Island

U.S. Hwy. 278, Pinckney Island, about 1 mile Northwest of Hilton Head Island

(FRONT) Inhabited for some 10,000 years, Pinckney Island was known as Espalanga, Look-out, and Mackey's prior to about 1775. Alexander Mackey received two Proprietary grants for land on the island in 1710. Charles Pinckney later owned the island and willed it in 1769 to his son, Charles Cotesworth, who became a successful planter here.
(REVERSE) James Bruce, former military aide to President Woodrow Wilson, purchased this island from the Pinckneys in 1937 and developed it into a small-game hunting preserve. In 1975 Margaret and James Barker and Edward Starr, Jr. donated the island to the United States for a wildlife refuge and a nature and forest preserve. *Erected by Beaufort County Historical Society, 1987*
GPS Coordinates: 32° 13.821' N, 80° 47.062' W

7–21 Beaufort Female Benevolent Society

308 Scott St., Beaufort

The Society, founded in 1814 to educate and provide relief for destitute children, built this house in 1895 and leased it for many years, using the income to help the needy. Tenants included the Clover Club, which operated a circulating library here (1910–1917); and an infirmary (1917–1925). Funds from the 1982

sale of the house continue to provide relief for people in need. *Erected by Beaufort County Historical Society and Beaufort Female Benevolent Society, 1989*
GPS Coordinates: 32° 25.933' N, 80° 40.259' W

7–22 St. Helena's Church

505 Church St., Beaufort

(FRONT) This Episcopal Parish was established by Act of the Assembly June 7, 1712. The first known rector, William Guy, conducted early worship services in homes of settlers. The parish suffered greatly during the 1715 Yemassee Indian attack; constructed the present building in 1724 (enlarged 1817 & 1842); and was given communion silver in 1734 by John Bull, a captain in the militia. According to local tradition, the [. . .]
(REVERSE) [. . .] church was used by British to stable horses during the Revolution and as a hospital in the Civil War. In 1823 Dr. Joseph R. Walker became rector, serving 55 years, during which time at least 25 parishioners entered the ministry. Among those buried in the churchyard are 2 British officers, 3 American generals, and 17 ministers of the gospel. The 1962 parish house serves the community for various functions. *Erected by Beaufort County Historical Society and Preservation Trust for Historic St. Helena's Episcopal Church, 1992*
GPS Coordinates: 32° 26.042' N, 80° 40.507' W

7–23 Mitchelville Site

Beach City Rd. (S.C. Sec. Rd. 7-333), Northeast of its intersection with Dillon Rd. (S.C. Sec. Rd. 7-334), Hilton Head Island

In 1862, after Hilton Head's fall to Union forces in 1861, this town, planned for the area's former slaves and named for General Ormsby M. Mitchel, began. *Erected by Town of Hilton Head Island and Chicora Foundation, Inc., 1995*
GPS Coordinates: 32° 14.084' N, 80° 41.507' W

7–24 Emancipation Day /Camp Saxton Site

Near the banks of the Beaufort River at the U.S. Naval Hospital Beaufort, Pinckney Blvd., Port Royal

Emancipation Day (FRONT)
On New Year's Day 1863 this plantation owned by John Joyner Smith was the scene of elaborate ceremonies celebrating the enactment of the Emancipation Proclamation. Hundreds of freedmen and women came from Port Royal, Beaufort, and the sea islands to join Federal military and civil authorities and others in marking the event. After the proclamation was read, the 1st South Carolina Volunteers (Colored), the first black regiment formed [. . .]
Camp Saxton Site (REVERSE)
[. . .] for regular service in the U.S. Army during the Civil War, received its national and regimental colors. Col. Thomas W. Higginson of the regiment wrote, "Just think of it!—the first day they had ever had a country, the first flag they had seen which promised anything to their people." This plantation was also the site of Camp Saxton, where the regiment (later the 33rd U.S. Colored Troops) organized and trained from late 1862 to early 1863. *Erected by Penn Center and the Michigan Support Group, 1996*
GPS Coordinates: 32° 23.393' N, 80° 40.863' W

7–25 St. Luke's Church

1 ½ mile South of the intersection of S.C. Hwy. 170 and U.S. Hwy. 278, 3 miles North of Pritchardville

This sanctuary, built 1824 as St. Luke's Episcopal Church, housed an active Episcopal congregation until just before the Civil War. It was sold to the trustees of St. Luke's Methodist Church in 1875 and has served that congregation since. St. Luke's is listed in the National Register of Historic Places for its architectural significance as a blend of the Georgian and Greek Revival styles. *Erected by the Congregation, 1996*
GPS Coordinates: 32° 16.42' N, 80° 56.964' W

7–26 Beaufort College

[Replaced by marker 7–62 in 2019.]

800 Carteret St., Beaufort

(FRONT) Beaufort College, a college preparatory academy founded in 1795, occupied this Greek Revival building from 1852 to 1861. The

school opened in 1804 at Bay and Church
Sts. but closed in 1817 after a yellow fever
epidemic, reopening in 1820 at Newcastle and
Craven Sts. This building, designed by John
Gibbes Barnwell II featured two classrooms,
two offices, and a library modeled after the
one at S.C. College, now the South Caroliniana Library at the University of S.C.
(REVERSE) Beaufort College closed its doors
in the fall of 1861 when Beaufort was occupied by Federal troops. For the rest of the
Civil War it was a school for former slaves
and part of a hospital complex serving both
freedmen and Federal soldiers. It also served
as headquarters of the Freedmen's Bureau
here during Reconstruction, then became a
public elementary school in 1909. In 1959 the
University of S.C. acquired this building for
its new Beaufort campus. *Erected by the Beaufort Historical Society and the Beaufort College
Board of Trustees, 2001*
GPS Coordinates: 32° 26.198' N, 80° 40.191' W

7–27 Sheldon Union Academy /Sheldon School

**Trask Parkway (U.S. Hwy. 21), just East of Sheldon
Dr., Sheldon community**

Sheldon Union Academy (FRONT)
Sheldon Union Academy, later Sheldon
School, opened in 1893 on this site and educated the black children of rural Sheldon
community for almost fifty years. The original Sheldon Union Academy board, which
founded and governed the school from 1893
to 1918, included S. T. Beaubien, M. W. Brown,
P. R. Chisolm, H. L. Jones, S. W. Ladson, F. S.
Mitchell, and N. D. Mitchell.
Sheldon School (REVERSE)
Sheldon Union Academy, founded by an independent group of community leaders, was
a private school until 1918. That year its board
deeded the property to Beaufort County,
which built a new public school on this site.
Sheldon School, which taught grades 1–7,
closed in 1942 when the county consolidated
its rural black schools. *Erected by the Committee for the Preservation of African-American
Landmarks, 2001*
GPS Coordinates: 32° 36.246' N, 80° 48.184' W

7–28 Battery Saxton

2226 Boundary St., Beaufort

(FRONT) Battery Saxton, constructed here in
1862, was in the second line of earthworks
built by Federal troops occupying Beaufort
during the Civil War. Laid out by the 1st New
York Engineers with the assistance of black
laborers, it held 3 8-inch siege howitzers and
was occupied 1862–65 as one of two batteries
anchoring a line from Battery Creek to the
Beaufort River, the remnants of which are visible here just south of U.S. Hwy. 21 (known as
Shell Rd. during the war).
(REVERSE) Battery Saxton was named for Brig.
Gen. Rufus Saxton (1824–1908), a native of
Massachusetts. Saxton, an ardent abolitionist, served for most of the war in and around
Beaufort in the Union Dept. of the South.
As military governor of the Ga. and S.C. sea
islands 1862–65 he led the way in educating
freedmen and in raising and training black
units for service in the U.S. Army. Saxton was
later assistant commissioner of the Freedmen's
Bureau for S.C., Ga., & Fla., 1865–66. *Erected
by the Historic Beaufort Foundation, 2001*
GPS Coordinates: 32° 26.473' N, 80° 42.005' W

7–29 Michael C. Riley Schools

**Goethe Rd. between Hilderbrand Rd. and Schultz
Rd., Bluffton**

(FRONT) This is the site of two schools that
served the black community of southern
Beaufort County for most of the twentieth
century. Bluffton Graded School, a small
frame building constructed about 1900, was
followed in 1954 by an elementary and high
school named for Michael C. Riley (1873–
1966), longtime trustee of Beaufort County
School District # 2.
(REVERSE) From 1954 to 1970 the elementary
school educated Bluffton's black students
in grades 1–8 and the high school educated
Bluffton's and Hilton Head's black students in
grades 9–12. After county schools were desegregated in 1970, it was an elementary school
for Bluffton's black and white students until
1991. A new Michael C. Riley Elementary
School opened nearby that same year. *Erected*

*by the Michael C. Riley High School Alumni
Association, 2002*
GPS Coordinates: 32° 14.462' N, 80° 51.752' W

7–30 Maxcy-Rhett House /"Secession House"

1113 Craven Street, Beaufort

Maxcy-Rhett House (FRONT)
This house was built circa 1810 for Milton
Maxcy (1782–1817), who came here from Massachusetts in 1804. Maxcy and his brother Virgil, who founded a school for young men in
Beaufort, later taught at Beaufort College. In
the 1850s Edmund Rhett (1808–1863), lawyer,
planter, state representative, and state senator,
bought the house and extensively remodeled
it in the Greek Revival style, featuring an
elaborate two-story portico.
"Secession House" (REVERSE)
Edmund Rhett, along with his brother Robert Barnwell Rhett (1800–1876), lawyer, state
representative, state attorney general, U.S.
congressman and senator, was an outspo-
ken champion of state rights and Southern
nationalism from the 1830s to the Civil War.
This house, long known as "Secession House,"
was the scene of many informal discussions
and formal meetings during the 1850s by the
Rhetts and their allies advocating secession
and Southern independence. *Erected by the
General Richard Anderson Camp # 47, Sons of
Confederate Veterans, 2005*
GPS Coordinates: 32° 25.963' N, 80° 40.496' W

7–31 Rose Hill

**Rose Hill Way on the Colleton River, just off Fording
Island Rd. (U.S. Hwy. 278), Bluffton vicinity**

(FRONT) This plantation was part of the
barony of Lords Proprietor Sir John Colleton;
his descendants sold this portion to Dr. James
B. Kirk in 1828. Kirk was one of the wealthiest cotton planters in antebellum St. Luke's
Parish. He gave Rose Hill to his daughter
Caroline (1817–1864) in the 1830s when she
married her cousin Dr. John W. Kirk (1803–
1868), also a physician and cotton planter.
(REVERSE) The Kirks began building this
Gothic Revival house shortly before the Civil

War. The house was unfinished for many years
until John Sturgeon III (d. 1978) bought it in
1946; architect Willis Irvin completed much
of the interior in 1946–49. It was listed in the
National Register of Historic Places in 1983,
damaged by a fire in 1987, and restored by the
White family in 1996–2007. *Erected by the
Gen. Richard H. Anderson Camp #47, Sons
of Confederate Veterans, 2007*
GPS Coordinates: 32° 17.087' N, 80° 52.887' W

7–32 The Great Sea Island Storm

**Penn Center, Martin Luther King, Jr., Dr. (S.C. Sec.
Rd. 7–45), St. Helena Island**

(FRONT) On the night of August 27, 1893, a
huge "tropical cyclone," the largest and most
powerful storm to hit S.C. until Hurricane
Hugo in 1989, made landfall just E of Savannah, Ga. With gusts as high as 120 mph and a
storm surge as high as 12 ft., the worst of the
storm struck the Sea Islands near Beaufort—
St. Helena, Hilton Head, Daufuskie, Parris,
and smaller islands were devastated.
(REVERSE) The storm killed more than 2,000
and left more than 70,000 destitute in coastal
S.C. and Ga. Losses in lives and property were
most catastrophic among blacks who were
former slaves or their descendants. Clara Barton and the American Red Cross launched a
massive relief effort, the first after a hurricane
in U.S. history. Donations in 1893–94 fed,
clothed, and sheltered thousands. *Erected by
the Beaufort County Historical Society, 2008*
GPS Coordinates: 32° 23.295' N, 80° 34.605' W

7–33 St. James Baptist Church

209 Dillon Rd., Hilton Head Island

This church, founded in 1886 by former members of First African Baptist Church, is one
of the oldest surviving institutions remaining
from the town of Mitchelville, a freedmen's
village established here by the United States
Army in 1862. The present brick sanctuary,
covered in stucco, is the third to serve this
congregation. It was built in 1972 and renovated in 2005. *Erected by the Congregation,
2011*
GPS Coordinates: 32° 14.076' N, 80° 41.491' W

7–34 Fort Howell

Beach City Rd., just Southwest of its junction with Dillon Rd., Hilton Head Island

(FRONT) This Civil War fort, named for Gen. Joshua Blackwood Howell (1806–1864), was built by the U.S. Army to defend Hilton Head Island and the nearby freedmen's village of Mitchelville from potential Confederate raids or expeditions. That village, just east of here, had been established by Gen. Ormsby M. Mitchel in the fall of 1862 and was named for him after his death.

(FRONT) This fort was an enclosed pentagonal earthwork with a 23' high parapet and emplacements for up to 27 guns. It was built from August to November 1864 by the 32nd U.S. Colored Infantry and the 144th N.Y. Infantry. Though Fort Howell never saw action, it is significant for its design and its structural integrity. It was listed in the National Register of Historic Places in 2011. *Erected by the Hilton Head Island Land Trust, Inc., 2011*
GPS Coordinates: 32° 14.056' N, 80° 41.526' W

7–35 William Simmons House

Gullah Museum of Hilton Head Island, 187 Gumtree Dr., Hilton Head Island

(FRONT) This house, built in 1930, is typical in materials and methods of construction of those built on the S.C. Sea Islands from the end of the Civil War to the mid-20th century. It was built on land bought after 1865 by William Simmons (ca. 1835–1922). Simmons, born a slave, had served in the U.S. Army during the war, enlisting in the 21st U.S. Colored Infantry as Ira Sherman.

(REVERSE) William Simmons's granddaughter Georgianna Jones Bryan (1900–1989) built this house in 1930 for her brother, William "Duey" Simmons (1901–1966). It illustrates everyday life and the persistence of Gullah culture in an African-American farm community until after a bridge was built from the mainland in 1956. It was renovated in 2010–11 as the Gullah Museum of Hilton Head Island. *Erected by the Gullah Museum of Hilton Head Island, 2011*
GPS Coordinates: 32° 13.607' N, 80° 44.487' W

7–36 First Presbyterian Church

Corner of Church & North Sts., Beaufort

(FRONT) Early attempts to establish a Presbyterian church in Beaufort, in the 1740s and 1880s, were unsuccessful. The first permanent congregation was founded in 1912 by 16 charter members. In 1921, when it acquired this lot, Rev. A. P. Toomer put up a sign with the Old Testament verse "the people had a mind to work." This Colonial Revival church, built in 1928–29, was designed by architect James H. Sams (1872–1935).

(REVERSE) Notable architectural features include simple clapboard siding and clear arched windows. Members completed the interior, with Rev. F. B. Mayes (minister 1929–1949) as chief carpenter and Elder J. W. Logan in charge. The 1947–48 chancel arches were built by the craftsmen who built the U.S. Naval Hospital. In 1988 First Presbyterian gave funds and members to help found Sea Island Presbyterian Church. *Sponsored by the Congregation, 2012*
GPS Coordinates: 32° 25.999' N, 80° 40.517' W

7–37 First African Baptist Church

70 Beach City Rd., Hilton Head Island

(FRONT) This church, organized in 1862, was first located in the town of Mitchelville, a freedmen's village established on Hilton Head by the United States Army. Rev. Abraham Murchinson, its first pastor, was a former slave. The congregation numbered about 120 members when it was organized in August 1862.

(REVERSE) The church moved to the Chaplin community after the Civil War and was renamed Goodwill Baptist Church. It moved to this site by 1898 and was renamed Cross Roads Baptist Church before retaking its original name; it is the mother church of five Beaufort County churches. The present building was built in 1966. *Sponsored by the Congregation, 2012*
GPS Coordinates: 32° 13.434' N, 80° 42.407' W

7–38 Fort Fremont

At Bay Point, .3 miles from Land's End Rd., St. Helena Island

(FRONT) These batteries, built by the U.S. Army in 1898 in response to the Spanish-American War, were part of Fort Fremont, which defended the coaling station and dry dock at the Port Royal Naval Station on nearby Parris Island. The fort, built 1898–99, was named for Maj. Gen. John C. Frémont (1813–1890), explorer, 1856 Republican presidential candidate, and Union Civil War general.

(REVERSE) The fort active 1898–1911, covered 170 acres and was manned by a Coast Artillery company numbering 112 men. It was armed with three 10" guns, two 4.7" guns, and submarine mines. Fort Fremont, which never saw action, was decommissioned in 1911 and sold in 1930. Part of the fort was acquired by Beaufort Co. in 2004, and listed in the National Register of Historic Places in 2010. *Sponsored by the Beaufort County Historical Society, 2013*
GPS Coordinates: 32° 18.009' N, 80° 38.545' W

7–39 Combahee River Raid /Freedom Along the Combahee

At Steel Bridge Landing, U.S. Hwy.17 N over the Combahee River at the Beaufort Co.–Colleton Co. line, Gardens Corner vicinity

Combahee River Raid (FRONT)
On June 1–2, 1863, a Federal force consisting of elements of the 2nd S.C. Volunteer Infantry (an African-American unit) and the 3rd Rhode Island Artillery conducted a raid up the Confederate-held Combahee River. Col. James Montgomery led the expedition. Harriet Tubman, already famous for her work with the Underground Railroad, accompanied Montgomery on the raid.
Freedom Along the Combahee (REVERSE)
Union gunboats landed 300 soldiers along the river, and one force came ashore here at Combahee Ferry. Soldiers took livestock and supplies and destroyed houses, barns, and rice at nearby plantations. More than 700 enslaved men, women, and children were taken to

freedom in perhaps the largest emancipation event in wartime S.C. Some freedmen soon enlisted in the U.S. Army. *Sponsored by the South Carolina Department of Transportation, 2013*
GPS Coordinates: 32° 39.112' N, 80° 41.114' W

7–40 First African Baptist Church

601 New St., Beaufort

(FRONT) This church, founded in 1865, grew out of an antebellum praise house for black members of the Baptist Church of Beaufort. During the Civil War, after the Federal occupation of the town, it hosted a school for freedmen. Rev. Arthur Waddell (1821–1895), its founding pastor, had come to S.C. from Savannah, Ga. In 1867 Rev. Waddell and two black ministers from Savannah formally organized this church.

(REVERSE) In 1885 the congregation, with more than 900 members, built this "handsome and commodious" Carpenter Gothic church. Rev. Waddell continued to serve this church until he retired in 1894. At his death in 1895 First African Baptist was described as "one of the most aristocratic colored churches." Robert Smalls (1839–1915), Civil War hero, state legislator, and U.S. Congressman, was its most prominent member. *Sponsored by the Beaufort County Historical Society, 2013*
GPS Coordinates: 32° 26.074' N, 80° 40.120' W

7–41 Grand Army of the Republic Hall

706 Newcastle St., Beaufort

(FRONT) This building was built ca. 1896 by the David Hunter Post No. 9, Grand Army of the Republic (G.A.R.). The G.A.R., founded in 1866, was a fraternal society for veterans of the Union army and navy, with white and black posts. David Hunter Post was founded in 1888 by African-American veterans, many of them former slaves on Sea Island plantations who had been soldiers in the United States Colored Troops in the Civil War.

(REVERSE) The post was named for Gen. David Hunter (1802–1886), who had organized the nucleus of the 1st S.C. Volunteers (Colored)

in 1862. Robert Smalls (1839–1915), Civil War hero, state legislator, militia general, and U.S. Congressman, was a post officer. The post hosted annual Decoration Day services at Beaufort National Cemetery and the Sons of Union Veterans of the Civil War continue that tradition. *Sponsored by the Beaufort County Historical Society, 2013*
GPS Coordinates: 32° 26.128' N 80° 40.454' W

7–42 Cherry Hill School

210 Dillon Rd., Hilton Head Island

(FRONT) This one-room frame school, built ca. 1937, was the first separate school building constructed for African-American students on Hilton Head Island. It replaced an earlier Cherry Hill School, which had held its classes in the parsonage of St. James Baptist Church. After the black community on the island raised funds to buy this tract, Beaufort County agreed to build this school.
(REVERSE) This was an elementary school with one teacher, with an average of about 30 students. It had grades 1–5 when it opened in 1937, adding grade 6 the next school year. The black community helped pay for maintenance of the school and also supplemented teacher salaries. Cherry Hill School was listed in the National Register of Historic Places in 2012. *Sponsored by St. James Baptist Church, 2013*
GPS Coordinates: 32° 14.082' N 80° 41.476' W

7–43 The Burning of Bluffton

DuBois Park, W. side of Boundary St., Bluffton

(FRONT) Bluffton, an antebellum planters' summer village, was virtually abandoned by its seasonal and year-round inhabitants when Federal forces captured Beaufort and Port Royal in November 1861. Confederate forces used it as an outpost to watch Port Royal Sound and the Charleston & Savannah RR. Early on June 4, 1863, an expedition of some 1,000 Federals landed at Hunting Island Plantation, then marched to Bluffton.
(REVERSE) Confederate pickets raised the alarm but could not offer immediate resistance and the Federals surprised a small Confederate force camped on the May River. A brief skirmish ended when shells from a Federal gunboat drove the Confederates away. Federal infantry then burned some 40 houses and other outbuildings, about two-thirds of the village. The Charleston Mercury called the Federal raid on Bluffton "an outrage." *Sponsored by the Lowcountry Civil War Round Table, 2013*
GPS Coordinates: 32° 14.065' N, 80° 51.678' W

7–44 Beth Israel Synagogue

401 Scott St., Beaufort

(FRONT) Beth Israel (House of Israel) Congregation was founded and chartered in 1905. Beaufort's Jewish community dates before the American Revolution, but grew most rapidly from the 1880s to the 1930s as more families arrived from Eastern Europe. Services were held in private homes and later in the Masonic Hall on Bay St., with some ceremonial functions held in the Beaufort Arsenal on Craven St.
(REVERSE) This frame synagogue was built by members of the congregation and dedicated in 1908, in ceremonies conducted by Rabbis J. J. Simonhoff of Charleston and George Solomon of Savannah. In 1910 the congregation bought a tract on Bladen St. for a cemetery that was established in 1912 and is still in use today. Founded as an Orthodox congregation, Beth Israel became a Conservative congregation in 1949. *Sponsored by the Beaufort County Historical Society, 2013*
GPS Coordinates: 32° 25.958' N 80° 40.250' W

7–45 St. Peter Catholic Church

Corner of Carteret and Duke Sts., Beaufort

(FRONT) This Greek Revival church, built in 1846, dedicated as "St. Peter the Apostle Church," is the oldest Catholic church in Beaufort County. Michael O'Connor (1798–1850), a native of Ireland who came to Beaufort in 1822, built it and deeded the church and lot to the bishop. Its first pastor was Rev. J. J. O'Connell (1821–1894), author of Catholicity in the Carolinas and Georgia (1879).
(REVERSE) The brick wall was built in 1857 by local craftsman Franklin Talbird Jr. During

the Civil War, the church housed a school for freedmen. The Gothic trefoil window was added in 1899. Though the parish moved to Lady's Island in 1987, this church has been used for special events since and was handsomely restored in 2012. The churchyard includes several fine examples of 19th and 20th century gravestone art. *Sponsored by the Beaufort County Historical Society, 2013*
GPS Coordinates: 32° 26.157' N, 80° 40.200' W

7–46 Daufuskie Island

At the Beaufort County Boat Landing, Daufuskie Island

(FRONT) This 5,200-acre island lies between the Cooper and New Rivers. Spanish and English explorers saw it in 1521 and 1663; English arrivals received grants ca. 1700. Indigo was the main crop before the American Revolution, when most planters here were Loyalists. Sea island cotton was the main crop after 1790. In 1861, when Union forces captured the sea islands, planters abandoned Daufuskie Island. (REVERSE) Freedmen during and immediately after the Civil War, and then their descendants, made up almost all of the population here until near the end of the 20th century. Many owned small farms or worked in the oyster industry. The island, listed in the National Register of Historic Places in 1982, is also part of the Gullah Geechee Cultural Heritage Corridor, designated by Congress in 2006. *Sponsored by the South Carolina Society Colonial Dames XVII Century, 2013*
GPS Coordinates: 32° 6.240' N, 80° 53.638' W

7–47 Gardens Corner

Junction of U.S. Hwys. 17 and 21, Gardens Corner

(FRONT) Gardens Corner was a junction of two significant roads long before the American Revolution. The King's Highway (now U.S. Hwy. 17) ran from Charleston to Savannah, while Shell Road (now U.S. Hwy. 21) ran from here to the Port Royal Ferry and on to Beaufort and Port Royal. By 1795 the junction was named for Benjamin Garden (1736–1789), whose Fairfield Plantation was nearby. (REVERSE) Elements of opposing armies

camped, marched, and skirmished nearby during the American Revolution and again during the Civil War. Gardens Corner, long a popular stop for travelers, boasted a store and inn for most of the 19th century and the Gardens Corner Restaurant and Court 1948–1970. The historic corner was replaced by a new highway interchange built 2007–2011. *Sponsored by Beaufort County and the Friends of Gardens Corner, 2014*
GPS Coordinates: 32° 36.050' N, 80° 45.558' W

7–48 Fairfield Plantation

Junction of U.S. Hwys. 17 and 21, Gardens Corner

(FRONT) This 756-acre plantation was established before the American Revolution by planter Benjamin Garden (1736–1789), for whom Gardens Corner was later named. Garden was also an avid sportsman, well known in the lowcountry for raising and racing thoroughbred horses. He served in the Lower Granville County Regiment of the S.C. Militia as early as 1756.
(REVERSE) Benjamin Garden represented Prince William's Parish in the 1st and 2nd Provincial Congresses 1775–76 and the 1st General Assembly in 1776. He was Lt. Colonel of the Lower Granville County Regiment ca. 1775–78, then colonel 1778–80. Captured and paroled when the British took Charleston in 1780, Garden later gave aid to the Loyalists before the end of the Revolution. *Sponsored by Beaufort County and the Friends of Gardens Corner, 2014*
GPS Coordinates: 32° 36.086' N, 80° 45.554' W

7–49 Wesley Methodist Church

701 West St. Beaufort

(FRONT) This church, established in 1833, was the first Methodist church in Beaufort and was founded as a mission to slaves and free blacks here and on the neighboring Sea Islands. The congregation had both black and white members but many more black members in the antebellum era. This church, first built in the "meeting house" form common to the Methodist church, was dedicated by Bishop William Capers in 1849.

(REVERSE) In 1861, after the Federal occupation of Beaufort and the Sea Islands, this church hosted a school for freedmen and continued to serve its black members. After the Civil War, it was formally affiliated with the Methodist Episcopal Church, the Northern Methodist church 1844–1939. Its first black minister was appointed in 1873, during Reconstruction. The church has flourished in the years since. *Sponsored by the Old Commons Neighborhood Association, 2014*
GPS Coordinates: 32° 26.138' N 80° 40.288' W

7–50 Port Royal Agricultural School /Beaufort County Training School

Shanklin Rd., Northeast of its intersection with Laurel Bay Rd., Burton

Port Royal Agricultural School (FRONT)
The Port Royal Agricultural School, later the Beaufort County Training School, operated nearby 1901–1955. Offering vocational and academic education for blacks, it was founded by Beaufort citizens led by Abbie Holmes Christensen (1852–1938). The school was modeled on Booker T. Washington's Tuskegee Institute, with his advice and support.
Beaufort County Training School (REVERSE)
Booker T. Washington called it "a model school of its kind" when he toured it in 1908. It was usually called "the Shanklin School" for Joseph S. Shanklin (1872–1957), Tuskegee alumnus and its principal 1903–1946. His wife India (1876–1939) was its matron, nurse, and a teacher. Renamed Beaufort Co. Training School, it became a public school in 1920 and closed in 1955. Shanklin Elementary School, 2.6 mi. W, opened in 1994. *Sponsored by Beaufort County, 2014*
GPS Coordinates: 32° 27.321' N, 80° 45.794' W

7–51 Bluffton

100 ft. W of SW Corner of May River Rd. and Calhoun St. intersection, Bluffton

(FRONT) Originally known as May River, and later as Kirk's Bluff, Bluffton was settled as a resort town where planters could escape the hot, malarial summers of lowcountry plantations. The streets were laid out in the 1830s and much of the early development took place along Calhoun and Bridge Streets. Bluffton's commerce was largely a result of the river trade, and a steamboat landing completed by the early 1850s served to increase traffic and spur growth.
(REVERSE) During the Civil War, Union forces set fire to much of the town during a raid and short battle on June 4, 1863. After the war, Bluffton emerged as a local commercial center with a number of general stores operating in the town. New transportation networks diverted traffic away from the river by the mid-20th century and trade declined. The rise in tourism since the 1990s has served as a catalyst for Bluffton's reemergence as a resort destination. *Sponsored by the Bluffton Historical Preservation Society, 2014, replacing a marker (7–2) placed by the Beaufort County Historical Society (n.d.)*
GPS Coordinates: 32° 14.233' N, 80° 51.748' W

7–52 Berean Church/J. I. Washington Branch Library

602 Carteret St., Beaufort

Berean Church (FRONT)
Berean Presbyterian Church was founded by Samuel J. Bampfield, an influential African American political figure during Reconstruction. Bampfield served in the S.C. House of Representatives, was Beaufort's postmaster, and clerk of the county court. In 1892 the congregation purchased this lot and constructed a church in the Gothic Revival style. Solomon P. Hood, who later was appointed U.S. Minister to Liberia, was the first pastor.
J. I. Washington Branch Library (REVERSE)
In 1931 the building was purchased by the Beaufort Township Library and converted for use as a segregated branch library for African Americans. It operated in that capacity until 1965 when this branch closed and Township Library was desegregated. The building was later used as headquarters for the Neighborhood Youth Corps and in 1993 was purchased by USC Beaufort for use as an art studio. *Sponsored by the Beaufort County Historical*

Society, the Old Commons Neighborhood Association, and USC Beaufort, 2014
GPS Coordinates: 32° 26.068' N, 80° 40.200' W

7–53 Intracoastal Waterway

Freeport Marina, 1 Freeport Rd., Daufuskie Island

(FRONT) Archeological evidence suggests human activity on Daufuskie Island as early as 12,000 B.C., with seasonal habitation tied to the harvesting of coastal resources. Early European inhabitants also realized the importance of the coastal waterways for navigation and transportation, utilizing the tidal waters as an intracoastal highway between Charleston and Savannah.
(REVERSE) Later improvements would formalize and extend this inland water route, and this section of the Cooper River is a small portion of what is now the Intracoastal Waterway (ICW), a 3,000 mile long inland shipping channel that stretches along the East and Gulf Coasts. The Atlantic portion of the ICW extends from Norfolk to Key West, traveling past Daufuskie Island on its journey south. *Sponsored by S.C. Society Colonial Dames XVII Century, Donald S. Russell Foundation, and U.S.C., 2014*
GPS Coordinates: 32° 7.043' N, 80° 51.005' W

7–54 Fort Mitchel

65 Skull Creek Drive, Hilton Head

(FRONT) Fort Mitchel was built by the U.S. Army in 1862. It was an earthen fortification of lunette design, open at the rear with two faces forming a salient angle and two flanking sides. It was designed to house five or six heavy guns and was positioned strategically to control Skull Creek and protect the approach to the U.S. Navy coaling station at Seabrook Landing, one mile NE of this spot.
(REVERSE) Originally named for its designer, Capt. Quincy Gillmore, Ft. Mitchel was renamed in honor of Maj. Gen. Ormsby Mitchel in 1863. Mitchel briefly commanded Union forces on Hilton Head before he died of yellow fever in Oct. 1862. The introduction of ironclad ships later in the war made the small battery at Ft. Mitchel ineffective and the

garrison was redeployed in 1864. *Sponsored by Beaufort County Historical Society, 2015*
GPS Coordinates: 32° 14.614' N, 80° 44.618' W

7–55 Queen Chapel A.M.E. Church

114 Beach City Rd., Hilton Head

(FRONT) The congregation of Queen Chapel can trace its roots to May 1865 when A.M.E. missionaries Rev. R. H. Cain, Rev. James H. A. Johnson, and James A. Handy arrived on Hilton Head Island. They visited the Freedmen's town of Mitchelville and preached a sermon before departing for Charleston. Missionaries like Cain, Johnson, and Handy represented the first official A.M.E. presence in S.C. since 1822.
(REVERSE) In 1865 Charleston born A.M.E. Bishop D. A. Payne returned to S.C. and brought with him a group of missionaries. When they arrived in Hilton Head they met with Rev. James Lynch, who had come to S.C. in 1863 to perform missionary work among the Freedmen. The A.M.E. denomination experienced rapid growth after the Civil War and Queen Chapel was among the early churches founded. *Sponsored by Beaufort County Historical Society and Queen Chapel A.M.E. Church, 2015*
GPS Coordinates: 32° 13.669' N, 80° 42.055' W

7–56 Parris Island

Malecon Dr. near entry gate to Parris Island Marine Corps Base, Parris Island

(FRONT) European occupation of Parris Island dates to the French Charlesfort, 1562–1563. The Spanish built Santa Elena 1566–1587 which was capital of Spanish Florida from 1571–1576. William III of England granted the island to Robert Daniel in 1698 and Col. Alexander Parris, the island's namesake, bought it in 1715. Union forces captured Port Royal Sound in 1861 and Parris Island served as a Quartermaster coaling station for the duration of the Civil War.
(REVERSE) Port Royal Naval Station opened in 1889. The base became dedicated to use by the Marine Corps in 1915. Parris Island served as the principal training facility for Marine

Corps recruits during WWI. After WWII, the Depot has served as the exclusive training site for enlisted women Marines. The base has played a pivotal role in regional development, both through improved infrastructure and direct and indirect economic benefits. *Sponsored by the Beaufort County Historical Society, 2016*
GPS Coordinates: 32° 22.527' N, 80° 43.013' W

7–57 Cyrus Garvin/Cyrus Garvin House

Bluffton Oyster Factory Park, Wharf St. near intersection with Bridge St., Bluffton

Cyrus Garvin (FRONT)
Little is known of Cyrus Garvin's early life. He was likely born into slavery, possibly on a plantation of the Baynard family. Garvin is notable for having amassed considerable status and property after emancipation. In 1868 he was acting as an agent on Ephraim Baynard's Montpelier plantation. By 1870 he was farming 75 acres and that number had risen to 100 ten years later. In 1878 he acted as an agent for St. Matthews Baptist Church, helping them to acquire land in Bluffton.
Cyrus Garvin House (REVERSE)
Cyrus Garvin built the house located here ca. 1870 and it is believed to be the oldest extant dwelling built by Freedpeople in Bluffton. The extended hall-and-parlor design was a vernacular form common to the low country. By 1880 Garvin lived here with his wife Ellen, their son Isaac, and Isaac's wife Janie and son Paul. Janie, who died in 1954, was the last person to inhabit the house, though the Garvins remained owners until 1961. The Beaufort Co. Land Trust acquired the land in 2001. *Sponsored by Town of Bluffton and Eugene and Melanie Marks, 2017*
GPS Coordinates: 32° 12.945' N, 80° 52.026' W

7–58 Baptist Church of Beaufort

600 Charles St., Beaufort

(FRONT) The Baptist Church of Beaufort descends from Euhaw Baptist Church on Edisto Island. In 1794 the first meeting house was built on this site. In 1795 Henry Holcombe moved to Beaufort and became the first mission pastor. The Beaufort Baptist Church was formally constituted as an independent church in 1804. The first burial was in 1809. Prior to the Civil War, 3,557 of 3,723 members were enslaved people.
(REVERSE) The current Greek Revival building dates to 1844 and was constructed under the pastorate of Richard Fuller, who served 1833–1847. During the Civil War the church was a Union Army hospital for black troops. In Dec. 1862, Rev. Solomon Peck read the preliminary Emancipation Proclamation from the pulpit to an audience of escaped slaves and black soldiers. After the war, nearly all black members left to join newly formed black churches. *Sponsored by the Beaufort County Historical Society, 2018*
GPS Coordinates: 32° 26.076' N, 80° 40.380' W

7–59 Lady's Island Oyster Factory

106 Sunset Blvd, Beaufort

(FRONT) The eastern oyster launched the Beaufort Co. commercial seafood industry. The first canning factory on this site, for which Factory Creek was named, was begun in 1883. Oysters were harvested from Sept. to May. Tomatoes and okra were canned in the summer. After the hurricane of 1893 the oyster industry became the largest employer in the county, providing jobs to approximately 3,500 Sea Islanders.
(REVERSE) By 1929, this factory was the largest producer of cove oysters in the world. L. P. Maggione bought the factory in 1917. In the 1950s it had over 300 employees, canning oyster products, tomatoes, and okra. African American migration to northern states in the early-to-mid 20th century, accompanied by die off in oyster beds, led to decline of the industry and the work force shrank to 25. The factory closed in 1986. *Sponsored by the Beaufort County Historical Society, 2018*
GPS Coordinates: 32° 25.489' N, 80° 38.781' W

7–60 Hilton Head Rear-Range Lighthouse

Leamington Ln., Hilton Head Island

(FRONT) The Rear Lighthouse of the Hilton Head Range Light Station was built in 1879–1880 by the U.S. Light House Board. Its light, which stood 92-feet above sea level, was visible from 15 miles away and once served to guide shipping vessels in Port Royal Sound. This tower was once part of a complex that also included a keeper's house and forward beacon, which was located more than 1 mile in front of this position.
(REVERSE) Sailors entering Port Royal Sound would steer their ships until the lights from the rear tower and forward beacon aligned. The frequently shifting channel required the forward beacon to be relocated numerous times. In 1884 a movable keeper's house with an integrated beacon was built to accommodate the frequent moves. Decommissioned in 1932, the lighthouse is listed in the National Register of Historic Places. *Sponsored by the Leamington POA, 2018*
GPS Coordinates: 32° 9.868' N, 80° 44.347' W

7–61 Mary Field School

203 School Rd., Daufuskie Island

(FRONT) Following Emancipation, education was a priority for African American families on Daufuskie. Adults and children attended school at First Union African Baptist Church 1872–1934. Church families purchased land in 1930 and by 1933 had raised funds to build a school. Workers from the island built the school. The two-room Mary Field School opened in 1934 with grades 1–6.
(REVERSE) Mary Field became a Beaufort Co. school in the 1950s. Miss Frances Jones taught on the island 1930–1969 and educated several generations of Daufuskie families. Author Pat Conroy was briefly a teacher here 1969–70 and his novel The Water is Wide was based on his experience. In 2009 the former school building was renovated to be used for church functions and as a community center. *Sponsored by Daufuskie Island Historical Foundation, 2018*
GPS Coordinates: 32° 6.281' N, 80° 52.660' W

7–62 Beaufort College

[Replaced marker 7-26 in 2019.]

801 Carteret St., Beaufort

(FRONT) Beaufort College, a college preparatory academy founded in 1795, occupied this Greek Revival building from 1852 to 1861. The School opened in 1804 on Bay Street, but closed in 1817 after a yellow fever epidemic, reopening in 1820 at Newcastle and Craven Sts. This building designed by John Gibbs Barnwell II featured two classrooms, two offices, and a library modeled after the one at S.C. College, now the South Caorlinian Library at the University of S. Carolina.
(REVERSE) Beaufort College closed in the fall of 1861 when U.S. troops occupied the city. Its library was sent north and stored at the Smithsonian Institution but the books burned. During the Civil War it was a school for former slaves and a hospital for Federal troops. The college trustees regained control after the war. It was a private school for whites until it became a public elementary school in 1909. It became the Beaufort campus of the University of S.C. in 1959.
GPS Coordinates: 32° 26.198' N, 80° 40.191' W

7–63 Tidalholm

1 Laurens St., Beaufort

(FRONT) This house was commissioned by Edgar Fripp (1806–1860) and completed ca. 1853. Based upon architect Samuel Sloan's designs, it was built in the Italianate style, with a prominent central cupola, and served as the "town home" for Fripp and his wife Eliza (1810–1861). Fripp was a substantial Sea Island Cotton planter, who owned Seaside Plantation on St. Helena Island. During the Civil War the house served as U.S. Hospital #7, which provided care for officers.
(REVERSE) The house suffered severe damage from the Sea Isand Hurricane of 1893. The cupola and gables were then incorporated into the roof, and a second floor piazza typical of the "Beaufort Style" was added. In the 1920s it was named "Tidalholm," meaning home by the river, and served as a popular seasonal guest house and retreat. In the late 20th century it was the backdrop for several

Hollywood films including "The Great Santini" (1979) and "The Big Chill" (1983). *Sponsored by Historic Beaufort Foundation, 2019*
GPS Coordinates: 32° 26.102' N, 80° 39.851' W

Berkeley County

No # Barnet's Tavern

S.C. Hwy. 6, Cross Vicinity

Near this spot stood Barnet's Tavern, called the Forty-Five Mile House, indicating its distance from Charleston. Here was the muster ground of the Eutaw State Volunteers, a company raised in 1833, to support the Ordinance of Nullification. From this tavern, on Sept. 11, 1781, Gen. Green sent to the President of Congress, despatches announcing the Battle of Eutaw Springs. [*Erected by the South Carolina Historical Commission, ca. 1929–1936.*]
GPS Coordinates: 33° 20.668' N, 80° 8.558' W

8–1 Stony Landing Plantation

Old U.S. Hwy. 52 at Stony Landing Rd., Moncks Corner

Here in 1863, the Confederate semi-submersible torpedo boat, Little David, first of its type, was constructed. It was designed by Dr. St. Julien Ravenel and built with funds raised by Theodore D. Stoney.
GPS Coordinates: 33° 11.826' N, 79° 59.579' W

8–2 Old Moncks Corner

Old U.S. Hwy. 52 at its intersection with U.S. Hwy. 17-A, Moncks Corner

Here was located the provincial town of Moncks Corner, deriving its name from Thomas Monck, an Englishman, who in 1735 purchased Mitten Plantation, and upon whose land the town was settled. It became an important commercial center prior to the Revolution. Upon the completion of the Northeastern Railroad in 1857, the new railroad station was called Moncks Corner after the old town.
GPS Coordinates: 33° 12.12' N, 79° 59.406' W

8–3 Santee Canal

Intersection of U.S. Hwy. 17 & U.S. Hwy. 52 at Stony Landing Plantation, Moncks Corner vicinity

(1) This canal, twenty-two miles in length, connects the Santee and Cooper Rivers. Chartered in 1786, construction was commenced in 1793, and completed in 1800, under the direction of Col. John Christian Senf, a native of Sweden, as Chief Engineer. The Canal was in operation until about 1850.
(2) The Santee Canal Company was chartered by act of March 22, 1786, organized the next day, with capital of £100,000 sterling, and the canal completed and opened to traffic from the Santee to the Cooper in 1800, being 22 miles, 20 feet wide at the bottom and 35 feet at the surface, 5 ½ feet deep, with 4 feet of water, capable of carrying boats of 22 tons burden. It ceased operations in 1850. [Originally there was a second Santee Canal marker located ½ mile North of intersection of Old U.S. Hwy. 52 & U.S. Hwy. 17-A. That second marker was replaced by marker 8-36 in 2005.]
GPS Coordinates: 33° 12.63' N, 79° 58.831' W

8–4 Mulberry Plantation

Old U.S. Hwy. 52, 5 Miles South of Moncks Corner

Originally granted to Sir Peter Colleton in 1679. Acquired in 1712 by Thomas Broughton, who erected the present mansion, said to be modeled after Seaton Hall in England, in 1714. Thomas Broughton was speaker of the Commons House of Assembly from 1726 to 1730 and Governor from 1735 to 1737.
GPS Coordinates: 33° 8.452' N, 80° 1.151' W

8–5 Goose Creek Chapel

[No longer extant, replaced by marker 8–48 in 2007.]

Old U.S. Hwy. 52, 9 mi. S of Moncks Corner

Here stood the chapel of ease of the Parish of St. James Goose Creek. [*Erected by the South Carolina Historical Commission, ca. 1929–1936.*]

8–6 Goose Creek Church

[Supplanted by marker 8–47 in 2007.]

Near St. James, Goose Creek Church, Snake River Rd., 0.2 miles South of Old State Rd., Goose Creek; Originally erected on U.S. Hwy. 52, 14.4 mi. S of Moncks Corner, in Charleston County

The Parish St. James was founded by Act of Assembly in 1706. The present edifice was begun in 1714 and completed in 1719. The royal arms of Great Britain can still be seen over the chancel, and here is preserved the Izard Hatchment, said to be one of only two in America. [*Erected by the South Carolina Historical Commission, ca. 1929–1936.*]
GPS Coordinates: 32° 58.622' N, 80° 1.968' W

8–7 Battle of Lenud's Ferry

U.S. Hwy. 17-A, North of Jamestown at the Santee River

Here, on May 6, 1780, Col. A. M. White was routed by Tarleton with the loss of 2 officers and 36 men killed and wounded and 7 officers and 60 dragoons taken; Tarleton lost 2 men. Two boys, Francis Deliesseline and Samuel Dupre, recaptured 14 of White's horses and delivered them to Maj. Jamison, Georgetown, refusing reward. *Erected by Berkeley County Historical Society* [Replaced a marker originally erected by the Georgetown Chapter D. A. R. in 1940.]
GPS Coordinates: 33° 17.837' N, 79° 41.064' W

8–8 Mepkin Plantation

S.C. Sec. Rd. 8-44, 4.9 mile South of its intersection with S.C. Hwy. 402, South of Moncks Corner

Home of Henry Laurens, born in Charleston in 1724, died at Mepkin in 1792. President of the first and second councils of safety,

1775–1776. President First Provincial Congress of S.C. 1775. Vice President of S.C. 1776. President of Continental Congress 1777–78. Elected minister plenipotentiary to Holland 1779. Confined 14 months in Tower of London, exchanged for Lord Cornwallis. Signed in Paris, with Adams, Jay and Franklin, preliminaries of peace, 1782.
GPS Coordinates: 33° 6.893' N, 79° 56.643' W

8–9 Biggin Church Ruins

[Replaced a marker ("Biggin Church") |erected by the South Carolina Historical Commission, 1929-1936.]

S.C. Hwy. 402, .8 mi. South of its intersection with U.S. Hwy. 52, Moncks Corner vicinity

(FRONT) These ruins are all that remains of Biggin Church, built soon after the American Revolution as the parish church of St. John's Berkeley Parish. This large parish, created in 1706 by the Anglican Church, was long and narrow, with distinct Upper, Middle, and Lower areas. The church here was named for nearby Biggin Creek, which flows into the Cooper River.
(REVERSE) The first church on this site was a log building. It was replaced ca. 1710–15 by a brick church, which burned in a forest fire in 1755. A brick church covered in stucco, built here ca. 1767, was burned by the British in 1781. These ruins are of the fourth and last church here, used infrequently after the Civil War. This church burned in a forest fire before 1899. *Sponsored by the Berkeley County Historical Society and the Biggin Cemetery Association, 2013*
GPS Coordinates: 33° 12.779' N, 79° 57.981' W

8–10 Quenby Bridge

Clements Ferry Rd. (S.C. Sec. Rd. 8-98), .3 mi. Southwest of its intersection with S.C. Hwy. 41, Huger

At this bridge, on July 17, 1781, British forces under Col. Coates, who was retreating from Moncks Corner, encountered pursuing Americans under Gen. Thomas Sumter. After the destruction of the bridge, Col. Coates sought refuge under cover of the buildings at Quimby

Plantation, where, that afternoon, he defeated an attack by the Americans. Those who fell in this engagement are said to have been buried near the road.
GPS Coordinates: 33° 5.656' N, 79° 48.478' W

8–11 Pompion Hill Chapel

Clements Ferry Rd. (S.C. Sec. Rd. 8–98), 2.3 m. Southwest of its intersection with S.C. Hwy. 41, Huger Vicinity

One quarter mile north, the first Church of England edifice outside Charleston was erected of cypress in 1703, largely through the efforts of Gov. Sir Nathaniel Johnson. The present brick structure was erected in 1763. The Parish of St. Thomas, of which this was a chapel of ease, was established by Act of Assembly, Nov. 30, 1706.
GPS Coordinates: 33° 4.853' N, 79° 50.151' W

8–12 Brabant Plantation

Clements Ferry Rd. (S.C. Sec. Rd. 8–98), 7.4 mile Southwest of its intersection with S.C. Hwy. 41, South of Huger

Residence of Rt. Rev. Robert Smith, who was born in Norfolk England, 1732. He was consecrated in Philadelphia in 1795 as the first Episcopal bishop of South Carolina. He died in 1801 and was buried in St. Philip's Churchyard, Charleston, S.C. On this plantation, on January 1782, an engagement took place between Americans under Col. Richard Richardson and British under Maj. Coffin.
GPS Coordinates: 33° 1.212' N, 79° 51.199' W

8–13 St. Thomas Church

Clements Ferry Rd. (S.C. Sec. Rd. 8–98), 11.9 mile Southwest of its intersection with S.C. Hwy. 41, South of Huger

The Parish of St. Thomas was established by Act of Assembly Nov. 30, 1706. The first church was erected in 1708 and destroyed by forest fire in 1815. The present edifice was erected in 1819.
GPS Coordinates: 32° 57.66' N, 79° 51.403' W

8–14 Spring Hill Methodist Church

S.C. Hwy. 27, about 2.5 miles South of its intersection with S.C. Hwy. 176, West of Moncks Corner

According to tradition Methodists worshiped here under a brush arbor as early as 1800. On August 2, 1814, Phillip Keller deeded one acre for a Methodist Church and burying ground. Eden and Rebecca Green Thrower deeded an additional acre in 1839. A new wooden structure replaced the original building in 1846–47. The present church was built in 1958. *Erected by The Williams Family Association, 1963*
GPS Coordinates: 33° 13.897' N, 80° 19.474' W

8–15 Thomas Sumter's Store

S.C. Hwy. 6, .5 miles south of Berkeley County-Orangeburg County line, north of Moncks Corner

About 1765–1767 Thomas Sumter, future hero of the American Revolution, kept a country store near this spot where the stream of colonial traffic to the Up Country divided in the fork where the Nelson's Ferry Road branched off from the Road to the Congarees. *Erected by The Cross Community Development Club, 1963*
GPS Coordinates: 33° 22.641' N, 80° 13.309' W

8–16 Lewisfield Plantation

Old U.S. Hwy. 52, about 1 miles Southwest of Moncks Corner

This land, part of Fairlawn Barony and known as Little Landing, was bought in 1767 by Sedgwick Lewis. His daughter Sarah married Keating Simons. They acquired the land in 1774 and are presumed to have built the present plantation house. Tradition has it that during the Revolution, Col. Wade Hampton took seventy-eight British prisoners and burned two boats with supplies and plunder at the nearby river landing. *Erected by Berkeley County Historical Society, 1978*
GPS Coordinates: 33° 10.059' N, 80° 0.888' W

8–17 Old Jamestown

S.C. Hwy. 45, about 1.5 miles Southeast of Jamestown

After receiving a proprietary land grant of 370 acres in 1705, French settlers laid out the town of Jamestown, c. 2 mi. N. By 1706, a church had been built known as the parish church of St. James, Santee. Jamestown never prospered and a number of settlers left before the Revolution, moving to the nearby parishes of St. Stephen's and St. John's, Berkeley. *Erected by the Berkeley County Historical Society, 1985* GPS Coordinates: 33° 16.172' N, 79° 40.12' W

8–18 Francis Marion/Francis Marion's Grave

S.C. Hwy. 45, 10 miles West of St. Stephen

Francis Marion (FRONT)
Brigadier General of S.C. Militia during the American Revolution, Francis Marion, was one of the partisan leaders who kept the war alive during the British occupation of the state. His elusive disappearances after surprise attacks against superior forces harassed and demoralized the enemy, earning for him the name, "Swamp Fox."
Francis Marion's Grave (REVERSE)
Francis Marion died Feb. 27, 1795, in his 63rd year, and was buried here at Belle Isle Plantation, home of his brother, Gabriel. His own plantation, Pond Bluff, was about 15 miles up river and is now under Lake Marion. He was born in South Carolina, the descendant of French Huguenot emigrants. The exact date and place of his birth are unknown. *Erected by South Carolina Department of Parks, Recreation, and Tourism, 1975, replacing a marker erected by the S.C. State Commission of Forestry, 1965*
GPS Coordinates: 33° 27.232' N, 80° 5.194' W

8–19 Medway

Old Mt. Holly Rd. & U.S. Hwy. 52, Goose Creek

(FRONT) Medway, established in 1686, features a 1704–05 brick house which is one of the oldest in S.C. The Lords Proprietors gave 12,000 acres on Back River to Johan W. van Aerssen (1632–ca. 1687), a Dutch Huguenot. In 1688 van Aerssen's widow Sabina married Thomas Smith (ca. 1648–1694), who acquired the plantation in 1691 and built a one-story brick house here ca. 1692. Smith, who was later briefly governor of S.C. 1693–94, is buried at Medway.

(REVERSE) Edward Hyrne acquired Medway from Thomas Smith's son, but the house burned in 1704. Hyrne built a new brick house in the same style. Later owners added a second story and other additions from the 1820s to the 1870s. The Stoney family owned Medway from 1833 to 1930, when Sidney (1903–1948) and Gertrude Legendre (1902–2000) bought it. The Legendres restored the house and grounds, and Medway was listed in the National Register of Historic Places in 1970. *Erected by the City of Goose Creek, 2009, replacing a marker erected in 1965*
GPS Coordinates: 33° 2.242' N, 80° 2.014' W

8–20 Strawberry Chapel

S.C. Sec. Rd. 8–44, about 7 miles South of its intersection with S.C. Hwy. 402, between Moncks Corner and Goose Creek

Chapel of Ease to St. John's (Biggin Church), built about 1725 on land bequeathed by James Child, founder at this place, of the Town of Childbury. Strawberry Ferry was established here by Act of Assembly in 1705.
GPS Coordinates: 33° 5.751' N, 79° 55.983' W

8–21 Silk Hope Plantation

S.C. Hwy. 402, about 2.5 miles North of Huger

Home and burial place of Sir Nathaniel Johnson, born in the County of Durham, England, in 1644; knighted in 1680, was a member of Parliament and Governor of Leeward Islands. He came to South Carolina in 1683 and settled at Silk Hope. From here he sent, in 1699, samples of silk to England. He was Governor of South Carolina from 1702 to 1709. Lord Cornwallis had his headquarters here for several months during the American Revolution.
GPS Coordinates: 33° 6.847' N, 79° 48.257' W

8–22 Berkeley County

Ten (10) markers, on Berkeley County line at major entrances:

1: S.C. Hwy. 6 at Berkeley County-Orangeburg County line, 7 mi. E of Eutawville

2: U.S. Hwy. 176 at Berkeley County-Orangeburg County line, 6 mi. SE of Holly Hill

3: Old U.S. Hwy. 52 at Goose Creek at Berkeley County-Orangeburg County line

4: S.C. Hwy. 41 at Berkeley County-Charleston County line, at Wando River near Cainhoy

5: U.S. Hwy. 17-A & S.C. Hwy. 41 at Santee River, N of Jamestown

6: S.C. Hwy. 27 at Berkeley County-Dorchester County line, near I-26

7: U.S. Hwy. 17-A at Berkeley County-Dorchester County line, at Summerville

8: S.C. Sec. Rd. 8-133, about 7.4 mi. E of Huger

9: S.C. Hwy. 45 at Berkeley County-Charleston County line, 6.5 mi. NW of McClellanville

10: U.S. Hwy. 52 at Berkeley County-Williamsburg County line, Santee River

[Text #1, ca. 1940]
Berkeley County
Area 1,238 square miles
Established by order of the Lord Proprietors, May 10, 1682. Named for John (Lord) Berkeley and Sir William Berkeley. The largest county in the state, and part of the middle coastal highway district.
This highway and markers were financed by Berkeley and Charleston Counties with the cooperation of the S.C. Highway Commission, Charleston Chamber of Commerce and through the Board of Commissioners.
The inscriptions on the highway historical markers in Berkeley County were compiled by Henry R. Dwight.
Board of Commissioners
Charleston County
Jenkins M. Robertson, Chairman
John Hertz
Berkeley County
J. Russell Williams
William F. Burguson, Sec. & Treas. M. Rutledge Rivers, Atty.

[Text #2, 1976]
This county was designated a court and land conveyance district in 1682, and an election district in 1683. It was named for two brothers, Lord John and Sir William Berkeley, both Lords Proprietors of Carolina. Over the years, functions of this early county have changed.

Modern Berkeley was created in 1882. Several boundary changes occurred 1893–1921. *Erected by Berkeley County Historical Society, 1976*

8–23 Wadboo Barony

S.C. Hwy. 402, Northwest side of Wadboo Bridge, Moncks Corner vicinity

Near this point was the SW corner of Wadboo Barony, a 12,000-acre tract about 4 miles square, granted in 1683 to James Colleton, son of an original Lord Proprietor, as part of the land due him as a landgrave of Carolina. Colleton's heirs were Loyalists during the Revolution; the Barony was confiscated, divided, and sold to Patriot citizens. *Erected by Berkeley County Historical Society, 1976*
GPS Coordinates: 33° 11.747' N, 79° 57.203' W

8–24 Cherokee Path

S.C. Hwy. 6 at its intersection with S.C. Sec. Rd. 8-132, Northwest of Moncks Corner

The main Cherokee Path, which extended from the overhill towns of the Cherokee Indians in present Tennessee to Charleston, passed near here. In existence before 1730, this early trade and transportation route played a significant role in the expansion of the North American frontier. *Erected by Berkeley County Historical Society, 1977*
GPS Coordinates: 33° 20.71' N, 80° 8.602' W

8–25 Francis Marion

S.C. Sec. Rd. 8-44 about 2.5 miles below Wadboo Bridge, Moncks Corner vicinity

According to family information, Francis Marion, brigadier general of the S.C. Militia during the American Revolution, was born near here on Goatfield Plantation. He was a member of the First Provincial Congress, fought in the battles of Parker's Ferry and Eutaw Springs (both in 1781), and served eight years in the S.C. Senate. Marion died in 1795. *Erected by Berkeley County Historical Society, 1986*
GPS Coordinates: 33° 9.953' N, 79° 57.46' W

8–26 Cross Post Office

S.C. Hwy. 6, Cross

This post office, originally named Cross Mill, was established in 1879. Adam Cross, a local storekeeper and Civil War veteran, was first postmaster. *Erected by Berkeley County Historic Preservation Commission, 1992*
GPS Coordinates: 33° 19.795′ N, 80° 9.19′ W

8–27 Otranto Plantation

Otranto Blvd. (extension of Otranto Rd., S.C. Sec. Rd. 8-542), at the railroad tracks, just Southwest of Goose Creek

Originally known as "Yeshoe," this plantation was granted in 1679 to Arthur Middleton, great-granduncle of the signer of the Declaration of Independence. Called "Otranto" after 1771, when it was bought by Dr. Alexander Garden, noted physician and botanist, for whom the "Gardenia" was named. In recent times, the estate was used as a hunt club. *Erected by Garden Club of Otranto, 1986*
GPS Coordinates: 32° 57.9′ N, 80° 2.514′ W

8–28 St. John's Church

S.C. Sec. Rd. 8-315 about ¼ miles North of its intersection with S.C. Hwy. 6, Pinopolis vicinity

This Baptist Church, constituted 1851, constructed the present building here in 1881 on land donated by A. D. Hare, a church trustee. *Erected by Berkeley County Historical Society, 1993*
GPS Coordinates: 33° 12.662′ N, 80° 2.625′ W

8–29 Otranto Indigo Vat

East side of Brushy Park Rd. (S.C. Sec. Rd. 8-503), at Gate 1 of the Brushy Park Industrial Complex, South of Moncks Corner

Built 1750–1790 at Otranto Plantation and used to process dye from indigo, an important S.C. crop from 1747 to 1796. Moved here 1979. *Erected by Berkeley County Historical Society, 1994*
GPS Coordinates: 32° 59.031′ N, 79° 55.95′ W

8–30 Thomas Walter

U.S. Hwy. 52 just East of its intersection with Colonel Maham Dr., Cross vicinity

The grave of Thomas Walter (ca. 1740–1789), pioneer botanist, is 9 mi. W at his Santee River plantation. A native of England, Walter came to S.C. by 1769. He collected and catalogued many plants native to the lowcountry. His catalog *Flora Caroliniana*, published in London in 1788, was the first botany of an American region to use the Linnaean classification system. *Erected by the Garden Club of S.C., Inc., 2003, replacing a marker erected in 1994*
GPS Coordinates: 33° 26.33′ N, 79° 59.1′ W

8–31 Pinopolis

In front of Pinopolis Post Office on S.C. Sec. Rd. 8-5, Pinopolis

Plantation owners began this pineland village in the 1830s to escape lowcountry plantation summer nights, thought to cause "country fever" (malaria). By 1844 Pinopolis comprised about twelve homes. The village served as a shelter for refugees during the Civil War. The post office began in 1894 with Elizabeth Ravenel as postmaster. Pinopolis has two Historic Districts listed in the National Register of Historic Places. *Erected by Anne Sinkler Fishburne Foundation and Berkeley County Historical Society, 1995*
GPS Coordinates: 33° 13.847′ N, 80° 2.2′ W

83–2 Skirmish at Wambaw Bridge /Skirmish at Wambaw Creek

French Santee Rd. (S.C. Hwy. 45) near Wambaw Creek Bridge at the Berkeley County-Charleston County line, Honey Hill vicinity

Skirmish at Wambaw Bridge (FRONT)
On February 24, 1782, at Wambaw Bridge 6 mi. N, a force of British cavalry, regular infantry, and Loyalist militia under Col. Benjamin Thompson surprised, defeated, and scattered part of Gen. Francis Marion's brigade of S.C. militia and Continental dragoons, under Col. Archibald McDonald and Maj. William Benison. The Americans lost 44 killed and captured; the British, none.

Skirmish at Wambaw Creek (REVERSE)
When Marion, who had just left the S.C.
Assembly to return to the army, learned of
the disaster, he took a regiment of Continental dragoons and marched toward the Santee
River. On February 25th Thompson surprised
Marion's force and drove it from Tidyman's
plantation near Wambaw Creek. The Americans lost 32 killed and captured; the British
lost 1 man captured in two days' fighting.
Erected by the Berkeley County Historical
Society and the U.S. Forest Service, 1997
GPS Coordinates: 33° 12.441' N, 79° 28.125' W

8–34 Moss Grove

[Marker misnumbered, should have been
8-33.]

**Ranger Dr. (S.C. Hwy. 6) at Country Pond Ln.,
South of Cross**

John J. Cross (1810–1890) bought 500 acres
here in 1844 and soon expanded Moss Grove
into one of the most productive cotton plantations in antebellum Berkeley District. This
house was built ca. 1880 for Cross's son Adam
(1844–1906), who farmed here and served as
postmaster while also operating a store, cotton gin, grist mill, rice mill, saw mill, and turpentine still. *Erected by the Berkeley County
Historical Society, 2002*
GPS Coordinates: 33° 19.385' N, 80° 9.738' W

8–34 St. Stephen's Episcopal Church

**Mendel Rivers Rd. (S.C. Hwy. 45), just East of its
junction with U.S. Hwy. 52, St. Stephen**

(FRONT) St. Stephen's, built 1767–69, is a fine
example of the rural churches built in the
S.C. lowcountry before the Revolution. "The
Church is one of the handsomest Country
Churches in So. Ca. and would be no mean
ornament in Charleston," the Rev. Frederick Dalcho wrote in his 1808 history of S.C.
Episcopalians.
(REVERSE) Essentially Georgian in style, St. Stephen's features a gambrel roof with curvilinear
gables and ornate interior woodwork such as
its high pulpit. Services were suspended many
times over the years. The church was last

restored and regular services resumed in 1955.
It was designated a National Historic Landmark in 1970. *Erected by the Berkeley County
Historical Society, 2004*
GPS Coordinates: 33° 24.346' N, 79° 55.011' W

8–35 Rehoboth Methodist Church

**Macbeth Rd. (S.C. Sec. Rd. 8–52), just West of its
intersection with U.S. Hwy. 52, Macbeth**

(FRONT) This church grew out of services held
as early as 1811, at first in a brush arbor and
later at a campground nearby. Ministers riding the Cooper River and Berkeley circuits
served this congregation for many years. The
first sanctuary here was given to the Methodists by area Episcopalians in 1847. Called Black
Oak, it had been built in 1808 as a chapel of
ease for Biggin Church.
(REVERSE) In 1852 Charles Macbeth (1805–
1881), the planter and politician for whom this
community was named, donated a 15.3-acre
tract to the congregation. The cemetery, which
dates from the 1830s, includes the graves of
Revs. John Bunch, who served 1837–38, and
William J. Hutson, who served in 1870. The
present sanctuary was built in 1927, during the
pastorate of Rev. D. Tillman Rhodes; it was
renovated in 1977. *Erected in Memory of Barbara Weeks Goodrich by Family, Friends, and
the Berkeley County Historical Society, 2004*
GPS Coordinates: 33° 15.763' N, 79° 57.917' W

8–36 Santee Canal

[Replaced marker 8–3.]

**Stony Landing Rd., Old Santee Canal State Park,
Moncks Corner vicinity**

(FRONT) This canal, twenty-two miles in length,
connects the Santee and Cooper Rivers. It was
chartered by act of March 22, 1786, with capital of £100,000 sterling. Construction began
in 1793 and the canal was completed by 1800,
under the direction of Col. John Christian
Senf, a native of Sweden, as Chief Engineer.
The canal was in operation until about 1850.
(REVERSE) The Santee Canal was opened to
traffic from the Santee River to the Cooper
River in 1800. It was 22 miles long, 20 feet
wide at the bottom and 35 feet wide at the

surface. It was 5 ½ feet deep, carrying 4 feet of water, and was capable of carrying boats with loads of up to 22 tons. The canal ceased operations about 1850. *Erected by Santee Cooper, 2005, replacing a marker erected before 1954*
GPS Coordinates: 33° 11.633' N, 79° 58.44' W

8–37 L. Mendel Rivers House

Mendel Rivers Ave. and Brick Church Cir., St. Stephen

(FRONT) Lucius Mendel Rivers (1905–1970), state representative 1933–36 and U. S. Representative 1940–70, was born in nearby Gumville and grew up on the family farm on Bonneau Road (now Mendel Rivers Avenue). Rivers attended the College of Charleston and the University of S.C. School of Law, practicing law in Charleston before winning a special election to the S.C. legislature in 1933.
(REVERSE) Rivers served as a lawyer for the U. S. Justice Dept. 1936–40 before his election to Congress. A firm supporter of the military, Rivers was re-elected for fifteen terms. He was instrumental in expanding the Charleston Navy Base after World War II and served as chair of the House Armed Services Committee 1965–70, during the Vietnam War. He is buried nearby at St. Stephen Episcopal Church. *Erected by the Charleston Harbor Pilots, Maybank Shipping Company, and the William Gilmore Simms Literary Society, 2005*
GPS Coordinates: 33° 24.271' N, 79° 55' W

8–38 Casey (Caice)

Berkeley County Library, 325 Old Moncks Corner Rd., Goose Creek

(FRONT) This African-American community grew up around a Methodist church founded during Reconstruction by a freedman named Casey or Caice. Its early services were under a tent, but a log cabin served as its first permanent church. In 1868 T. W. Lewis and other trustees bought a 25-acre tract between S.C. Hwys. 176 and 52. After a frame church replaced the cabin, Rev. William Evans (1822–1887) became the first permanent ordained minister at Casey Methodist Church.

(REVERSE) Casey Methodist Church was destroyed by arson in 1977; the adjacent cemetery is all that remains. Casey School, a three-room frame school built next to the church in the 1930s, taught area children in grades 1–7 until it burned in 1966. The Goose Creek Branch of the Berkeley County Public Library was built on the site in 1991. The Casey Fellowship Hall, across Moncks Corner Road from the church, was also a vital institution in the Casey community for many years. *Erected by the City of Goose Creek, 2006*
GPS Coordinates: 33° 1.193' N, 80° 2.573' W

8–39 Dixie Training School /Berkeley Training High School

Intersection of Main St. and Old U.S. Hwy. 52 North, Moncks Corner

Dixie Training School (FRONT)
Berkeley Training High School, first called Dixie Training School, stood here from 1920 until the 1980s. The first public school for blacks in Moncks Corner was founded in 1880. It held classes in local churches until its first school was built in 1900. The three-room school built here 1918–1920 at a cost of $6,700 was one of almost 500 in S.C. funded in part by the Julius Rosenwald Foundation 1917–1932.
Berkeley Training High School (REVERSE)
Rev. James Van Wright led a local effort to fund and build the school, with its slogan "A Dollar or A Day." Rev. Harleston, the first principal, was succeeded in 1921 by R. A. Ready (d. 1952), principal for 29 years. The school, at first including grades 1–11, became Berkeley Training High School in the 1930s. It moved into a new school on U.S. Hwy. 17 in 1955 and closed in 1970 when county schools desegregated. *Erected by the Alumni and Friends of Berkeley Training High School, 2006*
GPS Coordinates: 33° 11.524' N, 79° 59.778' W

8–40 Springfield Plantation

Boulder Bluff Elementary School, 400 Judy Dr., Goose Creek

(FRONT) Springfield Plantation, an inland rice plantation, was established here by Paul

Mazyck (d. 1749), a planter and merchant who combined two large tracts on Foster Creek, a branch of Back River. His father Isaac, a French Huguenot planter, had come to S.C. in 1686. Paul Mazyck, who owned more than 40 slaves by the time of his death, grew rice and other crops here and also owned several businesses in Charleston.

(REVERSE) A two-story house once stood here, with a large oak avenue in front and an ornamental "pleasure garden" behind it. Paul Mazyck's son Alexander (d. 1786) inherited Springfield; his widow Elizabeth owned 100 slaves in 1790. The plantation was sold out of the Mazyck family by 1846. Its 940 acres were divided into tenant farms for the next hundred years until it was developed for housing in the 1950s. *Erected by the City of Goose Creek, 2007*
GPS Coordinates: 33° 1.438' N, 80° 1.599' W

8–4.1 Howe Hall Plantation /Howe Hall

Dogwood Park, 460 Liberty Hall Rd., Goose Creek

Howe Hall Plantation (FRONT)
Howe Hall Plantation, an inland rice plantation, was established here by Robert Howe, who came to S.C. in 1683. His first house here was later described as "tolerable." Howe's son Job (d. 1706) built a brick plantation house here once described as "commodious" but spent most of his time in Charleston. Howe served in the Commons House of Assembly 1696–1706 and was Speaker 1700–05. He died of yellow fever in 1706.

Howe Hall (REVERSE)
Howe Hall Plantation was later purchased by several planters, including Thomas Middleton in 1719 and Benjamin Smith in 1769. By the late antebellum period James Vidal owned it and other nearby plantations. During Reconstruction Vidal sold parcels to African American societies and to individual freedmen. This area became an African American farming community for many years. Dogwood Park was created here by the Goose Creek Recreation Commission in 1990. *Erected by the Goose Creek Recreation Commission, 2007*
GPS Coordinates: 32° 59.928' N, 80° 0.856' W

8–4.2 Howe Hall Plantation/Howe Hall Elementary School

Howe Hall AIMS Elementary School, 115 Howe Hall Rd., Goose Creek

Howe Hall Plantation (FRONT)
Howe Hall Plantation was established here by Robert Howe about 1683 and passed to his son Job Howe (d. 1706), Speaker of the Commons House of Assembly 1700–05. Later owned by such prominent lowcountry families as the Middletons and Smiths, it was owned by James Vidal before the Civil War. During Reconstruction Vidal sold parcels to African American societies and individual freedmen for small farms.

Howe Hall Elementary School (REVERSE)
Howe Hall became an African American community made up of small family farms in the 1870s. It was nicknamed "Hog Hall" by locals who belittled the area's lower status when compared to the old plantation. Howe Hall Elementary School, serving grades 1–8, consolidated several local black schools and was built here in 1954. Integrated in 1967, it has been Howe Hall AIMS (Arts Infused Magnet School) Elementary since 2002. *Erected by the City of Goose Creek, 2007*
GPS Coordinates: 32° 58.774' N, 80° 1.686' W

8–4.3 Varner Town Indian Community

S. Live Oak Dr. (U.S. Hwy. 17-A), 1.4 mi. North of its intersection with St. James Ave. near Carnes Crossroads, Moncks Corner vicinity

(FRONT) Varner Town (or Varnertown) is a distinct Native American community including descendants of the Etiwan, Catawba, Cherokee, Edisto, and other area tribes. This community, located near Carnes Crossroads and Goose Creek, was named for William Varner (d. 1927) and his wife Mary Williams Varner (d. 1924).

(REVERSE) Several Indian schools served this community. The Varner School, also called the Varner Indian School, was built here in 1939 and closed in 1963. The church nearby has been the center of the community for many years. Nearby Williams Cemetery was named in memory of William W. Williams,

an Indian ancestor. *Erected by the Berkeley County Historical Society, 2007*
GPS Coordinates: 33° 4.266' N, 80° 5.218' W

8–44 Liberty Hall Plantation

101 Woodward Rd., Goose Creek

(FRONT) This inland rice plantation has its origins in a 1683 grant. In 1726 Nathaniel Moore and his wife sold a 900-acre parcel to Isaac Mazyck (d. 1736). Mazyck's son Benjamin (d. 1800), a rice planter, cattleman, and merchant, consolidated several nearby plantations and lived here until his death, when his son Stephen (1787–1832) inherited the plantation. Stephen's widow Mary sold it to Dr. Charles L. Desel in 1834.
(REVERSE) Dr. Charles Lewis Desel (1795–1855), a planter and physician, owned this plantation for more than twenty years. His friend Rev. John Bachman (1790–1874), a Lutheran minister and naturalist, brought artist and naturalist John James Audubon (1785–1851) here several times to hunt and observe birds and wildlife. Liberty Hall declined after the Civil War, and was leased as a hunting preserve from 1912 to 1943. *Erected by the City of Goose Creek, 2007*
GPS Coordinates: 32° 59.988' N, 80° 0.636' W

8–45 Boochawee Hall

Lake Greenview Park, East Pandora Dr. between Wells Rd. and Paslay Dr., Goose Creek
(FRONT) Boochawee Hall, created in 1683 by a 2,400-acre grant, was owned by two colonial governors, father and son. James Moore (d. 1706), a trader and planter, served on the Grand Council and later led "the Goose Creek Men," an anti-proprietary faction. Appointed governor in 1700, Moore commanded an expedition to Florida, burning St. Augustine in 1702. Moore, replaced as governor by Sir Nathaniel Johnson in 1703, returned to the council and held a seat there until his death. (REVERSE) James Moore Jr. (d. 1724) served three terms in the Commons House of Assembly and as an officer in the Tuscarora War (1711–13) before commanding the provincial forces in the Yemassee War (1715). Moore was appointed governor when the proprietary

government was overthrown in 1719. He was essentially a caretaker until he was succeeded by provisional royal governor Francis Nicholson in 1721. Moore was Speaker of the House in the first Royal Assembly at his death. *Erected by the City of Goose Creek, 2007*
GPS Coordinates: 32° 59.759' N, 80° 1.713' W

8–46 Button Hall

City of Goose Creek Department of Public Works, 200 Brandywine Blvd., Goose Creek

(FRONT) This plantation was once part of Boochawee Hall, owned by Governor James Moore (d. 1706). Moore left 615 acres to his daughter Rebecca, who married Thomas Barker (d. 1715) in 1709. Barker, who planted inland rice here, served one term in the Commons House of Assembly. In 1715, at the outset of the Yemassee War, Barker raised and commanded a company defending Goose Creek. That spring Capt. Barker and 26 of his men were killed in a Yemassee ambush.
(REVERSE) Rebecca Moore Barker married planter William Dry (d. 1740), who served six terms in the Commons House of Assembly and was its Speaker 1728–29. In 1785 William Loughton Smith (1758–1812) acquired the plantation; he was a state representative and later U.S. Congressman and U.S. minister to Portugal. Button Hall was owned by two of Smith's grandsons after the Civil War, when it was subdivided and sold or rented to freedmen for small farms. *Erected by the City of Goose Creek, 2007*
GPS Coordinates: 33° 0.205' N, 80° 2.145' W

8–47 St. James, Goose Creek

Vestry Ln., just off Snake River Rd. (S.C. Sec. Rd. 8-208), Goose Creek

(FRONT) St. James, Goose Creek was one of the first Anglican parishes in the lowcountry, created by the Church Act of 1706. The first church here, built in 1707, was a frame building. This Georgian brick church, covered in stucco, was completed in 1719. Described in 1855 as "a romantically situated ancient church," it was restored after the Charleston Earthquake of 1886, in 1907, and in 1955.

(REVERSE) Exterior features include a hipped roof and a pediment with a relief of a pelican feeding her young, symbol of the Society for the Propagation of the Gospel, which sent missionaries here from London. Interior features include a tall pulpit, the Royal arms of George I, and a hatchment, or arms, of the Izard family. This church was designated as a National Historic Landmark in 1970. *Erected by the Vestry of the St. James, Goose Creek Church, 2007*
GPS Coordinates: 32° 58.545' N, 80° 1.983' W

8-48 St. James, Goose Creek Chapel of Ease/Bethlehem Baptist Church

[Replaced marker 8-5, erected by the South Carolina Historical Commission, ca. 1929–1946.]

Intersection of Old U.S. Hwy. 52 (S.C. Sec. Rd. 8-791) & Avanti Ln., North of Goose Creek

St. James, Goose Creek Chapel of Ease (FRONT) One of two chapels of ease for St. James, Goose Creek Parish stood here on the road to Moncks Corner, about 7 miles from the 1719 parish church. The chapel of ease was a brick building with a cruciform plan. It was completed by 1725, during the tenure of the Rev. Richard Ludlam, but was already in ruins by 1820.

Bethlehem Baptist Church (REVERSE) Bethlehem Baptist Church, founded in 1812, built a frame church on this site. Described as "a neat wooden church adjoining the ruin" just before the Civil War, it was moved 4.5 miles NW in 1880. The church was renamed Groomsville Baptist Church for the Groom family, which donated the land. Cemeteries laid out here by the Anglicans and Baptists are contiguous and intermingled. *Erected by Berkeley County, 2007*
GPS Coordinates: 33° 4.161' N, 80° 1.391' W

8-49 Thorogood Plantation /Mount Holly Plantation

At the entrance to Mount Holly Aluminum, 3575 St. James Ave. (U.S. Hwy. 52), Goose Creek

Thorogood Plantation (FRONT)

In 1682 the Lords Proprietors granted 3,000 acres here, on a branch of the Back River, to Joseph Thorogood (d. 1684). Though Thorogood only owned the plantation two years and his widow Jane sold it after his death, it was called "Thorogood" for most of the 19th century. By the 1720s Andrew Allen owned Thorogood, established a profitable rice plantation here, and was also engaged in the local fur trade.

Mount Holly Plantation (REVERSE) Thorogood passed to John Deas (d. 1788) and his son John, Jr. (1761–1790). It, Mount Holly, and Cyprus plantations remained in the Deas family until 1824. Subdivided after the Civil War, this area was the core of an African American farming community. H. Smith Richardson bought it as a hunting plantation in 1937, renaming it Mount Holly. Mt. Holly Aluminum has produced aluminum as its plant here since 1980. *Erected by Mt. Holly Aluminum, 2007*
GPS Coordinates: 33° 2.325' N, 80° 2.098' W

8-50 Goose Creek/City of Goose Creek

125 St. James Ave., Goose Creek
Goose Creek (FRONT)
This area has been called Goose Creek since the late 17th century. For almost 200 years after the Lords Proprietors granted large tracts to English, French Huguenot, and other planters, their plantations dominated the landscape. After the Civil War most plantations were subdivided into small farms, many of them owned by freedmen and their descendants. Rural farming communities grew up around area crossroads from the late 19th century to the mid-20th century.

City of Goose Creek (REVERSE) World War II and the Cold War brought dramatic growth to this area with the U.S. Ammunition Depot and Naval Weapons Annex in 1941 and 1959, respectively. The population grew so quickly that local leaders hoping to manage the influx chartered and incorporated the City of Goose Creek in 1961, with Hilton W. Bunch as its first mayor. In 1966 a building here, originally a laundry, was converted for use as the third Goose Creek City Hall,

serving the town from 1974 to 1999. *Erected by Advance Auto Parts, Inc., 2007*
GPS Coordinates: 32° 59.954' N, 80° 2.44' W

8–51 St. Stephen Colored School /St. Stephen High School

Russellville Rd./Old Mill Rd., St. Stephen

St. Stephen Colored School (FRONT)
St. Stephen Colored School, the first public African American school in St. Stephen, was built here in 1924–25. A three-room frame building, it was one of almost 500 schools in S.C. funded in part by the Julius Rosenwald Foundation 1917–1932. It opened with grades 1–7, but burned in 1935. A brick elementary and high school with grades 1–10 replaced it. Grades 11 and 12 were added in 1936–37 and 1948–49.
St. Stephen High School (REVERSE)
A nine-room brick high school was constructed here in 1944–45, with Woodrow Z. Wilson as its last principal. It closed in 1954, and its students transferred to the new Russellville High School. The elementary school, with grades 1–7, was replaced by a new St. Stephen Elementary in 1966. The buildings here were torn down in 1965, and their bricks and lumber donated to Allen A.M.E. Church. *Erected by the Alumni and Friends of St. Stephen Colored Elementary and High School, 2008*
GPS Coordinates: 33° 24' N, 79° 55.605' W

8–52 The Village of Pineville

Matilda Cir. (S.C. Sec. Rd. 204), just South of its junction with S.C. Hwy. 45, Pineville

(FRONT) Pineville, established in 1793–94, was one of the first planters' retreats in the South. James Sinkler built the first summer house here in 1793. Pineville, named for its "religiously preserved" pines and known for its "sweet and balmy air," became a village in 1794 after John Cordes, Peter Gaillard, John Palmer, and Peter, Philip, and Samuel Porcher built houses here as well.
(REVERSE) By 1830 Pineville had more than 60 houses, a chapel, an academy, a library, and a race track. Frederick Porcher wrote in 1858, "the prestige of its ancient fame remains."

Union troops burned most of the village in 1865, except the chapel, library, post office, and Gourdin House (ca. 1820). The Pineville Historic District was listed in the National Register of Historic Places in 1992. *Erected by The Village of Pineville, 2008*
GPS Coordinates: 33° 25.616' N, 80° 1.744' W

8–53 Mount Holly Station /Mount Holly

Old Mt. Holly Rd., just South of its intersection with U.S. Hwy. 52, Mount Holly
Mount Holly Station (FRONT)

Mount Holly Station, a depot on the Northeastern Railroad between Florence and Charleston, was built here about 1853. It was named for nearby Mount Holly Plantation, carved out of Thorogood Plantation shortly before the American Revolution by John Deas, Jr. (1761–1790), a planter and state representative. The railroad tracks crossed the main oak avenue to the plantation, just south of the station and platform.
Mount Holly (REVERSE)
Otranto (or Porcher) was the next station toward Charleston, 19 mi. SSE. After the Civil War this vicinity, which kept the name Mount Holly, was a predominantly white rural community, in contrast to black rural communities nearby at Casey, Howe Hall, and Liberty Hall. Rice plantations were replaced by subsistence farms worked by families, tenants, or sharecroppers. Mount Holly was incorporated into the City of Goose Creek when it was created in 1961. *Erected by the Goose Creek Tea Ladies, 2009*
GPS Coordinates: 33° 1.743' N, 80° 2.1' W

8–54 The Oaks

The Oaks Plantation Golf & Country Club, 130 The Oaks Ave., Goose Creek

(FRONT) The Oaks, an inland rice plantation, was established here by Edward Middleton (d. 1685) on a 1678 grant from the Lords Proprietors. Middleton, a planter who came to S.C. from Barbados, received 1,630 acres on Yeaman's Creek, later renamed Goose Creek. Middleton served in several colonial offices,

including as a member of the Grand Council. The Oaks passed to Middleton's son Arthur (1681–1737), also on the Council, later President of the first Royal Council.
(REVERSE) Arthur Middleton's son Henry (1717–1784) served in the Continental Congress 1774–75 and was briefly its President. He later served in the Provincial Congress and first General Assembly of S.C. The original house here burned in 1840, long after the Middletons sold the property. The present house was built 1892 for Maine businessman Edwin Parsons, and renovated in 1930 by New York banker Charles Sabin. It has been The Oaks Plantation Golf & Country Club since 1964. *Erected by the Rotary Club of Goose Creek, 2008*
GPS Coordinates: 32° 59.031' N, 80° 2.135' W

8–55 Broom Hall Plantation

Bloomfield Park, off Westview Dr., Goose Creek

(FRONT) Broom Hall Plantation, later called Bloom Hall and still later Bloomfield, was first granted to Edward Middleton in 1678. By 1710 this property passed to Benjamin Gibbes (d. 1722), who named it for Broom House, his ancestral home in England. Gibbes's widow Amarinthia later married Peter Taylor (d. 1765), a longtime member of the Royal Assembly and rice planter, who built a large two-story brick house here.
(REVERSE) Broom Hall passed to Thomas Smith (1720–1790), member of the Royal Assembly and the Provincial Congress. An 1828 visitor called its gardens "the most interesting spot I have seen in Carolina." Sold to Henry Arthur Middleton in 1856, the house was virtually destroyed by the Charleston earthquake of 1886. Later owned by Westvaco, Broom Hall was subdivided for residential development in 1980. *Erected by the City of Goose Creek, 2008*
GPS Coordinates: 33° 0.154' N, 80° 3.881' W

8–56 Crowfield Plantation

Crowfield Golf & Country Club, 300 Hamlet Cir., Goose Creek

(FRONT) Crowfield Plantation, on the headwaters of Goose Creek, was originally granted to John Berringer in 1701. John Gibbes (1696–1764), a member of the Royal Assembly, sold it in 1721 to Arthur Middleton (1681–1737), also a member of the Royal Assembly. Middleton's son William (1710–1785) built a large two-story brick house here ca. 1730, naming it for Crowfield Hall, his great-aunt's English manor.
(REVERSE) William Middleton grew rice and indigo, raised cattle, made bricks, and laid out an elaborate formal garden. Rawlins Lowndes (1721–1800) bought Crowfield during the American Revolution; he sold it in 1783, describing it as "that elegant most admired seat." The house was virtually destroyed by the Charleston earthquake of 1886. Later owned by Westvaco, Crowfield became part of the Crowfield Golf & Country Club in 1990. *Erected by the City of Goose Creek, 2008*
GPS Coordinates: 33° 0.21' N, 80° 4.674' W

8–57 Early Indian Trading Paths /The Goose Creek Men

Goose Creek Municipal Center, 519 N. Goose Creek Blvd., Goose Creek

Early Indian Trading Paths (FRONT)
One of the earliest major trading paths in the Carolina colony, dating from the first decade of English settlement 1670–1680, ran nearby. The colonists traded guns and ammunition, cloth, rum, and other goods for furs and skins, trading with the Catawbas, Coosas, Westos, and Yamasees in the lowcountry and the Cherokees, Creeks, Choctaws, and Chickasaws farther in the backcountry.
The Goose Creek Men (REVERSE)
The "Goose Creek Men" were English planters, some who came to S.C. from Barbados. They settled nearby, soon became wealthy through the Indian trade, and conducted an illegal trade in Indian slaves and with pirates. The Goose Creek Men formed a faction opposing the Lords Proprietors between 1670 and 1720. Two of them, James Moore, Sr. (d. 1706) and his son James Moore, Jr. (d. 1724) served as governor of the colony. *Erected by the City of Goose Creek, 2008*
GPS Coordinates: 33° 1.664' N, 80° 2.132' W

8–58 Bowen's Corner

Intersection of Foster Creek Rd. & Tanner Ford Blvd., Hanahan

(FRONT) Bowen's Corner, an African-American farming community from the mid-19th century through the late-20th century, was originally part of a rice plantation established along Goose Creek in 1680. That tract was granted by the Lords Proprietors to Barnard Schenckingh (d. 1692). It was later owned by Benjamin Coachman (d. 1779), member of the Royal Assembly. By 1785 it passed to John Bowen (d. 1811), a state representative, for whom Bowen's Corner is named.

(REVERSE) Bowen and later absentee owners through the antebellum and post-Civil War era often employed slaves and freedmen as overseers or managers, giving them an opportunity to work toward self-sufficiency. "Bowen's Old Place" was subdivided into small farms after the war. By 1936 the Bowen's Corner community, between the railroad and the Goose Creek Reservoir, was centered on Bethel A.M.E. Church and Bowen's Corner School, for grades 1–8, which closed in 1954. *Erected by the City of Hanahan, 2008*
GPS Coordinates: 32° 56.224' N, 80° 0.507' W

8–59 Goose Creek Bridge

At the intersection of The Oaks Ave. and NAD Rd. (Naval Ammunition Depot Rd.), Goose Creek

(FRONT) The first bridge here, in use by 1680, had a raised road at either end and was built from split logs with the flat sides up, covered by sand or clay. Traffic over Goose Creek increased significantly after St. James, Goose Creek Church was built 200 yds. S in 1714–19. By the 1750s the bridge had to be replaced every few years. In 1780 British troops occupying The Oaks Plantation nearby guarded the bridge, a strategic point on the road to and from Charleston.

(REVERSE) The bridge was torn down and replaced by a larger covered one shortly after the Revolution. A later covered bridge, built in 1851, was 200 ft. long, on brick piers, with a plank floor and cypress shingle roof. It was burned in 1865 by Confederates attempting to delay Federals in the area. Another bridge here, built some years after the Civil War, was uncovered, with a simple railing. By 1925 a new U.S. Highway 52 included a bridge upstream and W. of this crossing. *Erected by the City of Goose Creek, 2008*
GPS Coordinates: 32° 58.85' N, 80° 1.961' W

8–60 Spring Grove Plantation

Cypress Gardens Rd. at the Spring Grove Plantation Clubhouse, Moncks Corner

(FRONT) Spring Grove, an inland rice plantation on the Back River, was part of a 1706 grant by the Lords Proprietors to John Barnwell. By 1727 the tract passed to planter and state representative Joseph Wragg (d. 1751) as part of his Dockton plantation. Spring Grove was not a separate plantation until 1793, when it included 1,406 acres, owned by planter and state representative George Keckley (d. 1829).

(REVERSE) Spring Grove remained in the Keckley family until 1843, when it was purchased by William Bell, who owned Cypress Grove and Pine Grove plantations nearby. Bell's son sold it soon after the Civil War. Spring Grove was later owned by the E. P. Burton Lumber Co., then the Cooper River Mining & Manufacture Co., and later the Pine Grove Hunting Club. It was subdivided for development as Pendley Homes in 2003. *Erected by Pendley Homes, 2008*
GPS Coordinates: 33° 4.693' N, 80° 0.640' W

8–61 The Yamasee War at Goose Creek, 1715

Foster Creek Park, adjacent to Goose Creek Primary School, 200 Foster Creek Rd., Goose Creek

(FRONT) In April 1715 Yamasee warriors killed government agents and traders who had come to meet with them at Pocotaligo, in present-day Beaufort County. Others killed colonists and raided plantations and farms at Port Royal, initiating the Yamasee War. Catawbas and Cherokees soon launched raids on other white towns and settlements, and many whites in Goose Creek fled to Charleston or barracaded themselves in their houses.

(REVERSE) Capt. Thomas Barker, who lived 1.5 mi. N, left Goose Creek on May 15 with 102

militia, intending to meet the Congarees near the Santee River. He and 26 men were killed in an ambush on May 16. On June 13 Capt. George Chicken and 120 cavalrymen of the Goose Creek militia ambushed a war party 20 mi. W near Wassamassaw, killing 40–60 and scattering the rest. The Catawbas would not threaten Goose Creek again. *Erected by the City of Goose Creek, 2008*
GPS Coordinates: 32° 58.309' N, 80° 1.844' W

8–62 Wassamassaw

At the intersection of State Rd. (U.S. Hwy. 176) and Jedburg Rd., Jedburg vicinity

(FRONT) Wassamassaw, with several variant spellings during the colonial era, is a Native American word thought to mean "connecting water." It first referred to the large cypress swamp here, but eventually referred to the community that grew up nearby in the Anglican parish of St. James, Goose Creek. Plantations laid out by the English and later by the Huguenots flourished before the Revolution. (REVERSE) The swamp was almost impassible for most of the colonial period, but the Wassamassaw Road ran just below the swamp between here and Goose Creek. A Chapel of Ease was built nearby shortly after the Yamasee War of 1715, and a free school was founded in 1728. The "Wassamassaw Cavalry," a militia company founded in 1857, later saw Confederate service as Company D, 2nd S.C. Cavalry. *Erected by Berkeley County, 2009*
GPS Coordinates: 33° 9.288' N, 80° 10.188' W

8–63 French Huguenot Plantation /Freedmen's Plantation

112–114 Westover Dr., Goose Creek

French Huguenot Plantation (FRONT)
Abraham Fleury, sometimes called Abraham Fleury Sieur De La Plaine, settled here about 1680. He was one of the first French Huguenot planters in Carolina. The Huguenots, Protestants who escaped the persecution of Catholic France, immigrated with encouragement from the Lords Proprietors, who promised them opportunity and religious freedom. They later assimilated into the predominantly Anglican society of the lowcountry.

Freedmen's Plantation (REVERSE)
This tract was often called Cherry Hill after it was merged into that plantation before the Revolution. In 1858 freedman and planter Lamb Stevens (1766?–1868) added it to his extensive holdings. Stevens, born into slavery in N.C., later purchased his freedom and moved to S.C. He owned as many as 30 slaves, some of them relatives he bought in order to protect them and their families. Lamb died in 1868 at the age of 102. *Erected by the City of Goose Creek, 2010*
GPS Coordinates: 33° 0.12' N, 80° 4.941' W

8–64 White House Plantation

At the Naval Weapons Station Charleston, Goose Creek

(FRONT) The first plantation here was established in 1731 by Alexander Vanderdussen (d. 1759), British army officer and member of the Royal Assembly. William Johnson (d. 1818), later a planter and state representative, bought it in 1769. Johnson demolished Vanderdussen's ruined house and built a new one, which he named "White House," on the old foundation. He grew rice and indigo here for many years.
(REVERSE) Johnson, an ardent Patriot, served in the Provincial Congress and the S.C. House of Representatives during the Revolution. He was an artilleryman during the Siege of Charleston in 1780, was held prisoner in exile for more than a year, then was reelected to the S.C. House several times after the war. White House eventually fell into ruins, and in 1941 the U.S. Navy acquired this property for its Naval Weapons Station. *Erected by the City of Goose Creek, 2010*
GPS Coordinates: 32° 50.772' N, 79° 56.649' W

8–65 Steepbrook Plantation

At Hanahan Elementary School, 4000 Mabeline Rd., Hanahan

(FRONT) This plantation was established in 1701 by a grant of 500 acres near Goose Creek to Lewis Lansac from the Lords Proprietors. In 1757 the original grant, with an additional 1,000 acres that had been owned by the Wilson and Godin families, was acquired by rice planter and legislator Peter Manigault (1731–1773). Manigault named his plantation for a stream that ran through his rice fields down to Goose Creek.

(REVERSE) Peter Manigault's two-story house sat on a nearby ridge on the bank of Goose Creek. Manigault, longtime member of the Commons House of Assembly, was Speaker of the House 1765–1772 and at his death the wealthiest man in North America. His son Gabriel (1758–1809), a planter and legislator, was best known as an amateur architect. W. J. Sineath acquired the 633-acre core of the plantation in 1833 and renamed it "The Oaks." *Erected by the Town of Hanahan, 2010*
GPS Coordinates: 32° 56.01' N, 80° 1.701' W

8–66 Berkeley Training High School

320 N. Live Oak Dr., Moncks Corner

(FRONT) Berkeley Training High School, located here from 1955 to 1970, replaced a four-room wood school 1 mi. S at Main St. and Old U.S. Hwy. 52. That school, built in 1918–1920 at a cost of $6,700, had been partially funded by the Julius Rosenwald Foundation. The new brick school, built here in 1955 at a cost of almost $400,000, opened with an enrollment of more than 500 students in grades 8–12.

(REVERSE) Joseph H. Jefferson, Sr. (1919–1983) was the only principal of Berkeley Training High School at this location, from 1955 to 1970. By the 1964–65 school year this school reached its peak of 723 students in grades 8–12. Its enrollment was reduced to grades 9–12 in 1965–66 and then to grades 10–12 in 1968–69. Berkeley Training High School closed in 1970 after the desegregation of Berkeley County schools. *Erected by the Berkeley Training High School Alumni Association, 2010*
GPS Coordinates: 33° 12.05' N, 79° 59.693' W

8–67 Friendship Methodist Church

1315 Ranger Dr. (S.C. Hwy. 6), Cross vicinity

(FRONT) This church, one of the oldest Methodist organizations in Berkeley County, was formally organized about 1825. Circuit riders

had preached in the area for more than forty years, and services held under a brush arbor here inspired participants to form a congregation and build their first church, a pole building.

(REVERSE) By 1843 the church built a large frame sanctuary, later remodeled in 1914–16. During Reconstruction its black members left to form their own congregations, among them Jerusalem Methodist Church. The present brick sanctuary, its construction delayed by the Santee Cooper project, was built in 1938 and dedicated in 1939. *Erected by the Congregation, 2011*
GPS Coordinates: 33° 17.964' N, 80° 10.001' W

8–68 Fairlawn Plantation/Fort Fairlawn

Rembert C. Dennis Blvd. (U.S. Hwy. 52), just S of Edward Dr. (S.C. Sec. Rd. 8-757), Moncks Corner

Fairlawn Plantation (FRONT)
Fairlawn Barony, sometimes called "Fair-Lawn," was granted to Peter Colleton, whose father John had been one of the original Lords Proprietors of the Carolina colony. John's grandson John (1679–1754), known as "The Honorable," was a planter and member of the Grand Council and the first Colleton to live in S.C. He built a large brick house here, later described by his granddaughter as "of course very magnificent."

Fort Fairlawn (REVERSE)
In April 1780, after their victory at Moncks Corner, British and Loyalist troops occupied Fairlawn and built an earthwork fort ½ mi. E. On November 17, 1781, Patriot militia under Cols. Hezekiah Maham and Isaac Shelby, on orders from Gen. Francis Marion, attacked the outpost commanded by Capt. Neal McLean. They took about 150 prisoners. The house, used as a hospital and storehouse, was burned. Contemporary accounts, however, disagree on which force burned it. *Sponsored by the Berkeley County Historical Society and the General Marion's Brigade Chapter, Daughters of the American Revolution, 2011*
GPS Coordinates: 33° 11.341' N, 79° 59.524' W

8–69 Carnes Crossroads

Near intersection of 1st Avenue and N Main St., Goose Creek vicinity

(FRONT) Carnes Crossroads was part of a 3,000 acre royal grant to Joseph Thorowgood in 1682. Later, the Etiwan, Native Americans who had lived on Daniel Island, moved here after European settlement pushed them from the Ashley-Cooper drainage basin. The Etiwan, part of the Cusabo group, had fewer members and were less powerful than the Westo and Cherokee to the west. They formed strategic alliances with British colonists and sided with the Carolina colony in the Yemassee War.

(REVERSE) By the early 20th century Dallas Carn, for whom the intersection is named, had acquired substantial land surrounding the crossroads. Carn had a homestead, farm, and business interests that he operated near this spot. As automobile traffic grew by mid-century, Carnes Crossroads remained a hub for rural commerce. Smith's Store, located just south of here, sold fuel and dry goods to locals and also operated as a dance hall that catered to military personnel stationed nearby. *Sponsored by the City of Goose Creek, 2014*
GPS Coordinates: 33° 3.259' N, 80° 6.076' W

8–70 Cherry Hill Classroom

1386 Cherry Hill Rd., Moncks Corner

(FRONT) This school was built ca. 1876 on land donated by John Campbell for a building that would serve as both a school for African American students and as a church for the Cherry Hill community. A one-room school for grades 1–6 with Aaron Cooper and St. Julian Manigault as its first teachers, it became a public school within the Berkeley County school district in the early 20th century.

(REVERSE) By the 1920s attendance here had grown enough to require a one-room addition, which was built on land donated by Mary Ann Cooper. Daisy Pasley and Pansy Cooper were the first teachers in the expanded school. The school closed after the 1954–55 school year, when many rural schools in Berkeley County were consolidated. It was rededicated as Cherry Hill Community Center in 2011. *Sponsored by Cherry Hill Community Center, 2014*
GPS Coordinates: 33° 13.726' N, 79° 56.580' W

8–71 Eighteen Mile House Tavern

NE of Intersection of Wilmer Ave. and St. James Ave., Goose Creek

(FRONT) From the 18th century, the State Road from Charleston and the Road to Dorchester met near here. These paths connected Charleston to the S.C. interior. Travelers from Charleston would have crossed Goose Creek, two miles south, before reaching this point. By the early 18th century a tavern complex developed here providing travelers with room, board, pasturage, and other services, such as coopering and blacksmithing.

(REVERSE) By the turn of the 19th century, Lewis Breaker owned the business. Later, Carston Vose, who also owned the Oaks Plantation, ran the tavern. In April 1865 African American troops of the 55th MA Infantry camped near here. They skirmished with Confederate cavalry and liberated slaves living on nearby plantations. After the war the Road to Dorchester was abandoned and a farm family occupied the site. *Sponsored by the City of Goose Creek, 2016*
GPS Coordinates: 33° 0.166' N, 80° 2.552' W

8–72 Maude E. Callen Clinic

2669 S.C. Hwy. 45, Pineville

(FRONT) Maude E. Callen (1898–1990) was born in Quincy, FL. She received formal training at Florida A&M Univ. and the Tuskeegee Institute. In 1923, she and her husband moved to Pineville, S.C., where she worked as an Episcopal missionary and one of the few nurse-midwives in S.C. She alone delivered over 800 babies and taught community women midwifery. Callen served poor patients throughout Berkeley Co.

(REVERSE) In 1951 Callen was featured in a LIFE magazine photo essay. The attention led to donations from across the nation, enabling the construction of the health clinic that she had long envisioned. The façade remains today as a reminder of her work. The clinic operated

from 1953–1986. Callen retired in 1971, but continued to serve the people of Berkeley County until her death in 1990. *Sponsored by Friends of Maude Callen and Berkeley County Historical Society, 2017*
GPS Coordinates: 33° 26.394' N, 80° 3.640' W

8–73 New Hope Methodist Church

1036 Cainhoy Rd., Huger

(FRONT) The congregation of New Hope Methodist Church dates to 1837. At that time the congregation consisted of both white members and enslaved African American members from surrounding plantations. After the Civil War the African American members purchased the church building and reorganized as an A.M.E. congregation. A new church, a frame building, was completed in 1910.
(REVERSE) In the 20th Century the congregation converted from an A.M.E. Church and joined the United Methodist Church. Traditionally, worship services are held during 5th Sunday, when local ministers hold an "All Day Meeting." During the 1960s members of the community would gather as "Joshua's Army" and march from Loretta Bridge to New Hope. The current sanctuary was completed in the 1950s. *Sponsored by New Hope United Methodist Church and Elder Lillie K. Davis & Charles Davis, 2017*
GPS Coordinates: 33° 5.352' N, 79° 49.009' W

8–74 St. Stephen (White) High School

113 Ravenell Dr., St. Stephen

(FRONT) St. Stephen High School was the first public white H.S. for the town of St. Stephen. The current building was built 1928–29 and designed by Florence-based architect Leon McDuff Hicks. Bricks for the project were made locally at the brickyard owned by Walker R. Funk. Construction was part of a state-wide movement to consolidate rural schools into larger, regional schools with bus service available to students.
(REVERSE) In 1930, the school complex was completed with the addition of an agriculture building and an athletic field house. In 1959

the field house was converted into the first public library for the area. St. Stephen H.S. remained segregated throughout its time as a H.S. (1928–56). It then was an elementary school for white students, 1957–70. In 2013 it was converted for use as a public library. *Sponsored by the St. Stephen Historical and Cultural Committee, 2018*
GPS Coordinates: 33° 24.298' N, 79° 55.570' W

8–75 Cordesville Rosenwald School

Doctor Evans Rd. S. of Umps Ln., Cordesville

(FRONT) Cordesville Rosenwald School, the first African American public school in Cordesville, S.C., was built on this site in 1923–24 at a total cost of $5,400. Constructed as a four-room frame building, it was one of almost 500 schools in S.C. funded in part by the Julius Rosenwald Foundation, 1917–1932.
(REVERSE) The Rosenwald Foundation provided $1,100 with the balance coming from public contributions, including $2,000 from the African American community. The original frame school burned in the 1930s and was replaced by a brick schoolhouse. Students here would go on to Dixie Training School, later known as Berkeley High School. *Sponsored by Alumni and Friends of Cordesville School, 2019*
GPS Coordinates: 33° 10.674' N, 79° 57.278' W

8–76 Quintyne Plantation

Intersection of Clements Ferry Rd. and Sweet Pl., Charleston

(FRONT) Richard Quintyne (d.1695) established a plantation near here and a creek .5 miles east in the 1680s. Likely born in England, Quintyne was a prominent planter in Barbados and one of many early Carolina colonists who moved here from the island. He arrived 1679 on the ship Plantation with indentured servant James Mahone and probably a number of enslaved Africans who later worked this land.
(REVERSE) Richard Quintyne lived here with his wife Elizabeth, five children, and an unknown number of enslaved people. The property was later owned by his son Henry who was killed in 1716 during the Yamasee War

(1715–17). Also near here was the Wading Place, where by 1709 a bridge owned by Col. Robert Daniell, Jr., connected this west bank of the creek to what was later known as Daniel Island. *Sponsored by Sweetwater Apartments, 2019*

GPS Coordinates: 32° 54.038' N, 79° 55.038' W

Calhoun County

No # Savany Hunt

In the collection of the South Carolina Department of Archives and History; Originally erected on U.S. Hwy. 21, 20 mi. N of St. Matthews

This stream was originally called Savannah Hunt, but German-speaking settlers about 1740 corrupted the first word and Savany Hunt became the permanent name. [*Erected by the South Carolina Historical Commission, ca. 1929–1936.*]

9–1 First Land Granted in Calhoun County Area

S.C. Hwy. 6, about 4 mi. Southeast of St. Matthews

George Sterling was granted 570 acres of land here on March 14, 1704. During the lifetime of his daughter, Mary Sterling Heatly Russell, the plantation was a stopping place for Indians and travelers on the Cherokee Path. The Rev. John Giessendanner held early religious services in the house (1750–1754).

GPS Coordinates: 33° 38.178' N, 80° 42.341' W

9–2 St. Matthew's Parish Episcopal Church

[No longer extant. Replaced by marker 9–11 in 2015.]

Intersection of U.S. Hwy. 601 & S.C. Hwy. 419, Northeast of St. Matthews

Stands 0.4 mile NW of this spot. An act creating the parish in 1765 was disallowed by the king. A second act was approved in 1768. The first of four buildings, each on a different site, was erected in 1766. The present edifice was built in 1852. The congregation was incorporated in 1788 as a member of the Protestant Episcopal Church.

9–3 Jericho Methodist Church [Mile and a Half East]

Intersection of U.S. Hwy. 176 and Jericho Rd., 2.5 miles South of Cameron

Bishop Francis Asbury stopped in this region in 1801 and 1803. About 1811, a congregation was organized and by 1815 Jericho Meeting House was standing on land given by Jacob Felkel. The present building there was apparently erected before 1850. A low partition separating the men and women and a slave gallery were removed in 1890 and a porch was added. Two annexes were built later.

GPS Coordinates: 33° 31.874' N, 80° 41.225' W

9–4 St. Matthew's Lutheran Church/Parent Lutheran Church of this Area

S.C. Hwy. 6, about 7 miles South of St. Matthews

In 1737–38, the elder Rev. John U. Giessendanner from Orangeburg began Lutheran work in this area; this was continued by his nephew until 1749. By the 1760s, St. Matthew's Lutheran Church near here was in use. A later building erected at this site in 1826 was replaced by the present church in 1900.

GPS Coordinates: 33° 37.069' N, 80° 40.294' W

9–5 Calhoun County

Calhoun County Courthouse, S. Railroad Ave., St. Matthews

First settled in 1704, this region by 1733 included Amelia and lower Saxe Gotha townships. In 1765 much of it was made part of the new St. Matthew's Parish and was so named until 1865. Efforts in 1890 and 1896 led to an act signed on Feb. 14, 1908, forming a new county from parts of Orangeburg

and Lexington, named for John C. Calhoun. *Erected by the Calhoun County Historical Commission*
GPS Coordinates: 33° 39.793' N, 80° 46.71' W

9–6 Shady Grove Church

Cameron Rd. (S.C. Hwy. 33), 3 miles Northeast of Cameron

Shady Grove Methodist Church was an outgrowth of Tabernacle Church, the parent Methodist body of this area. It was built in the early 1800s on land of Adam Holman, has a framework of hewn logs held together with wooden pegs, and has been remodeled three times. Ministers of Orangeburg Circuit, St. Matthews Circuit, and Cameron Charge have served Shady Grove. *Erected by the Calhoun County Historical Commission, 1970*
GPS Coordinates: 33° 37.069' N, 80° 40.294' W

9–7 Sandy Run Church/Christian Theus

1927 Old State Rd. (U.S. Hwy. 176), just Southeast of its intersection with Big Beaver Creek Rd., Sandy Run vicinity

Sandy Run Church (FRONT)
This Lutheran church, one of the oldest in the state, is thought to have been organized ca. 1765. By 1774, the Rev. Lewis Hochheimer was minister here. The church was incorporated 1788 as "The German Lutheran Church of Salem, on Sandy Run" and located at the present site by 1806. The S.C. Synod has met here several times.
Christian Theus (REVERSE)
Buried in this cemetery is the Reverend Christian Theus, whose grave was moved here in 1932 from its original location near the Reformed Lutheran Church of the Congarees, once standing about 7 miles northwest in old Saxe-Gotha Township. From 1739 to 1789, Theus was pastor of the Congarees church and also the local school teacher. *Erected by the Congregation, 1983*
GPS Coordinates: 33° 48.02' N, 80° 57.869' W

9–8 Mt. Lebanon Cemetery

Mt. Lebanon Rd., just SW of its intersection with Old State Rd. (U.S. Hwy. 176), Cameron vicinity

This is the original site of Mt. Lebanon Lutheran Church, organized January 13, 1844, as an extension of the St. Matthew's Church, Creston. Later, Mt. Lebanon Church moved to Cameron about 2 miles NW, dedicated its new building in 1917, and was renamed the Lutheran Church of the Resurrection. The congregation maintains the old cemetery here. *Erected by the Calhoun County Historical Commission, 1983*
GPS Coordinates: 33° 32.241' N, 80° 42.119' W

9–9 Mount Pleasant Baptist Church

Fort Motte Rd. (S.C. Hwy. 419) near its intersection with Adams Rd. (S.C. Sec. Rd. 9–80), Fort Motte

(FRONT) The first church built by African Americans at Fort Motte grew out of services held by slaves at nearby Bellville, Goshen, Lang Syne, and Oakland plantations. It was formally organized in 1867 by Caleb Bartley, Israel Cheeseborough, Cudjo Cunningham, Anderson Keitt, William McCrae, John Spann, and Harry Stuart.
(REVERSE) Rev. S. A. Evans, the first minister, was succeeded by Rev. Henry Duncan, who served until his death in 1905. The sanctuary, built in 1869 on land donated by Augustus T. and Louisa McCord Smythe, was remodeled in the 1970s and the 1990s. Mount Pleasant School educated students here from the 1870s into the 1920s. *Erected by the Congregation and the United Family Reunion, 2002*
GPS Coordinates: 33° 41.656' N, 80° 39.001' W

9–10 Good Hope Picnic

McCord's Ferry Rd. (S.C. Hwy. 267), Lone Star vicinity, between Lone Star and Elloree

The Good Hope Picnic, a celebration of the end of the planting season, is the oldest African-American event in the Lone Star community. Founded in August 1915 by farmers to market their produce and held on the second Friday in August, it has often included games

and music. Members of several African-American churches in and around Lone Star helped found the picnic and still support it. *Erected by the Good Hope Picnic Foundation, 2008*
GPS Coordinates: 33° 36.478' N, 80° 34.803' W

9–11 St. Matthew's Parish

1164 Fort Motte Rd., Fort Motte

St. Matthew's Parish was established by the S.C. Colonial Assembly between 1765 and 1768. The first of four church buildings was erected in Amelia Township ca. 1765. The parish church was incorporated by the S.C. General Assembly in 1788 as the Vestry and Church Wardens of the Parish of St. Matthew. The current sanctuary, known for many years as "The Red Church," was built in 1852. *Sponsored by Calhoun County Museum and Cultural Center, 2015*
GPS Coordinates: 33° 42.829' N, 80° 40.266' W

9–12 Lang Syne Cemetery

Near the intersection of Old Lang Syne Rd. and Adams Rd., Fort Motte vicinity

(FRONT) Established by the Peterkin family ca. 1905, buried here are many former slaves and their descendants. Among those interred here are African American inhabitants of Lang Syne depicted in Julia Mood Peterkin's novels: Mary Weeks Bryant (Scarlett Sister Mary), Daniel Anderson (Bree-dee), Louvenia Berry (Maum Vinner), Anniker Spann Bryant (Maum Aneky), and Hannah Jefferson (Maum Hannah).
(REVERSE) Several graves are marked by Holley Burial Aid Society tombstones. The area around the cemetery was also known as Sunday School Woods because it was the place where slaves from Lang Syne met for religious worship. Near here is Lang Syne School, the plantation's slave cemetery, known as The Yard, the African American Bellville Cemetery, and the Heatley-Dulles-Cheves-McCord family cemetery. *Sponsored by the United Family Reunion, 2016*
GPS Coordinates: 33° 43.539' N, 80° 39.632' W

9–13 True Blue Cemetery

True Blue Rd. (State Rd. S-9-132), between S.C. Hwy. 601 and Fort Motte Rd. (State Rd. S-9-25), Fort Motte vicinity

(FRONT) True Blue cemetery was established as the burial ground for slaves, former slaves, and their descendants from True Blue Indigo Plantation (ca. 1700), as well as the Singleton, Hanes, Weinges (Winsey) Street, and Fort Motte communities. This cemetery also served as the original burial ground for nearby Mt. Zion, Mt. Salem, and Jerusalem (Ancestors of True Blue) Baptist Churches.
(REVERSE) Those buried here are members of the Brizz, Brown, Cannon, Cokley, Colter, Garner, Glover, Heyward, Jones, Kirkland, Lavan, Logan, Milligan, Mitchell, Moultrie, Mosely, Owens, Palmer, Ravanel, Sasportas, Scott, Snipes, Switzer, Turquand (Turkvan), and White families. Some graves are marked by field stones while others have Holley Burial Aid Society tombstones. *Sponsored by the United Family Reunion, 2016*
GPS Coordinates: 33° 42.828' N, 80° 42.632' W

9–14 Bethel A.M.E. Church and School

410 S. Railroad Ave., St. Matthews

(FRONT) Bethel A.M.E. Church was established in 1865 and held its early services under a brush arbor. Bethel was the first A.M.E. Church in Lewisville (now St. Matthews). Trustees Robin Amaker, Jack Dantzler, and Frank Keitt purchased land from Jacob G. Keitt to build the first permanentsanctuary and school house in 1867. The church was dedicated in June 1867 with Rev. Abraham J. C. Hamilton serving as the first pastor.
(REVERSE) The Freedmen's Bureau contributed $250 to aid in the construction of a school for use by African American students. Known originally as the African Methodist Episcopal Church School, it was later renamed Bethel School. Mary Spiessegger was the first teacher, followed soon after by Charlotte S. Riley in Oct. 1867. The school served African American students from 1867 until the early 20th

century. *Sponsored by the Calhoun County Museum and Cultural Center, 2016*
GPS Coordinates: 33° 39.687' N, 80° 46.771' W

9–15 Oakland Cemetery
New Bethany Rd., Fort Motte vicinity

(FRONT) This cemetery was named for nearby Oakland Plantation (ca. 1800), the home of William Sabb Thomson (1785–1841), a planter and state senator. This cemetery served as the original burial grounds for Mt. Pleasant Church (1867) and New Bethany Church (1914). Buried here are former slaves who organized Mt. Pleasant and New Bethany Churches and their descendants.
(REVERSE) Families buried here include Bartley, Bates, Brown, Buckman, Cheeseboro, Davis, Esaw, Fogle, Ford, Glover, Gold, Goodwine, Govan, Green, Hart, Heatley, James, Keitt, Lomas, Lucas, Major, Miller, Morant, Noble, Pinckney, Reese, Seawright, Smith, Stewart, Stuart, Taylor, Wallace, Wolfe, and Wright. Fieldstones and Holley Burial Aid Society tombstones mark several graves. *Sponsored by the United Family Reunion, 2018*
GPS Coordinates: 33° 41.333' N, 80° 39.594' W

9–16 St. John Good Samaritan Lodge Hall and Cemetery
S.C. Hwy. 419, directly across from Mt. Pisgah A.M.E. Church, Fort Motte

(FRONT) St. John Good Samaritan Lodge Hall and Cemetery were established ca. 1900 on land sold by Jack Johnson. Among the early trustees was S.C. Senator Samuel Duncan. African American families buried here include Brown, Duncan, Green, Hanes, Lemon, McDuffie, Patterson, Slaffey, Spann, Stewart, Stuart, and Wright.
(REVERSE) African American benevolent and fraternal societies grew in number during the late 19th century as a way of providing support to members in times of need. Many also sponsored church construction and maintained cemeteries. They also supported education and "The Hall" served as a school through the late 1920s. *Sponsored by the United Family Reunion, 2018*
GPS Coordinates: 33° 44.029' N, 80° 41.229' W

Charleston County

No # St. Andrew's Parish Church
2604 Ashley River Rd.

Built in part in 1706, the year the Church of England was established here by law. Enlarged 1723. Burned out and rebuilt 1764. Scene of early missionary work among the Negroes. [*Erected by the South Carolina Historical Commission, ca. 1929–1936*]
GPS Coordinates: 32° 50.276' N, 80° 2.984' W

No # John's Island
U.S. Hwy. 17 at S.C. Hwy. 20, 1 mile North of John's Island

1 mile. Once St. John's Island. One of the earliest racing studs in the province started here at Fenwick Hall. 1779, Prevost's British force occupied this island after their unsuccessful attempt on Charlestown. 1780, Sir Henry Clinton here disembarked the army which besieged and captured Charlestown. [*Erected by the South Carolina Historical Commission, ca. 1929–1936. Missing as of July 2009.*]

10–1 South Carolina Canal & Rail Road Company [Original Track Location]
[Last known to have been on exhibit in 2012 at the now closed Best Friend of Charleston Railway Museum at Citadel Mall.]
Began its first successful scheduled steam railroad service in America on December 25, 1830, and by 1833 its 136 miles from Charleston to Hamburg made it the world's longest railroad. Now a part of Southern Railway System. [*Erected by the American Society of*

Civil Engineers at the track site at Camden Depot, 1970.]
GPS Coordinates: 32° 47.843' N, 80° 1.962' W

10–2 John's Island Presbyterian Church

Bohicket Rd. (S.C. Sec. Rd. 10–20), about 3 miles East of S.C. Hwy. 700, Johns Island

Founded by early English, Scottish, and French settlers about 1710, this is one of the oldest Presbyterian congregations in South Carolina. The original sanctuary, believed to have been built about 1719, was enlarged in 1823. *Erected by the Congregation in 1960*
GPS Coordinates: 32° 41.141' N, 80° 4.926' W

10–3 Thomas Smith

Corner of East Bay St. & Longitude Ln., Charleston

Governor of Carolina,/1693–1694/Planter, Merchant, Surgeon,/arrived in Charles Town in 1684 with his first wife, Barbara Atkins, and sons, Thomas and George. A cacique by 1690, he was created Landgrave by the Lords Proprietors on May 13, 1691. He died in his 46th year on November 16, 1694. His brick town house with a wharf on Cooper River was here on the corner of East Bay & Longitude Lane. *Erected by his descendants and South Carolina Colonial Dames XVII Century, 1967*
GPS Coordinates: 32° 46.477' N, 79° 55.637' W

10–4 Old Bank Building

Northwest corner of Church & Broad Sts., Charleston

Construction having begun in 1797, this building was occupied by the Bank of South Carolina on December 10, 1798, making it one of the oldest bank buildings in the U.S. It served as a bank until 1835. The Charleston Library Society used it 1835–1916. It was owned and occupied for the next fifty years by the Charleston Chamber of Commerce. In 1967 it reverted to its first use and became a bank again. *Erected by The Citizens and Southern National Bank of South Carolina, 1967*
GPS Coordinates: 32° 46.602' N, 79° 55.77' W

10–5 [St. Michael's Church]

Corner of Broad & Meeting Sts., Charleston

Here in the churchyard of/St. Michael's lie buried/two Signers of the/U. S. Constitution/CHARLES COTESWORTH/PINCKNEY/(1746–1825)/Lawyer and Legislator/Major General, U. S. Army/Minister to France/Presidential candidate-/JOHN RUTLEDGE/(1739–1800)/Lawyer and Statesman/Governor of South Carolina/Chief Justice of the U. S./Their years of public/service, 1762–1825, saw/both State and Nation well/on the road to greatness. *Erected by the Society Daughters of Colonial Wars in the State of South Carolina, 1968*
GPS Coordinates: 32° 46.569' N, 79° 55.855' W

10–6 [St. Philip's Church]

146 Church St., Charleston

Here in the churchyard of St. Philip's are buried/CHARLES PINCKNEY/(1757–1824)/Signer of the United States Constitution and author of the famous/"Pinckney Draught"/Governor of South Carolina/U. S. Senator and Congressman/Minister to Spain/EDWARD RUTLEDGE/(1749–1800)/Signer of the Declaration of Independence/Delegate to First and Second Continental Congresses/S.C. Legislator & Senator/Governor of South Carolina. *Erected by South Carolina Society Daughters of American Colonists, 1969*
GPS Coordinates: 32° 46.728' N, 79° 55.767' W

10–7 Christ Church

U.S. Hwy. 17 at its intersection with S.C. Sec. Rd. 10-97, Northeast of Mount Pleasant

The Church Act of 1706 created Christ Church Parish. The first church, a wooden structure built in 1707, accidentally burned in 1725. A brick church was erected in 1726, and although the British burned it in 1782 and the interior was destroyed by Union Troops in 1865, the original walls still stand. In 1874, the church was restored and consecrated. *Erected by the Congregation, 1970*
GPS Coordinates: 32° 50.659' N, 79° 48.843' W

10–8 Trinity Methodist Church Original Site/William Hammet

Hasell St. and Maiden Ln., Charleston

Trinity Methodist Church Original Site (FRONT)
The first Trinity Church building was erected on this site in 1792. By 1813, Trinity had joined the S.C. Conference, and in 1874 it merged with Cumberland Church, the oldest Methodist church in Charleston, founded in 1786. In 1926, Trinity moved to its present location at 273 Meeting Street where the church and cemetery records are now located.
William Hammet (REVERSE)
An Irishman from Belfast who was ordained by John Wesley, William Hammet was a missionary sent to America by the British Conference. He came to Charleston in 1791 from Jamaica and founded Trinity Methodist Church after a schism occurred within Cumberland Church between his followers and those of Bishop Francis Asbury. Hammet called his church the "Primitive Methodist Church" and was pastor of Trinity until his death in 1803. *Erected by Trinity United Methodist Church, 2005, replacing a marker erected in 1970 by the Pee Dee Chapter, Colonial Dames of the XVII Century*
GPS Coordinates: 32° 46.968' N, 79° 55.848' W

10–9 Chamber of Commerce

17 Lockwood Dr., Charleston

On December 9, 1773, the first Chamber of Commerce in the City of Charleston was organized on Broad Street at Mrs. Swallow's Inn. John Savage was its first President. After the Revolution and six months after Charleston was incorporated, the Chamber was reorganized. Of the postwar presidents, Alexander Gillon and John Lewis Gervais each served for a year, Edward Darrell for a number of years. The Charleston Chamber of Commerce was organized in 1773 in a tavern near the eastern end of Broad Street. For many years after the Civil War, the Chamber occupied the Riggs Building, formerly at East Bay and Broad. It was later located on Meeting Street, and from 1916 to 1966, it occupied the Old Bank Building at 50 Broad Street. Its present home is the old West Point Rice Mill, built in 1861. *Erected*

by Governor Robert Gibbes Chapter Colonial Dames XVII Century, 1970
GPS Coordinates: 32° 46.750' N, 79° 57.057' W

10–10 War of 1812 Encampment

Confederate Cemetery, Carr St., Mount Pleasant

(FRONT) On June 18, 1812, the United States declared war against Great Britain. One of the first units to be mustered into service was the Third Regiment of South Carolina Militia, which was stationed at Haddrell's Point, west of here, to aid in the defense of Charleston harbor. Their barracks stood within the present town limits of Mount Pleasant, and they were equipped with State funds.
(REVERSE) The 1812 monument in this cemetery originally marked a burial plot of the Third Regiment of State troops. The soldiers who were buried there apparently died from disease while stationed at Haddrell's Point, nearby. Before the Civil War, the monument is said to have stood at the corner of Pitt and King Streets. It was moved to this Confederate cemetery for protection from vandalism. *Erected by the United States Daughters of 1812, South Carolina Society, 1970*
GPS Coordinates: 32° 47.135' N, 79° 52.428' W

10–11 Lord Cornwallis

120 Charleston Blvd., Isle of Palms

(FRONT) Major General Charles Cornwallis established a brigade headquarters not far from this site on or around June 19, 1776. His brigade was part of a British army under the command of Sir Henry Clinton, which had occupied this island as a staging point for attacking the palmetto log fort on Sullivan's Island. This was Cornwallis's first major command in America.
(REVERSE) Cornwallis's troops were prevented from crossing Breach Inlet on June 28, 1776, by the fire of S.C. Rangers on the opposite shore. The British were defeated and sailed for New York. Cornwallis returned in 1780 as second in command of the army that captured Charles Town. Left in command of the South, he finally surrendered at Yorktown on October 19, 1781. Erected 2005, replacing a marker

erected in 1972 by the South Carolina Society, Sons of the American Revolution
GPS Coordinates: 32° 46.612' N, 79° 48.481' W

10–12 John Rutledge Home

116 Broad St., Charleston

This house, built before the American Revolution, was the residence of John Rutledge (1739–1800), first Governor of the State of South Carolina. He was President of South Carolina, 1776–78, and Governor, 1779–82, signer of the U. S. Constitution, 1787, Chief Justice of South Carolina 1791–95, and Chief Justice of the United States, 1795. The house was altered in 1853 by P. H. Hammarskold, who added the ornamental iron. *Erected by the South Carolina Society, Daughters of Colonial Wars, 1973*
GPS Coordinates: 32° 46.578' N, 79° 56.019' W

10–13 James F. Byrnes

[Reported missing.]

Marion Square, Charleston

James F. Byrnes, American statesman, was born in a house on nearby King Street and grew up in this neighborhood. He attended St. Patrick's parochial school and Bennett public school, both on St. Philip Street. He died April 9, 1972 and is buried in Trinity Cathedral churchyard, in Columbia, South Carolina. From humble beginnings, James F. Byrnes, born and brought up in this neighborhood, rose to eminence and handled affairs of worldwide importance. He served in both houses of Congress and as an associate justice of the U.S. Supreme Court. He was director of War Mobilization in World War II, Secretary of State and Governor of South Carolina. *Erected by Byrnes Centennial Committee, 1979*
GPS Coordinates: 32° 47.199' N, 79° 56.143' W

10–14 Drayton Hall/Drayton Family

Ashley River Rd. (S.C. Hwy. 61), 9 miles Northwest of Charleston

Drayton Hall (FRONT)
Seat of the Drayton family for seven generations, this land was acquired in 1738 by John Drayton (ca. 1715–1779) as the center of his extensive indigo and rice planting ventures. One of the finest examples of Georgian Palladian architecture in America, this is the only surviving colonial plantation house on the Ashley River.
Drayton Family (REVERSE)
This distinguished South Carolina family included among its members William Henry Drayton (1742–1779), Revolutionary War Patriot, Chief Justice of South Carolina, member of Continental Congress; Dr. Charles Drayton (1743–1820), Lieutenant Governor 1785–1787; and John Drayton (1767–1822), Governor of South Carolina 1800–1802, 1808–1812. *Erected by National Trust for Historic Preservation, 1984*
GPS Coordinates: 32° 51.88' N, 80° 4.967' W

10–15 The Grand Lodge of Ancient Freemasons of South Carolina

Corner of Church & Broad Sts., Charleston

Organized before August 18, 1737, this Grand Lodge met in Charles Shepheard's Tavern, an early meeting place of the colony, once located on this corner. *Erected by The Grand Lodge of Ancient Freemasons of S.C., 1987*
GPS Coordinates: 32° 46.617' N, 79° 55.754' W

10–17 The Elms Plantation

Elms Plantation Blvd., off U.S. Hwy. 78, about ½ mile from I-26, Ladson vicinity

Ralph Izard inherited The Elms after his father's death in 1749. During the Revolution he provided financial support to the Patriot cause. He also served as a foreign diplomat, advisor to George Washington, and U.S. senator. The Elms, which remained in the Izard family for generations, was established here by Izard's great-grandfather (also named Ralph), who settled in S.C. in 1682. *Erected by The Elms of Charleston and Jacob Van der Ver Chapter, S.C. State Society of the National Society Colonial Dames XVII Century, 1995*
GPS Coordinates: 32° 59.005' N, 80° 3.604' W

10–18 Laurel Hill Plantation

S.C. Hwy. 41, about ¾ mile North of U.S. Hwy. 17, Mount Pleasant vicinity

John Boone owned this land by 1694, and the plantation that developed here passed in 1864 to Dr. Peter P. Bonneau, signer of the Ordinance of Secession and Confederate Army surgeon. John D. Muller, Jr., a later owner, died in 1984 and set up a trust specifying that Laurel Hill be made available to benefit religious, charitable, scientific, literary, and educational groups. *Erected by Christ Church Parish Preservation Society, 1989*
GPS Coordinates: 32° 51.702' N, 79° 47.855' W
[Proposed location. Actual location is unknown. Entrance to Laurel Hill County Park is located at 32° 52.320' N, 79° 48.236' W.]

10–19 Thomas Pinckney, 1750–1828 /St. James, Santee

U.S. Hwy. 17, about 1 mi. S of South Santee River Bridge, NE of McClellanville

Thomas Pinckney, 1750–1828 (FRONT)
Distinguished planter-diplomat Thomas Pinckney owned nearby Fairfield and Eldorado plantations. A national figure, he was Governor of South Carolina; Minister to England; Envoy Extraordinary to Spain where he negotiated the "Pinckney Treaty," and major general in the War of 1812.
St. James, Santee (REVERSE)
One of the earliest settlements in S.C. and refuge for French Huguenots, St. James, Santee, Parish was a major agricultural area containing a number of large-scale rice plantations. At nearby Peach Tree Plantation, Jonathan Lucas, Sr. introduced a water mill for beating rice around 1787, which gave an impetus to rice culture in this area. *Erected by St. James, Santee, Parish Historical Society, 1989*
GPS Coordinates: 33° 10.665' N, 79° 24.893' W

10–20 Snee Farm

U.S. Hwy. 17 at entrance to Boone Hall Plantation, Mt. Pleasant

The country home of Charles Pinckney (1757–1824), Snee Farm stands about 0.7 mi. west of here. One of S.C.'s signers of the U.S.

Constitution, Pinckney also served in the General Assembly and in Congress. He was elected Governor of S.C. four times and was appointed minister to Spain in 1801 by Thomas Jefferson. George Washington visited Snee Farm in 1791 during his presidency. *Erected by U.S. Constitution Bicentennial Commission of S.C., 1990*
GPS Coordinates: 32° 50.679' N, 79° 48.843' W

10–21 Grave of Colonel William A. Washington

U.S. Hwy. 17, ¾ mile North of Rantowles at Live Oak Plantation

¾ mile on Live Oak Plantation at Sandy Hill Plantation, seven miles N.W, this Virginian made his home in the country through which he had led his American Cavalry. There, in 1791, he entertained his kinsman, George Washington, president of the United States. *Erected 1991 by The Arion Society of Charleston, replacing a marker destroyed in 1989*
GPS Coordinates: 32° 47.725' N, 80° 8.173' W

10–22 St. John's Church

5 Clifford St., Charleston

(FRONT) This church grew from services held for German inhabitants in Charleston by Rev. Johann Martin Boltzius in 1734 and Rev. Henry Melchior Muhlenberg in 1742. The cornerstone of the first house of worship was laid in 1759; the second and present church building was dedicated in 1818. Dr. John Bachman, noted clergyman, naturalist, and author, served as minister of St. John's 1815–1874. During this time, he [...]
(REVERSE) [...] helped his ornithologist and artist friend John James Audubon in producing Birds of America and the work entitled Viviparous Quadrupeds of North America. Bachman was influential in establishing the S.C. Lutheran Synod (1824), the Lutheran Theological Southern Seminary (1830), and Newberry College (1856). He died in 1874 and is buried in the church. *Erected by The Congregation, 1992*
GPS Coordinates: 32° 46.728' N, 79° 56.076' W

10–23 Belvidere School Site

S.C. Sec. Rd. 10–54 at its intersection with S.C. Sec. Rd. 10–1493, John's Island

In 1898 Charleston County School District No. 11 bought this land from J. S. Hart and built a public school on the site soon after. School closed in the early 1920s. *Erected by Children and Grandchildren of Alumni, 1994* GPS Coordinates: 32° 46.086′ N, 80° 7.08′ W

10–24 McClellanville

Corner of Charlotte St. and Pinckney St., McClellanville

(FRONT) McClellanville began in the late 1850s and early 1860s when local plantation owners A. J. McClellan and R. T. Morrison sold lots in the vicinity of Jeremy Creek to planters of the Santee Delta, who sought relief from summer fevers. The first store opened soon after the Civil War, and the village became the social and economic center for a wide area that produced timber, rice, […] (REVERSE) […] cotton, naval stores, and seafoods. Incorporated in 1926 and encircled by the Francis Marion National Forest and Cape Romain National Wildlife Refuge, McClellanville is best known for its shrimp fleet and seafood industries. Except for a period during the Civil War, two lighthouses in the Wildlife Refuge served as beacons to coastal shipping from 1827 to 1947. *Erected by St. James, Santee, Historical Society, 1995* GPS Coordinates: 33° 5.122′ N, 79° 27.635′ W

10–25 Mount Pleasant Presbyterian Church

302 Hibben St., Corner of Hibben and Church Sts., Mt. Pleasant

Erected about 1854 and originally a Congregational Church affiliated with Old Wappetaw Church, founded about 1699. Served as a Confederate hospital during the Civil War, then briefly housed the Laing School for freedmen during Reconstruction. Was accepted into Charleston Presbytery as a mission church and renamed Mount Pleasant Presbyterian Church in 1870. *Erected by the Congregation, 1996* GPS Coordinates: 32° 47.359′ N, 79° 52.692′ W

10–26 St. James Santee Parish Church

On the Santee River, North of U.S. Hwy. 17, McClellanville vicinity

(FRONT) Erected in 1768, this edifice, officially known as Wambaw Church, was situated on the King's Highway. It is the fourth church to serve St. James Santee Parish. The parish, founded in 1706 at the request of French Huguenot settlers, was the second oldest in the colony. The Rev. Samuel Fenner Warren served as parish rector from 1758 until his death in 1789.
(REVERSE) Thomas Lynch, Paul Mazyck, John Drake, Jonah Collins, Jacob Motte, Jr., Daniel Horry, and Elias Horry were appointed commissioners to build the church. The sanctuary combines elements of the Georgian and Classical architectural styles and reflects a late-18th century trend toward a more sophisticated design for parish churches. It was designated a National Historic Landmark in 1973. *Erected by St. James Santee Historical Society, 1996* GPS Coordinates: 33° 10.303′ N, 79° 27.926′ W

10–27 CS *H.L. Hunley*

Poe Ave., near Ft. Moultrie, Sullivans Island

(FRONT) The CS H. L. Hunley, the first submarine to sink an enemy warship, left from a point near here on the evening of February 17, 1864, and proceeded out Breach Inlet toward the USS Housatonic, anchored nearby. The Hunley rammed a fixed torpedo into the Housatonic's hull below the waterline, sinking it within an hour with a loss of 5 Union sailors. The Hunley itself sank as well about 3.5 mi. offshore with its entire 9-man crew of Confederate volunteers.
(REVERSE) The Hunley, named for Horace L. Hunley (1823–1863), an early promoter of Confederate submarines, had already lost a 5-man crew in August 1863 and an 8-man crew, including Hunley, in October 1863 during trial runs in Charleston Harbor. Its last crew, commanded by Lt. George E. Dixon of the 21st Alabama, included Fred Collins, James A. Wicks, C. Simkins, Arnold Becker, and ___ Ridgeway of the Navy, C. F. Carlson of Wagner's Co., S.C. Arty., ____ White, and

____ Miller. *Erected by Palmetto Soldiers Relief Society, 1997*

GPS Coordinates: 32° 45.549' N, 79° 51.394' W

10–28 Sweetgrass Baskets

U.S. Hwy. 17 N at Hamlin Rd., Northeast of Mt. Pleasant

Coil baskets of native sweetgrass and pine needles sewn with strips of palmetto leaf have been displayed for sale on stands along Highway 17 near Mount Pleasant since the 1930s. This craft, handed down in certain families since the 1700s, originally was used on plantations in rice production. Unique to the lowcountry it represents one of the oldest West African art forms in America. *Erected by the Original Sweetgrass Market Place Coalition and the Christ Church Parish Preservation Society, 1997*

GPS Coordinates: 32° 51.274' N, 79° 48.074' W

10–29 Old Wappetaw Church

James Mitchell Graham Hwy. (U.S. Hwy. 17 N), near Fifteen Mile Landing Rd., about 14 miles northeast of Mt. Pleasant between Woodville and Awendaw

Congregationalists from New England built a church near here around 1700. Troops from both sides camped on the grounds during the American Revolution. Burned by the British in 1782, it was rebuilt in 1786. The building was abandoned during the Civil War and its members organized Presbyterian churches in Mount Pleasant and McClellanville. *Erected by the Christ Church Parish Preservation Society and the St. James, Santee Parish Historical Society, 1998*

GPS Coordinates: 32° 55.659' N, 79° 42.871' W

10–30 Jacob Bond I'On (1782–1859)

At the entrance to the I'On Community, Mathis Ferry Rd., Mt. Pleasant

(FRONT) Jacob Bond I'On (1782–1859), planter, U.S. Army and militia officer, and state legislator, is buried in the family cemetery ½ mi. north. I'On, a contemporary of John C. Calhoun at Yale University, represented St. James Santee Parish in the S.C. House 1810–12, then resigned to become a captain in the 2nd U.S. Artillery, serving with distinction during the War of 1812.

(REVERSE) I'On, described at his death in 1859 as "a representative of the true Carolina gentleman," was elected to the S.C. Senate in 1816, serving until 1831 and representing first St. James Santee Parish, then Christ Church Parish; he was President of the Senate 1822–28. He was also intendant, or mayor, of Sullivan's Island in 1823 and a delegate to the Nullification Convention of 1832–33. *Erected by the I'On Company, 1998*

GPS Coordinates: 32° 48.711' N, 79° 52.764' W

10–31 Boone Hall Plantation

Long Point Rd., west of U.S. Hwy. 17 intersection, Mt. Pleasant

Boone Hall Plantation, established in 1681 by a grant to Major John Boone, remained in the family for 130 years. The plantation, purchased by the Horlbeck family in 1817, produced primarily Sea Island cotton. A cotton gin, smokehouse, and nine slave cabins, all built of brick made here, survive from the antebellum period. The present main house at Boone Hall was built for Thomas A. Stone in 1936. *Erected by Boone Hall Plantation and Gardens, 1999*

GPS Coordinates: 32° 50.783' N, 79° 49.016' W

10–32 Rifle Range Road

Intersection of Rifle Range Rd. and Coleman Blvd./Ben Sawyer Blvd. (S.C. Hwy. 703), Mt. Pleasant

A U.S. Navy rifle range was built near here during World War I on the site of an old S.C. National Guard firing range. Included were 100 targets, 2 armories, a 600-seat mess hall, 12 barracks and auxiliary buildings. After 1919 the 100-acre site leased from George F. Goblet, now Harborgate Shores, was used by the National Guard, Army Reserves, and Citadel cadets until 1937. *Erected by the Christ Church Parish Preservation Society, 1999*

GPS Coordinates: 32° 47.617' N, 79° 51.374' W

10–33 Maryville

Emanuel A.M.E. Church, 5th Ave., Maryville, South of Ashley River Rd., (S.C. Hwy. 61), Northwest of Charleston

The town of Maryville, chartered in 1886, included the site of the original English settlement in S.C. and the plantation owned by the Lords Proprietors 1670–99. When the old plantation was subdivided into lots and sold to local blacks in the 1880s, they established a town named for educator and community leader Mary Mathews Just (d. 1902). Though Maryville was widely seen as a model of black "self-government," the S.C. General Assembly revoked the town charter in 1936. *Erected by the City of Charleston, 1999*
GPS Coordinates: 32° 47.706' N, 79° 59.58' W

10–34 Riversville/Battle of Secessionville

Eastern end of Fort Lamar Rd., James Island

Riversville (FRONT)
Riversville, an antebellum village of fourteen acres, with seven lots on Savannah (later Secessionville) Creek, was established here in 1851 by Constant H. Rivers (1829–1910), who believed that the sandy soils and marsh breezes of James Island would protect inhabitants from the "malarious gases" common to the coast during the summer months.
Battle of Secessionville (REVERSE)
The village, renamed Secessionville by early 1861, gave its name to the battle fought nearby on June 16, 1862, in which Confederates repulsed numerous Federal assaults on an earthwork built across the peninsula and crushed Union hopes for an early occupation of Charleston. A water battery overlooking the marsh to the northeast was one of several earthworks built here in 1862 and 1863. *Erected by Chicora Foundation, Inc., 1999*
GPS Coordinates: 32° 42.365' N, 79° 56.339' W

10–35 Archibald Rutledge Birthplace

Corner of Pinckney St. and Rutledge Ct., McClellanville

(FRONT) Archibald Hamilton Rutledge (1883–1973), educator, man of letters, and the first poet laureate of S.C., was born at this site, in a house known to the Rutledge family as "Summer Place." Rutledge, who grew up here and at Hampton Plantation, taught English for 33 years at Mercersburg Academy, in Mercersburg, Pa. By the 1920s he was well known for his poems, nature articles, hunting tales, essays, and other writings.
(REVERSE) Appointed poet laureate in 1934, Rutledge retired in 1937 to the family home at Hampton Plantation, where he graciously received many visitors (Hampton, 7 mi. N, is now a state historic site). He is perhaps best known for Home by the River (1941), his affectionate memoir of Hampton and the people, wildlife, and landscape of the Santee Delta. Rutledge died here in 1973 and was inducted into the S.C. Hall of Fame in 1984. *Erected by the St. James-Santee Parish Historical Society, 2000*
GPS Coordinates: 33° 4.959' N, 79° 27.553' W

10–36 St. Paul's, Stono/St. Paul's Churchyard

Church Flats Rd., off S.C. Hwy. 162 just West of Stono Plantation Dr., Meggett vicinity

St. Paul's, Stono (FRONT)
St. Paul's Parish, one of the ten original parishes of colonial S.C., was created by the Church Act of 1706. The first parish church was built in 1708 on a bluff overlooking the Stono River. The parsonage and outbuildings were destroyed during the Yamasee War of 1715. After St. John's Colleton Parish was created in 1734, a new parish church for St. Paul's was built 8 mi. NW in 1736.
St. Paul's Churchyard (REVERSE)
Foundation ruins and a few graves are all that remain of the first St. Paul's, Stono. Robert Seabrook (1652–1710), buried here, served as high sheriff of Colleton County in 1698; as a captain of militia in 1706; and as a member of the Commons House of Assembly 1706–09, serving as Speaker in 1706. His wife Sarah (d. 1715) and their son Benjamin (d. 1717) are also buried here. *Erected by the Charles Towne Chapter, Colonial Dames of the XVII Century, 2002*
GPS Coordinates: 32° 44.923' N, 80° 10.952' W

10–37 Laing School

King St. and Royall Ave., Mt. Pleasant

(FRONT) Laing School, located here from 1868 to 1953, was founded in 1866 by Cornelia Hancock, a Quaker who had served as a nurse with the Union Army during the Civil War. First housed in Mount Pleasant Presbyterian Church, Laing Industrial School was named for Henry M. Laing of the Friends' Association for the Aid and Elevation of Freedmen. The 1868 school, destroyed by the Charleston earthquake of 1886, was replaced by a school which stood here until 1954.

(REVERSE) Early instruction at Laing, with its motto, "Try To Excel," combined academics with instruction in industrial, farming, and homemaking skills. A new Laing Elementary opened at King & Greenwich Streets in 1945; the high school remained here until a new Laing High opened on U.S. Hwy. 17 North in 1953. Laing High closed in 1970 with the desegregation of county schools. That building later housed Laing Middle School when it opened in 1974. *Erected by the Laing School Alumni Association, 2002*
GPS Coordinates: 32° 47.19' N, 79° 52.424' W

10–38 Friendship A.M.E. Church

204 Royall Ave., Mt. Pleasant

(FRONT) This church, founded during Reconstruction, has been at this site since 1890. The first sanctuary serving this congregation was located on Hibben St. and built on a lot leased from the town of Mount Pleasant in 1877. After moving here and building a new church under the pastorate of Rev. F. E. Rivers in 1890, the congregation grew so quickly that it built its third sanctuary, a large frame church, by 1895.

(REVERSE) A 1911 storm during the pastorate of Rev. Frank Woodbury nearly destroyed the sanctuary, which was essentially rebuilt. Later renovations, including the application of a brick veneer in 1961 during the pastorate of Rev. J. A. Sabb, Jr., gave the church its present appearance. Friendship A.M.E. Church also hosted the graduation exercises of nearby Laing School for many years until the school closed in 1953. *Erected by the Congregation, 2001*
GPS Coordinates: 32° 47.162' N, 79° 52.391' W

10–39 Confederate Lines

East side of U.S. Hwy. 17 N, just North of Long Point Rd. Mt. Pleasant

The earthworks nearby are remains of the 1861 fortifications built to defend Mount Pleasant. They extended east 2.5 miles from Butler's Creek at Boone Hall Plantation to Fort Palmetto on Hamlin Sound. Supporting this line were Battery Gary and those at Hobcaw Point, Hog Island, Hibben Street, and Venning's and Kinloch's Landings. Federal troops occupied the town 18 February 1865. *Erected by the Christ Church Parish Preservation Society, 2003*
GPS Coordinates: 32° 50.687' N, 79° 48.778' W

10–40 Hampton Plantation

Hampton Plantation State Park, 1950 Rutledge Rd., at its intersection with U.S. Hwy. 17, McClellanville

(FRONT) Hampton Plantation, 2 mi. NW, was established by 1730 and was one of the earliest rice plantations on the Santee River, in an area settled by Huguenots and often called "French Santee." The house, built in the 1730s for Elias Horry, later passed to his granddaughter Harriott Horry, who married Frederick Rutledge in 1797. The plantation remained in the Rutledge family until 1971.

(REVERSE) One of Hampton's best-known owners was Archibald Rutledge (1882–1973), educator, man of letters, and first poet laureate of S.C. He wrote of life there in Home By The River (1941), calling it "the mother plantation of this old plantation country." Designated a National Historic Landmark in 1970, it has been Hampton Plantation State Park since the state acquired it in 1971. *Erected by the St. James-Santee Parish Historical Society, 2001*
GPS Coordinates: 33° 10.444' N, 79° 25.04' W

10–41 Liberty Hill

At the Felix Pinckney Community Center, 4790 Hassell St., North Charleston

Liberty Hill, established in 1871, is the oldest community in what is now North Charleston. In 1864 Paul and Harriet Trescot, "free persons of color" living in Charleston, owned 112 acres here. They sold land to Ishmael Grant, Aaron Middleton, and Plenty and William Lecque for a settlement for freedmen. These men donated an acre of the southeast corner to "the African Church," now African Methodist Episcopal Church. *Erected by the City of North Charleston and the North Charleston Heritage Corridor, 2005*
GPS Coordinates: 32° 52.825' N, 79° 59.787' W

10–42 Park Circle

Park Circle, North Charleston

Park Circle is the focus of the master plan for North Charleston, designed by W. B. Marquis in 1912. One of the first modern planned communities in S.C., this 1500-acre development was completed shortly before World War II and grew with the wartime activity at the Charleston Navy Yard. Its four major avenues—Buist, Dupont, Montague, and Rhett—radiate from within Park Circle and were named for the developers who acquired and planned the neighborhood. *Erected by the City of North Charleston and the North Charleston Heritage Corridor, 2002*
GPS Coordinates: 32° 52.819' N, 79° 59.122' W

10–4[3] William Rhett House

[Marker erroneously numbered 10-4. It should read 10-43.]

54 Hasell St., Charleston

(FRONT) This house, built ca. 1712, is believed to be one of the oldest houses in Charleston. It was built for William Rhett (1666–1723), a merchant, sea captain, militia officer, and speaker of the Commons House of Assembly famous for capturing the pirate Steed Bonnet. In 1807 Christopher Fitzsimons (d. 1825), a merchant and planter, bought the house, renovating and enlarging it and adding its piazzas.

(REVERSE) The asymmetrical plan of the house includes a central hall with two large rooms on the western side and two slightly smaller rooms on the eastern side. With the relative decline of "Rhettsbury" in the early 20th century the house was a boarding house during the 1920s and 30s. Its restoration by Mr. and Mrs. Benjamin R. Kittredge, Jr., who bought it in 1941, was one of the first in this part of Charleston. *Erected by the Historic Charleston Foundation, 2002*
GPS Coordinates: 32° 46.983' N, 79° 55.827' W

10–44 The Parsonage/Miss Izard's School

5 & 7 President's Place, Charleston

The Parsonage (FRONT)
"The Parsonage," the home of Rev. James B. Middleton (1839–1918), stood here at 5 Short Court (now President's Place) until 1916. Middleton and his siblings, born slaves, were taught to read and write by their father, Rev. James C. Middleton (1790–1889). After the Civil War the elder Middleton, his son Rev. Abram Middleton (1827–1901), and Rev. James B. Middleton organized and served as pastors of many Methodist churches in the lowcountry.
Miss Izard's School (REVERSE)
This house, the home of the Frazer and Izard families, was built at 7 Short Court (now President's Place) by 1872. Anna Eliza Izard (1850–1945), niece of Revs. James B. and Abram Middleton, was a graduate of the Avery Normal Institute and taught school here for many years. Mamie Garvin Fields (1888–1987), a Middleton descendant, described life at 5 & 7 Short Court in *Lemon Swamp and Other Places* (1983). *Erected by the Avery Research Center for African American History and Culture, 2004*
GPS Coordinates: 32° 47.274' N, 79° 57.075' W

10–45 Mills House Hotel

Corner of Meeting and Queen Sts., Charleston

The original Mills House Hotel, later the St. John Hotel, stood on this site for 115 years. Built in 1853 for Otis Mills and designed by

architect John E. Earle, the hotel was described in 1857 as "costly in furniture, rich in decoration," and favored by "all the fashionable gentry." For many years one of Charleston's most popular hotels, it was torn down in 1968. The present Mills House Hotel, designed to resemble the original, was completed in 1970. *Erected by the Mills House Hotel, 2004*
GPS Coordinates: 32° 46.686' N, 79° 55.868' W

10–46 Battle of Fort Sullivan

Junction of Poe Ave. and Palmetto St., adjacent to Battery Jasper at Fort Moultrie National Monument, Sullivan's Island

(FRONT) On June 28, 1776, a British and Loyalist force seeking to capture Charleston advanced to Sullivan's Island with 9 ships and 2,500–3,000 infantry. The American defenders, 435 men under Col. William Moultrie of the 2nd S.C. Regiment, occupied a fort nearby, built from palmetto logs. Still unfinished when the fighting began, it is sometimes referred to as "Fort Sullivan" in contemporary accounts.
(REVERSE) As Adm. Peter Parker's ships shelled the fort its log walls absorbed or deflected the British shells and the Americans lost only 37 men killed or wounded. Moultrie's shells damaged every ship, inflicted 219 losses, and forced Parker's withdrawal. A British land attack at Breach Inlet also failed. The first major Patriot victory of the war also gave S.C. its nickname, "The Palmetto State." *Erected by the Fort Sullivan Chapter, National Society of the Daughters of the American Revolution, 2005*
GPS Coordinates: 32° 45.55' N, 79° 51.398' W

10–47 Lincolnville School /Lincolnville Elementary School

141 West Broad St., Lincolnville, West of Ladson
Lincolnville School (FRONT)
Lincolnville School, the first public school for black students in this community, stood here from 1924 to 1953. Built at a cost of $6,100, it was one of more than 5000 schools in the South funded in part by the Julius Rosenwald Foundation between 1917 and 1932. Four

teachers taught grades 1–8 in a frame school with four classrooms and an auditorium, on a four-acre lot on Broad Street.
Lincolnville Elementary School (REVERSE)
In 1953 Lincolnville School was covered with brick veneer and expanded to become Lincolnville Elementary School, with four classrooms, a library, and a cafeteria/auditorium. Students attended grades 1–7 there until Charleston County schools were desegregated in 1969. *Erected by the Lincolnville Elementary School Alumni Association, 2019*
GPS Coordinates: 33° 0.535' N, 80° 9.501' W

10–48 The Stono Rebellion (1739)

4246 Savannah Highway (U.S. Hwy. 17), just North of its intersection with S.C. Hwy. 162, Rantowles
(FRONT) The Stono Rebellion, the largest slave insurrection in British North America, began nearby on September 9, 1739. About 20 Africans raided a store near Wallace Creek, a branch of the Stono River. Taking guns and other weapons, they killed two shopkeepers. The rebels marched south toward promised freedom in Spanish Florida, waving flags, beating drums, and shouting "Liberty!"
(REVERSE) The rebels were joined by 40 to 60 more during their 15-mile march. They killed at least 20 whites, but spared others. The rebellion ended late that afternoon when the militia caught the rebels, killing at least 34 of them. Most who escaped were captured and executed; any forced to join the rebels were released. The S.C. assembly soon enacted a harsh slave code, in force until 1865. *Erected by the Sea Island Farmers Cooperative, 2006*
GPS Coordinates: 32° 47.111' N, 80° 8.83' W

10–49 Pollitzer House

5 Pitt St., Charleston
(FRONT) This was the home of sisters Carrie (1881–1974), Mabel (1885–1979), and Anita Pollitzer (1894–1975), longtime activists for women's rights. Anita, an artist and wife of press agent Elie C. Edson, played a pivotal role in the passage and ratification of the 19th Amendment, which allowed women to vote. She was national secretary, then chair of the

10-49 Pollitzer House, Charleston.
IMAGE COURTESY OF SCDAH

National Woman's Party (the forerunner of the National Organization for Women) from 1921 to 1949.
(REVERSE) In 1918 Carrie Pollitzer, co-founder and assistant principal of the S.C. Kindergarten Training School, led a successful effort to enroll women in the College of Charleston. Mabel, a science teacher at Memminger High School, organized an early school lunch program there. She also served as chair and publicity director of the state National Woman's Party and helped found the first free public library in Charleston County, which opened in 1931. *Erected by The Center For Women, 2006*
GPS Coordinates: 32° 46.795' N, 79° 56.312' W

10-50 Federal Expedition on John's Island/Battle of Burden's Causeway

River Rd. at Burden Creek Rd., John's Island
Federal Expedition on John's Island (FRONT)
The Battle of Burden's Causeway was the climax of a Federal expedition against John's Island, July 2–9, 1864. 5000 Federals under Brig. Gen. John P. Hatch crossed the Stono River and advanced along it. By July 6th they occupied a strong position here, where a bridge on Burden's Causeway crossed Burden's Creek.
Battle of Burden's Causeway (REVERSE)
Fewer than 2000 Confederates under Brig. Gen. B. H. Robertson opposed the Federals. Brief skirmishing and shelling occurred on

July 7th and 8th. On July 9, 1864, the Confederates attacked, were repulsed, were reinforced, and attacked again. Hatch, compelled to withdraw, evacuated John's Island late that night. *Erected by the Carolina Historical Site Preservation Foundation, Inc., and Secession Camp #4, Sons of Confederate Veterans, 2006*
GPS Coordinates: 32° 43.108' N, 80° 1.295' W

10-51 Battery Haig

Just off East Shore Dr., Oakland Subdivision, James Island
This Confederate earthwork, named for the owner on whose plantation it was built, was constructed in 1863. It and other works on the north bank of the Stono River were intended to help defend Charleston's western approaches along the Charleston & Savannah Railroad. In late 1864 Battery Haig was armed with two 24-pounder rifled cannon. It and the rest of the Confederate defenses of Charleston were abandoned when the city was evacuated February 17, 1865. *Erected by the South Carolina Battleground Preservation Trust, 2006*
GPS Coordinates: 32° 46.584' N, 80° 2.144' W

10-52 Maybank Green/Hobcaw Plantation

N. Shelmore Blvd. at Maybank Green, I'On Village, Mount Pleasant
Maybank Green (FRONT)
In 1697 David Maybank II (1660–1713) acquired 200 acres along Hobcaw Creek from the Lords Proprietors. Maybank, a carpenter, built a house on this site which he named Hobcaw Plantation. The plantation passed to his daughter Susannah (1700–1746) and her husband Capt. Jacob Bond (1695–1766), planter and member of the Commons House of Assembly. After Bond's death the plantation was owned by his daughter Rebecca Bond Read (1730–1786).
Hobcaw Plantation (REVERSE)
Rebecca and James Read's son Dr. William Read (1754–1845) was a deputy surgeon general in the Continental Army, serving under both George Washington and Nathanael Greene. This was one of Read's several

lowcountry plantations; his principal residence was in Charleston. In 1819 Read's cousin Jacob Bond I'On (1782–1859), planter, army officer, and legislator, hosted President James Monroe and Secretary of State John C. Calhoun at Hobcaw Plantation. *Erected by The I'On Company, 2007*
GPS Coordinates: 32° 49.006' N, 79° 52.845' W

10–53 Magnolia Cemetery

Meeting St. (U.S. Hwy. 52), Charleston, just North of its intersection with Mt. Pleasant St. and just South of its intersection with Cunnington St.

(FRONT) Magnolia Cemetery, established in 1850, was named for Magnolia Umbra Plantation, dating back to 1784. The ca. 1800 house built by Col. William Cunnington serves as the cemetery office. This is a fine example of the "rural cemetery" movement, with winding streets and paths, a lake, view of the Cooper River and marsh, and magnolias, live oaks, and other landscaping.
(REVERSE) Charleston architect Edward C. Jones designed the cemetery plan, and stonecutters William T., Edwin R., and Robert D. White sculpted many of its fine gravestones and monuments. Notable persons buried here include William Gregg, Robert Barnwell Rhett, William Gilmore Simms, George A. Trenholm, and Horace L. Hunley and three crews of the Confederate submarine H. L. Hunley. *Erected by the Magnolia Cemetery Trust, 2007*
GPS Coordinates: 32° 48.93' N, 79° 57.042' W

10–54 French Botanical Garden

W. Aviation Ave., just East of its intersection with S. Aviation Ave., West of I-26 at Exit 211A, North Charleston

André Michaux (1746–1802), botanist to Louis XVI of France, lived here 1786–96. He established a botanical garden 300 yards north in order to export native American trees and plants to France. Michaux was the first to import the camellia, crape myrtle, mimosa, parasol tree, and sweet olive to North America and the gingko and tea plants to this area. His son closed the garden in 1803. *Erected by*

the Michaux Garden Committee of the Charleston Horticultural Society, 2008
GPS Coordinates: 32° 54.044' N, 80° 1.785' W

10–55 Point Plantation

533 Pinckney St., McClellanville

(FRONT) The McClellan family for which McClellanville was named acquired this land shortly before the American Revolution. A 490-acre tract on Jeremy Creek was originally granted to John Whilden in 1705. In 1771 master carpenter Archibald McClellan, Sr. (1740–1791) bought the tract, built a house on the marsh, and named it Point Plantation. He planted an avenue of live oaks that still stand and expanded the plantation to 1350 acres, primarily raising cattle.
(REVERSE) Point Plantation passed to Archibald McClellan, Jr. (1764–1846), then to his sons William and Archibald. Archibald J. McClellan (1814–1880) grew cotton and produced lime and salt here after his brother's death. By the 1850s he and Richard T. Morrison (1816–1910) leased, then later sold, lots to area planters. The village here was named for the McClellan family by 1860. The old house at Point Plantation burned in 1902 and was replaced by the present house. *Erected by The Village Museum, 2008*
GPS Coordinates: 33° 5.018' N, 79° 27.585' W

10–56 Battery Number 5

Seaside Plantation Dr. between Secessionville Rd. and Planters Trace Dr., James Island

(FRONT) This was one of several Confederate earthworks constructed on the southwest portion of James Island in the summer of 1863. It was a significant part of the "New Line" or "Siege Line" intended to defend Charleston from Federal attacks up the Stono or Folly Rivers. This line replaced the 1861–62 lines that ran across James Island from Clark Sound to Wappoo Creek.
(REVERSE) In April 1864 Battery Number 5 was manned by Company H of the 2nd S.C. Artillery, commanded by Capt. W. H. Kennady. Its armament at that time was three 24-pounder smoothbore cannon and one 12-pounder

smoothbore cannon. This battery and the rest of Charleston's defenses were evacuated February 17, 1865. Battery Number 5 was listed in the National Register of Historic Places in 1982. *Erected by the South Carolina Battleground Preservation Trust, 2008*
GPS Coordinates: 32° 42.473' N, 79° 57.208' W

10–57 Jenkins Orphanage

3923 Azalea Dr., North Charleston

(FRONT) Since 1937 this has been the campus of the Jenkins Orphanage, established in Charleston in 1891 by Rev. Daniel Joseph Jenkins (1862–1937). Jenkins, a Baptist minister, founded this orphanage for African American children with aid from the city. Housed in the old Marine Hospital on Franklin Street downtown 1891–1937, it also included an institute to teach and train children between the ages of 3 and 20. More than 500 lived there by 1896.
(REVERSE) The Jenkins Orphanage Band played concerts across the U.S. and Europe for more than 30 years to help fund the orphanage. The band, taught by Hatsie Logan and Eugene Mikell, is prominent in the early history of jazz; alumni Cat Anderson, Freddie Green, and Jabbo Smith played for Duke Ellington, Count Basie, and others. The orphanage moved here in 1937, and its offices and dorms were built by the City of Charleston. Those historic buildings burned in the 1980s. *Erected by the Daniel Joseph Jenkins Institute for Children, a program of the Orphan Aid Society, Inc., 2008*
GPS Coordinates: 32° 50.816' N, 79° 59.788' W

10–58 Battery Haskell

Adjacent to Schooner Dr., Lighthouse Point, James Island

(FRONT) This two-gun Confederate artillery battery and magazine is all that remains of Battery Haskell, a large fortification built on Legare's Point in 1863 to help defend James and Morris Islands. This two-gun battery was just behind the left flank of Battery Haskell, named for Capt. Charles T. Haskell, Jr. of the 1st S.C. Infantry, mortally wounded on Morris Island July 10, 1863.

(REVERSE) Battery Haskell, "a massive open work," was built for twelve guns. In early 1865 its armament was one 8-inch smoothbore cannon, one 32-pounder smoothbore cannon, and two 10-inch mortars. It and the rest of Charleston's defenses were evacuated February 17, 1865. Battery Haskell was gradually demolished from the 1920s to the 1960s for farm use and later for residential development. *Erected by the South Carolina Battleground Preservation Trust, 2008*
GPS Coordinates: 32° 43.717' N, 79° 54.648' W

10–59 Battery Cheves

At the Southeasternmost curve of Robert E. Lee Blvd., Ft. Johnson Estates, James Island

(FRONT) This four-gun Confederate artillery battery was one of several earthworks built on the southeastern shore of James Island in the summer of 1863. Built between Battery Simkins and Battery Haskell, this battery was named for Capt. Langdon Cheves, an engineer who designed Battery Wagner on Morris Island and who was killed during the Federal assault there on July 10, 1863.
(REVERSE) The battery assisted in the defense of James and Morris Islands, and its armament in 1863 was four 8-inch smoothbore naval guns. A magazine explosion on September 15, 1863 killed five men and wounded two. Battery Cheves and the rest of Charleston's defenses were evacuated February 17, 1865. The battery was listed in the National Register of Historic Places in 1982. *Erected by the South Carolina Battleground Preservation Trust, 2008*
GPS Coordinates: 32° 44.267' N, 79° 54.43' W

10–60 The Elms

At the L. Mendel Rivers Library, 9200 University Blvd., Charleston Southern University Campus, North Charleston

(FRONT) The Elms, an inland rice plantation on the headwaters of Goose Creek, was owned by the Izard family for more than 150 years. In 1704 Ralph Izard (d. 1711), member of the Commons House of Assembly, bought a 250-acre tract here, expanding it to more than 500 acres. His son Ralph II (d. 1743) also served in the Assembly and on the Royal Council. The first to plant rice at The Elms, he enlarged it to more than 2,700 acres.

(REVERSE) Ralph Izard III (1742–1804) lent money to the Patriot cause and later served in the Continental Congress. A state representative after the war, then U.S. Senator, Izard was briefly President Pro Tempore of the Senate. An 1818 visitor to The Elms described its "avenue of lofty elms & of loftier live oaks." Its ca. 1718 house, later rebuilt after a fire, was virtually destroyed by the Charleston earthquake of 1886. *Erected by the City of North Charleston, 2008*
GPS Coordinates: 32° 58.782' N, 80° 4.38' W

10–61 Redoubt Number 3

South of Ft. Johnson Rd., Patriot Plantation, James Island

(FRONT) Redoubt Number 3, built here in 1861–62, was one of six identical Confederate earthworks built across the center of James Island, known collectively as the East Lines. Intended to help defend Charleston from Federal attacks up the Stono River, they were 60 yds. square and built for two guns each. In November 1863 this redoubt was armed with a single 24-pounder smoothbore cannon.

(REVERSE) The East Lines stretched south from a tributary of James Island Creek, on Croskey Royall's plantation, to Clark Sound, on the Rev. Stiles Mellichamp's plantation. By late 1863, stronger earthworks, called the New Lines, were built nearer the Stono River, making these lines obsolete. This redoubt and the rest of Charleston's defenses were evacuated February 17, 1865. *Erected by the South Carolina Battleground Preservation Trust, 2008*
GPS Coordinates: 32° 43.593' N, 79° 56.289' W

10–62 Fort Pemberton

221 Yates Ave., Riverland Terrace, James Island

Fort Pemberton, a large five-sided Confederate earthwork on the James Island side of the Stono River, was built in the spring of 1862 to defend Charleston from a Federal attack via Elliott's Cut and Wappoo Creek. Named for Maj. Gen. John C. Pemberton, commander

of the Dept. of S.C. and Ga., it was designed for as many as twenty-one guns but never held more than eight. Fort Pemberton was described in 1865 as "a large well-built work, heavily armed." In June 1864 it was manned by Co. B, 15th Battalion S.C. Heavy Artillery, commanded by Capt. Guignard Richardson. Its armament at that time was two 32-pounder banded rifled guns and two 32-pounder smoothbore cannon. It and the rest of Charleston defenses were evacuated on February 17, 1865. *Erected by the South Carolina Battleground Preservation Trust, 2008*
GPS Coordinates: 32° 45.576' N, 79° 59.983' W

10–63 Windsor Hill Plantation

3790 Ashley Phosphate Rd. at Windsor Hill Blvd., North Charleston

(FRONT) This inland rice plantation was established in 1701 by a grant of 500 acres to Joseph Child. The original grant was between the headwaters of Goose Creek and the Ashley River, and Child soon acquired an additional 300 acres. His son Benjamin added acreage and continued planting rice. In 1749 Benjamin and Hannah Child's daughter Mary inherited Windsor Hill and married rice planter John Ainslie (d. 1774).

(REVERSE) John and Mary Ainslie built a two-story house here about 1750. In 1776 their daughter Hannah married William Moultrie, Jr. (1752–1796). The plantation declined by the 1830s, and the house burned in 1857. Gen. William Moultrie (1730–1805), victor at the Battle of Sullivan's Island in 1776 and governor 1785–1787 and 1792–94, was first buried here but reburied on Sullivan's Island, at Fort Moultrie, in 1977. *Erected by the City of North Charleston, 2010*
GPS Coordinates: 32° 55.432' N, 80° 5.39' W

10–64 Camp of Wild's "African Brigade," 1863–1864/Wild's Brigade Cemetery

Folly Beach Community Ctr., 55 Center St., Folly Beach

Camp of Wild's "African Brigade," 1863–1864 (FRONT)

Folly Island was occupied by Union troops April 1863-February 1865. Gen. Edward A. Wild's "African Brigade" camped nearby from November 1863 to February 1864. The two regiments in Wild's brigade were the 55th Massachusetts, made up largely of free blacks, and the 1st North Carolina, made up of former slaves.
Wild's Brigade Cemetery (REVERSE)
A cemetery was laid out nearby for soldiers in Wild's Brigade who died here in 1863–64. Most graves were removed after the war. In 1987 relic hunters discovered additional graves of U.S. Colored Troops. In 1987–88 archaeologists removed 19 burials and published their findings. These soldiers were reburied with full military honors at Beaufort National Cemetery in May 1989. *Erected by The Friends of the 55th Massachusetts, 2010*
GPS Coordinates: 32° 39.495' N, 79° 56.526' W

10–65 The Siege of Charleston, 1780

King St., at the Northwest corner of Marion Square near Hutson St., Charleston

(FRONT) The British capture of Charleston in May 1780 was one of the worst American defeats of the Revolution. On March 30–31 Gen. Henry Clinton's British, Hessian, and Loyalist force crossed the Ashley River north of Charleston. On April 1 Clinton advanced against the American lines near this site, held by Gen. Benjamin Lincoln's Continentals and militia. The 42-day siege would be the longest of the war.
(REVERSE) As Gen. Charles Cornwallis closed off Lincoln's escape routes on the Cooper River, Clinton advanced his siege lines and bombarded Charleston. On May 12, 1780, in front of the American works near this spot, Lincoln surrendered the city and his force of 6,000 men, after what one British officer called "a gallant defense." The British occupied Charleston for more than 2 ½ years, evacuating Dec. 14, 1782. *Erected by the South Carolina Societies of the Daughters of the American Revolution and Sons of the American Revolution, and the Maj. Gen. William Moultrie Chapter, Sons of the American Revolution, 2010*
GPS Coordinates: 32° 47.187' N, 79° 56.198' W

10–66 Calvary Episcopal Church

104–106 Line Street, Charleston

(FRONT) This church, located on Beaufain Street for 91 years, was organized in 1847 to give free blacks and slaves in antebellum Charleston a separate Episcopal congregation of their own. The Rev. Paul Trapier was its first minister, and the church met in the St. Philip's Episcopal Church parsonage, then in Temperance Hall, before acquiring a lot at the corner of Beaufain and Wilson Streets.
(REVERSE) A stuccoed brick church on Beaufain Street was completed and consecrated in 1849. In 1940 Charleston Housing Authority bought the historic church and lot to build the Robert Mills Manor housing project. The congregation bought this lot on Line Street from the city and dedicated this sanctuary in 1942. Three African-American cemeteries have been on this site: one "Colored," one Baptist, and Calvary Episcopal. *Erected by the Congregation, 2010*
GPS Coordinates: 32° 47.639' N, 79° 56.744' W

10–67 Burke High School

Burke High School, 144 President St., Charleston

(FRONT) This school, founded in 1910, was the first public high school for African-Americans in Charleston. It succeeded the Charleston Normal & Industrial School, a private school at Bogard & Kracke Streets, which had been founded in 1894 by Rev. John L. Dart. The new Charleston Colored & Industrial School, built here at President and Fishburne Streets by the City of Charleston, opened in January 1911 with 375 students.
(REVERSE) David Hill became the first African-American principal in 1919. The school was renamed Burke Industrial School in 1921 in memory of J. E. Burke, vice chairman of the public school board. By 1930 Burke, with 1,000 students, had a full elementary and high school curriculum in addition to its vocational curriculum. Burke merged with Avery High School in 1954, was accredited, and was renamed Burke High School, in a new complex on this site. It was rebuilt in 2005. *Erected by the Burke High School Foundation, Inc., 2010*
GPS Coordinates: 32° 47.563' N, 79° 57.224' W

10–68 Cannon Street Hospital/ McClennan-Banks Memorial Hospital

135 Cannon St., Charleston

Cannon Street Hospital (FRONT)
Cannon Street Hospital, established here in 1897, served the African-American community of Charleston until 1959. Officially the Hospital and Training School for Nurses, it occupied a three-story brick building constructed ca. 1800. Dr. Alonzo C. McClennan (1855–1912), then one of only six black physicians in Charleston, was one of its founders and also edited The Hospital Herald 1898–1900.
McClennan-Banks Memorial Hospital (REVERSE)
By 1956 Dr. Thomas C. McFall, director of the Cannon Street Hospital, led a campaign to build a new hospital. McClennan-Banks Memorial Hospital, which opened on Courtenay Street in 1959, was named for Dr. McClennan and Anna DeCosta Banks (1869–1930), first head nurse of the Cannon Street Hospital. The old hospital here was torn down in 1961; the new hospital closed at the end of 1976 and was torn down in 2004. *Erected by the Waring Historical Library, Medical University of South Carolina, and the Avery Research Center for African American History and Culture, College of Charleston, 2010*
GPS Coordinates: 32° 47.268' N, 79° 56.972' W

10–69 Institute Hall/"The Union is Dissolved!"

134 Meeting Street, Charleston

Institute Hall (FRONT)
Institute Hall, built here in 1854, stood until 1861. An Italianate building, it was designed by Jones and Lee for the South Carolina Institute, a progressive organization promoting "art, ingenuity, mechanical skill, and industry." The Grand Hall, Charleston's largest public space, seated 3,000 and hosted fairs, exhibits, concerts, balls, and conventions. It hosted the 1860 Democratic convention, which split over the mention of slavery in the platform.
"The Union is Dissolved!" (REVERSE)
Abraham Lincoln's election as president in Nov. 1860 was the catalyst for a secession convention in S.C. The convention met in Columbia on Dec. 17, but moved to Charleston the next day. On Dec. 20, 1860, S.C. became the first state to secede from the Union. That night delegates signed the Ordinance of Secession before a huge crowd in the Grand Hall. Institute Hall later burned in the "Great Fire" of Dec. 1861. *Erected by the Fort Sumter-Fort Moultrie Historical Trust and the S.C. Civil War Sesquicentennial Advisory Board, 2010*
GPS Coordinates: 32° 46.704' N, 79° 55.873' W

10–70 Hampstead Cemetery

46 Reid St., Charleston

(FRONT) A cemetery established here in 1841, also known as "God's Acre" and later "the German Cemetery," was maintained by St. Matthews Evangelical Lutheran Church until about 1860. That church, founded in 1840 by the rapidly-growing community of Germans in Charleston, was originally the German Evangelical Church of Charleston. Its founders purchased land here for a cemetery shortly before they built their church at the corner of Anson and Hasell Streets.
(REVERSE) Hampstead Cemetery, laid out between cemeteries owned by the African Society and the Hebrew Congregation, sold half-plots and quarter-plots to church members and others. Yellow fever epidemics in 1849, 1852, and 1856 killed so many Germans that the cemetery was almost full by 1857, when the church dedicated Bethany Cemetery, a new cemetery in North Charleston, near Magnolia Cemetery. Several graves found herre in 1982 were removed to Bethany in 2009. *Erected by the Housing Authority of the City of Charleston, 2011*
GPS Coordinates: 32° 47.604' N, 79° 56.165' W

10–71 Hampton Park Terrace

Huger St., just Southwest of Rutledge Ave., Charleston

(FRONT) Hampton Park Terrace, an early 20th-century planned suburb, was laid out in 1912 along Huger Street between Rutledge and Hagood Aves. Its success coincided with the economic boom that following the opening of the Charleston Navy Yard in 1901. It was also aided by its location immediately south of Hampton Park, a large municipal park built on the site of the 1901–02 Charleston and West-Indian Exposition.

(REVERSE) Developers praised "the open fresh beauty of Hampton Park Terrace" and called it "the ideal home overlooking both river and Park." Most houses dates from 1912 to 1922 and include excellent examples of the American Foursquare, Colonial Revival, Prairie, Craftsman, and Bungalow styles. The Hampton Park Terrace Historic District was listed in the National Register of Historic Places in 1997. *Erected by the Hampton Park Terrace Neighborhood Council, 2011*
GPS Coordinates: 32° 47.93' N, 79° 57.084' W

10–72 Old Bethel Methodist Church

222 Calhoun Street, Charleston

(FRONT) This church, built in 1797 in the meeting-house form, was dedicated in 1798 and completed in 1809. It is the oldest Methodist church standing in Charleston. Originally at the corner of Pitt and Calhoun Streets, Bethel Methodist Church was a congregation of white and black members, both free blacks and slaves. Many blacks left the church in 1833 during a dispute over seating. Though some later returned, many did not.

(REVERSE) In 1852 the congregation moved this building west to face Calhoun Street, to make room for a new brick church, completed the next year. This church, called "Old Bethel," was used for Sunday school before its black members acquired it in 1876. They kept the name Old Bethel and moved the church to this location in 1882. Old Bethel Methodist Church was listed in the National Register of Historic Places in 1975. *Erected by the Congregation, 2011*
GPS Coordinates: 32° 47.057' N, 79° 56.517' W

10–73 Plainsfield Plantation

4611 Towles Rd., Meggett

(FRONT) Plainsfield Plantation, on this site, and Pawletts Plantation, nearby, were established

ca. 1690 by Joseph Blake (1663–1700), one of Carolina's Lords Proprietors and governor of the colony 1694 and 1696–1700. Blake, who had come to the colony ca. 1685 and was soon a member of the Grand Council, named his plantations for locales in his native Somersetshire, England.

(REVERSE) Blake was governor when he purchased Sir John Berkeley's proprietary share in 1694. Blake, a Dissenter who supported religious liberty and citizenship for French Huguenots and other non-English settlers, died in office. The "Goose Creek Men," planters who opposed his and the Proprietors' policies on settlers and Indian trade, took control of the government after Blake's death. *Sponsored by The Society of First Families of South Carolina 1670–1700, 2011*
GPS Coordinates: 32° 43.239' N, 80° 11.075' W

10–74 Cook's Old Field Cemetery /Copahee Plantation and Hamlin Beach

Just North of Rifle Range Rd., Mt. Pleasant vicinity

Cook's Old Field Cemetery (FRONT)
This plantation cemetery predates the American Revolution. It was established by early members of the Hamlin, Hibben and Leland families. James Hibben (d. 1835), one of the founders of Mount Pleasant, is buried here. Generations of both white and black families are interred here. In 2003 this cemetery was listed in the National Register of Historic Places.

Copahee Plantation and Hamlin Beach (REVERSE)
Thomas Hamlin established Copahee Plantation here in 1696. Later divided into Copahee and Contentment Cottage, it is now known as Hamlin Farms. In 1881 African American farmers bought 31 ten-acre lots from the Hamlins and founded the Hamlin Beach community. White and black descendants still live here today. *Sponsored by the Christ Church Parish Preservation Society, 2011*
GPS Coordinates: 32° 50.483' N, 79° 47.865' W

10–75 Inland Rice Fields, ca. 1701–1865

Palmetto Commerce Parkway, Northwest of Ashley Phosphate Rd., North Charleson vicinity

Embankments and ditches dating from the early 18th century are still visible here and show the elaborate layout of rice fields that were part of Windsor Hill and Woodlands plantations. Before the American Revolution, lowcountry planters grew rice in inland fields that did not use the tides for flood waters. Windsor Hill was established ca. 1701 by Joseph Child (d. 1717), and Woodlands was established ca. 1800 by Thomas Parker (d. 1821). The remnants of these rice fields are a tangible reminder of the skill and labor of the enslaved people who constructed them, many of whom had been rice farmers in Africa. *Sponsored by Charleston County, 2012*
GPS Coordinates: 32° 56.488' N, 80° 4.571' W

10–76 The Seizure of the *Planter*

Historic Charleston Foundation, 40 E. Bay St., Charleston

(FRONT) Early on May 13, 1862, Robert Smalls, an enslaved harbor pilot aboard the Planter, seized the 149-ft. Confederate transport from a wharf just east of here. He and six enslaved crewmen took the vessel before dawn, when its captain, pilot, and engineer were ashore. Smalls guided the ship through the channel, past Fort Sumter, and out to sea, delivering it to the Federal fleet which was blockading the harbor.

(REVERSE) Northern and Southern newspapers called this feat "bold" and "daring." Smalls and his crew, a crewman on another ship, and eight other enslaved persons including Smalls's wife, Hannah, and three children, won their freedom by it. Smalls (1839–1915) was appointed captain of the U.S.S. Planter by a U.S. Army contract in 1863. A native of Beaufort, he was later a state legislator and then a five-term U.S. Congressman. *Sponsored by Historic Charleston Foundation and the African American Historical Alliance, 2012*
GPS Coordinates: 32° 46.385' N, 79° 55.637' W

10–77 Cigar Factory/"We Shall Overcome"

701 E. Bay St., Charleston

Cigar Factory (FRONT)
This five-story commercial building, built ca. 1882 as a textile mill, was known as the Charleston Manufacturing Company, then Charleston Cotton Mills, in its early years. Leased to the American Tobacco Company in 1903, the plant was sold to that company in 1912. Popularly called "the Cigar Factory," it produced cigars such as Cremo and Roi-Tan until it closed in 1973. The Cigar Factory was listed in the National Register of Historic Places in 1980.

10–76 The Seizure of the *Planter*, Charleston.
IMAGE COURTESY OF SCDAH

"We Shall Overcome" (REVERSE)
By the end of World War II the factory employed 1,400 workers, 900 of them black women. In October 1945, 1,200 workers walked out over discrimination and low wages. Strikers sang the gospel hymn "I'll Overcome Some-day." Later revised as "We Shall Overcome," it would become the anthem of the Civil Rights Movement. The strike ended in March 1946 with a settlement giving workers raises and promising better treatment. *Sponsored by the Preservation Society of Charleston, 2013*
GPS Coordinates: 32° 47.828' N, 79° 56.043' W

10–78 James Simons Elementary School/Desegregation of Charleston Schools

West of intersection of King St. and Moultrie St., Charleston

James Simons Elementary School (FRONT)
This school, built in 1919 and designed by local architects Benson & Barbot, was the fifth public elementary school in the city. It opened for the 1919–1920 school year with an enroll-ment of 600. In 1955 the Charleston Branch of the National Association for the Advance-ment of Colored People (NAACP) petitioned the Charleston school board to desegregate all public city schools, including this one.
Desegregation of Charleston Schools (REVERSE)
In 1960 nine parents, with support from the NAACP, applied for their children's transfer to four white schools, including James Simons Elementary School. Denied by the board and on appeal, they sued in federal court in 1962 and won their case the next year. On Septem-ber 3, 1963, eleven black students entered this school and Memminger Elementary School and Charleston and Rivers High Schools. *Sponsored by the Preservation Society of Charleston, 2013*
GPS Coordinates: 32° 48.053' N, 79° 56.998' W

10–79 Kress Building/Civil Rights Sit-Ins

281 King St., Charleston

Kress Building (FRONT)
This three-story Art Deco building, built in 1930–31 was a 5- and 10-cent store owned by S. H. Kress & Co. until 1980. Kress, with about 400 American stores, designed its own build-ings. This store features a yellow brick façade with colorful and decorative glazed terracotta details typical of Kress's Art Deco designs. A 1941 two-story addition faces Wentworth Street. McCrory Stores bought this building in 1980, operating it under the Kress name until 1992.
Civil Rights Sit-Ins (REVERSE)
On April 1, 1960, the lunch counter here and those at the Woolworth's and W. T. Grant's stores on King St. were the targets of the city's first civil rights "sit-in." Black students from Burke High School were denied service but refused to leave. Arrested for trespassing, they were later convicted and fined. This youth-led protest was the beginning of a broader civil rights movement in Charleston. *Sponsored by the Preservation Society of Charleston, 2013*
GPS Coordinates: 32° 46.957' N, 79° 56.055' W

10–80 Hospital Strike of 1969

Ashley Ave., Charleston

(FRONT) Civil rights marches on Ashley Ave. and elsewhere occurred during strikes at two hospitals from March 20 to July 18, 1969. Workers, mostly black women, cited unequal treatment and pay when they organized and walked out of the Medical College Hospi-tal (MCH) on Doughty St. and Charleston County Hospital (CCH) on Calhoun St. Some picketers were arrested, the state of S.C. re-fused to sanction a union, and talks stalled. (REVERSE) The Southern Christian Leadership Conference joined the strike in its first major campaign since the death of Martin Luther King, Jr. Protests were marred by violence, and Gov. Robert McNair called out the Na-tional Guard and set a curfew. In May King's widow Coretta Scott King led 5,000 marchers down Ashley Ave. A settlement at MCH in June and CCH in July gave workers raises and promised better treatment. *Sponsored by the Preservation Society of Charleston, 2013*
GPS Coordinates: 32° 47.128' N, 79° 56.801' W

10–81 The Progressive Club

River Rd. & Royal Oak Dr., Johns Island

(FRONT) The Progressive Club, built in 1962–63, was a store and community center for Johns Island and other Sea Islands until it was badly damaged by Hurricane Hugo in 1989. The club had been founded in 1948 by civil rights activist Esau Jenkins (1910–1972), who worked to improve educational, political, economic, and other opportunities for blacks on the island and in the lowcountry.
(REVERSE) Jenkins, Septima Clark (1898–1987), and Bernice Robinson (1914–1994) founded the first Citizenship School in 1957 to encourage literacy and voter registration. Its success led to many similar schools across the South, called "the base on which the whole civil rights movement was built." The Progressive Club was listed in the National Register of Historic Places in 2007. *Sponsored by the Preservation Society of Charleston, 2013*
GPS Coordinates: 32° 40.626' N, 80° 2.445' W

10–82 Jonathan Jasper Wright Law Office

84 Queen St., Charleston

(FRONT) Jonathan Jasper Wright (1840–1885), the first African American in the U.S. to sit as a justice on a state supreme court, practiced law here from 1877 until his death in 1885. Wright, a native of Pa., was educated at Lancasterian Academy in Ithaca, N.Y. He came to S.C. in 1865 as a teacher for the American Missionary Association and also worked as an attorney for the Freedmen's Bureau.
(REVERSE) Wright wrote that he hoped to "vindicate the cause of the downtrodden." He was a delegate to the S.C. constitutional convention of 1868 and a state senator 1868–70. Wright, elected to the S.C. Supreme Court in 1870, resigned in 1877 due to political pressure. After he left the bench he practiced law, helped Claflin College found its Law Department, and became its Chair in Law. He died of tuberculosis in 1885. *Sponsored by the S.C. Black Lawyers Association, 2013*
GPS Coordinates: 32° 46.670' N, 79° 55.949' W

10–83 Union Heights/Howard Heights

Meeting St., just South of Beech Ave., North Charleston

Union Heights (FRONT)
This community, subdivided into lots in 1919, was named for the nearby union station of three railroads. It had been part of Belmont Plantation from the colonial period to the mid-19th century and became an African-American community after the Civil War. Union Heights, a thriving neighborhood of houses, churches, and shops, grew with the dramatic expansion of the Charleston Navy Yard from 1935 through World War II and into the 1960s.
Howard Heights (REVERSE)
This community, subdivided into residential lots for African Americans in 1943, was named for Howard University. It had been part of Windsor Plantation in the early 19th century, then was part of the phosphate operations of the Virginia-Carolina Chemical Co. The Charleston Housing Authority developed this area with federal funding during World War II. Though smaller than Union Heights, Howard Heights flourished from 1943 into the 1960s. *Sponsored by the Union Heights Community Council, 2014*
GPS Coordinates: 32° 50.324' N, 79° 57.709' W

10–84 Charles Towne/Old Town Plantation

Charles Towne Landing State Historic Site, Charleston

Charles Towne (FRONT)
The first permanent English settlement in what is now S.C. was established here in 1670. Named for King Charles II, the town was built on Albemarle Point, on the W bank of the Ashley River. It began in 1670–71 with a palisaded fort and a few houses. As it grew, additional lots were laid out across the Ashley River on Oyster Point. In 1680 the proprietors of the colony moved the capital to that site, in present-day downtown Charleston.
Old Town Plantation (REVERSE)
By 1700 this site was known as "Old Town Plantation," and it was used for farming for

almost 300 years. The last owners, Dr. and Mrs. Joseph I. Waring, renovated the overseer's house as their home and created 80 acres of landscaped gardens. In 1969 they sold more than 650 acres to the state of S.C., which developed a park here for the S.C. Tricentennial of 1970. The site became a state park in 1971. *Sponsored by the South Carolina Society, Children of the American Revolution, 2014*
GPS Coordinates: 32° 48.450' N, 79° 59.287' W

10–85 U.S. Courthouse and Post Office/*Briggs v. Elliott*

U.S. Courthouse, 83 Broad St., Charleston

U.S. Courthouse and Post Office (FRONT)
This Renaissance Revival building, opened in 1896, is notable for its association with U.S. District Judge J. Waties Waring (1880–1968). Waring, a Charleston native who served here 1942 to 1952, issued some of the most important civil rights rulings of the era. *Briggs v. Elliott,* the first suit to challenge public school segregation in the U.S., was heard here before three judges on May 28–29, 1951.
Briggs v. Elliott (REVERSE)
Thurgood Marshall and other NAACP Legal Defense Fund lawyers represented Harry and Eliza Briggs and 19 other courageous parents from Clarendon County. In a bold and vigorous dissent opposing the prevailing doctrine of separate but equal, Waring declared that segregation "must go and must go now. *Segregation is per se inequality.*" The U.S. Supreme Court followed his analysis as a central part of its groundbreaking decision in *Brown v. Board of Education* (1954). *Sponsored by the Charleston County Bar Association, 2014*
GPS Coordinates: 32° 46.579' N, 79° 55.907' W

10–86 Plymouth Church/Plymouth Parsonage

41 Pitt St., near intersection with Bull St., Charleston

Plymouth Church (FRONT)
In 1867 over 100 African Americans, most former members of the Circular Church, founded Plymouth Church, among the oldest black Congregational Churches in the South.

Plymouth is an example of the independent black churches formed at the dawn of emancipation. Early pastor Francis L. Cardozo was also involved in the operation of Avery Normal Institute, a school for black students. This Gothic Revival church building was completed in 1872.
Plymouth Parsonage (REVERSE)
Plymouth parsonage, built in 1886, was home to church leaders. Pastors who lived here were active in anti-lynching and equal rights campaigns. Plymouth also hosted a number of prominent black figures. W. E. B. Du Bois, a founding NAACP member, visited in 1925, and Paul Robeson, a singer and activist, stayed here while campaigning for presidential candidate Henry Wallace in 1948. In 1957 the congregation moved to a new location one mile north on Spring Street. *Sponsored by the Avery Research Center for African American History and Culture, 2014*
GPS Coordinates: 32° 46.977' N, 79° 56.417' W

10–87 Harmon Field/Cannon Street All-Stars

President St. at Fishburne St. (Harmon Field), Charleston

Harmon Field (FRONT)
Harmon Field, established in 1927, was one of many parks across the country created with support from the Harmon Foundation, a national philanthropic organization. Though dedicated to the "Recreation of All," state law mandated the racial segregation of public parks and Harmon Field remained a facility for African Americans until it was desegregated in 1964. Among other uses, the park was a venue for games played by amateur and semi-pro baseball teams.
Cannon Street All-Stars (REVERSE)
In 1953 the Cannon St. YMCA established the first African American Little League in S.C. and played games at Harmon Field. In 1955 the Cannon St. YMCA entered a team in the state Little League tournament. Rather than integrate, white teams boycotted and the Cannon St. All-Stars were state champions by forfeit. The All-Stars were invited to the Little League World Series, but not allowed to

compete. *Sponsored by the City of Charleston, 2014*

GPS Coordinates: 32° 47.567' N, 79° 57.185' W

10–88 Charleston Tea Plantation

6617 Maybank Hwy., Wadmalaw Island

(FRONT) The first confirmed cultivation of tea in the U.S. occurred when French botanist André Michaux brought tea plants to Middleton Barony on the Ashley River between 1799–1802. Large-scale production, however, was not attempted. Beginning in 1880 the U.S. Congress subsidized renewed cultivation efforts. The Pinehurst Plantation in Summerville was the most successful of these attempts.

(REVERSE) In 1963, cuttings from Pinehurst Plantation were transferred to 127 acres on Wadmalaw Island; land that is now the Charleston Tea Plantation. Because the Pinehurst plants had grown wild and cross-pollinated for decades prior to transfer they are now considered "South Carolina hybrids." Charleston Tea Plantation remains the only site of large-scale commercial tea production in the U.S. *Sponsored by Fort Sullivan Chapter, National Society of the Daughters of the American Revolution, 2014*

GPS Coordinates: 32° 37.129' N, 80° 11.115' W

10–89 Blake-Grimké House

321 East Bay St., Charleston

(FRONT) This Charleston double house was built before 1789 by William Blake, a planter and descendant of former Proprietary Governor Joseph Blake. By 1803 Mary Smith Grimké, descendant of Landgrave Thomas Smith, and Judge John F. Grimké, a planter and state Supreme Court justice, and their 11 children occupied the property. Among them were Sarah (1792–1873) and Angelina (1805–1879) Grimké who became leading advocates for equal rights for African Americans and women.

(REVERSE) From 1836–1838 the sisters, the first female agents of the abolitionist movement, traveled the Northeast as lecturers and organizers. In 1837 they helped organize the

first national convention of white and black women. Also in 1837 Sarah published a full-fledged argument for women's equal rights. The next year Angelina became the first American woman to address a legislative body, speaking to a committee of the Mass. legislature. Neither sister ever returned to Charleston. *Sponsored by College of Charleston Friends of the Library, 2015*

GPS Coordinates: 32° 47.216' N, 79° 55.756' W

10–90 Coastal Patrol Base #8

Riverland Dr. approximately ½ mile west of intersection with Grimball Road, James Island

(FRONT) The Civil Air Patrol (C.A.P.) was formed in 1941, just prior to U.S. entrance into WWII. C.A.P. air bases were located from Maine to Mexico and the James Island base was the 8th constructed. Its 3 runways were carved from a 108-acre cotton field and operations began in May 1942. This base remained in service until C.A.P. operations were moved to Charleston AFB after the war.

(REVERSE) From May 1942 to August 1943 almost 100 volunteers at Base 8 flew daily patrol missions. Aircrews primarily hunted enemy submarines, protected shipping lanes, and performed search and rescue. South Carolina natives Drew L. King and Clarence L. Rawls died at sea when their plane crashed off Myrtle Beach on Feb. 9, 1943. *Sponsored by S.C. Wing–Civil Air Patrol, 2016*

GPS Coordinates: 32° 42.839' N, 79° 58.743' W

10–91 Slave Auctions

Southeast corner of East Bay St. and Gillon St. intersection, Charleston

(FRONT) Charleston was one of the largest slave trading cities in the U.S. In the 1800s, the area around the Old Exchange Building was one of the most common sites of downtown slave auctions. Along with real estate and other personal property, thousands of enslaved people were sold here as early as the 1770s. Most auctions occurred just north of the Exchange, though some also took place inside. Merchants also sold slaves at nearby stores on Broad, Chalmers, State, and East Bay streets.

(REVERSE) Enslaved Africans were usually sold at wharves along the city harbor. Some Africans were sold near the Exchange, but most people sold here were born in the U.S., making this a key site in the domestic slave trade. In 1856, the city banned auctions of slaves and other goods from the Exchange. Indoor sales grew elsewhere, and Ryan's Mart, a complex of buildings between Queen and Chalmers streets, became the main downtown auction site. *Sponsored by the Old Exchange Building and Friends of the Old Exchange Building, 2016*
GPS Coordinates: 32° 46.620' N, 79° 55.615' W

10–92 Fireproof Building

100 Meeting St., Charleston

(FRONT) Constructed 1822–26, the County Records Building, known as the Fireproof Building, was designed by Charleston-born architect Robert Mills. Mills eliminated combustible materials from the design. Stone steps, flagstone flooring, and brownstone sills were used in place of wood. The brick vaulting on the interior carried the weight of the upper floors and eliminated the need for joists. The roof was clad in copper and all window sashes and frames were iron.
(REVERSE) Massive brownstone columns with roughcast stucco adorn the matching porticos on the north and south elevations. These porticos place this building within the Greek Revival style and it was the first public building in the city designed in that form. Home to the S.C. Historical Society since 1943, the Fireproof Building was listed in the National Register of Historic Places in 1969 and was declared a National Historic Landmark in 1973. *Sponsored by the South Carolina Historical Society, 2016*
GPS Coordinates: 32° 46.641' N, 79° 55.860' W

10–93 Battle of Dills Bluff

Harbor View Rd. at North Shore Dr., James Island

(FRONT) The Battle of Dills Bluff, the last engagement in S.C. during the American Revolution, took place on Nov. 14, 1782. Continental Army forces under command of Col. Thaddeus Kosciusko, and led by Capt. William

Wilmot's 2nd Maryland and Lt. John Markland's 1st Pennsylvania Regiments, attacked a force of British infantry and cavalry on the south side of James Island Creek.
(REVERSE) The British regulars were prepared for the attack, possibly through advance intelligence, and able to rush reinforcements to the field. The Continentals were outnumbered five to one and quickly overwhelmed. Markland was wounded; Wilmot and Lt. Moore of the Maryland line were killed. A slave named William Smith was wounded and taken prisoner. The British would evacuate Charleston in Dec. 1782. *Sponsored by Town of James Island, 2016*
GPS Coordinates: 32° 44.991' N, 79° 56.813' W

10–94 Charleston Public Water System

Marion Square, Charleston

(FRONT) In 1823, after learning of London's success with artesian wells, City Council agreed that deep artesian wells would be feasible for the city and its growing population. Several pilot projects followed and in 1879 a 1,970-feet deep well was drilled near this site. With an impressive 700,000 gallons per day yield, it is reported to be the first successful artesian supply in the region.
(REVERSE) The artesian supply was Charleston's primary water source until 1903 when a franchise was granted to the Charleston Light and Water Co. to take over the city system and construct a new plant and reservoir by damming Goose Creek. In 1917, the city acquired the plant and properties, forming the Commissioners of Public Works, now Charleston Water System, to manage and operate the city water system. *Sponsored by Charleston Water System, 2017*
GPS Coordinates: 32° 47.15.28' N, 79° 56.06.63' W

10–95 Laing School

Highway 17 N. at Six Mile Rd., Mt. Pleasant

(FRONT) The original Laing School was founded in Mt. Pleasant by the Abolition Society of Pennsylvania in 1866. In 1953, Laing H.S., the last segregated school in Mt. Pleasant

to graduate African American students from the 12th grade, was dedicated at this site in the Six Mile Community. From its inception, Laing students have made significant contributions to the state, nation, and world. (REVERSE) Laing H.S. closed in 1970 when Charleston Co. schools desegregated. Ten principals served Laing School, 1866–1970: Cornelia Hancock, 1866–76; Abby D. Munro, 1876–1913; Marie A. O'Neill, 1913–19; Charlotte Powell, 1919–43; James Graves, 1943–45; John Collins, 1945–48; William Swinton, 1948–56; William Rouse, 1956–61; Fletcher Linton, 1961–70; and Miriam M. Brown, 1953–69. *Sponsored by Laing School Association, 2017*
GPS Coordinates: 32° 50.501' N, 79° 49.003' W

10–96 Simeon Pinckney Homestead

Fort Johnson Road, James Island

(FRONT) Simeon Pinckney, who was born a slave in Manning, S.C., enlisted in the 3rd S.C. Inf. (Colored) in 1863, and also served in the 21st U.S. Colored Infantry during the Civil War. Later, Pinckney settled on James Island with wife Isabella, stepson Daniel, and sons Alex and Samuel. In 1874 he purchased twenty acres of land for $350. Here he built a house and farmed the land on his own account. (REVERSE) Simeon Pinckney died in Nov. 1921 and is buried in the Fort Johnson area. Remarkably, Pinckney was not only able to purchase land during Reconstruction, but the family was also able to retain ownership of at least a portion of the tract for nearly 150 years. The Town of James Island purchased 7 acres of the Pinckney homestead for use as a public park in 2016. *Sponsored by Town of James Island, 2017*
GPS Coordinates: 32° 44.794' N, 79° 54.474' W

10–97 Septima Clark Birthplace

105 Wentworth St., Charleston

(FRONT) Septima Poinsette Clark, who Martin Luther King Jr. called "the Mother of the Movement," was a nationally influential Civil Rights activist. She was born at 105 Wentworth St. on May 3, 1898 to Peter Poinsette, a former slave, and Victoria Anderson, who was

of Haitian descent. Clark earned her teacher's certificate from Charleston's Avery Normal Institute and her master's from Hampton Institute. She taught for nearly 40 years. (REVERSE) In 1953, Clark visited the Highlander Folk School in TN, which was dedicated to training community organizers and pursuing equality for all. Here she developed the "citizenship school" model, which promoted literacy and political education. By 1965 Clark had helped to organize nearly 900 citizenship schools, including the first one on nearby Johns Island, and had helped to register more than 50,000 Black voters. *Sponsored by College of Charleston Teaching Fellows, 2018*
GPS Coordinates: 32° 46.888' N, 79° 56.177' W

10–98 John L. Dart Library

1067 King St., Charleston

(FRONT) Dart Hall, at Kracke and Bogard Sts., was founded in 1927 by Susan Dart Butler (1888–1959) as the first public library for African Americans in Charleston. She was the daughter of Rev. John L. Dart (1844–1947), who in 1894 established the Charleston Normal and Industrial Institute, later Burke H.S. The library began as a reading room in the printing office of the Institute, relying on Rev. Dart's personal collection. (REVERSE) In 1931, with support of the Julius Rosenwald Fund, the collection and building expanded, and Dart Hall became a branch of the Charleston Free Library. The Dart family leased the building to the county for $1 a year until the county bought the building in 1952. Susan Dart Butler continued to serve as librarian until 1957. In 1968 a new library was completed here and the original Dart Hall Library was razed. *Sponsored by the Charleston County Public Library, 2017*
GPS Coordinates: 32° 48.31' N, 79° 57.056' W

10–99 First Memorial Day

Hampton Park, Charleston

(FRONT) Hampton Park was once home to the Washington Race Course and Jockey Club. In 1864 this site became an outdoor prison for Union soldiers. Before Charleston fell in

Feb. 1865, more than 250 prisoners died and were buried in mass graves. After Confederate evacuation, black ministers and northern missionaries led an effort to reinter bodies and build a fence around a newly established cemetery. Over the entrance workmen inscribed the words "Martyrs of the Racecourse."
(REVERSE) On May 1, 1865 a parade to honor the Union war dead took place here. The event marked the earliest celebration of what became known as "Memorial Day." The crowd numbered in the thousands, with African American school children from newly formed Freedmen's Schools leading the parade. They were followed by church leaders, Freedpeople, Unionists, and members of the 54th Mass., 34th, and 104th U.S. Colored Infantries. The dead were later reinterred in Beaufort. *Sponsored by the City of Charleston, 2017*
GPS Coordinates: 32° 48.019' N, 79° 57.468' W

10–100 Constitutional Convention of 1868

Meeting St., between Broad and Tradd St., Charleston

(FRONT) In January 1868 delegates met to rewrite the S.C. Constitution. They convened at the Charleston Club House, which once stood near here. Before the Civil War the Club House was reserved for Charleston's planter elite, but a majority of the delegates in 1868

were African American, some of them former slaves. The election of delegates to the convention was the first time that African American men voted in S.C.
(REVERSE) The 1868 Constitution was a remarkable document for its time. The Declaration of Rights made no distinctions based on race. It created the basis for the state's first public school system, as proposed by Robert Smalls, and guaranteed black male suffrage two years ahead of the 15th Amendment. In 1895, a new constitution would mandate segregated schools, outlaw interracial marriages, and disenfranchise black men. *Sponsored by the S.C. Civil War Sesquicentennial Advisory Board, 2018*
GPS Coordinates: 32° 46.535' N, 79° 55.862' W

10–101 "Porgy House"

Center St. and West Ashley Ave., Folly Beach

(FRONT) In the 1930s author DuBose Heyward and his wife, playwright Dorothy Heyward, owned a cottage 7 blocks W of this location. During the summer of 1934 American composer and pianist George Gershwin stayed at Folly Beach and collaborated with the Heywards on his folk opera Porgy and Bess (1935), which was based upon DuBose Heyward's 1925 novel Porgy. The house where Gershwin stayed was destroyed by a hurricane, but the Heyward home remains and is known locally as the "Porgy House."

10-100 Constitutional Convention of 1868, Charleston.
IMAGE COURTESY OF SCDAH

(REVERSE) Both Heyward's novel and Gershwin's opera were rare for their time as examples of white writers treating African American subjects as complex figures. During his stay in the Lowcountry Gershwin visited Black churches on James Island and incorporated some of what he saw and heard into his musical production. Porgy and Bess opened on Broadway in 1935 and ran for 124 performances. Today, the opera is perhaps best remembered for the song "Summertime." *Sponsored by the Folly Beach Exchange Club and the City of Folly Beach, 2018*
GPS Coordinates: 32° 39.320' N, 79° 56.452' W

10–102 Sullivans Island Quartermaster Dock

Thompson Ave. between Station 15 St. and Station 17 St., Sullivans Island

Fort Sullivan, first built in 1796, was left vacant after the Civil War. In 1897 a new building campaign began and in 1902 the U.S. Government began expanding the fort to include housing and support facilities. The ca. 1915 Quartermaster Dock and ca. 1930 warehouse here were part of the expansion, which also included an NCO Club and theatre. The fort was deactivated in 1947 and the property was sold by the War Assets Administration. *Sponsored by Cove Creek Properties, 2018*
GPS Coordinates: 32° 45.587' N, 79° 51.093' W

10–103 Lincolnville

Corner of W. Broad and Lincoln Sts. (State Rd. S-10–881), Lincolnville

(FRONT) The Town of Lincolnville was founded in 1867 by seven African American leaders: Daniel Adger, Marc Buffett, Rev. Richard H. Cain, Hector Grant, Rev. Lewis Ruffin Nichols, Rev. M. B. Salters, and Walter Steele. The town was located along the S.C.R.R. and was originally known as Pump Pond because the steam engines would stop here to refill their tanks. It was renamed Lincolnville in honor of Abraham Lincoln. The town was formally incorporated in 1889.
(REVERSE) Lincolnville was established as an African American enclave. Rev. R. H. Cain

purchased 500 acres, divided it into town lots, and sold to black settlers. By 1884 there were approximately 120 families living here and the town government was composed entirely of African American men. In addition to founding the town, Cain also served in the S.C. Senate and the U.S. House (1873–5, 1877–9). He was the first pastor of Emanuel A.M.E. Church after the Civil War and was appointed bishop in 1880. *Sponsored by the Town of Lincolnville, 2018*
GPS Coordinates: 33° 0.632' N, 80° 9.441' W

10–104 Carolina Art Association /James S. Gibbes Memorial Art Gallery

135 Meeting St., Charleston

Carolina Art Association (FRONT)
In 1857, a group of civic-minded Charlestonians established the Carolina Art Association. The goal of the CAA was to promote fine arts in S.C. The CAA was awarded its official state charter in 1858. The CAA is today the oldest surviving arts association in the Southeast. Upon his death in 1888, patron of the arts James S. Gibbes left a bequest that allowed the city and the CAA to build a museum of fine art. James S. Gibbes Memorial Art Gallery (REVERSE)
Designed by Frank Milburn, the James S. Gibbes Memorial Art Gallery, now the Gibbes Museum of Art, opened in 1905. The Beaux Arts-style building is the oldest purpose-built museum in S.C. and the oldest permanent structure designed for the display of art in the South. In 1936, the museum became the first to exhibit the Solomon R. Guggenheim Collection of modern art. It was expanded in 1978 and again in 2016. *Sponsored by the Gibbes Museum of Art, 2019*
GPS Coordinates: 32° 46.710' N, 79° 55.883' W

10–105 Pinckney Mansion

235 East Bay St., Charleston

(FRONT) The Pinckney Mansion was a Colonial double house built ca. 1746 at this site, then a large waterfront lot known as Colleton Square. It is believed to have been designed by

owner Charles Pinckney (ca. 1699–1758), a planter and Chief Justice of Provincial S.C. His wife Eliza Lucas (1722–1793) lived here after helping found colonial S.C.'s indigo industry. Enslaved people and free workers, skilled and unskilled, built the house. Colonial governors leased the property 1753–69. (REVERSE) Charles Cotesworth Pinckney (1746–1825), a framer of the U.S. Constitution, was among the mansion's residents. The house was one of the first in the U.S. with a Classical temple front façade. Among the first Palladian villas in Charleston, it helped set a new trend of planters keeping their main dwelling in town instead of at the plantation. Also at the site was a graden and a long row of outbuildings, including slave quarters and stables. Pinckneys owned the house until it burned in 1861. *Sponsored by Eliza Lucas Pinckney Chapter NSDAR, 2019*
GPS Coordinates: 32° 46.683' N, 79° 55.662' W

10–106 Memminger House /McAlister Funeral Home

150 Wentworth St., Charleston

Memminger House (FRONT)
Christopher Memminger (1803–1888) lived in a home at this site as early as 1830. A German immigrant orphaned at age 4, Memminger was adopted by future S.C. Governor Thomas Bennett. Memminger served in the S.C. legislature and championed public education before and after the Civil War. He helped draft the Confederate Constitution and was the Confederacy's Secretary of the Treasury 1861–1864. He returned to Charleston after the war and lived here until his death.
McAlister Funeral Home (REVERSE)
John McAlister was one of the city's first licensed embalmers and began an undertaking business on Meeting St. in the 1880s. In 1960, McAlister Funeral Home moved to this location and replaced the Memminger House with a purpose-built funeral home designed by Charleston architect Augustus Constantine (1898–1976). Its design offered a modern interpretation of the Colonial Revival style. It was razed in 2016. *Sponsored by the U.S. Department of Veterans Affairs, 2019*
GPS Coordinates: 32° 46.793' N, 79° 56.447' W

10–107 Federal Building

334 Meeting St., Charleston

(FRONT) Built 1964–65, this was originally a federal office building that housed more than 30 agencies of the U.S. government. Plans to locate a federal building here began as early as 1939, but World War II delayed the effort into the 1950s. It was the first major federal building project completed in postwar S.C. Designed by Charlestonian John Califf of Lyles, Bissett, Carlisle, and Woolfe, the seven-story Modernist building both praise and criticism upon its completion.
(REVERSE) In 1972, Congress officially renamed the building for Lucius Mendel Rivers (1905–1970). A Berkeley County native and 29-year U.S. Congressman, Rivers secured valuable military projects for the Charleston area and helped ensure the building's completion, later keeping an office here. Federal agencies and legislators occupied the building until 1999, after which it was threatened with demolition. It remained vacant until being reopened as a hotel in 2016. *Sponsored by The Charleston Museum and the L. Mendel Rivers Library at Charleston Southern University, 2019*
GPS Coordinates: 32° 47.271 ' N, 79° 56.096' W

10–108 Hunter's Volunteers

SW Corner of Grimball Rd. and Riverland Dr., Charleston vicinity

(FRONT) This site once beloned to Hunter's Volunteers, an African American militia est. on James Island by 1877. Part of the S.C. National Guard, the unit kept an enlistment of 30–40 men tasked with helping preserve civil order. Most of them were farmers or laborers. The unit was disbanded in 1891 after trying to stop the arrest of a Black man in Charleston but was reinstated in 1892.
(REVERSE) In 1899, Hunter's Volunteers bought this site from Sarah Grimball and Henry Grimball. Over time, the unit became more of a mutual aid society and social club than a military outfit. In 1897, a year after being disarmed by the state, members chartered the Hunter Volunteer Charitable Society. A two-story wooden building razed in the 1960s served as their lodge and may have originally

been an armory. *Sponsored by Canter Construction, 2019*
GPS Coordinates: 32° 42.879' N, 79° 58.096' W

10–109 Mosquito Beach

Intersection of Sol Legare Rd. & Folly Rd., Charleston vicinity

(FRONT) Located 1.5 mi. SW of here, Mosquito Beach is a .13-mile strip of land that served African Americans during the Jim Crow era, when nearby Folly Beach was segregated. The beach began as a gathering spot for workers at a nearby oyster factory in the 1920s and 1930s. A store selling seafood and drinks first opened in the 1930s. Other businesses followed in the 1940s and 1950s.
(REVERSE) Mosquito Beach lies along a tidal marsh historically known for the large mosquito population that gave the beach its name. By the 1960s, the beach provided African American leisure-seekers with music venues, pavilions, restaurants, and a hotel. Mosquito Beach's businesses as well as the land were owned by African Americans. Listed in the National Register of Historic Places in 2019. *Sponsored by Historic Charleston Foundation and Mosquito Beach Business Association, 2019*
GPS Coordinates: 32° 41.115' N, 79° 57.575' W

10–110 Charleston Station

North Charleston Intermodal Transportation Center, 4656 Gaynor St., North Charleston

(FRONT) The Charleston Station was built in 1956 by the Atlantic Coast Line (ACL). ACL hoped the new station would attract customers, particularly tourists traveling on its Florida-bound trains. In 1967, ACL merged with Seaboard Air Line to become the Seaboard Coast Line, which later merged with CSX. In 1970, Congress passed an act to prevent the financial collapse of several U.S. railroads by creating Amtrak, a national railroad corporation.
(REVERSE) Charleston Station was a two-story building designed in the International style and was emblematic of mid-century modern architecture. It was long and linear, with a low-sloped roof. The most distinctive feature was the green Mo-Sai pre-cast concrete panels used at the entrance and around the windows. When it opened in 1956, the station was segregated by race, with separate waiting rooms, bathrooms, and drinking fountains. The Charleston Station was razed in 2018. *Sponsored by City of North Charleston, 2019*
GPS Coordinates: 32° 52.468' N, 79° 59.877' W

Cherokee County

11–1 Limestone Springs

Griffith St. just Southwest of its intersection with O'Neal St., Limestone College Campus, Gaffney

Used as early as the American Revolution, this site became a "Summer Watering Place" in 1835. Low Country Aristocrats such as Governor David Johnson were attracted here by the climate and therapeutic waters. A post office was here from 1836 to 1879. Limestone College was established in 1845 as the Limestone Springs Female High School. *Erected by Limestone College Alumnae Association, 1969*
GPS Coordinates: 35° 3.317' N, 81° 38.983' W

11–2 Gaffney

115 North Granard St., Gaffney

The Grindal Shoals and Cherokee Ford roads crossed here when this land was originally granted to John Sarratt in 1799 by the State of South Carolina. Michael Gaffney purchased the land in 1804 and by 1820 Gaffney's Tavern was located at the crossroads. In 1873, John R. Logan laid out the present street plan, and Gaffney was incorporated as a town in 1875. *Erected by The Cherokee Historical and Preservation Society, 1977*
GPS Coordinates: 35° 4.412' N, 81° 39.026' W

11–3 Limestone College

Near intersection of College Dr. and Griffith St. at the entrance to Limestone College, Gaffney

Founded in 1845 as the Limestone Springs Female High School by Dr. Thomas Curtis and his son Dr. William Curtis, distinguished Baptist clergymen. The school thrived until falling on hard times during the Civil War and Reconstruction. In 1881 the institution was revived by New York benefactor Peter Cooper as CooperLimestone Institute. Renamed Limestone College in 1898. *Erected by Limestone College, 1998*
GPS Coordinates: 35° 3.434' N, 81° 38.9' W

11–4 Whig Hill

Union Hwy. (S.C. Hwy. 18), South of its junction with Round Tree Rd., approximately 5 miles South of Gaffney

This plantation, 1.5 mi. S. near Thicketty Creek, was settled about 1767 by John Nuckolls, Sr. (1732–1780), a native of Virginia. During the American Revolution, as the war in the backcountry became a vicious civil war, the plantation became known as "Whig Hill" for Nuckolls's support of the patriot cause. He was murdered by Tories in December 1780 and is buried on his plantation. *Erected by Cherokee County Historical and Preservation Society, 1998*
GPS Coordinates: 34° 59.367' N, 81° 39.067' W

11–5 Frederick Hambright

Battleground Dr. (S.C. Hwy. 216), approximately 75 yards from the Northwest entrance to Kings Mountain National Military Park

(FRONT) Frederick Hambright (1727–1817), a prominent militia officer of the American Revolution, lived his last 25 years in a house which stood 200 yds. NE. Hambright, born in Germany, emigrated to America as a boy, and settled in N.C. by 1750. He held several Tryon Co. offices from 1774 to 1776, most notably a brief term as a member of the N.C. Provincial Congress in 1775.
(REVERSE) Hambright, after several campaigns, was promoted to lt. col. by 1779. He commanded the Lincoln Co. (N.C.) troops

at Kings Mtn. Oct. 7, 1780, and was severely wounded. After recuperating at a log cabin near the battlefield he returned to N.C. but soon moved to S.C. and built a two-story house near the cabin; it burned in 1927. He is buried 1 mi. E of Grover, N.C. at Shiloh Cemetery. *Erected by the Cherokee County Historical and Preservation Society, 1999*
GPS Coordinates: 35° 9.221' N, 81° 23.802' W

11–6 Carnegie Library

210 N. Limestone St., Gaffney

This Classical Revival building, built in 1913–14 and designed by Arthur W. Hamby, was one of 14 public libraries built in S.C. between 1903 and 1916 with funding from Andrew Carnegie and the Carnegie Foundation. A 1937 addition compatible to the original design doubled its size. It served as the Cherokee County Public Library until 1972 and has housed county offices since that time. It was listed in the National Register of Historic Places in 2000. *Erected by the City of Gaffney and the Cherokee County Council, 2001*
GPS Coordinates: 35° 4.404' N, 81° 38.916' W

11–7 Granard Graded and High School/Granard High School

Granard St. (U.S. Hwy. 29) near its intersection with Logan St., Gaffney

Granard Graded and High School (FRONT)
This is the original location of Granard Graded and High School, also known as Granard Street School. It was built here between 1905 and 1914 and included the first black high school in Gaffney. The first high school graduating class numbered two students in 1923. J. E. Gaffney served as Granard's principal for more than thirty years. A new Granard High, a brick building, was built on Rutledge Avenue in 1937.
Granard High School (REVERSE)
The 1937 Granard High School included grades 1–11 until 1947, then added grade 12. Standard courses for grades 8–11 were supplemented by industrial and home economics courses, sports, music, art, and other activities. Granard High School organized its first

sports team in 1928 and its first band and chorus in 1947. The school closed in 1968 when Cherokee County schools were desegregated. *Erected by the Cherokee Historical and Preservation Society and the Cherokee County African-American Heritage Committee, 2008*
GPS Coordinates: 35° 3.935' N, 81° 39.7' W

11–8 Nuckolls-Jefferies House

571 Asbury Rd. (S.C. Hwy. 211), Pacolet vicinity

(FRONT) This house was built in 1843 for William Thompson Nuckolls (1801–1855) and later owned for many years by John D. Jefferies (1838–1910). Built in the Greek Revival style of the antebellum period and altered in the Neo-Classical style of the post-Civil War era, it is a fine example of a mid-19th century plantation house with significant late-19th century alterations.
(REVERSE) William T. Nuckolls, a lawyer and politician, had represented what was then Spartanburg District in the U.S. House of Representatives 1827–1833. This house passed through several owners after his death until 1875, when Capt. John D. Jefferies, a Confederate veteran and businessman, acquired it. The house was listed in the National Register of Historic Places in 2007. *Erected by the Cherokee Historical and Preservation Society, Inc., 2008*
GPS Coordinates: 34° 55.815' N, 81° 39.444' W

11–9 Mulberry Chapel Methodist Church

Asbury Rd. (S.C. Hwy. 211), 1 mile West of its intersection with Union Hwy. (S.C. Hwy. 18), Pacolet vicinity

(FRONT) This African American church, the first in what is now Cherokee County, was most likely built between 1880 and 1890. It served the Whig Hill, Asbury, and Thicketty communities of what was Union County before Cherokee County was created in 1897. Jack Littlejohn donated land for the chapel and cemetery.
(REVERSE) Regular services ended in the 1940s, but in 1953 Carl E. Littlejohn and others founded the Littlejohn Family Reunion,

which holds annual services here every fall. Several members of the Littlejohn family are buried here, as well as Samuel Nuckles (d. ca. 1900), state representative from Union County 1868–1872. *Erected by Mr. and Mrs. James West and the Cherokee Historical and Preservation Society, 2008*
GPS Coordinates: 34° 55.802' N, 81° 39.25' W

11–10 Steen Family Cemetery

El Bethel Rd. (S.C. Sec. Rd. 11-15) at the bridge over Thicketty Creek, Gaffney vicinity

The family cemetery of Lt. Col. James Steen (d. 1781), S.C. militia officer during the American Revolution, is on his plantation nearby, along Thicketty Creek. Steen, who commanded units in several campaigns from 1775 to 1781, was killed in 1781 while attempting to arrest a Loyalist in N.C. *Erected by the Cherokee Historical and Preservation Society, Inc., 2011*
GPS Coordinates: 34° 56.05' N, 81° 35.467' W

11–11 Goucher Baptist Church

415 Goucher Creek Rd., Gaffney vicinity

(FRONT) This church, the oldest in the Broad River Association, was founded in 1770 and was first called Thicketty Branch Baptist Church. After meeting in a brush arbor and area houses, it built its first permanent church, a log building, about 1 mi. N. Another log church replaced it on that site shortly after the Revolution, and the congregation was renamed Goshen Baptist Church in 1794. (REVERSE) The church, renamed Goucher Creek Baptist Church in 1800, acquired this site in 1883. A frame sanctuary here was replaced by a larger frame church in 1902. The congregation was renamed Goucher Baptist Church by 1930. Services were once a month until 1917, then twice a month until Rev. C. C. Alsbrooks became its first full-time pastor in 1949. The present church was built in 1960. *Erected by the Congregation, 2011*
GPS Coordinates: 34° 58.533' N, 81° 42.599' W

11–12 Limestone Quarry

Quarry Dr., Limestone College, Gaffney

(FRONT) Limestone deposits here furnished lime used in the production of iron during the American Revolution and throughout the 19th century. By the 1820s this open pit was a quarry owned by U.S. Congressman Wilson Nesbitt and was on a large tract including Limestone Springs, which later became a popular antebellum resort. Limestone Springs Female High School, founded in 1845, became Cooper-Limestone Institute in 1881 and Limestone College in 1898.

(REVERSE) This quarry, often called "Nesbitt's Quarry," was acquired by the school before the Civil War. Sold to help pay debts in 1883, it operated until World War I, when it was closed and filled with water. It was reopened in 1933 after pumping the water out, mining limestone and producing lime until the deposit here was finally exhausted in 1953. The quarry, filled with water since, was listed in the National Register of Historic Places in 1986. *Sponsored by Limestone College, 2014*
GPS Coordinates: 35° 3.290' N, 81° 38.927' W

11–13 Gaffney's Old Field/Central School

301 College Dr., Gaffney

Gaffney's Old Field (FRONT)
Much of the land in this area once belonged to Michael Gaffney, proprietor of Gaffney's Crossroads. The area also served as a militia encampment for many years with the company reporting for duty in Charleston during the war of 1812. The development of nearby Limestone Springs as a resort attraction resulted in increased tourism and Michael Gaffney allowed for the construction of a horse track here in his old field, as it was known locally.

Central School (REVERSE)
The Gaffney Male and Female Seminary moved into a new building at this site in 1887. In 1898, the seminary became the local high school. Central High School became Central Graded School when a new Gaffney High School building was opened in 1925. The current building replaced the original school in 1958. It remained in use as Central Elementary School until 1999. Today, the building is home to the Cherokee County History and Arts Museum. *Sponsored by friends and family of Janeen "C. J." Waters Aaltonen, Cherokee Historical & Preservation Society, Inc., and L'Etoile Club, 2016*
GPS Coordinates: 35° 4.046' N, 81° 38.934' W

11–14 Dunton Chapel Methodist Church

320 E. Buford St., Gaffney

(FRONT) Dunton Chapel Methodist Church can trace its origins to 1870, when Rev. J. R. Rosemond began preaching in the home of Milton Hardy. The church was built ca. 1878, but has undergone many renovations, including being brick veneered in 1937. Originally known as the "Church of Gaffney," it was named Dunton Chapel in 1888 to honor Dr. Lewis M. Dunton, presiding elder of the Greenville District of the M.E. Church (1879–82).

(REVERSE) The first school for African American students in Gaffney was opened at Dunton Chapel Methodist Church in 1899 under the direction of Rev. R. C. Campbell. By 1920 it remained as one of only ten schools in the county that served African American students. A public night school serving adult students was also operated at Dunton Chapel. The grade school remained in operation into the 1920s. *Sponsored by Dunton United Methodist Church, 2016*
GPS Coordinates: 35° 4.230' N, 81° 38.796' W

Chester County

12–1 Catholic Presbyterian Church

Old Catholic Church Rd. (S.C. Sec. Rd. 12-355) at Great Falls Rd. (S.C. Hwy. 97), Blackstock vicinity

One mile south. Divergent Presbyterian groups held services in this area as early as 1759. Rev. William Richardson, active in the area, is credited with unifying and naming them in 1770. The cemetery contains many graves of Revolutionary and Confederate soldiers. The present building was dedicated in 1842. *Erected by Chester County Historical Commission, 1964*

GPS Coordinates: 34° 36.606' N, 81° 2.478' W

12–2 Battle of Fishdam Ford

S.C. Hwy. 215, Leeds vicinity, just East of the Broad River near the Chester County-Union County line

On the east side of Broad River by an old Indian fish dam, General Thomas Sumter's camp was attacked before dawn on November 9, 1780 by the British 63rd Regiment and a detachment of the Legion, led by Major James Wemyss. The American campfires made excellent targets of the mounted British, who were severely defeated. Wemyss was taken prisoner by General Sumter. *Erected by Chester County Historical Society, 1974*

GPS Coordinates: 34° 35.676' N, 81° 24.99' W

12–3 Battle of Fishing Creek

U.S. Hwy. 21, about 2 miles North of Great Falls

At this site on August 18, 1780 General Thomas Sumter camped with captured booty and 800 men. He was surprised and defeated by Lt. Col. Tarleton and 160 soldiers. The disaster followed by only two days General Gates's defeat by Lord Cornwallis at Camden. The patriots lost 150 men killed and many captured, but Sumter escaped and soon rallied another large force. *Erected by Chester County Historical Society, 1974*

GPS Coordinates: 34° 38.172' N, 80° 54.27' W

12–4 Home Site of Justice John Gaston

S.C. Hwy. 9, just West of bridge over Fishing Creek, Fort Lawn vicinity

Two miles south, at Cedar Shoals on the south side of Fishing Creek, was the home of John Gaston, Esq., Justice of the Peace under both the Royal and State governments. Though advanced in years, he was the leading spirit in arousing resistance to the British in this area. All nine of his sons fought for freedom; four died in service. *Erected by Chester County Historical Society, 1974*

GPS Coordinates: 34° 41.562' N, 80° 57.072' W

12–5 Landsford in the Revolution /Landsford

Intersection of U.S. Hwy. 21 & S.C. Sec. Rd. 12-327, Rowell vicinity

Landsford in the Revolution (FRONT)
Thomas Sumter, William R. Davie, and Andrew Jackson all camped or quartered near here during up-country skirmishes after the fall of Charleston. The British General Cornwallis crossed here in Oct. 1780, on his way to Winnsborough after his plans to advance into N.C. were frustrated by Ferguson's defeat at King's Mountain.

Landsford (REVERSE)
Located about 4 mi. E, this ford, an early Indian crossing, was probably named for Thomas Land who received a nearby land grant from the Crown in 1755. Used by Patriot and British armies during the American Revolution. Later home of Wm. R. Davie, founder of University of N.C. The 1823 Landsford Canal bears witness to S.C.'s first great period of public works. *Erected by Chester County Historical Society, 1975*

GPS Coordinates: 34° 47.646' N, 80° 55.236' W

12–6 Alexander's Old Fields

Intersection of Richburg Rd. (S.C. Hwy. 99) &
Great Falls Hwy. (S.C. Hwy. 97), about 3 miles
North of Great Falls

The skirmish which took place here at Alexander's Old Fields, now Beckhamville, on June 6, 1780, was the first victory for S.C. Patriots after the fall of Charleston. A band of Whigs under the command of Captain John McClure attacked and routed an assembly of Loyalists. The victory helped solidify resistance to the Crown in this up country area. *Erected by Chester County Historical Society, 1976*
GPS Coordinates: 34° 35.43' N, 80° 55.2' W

12–7 Fishing Creek Church

3087 Fishing Creek Church Rd. (S.C. Sec. Rd.
12-50), Edgemoor vicinity

Presbyterian church reportedly est. 1752. Present building, enclosed with brick in 1958, dates from 1785. Cemetery contains pioneer settlers and veterans of many wars. *Erected by The Congregation, 1995*
GPS Coordinates: 34° 47.994' N, 81° 4.056' W

12–9 Chester County Courthouse

Main St. (S.C. Hwy. 72) between Center St. (U.S.
Hwy. 321) and Wylie Sts., Chester

This courthouse, built in 1852, was designed by Edward Brickell White (1802–1888) of Charleston, whose work was greatly influenced by Robert Mills. Additions by Alfred D. Gilchrist of Rock Hill in 1896 and 1928 included three-story rear wings and a rotunda. An elevator tower added to the rear wing, designed in 1994 by Frank M. Williams, complements the designs of White and Gilchrist. *Erected by Chester County Historical Society, 1997*
GPS Coordinates: 34° 42.36' N, 81° 12.792' W

12–10 Brainerd Institute

Lancaster St., Chester

This institute grew out of an 1866 school for freedmen; it became Brainerd Institute in 1868 when the Board of Missions of the Presbyterian Church in New York appointed Rev. Samuel Loomis to help establish churches and schools among the blacks near Chester. At first an elementary school, Brainerd grew to ten grades by 1913 and was a fouryear high school by the 1930s. Renamed Brainerd Junior College about 1935, it emphasized teacher training until it closed in 1939. *Erected by Chester Middle School Junior Beta Club, 1997*
GPS Coordinates: 34° 42.33' N, 81° 11.904' W

Chesterfield County

13–1 Old St. David's

100 Church St., Cheraw

St. David's, authorized by the General Assembly in 1768, was the last parish established in colonial S.C. Said to be buried in its churchyard are soldiers of British forces occupying the Cheraws in 1780. The steeple and vestibule of this Episcopal church were added ca. 1827 and services were held here until a new church was built in 1916. *Erected by Chesterfield County Historical Society, 1979*
GPS Coordinates: 34° 41.766' N, 79° 52.782' W

13–2 W.D. Craig House

Corner of Page & Main Sts., Chesterfield

One of Chesterfield's earliest houses, the Wm. Duke Craig House, ca. 1820, stood here before it was moved in 1975. Craig (1845–1935), farmer and merchant, also owned nearby Craig's Grist Mill. He fought in the Civil War with the 21st Regiment, S.C. Infantry, Co. E. In 1933, he donated the land for Craig Park, just north on Page Street. Altered through the years, the house now stands on county property, some 500 yds. N. *Erected by Chesterfield County, 1985*
GPS Coordinates: 34° 44.166' N, 80° 5.31' W

13–3 Chesterfield Courthouse

100 Main St., Chesterfield

Chesterfield County's first courthouse was built here soon after the county was established in 1785. The second courthouse on this site was built 1825–1829 from plans by architect Robert Mills, designer of the Washington Monument. According to local tradition it was burned by troops under William T. Sherman in 1865. The current structure, built ca. 1884, was used as a courthouse until 1978. *Erected by Chesterfield County, 1985*
GPS Coordinates: 34° 44.151' N, 80° 5.12' W

13–4 Cash Homesite/Capt. Thomas Ellerbe

U.S. Hwy. 52 about 5 mi. S of Cheraw, Cash community

Cash Homesite (FRONT)
About 100 yards east of here was the home of General Ellerbe Boggan Crawford Cash, widely known for his 1880 duel with challenger Colonel William M. Shannon, whom he killed. Subsequently, all officers of the state and members of the bar were required to take oath that they had not participated in a duel since January 1, 1881. This proviso was placed in the 1895 S.C. Constitution.
Capt. Thomas Ellerbe (REVERSE)
About three miles northeast of here is the Ellerbe Burial Ground (Red Hill Cemetery) where Captain Thomas Ellerbe (1743–1802) is buried. In 1768 he was appointed commissioner to build a church and parsonage for the Parish of St. David. Ellerbe later served in the Revolution as captain under General Francis Marion. *Erected by Historical Society of Chesterfield County and Chesterfield County Historic Preservation Commission, 1988*
GPS Coordinates: 34° 36.489' N, 79° 52.518' W

13–5 Coulter Memorial Academy Site

On Second St., between Powe and Kershaw Sts., Cheraw

Organized in 1881, this Negro Presbyterian (USA) school was founded by the Rev. J. P. Crawford with support from Mrs. C. E. Coulter from whom it received its name. The

Rev. G. W. Long was academy president from 1908 until 1943, and Coulter offered junior college credit, 1933–1947. The academy merged with the public school system, 1949. *Erected 1991 by the Coulter Memorial Academy National Alumni Association, Inc.*
GPS Coordinates: 34° 42.046' N, 79° 53.151' W

13–6 Dizzy Gillespie Birthplace

Dizzy Gillespie Birthplace Park, 337 Huger St., Cheraw

(FRONT) John Birks "Dizzy" Gillespie was born in a house on this site on Oct. 21, 1917. His family lived here until they moved to Philadelphia in 1935. A founder of modern jazz, Gillespie was an innovative trumpeter and bandleader known for his bent horn, bulging cheeks, sense of humor, and showmanship. In the 1950s he became a good will ambassador for the U.S. State Dept., playing concerts around the world.
(REVERSE) Gillespie was invited to perform at the White House by eight presidents from Eisenhower to George Bush. He received the National Medal of Arts, the highest prize awarded to an American artist, in 1989 and received the Kennedy Center Honors in 1990 for his lifetime contributions to American culture. Among his best-known songs were "A Night in Tunisia" and "Salt Peanuts." He died in New Jersey Jan. 6, 1993. *Erected by the Pee Dee Committee, Colonial Dames of America in the State of South Carolina, 2001*
GPS Coordinates: 34° 41.922' N, 79° 53.574' W

13–7 Seaboard Airline Railway Depot

W. Pine Ave. at the railroad tracks, one block west of N. 7th St. (U.S. Hwy. 1), McBee

This depot, built in 1914, was the second station built by the Seaboard Air Line Railway in McBee. The town, the most successful of those established along Seaboard's Columbia-to-Cheraw line after it was completed in 1900, grew so quickly that a new depot became a high priority by the end of the decade. This depot was both a passenger and freight depot until it closed in 1971. Now the McBee Library and Railroad Museum, it was listed

in the National Register of Historic Places in 1998. *Erected by the Town of McBee, 2001*
GPS Coordinates: 34° 28.158' N, 80° 15.456' W

13–8 Pee Dee Union Baptist Church

92 Chestnut St., at its junction with ACL Ave. and Washington St., Cheraw

(FRONT) This church, formally organized in 1867, had its origins in Cheraw Baptist Church, founded in 1837. Shortly after the Civil War 285 black members there received permission to organize a separate church. Rev. Wisdom London, the first pastor here, preached from a platform erected on this site until a new sanctuary was built. The first church here, a frame building, was destroyed by a tornado in 1912. (REVERSE) The present brick church, replacing the original one destroyed by the tornado, was built in 1912 during the pastorate of Rev. Isaiah Williams. Three ministers have served Pee Dee Union Baptist Church for twenty years or more: Rev. F. W. Prince, who served here from 1915 to 1940; Rev. J. C. Levy, who served here from 1953 to 1974; and Rev. Thomas Dawkins, who served here from 1974 to 1999. *Erected by the Congregation, 2003*
GPS Coordinates: 34° 41.805' N, 79° 52.689' W

13–9 John Craig House

E. Main St., Chesterfield

(FRONT) This house, the oldest in Chesterfield, was built ca. 1798 for John Craig (1755–1839), veteran of the American Revolution, merchant and miller, and county official. Craig's father Hugh moved his family from Ireland to Virginia in 1760; John and his older brother Alexander came to S.C. soon after the war and helped organize Chesterfield District, later Chesterfield County. Craig was also Clerk of the Court of Common Pleas and Commissioner of Locations.
(REVERSE) Craig, his wife Sarah Chapman (1778–1852), and their eleven children lived in this 14-room house, which often entertained travelers and distinguished guests. Craig ran a general store, tannery, and shoe shop in Chesterfield, and Craig's Mill on Thompson's Creek. His son William E. lived

here on March 2, 1865, when Federal Gen. W. T. Sherman used the house as his overnight headquarters in Chesterfield. *Erected by the Town of Chesterfield, 2009*
GPS Coordinates: 34° 44.151' N, 80° 5.112' W

13–10 Austin-Craig-Laney House

302 W. Main St., Chesterfield

(FRONT) This Carpenter Gothic house was begun ca. 1858 for Aaron Austin (1831–1863) and his wife Margaret Jane Craig. Austin, a Northerner who settled in Chesterfield in the 1850s, was a lawyer and also a Chesterfield District magistrate. He joined the Confederate army in 1862, became 2nd lt. of Co. D, 6th S.C. Cavalry, and died in 1863 in Charleston County. This house remained unfinished until after the war.
(REVERSE) In 1903 Aaron Austin's widow Margaret gave this house to George Kershaw Laney (1872–1959) and Sarah Louise Tiller (1883–1963) as a wedding present. Laney was a lawyer and teacher, then a longtime state representative and senator, serving in the S.C. House 1903–06 and the S.C. Senate 1907–1922 and 1931–1942. He was a member of the Senate judiciary committee 1911–1922 and 1931–1942, and committee chair 1919–1922. *Erected by the Town of Chesterfield, 2010*
GPS Coordinates: 34° 44.174' N, 80° 5.409' W

13–11 Francis Asbury's First Visit to S.C.

St. David's Episcopal Church, Church St., Cheraw

(FRONT) Francis Asbury (1745–1816), pioneer bishop of American Methodism, came to Cheraw in 1785, on his first visit to S.C. Asbury had just been ordained a superintendent at the first General Conference in Baltimore on December 27, 1784. He was on his way to Charleston with Revs. Woolman Hickson, Jesse Lee, and Henry Willis. They crossed the Great Pee Dee River and arrived in Cheraw on February 17, 1785.
(REVERSE) Asbury's party spent the night with a merchant here, a Methodist. Their host's clerk told Rev. Jesse Lee (1758–1816) that his native New England needed circuit riders to preach

the gospel there. He so impressed Lee with his earnestness that Lee established churches from Connecticut to Maine. Asbury and his party spent "some time" in prayer here at St. David's Episcopal Church before continuing south. *Erected by the First United Methodist Church of Cheraw, 2010*
GPS Coordinates: 34° 41.753' N, 79° 52.802' W

13–12 Thomas E. Lucas House

716 W. Main St, Chesterfield

(FRONT) This two-story house with a central-hall plan was built about 1868 for Dr. Thomas Ephraim Lucas (1836–1920), physician, Confederate officer, and state representative. Lucas graduated from the Citadel and the Medical College of S.C. in 1859. During the Civil War he was major of the 8th S.C. Infantry, then a lieutenant in the 15th Battalion S.C. Artillery. Lucas also represented Chesterfield in the S.C. House in 1864.
(REVERSE) Lucas, who had married Dorothy C. Hanna (1841–1921) in 1859, returned to Chesterfield after the war and resumed his medical practice, also serving as a school commissioner in 1870. His office, next to the house, was later attached to it for use as a kitchen. Thomas and Dorothy Lucas raised their four sons and three daughters here. This house was listed in the National Register of Historic Places in 1982. *Erected by the Town of Chesterfield, 2011*
GPS Coordinates: 34° 44.129' N, 80° 5.790' W

13–13 Chesterfield Post Office

Corner of E. Main St. & Scotch Rd., Chesterfield

(FRONT) This post office, built in 1937–38, is one of several New Deal-era post offices in S.C. designed by the Public Works Division of the U.S. Department of the Treasury. Its architecture, a restrained version of the Colonial Revival style, is typical of later New Deal-era post offices. It also included offices for the county extension agent and county home demonstration agent, under the U.S. Department of Agriculture.
(REVERSE) This post office features Bruno Mankowski's 1939 sculpture "The Farmer's

Letter," a plaster relief commissioned by the Section of Fine Arts of the U.S. Department of the Treasury. The section commissioned art in many New Deal-era public buildings, including 13 murals and 3 sculptures in S.C. Mankowski intended his sculpture to highlight the relationship between the people and their government. *Sponsored by the Town of Chesterfield, 2013*
GPS Coordinates: 34° 44.140' N, 80° 5.107' W

13–14 Craig Park

Page St. & Park Dr., Chesterfield

(FRONT) This park was built in 1933–35 by three New Deal-era programs of Franklin D. Roosevelt's first term. The land was donated by William D. Craig (1845–1935), once described as "one of Chesterfield's busiest citizens." Craig, a Confederate veteran, ran Craig's Mill on Thompson Creek, owned a general store downtown, and founded the Chesterfield Light and Power Co. in 1910 to bring electric lights to Chesterfield. He died just as the park was being completed.
(REVERSE) The land was cleared by the Civil Works Administration and the Federal Emergency Relief Administration built the "community hut," a rustic log building finished in 1935. The Works Progress Administration completed the park. Notable plantings include dogwood (the town tree), mountain laurel, and azalea, and the park features a playground and an amphitheater. The WPA Guide to the Palmetto State (1941) calls the park "a municipal playground for old and young." *Sponsored by the Town of Chesterfield, 2014*
GPS Coordinates: 34° 44.476' N, 80° 5.358' W

13–15 Chesterfield High School

Crescent Dr., Chesterfield

(FRONT) Chesterfield High School, which stood here from 1908 to 1992, was the successor to Chesterfield Academy, an antebellum school burned by Federal troops in 1865. A new academy, built in 1889, later became Chesterfield School. By 1907 it had three teachers and so many students in grades 1–11 that a new school was necessary. The 1908 school, designed by

E. V. Richards, was a two-story brick Classical Revival building.

(REVERSE) Enrollment grew after 1908, requiring additions in 1918 and 1923 and remodeling in the late 1950s. A gymnasium was built by the Works Progress Administration in 1934–39. Grade 12 was added in 1948. A new Chesterfield High School on N. Page St. was built in 1969 for students from Chesterfield, Ruby, and Gary in grades 10–12. The old school here, a junior high school until 1981, burned in 1992; the gymnasium burned in 2004. *Sponsored by the Town of Chesterfield, 2014*

GPS Coordinates: 34° 44.251' N, 80° 5.661' W

13–16 Robert Smalls School

316 Front St., Cheraw

(FRONT) Robert Smalls School was built in 1953 as a segregated school for African American students. Construction was funded as part of South Carolina's school equalization program. While both white and black schools were funded by this program, the purpose was to equalize African American educational facilities and conform with the doctrine of "separate but equal" in order to avoid racial integration.

(REVERSE) Designed by the firm of Hopkins, Baker & Gill of Florence, S.C., the school's Colonial Revival aesthetic was heavily influenced by Cheraw, Incorporated, a group of local leaders who worked to ensure that new construction in the area was consistent with Cheraw's historic character. The architecture of the building sets it apart from other equalization schools, which were usually built in a mid-century modern style. *Sponsored by Pathfinders United, 2015*

GPS Coordinates: 34° 42.126' N, 79° 53.044' W

13–17 Chesterfield Academy

601 W. Main St., Chesterfield

(FRONT) The building that stands here once served as the Chesterfield Academy. The first Chesterfield Academy building was located nearer to downtown. Local tradition holds that the Union 20th Corps burned the school, along with other buildings in Chesterfield, in March 1865. A new building was not erected until 1889, possibly from materials salvaged from the old St. Paul Methodist (later Chesterfield Baptist) Church.

(REVERSE) Chesterfield Academy operated as a private school, serving students from both Chesterfield and elsewhere. The school offered a two-year preparatory course of study with instruction in Latin, mathematics, ancient and modern history, and physical science. Also offered was instruction at the primary and intermediate levels. In 1909 S. M. Jackson purchased the building and converted it to a residence. *Sponsored by the Town of Chesterfield and Historical Society of Chesterfield County, 2016*

GPS Coordinates: 34° 44.127' N, 80° 5.634' W

13–18 Long High School Site

1010 W. Greene St., Cheraw

(FRONT) Long H.S. was completed in 1955 and replaced Coulter Academy as the primary African American H.S. in Cheraw. The school was named in honor of Rev. G. W. Long, Coulter's President from 1908 until 1943. Mr. Henry L. Marshall was the first principal. The new school was praised as a thoroughly modern facility, with a library, science lab, agriculture, woodworking/masonry workshops, and home economics classrooms.

(REVERSE) Long High played an integral role in the African American Community by providing cultural events and serving as a venue for strategic political planning during the 1960s. It would remain segregated by race from its opening until Chesterfield County complied with federal desegregation requirements in 1970. The last class graduated in 1970 with Mr. Otis L. Ford serving as the principal. The original school was razed in 1999. *Sponsored by the Long High Class of 1970 Legacy Committee, 2017*

GPS Coordinates: 34° 41.806' N, 79° 54.326' W

13–19   Dr. Duett Thompson Teal House

508 W. Main St., Chesterfield

(FRONT) The Dr. Duett Thompson Teal House was built in 1921. It is a large, asymmetrical home with a circular tower at its S.W. corner. Seven chimneys with corbelled caps pierce the roof. A spindle frieze over the stairway and patterned metal ceiling are among the interior embellishments. The house was listed in the National Register of Historic Places as part of the West Main St. Historic District in 1982. (REVERSE) Teal (1871–1954) graduated from Baltimore Medical College in 1893 and practiced medicine for 60 years. Teal was influential in bringing the railroad to Chesterfield. He also established the Teal Light and Power Co. in 1917, which delivered power to the town from 1917–1921. A dam and powerhouse generated power, which was carried to Chesterfield by six miles of transmission lines. *Sponsored by the Historical Society of Chesterfield and the Town of Chesterfield, 2017*
GPS Coordinates: 34° 44.169' N, 80° 5.558' W

13–20   Mt. Tabor Methodist Church

510 West Blvd., Chesterfield

(FRONT) Mt. Tabor Methodist Church dates to the early days of emancipation when, according to local tradition, a group of freedpeople met here under a brush arbor before the first church was built in 1868. The present church dates to ca. 1878 and was built by members of the congregation. The frame building features an off-center tower with pyramidal roof. The original bell has been removed but remains on the church grounds.
(REVERSE) The church is oriented on a north-south axis with its principal façade and bell tower facing north. It originally fronted an unpaved lane that passed in front, with the Chesterfield & Lancaster R.R. passing behind. S.C. Hwy. 9 (West Blvd.) was completed in the late 1920s and roughly follows the old rail line here. Mt. Tabor was listed in the National Register of Historic Places in 1982 as part of the West Main St. Historic District.

Sponsored by the Historical Society of Chesterfield and the Town of Chesterfield, 2018
GPS Coordinates: 34° 44.082' N, 80° 5.594' W

13–21   Carolina Hotel/Chesterfield and Lancaster R. R.

109 Church St., Chesterfield

Carolina Hotel (FRONT)
Constructed ca. 1905, this two-story building originally housed the Carolina Hotel. Then made of exposed brick, the hotel was likely built by owners James B. Streater and John T. Hurst, who hoped to serve passengers on the nearby Chesterfield and Lancaster Railroad. The building also served as a commercial mall and is believed to have housed a general store, bank, market, and, in the 1920s, an automobile dealership located on the first floor. Chesterfield and Lancaster R. R. (REVERSE) Chesterfield and Lancaster Railroad, chartered in 1887, operated a depot 500 ft. E. Work on the line began in 1900. It reached the town in 1901, becoming the first railroad to pass through Chesterfield. It carried passengers as well as freight, especially lumber products. Later part of the Seaboard Air Line, the 35 mi. track spanned Cheraw (east) and Crowburg (west), never reaching Lancaster. The line was abandoned in 1941. *Sponsored by Chesterfield Historical Society and Town of Chesterfield, 2019*
GPS Coordinates: 34° 44.088' N, 80° 5.455' W

13–22   Chesterfield Colored School

North side of Toatley Dr., Chesterfield

(FRONT) This was the site of the Chesterfield Colored School, a segregated school built in 1937 to serve African Americans. The wood frame building originally had eight classrooms and enrolled students in grades 1–8. Additional classrooms and an auditorium were built in 1943–44, and grades 1–12 attended by 1948. Student activities included basketball, chorus, clubs, a newspaper, literary society, and student council.
(REVERSE) By the early 1950s, more than 500 students were enolled at Chesterfield Colored School. The campus burned down on

November 21, 1952. The school reopened in temporary housing, where it remained until 1954–55, when pupils transferred to Gary High School (formerly Zoar School) and Edwards Elementary. The latter was built as part of S.C.'s equalization campaign to preserve segregation. *Sponsored by Chesterfield Historical Society and Town of Chesterfield, 2019*
GPS Coordinates: 34° 44.394' N, 80° 5.450' W

Clarendon County

14–1 Fort Watson

U.S. Hwy. 301-15, 1 mi. N of Lake Marion, St. Paul vicinity

The first post in S.C. retaken from the British, the stockade fort on this old Indian mound had controlled the road from Charleston to Camden as well as the Santee River. On April 15, 1781, Gen. Francis Marion and Lt. Col. Henry Lee encircled it with troops while Major Hezekiah Maham built a log tower whose fire could command it. On April 23, the Americans undermined the works and forced its surrender. *Erected by S.C. Forestry Commission, Parks Division, 1963*
GPS Coordinates: 33° 31.966' N, 80° 25.91' W

14–2 Midway Church

S.C. Hwy. 527, about .7 mi. N of its intersection with S.C. Sec. Rd. 14-19, S of Sardinia

Midway Presbyterian Church, named because of its location halfway between Salem and Williamsburg Churches, traces its beginning to 1801, when services were being held under a brush arbor. The earliest building was erected in 1802, and the Rev. G. G. McWhorter delivered the first sermon on January 10, 1803. The present structure was built in 1850. *Erected by Clarendon County Historical Commission, 1970*
GPS Coordinates: 33° 46.006' N, 80° 2.201' W

14–3 Richardson Graves

Old River Rd. (S.C. Sec. Rd. 14-76), 2.2 mi. S of Rimini

Three hundred yards west is the site of one of the earliest graveyards in St. Mark's Parish. In the cemetery are buried Richard Richardson, Brigadier in the Revolution, James Burchell Richardson, South Carolina Governor 1802–04, and John Peter Richardson, South Carolina Governor, 1840–42, and founder of the Citadel. *Erected by Clarendon County Historical Society, 1970*
GPS Coordinates: 33° 38.299' N, 80° 29.323' W

14–4 Anne Custis Burgess

Corner of S. Church & Burgess Sts., Summerton

This is the childhood home of Anne Custis Burgess, who was born in 1874 in Mayesville. After receiving a diploma from Converse College, she taught music at Summerton, Williamston, and Winthrop College. At the time of her death in 1910 she was employed by Thornwell Orphanage. Miss Burgess composed the music and Henry Timrod the lyrics for "Carolina," which became the state song in 1911. *Erected by the Clarendon County Historical Society, 1980*
GPS Coordinates: 33° 36.217' N, 80° 21.211' W

14–5 Revolutionary Skirmish Near Tearcoat Branch

Brewington Rd. (S.C. Sec. Rd. 14-50), .9 mile N of I-95, Sardinia vicinity

On the night of October 25, 1780, Col. Francis Marion with 150 men surprised and completely routed 200 Tories under Col. Samuel Tynes near here. Marion's forces suffered no casualties. With the dispersion of Tynes's troops, Lord Cornwallis became apprehensive of losing British supplies on the Santee River. *Erected by Clarendon County Historical Society, 1980*
GPS Coordinates: 33° 48.854' N, 80° 8.556' W

14–6 Encounter at Halfway Swamp /Site of Original St. Mark's Church

S.C. Sec. Rd. 14–76, about 1 mi. S of Rimini

Encounter at Halfway Swamp (FRONT)
On December 12, 1780, according to tradition, British Maj. Robert McLeroth was surprised near here by Gen. Francis Marion. The British first agreed to a staged combat with twenty men on each side, but slipped away during the night, escaping an all-out battle. Credence is given to the event by the skirmish on December 13th at Singleton's Mill, 10 miles north.
Site of Original St. Mark's Church (REVERSE)
The first church of St. Mark's Parish, established in 1757 by commissioners Isaac Brunson, John, Joseph, and William Cantey, James McGirt, Mathew Nelson, and Richard Richardson, stood nearby at Halfway Swamp. Burned by the British during the Revolution, it was rebuilt four times and now stands near Pinewood. *Erected by the Clarendon County Historical Society, 2010, replacing a marker erected by the society in 1980*
GPS Coordinates: 33° 39.301' N, 80° 29.724' W

14–7 Revolutionary Skirmish Near Wyboo Swamp

S.C. Sec. Rd. 14–410, 1.1. mi. W of its intersection with S.C. Hwy. 260, S of Manning near Lake Marion Dam

During Francis Marion's 1781 campaign to drive the British from the Pee Dee, he and his men clashed near here in March with British and Tory forces numbering more than 500 men. During the Wyboo skirmish, a Marion private, Gavin James, single-handedly held back an enemy advance. Marion's men finally dispersed the British and Tories. *Erected by Clarendon County Historical Society, 1980*
GPS Coordinates: 33° 32.368' N, 80° 13' W

14–8 Liberty Hill Church/Pioneers in Desegregation

2310 Liberty Hill Rd. (S.C. Sec. Rd. 14–373), about 1 mi. N of St. Paul, Summerton vicinity

Liberty Hill Church (FRONT)
In 1867, five years after the Emancipation Proclamation, Thomas and Margaret Briggs gave four acres of land to this African Methodist Episcopal church. The present building, completed in 1905, has been brick veneered. Meetings held here in the 1940s and 1950s led to local court cases, which helped bring about the U.S. Supreme Court's 1954 ruling desegregating public schools.
Pioneers in Desegregation (REVERSE)
Nineteen members of this congregation were plaintiffs in the case of Harry Briggs, Jr., vs. R. W. Elliott, heard in U.S. District Court, Charleston, in 1952. Although this court refused to abolish racial segregation in S.C. schools, this case, with others, led to the U.S. Supreme Court's 1954 landmark decision desegregating public schools. *Erected by The Congregation, 1985*
GPS Coordinates: 33° 35.46' N, 80° 23.372' W

14–9 Andrews Chapel Church

Mt. Everett Rd. (S.C. Sec. Rd. 14–306), 6.2 mi. N of Summerton, Panola vicinity

According to local tradition, this Methodist congregation was organized in 1786 and pioneer American bishop Francis Asbury later visited the area a number of times. The church stands today on land given by Ellis R. and Mary A. Richbourg in 1880. Bessie B. Parker, first woman to be ordained a Methodist minister in S.C., served here 1959–1962 and is buried in the cemetery. *Erected by The Congregation, 1986*
GPS Coordinates: 33° 39.281' N, 80° 23.067' W

14–10 Clarendon County/Manning

Clarendon County Courthouse, Town Square, Manning

Clarendon County (FRONT)
Five S.C. governors have come from this area, which was part of the Parish of St. Mark (1757) and Camden District (1769) before becoming Clarendon County in 1785. The county was then part of Sumter circuit court district (1799) before becoming Clarendon District (1855) and finally Clarendon County again in 1868, taking its name from the Earl of Clarendon, one of the original Lords Proprietors of Carolina.

Manning (REVERSE)

Manning, established in 1855 as the seat of Clarendon District, was incorporated in 1861, its town limits extending ½ mile from the courthouse in all directions. In 1865, the town was partially burned by Union troops under General Edward E. Potter. About two blocks N. of here on Church St. is the grave of Pvt. Josiah B. Pratt, one of Potter's soldiers, who was killed in this foray only a few days before Lee's surrender at Appomattox. *Erected by Clarendon County Historical Society, 1988*
GPS Coordinates: 33° 41.702' N, 80° 12.709' W

14-11 Taw Caw Church

301 E. Main St. (U.S. Hwy. 301), just E of Summerton town limits

In 1885 this black baptist church bought the building here, said built about 1860, from white Taw Caw church, now Summerton. Building additions have been made over the years. *Erected by The Congregation, 1992*
GPS Coordinates: 33° 36.48' N, 80° 20.111' W

14-12 Pleasant Grove School

U.S. Hwy. 301, about 2 mi. N of its intersection with S.C. Sec. Rd. 14-123, Alcolu vicinity, 4 mi. N of Manning

Black institution built soon after school district purchased the land 1933. School closed 1953 with 5 teachers/159 students. Now a community center. *Erected by Pleasant Grove School Committee, 1993*
GPS Coordinates: 33° 45.676' N, 80° 9.29' W

14-13 Mt. Zion A.M.E. Church

Camp Bob Cooper Rd., S of Summerton

(FRONT) This church, organized about 1865, held its early services in a nearby brush arbor but built a permanent sanctuary here soon afterwards. Rev. Daniel Humphries, its first pastor, served both Mt. Zion and its sister church St. James 1865-1879. The original sanctuary was torn down in 1918 and the present sanctuary was built that year with lumber from the old sanctuary.
(REVERSE) Mt. Zion School, once located here, served the community for many years with

church member I. S. Hilton as principal. Mt. Zion A.M.E. hosted several meetings from 1948 to 1954 on the desegregation of the public schools, and member Levi Pearson was the plaintiff in *Pearson v. County Board of Education* (1948), which led to the landmark decision in *Brown v. Board of Education* (1954). *Erected by the Congregation, 1999*
GPS Coordinates: 33° 32.045' N, 80° 14.723' W

14-14 Summerton Presbyterian Church

16 Cantey St., Summerton

(FRONT) This church, founded in 1875 as a mission of the Presbyterian Church in Manning, grew out of occasional services held in the Methodist church before the Civil War. The first worship site, a renovated carriage house, was located ½ mi. east at Wildwood Plantation, on Taw Caw Road.
(REVERSE) Summerton Presbyterian Church was formally organized in 1883 with twenty-one charter members. A frame church was built on Main St. in 1885, but by 1905 the congregation wished to move from the downtown business district and began work on the present brick sanctuary here, completed in 1907. *Erected by the Congregation for the 125th Anniversary and in Memory of C. Alex Harvin, Jr., 2001*
GPS Coordinates: 33° 36.324' N, 80° 21.086' W

14-15 Senn's Mill

3 Cantey St., Summerton

This complex, featuring a blacksmith shop (ca. 1903), grist mill (ca. 1905), and bottling plant (ca. 1921), was operated for many years by John G. Senn (1851-1942) and his son-in-law Frank W. Josey (1872-1959). Senn's grandson Walter B. Senn, Jr. (1917-1999) then ran the mill for almost fifty years. A significant example of a type of commercial complex once common in the towns of the rural South, it was listed in the National Register of Historic Places in 2000. *Erected by the Town of Summerton, 2001*
GPS Coordinates: 33° 36.542' N, 80° 21.08' W

14–16 Hannah Levi Memorial Library/Manning Library

211 N. Brooks St., Manning

Hannah Levi Memorial Library (FRONT)
The Hannah Levi Memorial Library, built in 1909–10 grew out of a library fund begun in 1905 by the children of Moses and Hannah Levi, along with proceeds from the sale of the Moses Levi Memorial Institute. A matching grant from the city of Manning and a public fund raising effort helped complete this Classical Revival building. It was possibly designed by Shand & Lafaye, architects for the county courthouse.

Manning Library (REVERSE)
Managed by the Manning Civic League, this building served as the Manning Library and as a social hall 1910–1976. Deeded to the county in 1976, it was the Clarendon County Public Library until 1984. The library was listed in the National Register of Historic Places in 1979. The Clarendon County Archives & History Center, established to collect, preserve, and display documents and artifacts, opened here in 1996. *Erected by the Wendell M. Levi Trust, 2005*
GPS Coordinates: 33° 41.955' N, 80° 12.644' W

14–17 Trinity A.M.E. Church

39 W. Rigby St., Manning

(FRONT) This church was founded soon after the Civil War by 50 freedmen and women who held their first services in a stable donated to them by S. A. Rigby. In 1869 the church trustees bought a half-acre lot for a school, and in 1870 they bought a one-acre lot for "the African Methodist Episcopal Church of Manning" on what is now Rigby Street, named for Rigby. The first church here, a frame building, was completed in 1874.
(REVERSE) The congregation, first called simply "Our Church" by its members, was renamed Trinity A.M.E. Church when its first building was completed in 1874. That building was replaced by a larger frame church, which burned in 1895. The present church, also a frame building, was built that year and covered in brick veneer in 1914. The Central S.C. Conference of the A.M.E. Church was

organized here in 1921. *Erected by the Congregation, 2006*
GPS Coordinates: 33° 41.796' N, 80° 12.746' W

14–18 Ebenezer Baptist Church

105 Dinkins St., Manning

(FRONT) This church was founded about 1869 by Mary Scott "Aunt Mary" Harvin, and held its first services in a nearby brush arbor. In 1881 church trustees purchased a one-half acre lot here from Dr. J. G. Dinkins for $35.00. The present church, built in 1901, was described as "enlarged and beautified on a very modern style" when two towers, a gallery, and anterooms were added in 1912.
(REVERSE) This was one of several churches in Clarendon County to host meetings between 1949 and 1954 on the desegregation of public schools. On April 20, 1949, plaintiffs in the suit that became *Briggs v. Elliott* met here. That case was later part of the landmark decision in *Brown v. Board of Education* (1954). By late 2009 Rev. George P. Windley, Sr. was Ebenezer's longest-tenured pastor, serving more than 30 years. *Erected by the Congregation, 2010*
GPS Coordinates: 33° 41.808' N, 80° 12.501' W

14–19 Cantey Family Cemetery

.2 mi S of S.C. Sec. Rd. 14–28, and 1.7 mi. E of S.C. Sec. Rd. S-351, Jordan vicinity

(FRONT) This cemetery was established about 1739 by Joseph Cantey (d. 1763), planter and member of the Commons House of Assembly. It is on the site of Mount Hope, Cantey's plantation near the Santee River. Cantey served what was then Craven County as a captain in the militia and justice of the peace, then served Prince Frederick's Parish in the Commons House of Assembly 1754–1757.
(REVERSE) Several generations of Canteys, as well as members of the Burgess, Clemons, Keels, McDonald, Montgomery (McGomery), Oliver, and Rhodus families related to the Canteys, are buried here. In 1883 Joseph Cantey's great-great grandson Joseph Samuel Cantey deeded this two-acre tract to eight trustees. The cemetery is owned and maintained by the Cantey Cemetery Association.

Erected by the Cantey Cemetery Association,
2010
GPS Coordinates: 33° 32.652' N, 80° 5.35' W

14–20 Manning Schools

Weldon Auditorium, Old Georgetown Rd. & N.
Brooks St., Manning

(FRONT) The Manning Collegiate Institute, the town's first public school opened here in early 1890. The two-story frame school with a bell tower, built in 1889–1890, was called "one of the most handsome and imposing" buildings in Manning. By 1899, however, the school was in debt and the building and property were endangered. The family of Moses Levi (1826–1899), farmer, merchant, and civic leader, bought it, cleared the debt, and donated it to the town.

(REVERSE) The school, renamed the Moses Levi Memorial Institute, operated here 1899–1910. In 1910 a new two-story brick school was built here as Manning Graded School and the old school was moved to West Boyce St. to house the Manning Training School. The new school, designed by Edwards, Walter, & Parnham of Atlanta, was later Manning High School for many years. Manning High moved to a new building in 1982. The old school here burned in 1983. *Sponsored by the Wendell M. Levi Trust, 2012*
GPS Coordinates: 33° 42.156' N, 80° 12.629' W

14–21 St. Mary Catholic Church

14 N. Cantey St., Summerton

(FRONT) This Carpenter Gothic church, dedicated in 1914, is the oldest Catholic church in Clarendon County. Established as a mission of St. Ann Catholic Church in Sumter, it grew out of masses held in the homes of Lebanese immigrants who came to Summerton beginning in 1899. Members of the Shaleuhy, Joseph, Nimmer, and other Catholic families organized this congregation in 1913 and acquired this lot for their new church.

(REVERSE) This church was dedicated in 1914 by Bishop H. P. Northrop and blessed by Bishop W. T. Russell in 1917. Its columned front porch was enclosed when the church was expanded in the 1950s. The founders of St. Mary were

members of the Maronite Church, an Eastern rite of the Roman Catholic Church. The stained glass window above the altar honors St. Sharbel Makhlouf (1828–1898) of Lebanon, a Maronite monk and hermit. *Sponsored by The Ladies Club of Our Lady of Hope Catholic Church, 2014*
GPS Coordinates: 34° 44.129' N, 80° 5.790' W

14–22 Brewington Presbyterian Church

2056 N. Brewington Rd. (S.C. State Rd. S-14-50),
Manning vicinity

Established ca. 1811 on the Black River, near Brewington Lake, by five members on land donated by James Evans family. It is believed to be the oldest church still standing on it's [sic] original site in Clarendon County. It was closed in 1951. Since then it has been maintained by the Brewington Cemetery Association. *Sponsored by Brewington Cemetery Association, 2016*
GPS Coordinates: 33° 42.128' N, 80° 3.167' W

14–23 Manning Training School

311 West Boyce St., Manning

(FRONT) Manning Training School has origins in the early 20th century with the Slater Fund helped finance Clarendon County Training School. This facility provided both education for black students and advanced training for African American teachers who taught in the rural South. Schools that performed this teacher-training function were known as "training schools." The first school burned in the 1920s.

(REVERSE) A new school was built in 1927–28 and was financed in part by the Rosenwald Fund. This Rosenwald School, the first Manning Training School, burned in 1941. It was replaced by temporary buildings until a new school was built in 1953 with funds from S.C.'s school equalization program. Mr. William M. Parker served as principal of Manning Training School from 1942 until it was consolidated with Manning H.S. in 1970. *Sponsored by Manning Training School Alumni, 2016*
GPS Coordinates: 33° 41.772' N, 80° 13.171' W

Colleton County

15–1 Old Jacksonborough First known as Pon Pon

S.C. Hwy. 64 just N of the Edisto River, Jacksonboro

Founded about 1735 on lands granted John Jackson in 1701. County Seat of Colleton District from 1799 to 1822. Provisional Capital of State while Charleston was under siege in the closing months of the American Revolution. First South Carolina Legislature met here Jan.-Feb. 1782. Sessions held in Masonic Lodge and Tavern. Passed Confiscation and Amercement Acts. *Erected by The Colleton County Historical Society, 1959*
GPS Coordinates: 32° 45.966' N, 80° 26.915' W

15–2 Colonel John Laurens

U.S. Hwy. 17 at the Combahee River, SW of Green Pond

Col. John Laurens, former aide of Washington and envoy to France, was killed Aug. 27, 1782, near Tar Bluff on Combahee River in one of the last battles of the Revolutionary War and buried temporarily 7 miles east in the Stock family cemetery. "For injured rights he fell and equal laws, the noble victim of a noble cause." *Erected 1995 by Colleton County Historical Society, replacing a marker originally erected in 1960*
GPS Coordinates: 32° 39.147' N, 80° 40.970' W

15–3 Edmundsbury

U.S. Hwy. 17 at the Ashepoo River, Green Pond vicinity

A brick Chapel of Ease for St. Bartholomew's Parish was built here in 1785 in a town laid out in 1740 and named for Landgrave Edmund Bellinger. The Vestry reported the Chapel unfit for use in 1786, and in 1810 it fell in ruins. A new Chapel built in 1819, burnt 1852, rebuilt 1854, was wrecked by Union troops in 1865. *Erected by Colleton County Historical Society, 1961*
GPS Coordinates: 32° 44.549' N, 80° 33.509' W

15–4 General Greene at the Round O

U.S. Hwy. 17-A, about 3 mi. W of Cottageville

General Nathanael Greene advanced into the Low Country with the Continental Army under his command and set up headquarters in this vicinity on the Round O in December 1781 before moving down to protect the General Assembly convened at Jacksonborough in January 1782 in defiance of the British who were confined to Charles Town. *Erected by Colleton County Historical Society, 1962*
GPS Coordinates: 32° 56.273' N, 80° 32.478' W

15–5 Island Creek Meeting House

U.S. Hwy. 15, N of Walterboro

The cemetery one-half mile west is on the site of a meeting house deeded to the Methodist Society by John Fontaine in 1802. Bishop Francis Asbury had held services at Island Creek on March 4, 1796, in "a pole house." In 1882 the members had moved to other churches. Annual services were held for a time by the Island Creek Memorial Association. *Erected by Colleton County Historical Society, 1964*
GPS Coordinates: 33° 0.128' N, 80° 38.228' W

15–6 Martyr of the Revolution /Hayne Hall

S.C. Hwy. 64, 13 mi. E of Walterboro

Martyr of the Revolution (FRONT)
When Loyalist soldiers attacked the camp of Col. Isaac Hayne's S.C. militia about 5 mi. W on July 7, 1781, they captured Hayne. He was soon condemned as a traitor because he had previously declared allegiance to Great Britain after the fall of Charleston. Hayne, hanged in Charleston on August 4, 1781, became a martyr to those fighting for America's independence.
Hayne Hall (REVERSE)
The surrounding land was part of Hayne Hall plantation, home of the Hayne family

in South Carolina and Colonel Isaac Hayne (Sept. 23, 1745–Aug. 4, 1781). Rice planter, iron manufacturer, church leader, and Patriot soldier, Colonel Hayne was executed by the British during the Revolution and buried here in the family cemetery. *Erected by the South Carolina Department of Parks, Recreation, and Tourism, State Park Service, 2007, replacing a marker erected in 1964*
GPS Coordinates: 32° 48.415' N, 80° 28.75' W

15–7 Walterborough Academy

Hampton St., W of its intersection with S. Miller St., Walterboro

Incorporated December 17, 1834, Walterborough Academy was the forerunner of the present city school system. Its trustees were Malachi Ford, John G. Godfrey, Thomas Riggs, James C. McCants, John D. Edwards, David Campbell, and Archibald Campbell. The Reverend John B. Van Dyck served as Preceptor until his death on February 17, 1840. *Erected by the Colleton County Historical Society, 1964*
GPS Coordinates: 32° 54.104' N, 80° 39.628' W

15–8 Bethel Presbyterian Church

S.C. Hwy. 64, 12 mi. E of Walterboro

Founded on this site in 1728 by the Reverend Archibald Stobo, Bethel or Pon Pon Church served a large Presbyterian congregation until replaced by Bethel Presbyterian Church in nearby town of Walterboro early in the nineteenth century. The original bell was moved to the new church in Walterboro. The old building burned in 1886. *Erected by Colleton County Historical Society, 1964*
GPS Coordinates: 32° 47.929' N, 80° 29.748' W

15–9 Walterboro Jail

N. Jeffries Blvd., between Benson St. & W. Washington St., Walterboro

This neo-Gothic building, designed by Jones & Lee, noted architects of Charleston, and constructed by J. & B. Lucas in 1855–56, replaced the jail built in 1822 when Walterboro became the seat of justice of Colleton District. It served as a jail until 1937, since which time,

it has been used by Colleton County to house various offices. *Erected by Colleton County Historical Society, 1965*
GPS Coordinates: 32° 54.221' N, 80° 40.039' W

15–10 Catholic Hill

S.C. Sec. Rd. 15–41, 2.5 mi. W of its intersection with S.C. Hwy. 303, S of Walterboro

Settlers from Ireland of the Roman Catholic faith in this area helped form the ecclesiastical territory of Colleton, Beaufort, and Barnwell Districts under Bishop John England in 1831. The Church of St. James the Greater was dedicated on this site on January 30, 1832, and remained in use until destroyed by fire on April 12, 1856. *Erected by Colleton County Historical Society, 1966*
GPS Coordinates: 32° 46.592' N, 80° 39.739' W

15–11 Hickory Valley

Wichman St., just W of its intersection with Fishburne St., Walterboro

Near here in a hickory grove Paul and Jacob Walter built in 1784 summer houses, which formed the nucleus of a summer colony which grew into the town of Walterboro. The first store in the town was here and later the first drug store. The park here was the center of community life until the cyclone of 1879 leveled most of the trees. *Erected by Colleton County Historical Society, 1967*
GPS Coordinates: 32° 54.259' N, 80° 39.549' W

15–12 Battle of Parker's Ferry

S.C. Hwy. 64, 11 mi. E of Walterboro

Sent to intercept a raid by 540 Hessians, British, and Tories, General Francis Marion with a force of 400 men, on August 30, 1781, set up an ambuscade along this road about 1 mile from the ferry. The enemy advancing along the narrow causeway were surprised and suffered heavy losses forcing them to withdraw to Charles Town. *Erected by Colleton County Historical Society, 1962*
GPS Coordinates: 32° 48.072' N, 80° 30.175' W

15–13 Temple of Sport

U.S. Hwy. 17, just W of its junction with S.C. Hwy. 303, Green Pond vicinity

On top of this ridge stood a sylvan temple erected before the Revolution by Colonel Barnard Elliott, patriot and sportsman. The structure was supported by columns in the classic manner. The site, a part of Colonel Elliott's Plantation "Bellevue," afforded an excellent stand for hunting deer. *Erected by Colleton County Historical Society, 1969*
GPS Coordinates: 32° 42.574' N, 80° 36.612' W

15–14 Pon Pon Chapel

Intersection of S.C. Hwy. 64 & S.C. Sec. Rd. 15–40, Jacksonboro vicinity

On Parker's Ferry road one mile northeast of here are the ruins of Pon Pon Chapel of Ease, established in 1725 by an Act of the General Assembly after the Yemassee War aborted plans for St. Bartholomew's Parish Church. John Wesley preached here in 1737. The brick building erected in 1754 was burned in 1801 and has since been known as "the Burnt Church." *Erected 1994 replacing a marker erected 1970 by Colleton County Historical Society*
GPS Coordinates: 32° 47.752' N, 80° 29.288' W

15–15 Salkehatchie Presbyterian Church

Hendersonville Hwy. (U.S. Hwy. 17-A) near its intersection with U.S. Hwy. 21, Salkehatchie vicinity

This was formerly the site of a Presbyterian church organized in 1766 by the Reverend Archibald Simpson, minister from Scotland. The church was incorporated on December 17, 1808. Serving the church were the Reverends Simpson, Edward Palmer, and J. B. Van Dyck. In the cemetery are the graves of early Scotch-Irish settlers. *Erected by Colleton County Historical Society, 1973*
GPS Coordinates: 32° 43.391' N, 80° 47.883' W

15–16 Hendersonville/Arab the Horse

Salem United Methodist Church, 7191 Hendersonville Hwy. (U.S. Hwy. 17A), Hendersonville

Hendersonville (FRONT)
Settled by 1791 and known as Godfrey Savanna, this area later was the summer home for a colony of Combahee River rice planters. The settlement, known as Hendersonville by 1862, was named for Dr. Edward Rogers Henderson, a local landowner and signer of the 1860 Ordinance of Secession from Colleton County.
Arab the Horse (REVERSE)
The book *Autobiography of Arab* was written by his master Corporal Edward Prioleau Henderson, and included their experiences in the Civil War. Henderson of the 2nd S.C. Cavalry, rode Arab extensively with Gen. James "Jeb" Stuart in MD, PA and VA and around Union Gen. George McClellan's army. Arab is buried west of here on the plantation where he was foaled and raised, which once belonged to Dr. Edward Rogers Henderson. *Erected by Salem United Methodist Church and Colleton County Historical Society, 1993*
GPS Coordinates: 32° 47.623' N, 80° 43.501' W

15–17 Anderson Field/Walterboro Army Air Field

Aviation Way, at the Lowcountry Regional Airport, Walterboro

Anderson Field (FRONT)
This airfield, the first in Colleton County, was built and dedicated in 1933 on 60 acres leased to the town of Walterboro by the estate of C. C. Anderson, for whom it was named. By 1937 the town purchased the field and its 3 unpaved landing strips. Local, state, and federal sources combined to fund a large hangar and paved runways by 1941. The U.S. Army Air Corps leased the field from the town in early 1942 and purchased an additional 3,712 acres to create a new Walterboro Army Air Field.
Walterboro Army Air Field (REVERSE)
The Walterboro Army Air Field, opened in August 1942, was a sub-base of the Columbia Army Air Base and the largest sub-base in the 3rd Air Force. It served as a final training base for pilots prior to overseas duty and housed

a military population of as many as 6,000 as well as hundreds of German POWs. When the base closed after the war the field was deeded back to Walterboro and Colleton County. *Erected by the Walterboro/Colleton County Airport Commission & the Colleton County Historical and Preservation Society, 1997* GPS Coordinates: 32° 54.981' N, 80° 38.274' W

15–18 Colleton County Courthouse

Corner of Hampton St. (S.C. Hwy. 63) and S. Walter St., Walterboro

(FRONT) The original section of this courthouse, completed in 1822 after the county seat moved to Walterborough from Jacksonborough, was built by contractor William Thompson. The front portico is attributed to Robert Mills, who completed an unfinished design by William Jay. The courthouse was in such poor condition within a few years, however, that it was extensively renovated in 1843–44.
(REVERSE) This courthouse, listed in the National Register of Historic Places in 1971, is built of brick covered in stucco to imitate stone. It was enlarged in 1916 by a frame wing on the west elevation. In 1937–39 a project of the Works Progress Administration covered the west wing with brick, built a new brick wing on the east elevation and an addition on the north entrance, and remodeled the interior. *Erected by the Colleton County Historical and Preservation Society, 2001* GPS Coordinates: 32° 54.132' N, 80° 39.984' W

15–19 Bethel Presbyterian Church

403 Church St., Walterboro

(FRONT) This church, originally located at Jacksonboro, was founded in 1728 by Rev. Archibald Stobo (d. 1741), father of the Presbyterian church in S.C. The first building at Jacksonboro was replaced in 1746 by a "handsome sanctuary" that stood until it was destroyed by a forest fire in 1886. A summer chapel built on this site in 1821 was a branch of the Jacksonboro church.
(REVERSE) By the 1830s the Walterboro church became the main sanctuary under the leadership of Rev. Edward Palmer (1788–1882),

minister here 1827–32, 1844–45, and 1862–74. A second frame church, built here in 1860–61, was destroyed by a tornado in 1879. It was replaced by another frame church in 1880, which burned in 1966. The present brick sanctuary, the fourth on this site, was built in 1969. *Erected by the Colleton County Historical and Preservation Society, 2003* GPS Coordinates: 32° 54.308' N, 80° 39.482' W

15–20 Cross Swamp Methodist Church

Lively Stone Rd., just N of its intersection with Cross Swamp Rd. (S.C. Sec. Rd. 15–27), Islandton vicinity

(FRONT) Cross Swamp Methodist Church, the first Methodist congregation in upper Colleton County, was founded in 1808. James and Asia Sineath deeded an acre on this site to church trustees in April and the first sanctuary, which was a log pole building, appears as a "meeting house" on a November 1808 plat.
(REVERSE) The second sanctuary, a hewn log building, was replaced by a frame sanctuary shortly before the Civil War. That church burned in 1910; this sanctuary was built and dedicated in 1911. Cross Swamp was on the Lodge Circuit when regular services ended in 1969. The cemetery here dates from the 19th century. *Erected by the Cross Swamp Cemetery Association, 2008* GPS Coordinates: 32° 58.276' N, 80° 56.457' W

15–21 Training the Tuskegee Airmen

1447 Mighty Cougar Drive, Walterboro, near the Colleton County High School Student Parking Lot

(FRONT) Graduates of the Tuskegee Army Flying School, who belonged to the first African-American units in the U.S. Army Air Corps, took further combat flight training at Walterboro Army Air Field from May 1944 to October 1945. Many of the first "Tuskegee Airmen" had already won distinction and fame in missions over North Africa, Sicily, and Italy in 1943–44, and several of them were assigned here as combat flight instructors.
(REVERSE) Trainees here flew the P-39, P-47, and P-40 fighter planes and the B-25 bomber. The officers' quarters and enlisted men's

barracks stood just east and just west of this spot, respectively. Segregation on American military posts, in place until 1948, was made worse by the fact that German POWs held here could use "White" facilities but the "Colored" officers and men of the U.S. Army Air Corps could not. *Erected by the Hiram E. Mann Chapter, Tuskegee Airmen, Inc., 2011*
GPS Coordinates: 32° 56.376' N, 80° 38.162' W

15–22 Colleton Training School /Gruber Street USO

229 Gruber St., Walterboro

Colleton Training School (FRONT)
Colleton Training School opened in 1925 and served African American students in the elementary and high school grades. In 1954 it was renamed Colleton High and remained in use until 1970 when Colleton County schools were desegregated. During World War II the school was temporary home of the USO established for ue by black servicemen, including the Tuskegee Airmen, who were trained at Walterboro Army Airfield.
Gruber Street USO (REVERSE)
In 1944 a federal grant allowed for the construction of a purpose-built USO for black servicemen. Built adjacent to the original Colleton Training School it included an auditorium and dance floor. The USO hosted weekly dances, live music, and games. It was necessary to have a USO for black soldiers because other facilities in Walterboro were segregated and did not admit black troops. After the war the building was repurposed for use by Colleton Training School. *Sponsored by the Colleton Training School/Colleton High School Alumni Association, Inc., 2019*
GPS Coordinates: 32° 54.536' N, 80° 39.067' W

15–23 Destruction of the *Boston*

Frank E. Baldwin Jr. Bridge Landing, Ashepoo River, Bennetts Point

(FRONT) On May 23–24, 1864, Union forces attempted an amphibious operation to destroy a railroad trestle across the Ashepoo River. Soldiers from the 34th U.S.C.T. were carried up the Ashepoo on the steamer Boston. The boat was grounded on an oyster bed 300 yds. in front of a Confederate position at Chapman's Fort (approx. 1/2 mile west of this spot) and C.S.A. artillery would lob 200 shells at the Boston.
(REVERSE) Using one small rowboat, Lt. George Brush of the 34th U.S.C.T. made multiple trips under fire to ferry 400 members of his command to safety. 13 were killed. After the Boston was evacuated it was set afire. Brush and four other men, William Downey, John Duffy, David Gifford, and Patrick Scalan, all of the 4th MA Cavalry, were awarded the Medal of Honor for their actions during the engagement. *Sponsored by Bennetts Point Fire and Community Services, 2016*
GPS Coordinates: 32° 36.801' N, 80° 28.909' W

15–24 Walterboro Water Tower

SE of intersection of N. Memorial Ave. and E. Washington St., Walterboro

(FRONT) This concrete water tower was built in 1915 as part of a program to improve Walterboro's water, sewer, and electrical infrastructure. Constructed to replace a smaller water tower at the Colleton Co. Courthouse (.3 mi. W), it stands 132-feet-tall and has a capacity of 100,000 gallons. When in operation, its water supply was steam-pumped from a reservoir after being drawn from an artesian well.
(REVERSE) In 1930, the town council had three cells added to the tower's base and used it as a jail. In the years that followed, the tower became a Walterboro landmark. Young residents made a tradition of the climbing the tower until an exterior ladder was removed in the 1970s. The town stored water in the tower until 2009, when it was decommissioned and replaced. It is one of the last towers of its type and era that survives in S.C. *Sponsored by City of Walterboro, 2019*
GPS Coordinates: 32° 54.140' N, 80° 39.738' W

Darlington County

16–1 Major Robert Lide

[Marker no longer extant.]

Cashua Ferry Rd. (S.C. Hwy. 34) near its intersection with Georgetown Rd. (S.C. Sec. Rd. 16–495), Mechanicsville

Born May 19, 1734/Died March 12, 1802/ Served in the militia of South Carolina under General Francis Marion during the Revolutionary War and was for many years deacon of Cashway Baptist Church/is buried in Lowders Hill Cemetery/.2 mile east. *Erected by Major Robert Lide Chapter, D.A.R. and the County of Darlington, 24 September 1960*
GPS Coordinates: 34° 21.113' N, 79° 44.637' W

16–2 David Rogerson Williams

Society Hill Rd. (S.C. Sec. Rd. 16–133), 3 mi. S of Society Hill

March 8, 1776-November 17, 1830/Statesman, educator,/pioneer manufacturer,/scientific farmer,/State Senator, Congressman,/Governor 1814–1816,/Brigadier General in/the War of 1812./His residence, "Center Hall,"/was ½ mile east. His grave is in/the family cemetery 2 ½ miles east. *Erected by Darlington County Historical Society, 1962*
GPS Coordinates: 34° 27.008' N, 79° 50.6' W

16–3 Long Bluff

Welsh Neck Baptist Church, 112 Church St. (U.S. Hwy. 15–401), Society Hill

(FRONT) Long Bluff, ¾ mile east on Great Pedee River, was the site of the first courthouse and jail for old Cheraws District in 1772. The town was known as Greeneville after the Revolution and remained the seat of justice until the formation of Darlington, Marlboro and Chesterfield Districts. Circuit courts and elections were conducted for a while longer.
(REVERSE) At a Circuit Court held here on November 15, 1774, more than a year before the Declaration of Independence, the Grand Jury of Cheraws District denied the right of

Parliament to levy taxes on them and declared themselves ready to defend with their lives and fortunes the right to obey only those laws made by their own elected representatives. *Erected by Darlington County Historical Society, 1965*
GPS Coordinates: 34° 30.789' N, 79° 51.003' W

16–4 Evan Pugh

Near intersection of Lide Springs Rd. (S.C. Sec. Rd. 16–29) & Mechanicsville Hwy. (S.C. Sec. Rd. 16–892), 2 mi. N of Mechanicsville

One half mile east of this site Evan Pugh (1729–1802) is buried at Pugh Field, near his homesite. He moved to this Pee Dee section in 1762 from Pennsylvania and served as a Minister for the Welsh Neck, Cashaway, and Mount Pleasant Churches of the Charleston Baptist Association, 1766–1802. He was an American Revolutionary patriot. *Erected by Darlington County Historical Society, 1967*
GPS Coordinates: 34° 30.789' N, 79° 51.003' W

16–5 Lamuel Benton

Cashua Ferry Rd. (S.C. Hwy. 34), East of intersection with Georgetown Rd. (S.C. Sec. Rd. 16–495), Mechanicsville

Owner of many acres north of here, Lamuel Benton was prominent in the Revolution as Colonel of the Cheraws militia under Francis Marion and as forager for Greene's Continental Army. Member S.C. House of Representatives, 1781–87; Delegate to the S.C. Constitutional Convention of 1790; Sheriff of Cheraws District, 1798 and 1791; Member of Congress, 1793–1799. *Erected by Darlington County Historical Commission, 1968*
GPS Coordinates: 34° 21.155' N, 79° 44.58' W

16–6 George W. Dargan 1802–1859

Weaver St. at Smith Ave., Darlington

Near this site stood the home of George W. Dargan, antebellum leader of this area, who

served as State Senator, 1842–1847 and Chancellor of the S.C. Court of Equity, 1847–1859. He was a trustee of the S.C. College and a member of the Southern Rights Convention of 1852. The mansion burned down on May 14, 1898. *Erected by Darlington County Historical Commission, 1968*
GPS Coordinates: 34° 18.544' N, 79° 53.718' W

16–7 Darlington District Agricultural Society/The Mineral Spring

Just off Mineral Springs Rd. (S.C. Sec. Rd. 16–177), at its intersection with Georgeanna Dr., just N of Darlington

Darlington District Agricultural Society (FRONT)
On May 5, 1846, a society was organized for "mutual improvement in agriculture and to promote the planting interest of the country." Most of the annual meetings since that time have been held at this spring. The first officers were W. E. James, Rev. J. M. Timmons, Isaac W. Wilson, Robert Rogers, and Rev. Robert Campbell.
The Mineral Spring (REVERSE)
On July 17, 1819, this spring and the surrounding lands were purchased from Henry King by the Darlington Mineral Springs Company, intent upon developing the site as a beneficial spa. The enterprise was abandoned soon after the death of the chief promoter. *Erected by Darlington County Historical Commission, 1969*
GPS Coordinates: 34° 19.626' N, 79° 53.022' W

16–8 Jacob Kelley House

Kelleytown Rd. (S.C. Sec. Rd. 16–12), Kelleytown, 3 mi. W of Hartsville

This house, home of Jacob Kelley (1780–1874), was used as a Union headquarters on March 2–3, 1865 by Major-General John E. Smith, Commander of the Third Division, Fifteenth Army Corps. During the encampment by Federal forces, the mills near Kelley Town were run for the benefit of the Third Division and foraging parties roamed the area. *Erected by Darlington County Historical Commission, 1969*
GPS Coordinates: 34° 20.996' N, 80° 8.525' W

16–9 St. David's Academy

At modern St. David's Academy, S. Main St. (U.S. Hwy. 15–401), Society Hill

The St. David's Society, organized in 1777 and chartered in 1778, built the first public academy in St. David's Parish ¾ mile northeast in 1786. Alexander McIntosh, George Hicks, Abel Kolb, William Pegues, and Thomas Evans were early officers. The academy was removed to this site about 1840 and the present building was erected in 1957. *Erected by Darlington County Historical Commission, 1970*
GPS Coordinates: 34° 30.36' N, 79° 51.47' W

16–10 Thomas E. Hart House

1624 W. Carolina Ave. (S.C. Sec. Rd. 16–10), Hartsville

This house was the residence of Captain Thomas Edwards Hart, who settled on these lands in 1817, and for whom Hartsville was named. He was a Justice of the Peace, Chairman of the Board of Free Schools, planter, merchant, and was appointed first Postmaster when the Hartsville Post Office was established in 1838. He died in 1842 at the age of 46. *Erected by Darlington County Historical Commission, 1970*
GPS Coordinates: 34° 21.937' N, 80° 6.975' W

16–11 Samuel Bacot 1745–1795

S.C. Sec. Rd. 16–179, 2 mi. SE of Darlington

Early land records indicate that Samuel Bacot settled in the back country of South Carolina about 1770. He served in the State Militia during the Revolution, was taken prisoner by the British in 1780, but with his companions made his escape, avoiding confinement in a Charles Town prison. His grave is one half mile northeast. *Erected by Darlington County Historical Commission and Samuel Bacot Chapter, Daughters of the American Revolution, 1972*
GPS Coordinates: 34° 16.311' N, 79° 49.289' W

16–12 Attempted Ambush

S.C. Sec. Rd. 16-49, about ½ mi. from U.S. Hwy. 52 and just N of the railroad, S of Darlington

On March 5, 1865, near the point where the Ebenezer Road crossed the Cheraw and Darlington Railroad, the 29th Missouri Mounted Infantry, of Col. Reuben Williams's command, deployed on either side of the tracks to capture a Confederate train approaching from Florence. The attempt failed when the engineer, discovering the trap, reversed his engine and escaped. *Erected by Darlington County Historical Commission, 1975*
GPS Coordinates: 34° 16.216' N, 79° 51.069' W

16–13 Welsh Neck Church

112 Church St. (U.S. Hwy. 15-401), Society Hill

(FRONT) This church, the pioneer center of Baptist influence in the area, was constituted January 1738 by Welsh from Pennsylvania and was originally located about two miles northeast of here. The first pastor was Philip James. It was incorporated March 17, 1785, as the "Baptist Church at the Welsh Neck on Pedee River."
(REVERSE) Seat of worship of this Baptist church was relocated here about 1799, on land acquired from Capt. William Dewitt. The second meeting house on this spot, dedicated in 1843, was destroyed by lightning July 5, 1928 and was replaced by the present structure in 1938. *Erected by Welsh Neck Baptist Church and The Darlington County Historical Commission, 1976*
GPS Coordinates: 34° 30.761' N, 79° 51.041' W

16–14 Augustin Wilson

Lake Swamp Baptist Church Cemetery, 6558 Oats Hwy. (S.C. Hwy. 403), Lake Swamp community, Timmonsville vicinity

Augustin Wilson, whose grave is about 150 ft. E. and marked by a partially embedded cannon barrel, was born 1755 in Va. During the American Revolution, he served with N.C. troops protecting S.C. against Tories and Indians and as an Ensign at the 1779 Battle of Brier Creek, Ga. He moved to South Carolina before 1820, where he died in 1848. *Erected by Darlington County Historical Society, 1976*
GPS Coordinates: 34° 10.166' N, 79° 57.957' W

16–15 Macedonia Church

400 S. Main St. (U.S. Hwy. 52), Darlington

(FRONT) Tradition says first meetings of this Baptist Church were held in the home of Laura Brown. A house of worship was constructed on the N.E. corner of present S. Main and Hampton streets on land purchased during 1866–1874. The present site was acquired in 1922 and the building occupied Feb. 3, 1935.
(REVERSE) This Baptist Church was constituted when a group of black members led by Rev. Isaac Brockenton withdrew from the Darlington Baptist Church on Feb. 11, 1866. Brockenton became the first pastor and served until his death in 1908. The first trustees were Evans Bell, Peter Dargan, Lazarus Ervin, Antrum McIver, Samuel McIver, Samuel Orr, and Samuel Parnell. *Erected by Darlington County Bicentennial Commission for Ethnic Participation, 1977*
GPS Coordinates: 34° 17.872' N, 79° 52.048' W

16–16 St. James Church

312 Pearl St., Darlington

(FRONT) This United Methodist Church was originally named Pearl Street Methodist Episcopal Church. The first trustees were Henry Brown, Abner Black, Wesley Dargan, Zeddidiah Dargan, January Felder, Randolph Hart and Rev. B. Frank Whittemore. Tradition says Federal occupation troops supplied the church bell, which they had taken from nearby St. John's Academy.
(REVERSE) In 1866, this United Methodist Church was founded by freedmen with aid from the Methodist Episcopal Church Missionary Society. The first minister was Rev. Liverus Ackerman, and the first building, also used as a school for freedmen, was completed by April 1866. The second house of worship dates from about 1883; the present building was completed in 1960. *Erected by the Congregation, 1976*
GPS Coordinates: 34° 18.059' N, 79° 52.484' W

16–17 Lower Fork of Lynches Creek Baptist Church/Gum Branch Church

1504 Clyde Rd. (S.C. Sec. Rd. 16-53), near its intersection with S.C. Sec. Rd. 16-23, Clyde community, about 5 mi. NW of Hartsville

Lower Fork of Lynches Creek Baptist Church (FRONT)
This church, which probably evolved from a branch meeting house built nearby in 1770 by First Lynches Creek Church, was constituted in 1789; Joshua Palmer became minister in the same year. The church held early meetings at Lower Fork of Lynches Creek, Boggy Swamp and Witherinton's Mill. By 1798, the church was located here.

Gum Branch Church (REVERSE)
In 1797, David Kelly was deacon and Cornelius Keith was clerk of Lower Fork of Lynches Creek Church. Originally in the Charleston Association and later the Moriah Association, the church joined the Welsh Neck Association in 1837. The name was changed to Gum Branch in 1844, and the present sanctuary was completed in 1955. *Erected by The Congregation, 1989*
GPS Coordinates: 34° 22.952' N, 80° 11.125' W

16–18 Edmund H. Deas

2nd block of Ave. E, off South Main St., Darlington

After moving to Darlington County in the 1870s, Edmund H. Deas served as county chairman of the Republican Party for a number of years and was a delegate to four national conventions. A black candidate for Congress in 1884 and 1890, Deas was Deputy Collector of Internal Revenue in S. C., 1889–94 and 1897–1901. This house was his residence at his death in 1915. *Erected by Darlington County Bicentennial Committee for Ethnic Participation, 1977*
GPS Coordinates: 34° 17.727' N, 79° 51.751' W

16–19 Wilson Crossroads /Dr. Peter A. Wilson

Intersection of Timmonsville Hwy. (S.C. Hwy. 340) & Hoffmeyer Rd. (S.C. Hwy. 19), about 4 mi. S of Darlington

Wilson Crossroads (FRONT)
At this point the Camden-Mars Bluff road intersected the road to Darlington on property granted to the Reverend John Wilson (1790–1869) by the state of South Carolina in 1837. Wilson, a North Carolinian, settled here, and after his death his grandson, Dr. Peter A. Wilson, lived on a portion of the land and practiced medicine.

Dr. Peter A. Wilson (REVERSE)
Peter Wilson (1846–1913) was born in Darlington County and served in the Confederate Army. He graduated from Washington University School of Medicine in Maryland (1869) and upon the death of his grandfather, the Reverend John Wilson, settled near here and practiced medicine. Dr. Wilson is buried in High Hills Baptist Church Cemetery, about one mile north of here. *Erected by The Dr. Henry Woodward Chapter of the S.C. State Society, Daughters of the American Colonists, 1979*
GPS Coordinates: 34° 13.405' N, 79° 53.851' W

16–20 William Andrew Dowling

E. Seven Pines St. (S.C. Hwy. 19) and S. Center Rd., about 1.5 mi. W of Dubose Crossroads and about 4 mi. E of Oats, SW of Darlington

Born in Darlington County in 1859, William Dowling was a descendant of Robert Dowling, who had settled in S.C. in the Parish of St. David by 1773. William served as a member of the South Carolina House of Representatives, 1899–1900, and was Darlington County Supervisor when the 1902–1903 courthouse was built. Dowling's home stood about one-half mile east of here. *Erected by The Dr. Henry Woodward Chapter of the S.C. State Society, Daughters of American Colonists, 1979*
GPS Coordinates: 34° 16.053' N, 80° 0.915' W

16–21 Zachariah W. Wines

Cheraw St., Society Hill

Black merchant and educator Zachariah Wines, born 1847 in Society Hill, represented Darlington County in the S.C. House 1876–78 and was commissioned Captain in the National Guard by Gov. Wade Hampton in 1877.

He taught at nearby Waddell School and later served as Society Hill Postmaster, 1897–1904. He died in 1920 and is buried about ⅓ mile northeast. *Erected by Darlington County Bicentennial Committee for Ethnic Participation, 1979*
GPS Coordinates: 34° 30.454' N, 79° 51.065' W

16–22 Darlington County/ Darlington County Courthouse

Darlington County Courthouse, 1 Public Square, Darlington

Darlington County (FRONT)
This area became part of St. David's Parish in 1768, Cheraws District in 1769, and then Darlington County on March 12, 1785. In 1800 Darlington became a circuit court district, and again a county in 1868. Extensive territory was lost in 1888 and 1902 with the creation of new counties.
Darlington County Courthouse (REVERSE)
The first courthouse at this site was destroyed by fire March 19, 1806. A later building, thought to have been designed by architect Robert Mills, burned in 1866 and in 1873 was rebuillt. The subsequent courthouse, built 1903–1904, was in use until 1964 when the present structure was completed. *Erected by Darlington County Bicentennial Commission, 1985*
GPS Coordinates: 34° 18.19' N, 79° 52.279' W

16–23 John L. Hart/John Hart House

E. Home Ave., just E of N. 5th St., in front of First Baptist Church, 104 E. Home Ave., Hartsville

John L. Hart (FRONT)
In 1845, John Lide Hart (1825–1864) bought a 491-acre plantation here. Along what is now Home Avenue, he built a carriage factory, a store, a steam-powered sawmill and grist-mill, and houses for himself and his workers. Hart also donated land for the First Baptist Church, which he helped establish. The property here left his ownership in 1854. Hart, a Confederate lieutenant, died in action near Petersburg, Virginia.
John Hart House (REVERSE)

This example of regional vernacular architecture of the mid-19th century is the last antebellum structure known to remain on the site of John Hart's plantation and carriage factory. Many of Hartsville's leading citizens have owned or lived in the house since it left Hart's ownership in 1854. In 1981, the house was acquired by the Hartsville Heritage Foundation. *Erected by Hartsville Heritage Foundation, 1986*
GPS Coordinates: 34° 22.602' N, 80° 4.427' W

16–24 Wesley Chapel

Intersection of Wesley Chapel Rd. (S.C. Sec. Rd. 16–170) and Indian Branch Rd. (S.C. Sec. Rd. 16–28) about 1.3 mi. SE of Lydia

Said to be Darlington County's oldest Methodist church, Wesley Chapel, thought to be founded in 1789, was the site of early camp meetings. By 1802, the church was known as Gully Meetinghouse and was located about 1 ½ miles N. The site here was obtained from Jesse & John Clements in 1832; the church renamed Wesley Chapel in 1834; and the present sanctuary built in 1908. *Erected by The Congregation, 1989*
GPS Coordinates: 34° 16.407' N, 80° 5.735' W

16–25 Lawrence Faulkner/Simon Brown

Main St. (U.S. Hwy. 15/401), at its intersection with U.S. Hwy. 52, Society Hill

Lawrence Faulkner (FRONT)
Born ca. 1840 and a resident of Darlington County by 1871, Lawrence Faulkner was a black school teacher, later merchant, and Society Hill's postmaster from 1877 to 1889. A trustee of nearby Union Baptist Church, Faulkner died in 1898. His store and dwelling were located on this site.
Simon Brown (REVERSE)
A former slave from Virginia, Brown lived in Society Hill around 1900 and for years was employed by Lawrence Faulkner's widow to work on her farm. His small house was adjacent to the Faulkner house on this site. A gifted story-teller of black folk tales, Brown's allegories were posthumously recorded by the

Smithsonian Institution. *Erected by Darlington County Historical Commission, 1989*
GPS Coordinates: 34° 30.708' N, 79° 51.096' W

16–26 Society Hill Library Society

Academy St., just off Main St. (U.S. Hwy. 15/401), Society Hill

(FRONT) On June 5, 1822, twelve men paid $20 each to purchase books for a library. These men were J. J. Evans; David and Elias Gregg; D. R. W., J. K. and T. E. McIver; Thomas Smith; Alexander Sparks; D. R. and J. N. Williams; J. F. Wilson; and J. D. Witherspoon. On December 7, 1822 the men formed the Society Hill Library Society.
(REVERSE) This society was incorporated Dec. 20, 1823 and by 1826 was located in a structure about 900 ft. N. on land given by John D. Witherspoon. Elias Gregg is thought to have been the first librarian, serving until 1844. The library building was moved from its original site on Main St. to the St. David's Academy lot here about 1932. It was taken into the county library system in 1971. *Erected by South Carolina Society of Colonial Dames XVII Century, 1990*
GPS Coordinates: 34° 30.545' N, 79° 51.292' W

16–27 James Lide Coker

E. Home Ave. at S. 4th St., Hartsville

(FRONT) James L. Coker (1837–1918) came here from Society Hill ca. 1858 as a planter. While serving in the Civil War as a captain in Co. E, 6th Regiment S.C. Volunteers, he was seriously wounded. Promoted to major in 1864, he was a member of the S.C. House 1865–66. In 1865 he founded J. L. Coker & Co. and was a founder of the Bank of Darlington (1881); Darlington Manufacturing [. . .]
(REVERSE) [. . .] Co. (1881); Hartsville Railroad (1884); Carolina Fiber (1890) and Southern Novelty (1899), both now Sonoco; Hartsville Oil Mill (1900); Hartsville Cotton Mill (1900); Coker's Pedigreed Seed Co. (1902); and the Bank of Hartsville (1903). Major Coker's generosity resulted in the founding of Coker College in 1908. His home, which burned in 1922, was located here. *Erected by Hartsville Heritage Foundation, 1991*
GPS Coordinates: 34° 22.667' N, 80° 4.252' W

16–28 David Robert Coker 1870–1938

E. Home Ave. between 3rd St. and S. 4th St., on the Coker College campus, Hartsville

Known world-wide for developing new varieties and for perfecting superior strains of agricultural crops (including cotton), Coker, for years was pres. Pedigreed Seed Co., chartered 1918. He was intendant (mayor) of Hartsville 1900–1901; member National Agricultural Advisory Commission; trustee of University S.C. and Coker College. His 1916 home here is now part of Coker College. *Erected by Hartsville Centennial Commission, 1992*
GPS Coordinates: 34° 22.65' N, 80° 4.268' W

16–29 Carolina Fiber Co./Sonoco Products Company

E. Home Ave. at 3rd St., Hartsville

Carolina Fiber Co. (FRONT)
One of the first methods for producing paper from native pine wood pulp was developed by J. L. Coker, Jr. As a result, he with Maj. J. L. Coker and C. J. Woodruff formed the Carolina Fiber Company, March 20, 1890, to manufacture and market wood pulp and paper. Their mill was on nearby Black Creek. In 1941 the entire operation merged with adjacent Sonoco Products Company.
Sonoco Products Company (REVERSE)
This enterprise was chartered as Southern Novelty Company in 1899; first directors were: Maj. J. L. Coker, J. L. Coker Jr., D. R. Coker, J. J. Lawton, and W. F. Smith. The name was changed to Sonoco Products Company in 1923. Today Sonoco is a leading global manufacturer of packaging products for major industries and employs approximately 16,000 people in 22 countries. *Erected by Hartsville Centennial Commission, 1993*
GPS Coordinates: 34° 22.752' N, 80° 4.037' W

16–30 Trinity Church

Corner of N. Main St. (U.S. Hwy. 15/401) and Burns St., Society Hill

This Episcopal church, located about 800 ft. N., was incorporated 1833. Early members associated with the church are said to have been from the Dewitt, Edwards, Evans, Hanford,

Hawes, McCollough, Williams and Witherspoon families. In 1834 the present structure was consecrated by Bishop Nathaniel Bowen. After many years, the church became inactive and was officially listed as dormant 1931. The building is now maintained by private benefactors. *Erected by Pee Dee Committee, National Society of Colonial Dames of America in the State of South Carolina, 1993*
GPS Coordinates: 34° 30.662' N, 79° 51.153' W

16–31 Eastern Carolina Silver Company

Intersection of E. Home Ave. & N. 2nd St., Hartsville

This silver co., chartered March 5, 1907, manufactured and sold coffee and tea sets, bread trays, bowls, candelabra, and cups. J. L. Coker served as pres., W. F. Smith as vice pres., and C. W. Coker as sec. & treas. By 1908 the company had begun to manufacture classically-designed quadruple plate, some ornamented with cotton blossom motifs. The enterprise, located 3 blocks NE, dissolved Nov. 25, 1909. *Erected by Hartsville Centennial Commission, 1994*
GPS Coordinates: 34° 22.75' N, 80° 4.019' W

16–32 Welsh Neck High School/ Coker College

Facing Coker College property in front of Allston House, E. Home Ave., Hartsville

Welsh Neck High School (FRONT)
The Welsh Neck Baptist Association initiated this institution as a coeducational boarding school. It opened Sept. 17, 1894, through the generosity of Maj. James Lide Coker, Civil War veteran, local industrialist, and the school's first chairman of the board of trustees. Enrollment peaked at 267 in 1902. When the 1907 public high school act reduced the need for this school, it became a four-year college for women.
Coker College (REVERSE)
The trustees of Welsh Neck High School converted their institution into a non-sectarian Baptist college. It opened Sept. 30, 1908, as "Coker College for Women, founded by James L. Coker." Baptist control ended in

1944, and in 1969, the college became coeducational. The Governor's school for Science and Mathematics opened on the campus in 1988. Throughout its history, Coker has emphasized liberal arts. *Erected by the Hartsville Centennial Commission, 1995*
GPS Coordinates: 34° 22.69' N, 80° 4.158' W

16–33 Laurie M. Lawson

Intersection of E. Seven Pines St. (S.C. Sec. Rd. 16–19) and S.C. Sec. Rd. 16–360, about 1.8 mi. E of Oats

Birthplace of L. M. Lawson (1873–1943), attorney, farmer, Methodist layman. Served in S.C. House 1905–10, S.C. Senate 1911–14, Pres. Darlington Agricultural Soc. 1938–39. *Erected by Darlington County Historical Commission, 1995*
GPS Coordinates: 34° 15.805' N, 80° 2.949' W

16–34 First Baptist Church

104 E. Home Ave., Hartsville

(FRONT) Members of New Providence and Gum Branch Baptist churches under John L. Hart's leadership began Hartsville Baptist, the first church in town, 16 November 1850. A union Sunday school met on the site as early as July 1849. John L. Hart donated land on which the congregation built a sanctuary in 1851. Rev. J. W. Burn served as first pastor for many years. The church joined Welsh Neck Association in 1851, and the S.C. General [. . .]
(REVERSE) [. . .] Assembly chartered the congregation in 1853. By 1906 name changed to First Baptist Church. Dr. E. V. Baldy, pastor in 1909, served as first president of Coker College. New congregations established by this church are: Fourth Street 1906; Eastside (now Emmanuel) 1926; Lakeview 1944; South Hartsville 1951; West Hartsville 1952; and North Hartsville 1959. The congregation completed the present sanctuary 1964. *Erected by Hartsville Centennial Commission, 1995*
GPS Coordinates: 34° 22.592' N, 80° 4.448' W

16–35 Butler School

6th St., Hartsville

Butler School, located on this site since 1921, was the second public school to serve Hartsville's black community and operated for over sixty years. Known as the Darlington Co. Training School until 1939, it was renamed for Rev. Henry H. Butler, its principal 1909–1946. The first building on this site burned in 1961; extant buildings date from 1936 to the mid-1960s. Butler School was a junior high and high school when it closed in 1982. *Erected by Hartsville Centennial Commission, 1996*
GPS Coordinates: 34° 21.539' N, 80° 4.207' W

16–36 Society Hill Presbyterian Church

3/10 mi. N of the church, Main St. (U.S. Hwy. 15/401) at its intersection with Pressley Ave., Society Hill

(FRONT) Located 3/10 mi. north. Was organized August 12, 1891 with 17 charter members, by a commission of the Pee Dee Presbytery under Revs. J. G. Law, J. G. Richards, and W. B. Corbett. Elders H. A. Womack and J. S. McCall and deacon L. M. Crosswell were appointed church officers. Services were held in the school until the sanctuary was built 1892–93; a manse was built 1922. Rev. J. P. Marion, the first full-time minister, served 1892–1902.
(REVERSE) For several years in the early twentieth century the church also sponsored seminary students preaching at as many as six mission stations in the Pee Dee region without financial aid from the Presbytery. Society Hill Presbyterian Church is in the Welsh Neck-Long Bluff-Society Hill Historic District, listed in the National Register of Historic Places in 1974. *Erected by the Congregation, 1996*
GPS Coordinates: 34° 30.543' N, 79° 51.302' W

16–37 Darlington Raceway

At the NMPA Stock Car Hall of Fame/Joe Weatherly Museum, Darlington Raceway, S.C. Hwy. 151/34 West, 2 mi. W of Darlington

(FRONT) Darlington Raceway, the first superspeedway in NASCAR history, was constructed in 1950 by Harold Brasington, a local race promoter who saw an asphalt-paved track as an advance over the standard dirt tracks and wanted a 500-mile stock car race to rival the Indianapolis 500. On September 4, 1950, the new mile-and-a quarter raceway hosted the first Southern 500, a 400-lap race in which 75 cars raced at top speeds of 80 m.p.h.
(REVERSE) The egg-shaped track at Darlington quickly gained a reputation as "the track too tough to tame" and the Southern 500 became one of racing's most important events. The Plymouth which Johnny Mantz drove to win the first race is one of several historic cars on display with other racing memorabilia at the NMPA Stock Car Hall of Fame/Joe Weatherly Museum, which opened here in 1965 to honor the pioneers of NASCAR. *Erected by Darlington Raceway, 1997*
GPS Coordinates: 34° 17.844' N, 79° 54.296' W

16–38 First Baptist Church

246 S. Main St., Darlington

(FRONT) Established in 1831 as Darlington Baptist Church of Christ, with Rev. W. Q. Beattie as its first minister; joined the Welsh Neck Association in 1832. The first sanctuary, built in 1830 just before the church was formally organized, was replaced in 1859 by a second building. During the Civil War the church offered its bell to be melted down to cast cannon for the Confederacy.
(REVERSE) This church, which has licensed or ordained 14 clergymen since 1831, was renamed First Baptist Church of Darlington in 1912; the present brick sanctuary was dedicated that December. The Hardin Building was built in 1924; the Jones Building in 1956, the Illy McFall Memorial Building in 1975, and the E. S. Howle Fellowship Hall in 1983. Additional renovations were completed in 1997. *Erected by the Congregation, 1998*
GPS Coordinates: 34° 18.002' N, 79° 52.145' W

16–39 Japonica Hall/Maj. J. J. Lucas

S. Main St. (U.S. Hwy. 15/401), near its junction
with St. David's St., Society Hill

Japonica Hall (FRONT)

This house, built in 1896–97 and designed in
the Beaux Arts style by noted S.C. architect
Charles Coker Wilson, was the home of Maj.
James Jonathan Lucas (1831–1914). An earlier
house here, which burned in 1892, had been
the home of Dr. Thomas Smith (d. 1875), who
married the widow of Judge Samuel Wilds.
Lucas served Charleston District as a state
representative 1856–1862.

Maj. J. J. Lucas (REVERSE)

In 1862, Lucas, a Citadel graduate, organized
and became major of Lucas' Battalion of
Heavy Artillery, which spent most of the Civil
War on James Island near Charleston. Maj.
Lucas moved to Society Hill in 1865, and later
served as a director of the Cheraw & Darling-
ton RR and Atlantic Coast Line RR. Japonica
Hall was listed in the National Register of His-
toric Places in 1989. *Erected by the Darlington
County Historical Commission, 1999*
GPS Coordinates: 34° 30.338' N, 79° 51.508' W

16–40 Williamson's Bridge

S. Charleston Rd. (S.C. Sec. Rd. 16-35), at Williamson's Bridge over Black Creek, SE of Darlington

Williamson's Bridge was built over Black
Creek by 1771. In 1780 a part of Brig. Gen.
Francis Marion's S.C. militia brigade—the
"Pee Dee Regiment" or "Cheraws Militia"
under Lt. Col. Lamuel Benton (1754–1818)—
clashed with Loyalists here. Benton's militiamen forced the Tories from the bridge,
pursued them for some distance, and finally
routed them in hand-to-hand combat. *Erected
by the Darlington County Historical Commission, 2000*
GPS Coordinates: 34° 16.219' N, 79° 47.201' W

16–41 Caleb Coker House

S. Main St. (U.S. Hwy. 15/401) at Pressley Ave.,
Society Hill

This house, built ca. 1832, was the home of
Caleb Coker (1802–1869) and the birthplace
of his son Maj. James Lide Coker (1837–1918),
Confederate officer, industrialist, and founder
of Coker College. Caleb Coker, a merchant,
was also a director of the Cheraw & Darlington RR, librarian of the Society Hill Library
Society, and a charter member of the Darlington Agricultural Society. *Erected by the Darlington County Historical Commission, 2000*
GPS Coordinates: 34° 30.538' N, 79° 51.286' W

16–42 Hartsville Oil Mill

Hartsville Oil Mill Office, 201 S. Fifth St., (U.S.
Hwy. 15), Hartsville

(FRONT) The Hartsville Oil Mill, founded in
1900 by J. L. Coker, D. R. Coker, and J. J. Lawton, stood here until 1993. A cotton oil mill,
it crushed cottonseed to produce cooking oil;
meal and cake for feed and fertilizer; and lint
for stuffing and explosives. It was chartered in
1909 with Lawton as president, treasurer, and
general manager; Albert Jordan as secretary;
and C. G. Timberlake as superintendent.

(REVERSE) The mill office, still standing at this
site, was built in 1915. Under the leadership of
president E. H. Lawton, Sr., the mill was converted from hydraulic presses to screw presses
in 1954. The mill began extracting oil and
meal from soybeans by 1957. The company
sold the Hartsville mill in 1981 and moved its
headquarters to Darlington. In 2000 it was
the last cotton oil mill still operating in S.C.
Erected by the Hartsville Museum, 2000
GPS Coordinates: 34° 22.37' N, 80° 4.335' W

16–43 Henry "Dad" Brown

Corner of S. Gov. Williams Hwy. (U.S. Hwy. 52) &
Brockington Rd., Darlington

(FRONT) Henry "Dad" Brown (1830–1907), a
black veteran of the Mexican, Civil, and Spanish-American Wars, is buried 75' N with his
wife Laura. Variously said to have been born
free or born as a slave who purchased his and
Laura's freedom, he was born near Camden.
Brown, a brickmason, joined the Confederate
army in May 1861 as a drummer in the "Darlington Grays," Co. F, 8th S.C. Infantry.

(REVERSE) Brown enlisted as a drummer in Co.
H, 21st S.C. Infantry in July 1861 and served
for the rest of the war. He "captured" a pair
of Union drumsticks in battle. He was also a

member of the "Darlington Guards" 1878–1907. Described as "a man of rare true worth" at his death in 1907, Brown was honored shortly afterwards by Darlington citizens who erected the monument nearby. *Erected by the City of Darlington Historical Landmarks Commission, 2000*
GPS Coordinates: 34° 17.364' N, 79° 52.965' W

16–44 Fair Hope Presbyterian Church

E. Lynches River Rd., Carters Crossroads vicinity, S of Lamar

This church was organized in 1872 by Harmony Presbytery with Capt. Joseph Commander (1800–1883) as its first elder. This sanctuary, built on land donated by Commander, was moved here and remodeled about 1909. Fair Hope, a founding member of the Pee Dee Presbytery in 1889, withdrew in 1969 to become an independent church. *Erected by the Darlington County Historical Commission, 2001*
GPS Coordinates: 34° 6.671' N, 80° 4.667'

16–45 Lawrence Reese

Belk Funeral Home, 229 W. Broad St., Darlington

(FRONT) West Broad Street features several late-19th to early-20th century residences designed and built by Lawrence Reese (1865–1915), a native of Marlboro County who came to Darlington as a merchant by 1887. Reese, who had no formal training in architecture, was a self-taught master craftsman and designer. The Belk Funeral Home, at 229 West Broad, was built ca. 1900 as a residence for Abraham Hyman and was Reese's own favorite of the several houses he designed here.
(REVERSE) The West Broad Street Historic District, listed in the National Register of Historic Places in 1988, features 14 houses designed and built by Lawrence Reese between ca. 1890 and ca. 1910, most of them with elaborate Eastlake, Queen Anne, and other Victorian era architectural elements. Reese also designed and built the South Carolina Western Railway Station on Russell Street, built in 1911 and also listed in the National Register

in 1988. Erected by the St. John's Heritage Foundation, 2000
GPS Coordinates: 34° 17.918' N, 79° 52.275' W

16–46 Damascus Methodist Church

E. Home Ave., (S.C. Sec. Rd. 16–10), just E of Hartsville

The church organized as early as 1817 and known as "Wright's Meeting House, Black Creek" was the first Methodist congregation in the area. James D. Wright, an elder who was appointed "Exhorter" in 1826, preached here until his death in 1862. Damascus Methodist Church declined after 1893, when Wesley Methodist Church was founded in Hartsville; it disbanded by 1901. *Erected by the Darlington County Historical Commission, 2001*
GPS Coordinates: 34° 22.932' N, 80° 3.043' W

16–47 Execution of Adam Cusack

Main St. (U.S. Hwy. 15/401), at Bradshaw St., Society Hill

In August or September 1780 Major James Wemyss's 63rd Regiment of Foot marched from Georgetown to Cheraw burning and looting Patriot houses and farms. When Adam Cusack, who ran a ferry over Black Creek, refused to take some British officers across he was arrested. Convicted in an extralegal court martial, he was hanged nearby as his wife and children pleaded with Wemyss for mercy. *Erected by the Darlington County Historical Commission, 2002*
GPS Coordinates: 34° 31.117' N, 79° 50.637' W

16–48 Wilds-Edwards House/ Samuel Hugh Wilds

Edwards Ave., just S of Pearl St., Darlington

Wilds-Edwards House (FRONT)
This Italianate house, designed by J. L. Clickner, was built 1856–57 for planter Samuel H. Wilds (1819–1867). According to tradition Clickner returned in early 1865 as a Union soldier and persuaded his superiors not to burn the house during a raid in the area. In 1870 attorney B. W. Edwards (1824–1890), later a state senator, acquired the house; it

remained in the family until 1999.

Samuel Hugh Wilds (REVERSE)

Samuel H. Wilds was a member of the Darlington Agricultural Society, a colonel in the antebellum militia, and a state representative 1856–57 and again in 1864. He organized the "Wilds Rifles" (later Co. B, 21st S.C. Infantry) at the outbreak of the Civil War as its captain and rose to major by war's end. This house was listed in the National Register of Historic Places in 1988. *Erected by the City of Darlington Historical Landmarks Commission, 2001*

GPS Coordinates: 34° 17.942' N, 79° 52.518' W

16–49 Darlington Memorial Center

Pearl St. just S of its intersection with Edwards Ave., Darlington

This house was built in 1889 by Charles McCullough (1853–1908), who served as town councilman and later as mayor. It was for many years a recreation center for local youth. The Darlington Memorial Center, chartered in 1946 as a memorial to Darlington men who died in World War II, was funded primarily by area civic clubs. It was acquired by the city of Darlington in 1950. *Erected by the Darlington Landmarks Commission, 2002*

GPS Coordinates: 34° 18.006' N, 79° 52.583' W

16–50 Andrew Hunter

Intersection of E. McIver Rd. (S.C. Sec. Rd. 16–179/Old Darlington Hwy.) and Pisgah Rd. (S.C. Sec. Rd. 16–112), SE of Darlington

(FRONT) Andrew Hunter (d. 1823), planter, state representative, and county official, is buried in the Hunter family cemetery about 400 ft. south. During the American Revolution he ran a grist mill several miles south on High Hill Creek, supplying meal and corn to the Patriots in the Southern Department. He also served as a scout in the state militia under Gen. Francis Marion.

(REVERSE) In 1782 Hunter, scouting in N.C., was captured by Col. David Fanning, a prominent Loyalist. He escaped on Fanning's horse, taking his saddle, holsters, pistols, and papers. After the war he represented St. David's Parish (1787–88) and Darlington County (1796–97)

in the S.C. House of Representatives and served on commissions for roads, navigation, and a new courthouse and jail. *Erected by the Darlington County Historical Commission, 2002*

GPS Coordinates: 34° 15.615' N, 79° 47.834' W

16–51 "Yankee Hill"

N. Main St. (U.S. Hwy. 52) just N of Evangeline Dr., Darlington

(FRONT) In the summer of 1865, just after the end of the Civil War, Federal troops began their occupation of many cities and towns in S.C. Units in Darlington in 1865–66 included the 15th Maine Infantry, 29th Maine Veteran Volunteers, 1st Maine Battalion, and 30th Massachusetts Veteran Volunteers. They camped on the grounds of the nearby St. John's Academy and used it as a hospital.

(REVERSE) Four Federal privates (Patrick Gately and Ira J. Newhall of the 15th Maine and George Kinney and John Maloney of the 29th Maine) who died of disease while stationed in Darlington in 1865–66 were originally buried nearby. This area was called "Yankee Hill" for many years. Their remains were later removed and reburied at Florence National Cemetery. *Erected by the Darlington County Historical Commission, 2002*

GPS Coordinates: 34° 18.392' N, 79° 52.417' W

16–52 Julius A. Dargan House

488 Pearl St., Darlington

(FRONT) This house was built in 1856 for Julius A. Dargan (1815–1861). Built on land acquired from Jesse H. Lide in 1839, the house is a fine example of the Greek Revival style. Dargan briefly taught school and practiced law with his brother G. W. Dargan for many years; he was also a state representative 1850–52, delegate to the Secession Convention, and signer of the Ordinance of Secession.

(REVERSE) After Dargan's death in 1861 the house passed to several owners, most notably A. G. Kollock (1862–1930), editor of the Darlington News, and J. C. Stone (1900–1975), manager of the Darlington Coca-Cola Bottling Company. The house was listed in the

National Register of Historic Places in 1988. It was acquired by the City of Darlington in 1999 and restored by the city in 2003. *Erected by the Darlington Landmarks Commission, 2004*
GPS Coordinates: 34° 17.988' N, 79° 52.614' W

16–53 Lydia Rural Fire Dept.

W. Lydia Hwy. (U.S. Hwy. 15), Lydia

The Lydia Rural Fire Department, the first rural fire department in this county, was organized in 1954 after fires destroyed three houses in less than a month. Its organizers met at the store and gas station owned by E. Gay Bass (1913–1997). By mid-1955 the department had received a charter, built a fire station, and bought two trucks. Bass, its first fire chief, served 23 years. *Erected by the Lydia Rural Fire Department, 2005*
GPS Coordinates: 34° 17.346' N, 80° 6.46' W

16–54 Darlington Memorial Cemetery

At the entrance to the cemetery, Ave. D and Friendship St., Darlington

(FRONT) This cemetery, established in 1890, was originally a five-acre tract when it was laid out as the cemetery for the nearby Macedonia Baptist Church. The first African American cemetery in Darlington, it includes about 1,900 graves dating from the late 19th century to the present. In 1946 Bethel A.M.E. Church and St. James Methodist Church, both nearby, established their own cemeteries here as well.
(REVERSE) Among the prominent persons buried here are Rev. Isaac Brockenton (1829–1908), the founding pastor of Macedonia Baptist Church; Edmund H. Deas (1855–1915), prominent Darlington County politician; and Lawrence Reese (1864–1915), a self-taught designer and master craftsman who designed and built several houses on West Broad Street. This cemetery was listed in the National Register of Historic Places in 2005. *Erected by the Darlington Memorial Cemetery Association, 2006*
GPS Coordinates: 34° 18.084' N, 79° 51.38' W

16–55 John L. Hart House

Near the intersection of Society Hill Rd. (S.C. Sec. Rd. 16–133) and N. Springville Rd. (S.C. Sec. Rd.16–228), Springville, NE of Darlington

(FRONT) This house was built ca. 1856 for John Lide Hart (1825–1864), merchant and Confederate officer. Hart, who lived in Hartsville, named for his father Thomas E. Hart, founded a carriage and harness factory there in 1851. In 1853 he and partner William Shy founded Hart & Shy, a carriage factory in Darlington. Debts forced Hart to sell out and move here to Springville in 1855–56.
(REVERSE) Hart was a member of the Darlington District Agricultural Society and a captain in the antebellum militia. In 1861 he joined the Confederate army as a sergeant in the "Wilds Rifles," later Co. B, 21st S.C. Infantry. Hart, later promoted to lieutenant, was killed at Drewry's Bluff, Va., May 16, 1864. This house was listed in the National Register of Historic Places in 1985. *Erected by the Darlington County Historical Commission, 2007*
GPS Coordinates: 34° 20.741' N, 79° 51.141' W

16–56 John Westfield Lide House

Near the intersection of Society Hill Rd. (S.C. Sec. Rd. 16–133) & S.C. Sec. Rd. 16–29, Springville, NE of Darlington

(FRONT) This Greek Revival house was built ca. 1840 for John Westfield Lide (1794–1858), planter and state representative. Lide, the son of Maj. Robert Lide and Mary Westfield Holloway Lide, was a member of the third graduating class at S.C. College (now the University of S.C) in 1809. He returned to Darlington District, became a planter, and expanded his holdings in the area.
(REVERSE) Lide represented Darlington District in the S.C. House of Representatives 1822–25 and was later commissioner of public buildings and commissioner to approve public securities. This house features an unusual wraparound rain porch as well as Gothic Revival and Italianate architectural elements. It was listed in the National Register of Historic Places in 1985. *Erected by the Darlington County Historical Commission, 2008*
GPS Coordinates: 34° 21.292' N, 79° 50.869' W

16–57 Mont Clare Community Center

1632 Mont Clare Rd., Darlington

(FRONT) This community center, the first in Darlington County, was built in 1933 by area citizens. The land was donated by E. M. Williamson of Mont Clare Plantation, the cypress logs and other lumber were cut at T. C. Coxe's Skufful Plantation, and the sandstone for the foundation was quarried at Skufful Plantation. (REVERSE) The Mont Clare Mission was a nondenominational Sunday School and worship service organized in 1913 at nearby Mont Clare School. It met here from 1933 until Mont Clare Baptist Church was formally founded in 1960. This center, described as a "lovely log building," has hosted church, school, and other events. *Erected by the Welsh Tract Historic Properties Association, 2008*

GPS Coordinates: 34° 23.828' N, 79° 49.023' W

16–58 Society Hill Depot

W. Depot St. at its intersection with N. Main St. (U.S. Hwy. 15/401), Society Hill

(FRONT) This depot, built shortly after the Civil War, features a distinctive architectural design favored by the Cheraw & Darlington Railroad during its history as an independent line. The C & D, chartered in 1849, ran 40 miles between Cheraw and present-day Florence and began service in 1855. The first combined passenger and freight depot in Society Hill was built nearby on West Depot St. (REVERSE) Federal troops burned the original depot, a short distance north, in March 1865. This depot, constructed on the same plans, was built there by 1866. The Cheraw & Darlington RR was acquired by the Atlantic Coast Line RR in 1898. This was a freight and passenger depot until the 1940s and a freight depot until 1973. Now owned by the Town of Society Hill, it was moved here in 2002. *Erected by the Darlington County Historical Commission, 2008*

GPS Coordinates: 34° 31.115' N, 79° 50.641' W

16–59 Grove Hill Cemetery

Near the cemetery entrance on S. Warley St., just NW of its intersection with E. Broad St., Darlington

Grove Hill Cemetery, the first public cemetery in Darlington, was chartered in 1889. Citizens founded it "on account of the health of our town but also on account of the great scarcity of space in the church cemeteries." The original 26-acre tract on Swift Creek was later expanded, doubling the burial space. In 1896 a half-acre tract was designated as "Darlington Hebrew Cemetery." *Erected by the Grove Hill Cemetery Company, 2009*

GPS Coordinates: 34° 18.265' N, 79° 51.576' W

16–60 Darlington County Jail

204 Hewitt St., Darlington

(FRONT) This building, a New Deal project of Franklin D. Roosevelt's Public Works Administration (PWA), was built in 1937 at a cost of $60,000. Called "one of the most modern jails in the South," it was designed by Rock Hill architect Alfred D. Gilchrist (d. 1944). Its second floor featured separate cell blocks for black and white males and separate cells for black and white females. (REVERSE) The office, kitchen, and jailer's quarters were on the first floor; hospital and juvenile cells were on the third floor; and cells for minor offenders were in the basement. The jail closed in 1976. Since 1984 it has been the headquarters of the Darlington County Historical Commission. The commission, created in 1965 to maintain a county archives and research repository, also marks area historic sites. *Erected by the Darlington County Historical Commission, 2009*

GPS Coordinates: 34° 18.283' N, 79° 52.292' W

16–61 Mount Pleasant Baptist Church/Lowther's Hill Cemetery

Near intersection of Cashua Ferry Rd. (S.C. Hwy. 34) & Georgetown Rd., Mechanicsville vicinity

Mount Pleasant Baptist Church (FRONT) Mount Pleasant Baptist Church, organized by 1785, first met in a nearby school. It built a sanctuary here in 1791; that year Cashaway

Baptist Church merged with it. In 1818 the congregation moved about 2 mi. S to Mechanicsville, built a new sanctuary there, and was renamed Mechanicsville Baptist Church.

Lowther's Hill Cemetary (REVERSE)
This cemetery was established ca. 1789, after Mount Pleasant Baptist Church relocated here; burials continued until 1956. Prominent area leaders buried here include Maj. Robert Lide (1734–1802), an officer under Gen. Francis Marion; Capt. Thomas E. Hart (1796–1842), for whom Hartsville was named, and planter and state representative John Westfield Lide (1794–1858). *Erected by the Darlington County Historical Commission, 2010*
GPS Coordinates: 34° 21.181' N, 79° 44.469' W

16–63 Henry C. Burn House

163 South Main St., Society Hill

(FRONT) Henry C. Burn (1839–1912), state representative and Darlington County public servant, lived here from 1882 until his death. Burn, born in Chesterfield District, was educated at St. David's Academy in Society Hill, then at Furman University, before joining the Confederate army. He came back to S.C. and farmed briefly in Chesterfield District but returned to Society Hill by 1875.
(REVERSE) Burn represented Darlington District in the S.C. House 1890–92. He was later postmaster of Society Hill 1893–1900, a delegate to the S.C. Constitutional Convention of 1895, and Darlington County Superintendent of Education 1900–08. This house, built as a four-room cottage, was later enlarged by Burn's son Frank. Henry C. Burn also operated a carpenter's shop and a blacksmith shop on the property. *Erected by the Darlington County Historical Commission, 2010*
GPS Coordinates: 34° 30.683' N, 79° 51.125' W

16–64 Mt. Zion Baptist Church

3208 N. Governor Williams Hwy., Dovesville vicinity

(FRONT) This church, founded in 1869, was organized by 36 black members of nearby Black Creek Baptist Church, who received letters of dismissal to form their own congregation. Rev. William Hart, its first minister, served

until his death in 1872. He was succeeded by his son, Rev. Alfred Hart, who served here 1872–79, after representing Darlington County in the S.C. House 1870–72.
(REVERSE) The church held its first services in a brush arbor on this site, which its trustees bought from James C. McCallman in 1872. After worshipping under a frame shelter for several years, Mt. Zion built its first permanent sanctuary, a frame building, in 1890. The congregation grew enough to build a second frame church in 1908. The present brick sanctuary was dedicated in 1979. *Erected by the Darlington County Historical Commission, 2011*
GPS Coordinates: 34° 23.871' N, 79° 54.196' W

16–65 Coker's Pedigreed Seed Company/Coker Experimental Farms

S. 4th St. (S.C. Hwy. 151), just NW of its intersection with U.S. Hwy. 15, Hartsville

Coker's Pedigreed Seed Company (FRONT)
This company, incorporated in 1914 by David R. Coker (1870–1938), grew out of his pioneering work breeding plants and developing high-quality seeds. At first focusing on helping Southern farmers grow superior upland cotton, it later had great success with corn, wheat, oats, soybeans, tobacco, and other crops.

Coker Experimental Farms (REVERSE)
The trademark of the company was a red heart with the motto "Blood Will Tell." Coker Experimental Farms, begun on a 220-acre tract nearby, was designated a National Historic Landmark (NHL) in 1964 and included several thousand acres when it closed in 1988. The Coker Farms NHL Foundation was created in 1998 to preserve and interpret 35 acres of the historic farm complex. *Erected by the Coker Farms National Historic Landmark Foundation, 2010*
GPS Coordinates: 34° 21.49' N, 80° 3.564' W

16–66 John Wesley Methodist Church

304 E. Main St., Lamar

(FRONT) This church, founded about 1865, is the first African-American church in Lamar and was long known as Lamar Colored Methodist Episcopal Church. It was organized by Rev. John Boston, a former slave who was its first minister, serving here 1865–67. Boston, who also represented Darlington Co. in the S.C. House 1868–70 and 1872–74, is buried in the church cemetery. The old Boston Township was named for him.

(REVERSE) The church held its first services in a brush arbor, but completed a frame sanctuary here about 1866. That church burned in 1906 and was replaced later that year by the present frame sanctuary, a Gothic Revival building. In 1916 trustees donated a half-acre for the Lamar Colored School, later Spaulding High School. Electricity replaced gas lights in 1935 and the exterior was covered in brick veneer in the 1950s. *Erected by the Darlington County Historical Commission, 2011*
GPS Coordinates: 34° 9.822' N, 80° 3.647' W

16–67 New Providence Baptist Church

1884 Antioch Rd., Hartsville vicinity

(FRONT) This church, with its origins in meetings held in a brush arbor as early as 1804, was organized into a formal congregation in 1812, with Rev. Charles Williams as its first pastor. Its first permanent church, a log building about 2 mi. NE, was replaced by a "comfortable meeting house" on that site about 1832.

(REVERSE) In 1850, after the congregation voted not to relocate to a site near Hartsville, some members and some from Gum Branch Baptist Church left to found First Baptist Church in Hartsville. The church acquired this 1.5-acre site in 1890 and built the present frame sanctuary in 1891, with several later renovations. The New Providence School nearby taught grades 1–8 from 1902 to 1913. *Erected by the Congregation, 2011*
GPS Coordinates: 34° 25.570' N, 80° 1.910' W

16–68 Flat Creek Baptist Church

1369 Society Hill Rd., Darlington vicinity

(FRONT) This African-American church was founded in 1877, with Rev. Daniel Jesse as its first pastor. It held its first services in a brush arbor, and acquired a site about 2 mi. SE on Flat Creek Rd. in 1881, building a frame sanctuary there. The church, known through the years as Simmons' Flat, Summer's House, the Grove, and Marggie Branch, was renamed Flat Creek Baptist Church by 1927.

(REVERSE) In 1913 Rev. Henry Hannibal Butler (1887–1948), newly ordained, came to Flat Creek Baptist Church as his first pastorate. Butler, principal of Darlington Co. Training School / Butler School in Hartsville (renamed for him in 1939), was later president of the S.C. State Baptist Convention and president of Morris College. The congregation moved here and built the present brick church in 2000. *Erected by the Congregation, 2011*
GPS Coordinates: 34° 21.685' N, 79° 50.504' W

16–69 Bethlehem Methodist Church

2232 Bethlehem Rd., Hartsville vicinity

(FRONT) This church, on this site since 1889, grew out of Sardis Methodist Church, a mission station organized in 1887 with a small frame church on Old Camden Rd. 3 mi. E. When that church burned in 1889, its elders accepted a donation of 4 acres here from David Byrd for "New Sardis Methodist Church." This church was completed and dedicated in 1890 as Bethlehem Methodist Church.

(REVERSE) At first on the Clyde circuit, this church, averaging about 250 members in its early years, became the main church of the Bethlehem Circuit when that circuit was created in 1910. A parsonage built that year, on an acre donated by F. W. Howle, served as the circuit parsonage until 1953. Bethlehem School, across the road from the church, was a rural primary school from 1906 to 1913. *Sponsored by the Darlington County Historical Commission, 2012*
GPS Coordinates: 34° 27.224' N, 79° 59.342' W

16–70 Hartsville Graded School /Mt. Pisgah Nursery School

630 South 6th St., Hartsville

Hartsville Graded School (FRONT)
The first public school for the black children of Hartsville and vicinity operated on this site from about 1900 to 1921. It was renamed Darlington County Training School in 1918. A new school was built on 6th St. south of this site in 1921. Rev. Henry H. Butler (1887–1948) was principal at both sites for a combined 37 years. The 1921 school was renamed Butler School in Butler's honor in 1939.
Mt. Pisgah Nursery School (REVERSE)
Mt. Pisgah Presbyterian Church grew out of a Sunday school started on this site by Rev. T. J. James in 1922. The church was organized that same year, and a new church building was erected nearby in 1926. Rev. James also founded Mt. Pisgah Nursery School, which operated in the old graded school here for many years. Rev. James's family later donated this property to the city for Pride Park, established in 1986. *Sponsored by the South Carolina African American Heritage Commission, 2012*
GPS Coordinates: 34° 21.986' N, 80° 4.336' W

16–71 New Hopewell Baptist Church

3500 New Hopewell Rd., Hartsville vicinity

(FRONT) This church was formally organized soon after the Civil War. It was founded by 20 black members of Antioch Baptist Church, who received letters of dismissal to form their own congregation in 1869. Slaves and free blacks had belonged to Antioch Baptist Church since its organization in 1830.
(REVERSE) This church held its first services in a brush arbor. In 1871 Mrs. Lottie Cosom donated an acre on this site, later expanded to four acres for the church and cemetery. New Hopewell built its first permanent church here in 1886, renovated in 1887 and 1917–18. The present sanctuary was built in 1962. *Sponsored by the Darlington County Historical Commission, 2013*
GPS Coordinates: 34° 26.840' N, 79° 57.159' W

16–72 Swift Creek Baptist Church

413 N. Center Rd., Hartsville vicinity

(FRONT) The earliest record of this church dates to 1789, when it belonged to the Charleston Baptist Association and had 76 members. It took its name from, and built its first and later churches near, Swift Creek. The congregation grew after a revival in 1829 and the church joined the Welsh Neck Baptist Association in 1831. It soon became a central part of this rural community.
(REVERSE) The congregation acquired this site in 1844, during the long pastorate of Rev. William Beck from 1833 to 1876. The historic cemetery here dates from 1878. A large frame church built here in 1903, described by the Baptist Courier as "a model house" when it was dedicated, was replaced by the present brick church in 1950, during the pastorate of Rev. E. B. Bagby, Jr. *Sponsored by the Congregation, 2013*
GPS Coordinates: 34° 26.840' N, 79° 57.159' W

16–73 Rosenwald Consolidated School/Rosenwald High School

508 Church St., Society Hill

Rosenwald Consolidated School (FRONT)
The Julius Rosenwald Consolidated School, built in 1930, was a combined elementary and high school until 1953 and a high school until 1982. It brought in African-American students from three rural schools in and near Society Hill. A brick school built at a cost of $11,150, it was one of almost 500 in S.C. funded in part by the Julius Rosenwald Foundation 1917–1932. Arthur A. Prince was its first principal.
Rosenwald High School (REVERSE)
The school opened with pupils in grades 1–10; grade 11 was added in 1939 and grade 12 in 1948. A frame industrial education building was built in 1936. The school, accredited after World War II, became Rosenwald High School, though it continued to include elementary pupils until 1954, when a new Rosenwald Elementary School was built in Society Hill. The high school closed in 1982. *Sponsored by the Rosenwald School Reunion, 2014*
GPS Coordinates: 34° 30.301' N, 79° 51.101' W

16–74 Jerusalem Baptist Church

6th St. & Laurens Ave., Hartsville

(FRONT) This church, organized soon after the Civil War, is one of the oldest African-American churches in Darlington County. It held its first services a few miles E under a brush arbor on Snake Branch, a creek near E. Carolina Ave. The first permanent church, a log building, was built there. Trustees acquired this site in 1898, built the present church in 1907, and chartered the congregation in 1908. (REVERSE) This church, built in 1907 as a frame building, was described as "a splendid achievement" when it was covered in brick veneer and rededicated in 1939. It had a congregation of more than 350 during the Depression. Rev. Henry H. Butler (1887–1948), pastor from 1932 until his death, was also for many years the principal of the Darlington Co. Training School/Butler School and later president of Morris College. *Sponsored by the Darlington County Historical Commission, 2014*
GPS Coordinates: 34° 22.277' N, 80° 4.438' W

16–75 Round O

1901 Society Hill Road, Darlington

Much of the land in this vicinity was once part of Thomas Smith's Round O Plantation. The name derives from a large Carolina Bay in the area known as "The Round Owe." Round O was birthplace of former S.C. Representative (Dist. 73) and Senator (Dist. 19) Kay Patterson, who was among the first African Americans elected to the S.C. legislature since 1902 when he won election in 1974. *Sponsored by South Carolina African American Heritage Foundation, 2016*
GPS Coordinates: 34° 22.917' N, 79° 50.249' W

16–76 St. John Methodist Church

W. Seven Pines St. near intersection with Tomahawk Rd., Hartsville vic.

(FRONT) The first meetings of what would become St. John Methodist Church took place under a brush arbor. The congregation completed their first permanent sanctuary, a one-room frame structure, in 1867. Having outgrown that building, the members built a larger frame church in 1907. After nearly seventy years of service, that building was replaced by the current sanctuary in 1976. (REVERSE) The St. John Methodist Church Cemetery contains graves from as early as the 1890s and is still in use. The cemetery contains over 600 graves of church members and other African Americans from Hartsville, Darlington, Lamar, and surrounding areas. *Sponsored by St. John United Methodist Church, 2017*
GPS Coordinates: 34° 15.204' N, 80° 4.990' W

16–77 Hartsville Passenger Depot

114 South Fourth St., Hartsville

This passenger depot was built by the Atlantic Coast Line (ACL) Railroad in 1908 and is an example of an early 20th-century passenger depot. It serviced the town until 1940 when the ACL discontinued passenger service to Hartsville. The depot was remodeled in 1948 to house the office of the Chairman of the ACL Board. Former ACL Chairman A. L. M. Wiggins continued to occupy the office until his death in July 1980. *Sponsored by the City of Hartsville, 2017*
GPS Coordinates: 34° 22.474' N, 80° 4.238' W

16–78 Hartsville Colored Cemetery

417 Marion Ave., Hartsville

The cemetery was founded by two mutual aid associations representing Hartsville's African American Community. The first acre was acquired in 1904 by the Hartsville Colored Cem. Association. A second acre was acquired in 1931 by the Mutual Cem. Association. The burials chronicle former slaves and local residents including professionals and veterans who served from the Spanish American War to the Vietnam War. *Sponsored by the City of Hartsville, 2017*
GPS Coordinates: 34° 21.861' N, 80° 4.762' W

16–79 Hartsville Cotton Mill

250 Block of Coker Ave., Hartsville

The mill was chartered in 1900 with a capital stock of $250,000 on 100 acres purchased from J. L. Coker. The mill opened in 1903 with 10,000 spindles and 350 Draper looms. A mill

village with churches, shops, and a Y.M.C.A. was built by the mill. In 1962 ownership transferred to Pacolet Industries, Inc. The mill closed in 1984. Currently the site is home to the Governor's School for Science & Mathematics. *Sponsored by the City of Hartsville, 2018*
GPS Coordinates: 34° 22.402' N, 80° 4.027' W

16–80 St. Joseph's Catholic Church

307 W. Washington St., Hartsville

St. Joseph's began as a missionary parish to serve Hartsville's African American community. Established in 1945, the parish operated a school and convent in addition to the church. By 1953 the school, which served African American students, included grades K-7 and had 90 enrollees. In 1967 the school and convent closed. In 1980 the church merged with St. Mary the Virgin Mother. *Sponsored by the City of Hartsville, 2018*
GPS Coordinates: 34° 21.682' N, 80° 4.460' W

16–81 Mt. Rona Missionary Baptist Church

245 Lumber Rd., Society Hill

Mt. Rona was founded ca. 1903, when the first trustees purchased this site. Early members included the Bacote, Leek, Martin, Brock, Mills, and Moses families. Among the earliest church institutions were the Deacons Board, Senior Choir, and Missionary Society. In 2007, a new sanctuary was built next to the original chapel. *Sponsored by the Congregation, 2019*
GPS Coordinates: 34° 27.265' N, 79° 50.232' W

16–82 Bethel Church

2413 Bethel Rd., Hartsville

Bethel Methodist Church organized ca. 1856 as Jerusalem Church on land said to have been donated by Hardy M. Parrott (1816–1876). Early leaders included the Parrott, House, and DeWitt families. In 1885, Bethel merged with Snow Hill Church and moved west of Flinn's Crossorads under the name New Bethel. The church returned to this site in 1911 and dedicated the new building as Bethel. *Sponsored by the Darlington County Historical Commission, 2019*
GPS Coordinates: 34° 18.568' N, 80° 1.682' W

16–83 Arcade Hotel

W. College Ave., 100 ft. W of N. 5th St. intersection, Hartsville

(FRONT) This building first served as the Arcade Hotel, built in 1913 for $51,000 for J. J. Lawton & Associates. The hotel was designed by Ernest V. Richards and built by contractor J. M. Lawton. It offered a European plan with cold and hot water and a telephone in each of its 43 rooms, some of them with private baths and parlors. Other amenities included a barber shop, fine dining, a sample room, and retail space. The hotel's first manager was William H. McFall.
(REVERSE) For a time, the Arcade Hotel was Hartsville's leading social center. It underwent three major improvements between 1922 and 1988. It closed in 1976 but briefly reopened in 1983. SPC Cooperative Credit Untion bought the building in 1988 and undertook a $1.9 million renovation project, restoring the first floor largely to its 1913 appearance and converting the two upper floors into office space. Listed in the National Register of Historic Places on December 19, 1986. *Sponsored by SPC Credit Union, 2019*
GPS Coordinates: 34° 22.09' N, 80° 4.64' W

Dillon County

17–1 The Meeting House

Bear Swamp Baptist Church, 541 Bear Swamp Rd. (S.C. Sec. Rd. 17–56), Lake View vicinity

On December 22, 1801, one acre on the north side of Bear Swamp was deeded for the use of the Baptist Society. Local tradition says that the meeting house that stood on this tract was built in the 1780s and was used as a camp site by travelers between Fayetteville and Georgetown. In 1831, the Baptist Society was constituted as Bear Swamp church. *Erected by Bear Swamp Baptist Church and The Friday Afternoon Book Club of Lake View, S. C., 1970*
GPS Coordinates: 34° 20.898' N, 79° 8.551' W

17–2 James W. Dillon House Museum

1304 W. Main St., Dillon

This house was built in 1890 as the home of James W. Dillon, the father of Dillon County, and is on the National Register of Historic Places. Purchased by the Dillon County Historical Society in 1967, it was moved to this site and restored as a museum to preserve a record of those who contributed to the development of Dillon County. *Erected By Dillon County Historical Society, 1971*
GPS Coordinates: 34° 25.6' N, 79° 22.9' W

17–3 Early Cotton Press

S.C. Hwy. 38, just E of its junction with I-95 Exit 181 and .3 mi. W of its junction with S.C. Hwy. 917 W, Oak Grove vicinity, SE of Latta

This cotton press, built in 1798 according to tradition, is thought by many to be the oldest in existence. It was first owned and used by John Bethea, III, and later by Henry Berry. Powered by oxen or mules rotating the beam to tighten the press, it was rendered obsolete by modern machinery. A Berry descendant moved it to this site about 1948 to preserve it.

Erected by Dillon County Historical Society, 1974
GPS Coordinates: 34° 20.286' N, 79° 31.452' W

17–4 Joel Allen House

Intersection of Centerville Rd. (S.C. Sec. Rd. 17–38) & Skillet Rd., (S.C. Sec. Rd. 17–54), 7 mi. NW of Latta, Centerville community

This house, located ¼ mile E, was built about 1857 by Joel Allen, a Baptist minister who organized and served many churches in the Pee Dee area 1838–1884. He represented Marion County in the S.C. General Assembly 1870–1872. His son, W. B. Allen, added a second story to the 1 ½ story dwelling about 1891. The present kitchen was built about 1940 by J. J. Allen. *Erected by Dillon County Historic Preservation Commission, 1975*
GPS Coordinates: 34° 24.696' N, 79° 29.562' W

17–5 Selkirk Farm

Intersection of S.C. Hwy. 9 & Eli Branch Rd. (S.C. Sec. Rd. 17–38), E of Manning Crossroads

David Satterwhite was granted 177 acres here in 1789 by Charles Pinckney, Governor of S.C. In 1855 this tract passed into the hands of The Rev. James A. Cousar, who added a three-acre tract in 1858 on which he built the present house, gin house, and outbuildings. The name originated from a nearby post office, which was discontinued in 1901. *Erected by Dillon County Historic Preservation Commission, 1975*
GPS Coordinates: 34° 28.068' N, 79° 30.072' W

17–6 Catfish Creek Baptist Church

1495 Catfish Church Rd., near the Intersection of S.C. Sec. Rd. 17–63 (Catfish Church Rd.) & S.C. Sec. Rd. 17–41 (Dalcho Rd.), Latta vicinity

This Baptist church, constituted in 1802, has ordained eleven ministers, provided a

missionary to Brazil, and has helped to establish a number of other churches. The present house of worship, dedicated in 1883 with portico added in 1970, is on the National Register of Historic Places. *Erected by Dillon County Historic Preservation Commission, 1977*
GPS Coordinates: 34° 21.9' N, 79° 29.6' W

17–7 Saint Paul Methodist Church

Bradford Blvd. (S.C. Hwy. 9 W), 150 yds. E of its intersection with Harllees Bridge Rd. (S.C. Sec. Rd. 17–23), Little Rock

This church was established prior to 1803 and was known as Liberty Chapel. The present structure, built in 1871, is significant both for its architecture and as a reflection of Methodism in the Pee Dee area. A Victorian adaptation of the classic meeting-house form, St. Paul's was entered in the National Register of Historic Places in 1977. *Erected by Dillon County Historic Preservation Commission, 1978*
GPS Coordinates: 34° 28.65' N, 79° 24.133' W

17–8 Dillon County/Dillon County Courthouse

Dillon County Courthouse, 301 W. Main St., Dillon

Dillon County (FRONT)
Originally in colonial Craven County, this area became part of Georgetown District, 1769; Liberty County, 1785; Marion District, 1798; and Marion County, 1868. The movement to separate this county from upper Marion County began some years before the General Assembly enacted the bill creating Dillon County. It was signed by Governor Martin F. Ansel, Feb. 5, 1910, in the presence of Dillon citizens.

Dillon County Courthouse (REVERSE)
James W. Dillon and his son Thomas gave one-half of this block for erection of the Dillon County Courthouse; they also assisted financially in its construction. The cornerstone was laid October 30, 1911. Honoring James W. Dillon as Father of Dillon county, the granite monument on the grounds was unveiled June 29, 1938. *Erected by Dillon County Historic Preservation Commission, 1979*
GPS Coordinates: 34° 25.104' N, 79° 22.5' W

17–9 The Latta Library

101 N. Marion St. at its intersection with W. Main St., Latta

(FRONT) In 1911 W. C. Allen led a movement for a public library in Latta and was authorized by the town council to negotiate with Andrew Carnegie for funds. After the town complied with conditions set by Mr. Carnegie, he donated $5,000 and C. F. Bass of Latta gave land for the building, which opened as the Latta Library in 1914. Voters in a valid election levied a tax for maintenance. A rear portion and north wing were added later.

(REVERSE) This library initially served the Latta area and its schools, but in 1929 extended its service to all Dillon County schools. The cost led the library board to ask the county to provide aid. The county complied, although local control of library service continued. By statutory provision in 1973 a county library providing for countywide control was established; the Latta Library is the base of this operation. *Erected by Latta Rotary Club, 1979*
GPS Coordinates: 34° 20.317' N, 79° 26.07' W

17–10 Reedy Creek Springs

S.C. Hwy. 34, about 1 mi. S of Bingham near Dillon County-Marlboro County line

(FRONT) About 0.4 mile NW is Reedy Creek Springs, known for the medicinal value of its water. Here, before the turn of the century, William B. Allen laid out a quadrangle of a few acres, planted water oaks, and built a pavilion, hotel, cottages, and stables. The spa became popular as a gathering place for religious, educational, cultural, and social groups from a wide area.

(REVERSE) Reedy Creek Springs was a popular Pee Dee area resort for a number of years before and after 1900, and visitors traveled here by train and by horse. As automobiles became common, however, vacationers went further afield and the springs were neglected and suffered the ravages of time. Broken stones now mark the site of this once-popular spa. *Erected by Dillon County Historic Preservation Commission, 1982*
GPS Coordinates: 34° 25.368' N, 79° 33.24' W

17–11 Pee Dee Church

Dillon Hwy. (S.C. Hwy. 9), about 2 mi. E of Dillon

Duncan McIntire, a licensed minister who preached in Gaelic for those who could speak no other language, organized this Presbyterian congregation shortly before 1829. The present vernacular Gothic Revival structure was completed by 1851. A number of other congregations had their beginnings in this church. *Erected by Dillon County Historical Society, 1986*

GPS Coordinates: 34° 21.882' N, 79° 19.548' W

17–12 Town of Dillon/Florence Railroad Company

At the Seaboard Coast Line Railroad Depot, Main St., Dillon

Town Of Dillon (FRONT)
Dillon was laid out by civil engineers of the Florence Railroad Company following a plan by John H. David, a local physician. The town was incorporated by the General Assembly on December 22, 1888, and its boundaries extended in a half-mile radius from the railroad depot. The first mayor and postmaster of the town was Duncan McLaurin. In 1893 a freight station was constructed, and in 1904, the present passenger depot was built.
Florence Railroad Company (REVERSE)
In 1882 the Florence Railroad Company was chartered and authorized to build and operate a line east of Florence northward to the state border. Right-of-way problems here were solved when J. W. Dillon and his son Thomas offered half-interest in 63 acres if the railroad would use the land, build a depot, and lay out a town. The offer was accepted, and the railroad from Pee Dee to the state line was opened in 1888. *Erected by Dillon County Historic Preservation Commission, 1980*

GPS Coordinates: 34° 25.044' N, 79° 22.344' W

17–13 Main Street Methodist Church

401 East Main St., Dillon

(FRONT) This church, founded in 1892, built its first sanctuary at West Main St. and Third Ave., where the Dillon County Courthouse now stands. That lot was donated by James W. Dillon (1826–1913), for whom the town and county are named. The original church, a frame building, was moved to the corner of Third Ave. and Hudson St. in 1910 to make way for the new county courthouse, completed in 1911.
(REVERSE) The first sanctuary here, a brick cruciform church in the Gothic Revival style, was designed by Charlotte architect Oliver D. Wheeler (1864–1942). Completed in 1914, it only stood seven months before it burned in January 1915. The congregation worshipped in the courthouse until a new church was built. Wheeler also designed the present sanctuary, which duplicates his original design and was completed in 1916. *Erected by the Congregation, 2003*

GPS Coordinates: 34° 24.93' N, 79° 22.122' W

17–14 Ford's Mill & Page's Mill /Lake View

N. Main St. (S.C. Hwy. 41), Lake View

Ford's Mill & Page's Mill (FRONT)
In 1792 Major William Ford built a dam at each end of Bear Swamp, creating a millpond and building a grist mill. This area was known as Ford's Mill for many years. In 1870 Dr. C. T. Ford sold the property to his brother-in-law, Joseph N. Page, who soon opened a large general store. The community was renamed Page's Mill, and in 1877 a post office was opened with J. N. Page as its first postmaster.
Lake View (REVERSE)
After the railroad came through this area in 1900 the town of Page's Mill grew from the mill, general store, and post office toward the railroad tracks. The town of Page's Mill was incorporated February 26, 1907. The Ford's Mill / Page's Mill community, part of Marion County since the county was created in 1798, became part of Dillon County when that county was created in 1910. It was renamed Lake View in 1916. *Erected by the Town of Lake View, 2007*

GPS Coordinates: 34° 20.97' N, 79° 9.917' W

17–15 Pine Hill A.M.E. Church/Pine Hill Rosenwald School

2258 Centerville Rd., Latta

Pine Hill A.M.E. Church (FRONT)
This church, founded in 1876, was in Marion County before Dillon County was created in 1910. At first on S.C. Hwy. 34, the church acquired this site in 1891 when Alfred Franklin Page (1863–1929) and his wife Laura Willis Page (1886–1963) donated 1.97 acres here. The congregation built a new Pine Hill A.M.E. Church shortly afterwards. This sanctuary was built in 1977.

Pine Hill Rosenwald School (REVERSE)
Pine Hill Rosenwald School, one of the first ten Rosenwald schools in the state, was built here in 1917–18. One of 500 rural black schools in S.C. funded in part by the Julius Rosenwald Foundation 1917–1932, it was a frame two-room school. With two to four teachers, it reached a peak of 208 students in grades 1–7 in 1938–39. The school closed in 1957 and burned in 1977. *Erected by the Congregation, 2011*
GPS Coordinates: 34° 26.244′ N, 79° 29.19′ W

17–16 Leland Grove School

S.C. Hwy. 57, just N of Bakers Mill Rd., Leland Grove community, Clio vicinity

(FRONT) This is one of a few American Indian schools in S.C., built in 1934 as a one-room school. It averaged about 50 Lumbee Indian students a year, from the Carolinas community and other areas of Dillon and Marlboro Counties. At first for grades 1–7, it later added grades 8–12, building a second room in 1940. James Knox Braboy (1906–1976) was principal, teacher, and custodian 1934–1970.

(REVERSE) Braboy, a Lumbee Indian and native of N.C., was named S.C. Teacher of the Year in 1970 for his dedication to his students. He walked them to school across the McInnis Bridge over the Little Pee Dee River before the county bought a bus, then drove the bus for many years. Leland Grove School closed after the 1969–1970 school year with the desegregation of S.C. schools. *Sponsored by the Leland Grove School Society, 2014*
GPS Coordinates: 34° 34.975′ N, 79° 25.420′ W

17–17 Dillon Graded School and Dillon Public School

N. 3rd Ave. near intersection with W. Cleveland St., Dillon

(FRONT) The Dillon School Campus includes a unique collection of educational buildings from different periods, each representing the pedagogical and architectural styles of the age. The first building constructed on the campus was the 1896 Dillon Graded School. Built in the Italianate-style, the school was meant as a statement of the community's commitment to educating its children.

(REVERSE) Auditorium and gymnasium additions built in 1936 display a striped classicism typical of Public Works Administration (PWA) funded building projects. The 1957 cafeteria addition exhibits then-prevailing thinking that one-story schools with window walls for light and circulation were best. The complex was listed in the National Register of Historic Places in 2014. *Sponsored by Dillon Historic School Foundation, 2015*
GPS Coordinates: 34° 25.237′ N, 79° 22.385′ W

17–18 Kentyre Presbyterian Church

3150 Kentyre Rd., Hamer

(FRONT) Kentyre Presbyterian Church traces its origins to meetings held in the home of Peggy Edwards in the 1860s. The congregation was officially organized in 1871 and was named after the Kintyre region of Scotland. The first permanent sanctuary, which remains in use today, was begun in 1873 on land donated by J. S. Murphy. Charter members came from Reedy Creek and Pee Dee Presbyterian Churches.

(REVERSE) Also accepted into membership in 1871 were 21 African Americans who had no church. In 1895 a large two-story schoolhouse replaced the original school on the property. It was used until 1917 and later served as the educational building for the church. Renovations to the sanctuary were made in 1956 and the current educational building was added in 1963. *Sponsored by Kentyre Presbyterian Church, 2018*
GPS Coordinates: 34° 27.324′ N, 79° 18.517′ W

Dorchester County

18–1 Old Dorchester

Off S.C. Hwy. 642 in Old Dorchester State Park, S of Summerville

Laid out in 1697 as a market town for the Congregationalist colony from Dorchester, Mass., the village contained 116 quarter-acre lots and a town square and commons. An Anglican church was built in 1720, a fair was established in 1723, and a Free School in 1734. Dorchester became a trade center and by 1781 had about 40 houses. The town gradually declined after the Revolution. By 1788 it was abandoned. *Erected in 1963 by S.C. State Commission of Forestry, Division of State Parks* GPS Coordinates: 32° 57.008' N, 80° 10.26' W

18–2 Parish Church of St. George, Dorchester

Off Dorchester Rd. (S.C. Hwy. 642) in Old Dorchester State Park, S of Summerville

St. George's, an Anglican parish, was erected 1717. A brick church 50 ft. long and 30 ft. wide with a chancel 15 by 5 feet, begun in August 1719, was enlarged in the 1730's. The tower was built before 1753 and in 1766 held four bells. Burned by the British in the Revolution, the church was partially repaired and used afterwards, but as the congregation moved away, it fell into decay. *Erected in 1963 by S.C. State Commission of Forestry, Division of State Parks* GPS Coordinates: 32° 56.947' N, 80° 10.207' W

18–3 Fort Dorchester

Off Dorchester Rd (S.C. Hwy. 642) in Old Dorchester State Park, S of Summerville

A brick powder magazine enclosed by a tabby wall eight feet high was built here in 1757. During the Revolution, Dorchester was a strategic point. In 1775 the magazine was fortified and the garrison commanded by Capt. Francis Marion. British troops occupied the town in April 1780. They were driven out by cavalry and infantry under Col. Wade Hampton and Gen. Nathanael Greene on December 1, 1781. *Erected in 1963 by S.C. State Commission of Forestry, Division of State Parks* GPS Coordinates: 32° 56.853' N, 80° 10.206' W

18–4 Middleton Place/Arthur Middleton

Ashley River Rd. (S.C. Hwy. 61), 12 mi. NW of Charleston

Middleton Place (FRONT)

These famous gardens were laid out about 1741 by Henry Middleton (1717–84), President of Continental Congress. His son, Arthur, Signer of the Declaration of Independence, lived here as did his son Henry (1770–1846), Governor of S.C. and Minister to Russia, who introduced the camellias. His son William (1809–83) planted the first azaleas. The original residence was looted and burned by Federal forces in 1865.

Arthur Middleton (REVERSE)

Planter, Patriot, Signer/of the Declaration/of Independence./Born here June 26, 1742, Arthur Middleton, after receiving his education in England, returned to make his home here in 1763. He served in the Commons House of Assembly, the Council of Safety, the Continental Congress, the militia, and the state legislature. He died Jan. 1, 1787, and is buried in the garden here. *Erected by S.C. Societies of the Daughters of American Colonists and Daughters of Colonial Wars, 1964* GPS Coordinates: 32° 53.981' N, 80° 8.441' W

18–5 Old White Meeting House and Cemetery

Dorchester Rd. (S.C. Hwy. 642), just W of White Church Ln., Summerville vicinity

(FRONT) This church was established in 1696 by settlers from Dorchester, Mass., for which the town of Dorchester was named. This brick sanctuary, built ca. 1700, was occupied and then burned by British troops in 1781. The church was reorganized as "The United Independent Congregational Church of Dorchester and Beech Hill" in 1793 and the building rebuilt the next year. A summer church was built in nearby Summerville in 1831.

(REVERSE) In 1859 members of the Dorchester congregation established the Summerville Presbyterian Church, which was then admitted into the Charleston Presbytery. The church at this site, often called "Old White Meeting House," was almost abandoned and was in disrepair in 1886 when the Charleston earthquake reduced it to ruins. The cemetery here includes graves dating from the eighteenth century to the present. *Erected by Summerville Presbyterian Church, 1996*
GPS Coordinates: 32° 57.964' N, 80° 11.733' W

18–6 Newington Plantation

Plantation Cir., off Bacon's Bridge Rd (S.C. Hwy. 165), Summerville

(FRONT) Newington Plantation was established on this site in the 1680s after Daniel Axtell received a royal grant of 300 acres. Axtell died shortly after arriving in the colony and his widow Rebecca built a house on the grant by the 1690s. In 1711 Lady Axtell gave Newington, named after the family plantation in England, to her daughter Elizabeth, the widow of Gov. Joseph Blake. Mrs. Blake's son Col. Joseph Blake (1700–1751) inherited [. . .]

(REVERSE) [. . .] the plantation at her death in 1726 and built a large brick house on this site, one which was noted for its many windows, brick outbuildings, and rare double-row avenue of live oaks. Newington remained in the family until it was sold to Henry A. Middleton in 1837. The house burned in 1845 and was in ruins by 1876, when Middleton leased Newington Plantation to the United States government for use as an experimental tea farm. *Erected by Newington Plantation Estates Association, 1997*
GPS Coordinates: 32° 58.993' N, 80° 12.277' W

18–7 Four Holes Swamp Bridge/ Harley's Tavern

Near the Dorchester County Department of Public Works, 2120 E. Main St. (U.S. Hwy. 178) between Harleyville and Dorchester

Four Holes Swamp Bridge (FRONT)
The first bridge across Four Holes Swamp, a branch of the Edisto River, was built between 1770 and 1780 and was located about 200 ft. N. of the present bridge. The old bridge, on the road from Orangeburg to Charleston, was the site of several actions in 1781 and 1782 where S.C. militia and Patriot forces under Cols. Henry and Wade Hampton and William Harden clashed with Loyalists.

Harley's Tavern (REVERSE)
The first post office in what is now Dorchester County was opened in 1803 by William Harley at his tavern, a frequent stop for travelers on the Columbia Road. It stood near the present site of the Department of Public Works. Harley's son James (1801–1867) is buried just N. of the site on U.S. Hwy. 178; the town of Harleyville was named for William's grandson William W. (1825–1906). *Erected by Dorchester County, 1999*
GPS Coordinates: 33° 8.562' N, 80° 21.15' W

18–8 Old Town Hall

201 West Carolina Ave., Summerville

(FRONT) The Old Town Hall, built ca. 1860, is the oldest public building in Summerville. Rev. Robert I. Limehouse (1815–1881), a Methodist minister and the town intendant, or mayor, purchased the site for the town hall that year. A jail and market place also once stood here. In early 1865, in the final days of the Civil War, the village wardens left a meeting to defend Summerville from a band of raiders and killed one of them.

(REVERSE) At least sixteen intendants served Summerville in this building between ca. 1860 and 1892, when a new town hall was built on the Square. The Old Town Hall, described as the "heart of the old village," was later a school, polling place, community center, tea room, and residence. Though badly damaged by Hurricane Hugo in 1989, the building was purchased and restored by the Summerville

Preservation Society and is now the Society's headquarters and archives. *Erected by the Summerville Preservation Society, 2000*
GPS Coordinates: 33° 0.675' N, 80° 11.267' W

18–9 Alston Graded School/Alston High School

Corner of N. Cedar St. and W. 1st N. Sts., Summerville

Alston Graded School (FRONT)
Alston Graded School, one of the first African-American schools founded in Dorchester County, stood here from 1910 to 1954. Named for its founder, Dr. J. H. Alston, it included grades 1–11 until 1949 and 1–12 afterwards. The two-story wood frame school, which was designed by architects Burden and Walker of Charleston and built by N. A. Lee, was moved to Bryan Street in 1953.
Alston High School (REVERSE)
Alston High School, located on Bryan Street from 1953 to 1970, included grades 1–12. A new one-story brick school built on the new site in 1953 was constructed for about $200,000. It closed in 1970 after the desegregation of county schools. The present Alston Middle School, on Bryan Street, includes grades 6–8. *Erected by the Alston Heritage Foundation, 2000*
GPS Coordinates: 33° 1.352' N, 80° 10.536' W

18–10 Appleby's Methodist Church

Old Wire Rd. (S.C. Sec. Rd. 18–19), at its junction with Cowtail Rd. (S.C. Sec. Rd. 18–71), St. George vicinity

(FRONT) This church was organized shortly after the Revolution and this site was deeded to seven trustees in 1787. One of them, Jacob Barr, was the first minister to serve here. Appleby's Methodist Church was named for a prominent local family and the Greek Revival sanctuary here was most likely built between 1840 and 1850. It was listed in the National Register of Historic Places in 1978.
(REVERSE) The cemetery includes plots of the Appleby and other area families, and the graves of some slaves as well. Capt. Morgan T. Appleby's company was organized here for

Confederate service in the spring of 1862, using the churchyard as its muster ground. Later Company C of the 24th S.C. Infantry, it served in S.C., Miss., Tenn., Ga., and N.C. from 1862 to 1865. *Erected by the Generals Gordon-Capers Camp #123, Sons of Confederate Veterans, 2002*
GPS Coordinates: 33° 8.214' N, 80° 39.102' W

18–11 Archdale Hall

Archdale Blvd., S of Dorchester Rd. (S.C. Hwy. 161) between Lincoln Blvd. and Park Gate Dr., Summerville vicinity

Archdale Hall Plantation was established in 1681 by a royal grant of 300 acres to Richard Baker. The plantation, later expanded to more than 3000 acres, produced indigo and rice. The house which once stood here, built before 1750, was a fine example of Georgian residential architecture. It survived the Civil War only to be demolished by the Charleston earthquake of 1886. *Erected by the Archdale Civic Association, 2002*
GPS Coordinates: 32° 53.991' N, 80° 6.131' W

18–12 Koger-Murray-Carroll House

Old Wire Rd. (S.C. Sec. Rd. 18–19) just E of I-95, 2.5 mi. W of Grover

(FRONT) This house, an excellent example of early Federal era-architecture, was built about 1800 for Joseph Koger, Jr. (1779–1866), planter, state representative 1806–1812, Colleton District sheriff 1813–18, and state senator 1818–1838. Koger moved to Mississippi in 1838 and sold the house to his brother-in-law, John Soule Murray (1792–1844), planter and state senator 1840–43.
(REVERSE) In 1865 James Parsons Carroll (1809–1883), chancellor of the state court of equity, bought the house as a summer retreat. Carroll had been a state representative 1838–39, state senator 1852–53 and 1858–59, and a delegate to the Secession Convention. The house has long been called "the Old Carroll Place" and was listed in the National Register of Historic Places in 1974. *Erected by the Generals Gordon-Capers Camp #123, Sons of Confederate Veterans, 2003*
GPS Coordinates: 33° 7.716' N, 80° 38.118' W

18–13 Grover Methodist Church

U.S. Hwy. 15, 5 mi. S of Grover

(FRONT) This church was founded in the early 19th century as Murray's Church and served by ministers riding the Cypress Circuit. It was originally named for the Murray family, which also gave this town its first name of Murray's Crossroads. The first church here, damaged by a storm in 1878, was replaced by the present church, built of heart pine by Philip and Jim Liston in 1890–97.
(REVERSE) Murray's Church was renamed Grover Methodist Church in 1905, after the Murray's Crossroads post office was renamed Grover. The church undertook several renovations in the 1960s, covering the 1897 frame church with brick veneer, remodeling an early 20th century school for its Sunday school building and later a fellowship hall, and moving the 1912 bell from the steeple to a bell tower. *Erected by the Generals Gordon-Capers Camp # 123, Sons of Confederate Veterans, 2006*
GPS Coordinates: 33° 6.372' N, 80° 35.635' W

18–14 Cypress Methodist Camp Ground

Just S of Cypress Campground Rd./Myers Mayo Rd. (S.C. Sec. Rd. 18–182), between U.S. Hwy. 78 and I-26, Ridgeville vicinity

(FRONT) This camp ground, dating to 1794, is one of the oldest in S.C. Francis Asbury (1745–1816), circuit rider and the first Methodist bishop in America, preached here in 1794, 1799, 1801, and twice in 1803. The camp ground is supported by five local communities: Givhans, Lebanon, New Hope, Ridgeville, and Zion.
(REVERSE) "Tents," or rough-hewn cabins, form a rectangle around the "tabernacle," the open-sided shelter where services are held. The cemetery nearby includes graves as early as 1821. This camp ground, in session the week ending the fourth Sunday in October, was listed in the National Register of Historic Places in 1978. *Erected by the Upper Dorchester County Historical Society, 2009*
GPS Coordinates: 33° 6.204' N, 80° 16.397' W

18–15 Shady Grove Camp Ground

Off U.S. Hwy. 178, just SE of the Orangeburg County/Dorchester County line, St. George vicinity

(FRONT) This camp ground, established about 1870, is the largest of 4 Methodist camp grounds in Dorchester County. Tradition holds that Ceasar Wolfe and a group of former slaves, caught in a storm, stopped in a grove here for shelter. Rice planter S. M. Knight asked them to help harvest his fields, and after they did so he gave them this spot as a place of worship. They named it Shady Grove.
(REVERSE) The group first met under a brush arbor but later built "tents," the rough-hewn cabins typical of church camp grounds. The first tents burned in 1958 and were replaced; fires also occurred in 1969 and 1976. The "tabernacle" here is the centrally-located shelter where services are in session ending the fourth Sunday in October. A trumpet call on a ceremonial horn opens the meeting. *Erected by the Upper Dorchester County Historical Society, 2010*
GPS Coordinates: 33° 16.594' N, 80° 35.769' W

18–16 St. Paul Camp Ground

940 St. Paul Rd., Harleyville vicinity

(FRONT) This Methodist camp ground, one of four in Dorchester County, was established in 1880. African-American freedmen in this area held services in a brush arbor at the "Old Prayer Ground" nearby as early as 1869. By 1873 they acquired two acres nearby and founded St. Paul A.M.E. Church, building their first permanent sanctuary just southwest.
(REVERSE) In 1880 four community leaders purchased 113 acres here and deeded it to trustees for a new St. Paul Camp Ground. "Tents," or rough-hewn cabins, form a circle around the "tabernacle," the open-sided shelter where services are held. This camp ground, in session the week ending the third Sunday in October, was listed in the National Register of Historic Places in 1998. *Erected by the Upper Dorchester County Historical Society, 2011*
GPS Coordinates: 33° 12.285' N, 80° 28.938' W

18–17 Dorchester

Intersection of Schoolhouse Rd. & U.S. Hwy. 78, Dorchester

(FRONT) This town, in Colleton County before Dorchester was founded in 1897, dates to the early 19th century and the origins of railroading in S.C. By 1843, only ten years after the S.C. Canal & Rail Road Company completed its first 133 miles of track from Charleston to Hamburg, the station here was called Ross, sometimes known as Ross's, Ross's Station, or Ross's Turnout. The post office established here in 1854 was called Elmville until Reconstruction.

(REVERSE) The railroad, later the S.C.R.R. and by 1899 part of the Southern Railway, kept a station, a "turnout" or second set of tracks, and a water tower here for more than 100 years. It carried wood, turpentine, pulpwood, and livestock, and was instrumental in the town's development. The post office here was renamed Ross Station by 1875, then renamed Dorchester in 1903. The town, incorporated as Rosses in 1892, was incorporated again as Dorchester in 1912. *Sponsored by the Upper Dorchester County Historical Society, 2012*
GPS Coordinates: 33° 8.332' N, 80° 23.745' W

18–18 Badham House/Dorchester Lumber Company

6188 U.S. Highway 78, Reevesville

Badham House (FRONT)
This Neoclassical Revival house, called "one of the finest" in S.C. in 1920, was built in 1912 for Vernon Cosby Badham (1856–1947) and his second wife Lelia Johnston. Badham, a native of N.C., moved to S.C. in the 1880s and sold sawmill machinery in this area. In 1901 he built the Dorchester Lumber Company, across the highway and on the Southern Railway. The sawmill cut 50,000–100,000 feet of timber a day, hauling it from the swamps by a narrow-gauge railroad.
Dorchester Lumber Company (REVERSE)
The sawmill, in operation from 1901 to 1938, employed 500 men at its peak. A large complex here included a company office, company store, worker housing, a school, and a church.

The post office active here 1901–1945 was called Badham. Dorchester Lumber Company shut down during the Depression, and all that remains of the old mill across the highway is the brick ruin of the vault from the mill office. *Sponsored by the Upper Dorchester County Historical Society, 2012*
GPS Coordinates: 33° 11.708' N, 80° 36.731' W

18–19 Bacon's Bridge/"The Hill"

Bacon's Bridge Rd. (S.C. Hwy. 165) near the Ashley River, Summerville vicinity

Bacon's Bridge (FRONT)
An early bridge over the Ashley River near this site, built ca. 1696–1700, was first owned by John Stevens. Stevens sold this tract to Michael Bacon soon afterwards. Bacon's Bridge became a public bridge in 1722. During the American Revolution, Patriot and British/Loyalist commanders in the lowcountry considered Bacon's Bridge a strategic location.
"The Hill" (REVERSE)
In Feb. 1780 Gen. William Moultrie built an earthwork nearby to defend the bridge and the approaches to Charleston. Gen. Nathanael Greene's Southern Army, including Gen. Francis Marion's militia, camped at Bacon's Bridge March-July 1782. In 1850 Rev. Robert I. Limehouse (1815–1881), later intendant of Summerville, built a house on the redoubt and named his plantation "The Hill." *Sponsored by the Summerville Preservation Society, 2014*
GPS Coordinates: 32° 57.505' N, 80° 12.058'

18–20 Ridgeville

Ridgeville

(FRONT) This town, in Colleton County before Dorchester County was founded in 1897, dates from 1831. It was one of the first stations on the S.C. Rail Road from Charleston to Hamburg. This area was called Ridgeville as early as 1820, for its location on a ridge between Four Holes Swamp and Cypress Swamp. From the 1840s to the Civil War Ridgeville was a popular destination for "pleasure parties," day trips up from Charleston and back on the S.C. Rail Road.

(REVERSE) Town lots were laid out and sold here in 1849, and the town became a planters' summer retreat and a center of trade. One antebellum visitor called Ridgeville "a very pleasant, healthy village" and its citizens "industrious, prosperous and hospitable." It was incorporated in 1875, with its limits a half-mile radius from the depot. The town was centered along Railroad Ave. and Main St. The timber and turpentine industries here flourished into the 20th century. *Sponsored by the Upper Dorchester County Historical Society, 2013*
GPS Coordinates: 33° 8.101' N, 80° 18.676' W

18–21 Harleyville

Near intersection of S.C. Hwy 178 and N. Railroad Ave., Harleyville

(FRONT) Harleyville is named for the Harley family who owned much of the land that comprises the present town. William "Cow Bill" Harley owned substantial property in this vicinity and raised cattle for the Charleston market. In 1885 he sold a right of way across his land to the Eutawville Railroad, which built a road between Pregnall's and Eutaw Springs with Harleyville a regular stop. The railroad spurred development of the lumber industry and the town was incorporated in 1893.
(REVERSE) As automobile travel became more popular in the 20th century, Harleyville again benefitted from its location along what was then one of S.C.'s main thoroughfares. S.C. Hwy. 2 (now Hwy. 178) was the first hard-surfaced road in Dorchester County. When completed in 1932 it extended from upstate S.C. to Charleston. Considered "S.C.'s Main St.," Hwy. 2 allowed Harleyville to remain a trading center for surrounding farms. I-26 replaced S.C. Hwy. 2 as a main highway in the 1960s. *Sponsored by the Upper Dorchester County Historical Society, 2014*
GPS Coordinates: 33° 12.874' N, 80° 26.869' W

18–22 Pinehurst Tea Farm

Tea Farm Rd. near the intersection with Alt. Rt. 17, Summerville

(FRONT) In 1880 the U.S. government leased 200 acres of the former Newington Plantation from Henry Middleton for tea production. In 1888, Dr. Charles Shepard, a professor at the Medical College of S.C., used plants from the federal farm to create "Pinehurst," the first commercially viable tea farm in America. Production rose from 98 pounds in 1892 to 12,000 pounds in 1907.
(REVERSE) Shepard imported exotic plants to create beautiful gardens and roadways at Pinehurst. He established a school to educate the tea pickers' children. Dignitaries such as Teddy Roosevelt visited Pinehurst. Charles Shepard died in 1915 and tea production ceased in 1919 when the tea factory burned. In 1995 the S.C. General Assembly made tea the "Hospitality Beverage of S.C." *Sponsored by the Summerville Preservation Society, 2016*
GPS Coordinates: 33° 0.290' N, 80° 11.662' W

18–23 Guerin's Pharmacy

140 S. Main St., Summerville

(FRONT) Guerin's Pharmacy, founded in 1871 by Henry C. Guerin, is the oldest operating pharmacy in S.C. Guerin was a Charleston physician who served as Chief Commissary for S.C. during the Civil War. Afterwards he moved to Summerville and bought Schweatman Drug Store, which was operating from the home of Mrs. R. W. Myers. Guerin moved the business to a frame building at its current site. Henry's son Joseph Guerin received his pharmacy degree in 1892 and took over the business.
(REVERSE) About 1895 the one-story building was replaced by a two-story wooden structure that was brick veneered with a one-story addition in 1925. Herbert Dunning was hired as pharmacist in 1910 and eventually owned the drug store. After Herbert's death in 1975 his nephew Charles Dunning bought the drug store. Upon Charles' death in 2014 his daughter Barbara became pharmacist in charge. Guerin's Pharmacy is the oldest continuously operating business in Summerville. *Sponsored*

by the Summerville Preservation Society,
2016
GPS Coordinates: 33° 1.152' N, 80° 10.572' W

18–24 St. George Public High School

Corner of Raysor St. and Ridge St., St. George

(FRONT) St. George High School was built in
1927 on the corner of Raysor and Ridge Sts.
In 1936 the school district received a W.P.A.
grant to build a new gymnasium. The building continued as a high school until 1956,
when a new school was built nearby. It remained in use as an elementary school until
1972. In 2000 the building was renovated by
Dorchester County and became a county
service building.

(REVERSE) The first free school in St. George
was located at the corner of Whitridge and
George Sts. In 1884 it was moved to a two-
story building near this site. In 1907 a new
building replaced the first schoolhouse. It
housed grades 1–10. In 1927 St. George High
School was built adjacent to the 1907 building,
which then became St. George Elementary.
The 1907 school was closed in 1961 and razed
in 1962. *Sponsored by the Dorchester County*
Historical Society and the Class of 1954, 2017
GPS Coordinates: 33° 11.304' N, 80° 34.495' W

18–25 Jewish Life

Hutchinson Square, Summerville

(FRONT) Summerville became a renowned
health resort in the late 1800s. Many Jewish
merchants, drawn to the bustling settlement,
set up shop in Hutchinson Square. Among the
first were Philip Wineman, a pharmacist from
England, and Saul Alexander, a tailor from
Ukraine. On Short Central Samuel Lynch and
his son, Seymour, became major property and
business owners. Twentieth-century stores
included Kramer's Pharmacy, Barshay's, Seymour's, and Wolper's Dorchester Jewelers.

(REVERSE) Among other Jewish family names
in Summerville were Lazarus, Bernstein,
Meyers, Epstein, Bornstein, Mirmow, and
Friedberg. Seymour's, one of the last remaining Jewish-owned stores in town, closed in
1997. In the second half of the 20th century

descendants of Jewish merchants moved to
larger cities, but their legacy endures. The
Saul Alexander Foundation has funded parks
in the town as well as cultural and educational
organizations in the Lowcountry. *Sponsored*
by the Jewish Historical Society of South Caro-
lina, 2017
GPS Coordinates: 33° 1.197' N, 80° 10.520' W

18–26 Timrod Library

217 Central Ave., Summerville

(FRONT) In 1897, the Timrod Library was orga-
nized by 19 women as a Chautauqua Reading
Circle. It was chartered in 1908 as the Timrod
Literary and Library Association. In 1915,
Timrod's current home was erected on land
donated by the Town through efforts of Mayor
W. H. Richardson. The building was designed
by Henry Burden and the bricks donated by
T. W. Salisbury. The builder was Jim Cooper.
The library was named in honor of S.C. poet
Henry Timrod, best known for his Confeder-
ate poetry.

(REVERSE) Timrod Library is one of two remaining subscription libraries in S.C., meaning that it is supported primarily through
donations and membership dues. In 1927, a
kitchen and assembly room were added. Catherine "Catty" Stewart served as librarian from
1938 to 1953. Her generous bequest in 1979
enabled the library to expand in 1985 with the
addition of another room, aptly named the
"Catherine Stewart Room." *Sponsored by the*
Summerville Preservation Society, 2018
GPS Coordinates: 33° 1.076' N, 80° 10.785' W

18–27 Pine Forest Inn

Intersection of Linwood Ln. and Salisbury Dr.,
Summerville

(FRONT) The Pine Forest Inn opened in 1892. It
was owned and managed by F. W. and George
Wagener. The 60-acre resort and health spa
contained 150 steam-heated sleeping apartments. The dining room could hold 250
people. The Inn had a power plant, 50 horse
stable, a dairy and hennery, and telegraph and
telephone service. The Pine Forest Inn had an
amusement hall with 3 bowling alleys, shuffle

boards, and billiard tables. The resort also had an 18-hole golf course situated on 130 acres.
(REVERSE) Construction was overseen by the Charleston firm of Simons & Huger. Many early travelers were drawn to the Inn with the promise that the local climate would promote good health and it was celebrated as the world's finest sanitarium. Notable visitors included Presidents Teddy Roosevelt in 1902 and William Howard Taft in 1908. During WWII, T. W. Salisbury used the Inn to house defense workers and later it served as an "Adventure School." It was torn down ca. 1960. *Sponsored by the Summerville Preservation Society, 2018*
GPS Coordinates: 33° 0.575' N, 80° 11.513' W

18–28 Stallsville

255 Stallsville Loop, Summerville

(FRONT) The pineland village of Stallsville developed on the high ground above Saw Mill Creek and was named for the Stall family, who owned property and lived here by the early 19th C. Thomas D. Stall married Sarah Mary Rose, daughter of John Rose, who owned nearby Rose Hill plantation, in 1797. In 1816, Stall purchased 431 acres along Saw Mill Creek and settled here with his household, including his wife, five surviving children, and numerous enslaved people.
(REVERSE) The village grew up around a half circle with both ends of Stallsville Loop attached to Bacons Bridge Rd. The Le Bleu House, one of the oldest in Stallsville, was built ca. 1810. Construction of Stallsville Methodist Church began in 1887 on land

that had been part of the Le Bleu plantation. The church formed with a core of 21 initial members. Rev. Andrew D. Green was the first pastor and husband of Arabella Stall, one of the granddaughters of Thomas D. and Sarah Rose Stall. *Sponsored by the Summerville Preservation Society, 2018*
GPS Coordinates: 32° 59.707' N, 80° 11.125' W

18–29 Town of St. George

Intersection of U.S. Hwy. 78 and U.S. Hwy. 15, St. George

(FRONT) St. George developed as a stop on the S.C. Canal and Railroad known as "George's Station." It was named for James George (1789–1867), a plantation owner who gave land for the station when the railroad was built in the 1830s. He is believed to have operated a store in the area as early as 1810. The town was officially incorporated as George's Station in 1875 and was re-incorporated St. George's in 1889. In 1897, it was chosen as the seat of newly created Dorchester County.
(REVERSE) The new name recalled the old colonial parish of St. George's, Dorchester, as well as the town's founder, James George. The postal service first shortened the name to "St. George," which came into common use by mid-century. By 1910, the town was a commercial hub with two banks, two hotels, several mills, and numerous stores. The construction of U.S. Hwy. 15 in the 1920s brought even more business and traffic, as it was along the most direct route from New York to Miami. *Sponsored by Dorchester County Historical Society and Town of St. George, 2019*
GPS Coordinates: 33° 11.159' N, 80° 34.402' W

Edgefield County

19–1 Old Law Building

Simkins St., Edgefield

Site of law offices of/ELDRED SIMKINS/Congressman, Lt.-Governor./GEORGE MCDUFFIE/Congressman, Governor,/U.S. Senator./FRANCIS W. PICKENS/Congressman, Governor,/

Minister to Russia./FRANCIS H. WARDLAW,/Author of/Ordinance of Secession./JOHN C. SHEPPARD,/ Lt.-Governor, Governor./JAMES O. SHEPPARD, Lieutenant-Governor,/National Head "40 & 8." *Present building given in 1949 to Edgefield County Historical Society by Miss*

Anne L. Golightly [*Erected by Edgefield County Historical Society, 1962.*]
GPS Coordinates: 33° 47.383' N, 81° 55.383' W

19–2 Big Stevens Creek Baptist Church (Hardy's)

1850 W. Martintown Rd. (S.C. Hwy. 230), Morgana vicinity

Founded in 1762 by the Reverend Daniel Marshall, pioneer missionary and minister, this was the first church of the Baptist faith in the present Edgefield County. "Mother of Churches." *Erected by Edgefield Baptist Association on the Bicentennial of the church, 1962*
GPS Coordinates: 33° 36' N, 82° 1.059' W

19–3 First Baptist Church/ Village Cemetery

212 Church St., Edgefield

First Baptist Church (FRONT)
Founded in 1823 as Edgefield Village Baptist Church with Basil Manly, Sr., Pastor, Matthew Mims, Clerk, and Arthur Simkins, Moderator, this church led in the establishment here in 1826 of Furman Academy and Theological Institution. William Bullein Johnson, pastor here 1830–52, served as president of the Southern Baptist Convention 1845–51; Robert G. Lee, a former pastor, served in 1948–51.
Village Cemetery (REVERSE)
Burial place of three S.C. Governors/F. W. Pickens, 1807–1869/J. C. Sheppard, 1850–1931/ John G. Evans, 1863–1942/and the families of/ Gov. Pierce H. Butler/and Gov. M. L. Bonham./Also buried here are/Francis H. Wardlaw/1800–1861/Preston S. Brooks/1818–1857/ Matthew C. Butler/1836–1909/John Lake, 1870–1949,/Missionary to China. *Erected by First Baptist Church, Edgefield, S.C., 1967*
GPS Coordinates: 33° 47.45' N, 81° 55.65' W

19–4 Old Simkins Cemetery

Center Springs Rd. (S.C. Sec. Rd. 19-39), 3.5 mi. N of Edgefield

½ mile west, on "Cedar Fields" plantation, is buried the family of Captain Arthur Simkins, soldier in the American Revolution and a

founder of Edgefield. Born in Virginia on Dec. 10, 1742, he died Sept. 29, 1826. He was a county court judge, a member of the S.C. General Assembly, and was on the commission to divide Ninety Six District into counties. *Erected by Edgefield County Historical Society and Old 96 District Chapter, Daughters of the American Revolution, 1969*
GPS Coordinates: 33° 49.667' N, 81° 54.283' W

19–5 Richard Tutt Home/Tutt Cemetery

Corner of Gray & Penn Sts., Edgefield

Richard Tutt Home (FRONT)
The Tutt house which formerly stood on this site is believed to have been the first home at Edgefield Court House. Richard Tutt was one of the party who in October 1775 arrested Tory leader Robert Cunningham and escorted him to Charleston. Later, as a Lieutenant in the 5th S.C. Continentals, he served at Fort Rutledge. In the Siege of Ninety Six, he is said to have worked on the tunnel the Patriots projected under Star Fort.
Tutt Cemetery (REVERSE)
This family cemetery was located near the Tutt home. Among the seven graves are those of Lieutenant Richard Tutt, born in Culpeper County, Virginia, 1749, died in Edgefield, 1807, and his son-in-law, Matthew Mims (1780–1848), Clerk of Court, 1814. Richard Tutt settled near Liberty Hill before the Revolution, later served in Edgefield as village surgeon and Justice of the Peace. *Erected by The City of Edgefield and 96 Rangers Chapter, Children of the American Revolution, 1976*
GPS Coordinates: 33° 47.017' N, 81° 55.867' W

19–6 Horns Creek Baptist Church/ Revolutionary Skirmish at Horns Creek

Old Stage Rd. (S.C. Sec. Rd. 19-76), near its intersection with Yarborough Rd., 6 mi. S of Edgefield

Horns Creek Baptist Church (FRONT)
This church was constituted in 1768 by the Reverend Daniel Marshall, one of the founders of the Baptist faith in this part of South Carolina. Other early ministers of Horns

Creek included Hezekiah Walker, Samuel Marsh, and John Landrum. The church was incorporated on January 20, 1790.

Revolutionary Skirmish at Horns Creek (REVERSE)

Not far from this historic church a skirmish took place in 1781. Captain Thomas Key of Colonel LeRoy Hammond's regiment attacked a party of Tories under the command of Captain Clark. The Tories were defeated, their captain killed, and the entire company captured and paroled. *Erected by Edgefield County Historical Society and Edgefield County Council, 1974*

GPS Coordinates: 33° 43.283′ N, 81° 56.183′ W

19–7 Village Academy/Furman Academy and Theological Institution

Church St., 100 ft. S of its intersection with Brooks St., Edgefield

Village Academy (FRONT)

Organized in 1811, the Edgefield Village Academy was located for many years on this site acquired from Col. Eldred Simkins, in 1825. The South Carolina Coeducational Institute was located here from 1903 to 1913. During Reconstruction, many exciting political meetings were held in the grove near the Academy.

Furman Academy and Theological Institution (REVERSE)

This school, founded by the State Convention of Baptists of South Carolina on March 17, 1826, was originally located on this site. The Institution was the forerunner of both Furman University in Greenville, South Carolina and Southern Baptist Theological Seminary in Louisville, Kentucky. *Erected by The Edgefield County Historical Society and Edgefield County, 1975*

GPS Coordinates: 33° 47.667′ N, 81° 55.733′ W

19–8 Edgefield United Methodist Church/The Reverend Joseph Moore

Corner of Bacon & Norris Sts., Edgefield

Edgefield United Methodist Church (FRONT)

By 1841, this congregation was established and was a member of the Edgefield Circuit. The present structure was dedicated in November of 1892 by Bishop W. W. Duncan. The Reverend Joseph Moore sold to the church the land upon which it is presently built. A member of this church, Jennie Hughes Nicholson, was a missionary to China from September of 1901 until February of 1906.

The Reverend Joseph Moore (REVERSE)

Moore was an early Methodist minister who was preaching by 1791 and was a circuit rider in the states of South Carolina, North Carolina, Georgia, and Virginia. He died in Edgefield District in 1851 and bequeathed his estate to the Edgefield Circuit of the Methodist Church. Moore is buried in the Edgefield Village Baptist Cemetery. *Erected by Edgefield United Methodist Church, 1978*

GPS Coordinates: 33° 47.283′ N, 81° 55.667′ W

19–9 Bettis Academy

Edgefield Rd. (U.S. Hwy. 25) at S.C. Hwy. 37 (Bettis Academy Rd.), SW of Trenton

Established as a result of the inspiration and efforts of the Reverend Alexander Bettis, this educational institution was incorporated in 1889, and provided elementary, high school, and junior college training for blacks. A. W. Nicholson succeeded Bettis as president and served for about fifty years. The school, which was closed in the 1950s, was located about 1 ½ miles southeast. *Erected by Mt. Canaan Educational and Missionary Association, 1979*

GPS Coordinates: 33° 39.933′ N, 81° 52.85′ W

19–10 Sheppard's Crossroads

Intersection of U.S. Hwy. 25 and Long Cane /Sheppard Rd., Sheppard's Crossroads, about 8 mi. N of Edgefield

In 1828, this property, shown on Anderson's 1816 map as Kirksey's Tavern, was sold by John Kirksey to James Sheppard (1790–1859), state representative, merchant, and War of 1812 veteran. He and Louise Mobley, his third wife, were parents of John C. Sheppard (1850–1931), Governor of South Carolina in 1886. In rear of the house is the family cemetery.

Erected by Edgefield County Historical Society, 1972
GPS Coordinates: 33° 58.183' N, 82° 2.747' W.

19–11 Lt. General James Longstreet 1821–1904

Martintown Rd. (S.C. Hwy. 230) about 1.8 mi. N of I-20, Poverty Hill vicinity

Born 1 mi. E. Cmdr. 1st Corps, Army of Northern VA Confederate States Army; Lee's "Old Warhorse"; West Point graduate; Mexican War veteran. *Erected by 15th Regiment S.C. Volunteers, Camp # 51, Sons of Confederate Veterans, 1995*
GPS Coordinates: 33° 33.867' N, 82° 0.714' W

19–12 Johnston

Intersection of Lee St. (S.C. Hwy. 121) & Calhoun St. (S.C. Hwy. 23), Johnston

Johnston, founded in 1868 as Johnston's Station on the Charlotte, Columbia, & Augusta Railroad and also known as Johnson's Turn Out, was named for railroad president William Johnston. It was first incorporated in 1875 and rechartered with its present name of Johnston in 1897. The Johnston Historic District, a collection of 146 houses, businesses, and churches dating from ca. 1880 to ca. 1920, was listed in the National Register of Historic Places in 1983. *Erected by the Town of Johnston, S.C., 1997*
GPS Coordinates: 33° 49.9' N, 81° 48.067' W

19–13 J. Strom Thurmond Birthplace

305 Columbia Rd. (S.C. Hwy. 23), Edgefield

(FRONT) J. Strom Thurmond, by mid-1997 the longest-serving U.S. Senator in history, was born here to J. William and Gertrude Strom Thurmond Dec. 5, 1902. Educated at Clemson College, he taught high school 1923–29, was county superintendent of education 1929–33, state senator 1933–38, and circuit judge 1938–42. As a U.S. Army officer 1942–46, he participated in the D-Day invasion of Normandy and won the Bronze Star.
(REVERSE) Thurmond, governor of S.C. 1947–51, ran for president on the States Rights Democratic Party ticket in 1948. He was first elected to the U.S. Senate in 1954 as a write-in candidate but resigned his seat in early 1956 to fulfill a promise to voters. He was easily reelected that fall, then again in 1960, 1966, 1972, 1978, 1984, 1990, and 1996. He served as President Pro Tempore of the U.S. Senate 1981–86 and 1994-present. *Erected by the Edgefield County Historical Society, 2000*
GPS Coordinates: 33° 47.3' N, 81° 55.267'

19–14 Lott's Tavern & Post Office

1225 Calhoun St., Johnston

A house built for Emsley Lott about 1770, later Lott's Tavern and still later Lott's Post Office, stood here until it was demolished in 1918. Lott soon enlarged his one-room log house to become a tavern on the Columbia road. In 1839 his son John built a front room on the tavern and became the first postmaster of Lott's Post Office, the first post office in present-day Johnston. *Erected by the Ridge Heritage Association, 2001*
GPS Coordinates: 33° 50.616' N, 81° 47.204' W

19–15 Benjamin R. Tillman House

Pine House Rd. (S.C. Hwy. 121), Trenton

(FRONT) Benjamin Ryan "Pitchfork Ben" Tillman (1847–1918), governor of S.C. 1890–94 and U.S. senator 1894–1918, bought this farm just before he left the governor's office in 1894. He lived here until his death. Tillman, a farmer himself, grew deeply concerned about the economic problems facing agriculture in S.C. He became politically active in 1885 as the farmers' principal advocate.
(REVERSE) A spirited and controversial orator, Tillman was a champion to the many small farmers who elected him governor in 1890. He called the convention which drew up a new state constitution in 1895 and was also instrumental in establishing Clemson College and Winthrop College and in creating a state liquor dispensary system. He is buried at Ebenezer Church cemetery just south of here. *Erected by the Trenton Development Association and the Trenton Garden Club, 2002*
GPS Coordinates: 33° 44.819' N, 81° 50.827' W

19–16 Mt. Canaan Baptist Church

2451 Edgefield Rd. (U.S. Hwy. 25), S of Trenton

(FRONT) This church, founded in 1868, was one of the first black Baptist churches in this area. Alexander Bettis (1836–1895), a former slave, established this church with the assistance of three white ministers after the local Baptist association refused to ordain him. Mt. Canaan grew from seventeen charter members to more than 2,000 members in only three years. (REVERSE) This was the first of forty churches Rev. Alexander Bettis organized in Edgefield and Aiken Counties. He also founded Bettis Academy in 1881. He served Mt. Canaan and three other area churches until his death in 1895 and is buried here. Early services were held in a brush arbor. The original frame sanctuary was replaced by the present brick sanctuary in 1961. *Erected by the Congregation, 2004*
GPS Coordinates: 33° 40.117' N, 81° 52.717' W

19–17 Johnston Schools/Johnston Educators

At Johnston Elementary School, Lee St. (S.C. Hwy. 121), N of Academy St., Johnston

Johnston Schools (FRONT)
Johnston's first school opened on this site in 1873. The Male and Female Academy was a boarding school, with Rev. Luther Broaddus as its first principal. Alternately a private and public school during its early history, it was reorganized in 1884 as the Johnston Male and Female Institute. It became Johnston High School when it was sold to the town in 1906. A three-story brick high school was built here in 1910; it was torn down when the school closed in 1961.
Johnston Educators (REVERSE)
Henry Simms Hartzog (1866–1953), superintendent of the Institute 1895–97, left Johnston to become the third president of Clemson College. Dr. John Lake, who succeeded Hartzog as superintendent, was later a Baptist missionary to China. Joseph Earle Jacobs (1893–1971), a graduate of Johnston High School who taught there 1914–15, was a career diplomat in the U.S. Foreign Service 1915–57, most notably

as Ambassador to Czechoslovakia (1949) and to Poland (1955–57). *Erected by the Ridge Heritage Association, 2008*
GPS Coordinates: 33° 50.023' N, 81° 48.237' W

19–18 Edgefield

Main St. & Bacon St., near the Town Hall, Edgefield

(FRONT) Edgefield was founded in 1785 as the county seat and site of the new courthouse and jail for Edgefield County, created out of the old Ninety-Six District. Also called Edgefield Village or Edgefield Court House, it was described by Robert Mills as "a neat little village" in 1826, and was incorporated in 1830. Edgefield, with a reputation as a center of politics and law, gave the state many of its most prominent figures for more than 150 years. (REVERSE) Ten governors and five lieutenant governors of S.C. from 1812 to 1951 were natives or residents of Edgefield or the county. Cotton was the major crop in the area for many years. Commercial growth and a new prosperity that followed the arrival of the railroad in 1888 and the opening of the Edgefield Cotton Mill in 1898 lasted until the mid-20th century. The Edgefield Historic District was listed in the National Register of Historic Places in 1972. *Erected by the Edgefield Community Development Association, 2011*
GPS Coordinates: 33° 47.338' N, 81° 55.652' W

19–19 Halcyon Grove

406 Buncombe St., Edgefield

(FRONT) This Federal house with a later Classical Revival porch was the home of two governors of S.C. It was built ca. 1824 for planter Daniel Bird, who sold it in 1829 to Francis Wilkinson Pickens (1807–1869), then a lawyer and planter. Pickens lived here until the mid-1830s, when he deeded the house to his father, Andrew Pickens Jr. (1779–1838). The elder Pickens, a planter, was an officer in the War of 1812 and then governor 1816–18. He lived here until 1836.
(REVERSE) Francis W. Pickens, later a state representative and senator, U.S. Congressman, and U.S. Minister to Russia, was governor 1860–62, during the secession crisis and first

two years of the Civil War. In 1836 Andrew Pickens Jr. sold the house to John Lipscomb (1789–1856), a planter and merchant who also owned plantations in Florida but lived here. Descendants of the Bates/Hartley/ Feltham family owned Halcyon Grove for nearly 140 years, from 1869 to 2008. *Erected by the Edgefield County Historical Society, 2011*
GPS Coordinates: 33° 47.598' N, 81° 55.801' W

19–20 Darby

1150 Augusta Rd. (U.S. Hwy. 25), Trenton vicinity

(FRONT) This Greek Revival house was built for Nathan L. Griffin (1803–1853), lawyer, planter, and member of the S.C. House 1838–39 and S.C. Senate 1846–1853. Griffin's son-in-law Milledge L. Bonham (1813–1890) lived here with his wife Ann from their marriage in 1845 to 1861. Bonham, after serving in the S.C. House, was an officer during the Mexican War and a U.S. Congressman 1857–1860.
(REVERSE) Bonham, a Confederate general and C.S. Congressman during the Civil War, was governor of S.C. 1862–64. In 1863 he sold Darby to George A. Trenholm (1807–1876), Confederate Secretary of the Treasury 1864–65, whose relative Francis S. Holmes (1815–1882) of the Confederate Nitre & Mining Bureau lived here 1864–65. Darby was listed in the National Register of Historic Places in 1974. *Sponsored by the Edgefield County Historical Society, 2012*
GPS Coordinates: 33° 45.057' N, 81° 52.892' W

19–21 Philippi Baptist Church

125 Steeple Rd., Johnston

(FRONT) This church, established in 1814 and a charter member of the Ridge Baptist Association, is among the oldest in Edgefield County. Revs. Thomas DeLoach, Francis Walker, and John Landrum organized the church, with twenty-five white and black charter members, including three slaves. After the Civil War the black members left to form their own congregation.
(REVERSE) The first church, a log building, was 3 to 4 mi. SE and was replaced by a second log church, built here. The third church, a small

frame building, was replaced in 1897 by the present church, built at a cost of $850 and described as "one of the largest and handsomest churches in Western Carolina." Rev. J. C. Browne (1836–1914), the longest-serving minister, preached here 1885–1913. *Sponsored by the Congregation, 2014*
GPS Coordinates: 33° 46.870' N, 81° 45.947' W

19–22 Holly Hill

312 Gray St., Edgefield

(FRONT) Holly Hill sits on a tract of land originally granted to James Robeson in 1768 as part of England's expansion into the S.C. backcountry. Robeson sold this property in 1778 to Sarah and Jenkin Harris, whose sons, Jenkin Jr., John and Moses, became active in the development of Edgefield Village. Later, Charles Goodwyn, a lawyer and state senator, lived at the site until his death in 1824. Architectural study suggests that the eastern half of the house may date to the 18th century.
(REVERSE) The house had a series of owners in the 19th and 20th centuries including Sheriff Humphrey Boulware, Irish immigrant and Catholic leader Peter McHugh, planter and physician Dr. C. P. Devore, and Edgefield socialites Wallace and Adrienne "Dollie" Dugas Sheppard. In 1919 the property was purchased by Benjamin Tillman Lanham who operated a dairy here. The Lanham family lived in the house until the 1970s. *Sponsored by the Edgefield County Historical Society, 2015*
GPS Coordinates: 33° 47.116' N, 81° 56.069' W

19–23 Mt. Pleasant Baptist Church

115 Steeple Rd., Johnston

(FRONT) Mt. Pleasant Baptist Church was organized in 1869 when the African American members of Philippi Baptist Church requested permission to form an independent congregation. Fifty-two African American members, most of them recently emancipated freed people, formed the core of the original congregation.
(REVERSE) From the early days the church also supported a school for African American children. In 1939 the Baptist Young People's

Union formed a Johnston chapter in the small two-room schoolhouse that once stood on the property. Rev. E. M. Gordon served the longest tenure of any pastor here, from 1968 to 2014.

Sponsored by Mt. Pleasant Baptist Church, 2019
GPS Coordinates: 33° 46.877' N, 81° 45.925' W

Fairfield County

20–1 Confederate Headquarters

At the Century House, S.C. Hwy. 34, one block W of Main St., Ridgeway

During February 17–19, 1865, General P. G. T. Beauregard, with Wade Hampton's cavalry acting as rear guard, made his headquarters here, telegraphing General R. E. Lee in Virginia news of the evacuation of Columbia, 20 miles south, before retiring to Winnsboro. Following and destroying the railroad, Union troops arrived February 21. *Erected by Fairfield County Chamber of Commerce, 1962*
GPS Coordinates: 34° 18.372' N, 80° 57.63' W

20–2 Old Brick Church

S.C. Hwy. 213, 1.5 mi. NE of its its intersection with S.C. Hwy. 215, Jenkinsville vicinity

On May 9, 1803, the Associate Reformed Synod of the Carolinas was organized here at Ebenezer A.R.P. Church, built in 1788 by a congregation dating from colonial days. The rock wall was added in 1852. Damaged by Union troops in 1865, the church was repaired and remained in active use until 1920. *Erected by Fairfield County Chamber of Commerce, 1962*
GPS Coordinates: 34° 19.177' N, 81° 15.649' W

20–3 James Henry Carlisle
1825–1909

201 East Washington St., Winnsboro

(FRONT) Educator, Humanitarian, Religious Leader, College President. He believed that: "The student ought to be educated not simply or chiefly because he intends to be a farmer, lawyer, or statesman, but because he is a human being with capacities, and powers, with inlets of joy, with possibilities of effort and

action, which no trade or calling can satisfy or exhaust."
(REVERSE) Born in this house on May 24, 1825, the son of William and Mary Ann Carlisle, this noted teacher received his education at Mount Zion Institute and South Carolina College. A delegate in 1860 to the Secession Convention and a legislator in 1864, his greatest service was as the third President of Wofford College from 1875 to 1902, where he had taught since 1853. He died October 21, 1909. *Erected by Fairfield County Historical Society, 1965*
GPS Coordinates: 34° 22.857' N, 81° 5.07' W

20–4 William Porcher Dubose

Congress St., Winnsboro

This noted author-theologian, born at this site April 11, 1836, educated at Mt. Zion Institute, the Citadel, and the University of Virginia, served as an officer and as chaplain in the Confederate War. He was rector in Winnsboro and Abbeville, and in 1871 became Chaplain and Professor at the University of the South at Sewanee, Tenn. He died in 1918. *Erected by Fairfield County Historical Society, 1965*
GPS Coordinates: 34° 22.914' N, 81° 5.214' W

20–5 Nuclear Power

Parr Rd. (S.C. Sec. Rd. 20-16), 1.1 mi. E of its intersection with S.C. Hwy. 215, Parr vicinity

Two miles west of here at Parr Shoals on Broad River is the first atomic nuclear power plant in the Southeast. In 1954, the Atomic Energy Act was amended to allow the construction of nuclear power plants by private industry. Built by Carolinas Virginia Nuclear Power Associates, Inc., this plant was

dedicated on October 24, 1962. *Erected by Fairfield County Historical Society, 1965*
GPS Coordinates: 34° 15.862' N, 81° 18.256' W

20–6 Kincaid-Anderson House

Landis Rd. (S.C. Sec. Rd. 20-48), .9 mi. from its intersection with S.C. Hwy. 213, Jenkinsville vicinity

This two-story brick house was built by James Kincaid (1754–1801), Revolutionary War soldier, who came from Scotland in 1773 and acquired this land in 1775. It was completed according to his plans after his death by his son William Kincaid (1782–1834). Their descendants, the Andersons, lived here until about 1900. *Erected by Fairfield County Historical Society, 1966*
GPS Coordinates: 34° 19.046' N, 81° 14.478' W

20–7 Fairfield County/Winnsboro

Fairfield County Courthouse, Congress St., Winnsboro

Fairfield County (FRONT)
A center of activity in the Regulator movement to bring law and order to the backcountry, this area in 1769 was made part of Camden District under the Circuit Court Act. In 1775 it formed part of the District between the Broad and Catawba Rivers for election purposes. Laid out as the jurisdiction of a county court in 1785, Fairfield became a judicial district in 1800 and a county again in 1868.
Winnsboro (REVERSE)
Settled on land of the Winn family, by 1780 Winnsborough had about twenty houses when it was occupied by Cornwallis. On February 21, 1865, it was occupied again, by General W. T. Sherman. Chartered in 1785 by Richard and John Winn and John Vanderhorst, it was made the seat of justice for Fairfield District. Incorporated in 1832, Winnsboro became a social, religious, and educational center of this area. *Erected by Fairfield County Historical Society, 1967*
GPS Coordinates: 34° 22.816' N, 81° 5.188' W

20–8 Fairfield County Courthouse

On the wall of the Fairfield County Courthouse, Congress St., Winnsboro

This courthouse was built in 1822 by Wm. McCreight under the supervision of Robert Mills, South Carolina architect, then serving as Supt. of Public Works. Alterations and additions were made in 1844. It was renovated in 1939 with the addition of two rear wings and the flying stairways in front by G. Thomas Harmon, AIA, as supervising architect. *Erected by Fairfield County Historical Society, 1967*
GPS Coordinates: 34° 22.815' N, 81° 5.193' W

20–9 Thomas Woodward

S.C. Hwy. 34, about 1 mi. S of Rockton

1/4 mile east stood the home of Thomas Woodward, prominent leader of the South Carolina Regulator Movement, 1768–1769. He was a member of the First Provincial Congress and a Charter Member of the Mt. Zion Society. As Captain of Rangers in 1775–76 he led soldiers from this area in the Snow Campaign against Indians and Tories. *Erected by Fairfield County Historical Society, 1969*
GPS Coordinates: 34° 19.893' N, 81° 3.838' W

20–10 Battle of Mobley's Meeting House

S.C. Sec. Rd. 20-18, just N of its intersection with S.C. Hwy. 215, N of Salem Crossroads.

On May 26, 1780, one of the first victories for the Patriots after the fall of Charleston took place 1 ½ miles east on Little River. A body of Tories gathering at a Baptist meeting house in Mobley's settlement were attacked and dispersed by a band of Whigs under Col. Wm. Bratton, Maj. Richard Winn, and Capt. John McClure. *Erected by Fairfield County Historical Society, 1969*
GPS Coordinates: 34° 28.706' N, 81° 17.689' W

20–11 Feasterville Female and Male Academy

S.C. Hwy. 215, about 1 mi. S of intersection of S.C. Hwy. 215 & S.C. Sec. Rd. 20-33, NW of Salem Crossroads

Around 1840, an academy was established at this site by John Feaster, a noted landowner of this area, for the education of female and male students. By 1842, both an academy building and a boarding house (dormitory) had been erected. Mr. Feaster appointed as trustees his sons, Andrew, Jacob, and John M. Feaster. *Erected by Fairfield County Historical Society, 1970*
GPS Coordinates: 34° 30.134' N, 81° 21.614' W

20–12 Mt. Zion Society

Old Mt. Zion Institute Campus, Walnut St., Winnsboro

A social and benevolent group dedicated to the promotion of education, the Mt. Zion Society was organized in January 1777 at Charleston, S.C. John Winn was its first president. By the 1780s the society had founded a school for boys in Winnsboro. Under the leadership of J. W. Hudson, Mt. Zion Institute became an important educational force in antebellum South Carolina. It became a public school about 1878. *Erected by Fairfield County Historical Society, 1970*
GPS Coordinates: 34° 23.019' N, 81° 5.022' W

20–13 Mount Olivet Church

Mobley Hwy. (S.C. Sec. Rd. 20-20), .3 mi. W of its intersection with S.C. Hwy. 200, 7 mi. N of Winnsboro

Organized before 1785, this Presbyterian Church was originally known as Wolf Pit Church, later as Wateree, and was finally named Mt. Olivet in 1800. The Reverend William Martin, a Covenanter minister licensed by the Reformed Presbytery of Scotland, was an early minister here. The present house of worship was completed in 1869. *Erected by the Congregation, 1975*
GPS Coordinates: 34° 27.88' N, 81° 2.016' W

20–14 Cathcart-Ketchin House/ Catharine Ladd

231 South Congress St., Winnsboro

Cathcart-Ketchin House (FRONT)
Richard Cathcart purchased this lot from John McMaster in 1829, and it is thought he built the present federal-style house shortly thereafter. The house has had a number of owners including Priscilla Ketchin, who purchased it in 1874. The building was deeded to Fairfield County in 1969 by Ella Cathcart Wilburn and Carrie Cathcart Owings and was entered in the National Register of Historic Places in 1970.

Catharine Ladd (REVERSE)
Born in Virginia in 1810, playwright, poet, and educator Catharine Stratton Ladd married George Ladd, an artist who had studied with Samuel F. B. Morse. The Ladds owned this house from 1852 until 1862. Mrs. Ladd was principal of the Winnsboro Female Institute and during the Civil War was president of the Fairfield District Ladies' Relief Association. She died in 1899 and is buried in Salem Presbyterian churchyard. *Erected by Fairfield County Historical Society, 1979*
GPS Coordinates: 34° 22.641' N, 81° 5.13' W

20–15 John Hugh Means/William Harper

S.C. Sec. Rd. 20-18, 3 mi. N of Salem Crossroads

John Hugh Means (FRONT)
Governor of S.C. (1850–1852), president of the 1852 Secession Convention, and signer of the Ordinance of Secession in 1860, John Means was born near here in 1812. A colonel in the 17th Regiment, S.C. Volunteers, CSA, he died Sept. 1, 1862, from wounds received at the Second Battle of Manassas. He is believed to be buried in the Means Cemetery, about 50 yards east.

William Harper (REVERSE)
A graduate and trustee of S.C. College, William Harper immigrated here from Antigua in 1791. Admitted to the bar in 1813, he served in the S.C. House, was a U.S. Senator, court reporter, Chancellor, and judge of the Court of Appeals. He died in 1847 and is buried 50 yards east. The University of South Carolina's

Harper College takes its name from William Harper. *Erected by Fairfield County Historical Society, 1983*
GPS Coordinates: 34° 28.055' N, 81° 17.633' W

20-16 Fairfield Institute/Kelly Miller 1863-1939

Congress St., between Moultrie and Palmer Sts., Winnsboro

Fairfield Institute (FRONT)
This grade school and normal institute for blacks was founded in 1869 during Reconstruction by the Northern Presbyterian Church. The Reverend Willard Richardson was principal. In 1880, one- hundred of its students were studying to be teachers and twenty others to enter the ministry. The school closed in 1888 to merge with Brainerd Institute in Chester. The site is located one block west.
Kelly Miller 1863-1936 (REVERSE)
Born in Fairfield County, this renowned black educator attended Fairfield Institute, 1878-1880, and won a scholarship to Howard University, from which he graduated in 1886. After graduate work at Johns Hopkins, Miller received his A.M. and L.L.D. degrees (1901 and 1903) and was for many years professor and dean at Howard. His writings on race problems were widely read and used in major universities. *Erected by Fairfield County Historical Society, 1985*
GPS Coordinates: 34° 13.514' N, 81° 3.058' W

20-17 Graveyard of the Richmond Covenanter Church Reformed Presbyterian

S.C. Hwy. 901 at its intersection with S.C. Hwy. 52, .5 mi. S of Fairfield County-Chester County line and W of Mitford (A quarter mile east)
Here lie buried many of the Scotch Irish pioneers who in 1772, under the leadership of the Rev. William Martin, founded one of the first Covenanter churches in upper South Carolina. *Erected in 1959*
GPS Coordinates: 34° 32.715' N, 81° 1.446' W

20-18 First Methodist Church

109 W. College St., Corner of W. College St. and N. Congress St. (U.S. Hwy. 321), Winnsboro
First United Methodist Church was established in 1808 under the leadership of the Rev. James Jenkins, an early circuit-riding minister, and John Buchanan, a captain in the Revolution. Pioneer American Methodist bishop Francis Asbury visited here from 1809 to 1814. This building (1908) is the congregation's third structure; two earlier ones were located about two blocks SE. *Erected by The Congregation, 1990*
GPS Coordinates: 34° 22.962' N, 81° 5.238' W

20-19 Bethel Church

N. Zion St. & E. Washington St., Winnsboro
(FRONT) This Associate Reformed Presbyterian Church was incorporated in 1823. Early pastors were the Rev. James Lyle and the Rev. Thomas Ketchin, installed 1825 and 1844 respectively. The old cemetery, located at corner of Fairfield and Vanderhorst streets, is the traditional site of first church building; the second, located across Fairfield Street, was dedicated in 1873. The Women's Benevolent Society was organized 1871 and the Junior Christian [...]
(Revere) [...] Union in 1883. The congregation, under the Rev. Charles E. McDonald's leadership, moved to this site upon completing the present 1903 building. The Boag Memorial Educational Building, dedicated 1937, was a gift of Mr. & Mrs. James O. Boag. Buried in the cemetery are the Rev. Neill E. Pressly D.D., and Rachel Elliott Pressly, first ARP missionaries to Mexico 1878-1917; and the Rev. Oliver Johnson, D.D., pastor of this church 1908-1945. *Erected by The Congregation, 1993*
GPS Coordinates: 34° 22.86' N, 81° 5.088' W

20-20 Church of Jesus Christ of Latter-Day Saints

Centerville Rd. (S.C. Sec. Rd. 20-67), near its junction with Ridgeway Rd. (S.C. Hwy. 34), SE of Ridgeway
Site of 5 buildings 1897-1986. Enemies of

church burned two, tornado destroyed one.
1994 marks 100 years of Mormon presence in
this community. *Erected by The Congregation,
1994*
GPS Coordinates: 34° 16.919' N, 80° 51.572' W

20–21 St. Paul Baptist Church

207 N. Garden St., Winnsboro

This African American church was organized
in 1873 by Simon McIntosh, Henry Golden,
Lily Yarborough, Frances Kelly, Lizzie Hart,
and others. The first pastor, Rev. Daniel
Golden, served 1873–1891. The first sanctuary was built in 1876. The present sanctuary
was built in 1893 and remodeled during the
pastorate of Rev. C. L. McMillian, who served
1958–1989. *Erected by The Congregation, 1995*
GPS Coordinates: 34° 13.788' N, 81° 3.271' W

20–22 Saint John's Episcopal Church

Intersection of West Liberty St. and South Gadsden
St., Winnsboro

(FRONT) Organized in 1839 and named for
St. John's, Berkeley Parish, this was the third
Episcopal church established north of Columbia. The Rev. Josiah Obear became its first
rector in 1841, serving 1841–49 and 1875–82.
The first sanctuary, a wood-frame building,
was built on Fairfield St. in 1842. During the
Civil War many families who fled the lowcountry and lived in Winnsboro as refugees
worshipped at St. John's.
(REVERSE) The original sanctuary was burned
by Union troops in Feburary 1865. A second
wood-frame sanctuary was designed by a
former St. John's rector, the Rev. John DeWitt
McCullough, in the Carpenter Gothic style.
It was built on Liberty St. in 1869 and burned
in 1888. This brick sanctuary, designed by
architect R. S. Schuyler in the Gothic style
and constructed by contractor Gorge Waring,
was consecrated in 1889. *Erected by St. John's
Church, 1999*
GPS Coordinates: 34° 22.657' N, 81° 5.358' W

20–23 Camp Welfare

Camp Welfare Rd., 2.5 S. of Wateree Rd., Mitford

(FRONT) This camp ground, described by one
journalist as "picturesque, rugged, simple
with an overhanding air of festivity," has
hosted an annual camp meeting since 1876;
slaves had worshipped here before the Civil
War. The site was purchased in 1878 by trustees Carter Beaty, Charles Green, Jeff Gaither,
Henry Hall, and John Hall. It was deeded to
Camp Wllfair A.M.E. Zion Church in 1925.
(REVERSE) The small wood-frame or cinder-
block houses a Camp Welfare are typical of
"tents" at church camo grounds. An early 20th
century one-room school stood here until it
closed in 1955. The site also includes Camp
Wellfair A.M.E. Zion Church (built about
1930), an open-air arbor, and a cemetery.
Camp Welfare was listed in the National Register of Historic Places in 1984. *Erected by the
Fairfield County Historical Society, 2002*
GPS Coordinates: 34° 17.676' N, 80° 34.261' W

20–24 The Oaks

Monjicono Rd., ½ mi. W. of Jackson Creek Rd.,
Rion vicinity

(FRONT) This early Greek Revival house, built
about 1835, is notable for its central double-
tiered pedimented portico and double end
chimneys. It was named for the oak avenue
leading up to it and the oak grove surrounding it. The Oaks was built for Richard A. R.
Hallum (1809–1875), who sold it and its 1,000-
acre plantation to John Montgomery Lemmon
(1829–1906) in 1856.
(REVERSE) In Feburary 1865 John M. Lemmon
was in the Confederate army in Virginia when
elements of Gen W. T. Sherman's Federal army
advanced towards Winnsboro from Columbia. Foragers looted the plantation, taking
food, livestock, and valuables. The Oaks was
owned by the Lemmon family or their descendants until the 1980s. It was listed in the
National Register of Historic Places in 1984.
*Erected by the Fairfield County Historical
Society, 2006*
GPS Coordinates: 34° 21.234' N, 81° 11.274' W

Florence County

21–1 Moses S. Haynsworth

S. Charleston Rd. (S.C. Sec. Rd. 21–35), just N of
Cecil Rd., N of I-95 between Exits 164 and 169,
Florence vicinity

Born in Darlington District in 1845, this
Confederate War veteran witnessed the fir-
ing attack on the Union steamer "Star of the
West" as it attempted to reinforce Ft. Sumter
Jan. 9, 1861. He participated in skirmishes at
Tullifinny River near Yemassee Dec. 1864.
Owner of this plantation, "Idylwild," he died
in 1928, and is buried in Florence, S.C. *Erected
by Governor Robert Gibbes Chapter, National
Society Colonial Dames XVII Century, 1975*
GPS Coordinates: 34° 14.529' N, 79° 47.227' W

21–2 William Gee

W. Palmetto St. (U.S. Hwy. 76) at its junction
with S. Cashua Dr., 5 mi. W of Florence, Ebenezer
vicinity

A veteran of the Revolution, William Gee
served as a private with the Continental Line
of N.C. and moved to this area before 1797. He
was one of the original members of the Washington Society, organized in 1803 to establish
an academy on Jeffries Creek at Ebenezer. His
grave is located about 250 feet southwest of
here. *Erected by the Florence County Historical
Society, 1976*
GPS Coordinates: 34° 9.817' N, 79° 51.236' W

21–3 Witherspoon's Ferry /Johnsonville

Kingsburg Hwy. (S.C. Hwy. 51/41) between
American Legion Hut # 144 and Odell Venters
Landing, just N of Johnsonville

Witherspoon's Ferry (FRONT)
In use during the American Revolution,
Witherspoon's Ferry was the site where
Francis Marion accepted command of the
Williamsburg Militia in 1780. Ownership of
the ferry lands passed from Robert to John

Witherspoon in 1787; in 1802 John bequeathed
the land to Aimwell Presbyterian Church. The
church had closed by 1820.
Johnsonville (REVERSE)
In 1819, former South Carolina Governor
David R. Williams, son-in-law of John With-
erspoon, obtained these ferry lands. In 1842
William Johnson acquired the land and in
1843 a post office, named Johnsonville, was
established near here. *Erected by Three Rivers
Historical Society, 1979*
GPS Coordinates: 33° 50.217' N, 79° 26.917' W

21–4 Marion at Port's Ferry/Asbury at Port's Ferry

Kingsburg Hwy. (S.C. Hwy. 41/ 51), Kingsburg
vicinityabout 3 mi. N of Johnsonville

Marion at Port's Ferry (FRONT)
Port's Ferry, 3 miles NE on the Pee Dee,
was owned and operated by Frances Port (ca.
1725–1812), widow of Thomas Port, who was
a member of the Provincial Congress from
Prince Frederick's Parish. This was a strategic
crossing for Francis Marion, who fortified and
used it frequently in his fall campaign of 1780
against British and Tories.
Asbury at Port's Ferry (REVERSE)
During his journeys in S.C. from 1801 on,
Methodist Bishop Francis Asbury often used
the ferry and stayed at the homes of friends
nearby. In 1811, the year before Frances Port's
death, Asbury "found mother Port keeping
house at eighty-seven." His last crossing was
in January 1816, a few weeks before his own
death. *Erected by Three Rivers Historical Society, 1980*
GPS Coordinates: 33° 51.583' N, 79° 26.817' W

21–5 Ebenezer Church

524 S. Ebenezer Rd (S.C. Sec. Rd. 21–112), about
1.2 mi. N of U.S. Hwy. 76, Ebenzer vicinity

(FRONT) In January of 1778 Ebenezer Baptist
Church was constituted by pioneer minister

Evan Pugh and Richard Furman, for whom Furman University is named. Admitted to the Charleston Baptist Association in 1778, the church was incorporated in 1791 as "The Baptist Church, Ebenezer, Jeffries's Creek." Timothy Dargan was an early minister, who served the church until his death in 1783. (Revere) Through the years, this church has supported evangelism, missions, and education. One member, Neale C. Young, served 42 years as a missionary to Nigeria. Another, Ruth Pettigrew, was a missionary to China and Hong Kong for 39 years. Miss Young is buried in Ebenezer Cemetery and Miss Pettigrew in Hong Kong, where she chose to spend her last days. *Erected by The Congregation, 1982*
GPS Coordinates: 34° 10.738' N, 79° 51.14' W

21–6 Young Farm

W. Palmetto St. (U.S. Hwy. 76), about 1.5 mi. W of Florence and just S of I-95 Exit 157, Ebenezer vicinity

In 1925 U.S. Secretary of Commerce Herbert Hoover, later U.S. president, inspected Fred Young's dairy farm following recognition of one of its Jerseys, Sensation's Mikado's Millie, as a world champion butter-fat producer. The house here, built ca. 1877 according to family tradition, was remodeled 1968 by Edward L. Young, S.C. House member 1958–60, U.S. Congressman 1972–74. *Erected by Florence County Historical Commission, 1983*
GPS Coordinates: 34° 9.558' N, 79° 51.738' W

21–7 Dewitt Bluff

Near intersection of River Rd. (S.C. Sec. Rd. 21-40) and Old River Rd. (S.C. Sec. Rd. 21-57), just SE of Pamplico

(FRONT) Located about ½ mile east, this bluff, part of a Royal landgrant to Edward Crofts in 1740, was named for the DeWitt family, who settled nearby prior to 1767. This area of Prince Frederick Parish was known as Queensborough Township, one of 11 such townships planned by the British Crown in 1730 to foster settlement and protect the interior of the province.
(REVERSE) The bluff named for the DeWitt family who settled in this area before 1767 is located about ½ mile east of here. By 1840, an adjacent landing for steamboats plying the Pee Dee River was named for the bluff. Members of the DeWitt family served in the Revolution and in the War Between the States; the family still owns land in this area. *Erected by Florence County Historical Society, 1987*
GPS Coordinates: 33° 59.419' N, 79° 31.53' W

21–8 William W. Harllee

At Hopewell Presbyterian Church, 5314 Old River Rd. (S.C. Sec. Rd. 21-57), just E of the intersection of S.C. Sec. Rd. 21-57 & S.C. Sec. Rd. 21-327, Florence vicinity

President of Wilmington & Manchester Railroad and a founder of the city of Florence, Harllee (1812–1897) was also a general in the S.C. Militia, signer of Ordinance of Secession, Lt. Governor (1860–62), member of the General Assembly, and president of the S.C. Bar Association. Both he and his daughter, from whom Florence takes its name, are buried here in Hopewell Cemetery. *Erected by Florence Heritage Foundation, 1990*
GPS Coordinates: 34° 7.716' N, 79° 37.404' W

21–9 Browntown

At the Browntown Museum, 3114 Johnsonville Hwy. (U.S. Hwy. 341), about 10 mi. E of Lake City and 5 mi. W of Prospect Crossroads

This area is part of several royal landgrants to Moses Brown in 1768–69 which developed into a family community known as Browntown. Family holdings here eventually comprised over 8,000 acres. Many indications of pioneering ingenuity and farm-related industry remain, including a notable cotton gin with wooden gears which continued operating through the late 19th century. *Erected by the Three Rivers Historical Society, 1982*
GPS Coordinates: 33° 49.935' N, 79° 37.247' W

21–10 Christ Episcopal Church

2305 N. Williston Rd. (U.S. Hwy. 327), 2.5 mi. S of I-95, Mars Bluff vicinity

(FRONT) First organized as a chapel in 1843 by the Rev. N. P. Tillinghast of Trinity Church, Society Hill, this church was formally established as Christ Church, Mars Bluff, in 1856. The Rev. Augustus Moore, who took over the chapel in 1854, became the first rector of Christ Church and served until 1876. This sanctuary, on land donated by Dr. Edward Porcher, was consecrated in 1859.
(REVERSE) By the 1890s Christ Church became a mission church rather than a parish church, but continued monthly services until they were suspended in 1918. The church began an annual homecoming service in 1927 and held special services such as baptisms and weddings during the 1930s and 1940s; it was officially reorganized as a mission church in 1950. *Erected by the Pee Dee Committee, National Society of Colonial Dames of America in the State of South Carolina, 1997*
GPS Coordinates: 34° 14.555' N, 79° 41.532' W

21–11 Roseville Plantation

3636 N. Williston Rd. (Old Georgetown Rd./S.C. Hwy. 327), just N of its intersection with I-95 Exit 170, Florence vicinity

(FRONT) Roseville Plantation was established by a royal grant before the American Revolution and a house was built here ca. 1771 for the Dewitt family. Richard Brockinton (d. ca. 1843), planter and state representative, purchased Roseville in 1821. Most of the house burned ca. 1832, and a second house was built on the original foundation for Brockinton and his wife Mary Hart about 1835.
(REVERSE) In the 1850s the plantation passed to the Brockintons' nephew Peter Samuel Bacot (1810–1864), a planter, whose daughter Ada White Bacot Clarke (1832–1911) was born here and was later a Confederate nurse and diarist. The Clarkes remodeled the house ca. 1885 and ca. 1910. Roseville was restored by the Tucker family and listed in the National Register of Historic Places in 1997. *Erected by the Ellison*

Capers Chapter, United Daughters of the Confederacy, 1998
GPS Coordinates: 34° 16.625' N, 79° 42.177' W

21–12 William R. Johnson House/ The Columns

E. Old Marion Hwy. (S.C. Hwy. 24) at Rankin Plantation Rd., Mars Bluff vicinity

William R. Johnson House (FRONT)
This Greek Revival house was built ca. 1854 for William R. Johnson, (1813–1893), physician, planter, and legislator in what was then Marion District. Johnson, an 1838 graduate of the Medical College of S.C., later served in the S.C. House of Representatives 1852–55 and the S.C. Senate 1860–63; he died here in 1893 and is buried at nearby Hopewell Presbyterian Church.
The Columns (REVERSE)
After Walter L. Rankin of N.C. acquired the house in 1902, Mrs. Rankin named it "The Columns"; it is still owned by his descendants. It has been called "Carolina Hall" since 1934, when it was the model for the plantation house in the movie *Carolina,* starring Janet Gaynor and Lionel Barrymore. It was listed in the National Register of Historic Places in 1974. *Erected by the Pee Dee Committee, The National Society of The Colonial Dames of America in the State of South Carolina, 2000*
GPS Coordinates: 34° 13.637' N, 79° 38.896' W

21–13 Ney School/Back Swamp School

E. Pocket Rd. (S.C. Sec. Rd. 21-26), just W of its junction with Rogers Ct., Back Swamp community, Florence vicinity

Ney School (FRONT)
About 1843 Robert Rogers (1808–1882), a planter at "Blooming Grove" in the Back Swamp community of what was then Darlington District, built a plantation schoolhouse and hired Peter Stuart Ney (d. 1846) to teach his children. The original building, moved here in 1870, was later the library for Back Swamp School (1921–1950). In 1970 it was moved to the home of Evander McIver Ervin.

Back Swamp School (REVERSE)
This school, the second on the site, was built in 1921 by Back Swamp residents. An elementary school sometimes known as St. Winifred's, it boasted as many as two teachers and sixty students in some years. When it closed in 1950 its students were transferred to Florence schools; it has since served as the Back Swamp Community Center. *Erected by the Darlington County Historical Commission, 2000*
GPS Coordinates: 34° 16.439' N, 79° 43.087' W

21–14   Mt. Zion Rosenwald School

5040 Liberty Chapel Rd., Mars Bluff

(FRONT) This school, built in 1925, was the first public school for African American students in the Mars Bluff community. One of more than 5000 schools in the South funded in part by the Julius Rosenwald Foundation, it features a standard two-classroom plan typical of the rural schools built by the foundation between 1917 and 1932.
(REVERSE) The first school here, a private school built by Mt. Zion Methodist Church in 1870, burned in the early 1920s. Mt. Zion Rosenwald School usually operated on a four- or five-month calendar in which two or three teachers taught grades 1–6. It closed in 1952 when a new Mars Bluff Consolidated School opened. This school was listed in the National Register of Historic Places in 2001. *Erected by Mt. Zion United Methodist Church, 2002*
GPS Coordinates: 34° 10.773' N, 79° 38.618' W

21–15   Hewn-Timber Cabins

E. Palmetto St. /Christopher James Yahnis Hwy. (U.S. Hwy. 301/76) at Wallace Woods Rd., on the Francis Marion University Campus, Mars Bluff

(FRONT) The African Americans who built the two hewn-timber cabins that stand 200 yds. S on Wallace Woods Road were brought to Mars Bluff as slaves in 1836. They lived in these cabins on the cotton plantation of J. Eli Gregg, in what was then Marion District. These cabins are the last two of eight that originally stood in a cotton field at what is now the center of the university campus.

(REVERSE) The cabins, built of 4" × 9" hand-hewn timbers, feature precise full-dovetail joints and pine plank floors. They were enlarged after the Civil War. Freedmen and later tenant farmers lived in these houses until the 1950s. Relocated several times, one cabin was moved to this site in 1980, the other in 1990. They were listed in the National Register of Historic Places in 1974. *Erected by Francis Marion University, 2002*
GPS Coordinates: 34° 11.754' N, 79° 38.993' W

21–16   Greater St. James A.M.E. Church

339 Moore St., Lake City

(FRONT) This church was founded in 1883 by a Rev. Hill and twenty-five charter members. Early services were held in a member's house on E. Main Street. The congregation purchased a lot at the corner of Lake and N. Church Streets in 1885 and built its first sanctuary, a frame building, that year. That church was renovated and enlarged in 1917. It was further renovated, adding a steeple, in 1948–50.
(REVERSE) In 1951 Rev. J. A. DeLaine (1898–1974) was transferred from Pine Grove A.M.E. Church in Summerton after playing a leading role in *Briggs v. Elliott*, the Clarendon County school desegregation case that led to *Brown v. Board of Education* (1954). Unknown persons burned the church in October 1955. Rev. G. Lee Baylor was the pastor when a new sanctuary, named Greater St. James, was dedicated here in 1957. *Erected by the Congregation, 2004*
GPS Coordinates: 33° 51.995' N, 79° 45.902' W

21–17   Mt. Zion Methodist Church

5040 Liberty Chapel Rd., Mars Bluff

(FRONT) This church, founded in 1868 with Rev. James Wesley Johnson as its first minister, held its early services in a brush arbor. In 1870 trustees purchased this 1 ¾ acre tract to build a "Negro Schoolhouse" sponsored by the church, the first in the Mars Bluff community. This sanctuary, originally a frame building, was built in 1875 on a tract purchased from the school.

(REVERSE) The sanctuary was extensively re-modeled and covered in brick veneer in 1970. The cemetery nearby, established in 1876, includes the graves of such early church leaders as Anthony H. Howard (1840–1908), a former slave who served in the S.C. House of Representatives during Reconstruction. Howard was also one of several black farmers who grew rice here after the Civil War. *Erected by the Congregation, 2004*
GPS Coordinates: 34° 10.758' N, 79° 38.616' W

21–18 Roseville Plantation Slave and Freedman's Cemetery/Clarke Cemetery

Near Roseville Plantation, 3636 N. Williston Rd. (Old Georgetown Rd./S.C. Hwy. 327), just N of its intersection with I-95 Exit 170, Florence vicinity

Roseville Plantation Slave and Freedman's Cemetery (FRONT)
This was originally the slave cemetery for Roseville Plantation. Roseville, established about 1771 by the Dewitt family, was later owned by the Brockinton, Bacot, and Clarke families from the 1820s through the Civil War. A 1200-acre plantation, it had more than 100 slaves living and planting cotton here by 1850. Clarke Cemetery (REVERSE)
This cemetery is sometimes called "the Clarke Cemetery" after the family that owned Roseville from Reconstruction until 1948. It is about 150 ft. square, and though it contains relatively few gravemarkers it includes at least 150 and as many as 250 or more graves. Slaves, freedmen, and their descendants were buried here for two hundred years, from the 1770s to the 1970s. *Erected by the Roseville Slave Cemetery Committee, 2004*
GPS Coordinates: 34° 16.902' N, 79° 42.156' W

21–19 Florence Depot 1852/ Wilmington & Manchester RR

Hoffmeyer Rd. at W. Darlington St., Florence

Florence Depot 1852 (FRONT)
The original depot named Florence was built here in 1852, where the Wilmington & Manchester RR crossed present-day Hoffmeyer Rd. It was named for Florence Harllee

(1848–1927), daughter of the railroad's president, William W. Harllee (1812–1897). In 1855 a new depot was built 2 mi. E where the railroad crossed Coit St., the Cheraw & Darlington RR, and the North Eastern RR. Wilmington & Manchester RR (REVERSE)
The 1855 depot became the center of the city of Florence, incorporated in 1871. The Wilmington & Manchester RR, chartered in 1846, began operating in 1853 and ran from Eagle Island, N.C., to Manchester, S.C., passing within 10 mi. of Darlington, S.C. In 1870 it was reorganized as the Wilmington, Columbia, & Augusta RR. It became part of the Atlantic Coast Line RR in 1898. *Erected by the Florence County Historical Society, 2005*
GPS Coordinates: 34° 11.591' N, 79° 48.649' W

21–20 Hannah

U.S. Hwy. 378, Hannah

(FRONT) Hannah, named for the Hannah/Hanna family, was known as Cane Branch or Lynches River before a post office was opened here in 1887. William S. Hannah (1807–1876), a farmer and merchant, built his house nearby in 1847 and also ran a general store here; he later dropped the final "h" from the family name. This area was part of Marion County until Florence County was created in 1888. (REVERSE) The Hannah Post Office, open from 1887 to 1917, served a community of two churches, two general stores, a cotton gin, saw mill, grist mill, and cane mill. William S. Hanna's store, built ca. 1850, operated for more than 135 years, passing to his son Ervin (1840–1924), grandson Davis (1892–1978), and great-grandson Murdock (1920–1986). The old store was replaced in the 1960s. *Erected by the Florence County Historical Commission, 2005*
GPS Coordinates: 33° 53.009' N, 79° 34.675' W

21–21 William H. Johnson Birthplace

E. Palmetto St., just W of Kemp St., Florence

(FRONT) William Henry Johnson (1901–1970), one of the most important African-American artists of the 20th century, was born nearby on Cox Street. His family later lived on the corner of Cheves and Kemp Streets. In 1918, at the age of 17, Johnson moved to New York City. Johnson studied at the National Academy of Design and the Cape Cod School of Art, won several prizes, and studied art in Europe 1926–29.

(REVERSE) Johnson, back in America in 1929–31, had paintings in several exhibitions and a one-day show at the Florence Y.M.C.A. Visits to Florence inspired paintings of local people and places. In 1931 he married Danish artist Holcha Krake, living in Europe before returning to New York in 1938. After Johnson's wife died in 1944 his health declined; he was institutionalized in New York in 1947 and died there in 1970. *Erected by the Florence City Council and the Florence County Council, 2006*

GPS Coordinates: 34° 11.673' N, 79° 45.183' W

21–22 Jamestown

Jamestown community, S.C. Hwy. 24 near its intersection with Jamestown Rd., Mars Bluff vicinity

(FRONT) This African American community, which flourished here for 70 years, has its origins in a 105-acre tract bought in 1870 by former slave Ervin James (1815–1872). James, determined to own his own farm instead of being dependent on sharecropping or tenant farming, bought the tract from Eli McKissick and Mary Poston. His five sons and a son-in-law later divided the tract into individual farms.

(REVERSE) Between 1870 and 1940 Ervin James's descendants and other area families purchased additional land, creating a rural community of about 250 residents. Among its institutions were the Jamestown Cemetery, dating from its earliest days; the Summerville Methodist Church (renamed Bowers Chapel), established about 1880; and the Summerville Elementary School, built in 1926. *Erected by the Jamestown Reunion Committee, 2006*

GPS Coordinates: 34° 12.831' N, 79° 36.725' W

21–23 Pisgah Methodist Church

621 N. Ebenezer Rd., Florence

(FRONT) This church, founded in 1806 in what was Darlington District until Florence County was founded in 1888, grew out of an early Methodist "Society." Rev. Thomas Humphries (d. 1820), who served this and other area circuits, conducted the first service. In 1813 Dempsey Russell donated an acre to the congregation, which soon built a frame building here as its first permanent church.

(REVERSE) The church, often called "Russell's Meeting House" or "Russell's Church" for Dempsey Russell, changed its name to Pisgah Methodist Church in 1840. It moved to a site a few miles west after the Civil War but soon returned to this site and built a larger frame church in 1878–79. The present church, built in 1914, is a fine example of the Carpenter Gothic architectural style. *Erected by the Congregation, 2006*

GPS Coordinates: 34° 12.686' N, 79° 50.369' W

21–24 The Assassination of Rep. Alfred Rush

[Damaged and temporarily removed in 2020.]

Intersection of W. John Paul Jones Rd. (S.C. Sec. Rd. 21–35) and W. Cummings Rd. (S.C. Sec. Rd. 21–848), vicinity of Peniel Crossroads, NW of Effingham

(FRONT) Alfred Rush (d. 1876), a black state representative for two terms during Reconstruction, was assassinated near here, about 1/2 mi. from his home, on May 13, 1876. Rush, who represented what was then Darlington County in the S.C. House 1868–70 and 1874–76, was also a deacon at Savannah Grove Baptist Church.

(REVERSE) Rush and his wife, returning from a picnic at Mt. Carmel Church near Timmonsville, were ambushed by an unknown gunman. Alfred Rush was killed instantly. Several black Darlington County officials wrote Gov. D. H. Chamberlain, "this was a cold blooded murder and our people are very much excited over it." *Erected by the Florence County Historical Commission, 2008*

GPS Coordinates: 34° 5.073' N, 79° 50.923' W

21–25 Hopewell Presbyterian Church

5314 Old River Rd., Florence

(FRONT) This church, organized ca. 1770, is the first Presbyterian church in what is now Florence County. Many of its founding families came to S.C. from Scotland and Ireland. The first church here, a frame building, stood across Old River Road with the church cemetery around it, but burned soon after it was completed.

(REVERSE) The second church was replaced by this Greek Revival church in 1842, with its two-story portico, gallery, and original pews. Darlington (1827), Florence First (1861), and Effingham (1906) are daughter churches of Hopewell. The church and cemetery were listed in the National Register of Historic Places in 2000. *Erected by the Congregation in Memory of Mrs. W. H. (Lydia) Gregg, 2008* GPS Coordinates: 34° 7.703' N, 79° 37.41' W

21–26 Atomic Bomb Accident at Mars Bluff, March 11, 1958

E. Marion Hwy. (U.S. Hwy. 301/76) near the Francis Marion University Campus, Mars Bluff

(FRONT) In 1958, in the midst of the Cold War, the U.S. Air Force accidentally dropped an atomic bomb near here. The unarmed 7,600-lb., 10'8"-long bomb was aboard a B-47E bomber on a training mission headed for England. Its high-explosive trigger detonated on impact, making a crater as large as 35 feet deep and 70 feet wide.

(REVERSE) The bomb landed in the woods behind the asbestos-shingle-sided home of railroad conductor Walter "Bill" Gregg (b. 1921). Gregg, his wife, their three children, and a niece were injured by the concussion, which destroyed the house and outbuildings and did slight damage to buildings within a 5 mile radius. *Erected by the Florence City and County Historical Commission, 2008* GPS Coordinates: 34° 11.801' N, 79° 39.796' W

21–27 Red Doe

Francis Marion Rd. (S.C. Hwy. 327), .5 mi. S of Liberty Chapel Rd., approximately 3 mi. E of Florence

(FRONT) This house was built in 1846 for Evander A. Gregg (1818–1874), a planter in what was Marion District. Its high masonry basement and porch form, indigenous to northeastern S.C., make it a fine example of a raised Carolina cottage. It was acquired by R. L. Singletary (1830–1910) in 1867 and by J. W. Wallace (1861–1928) in 1912. The plantation was named Red Doe in the 1930s.

(REVERSE) "Red Doe" refers to an incident during the Revolution when Patriot scout Andrew Hunter escaped on "Red Doe," the horse of Loyalist Col. David Fanning. Red Doe, restored by Chisolm and Annie Wallace in 1940, was listed in the National Register of Historic Places in 1982. In 2006 Robert P. Wilkins donated it to a nonprofit group for preservation. *Erected by the Florence City and County Historical Commission, 2009* GPS Coordinates: 34° 10.513' N, 79° 38.903' W

21–28 Lake City

At the corner of Main St. (U.S. Hwy. 378 & S.C. Hwy. 341) & Church St., Lake City

(FRONT) This area, in what was then Williamsburg Township, was settled as early as 1754 by members of the Dick, Graham, McAllister, Scott, and other families. Several residents served under Francis Marion during the Revolution. By the 1820s this community was sometimes called "the crossroads" for the intersection of two major roads (one from Georgetown to Camden, the other from Charleston to Cheraw), now Main and Church Streets.

(REVERSE) This area was known as "Graham's Crossroads" for Aaron Graham, who built a house here ca. 1830. The post office opened here in 1848 was named "Lynches Lake." The town grew after the Northeastern RR was completed in 1857 and was chartered as Graham in 1874. Renamed Lake City in 1883, it was in Williamsburg County until 1912. Its tobacco market, opened in 1899, was among the largest in S.C. Its bean market, opened in 1936, was once the largest in the world.

Erected by the Florence City and County Historical Commission, 2009
GPS Coordinates: 33° 52.299' N, 79° 45.183' W

21–29 American Legion Post #1/2nd Lieutenant Fred H. Sexton

3631 E. Palmetto St., Florence

American Legion Post #1 (FRONT)
This post, organized in May 1919 and chartered by national headquarters in June 1919, was the first American Legion post in S.C. Florence County veterans J. D. Smyser, R. B. Fulton, and N. S. Lachicotte represented S.C. at the first national caucus. The American Legion of S.C. held its first state caucus in Florence in July 1919. A monument to Florence County WWI veterans was erected here in 1928.
2nd Lieutenant Fred H. Sexton (REVERSE)
American Legion Post #1 is named for 2nd Lieutenant Fred H. Sexton (1890–1918), killed in France in World War I. Sexton, a native of Union, moved to Florence in 1911. He enlisted in the S.C. National Guard and was promoted to 2nd lt., 113th Infantry, 29th Division, in 1918. He was killed in the Meuse-Argonne in Oct. 1918 and posthumously awarded the Distinguished Service Cross, the second highest American military honor. *Erected by the Fred H. Sexton Post # 1, American Legion, Department of South Carolina, 2010*
GPS Coordinates: 34° 11.816' N, 79° 41.467' W

21–30 Gregg-Wallace Farm Tenant House

310 Price Rd., Mars Bluff vicinity

(FRONT) This house, built as a one-room tenant house ca. 1890 and later enlarged several times, features a narrow front porch and rear shed addition typical of many tenant houses on plantations and farms in the post-Civil War South. Like the families who lived here, most tenants were African American.
(REVERSE) From 1890 to 1999 members of the Williams, Waiters, Frazier, Martin, and Gregg families lived here, working as wage laborers or sharecroppers, on land owned by the Gregg and Wallace families. This tenant house was

listed in the National Register of Historic Places in 2002. *Erected by the Florence City and County Historical Commission, 2010*
GPS Coordinates: 34° 12.078' N, 79° 39.155' W

21–31 Wilson School/Wilson High School

Corner of Palmetto & Dargan Sts., Florence

Wilson School (FRONT)
Wilson School, later Wilson High School, was the first public school in Florence, and stood here from 1866 to 1906. At first a private school for black children, it was established by the New England Branch of the Freedmen's Union Commission and operated by the Freedmen's Bureau. Thomas C. Cox, its first principal, later served as Darlington County sheriff. The school became a public school after the S.C. Constitution of 1868 authorized a system of free public schools.
Wilson High School (REVERSE)
Rev. Joshua E. Wilson (1844–1915), a Methodist minister, was an early principal of what was long called "the Colored Graded School." It was most likely named Wilson School for him. The school on this site, a frame building, was torn down in 1906 to make was for Central School. A new Wilson School was built on Athens Street. Wilson High School was on Athens Street 1906–1956 and on North Irby Street 1956–1982. It has been on Old Marion Highway since 1982. *Erected by the Wilson High School Alumni Association, Inc., 2010*
GPS Coordinates: 34° 11.613' N, 79° 45.957' W

21–32 Lawton-Chase House/ Florence Museum

558 Spruce St., Florence

Lawton-Chase House (FRONT)
This Art Moderne house, completed in 1939 for Joseph Maner Lawton, has housed the Florence Museum since 1953. It was designed by Sanborn Chase, then an engineering student influenced by Moderne architecture in France and later a prominent local businessman. The house features curved streamlined forms, a semicircular glass block entrance bay, and black glass bands just below the roofline.

When completed it was described as "the talk of Florence."

Florence Museum (REVERSE)

The Florence Museum, chartered in 1936, was founded by the Florence Museum Committee, a group of civic-minded women who had organized as the Blue Bird Tea Room Committee during World War I. It was housed in the basement of the Florence Public Library from 1939 to 1952, when the museum board acquired this house. Its collection of fine art, archaelogical and historical artifacts, and natural science exhibits was opened to the public here in 1953. *Sponsored by the Florence Museum, 2011*

GPS Coordinates: 34° 11.208' N, 79° 46.557' W

21–33 W.T. Askins House

178 S. Acline Ave., Lake City

This Folk Victorian house, with pierced brackets and fretwork on its two-tiered porch, was built ca. 1895 for William Thomas Askins (1859–1932). Askins, a merchant and farmer, built and operated five stores here beginning in the 1890s, including the general store W. T. Askins and Sons. He and three sons also owned several tobacco and truck farms on the outskirts of Lake City. This house was listed in the National Register of Historic Places in 1995. *Sponsored by Florence County, 2012*

GPS Coordinates: 33° 52.213' N, 79° 45.335' W

21–34 Mars Bluff

Near the intersection of Fore Rd. (S.C. Sec. Rd. 21-89) & Hunt Rd., Mars Bluff

(FRONT) This is the center of Mars Bluff, a rural community 8 mi. across in both directions, bounded by the Great Pee Dee River, Black Creek, & Jefferies Creek. A ferry across the Great Pee Dee began operation in 1767. Patriot and Loyalist militia later clashed in the area during the Revolution. Mars Bluff grew in both size and significance after the Wilmington & Manchester RR arrived in the 1850s. (REVERSE) By the 1830s J. Eli Gregg (1805–1873) ran a general store south of here. He built a new store on this site, across from the depot, when the railroad was completed in 1853. A

blacksmith shop, cotton gin, grist mill, and saw mill made this the focus of Mars Bluff life for many years. Gregg's original store burned by 1930, but a store operated on this site until the 1950s. *Sponsored by the Samuel Bacot Chapter, Daughters of the American Revolution, 2013*

GPS Coordinates: 34° 12.270' N, 79° 39.348' W

21–35 Joshua Braveboy Plantation

Ron E. McNair Blvd. (U.S. Hwy. 52) at the Lynches Lake Bridge, Lake City

This site was part of the 150-acre plantation of Joshua Braveboy (1740-fl. 1820), a free black who served in the S.C. militia during the American Revolution. Braveboy, a native of N.C., came to S.C. in 1771 and received a grant on Two Mile Branch at Lynches Creek. He served under Gen. Francis Marion in 1780–81, and in another militia unit in 1782. He spent the rest of his life here, in what was then Williamsburg Co. *Sponsored by the Florence County Historical Commission, 2013*

GPS Coordinates: 33° 53.069' N, 79° 45.452' W

21–36 The Lynching of Frazier Baker

Church St., S. of intersection with Deep River St., Lake City

(FRONT) In 1898 a building here was the scene of a lynching that sparked outrage across the nation. Frazier Baker, an African American who had recently been appointed postmaster of Effingham, was appointed postmaster of Lake City in 1897. Whites who resented Baker harassed him, even burning the post office in an attempt to make him resign and leave town. An old school on this site became a temporary post office and Baker's home. (REVERSE) On the night of Feb. 21–22, 1898, a mob set the house on fire and shot Baker and his family when they ran out. Baker and a baby daughter were killed, his wife and three of their children were wounded, and an editorial called it "the most horrible crime ever committed" in S.C. Local and state officials did nothing. Eleven men were tried in federal court in 1899, but a hung jury resulted in a

mistrial. *Sponsored by the Town of Lake City,*
2013
GPS Coordinates: 33° 51.784' N, 79° 45.535' W

21–37 Church Street/Main Street

Church & Main Sts., Lake City

Church Street (FRONT)
Before the 1820s this intersection of two major roads, one from Georgetown to Camden
and the other from Charleston to Cheraw, was
popularly called "the crossroads." After Aaron
Graham built a house here ca. 1830, the area
became known as "Graham's Crossroads."
Church Street, the main north-south road
through the town until 1924, was named soon
after Bethlehem Baptist Church (now Lake
City First Baptist Church) was built in 1828.
Main Street (REVERSE)
Main Street, the main east-west road through
the town, first appears by that name on an
1812 plat. Before the Civil War this cross-
roads featured an inn and post office, drug
store, cotton gin, and an academy. Graham's
Methodist Church (now Lake City Methodist
Church) was built on Main Street in 1876.
Stores and warehouses were built on Railroad
Avenue, renamed Acline Avenue in 1898 when
the Atlantic Coast Line Railroad bought the
Northeastern Railroad. *Sponsored by the Lake*
City Beautification Committee, 2014
GPS Coordinates: 33° 52.288' N, 79° 45.177' W

21–38 Lake City Tobacco Markets/
Imperial Tobacco Company

N. Acline Ave., just S of W. Thomas St., Lake City

Lake City Tobacco Markets (FRONT)
Farmers in this vicinity began growing
tobacco in the early 1890s, and by 1895 Lake
City opened its first tobacco market and warehouse. It built its second warehouse by 1903,
a third by 1909, and two more by 1917. In the
heart of the S.C. "tobacco belt," this was the
second-largest market in the state for most of
the 20th century, and one of the largest in the
five states producing flue-cured tobacco.
Imperial Tobacco Company (REVERSE)
This building was built in 1912 for the Imperial Tobacco Company of Great Britain

and Ireland to redry and process tobacco
after it was sold and before it was aged in
warehouses. Imperial bought and processed
flue-cured tobacco in five Southern states for
most of the 20th century. This plant, once
the largest redrying plant in S.C., was sold
to T. S. Ragsdale & Co. of Lake City in 1960
and closed in 1971. *Sponsored by the Florence*
County Historical Commission, 2014
GPS Coordinates: 33° 52.159' N, 79° 45.353' W

21–39 Lake City Produce Markets/
Lake City Bean Market

111 Henry St., Lake City

Lake City Produce Markets (FRONT)
Lake City was a significant produce market as
early as 1894, shipping fruits and vegetables
to Northern markets until World War I. The
market revived in the late 1920s and flourished during the Depression, when it shipped
beans, squash, cucumbers, peas, and other
vegetables. Lake City was one of the largest
truck markets in the U.S. and claimed to be
the largest string-bean or snap-bean market
in the world.
Lake City Bean Market (REVERSE)
This building, originally called "the Lake
City Municipal Auction Market," was built in
1936 with assistance from the Public Works
Administration. It was soon popularly called
"the Lake City Bean Market" to recognize
the town's claim as the largest bean market in
the world before World War II. Extensively
restored, it reopened in 2011 as a community
center and sponsors events year-round. *Spon-*
sored by the Lake City Beautification Commit-
tee, 2014
GPS Coordinates: 33° 52.268' N, 79° 45.243' W

21–40 H.H. Singletary Building

E. Main St. & S. Acline Ave., Lake City

(FRONT) This two-story commercial building
was built in 1910 by Henry Horace Singletary
(1848–1912) as the H. H. Singletary Company,
with a grocery store on the first floor. Singletary, perhaps the most prominent businessman and civic leader in the town from
Reconstruction into the 20th century, once

owned almost 600 acres in what is now downtown Lake City. He also ran a sawmill and brickyard.

(REVERSE) Singletary was a pioneer in the creation and early prosperity of Lake City's produce markets in the 1890s, shipping local strawberries to Northern markets. He gave assistance to many institutions in Lake City, donating lumber for the first school in 1878, land for the second school in 1888, and land for the first sanctuary of Lake City Presbyterian Church, built in 1888. *Sponsored by the Lynches Lake Historical Society, 2014*
GPS Coordinates: 33° 52.377' N, 79° 45.281' W

21–41 Whitehead Infirmary

238 East Main St., Lake City

(FRONT) Dr. James Whitehead (1906–2004) was a graduate of Lake City H.S. and the Medical University of S.C. After completing his internship at Spartanburg General, he returned to Lake City where he practiced medicine for 55 years. In 1938 he oversaw the construction of this two-story building, which was built as a 14-bed obstetric hospital. With few other local options for professional medical care, however, Whitehead Infirmary quickly became the primary acute care facility in town.

(REVERSE) Whitehead Infirmary was established at a time when childbirth was increasingly occurring outside of the home. By 1950 the majority of U.S. births took place in hospitals and Whitehead Infirmary was part of this shift in medical practice. In addition to obstetrics, Dr. Whitehead also performed general surgery and treated numerous victims of traumatic injuries. The infirmary closed in 1959, but Whitehead maintained a clinic here until his retirement in 1986. *Sponsored by Lynches Lake Historical Society, 2014*
GPS Coordinates: 33° 52.280' N, 79° 45.030' W

21–42 Palmetto State Bank Robbery

Corner of Main and Acline Ave., Lake City

(FRONT) Constructed in 1907, this building originally housed Farmers and Merchants Bank. In 1934 the newly formed Palmetto State Bank opened here. On Sept. 5, 1934 the bank was robbed by three armed men. The bank had larger than normal deposits on hand because it was the height of tobacco marketing season and the group stole a reported $114,082. Frank English and his wife Geneva were the only people tried for the crime.

(REVERSE) At trial it was alleged that English was an associate of George "Baby Face" Nelson, and that the notorious criminal was involved in the crime, but that was never proven. Frank English was sentenced to 25 years and Geneva English received one year as an accessory. Palmetto State failed due to the robbery, but depositors were repaid by the newly established FDIC. It was the first time an FDIC insured bank had closed in S.C. *Sponsored by Lynches Lake Historical Society, 2014*
GPS Coordinates: 33° 52.381' N, 79° 45.283' W

21–43 Willow Creek Baptist Church

3089 N. Old River Rd., Florence

(FRONT) The congregation of Willow Creek Baptist Church can trace its origins to the early 19th century when it was first associated with Lynch's Creek Church. The first meeting house was built in the neighborhood ca. 1815. Samuel Timmons, pastor at Lynch's Creek, provided itinerant service in the early years. In 1829 Willow Creek was officially organized and joined the Charleston Baptist Association.

(REVERSE) In 1832 Willow Creek was a founding member of the Welsh Neck Baptist Association and in 1890 was again a charter member, this time of the Florence Association. In 1841 church member Edward Burch deeded three and a quarter acres of land, including the meeting house, to the Willow Creek Congregation. The first burials in the adjacent cemetery date to the early 19th century. *Sponsored by Willow Creek Baptist Church, 2015*
GPS Coordinates: 33° 6.286' N, 79° 35.422' W

21–44 McLeod Medical Center

111 West Cheves St., Florence

(FRONT) The McLeod Infirmary was located here in 1906, inspired by the need to provide

access to local medical and surgical care for people of the region. Frank Hilton McLeod was born in Richmond Co., N.C. in 1868 and graduated from the Univ. of Tennessee Medical School. In 1891, he moved to Florence and chartered the Florence Infirmary. By the 1920s it was the third largest hospital in the state. (REVERSE) In 1930, with the assistance of the Duke Endowment, McLeod Infirmary became a non-profit institution. A new building opened in 1935 and expanded capacity to 190 beds. Renamed McLeod Memorial Hospital in 1971, expansion continued when 14 blocks of Urban Renewal land were acquired just east of this location. The new McLeod Regional Medical Center opened in 1979 with over 300 beds and improved acute care facilities. *Sponsored by McLeod Medical Center, 2016*
GPS Coordinates: 34° 11.728' N, 79° 45.951' W

21–45   Historic Downtown African American Business District

300 Block of N. Dargan St., Florence

(FRONT) The 200 and 300 blocks of N. Dargan St. were once the center of a thriving African American business district in Florence. A number of black-owned businesses operated here, including restaurants, barber shops, funeral parlors and pharmacies. These businesses provided services to African American customers who were often denied access to white-owned businesses.
(REVERSE) By the first decades of the 20th century North Florence had become the principal African American residential district as patterns of racial segregation became more fixed. The shops located on N. Dargan St., just north of the Atlantic Coast Line Railroad, served the predominantly African American residents who lived and worked here. *Sponsored by the City of Florence, 2017*
GPS Coordinates: 34° 12.058' N, 79° 45.976' W

21–46   Timmonsville

100 Block of E. Main St., Timmonsville

(FRONT) Timmonsville was founded in 1852 and named for Rev. J. Morgan Timmons. Initial growth was spurred by the Wilmington

and Manchester R.R., which carried cotton and forest productions to the port of Wilmington. J. M. Timmons established a turpentine distillery by 1854 and a steam-powered saw mill produced 5,000 feet of plank in that same year. The Timmonsville Tobacco Warehouse Co. organized in 1895, placing Timmonsville at the center of the growing Pee Dee tobacco belt.
(REVERSE) A fire in 1901 burned much of the downtown. Driven by profits from the tobacco industry, the town rebuilt and by 1910 population had doubled. The Atlantic Coast Line R.R., which absorbed the W.M.R.R. in 1898, built a brick depot on Railroad (now Main) St. The Seaboard Air Line R.R. was operating a second line through Timmonsville by 1914, testament to its place as the third largest tobacco market in the state. Leaf factories and warehouses all serviced the industry. *Sponsored by the Town of Timmonsville, 2017*
GPS Coordinates: 34° 8.087' N, 79° 56.501' W

21–47   Civil Rights Sit-Ins

Intersection of N. Dargan St. and W. Evans St., Florence

(FRONT) On March 3–4, 1960, members of the Florence Youth branch of the NAACP staged protest demonstrations here at the former S. H. Kress store. Wilson H.S. students marched from Trinity Baptist Church to sit at the store's lunch counter, but were refused service and asked to leave. The police were called and the students left peacefully. Store management closed the counter before reopening shortly after.
(REVERSE) On March 4, 1960, students planned to picket in front of the store, but were arrested while walking up the building. Forty-eight protestors were arrested and charged with "parading without a permit." The convictions were appealed to the S.C. Supreme Court and overturned in City of Florence v. George (1962). The lunch counter remained closed until the 1970s when it was reopened with service for all. *Sponsored by Florence County Museum, 2019*
GPS Coordinates: 34° 11.5' N, 79° 45.58' W

21-49 Trinity Baptist
Church, Florence.
IMAGE COURTESY OF
SCDAH

21–48 Frank Mandeville Rogers Jr. /Florence Tobacco Warehouse Company

On Darlington Street, east of intersection with
N. Dargan St.

Frank Mandeville Rogers, Jr. (FRONT)
Frank Mandeville Rogers Jr. (1857–1945) of
Florence Co. was influential in the development of Bright Leaf Tobacco in S.C. In 1884–
85, he raised, cured, and sold a plot of tobacco
on his Mars Bluff plantation, proving its potential to replace cotton as S.C.'s top cash crop.
Rogers built a tobacco factory on Day St. and
led efforts to open S.C.'s first tobacco auction
warehouse, helping revitalize S.C.'s agricultural market economy.
Florence Tobacco Warehouse Company
(REVERSE)
The first auction in S.C. of flue-cured tobacco
occurred on this site in Oct. 1891 at the Florence Tobacco Warehouse. Nearly 300 people
attended. Before the Warehouse, Pee Dee
farmers had to ship their crop to N.C. and
Va. to sell. Other local markets opened soon
after. By 1900, the Pee Dee produced over 90
percent of S.C.'s annual 20 million pound tobacco crop, leading *The State* to call the plant,
"the Pearl of the Pee Dee." *Sponsored by Florence County Museum, 2019*
GPS Coordinates: 34° 12.055' N, 79° 45.921' W

21–49 Trinity Baptist Church

124 W. Darlington St., Florence

(FRONT) Trinity Baptist organized in 1868,
with Rev. Wesley J. Parnell (d.1873) serving as
its first pastor. The church initially met at the
home of members Jacob and Sarah Lindsey
on Front St. before obtaining a property at
the corner of Dargan and Marlboro Sts. The
church acquired this site in 1884 and began
meeting in a small frame sanctuary. Construction began on the current church around 1893
and finished by 1909.
(REVERSE) One of the city's oldest historically
black churches, Trinity became an important site for African American religious and
civic life in 20th century Florence. Ministers
often held city and state leadership positions.
Beginning in the 1940s, the church was a hub
of activity related to the civil rights movement, hosting meetings, N.A.A.C.P. events,
and national figures like Thurgood Marshall
and Fannie Lou Hamer. *Sponsored by Trinity
Baptist Church, 2019*
GPS Coordinates: 34° 12.026' N, 79° 46.052' W

Georgetown County

22–1 Attacks Upon Georgetown

U.S. Hwy. 17, E of Georgetown, near the Hobcaw Point Fishing & Observation Pier, on the peninsula between the Pee Dee and Waccamaw Rivers

On January 24, 1781, Capts. Carnes and Rudulph, by orders from Gen. Marion and Col. Lee, surprised the British garrison at Georgetown and captured Col. Campbell. Upon Gen. Marion's second approach, June 6, 1781, the British evacuated the town. Gen. Marion seized the stores, demolished the works, and retired. *Erected by the Georgetown Chapter, D. A. R., 1938*
GPS Coordinates: 33° 21.99' N, 79° 15.6' W

22–1 Attacks upon Georgetown, Georgetown Co.
IMAGE COURTESY OF SCDAH

22–2 Georgetown

700 block of Highmarket St. between Broad and Screven Sts., Georgetown

Georgetown, the third oldest town in the state, was laid out in 1729 by Elisha Screven on land granted to John and Edward Perrie, Sept. 15, 1705, and deeded by him, Jan. 16, 1734, to George Pawley, William Swinton, and Daniel LaRoche, trustees. It was made a port of entry in 1732. *Erected by the City of Georgetown, 1940*
GPS Coordinates: 33° 22.095' N, 79° 16.833' W

22–3 Hopsewee

U.S. Hwy. 17/701 at Hopsewee Rd., just S of its junction with Powell Rd. (S.C. Sec. Rd. 22-24), about 14 mi. S of Georgetown, North Santee vicinity

Thomas Lynch, Jr., signer of the Declaration of Independence, was born here, Aug. 5, 1749. He was elected from St. James's Parish, Santee, to 1st Provincial Congress, Dec. 19, 1774; to 2nd Provincial Congress, Aug. 7–8, 1775; to the Continental Congress, Mar. 23, 1776; Commissioned Captain, Provincial Troops, June 17, 1775; served on committee to draft constitution for South Carolina, 1776. He was lost at sea, 1779. *Erected by Georgetown County. 1940*
GPS Coordinates: 33° 12.729' N, 79° 22.923' W

22–4 Prospect Hill

U.S. Hwy. 17, E of Georgetown, about 1.7 mi. E of the Waccamaw River

On his tour south to inspect the defenses of the Atlantic coast, President Monroe reached Prospect Hill, Col. Benjamin Huger's residence, April 21, 1819. During his stay, April 21–24, he was lavishly entertained by his host and by the citizens and the town council of Georgetown. *Erected by the Georgetown County Historical Society, 1991* [Replaced a marker erected in 1940 by the Georgetown Chapter, Daughters of the American Revolution.]
GPS Coordinates: 33° 22.067' N, 79° 13.267' W

22–5 Clifton Plantation

U.S. Hwy. 17, 0.8 mi. E of the Harrell Siau Bridge over the Waccamaw River, E of Georgetown

President George Washington on his southern tour traveled southward over this road, April

27–30, 1791. While in this vicinity the day and night of April 29, he was the guest of Captain William Alston on this plantation, Clifton, which originally was a part of the Hobcaw Barony. *Erected by the Georgetown County Historical Society, 1991* [Replaced a marker erected in 1940 by the Georgetown Chapter, Daughters of the American Revolution.]
GPS Coordinates: 33° 21.872' N, 79° 14.097' W

22–6 Gabriel Marion

Intersection of Highmarket St. (U.S. Hwy. 521) & White's Bridge Dr., Georgetown

When Capt. John Nelson, who was sent by Gen. Marion in Jan. 1781 to the Sampit Road to reconnoitre, met Capt. Barfield and his Tories near White's Bridge, a sharp fight ensued. Lieut. Gabriel Marion, nephew of Gen. Marion, was captured and inhumanely shot about a quarter of a mile north of here. His name was fatal to him. *Erected by Georgetown County, 1940*
GPS Coordinates: 33° 23.142' N, 79° 18.648' W

22–7 Skirmish at Sampit Bridge

At Sampit United Methodist Church, U.S. Hwy. 17A, Sampit

In the early evening about March 20, 1781, the last skirmish between Gen. Marion and Col. Watson was fought at Sampit Bridge, one-half mile west of this spot. Col. Watson's loss was twenty men killed and a large number wounded; Gen. Marion's reputed loss was one man killed. *Erected by Georgetown County, 1940*
GPS Coordinates: 33° 21.866' N, 79° 27.474' W

22–8 Lafayette

U.S. Hwy. 17, 0.8 mi. E of the Harrell Siau Bridge over the Waccamaw River, E of Georgetown

A lover of liberty, Lafayette left Bordeaux, France, March 26, 1777, "To conquer or perish" in the American cause, and arrived at Benjamin Huger's summer home near here, June 14, 1777, where he spent his first night in America. He rendered eminent service in our struggle for independence. *Erected by Georgetown County, 1940*
GPS Coordinates: 33° 21.87' N, 79° 14.1' W

22–9 Prince George's Parish Church, Winyah

708 Highmarket St., Georgetown

Prince George's Parish, Winyah, was created March 10, 1721, and the parish church was erected on Black River, 1726, at the present Brown's Ferry. After Prince Frederick's Parish was formed from Prince George's, April 9, 1734, the parish church was erected here, 1737–1750. The tower and chancel were added in 1824. *Erected under Auspices of the Georgetown Chapter, D. A. R., 1941*

22–10 Skirmish at Black Mingo Creek

County Line Rd. (S.C. Sec. Rd. 22–51/41), just N of Mingo Landing Trail, 1.6 mi. N of Rhems

On Sept. 14, 1780, Gen. Francis Marion's Patriots routed a Tory force commanded by Capt. J. Coming Ball. The Tories, attacked on one flank by Capt. Thomas Waties and on the other by Col. Peter Horry, fled into Black Mingo Swamp. The short but sharply-contested action cost each side nearly one-third of its men. *Erected by the Georgetown County Historical Society, 2005, replacing a marker erected by Georgetown County in 1941*
GPS Coordinates: 33° 37.35' N, 79° 25.992' W

22–11 Washington Allston

Inside Brookgreen Gardens on Allston Circle Dr., Murrells Inlet vicinity

Washington Allston, "the American Titian," artist and author, was born at Brookgreen, Nov. 5, 1779. He studied in London, Paris, and Venice. He had a studio in London, 1811–1818; in Boston, 1818–1830; in Cambridge, 1830–1843, where he died, July 9, 1843. Allston was, said Coleridge, "a painter born to renew the 16th century." *Erected by Georgetown County, 1941*
GPS Coordinates: 33° 31.08' N, 79° 5.746' W

22–12 Sergeant McDonald

Georgetown City Hall, 120 Fraser St., Georgetown

[Marker relocated in 2008 from original site at intersection of N. Fraser St. and Indigo Ave.] Here Sgt. McDonald bayoneted the fleeing Maj. Gainey, following the defeat of the Tories under Major Gainey by the Americans under Col. Peter Horry. This bloody skirmish took place January, 1781, between the Sampit and Black River Roads. *Erected by Georgetown County, 1938*
GPS Coordinates: 33° 23.376' N, 79° 17.331' W

22–13 Washington's Visit

Inside Brookgreen Gardens on Allston Circle Dr., Murrells Inlet vicinity

On his southern tour in 1791 President George Washington spent the night of April 28 here at Brookgreen Plantation. He was the guest of its owner, Dr. Henry Collins Flagg, a surgeon in the Revolution, and his wife, the former Rachel Moore Allston. Washington left Brookgreen at 6 A.M. April 29 to breakfast at Clifton Plantation near Georgetown. *Erected by Brookgreen Gardens, 1981*
GPS Coordinates: 33° 31.073' N, 79° 5.73' W

22–14 Joseph Alston

Inside Brookgreen Gardens on Allston Circle Dr., Murrells Inlet vicinity

Joseph Alston (1779–1816) was educated at the College of Charleston and at Princeton. He inherited The Oaks Plantation and in 1801, married Theodosia, daughter of Aaron Burr. Alston was a member of the S.C. House (1802–12), its speaker for 5 years, Governor (1812–14), and Senator (1814–16). He is buried at The Oaks Cemetery about 2 miles west. *Erected by The Aaron Burr Association, 1981*
GPS Coordinates: 33° 31.059' N, 79° 5.754' W

22–15 Methodists

Duncan Memorial United Methodist Church, 901 Highmarket St. near Orange St., Georgetown

William Wayne, nephew of Revolutionary General Anthony Wayne, was converted here by Bishop Francis Asbury on February 24, 1785, and a Methodist congregation was formed later that year. Woolman Hickson was appointed minister. This is the site of an early cemetery, parsonage, and church (ca. 1833), in use until 1903 when the present nearby structure, Duncan Memorial Methodist Episcopal Church, was dedicated. *Erected by The Congregation 1982 Honoring Elizabeth J. Ashford, Church Historian*
GPS Coordinates: 33° 22.162' N, 79° 16.971' W

22–16 Winyah Indigo Society

500 block of Prince St. near Cannon St., Georgetown

Springing from the fervor for indigo, the colony's vital new crop for making blue dye, the Winyah Indigo Society was begun in 1755 and incorporated 1757 to ensure stronger financial support for the free school which it had founded. Thomas Lynch was then president of the society, which also maintained a library and served as an intellectual center. The 1857 building here was used by Union forces during the Civil War. *Erected by Winyah Indigo Society, 1983*
GPS Coordinates: 33° 21.909' N, 79° 16.746' W

22–17 Antipedo Baptist Church/Old Baptist Cemetery

700 block of Church St. near Screven St., Georgetown

Antipedo Baptist Church (FRONT)
In the plan of Georgetown, laid out by 1730, this one acre lot was reserved for Antipedo Baptists by Elisha Screven. A brick building built before the Revolution for the Baptists, Presbyterians, and Independents, housed the area Baptists who were constituted 1794. By 1804 its congregation had built "a handsome and commodious wooden meetinghouse" on this lot, commanding a view of the whole town from the FRONT.

Old Baptist Cemetery (REVERSE)
Among the graves here are those of William Cuttino, Sr., treasurer and builder of the Antipedo Baptist Church; and John Waldo, minister and educator. Other early leaders buried here include the Rev. Edmund

Botsford, native of England who became minister of this church in 1796; and Savage Smith, president of the church in 1805. *Erected by First Baptist Church, 1983*
GPS Coordinates: 33° 22.2' N, 79° 16.667' W

22–18 Georgetown

[Reported missing in 2014.]

Francis Marion Park, Front St. at Broad St., Georgetown

(FRONT) Ships and boats have loaded and unloaded cargo at the Sampit River near Front Street since the founding of Georgetown, ca. 1729. In 1732 Georgetown became an official port of entry, shipping naval stores, rice, indigo, pork, and animal skins. In the mid-19th century, Georgetown was the principal rice-growing area of the U.S. and exported quantities of rice, as well as lumber and cotton. (REVERSE) Brig. Gen. Francis Marion spent his early life near Georgetown and it is for him that this park is named. During the American Revolution, Marion marched his forces to Georgetown, drove the British out, and occupied the town May 28, 1781. In August 1781, much of the town was burned during a raid by the British privateer Manson. Toward the end of the Revolution, Georgetown became a valuable supply port for the American army in the South. *Erected by the Georgetown County Chamber of Commerce and the Georgetown County Historical Society, 1983*
GPS Coordinates: 33° 21.986' N, 79° 17.020' W

22–19 Mount Tabor Church

Tabor Dr., just E of the junction of S.C. Sec. Rd. 22-264 (Exodus Dr.) & U.S. Hwy. 701, about 1.5 mi. S of Yauhannah

Organized as a result of the preaching of Elder James Singleton, the Mount Tabor congregation was constituted October 21, 1832 and admitted into Welsh Neck Baptist Association the same year. Samuel Hennecy and Uriah Woodard represented Mount Tabor at the association's meeting and reported the church's membership at eighty-four people. *Erected by The Congregation, 1984*
GPS Coordinates: 33° 36.7' N, 79° 11.767' W

22–20 Winyah Schools

1200 Highmarket St., Georgetown

Winyah Indigo School District was created in 1885 to maintain public education in Georgetown. In 1887, the district assumed the existing school owned by the Winyah Indigo Society, established 1755. Completed in 1908 was a building housing grades 1–10 which still stands. Winyah High, built here in 1938, was integrated 1970. It burned in 1981. The new high school, 1985, became Georgetown High when Winyah and Howard consolidated. *Erected 1985 by Senior Classes 1981–85*
GPS Coordinates: 33° 22.356' N, 79° 17.193' W

22–21 Howard School

Corner of Duke & King Sts., Georgetown

After purchasing this land January 1, 1866, Georgetown Colored Academy built a school here. By 1908 the old building had been torn down and a new school built, its name changed to Howard. The elementary department moved into a new structure on Kaminski Street in 1938; the high school followed in 1949. After the 1984 graduation, predominantly black Howard merged with mostly white Winyah School to form Georgetown High School. *Erected by Georgetown Chapter of Delta Sigma Theta, 1986*
GPS Coordinates: 33° 22.305' N, 79° 16.971' W

22–22 Bethel Church

Corner of Duke & Broad Sts., Georgetown

This African Methodist Episcopal church was the first separate black church in Georgetown County. It was established by the Rev. A. T. Carr shortly after the 1863 Emancipation Proclamation which freed the slaves. The church purchased this property Jan. 15, 1866, and remodeled the present building in 1908 when the Rev. R. W. Mance was minister. The educational building was built in 1949 under the pastorate of Rev. H. B. Butler, Jr. *Erected by Georgetown Chapter of Delta Sigma Theta, 1988*
GPS Coordinates: 33° 22.206' N, 79° 16.812' W

22–23 General Arthur M. Manigault

Highmarket St. (U.S. Hwy. 17-A) at S.C. Sec. Rd. 22-452, about 100 yds. W of Georgetown city limits

Volunteer aide-de-camp to Gen. Beauregard in April 1861, mustered into Confederate service at White's Bridge near here on July 19, 1861, as colonel of the 10th Regiment, S.C. Infantry, promoted to Brigadier General on April 26, 1863, wounded at the Battle of Franklin Nov. 30, 1864, Gen. Manigault died Aug. 16, 1886, at his South Island Plantation. *Erected by Pee Dee District UDC, 1967*
GPS Coordinates: 33° 23.306' N, 79° 19.022' W

22–24 Theodosia Burr Alston

Inside Brookgreen Gardens on Allston Circle Dr., Murrells Inlet vicinity

Daughter of Aaron Burr and one of the most learned women of her era; wife of Governor Joseph Alston, who is buried west of here, with Aaron Burr Alston, their ten-year-old son; sailed from Georgetown on Dec. 30, 1812 on the schooner "Patriot" to join her father in New York and disappeared off the N.C. coast during a terrific storm. *Erected by Theodosia Burr Chapter, Daughters of the American Revolution, 21 January 1970*
GPS Coordinates: 33° 31.053' N, 79° 5.736' W

22–25 Birthplace of Jeremiah John Snow/China Grove Plantation

S.C. Sec. Rd. 22-6, about 1.5 mi. SE of the intersection of S.C. Hwys. 512 and 513, Union Crossroads vicinity

Birthplace of Jeremiah John Snow (FRONT)
China Grove was the birthplace of the Reverend Jeremiah John Snow (1836–1892), a son of the third James Snow who lived here. He entered the Methodist Conference in 1863, and was a chaplain in the Third Regiment, South Carolina Troops, in the Civil War. Later he was a circuit-riding minister. His grave is at Union Church.
China Grove Plantation (REVERSE)
China Grove, located on the Old Stage Road to Indiantown near its junction with the Britton's Ferry Road, was for many years the home of the Snow family. The eighteenth century plantation house has been restored. Its construction is attributed to James Snow (1730–1793), whose grandfather, Dr. Nathaniel Snow, came to South Carolina in 1697. *Erected by Dr. Henry Woodward Chapter, South Carolina Society, Daughters of the American Colonists, 1974*
GPS Coordinates: 33° 37.122' N, 79° 24.368' W

22–26 Pawley's Island/Waccamaw Neck

At Pawley's Island Town Hall, 321 Myrtle Ave. near its intersection with 3rd St., Pawley's Island

Pawley's Island (FRONT)
This island, located about ½ mile east, was used by plantation householders who lived on the seashore from May to November to escape malaria, or "summer fever." A number of houses built about 1850, and the summer academy and rectory of All Saints' Parish remain. The hurricane of 1822 destroyed most earlier homes.
Waccamaw Neck (REVERSE)
Narrow strip of land from Atlantic Ocean to Waccamaw River. Rice plantations flourished by 1740. Remaining are ca. 1790 houses, Litchfield and Prospect Hill, and one slave chapel. All Saints Parish est. 1767. Area furnished salt for Revolutionary War. Visitors included Lafayette 1777, Washington 1791, J. Monroe 1819, Churchill 1932, F. Roosevelt 1944. *Erected by Waccamaw Garden Club, 1975*
GPS Coordinates: 33° 26.022' N, 79° 7.27' W

22–27 Hot and Hot Fish Club

Huntington Beach State Park, 16148 Ocean Hwy., Murrells Inlet

Established by and comprised of the planters of All Saints Parish, this social club was dedicated to epicurean pursuits. Although formed before 1816, the organization was probably dissolved during the Civil War. Nearby Drunken Jack Island was the first recorded of five different sites for the clubhouse. *Erected by Georgetown County Historical Society, 1979*
GPS Coordinates: 33° 21.978' N, 79° 16.842' W

22–28 William Screven/Elisha Screven

600 block of Prince St. between Screven and Queen Sts., Georgetown

William Screven (FRONT)

In this cemetery is buried William Screven, first pastor of the earliest Baptist church in the South. A native of England, he ministered to the Baptists there before migrating to Maine, establishing a Baptist church in Kittery, Maine, in 1682. By 1698, he had led his church to Charleston, S.C. He later moved to Georgetown, exerting his Christian influence until his death in 1713.

Elisha Screven (REVERSE)

Elisha Screven, founder of Georgetown, was a younger son of William, who owned and lived his final years on these Winyah lands. To promote settlement here, Elisha planned a town, to be called Georgetown, which reserved lots for Anglican, Presbyterian, and Baptist churches, as well as for a school and other public buildings. Retained in the plan was this Screven family cemetery. The town had been laid out by 1730. *Erected by First Baptist Church, City of Georgetown, Georgetown County Council, and the Georgetown Chamber of Commerce, 1980*
GPS Coordinates: 33° 21.978' N, 79° 16.842' W

22–29 Joseph Blyth Allston House (Pawley House)

441 Myrtle Ave., Pawleys Island

This house stands on land owned by R. F. W. Allston, governor of S.C. 1856–58. His nephew Joseph Blyth Allston obtained the land in 1866 and it is thought he then moved this circa 1800 house onto his property. After Hurricane Hugo struck S.C. in 1989, the house was extensively altered and placed on a higher foundation. Mortise and tenon joints with pegs can still be seen under the house. *Erected by Pawleys Island Civic Association, 1993*
GPS Coordinates: 33° 25.459' N, 79° 7.539' W

22–30 R.F.W. Allston House

458 Myrtle Ave., Pawleys Island

This summer residence was owned by Robert F. W. Allston (1801–1864) when the state of S.C. granted the marsh behind it to him in 1846. Allston was a large property and slave owner, a successful rice planter, and served as governor of S.C. 1856–58. The house remained in the family until 1901. After Hurricane Hugo struck S.C. in 1989, the house was placed on higher wooden posts. *Erected by Pawleys Island Civic Association, 1993*
GPS Coordinates: 33° 25.252' N, 79° 7.622' W

22–31 P.C.J. Weston House /Pelican Inn

506 Myrtle Ave., Pawleys Island

Plowden Weston, Lt. Gov. of S.C. 1862–64, obtained land here in 1844 and by 1858 had built this beach residence. The Weston family sold the property to William St. Julien Mazyck in 1864, who sold the house to Atlantic Coast Lumber Company in 1901. The company permitted its employees to vacation here. After an ownership change some years later, the house was named The Pelican Inn. *Erected by Pawleys Island Civic Association, 1993*
GPS Coordinates: 33° 25.169' N, 79° 7.69' W

22–32 All Saints Summer Parsonage/The Rectory

510 Myrtle Ave., Pawleys Island

This house, built by 1848, served as the summer parsonage for All Saints Episcopal Church for many years. Evening summer services were held here by the congregation, which included a number of rice plantation owners who spent summers at Pawleys Island. The parsonage/rectory was sold by the congregation in 1960 to its present owner. *Erected by Pawleys Island Civic Association, 1993*
GPS Coordinates: 33° 25.086' N, 79° 7.725' W

22–33 Ward House/Liberty Lodge

520 Myrtle Ave., Pawleys Island

This house, one of the oldest on Pawleys, was reputedly moved here after 1858. It stands on

land once owned by area rice planter Joshua J. Ward (1800–1853), who was Lt. Gov. of S.C. 1850–52. The house has hand-hewn sills and joists and mortise-and-tenon joints. It remained in the Ward family until 1912, when sold to Cornelia C. Ehrich, who named it Liberty Lodge. Ownership is still in this family. *Erected by Pawleys Island Civic Association, 1993*
GPS Coordinates: 33° 25.104' N, 79° 7.714' W

22–34 Nesbit/Norburn House

560 Myrtle Ave., Pawleys Island

By 1842 this house was here on Pawleys Island and was owned by Robert Nesbit (1799–1848). A native of Scotland and a rice planter in this area, Nesbit also owned nearby "Caledonia" plantation. The house on Pawleys remained in the Nesbit family until after the death of Ralph Nesbit in 1938. It was then sold to Dr. Charles Norburn of Asheville, North Carolina. *Erected by Pawleys Island Civic Association, 1993*
GPS Coordinates: 33° 24.995' N, 79° 7.77' W

22–35 All Saints Academy Summer House

566 Myrtle Ave., Pawleys Island

This house was built between 1838 and 1848 by All Saints Academy for the summer residence of its headmaster. Robert F. W. Allston, Governor of S.C. 1856–58, actively participated in leadership of the academy. After some years, the academy's dwelling passed to private, individual ownership. It was extensively damaged by Hurricane Hugo in 1989 but has been meticulously restored. *Erected by Pawleys Island Civic Association, 1993*
GPS Coordinates: 33° 25.056' N, 79° 7.74' W

22–36 LaBruce/Lemon House

546 Myrtle Ave., Pawleys Island

This house, built on 10 acres of beach land by 1858, was owned by the LaBruce family, who were successful rice planters in this area of All Saints Parish. According to local tradition, two small dwellings on the property were slave cabins. The residence was purchased by Calhoun Lemon of Barnwell, South Carolina, in 1952 and still remains in this family. Additions have been made to the house through the years. *Erected by Pawleys Island Civic Association, 1993*
GPS Coordinates: 33° 24.95' N, 79° 7.782' W

22–37 Joseph Hayne Rainey

909 Prince St., Georgetown

This National Historic Landmark was the family home of Joseph H. Rainey, the first African American elected to the U.S. House of Representatives, 1870–1879. Born in Georgetown County in 1832, Rainey, it is said, made blockade-running trips during the Civil War. He was a delegate to the Constitutional Convention of 1868, served two years in the S.C. Senate, and two years as internal revenue agent of S.C. He died in Georgetown, S.C., in 1887. *Erected by Georgetown Chapter Delta Sigma Theta, 1994*
GPS Coordinates: 33° 22.117' N, 79° 17.033' W

22–38 R.F.W. Allston Causeway

Intersection of S. Causeway Rd. (S.C. Sec. Rd. 22–266) & Myrtle Dr. (S.C. Sec. Rd. 22–10), Pawleys Island

This causeway was built between January 1845 and November 1846 by Robert Francis Withers Allston, who owned a summer residence on Pawleys Island. Known as Governor Allston's bank, it connected the island to the mainland. Allston was a large property and slave owner in the area, and he was governor of South Carolina 1856–58. The causeway and contiguous property remained in the Allston family until 1901. *Erected by Pawleys Island Civic Association, 1994*
GPS Coordinates: 33° 25.435' N, 79° 7.556' W

22–39 Retreat Rice Plantation

S.C. Sec. Rd. 22–18, about 1 mi. S of Belle Isle Garden

In 1711 the Lords Proprietors granted Winyah Barony to Robert Daniel, who sold it to Thomas Smith. By 1787 Retreat had been

carved from the 12000-acre grant. *Erected by Whites Bridge Garden Club, 1994*
GPS Coordinates: 33° 16.267' N, 79° 17.85' W

22-40 Hobcaw Barony

[No longer extant. Replaced by Marker 22-57, erected by the Belle W. Baruch Foundation, 2008.]

At the entrance to the Belle W. Baruch Foundation, Hobcaw Barony, U.S. Hwy. 17, 1 mi. N of Georgetown

Erected by the Belle W. Baruch Foundation, 1995

22-41 Bethesda Baptist Church

Wood St., between Prince and Haymarket Sts., Georgetown

Organized shortly after the Civil War with Rev. Edward Rhue as its first pastor, Bethesda Baptist Church purchased this site by 1867. Construction of this sanctuary began in 1922 during the pastorate of Rev. A. W. Puller and was completed and dedicated during the pastorate of Rev. G. Going Daniels in 1927. Rev. W. A. Johnson served as Bethesda's pastor from 1956 until his death in 1995. *Erected by Georgetown Alumnae Chapter, Delta Sigma Theta, 1996*
GPS Coordinates: 33° 22.252' N, 79° 17.13' W

22-41 Prince George Winyah Parish (1721)/Prince Frederick's Parish (1734)

S.C. Hwy. 51, 1 mi. from Georgetown side of Brown's Ferry Bridge, Georgetown vicinity

Prince George Winyah Paris (1721) (FRONT) Early settlement in this area near the Black River, based primarily on the Indian trade and the production of naval stores, prompted the creation of Prince George Winyah Parish in 1721. When the first Anglican church to serve the parish was built in 1726 Governor Francis Nicholson made a donation toward its construction. The Rev. Thomas Morritt became the first rector of Prince George Winyah in 1728.
Prince Frederick's Parish (1734) (REVERSE)

Within a few years successful rice production and the growth of Georgetown helped expand settlement inland and prompted the creation of a new parish. Prince Frederick's Parish included this area when it was established in 1734. A new parish church for Prince George Winyah was built in Georgetown by 1747 and the sanctuary here served Prince Frederick's Parish until a new parish church was built near the Pee Dee River in 1837. *Erected by the Georgetown Committee of the National Society of Colonial Dames of America in the State of South Carolina, 1996*
GPS Coordinates: 33° 32.083' N, 79° 23.439' W

22-42 First Baptist Church

219 Cleland St., corner of Cleland and Highmarket Sts., Georgetown

(FRONT) This congregation, founded in 1794 and long known as Antipedo Baptist Church, was the first separate Baptist congregation in Georgetown. Baptists had worshipped in the area as early as 1710, sharing the Black Mingo Meeting House with the Presbyterians and later sharing the Old Brick Church with other denominations during the period when the Church of England was the only officially-recognized church in South Carolina.
(REVERSE) Antipedo Baptist Church was located on Church St. by 1804. A later sanctuary, on Lot 130 on Highmarket St., was renamed First Baptist Church of Georgetown in 1911 and was occupied until 1915. In 1913 this lot was purchased for a new sanctuary, completed in 1915. First Baptist Church has occupied three sanctuaries on this site: the first 1915-1949, the second 1949-1996, and the present sanctuary, which was completed in 1997. *Erected by First Baptist Church, 1997*
GPS Coordinates: 33° 22.324' N, 79° 17.186' W

22-43 William Doyle Morgan House

732 Prince St., Georgetown

(FRONT) 732 Prince Street was the home of William Doyle Morgan (1853-1938), mayor 1891-1906 and the catalyst for much of Georgetown's growth and prosperity by the turn of the century. He helped give the city what one observer called "the snap and vim of twentieth century progress," such as a modern water and sewer system, electric lights, macadamized streets, sidewalks, a deepened harbor, and jetties in Winyah Bay. (REVERSE) When Morgan retired in 1906 citizens presented him a sterling silver punch bowl in recognition of his "Zeal and Energy" and "Untiring Efforts for the Improvement of the City and Her Harbor." He founded and was president of the Bank of Georgetown 1891–1927. Morgan, a devout Catholic, was also instrumental in the construction of St. Mary's Catholic Church, built in 1899–1901 and consecrated in 1902. *Erected by Georgetown County Historical Society, 1997* GPS Coordinates: 33° 22.05' N, 79° 16.933' W

22–44 Beth Elohim Cemetery

Corner of Broad & Duke Sts., Georgetown

(FRONT) This cemetery, established ca. 1772, is the second oldest Jewish cemetery in the state and serves a community which has been significant here since well before the American Revolution. Abraham Cohen and Mordecai Myers, who opened stores in the town in 1762 and 1772, are buried here, as is Heiman Kaminski, who arrived in Georgetown in 1856 and was one of its most prominent businessmen by the turn of the twentieth century. (REVERSE) The Jewish community has emphasized leadership and public service from the beginning; Abraham Cohen, for example, was a member of the committee welcoming President George Washington in 1791. Three of Georgetown's six Jewish mayors are also buried here: Louis S. Ehrich (Mayor 1886–88), Harold Kaminski (1930–35), and Sylvan L. Rosen (1948–1961). *Erected by Georgetown County Historical Society, 1997* GPS Coordinates: 33° 22.2' N, 79° 16.8' W

22–45 Robert Stewart House

1019 Front St., Georgetown

(FRONT) The Robert Stewart House was built between 1740 and 1770 by Robert Stewart (d. 1776), planter and militia captain; it was sold in 1787 to Daniel Tucker (d. 1797), prominent

Georgetown merchant. When President George Washington arrived in Georgetown during his southern tour on April 30, 1791, a militia company and local reception committee met him at the nearby boat landing and escorted him here, where he spent the night as Tucker's guest. (REVERSE) Washington was entertained lavishly and then honored by the Masons of Prince George Lodge No. 16 and the Winyah Indigo Society. This house, the only extant brick residence in Georgetown built before the American Revolution, was later owned by Benjamin Allston, Sr. (1765–1847). It remained in the hands of his descendants, the Pyatt and Parker families, until 1979. *Erected by Georgetown County Historical Society, 1997* GPS Coordinates: 33° 22.116' N, 79° 17.208' W

22–46 Georgetown County Courthouse

Georgetown County Courthouse, corner of Screven & Prince Sts., Georgetown

(FRONT) This courthouse, designed by prominent architect and South Carolina native Robert Mills (1781–1855), was built in 1823–24 to replace a courthouse which had been damaged by two hurricanes. Mills himself, who also designed the Washington Monument, called this courthouse "a great ornament to the town." A modern Mills scholar has described it as "the most sophisticated of his South Carolina courthouses." (REVERSE) An initial appropriation of $12,000 was approved for the new courthouse. The South Carolina Board of Commissioners for Public Buildings, including John Keith and Abraham Cohen of Georgetown, supervised its construction by contractor Russell Warren. This Mills design is an excellent example of the Classical Revival style so widely used in American public architecture during much of the nineteenth century. *Erected by Georgetown County Historical Society, 1997* GPS Coordinates: 33° 22.002' N, 79° 16.886' W

22–47 Town Clock/Kaminski Building

Front St., Georgetown, between the Town Clock and the Kaminski Building

Town Clock (FRONT)

This Greek Revival market and town hall was built in 1842 after a fire destroyed many of the frame buildings on Front Street. An open-air market occupied the first floor and the town hall occupied the second floor; the clock tower and belfry were added in 1845. On February 24, 1865 the town council, meeting here, surrendered Georgetown to officers of the U.S. Navy. The Rice Museum opened in this building during the S.C. Tricentennial in 1970.

Kaminski Building (REVERSE)

This store, constructed as a two-story building for Stephen W. Rouquie in 1842, features a cast-iron façade designed by Daniel Badger. In 1869 Heiman Kaminski, who had rented the building since 1867 to house his hardware store, acquired it. Over the next 30 years H. Kaminski and Co. became one of Georgetown's most successful businesses; by 1878 a third story and rear addition were added. The building is now part of the Rice Museum. *Erected by Georgetown County Historical Society, 1997*

GPS Coordinates: 33° 22.11' N, 79° 17.19' W

22–48 John and Mary Perry Cleland House

405 Front St., Georgetown

(FRONT) This house, one of Georgetown's earliest, was built ca. 1737 by John and Mary Perry Cleland. Mrs. Cleland inherited the property from her father John Perry, who had been granted a large tract in 1705 including the site of present-day Georgetown. This house is a raised tidewater residence with its main entrance facing the Sampit River. It features elements of the Georgian and Federal styles. (REVERSE) In 1753 the house was purchased by the Clelands' Nephew Archibald Baird. He made small additions to each end of the house and relocated the main entrance to Front Street. A porch was added there ca.

1780. Later prominent owners of the house included John Withers, Jr., Francis Withers, Dr. Joseph Blythe, and Robert F. W. Allston. *Erected by Georgetown County Historical Society, 1997*

GPS Coordinates: 33° 21.79' N, 79° 16.732' W

22–49 Kaminski House

1003 Front St., Georgetown

(FRONT) This house, probably built between 1750 and 1800, was for many years the home of Harold Kaminski (1886–1951), Georgetown County commissioner, mayor 1930–35, and U.S. Navy officer, and his wife Julia Bossard Pyatt (d. 1972). The house was originally owned by members of the Trapier and Keith families, including John Keith (d. ca. 1823), first intendant, or mayor, of Georgetown in 1806. It then passed through a succession of owners from 1853 to 1931.

(REVERSE) The Kaminski House, originally a single house with a central stairhall between two rooms, was significantly enlarged in the 1890s by George R. Congdon (1834–1909), also mayor in 1872, and in the 1930s and 1940s by Harold and Julia Kaminski. The house and its furnishings, including antiques from the 18th to the 20th centuries, was bequeathed to the City of Georgetown by Julia Pyatt Kaminski and has been open to the public as a house museum since 1973. *Erected by the Georgetown County Historical Society, 1998*

GPS Coordinates: 33° 22.11' N, 79° 17.19' W

22–50 The Oaks Plantation

U.S. Hwy. 17 N, Georgetown vicinity, near the entrance to the plantation on the North Santee River

The Oaks Plantation was established on the Santee River in 1705 by a grant from the Lords Proprietors to John Sauseau, a French Huguenot settler. It passed through several owners in the prominent Buchanan and Withers families before 1793, when brothers Isaac and William Mazyck acquired a tract of more than 1,000 acres and began producing rice here on the rich Santee River delta. *Erected by the St. James Santee Parish Historical Society, 1998*

GPS Coordinates: 33° 13.047' N, 79° 22.818' W

22–51 Pleasant Hill School

Pleasant Hill Dr. (S.C. Hwy. 513), Hemingway vicinity

Pleasant Hill Consolidated School opened in 1938 as an elementary and high school. It also included a cannery and a home economics/farm-shop building. Pleasant Hill housed a middle and high school 1970–1985 and closed in 2000 as Pleasant Hill Middle School. An excellent example of New Deal-era school architecture, it was listed in the National Register of Historic Places in 1998. *Erected by the Pleasant Hill Middle School Parent-Teacher Organization, 2001*
GPS Coordinates: 33° 40.85' N, 79° 22.05' W

22–52 Prince Frederick's Chapel

At the chapel ruins, Plantersville Rd. (S.C. Sec. Rd. 22-52), 4 mi. E of U.S. Hwy. 701, Plantersville

(FRONT) The first church on this site, known as Prince Frederick's Chapel, Pee Dee, was built in 1848 on a site donated by the Rev. Hugh Fraser in 1834. Most of its parishioners were rice planters along the Pee Dee River. These ruins are of the second church here, approved by a committee of R. F. W. Allston, Davison McDowell and Francis Weston and begun in 1859 but interrupted by the Civil War.
(REVERSE) This Gothic Revival church designed by Louis J. Barbot was completed in 1876 with a gift of $1700 by John Earle Allston. With the decline of rice planting the church gradually fell into disrepair and was eventually deemed unsafe. It was demolished in 1966, leaving only the front wall and tower. The ruins were listed in the National Register of Historic Places in 1974. *Erected by the Georgetown Committee of the National Society of the Colonial Dames of America in the State of South Carolina, 2001*
GPS Coordinates: 33° 30.351' N, 79° 10.832' W

22–53 Chicora Wood Plantation

Chicora Wood Ave., approximately 2 mi. SE of the intersection of Plantersville Rd. (S.C. Sec. Rd. 22-52) and Exodus Dr., Plantersville

(FRONT) This plantation, with its origins in several grants to John Allston in 1732, 1734, and later, was in the hands of his grandson

Benjamin, Jr., of Brookgreen, by 1806. The property passed first to Benjamin's widow Charlotte and then after her death in 1824 to her son Robert F. W. Allston (1801–1864), rice planter, state representative and senator 1828–56, and governor 1856–58.
(REVERSE) This house was completed in 1838 by Robert F. W. Allston and his wife Adele Petigru. Their daughter Elizabeth Allston Pringle (1845–1921) continued to plant rice here for 40 years after her father died in 1864 and wrote of life at Chicora Wood in A Woman Rice Planter (1913) and Chronicles of Chicora Wood (1922). She died here in 1921. *Erected by the Georgetown Committee of the National Society of the Colonial Dames of America in the State of South Carolina, 2001*
GPS Coordinates: 33° 31.035' N, 79° 10.863' W

22–54 All Saints Parish 1767/All Saints, Waccamaw

All Saints Parish, Waccamaw, Episcopal Church, 10172 Ocean Hwy. (U.S. Hwy. 17), Pawleys Island vicinity

All Saints Parish 1767 (FRONT)
Anglican services were held on Waccamaw Neck by 1737, with a chapel built on land purchased by Percival Pawley. All Saints Parish, Waccamaw, created out of Prince George Winyah Parish in 1767, was the third Anglican parish created in present-day Georgetown County. Though the parish declined somewhat after the American Revolution it was revived soon afterwards.
All Saints, Waccamaw (REVERSE)
The parish church of All Saints Parish, Waccamaw, has stood on this site since 1737. A brick Greek Revival sanctuary built in 1843 burned in 1915 and was replaced in 1917 by a church replicating that design on a smaller scale and which was listed in the National Register of Historic Places in 1991. The present sanctuary was built in 1988. *Erected by the Peedee Chapter, National Society Colonial Dames XVII Century, 2001*
GPS Coordinates: 33° 28.044' N, 79° 8.367' W

22–55 Mt. Olive Baptist Church

1043 Duke St., Georgetown

(FRONT) This church was founded in 1866 by Rev. James Smalls, its pastor for many years. The congregation, which built its sanctuary here on land owned by the Gospel Harp Society, grew to more than one hundred members by 1903. In 1914 trustees S. B. Belin, Neptune Boyd, Siward Dunmore, Joseph Gibson, I. J. McCottree, W. M. Salters, and Samuel White, Jr., purchased this property from the trustees of the Gospel Harp Society.

(REVERSE) The first church here, a frame building, was replaced by this brick sanctuary in 1920. Built during the pastorate of Rev. T. O. Mills, it features elaborate stained glass windows. Mt. Olive was also one of several Georgetown churches hosting graduation exercises for Howard High School in the 1940s. *Erected by the Georgetown Chapter, Delta Sigma Theta Sorority, 2001*

GPS Coordinates: 33° 22.339' N, 79° 17.034' W

22–56 Sampit Methodist Church

U.S. Hwy. 17A, Sampit

(FRONT) This church, formally organized in 1839, had its origins in a slave mission begun in 1786 on Gov. Thomas Boone's plantation, 3 miles SE. Rev. P. A. M. Williams became its first minister in 1840. The first church, a frame building built the same year, stood 1.5 miles S. The present sanctuary was built on a 5-acre plot donated to the church in 1887 by Benjamin D. Bourne, a member and trustee.

(REVERSE) The present sanctuary, built by the time the congregation acquired this site in 1887, was originally a frame church. It was extensively renovated in 1959–60 and completely covered in brick in 1975–76. Three members of the church later became Methodist ministers: Revs. C. D. Huggins, Jack D. Watts, and John Paul Watts, Sr. Sampit is also the mother church of Oak Grove Methodist Church, founded in 1890. *Erected by the Congregation, 2003*

GPS Coordinates: 33° 21.861' N, 79° 27.48' W

22–57 Hobcaw Barony

At the entrance to the Belle W. Baruch Foundation, Hobcaw Barony, U.S. Hwy. 17, 1 mi. N of Georgetown

(FRONT) In 1718 the Lords Proprietors granted 12,000 acres on Hobcaw Point, the southern portion of Waccamaw Neck, to John, Lord Carteret. The barony was subdivided beginning in 1766, creating several large rice plantations which flourished until the Civil War. In 1905–07 Bernard M. Baruch (1870–1965), Camden native and Wall Street financier, acquired these tracts for a winter retreat.

(REVERSE) Bernard Baruch was an advisor to presidents from Woodrow Wilson to Harry S. Truman. Belle Baruch (1900–1965), the oldest of his three children, was a sailor, pilot, and equestrian who shared her father's passion for the outdoors. She bought the property from him and created a trust devoted to research and education in forestry, wildlife, and marine biology by S.C. universities. *Erected by the Belle W. Baruch Foundation, 2008, replacing a marker erected in 1995*

GPS Coordinates: 33° 21.851' N, 79° 13.622' W

22–58 Sinking of the USS Harvest Moon

Behind 633 Front St., Georgetown

(FRONT) In early 1865 the USS Harvest Moon, a 193-foot, 5-gun side-wheel steamer, was the flagship of Adm. John A. Dahlgren of the South Atlantic Blockading Squadron, U.S. Navy. It arrived off Georgetown and anchored nearby on February 26th. Confederate Capt. Thomas W. Daggett, in charge of coastal defenses from Little River to Georgetown, made plans to sink the Harvest Moon with a "torpedo," or mine.

(REVERSE) Daggett, working on the 2nd floor of S. W. Rouquie's store here at 633 Front Street, built a keg torpedo and floated it out as the Harvest Moon steamed down the bay early on March 1, 1865. The blast blew a hole in the starboard quarter and main deck, and the ship sank in five minutes, with only one sailor killed. The smokestack of the Harvest Moon can still be seen at low tide in Winyah Bay, near Battery White. *Erected by the Arthur M.*

Manigault Chapter #63, United Daughters of the Confederacy, and the Battery White Camp #1568, Sons of Confederate Veterans, 2011
GPS Coordinates: 33° 21.923' N, 79° 16.932' W

22–59 Dissenter Meeting House and Cemetery

Off Pump House Landing Rd., just SE of the Black River, Andrews vicinity

(FRONT) This is the site of a "Dissenter" meeting house, built ca. 1726 by one of the first Baptist congregations in S.C. outside of Charleston. It was founded by Rev. Elisha Screven (d. 1754), son of Rev. William Screven (d. 1713). The elder Screven had founded a Baptist congregation in Charleston as early as 1696.

(REVERSE) Presbyterians and other "Dissenters" who did not belong to the Anglican church were also allowed to hold services here. Presbyterians soon outnumbered the rest. By about 1742 they built a new church 7 mi. N and named it Black Mingo Presbyterian Church. The historic cemetery here has lost most of its gravestones. *Sponsored by the First Baptist Church of Georgetown, 2012*
GPS Coordinates: 33° 28.875' N, 79° 26.904' W

22–60 Brookgreen Plantation

Grounds of Brookgreen Gardens, 1931 Brookgreen Drive, Murrells Inlet

(FRONT) Title to the land that comprised Brookgreen Plantation is traced to a patent for 48,000 acres granted to Robert Daniell in 1711. The property passed to the Allston family when William Allston bought it in ca. 1740. William Allston Jr. acquired it in 1764 and developed it as his home plantation. By 1799 title had passed to Joshua Ward, whose son, Joshua John Ward, was born here in 1800.

(REVERSE) Joshua John Ward was active in the Winyah and All Saints Agricultural Society and was noted for his development of long-grain rice. He would become among the wealthiest planters in the nation. In 1850 Ward's plantations, including Brookgreen, yielded 3,900,000 pounds of rice on land cultivated by 1,092 enslaved laborers. Ward and

his descendants lived here until 1938. *Sponsored by National Society of Colonial Dames XVII Century, Chicora Chapter, 2014*
GPS Coordinates: 33° 31.085' N, 79° 5.757' W

22–60 Georgetown County Stadium
[Marker mistakenly double numbered.]

1500 Emanuel St., Georgetown

(FRONT) The Atlantic Coast Lumber Company acquired the land on which Georgetown County Stadium now sits in 1900. The stadium was built by 1908 and games have been played here for more than a century. Originally known as Atlantic Coast Lumber Park, the City of Georgetown purchased the site in 1943. From 1948–1951 the stadium was home to the Georgetown Athletics, a semi-pro team that competed in the Palmetto Baseball League.

(REVERSE) In 1962 the stadium was converted to football-only use and was the home venue for both Winyah and Howard High Schools until the two were consolidated in 1982. In 1989 the facility was renamed Mike Johnson Park in honor of the long-time Georgetown High School baseball coach. Since 1991 it has been home to the International Paper Baseball Classic tournament. *Sponsored by the Georgetown Bulldog Booster Club, 2015*
GPS Coordinates: 33° 22.2193' N, 79° 17.702' W

22–61 DeBordieu Beach

Entrance to Old Carriage Rd., off of Luvan Blvd., approximately 2,100 ft. E. of U.S. Hwy. 17, DeBordieu Beach

(FRONT) Many Waccamaw Neck planters summered at the seashore from late May to early November to escape the malarial swamps of the rice fields. DeBordieu and Pawleys Islands were favorite destinations. Summer cottages were usually built on the banks of the early marsh behind the island. These early homes were constructed on high brick foundations that stood above the rise of gale tides along the creek.

(REVERSE) Much of what is now DeBordieu Beach was owned by William Alston, who built two seashore houses here by 1800. Each

May, Alston and other planters would move their entire households to the shore. Furniture, bedding, and provisions were packed first into boats and then transferred to wagon to complete the journey via narrow carriage roads. *Sponsored by DeBordieu Colony Community Association, 2015*
GPS Coordinates: 33° 22.460' N, 79° 12.382' W

22–62 Oak Grove Methodist Church

1676 Kent Rd., Andrews

(FRONT) Bishop Francis Asbury first arrived in Georgetown in Feb. 1785 and would return in 1786, at which time he established a slave mission at Boone Plantation on the Sampit River. Asbury would return many times over the years and his efforts would help lead to the establishment of Sampit Methodist Church in 1839. Oak Grove Methodist, which descended from Sampit, would follow in 1890.
(REVERSE) C. C. Mercer donated the land on which Oak Grove Methodist Church was built. The first church was lost to fire in 1932, though the pulpit survived and remains in use. Services were held in Oak Grove School while a new building was constructed. The present sanctuary began as a simple frame structure but grew over time. The stained glass windows were added in 1977, the steeple and bell in 1988. *Sponsored by Oak Grove Methodist Church, 2016*
GPS Coordinates: 33° 23.873' N, 79° 28.765' W

22–63 Beneventum Plantation

604 Beneventum Rd., Georgetown vicinity

(FRONT) The main house at Beneventum dates to ca. 1755. It was likely commissioned by William Fyffe, a surgeon and Scottish emigrant who acquired 500 acres from James Coachman in 1754. Fyffe's plantation was known as The Grove. Christopher Gadsden owned an adjacent plantation called Charing Cross Ferry. Gadsden was a statesman and Patriot, serving as a brigadier general in the Continental Army.
(REVERSE) John Julius Pringle acquired parts of The Grove and Charing Cross Ferry plantations in 1806. The land included ferry rights

across the Black River. In 1829 Pringle also acquired the house and would rename the plantation Beneventum, which is loosely translated from the Italian meaning "good wind." The name was meant to advertise that this was a favorable crossing site. *Sponsored by the Pee Dee Land Trust, 2016*
GPS Coordinates: 33° 26.740' N, 79° 15.582' W

22–64 Potter's Field

Highmarket St. near Dozier St., Georgetown from the 1880s to the 1930s

(FRONT) From the 1880s to the 1930s the block bordered by Highmarket, Dozier, Duke, and Church streets served as a cemetery for criminals, the indigent, and the unknown. These types of cemeteries were located in many towns and communities and were typically referred to as a Potter's Field. Many of the people buried here, most of whom were buried in unmarked graves, were African Americans.
(REVERSE) The earliest known burial here took place in 1881 after Frank Magrath was hung in a public execution after being convicted of murder. Another of the known burials was Edward Rainey. Rainey was the brother of Joseph Hayne Rainey, the first African American member of the U.S. House of Representatives. Burials continued here until the 1930s. By the 1950s most of the graves had been relocated and the land was redeveloped. *Sponsored by Delta Sigma Theta Sorority and Georgetown County Public Library, 2016*
GPS Coordinates: 33° 22.388' N, 79° 17.245' W

22–65 St. John A.M.E. Church

76 Duncan Ave, Pawleys Island

St. John A.M.E. Church was established in the spring of 1867 with Rev. Saby Green as the first pastor. Early meetings were held under a brush arbor until a log framed church was built at Litchfield in 1867. The current brick sanctuary replaced the original church in 1947. The church began as a member of the Waccamaw Circuit but became a station church in 1965. *Sponsored by St. John A.M.E. Church, 2017*
GPS Coordinates: 33° 27.187' N, 79° 7.428' W

22–66 James A. Bowley

231 King St., Georgetown

(FRONT) In the 1870s, this was the home of James Alfred Bowley (ca. 1844–1891). Born enslaved in Maryland, Bowley was the great nephew of Harriet Tubman (ca. 1822–1913). In 1850, Tubman and Bowley's free father organized a plan to free Bowley and his mother and sister, making them the first enslaved people who Tubman helped emancipate. Bowley attended school in Philadelphia before rejoining his family in Canada. During the Civil War, he served as a landsman in the United States Navy.
(REVERSE) After the war, Bowley moved to Georgetown and worked for the Freedmen's Bureau as a teacher. By 1870, he had married Laura Clark (1854–1932) and lived at this location. They sold the home in 1880. Bowley served in the S.C. House (1869–1874) and was trustee for the University of S.C. when it was briefly integrated. In 1874, a rivalry with another black Republican led to a violent clash that made national news. Bowley also founded the short-lived Georgetown Planet newspaper. *Sponsored by the Gullah Geechee Chamber, 2019*
GPS Coordinates: 33° 22.216' N, 79° 17.035' W

22–67 Friendly Aid Society /Rosemont School

809 Palm St., Georgetown

Friendly Aid Society (FRONT)
The Christian Friendly Aid Society (CFAS), an African American benevolent society, built a lodge here ca. 1947. The Society began in the early 20th century among neighborhood families descended from people once enslaved on Rosemont Plantation, approx. 10 mi. north of here. The Society assisted members with medical and funeral costs, while the lodge served as a place to socialize and discuss community issues.
Rosemont School (REVERSE)
Shortly after the CFAS constructed the lodge, the building housed the Rosemont School, a segregated elementary school in the Georgetown County School District. The school was previously located on the site of Rosemont Plantation and served black families still living on the plantation grounds. The school kept an enrollment of around 40–50 children attending the first and second grades. It closed in 1955 when J. B. Beck Elementary opened. *Sponsored by Alpha Kappa Alpha Sorority, Mu Phi Omega Chapter, 2019*
GPS Coordinates: 33° 23.005' N, 79°1 7.430' W

Greenville County

No # About 1765

South Main St. (S.C. Hwy. 124), at the Reedy River Bridge, Greenville

Near Reedy River Falls, stood the home, trading station, and grist mill of Col. Richard Pearis, first white settler of this section. He was a noted Indian trader and prominent Tory of the Revolution. *Erected by the Camps of Greenville County Woodmen of the World, 1948*
GPS Coordinates: 34° 50.761' N, 82° 24.077' W

23–1 The Old Record Building

South Main St., across from the Poinsett Hotel, Greenville

70 feet south of this point was erected, 1820, "the old record building," designed by Robert Mills (1781–1855), famous Charleston architect, designer of the Washington Monument. This building of classic design was county courthouse until 1855; then record building until removed, 1924. John C. Calhoun spoke from its portico on current issues. *Erected by the Greenville Life Underwriters Association, 1938*
GPS Coordinates: 34° 50.923' N, 82° 23.977' W

23–2 Camp Sevier

U.S. Hwy. 29 (Wade Hampton Blvd.), near Artillery Rd., Greenville

This camp, named in honor of John Sevier, Lieutenant Colonel, N. C. Militia, 1777, Col., 1781, Brig. Gen., U. S. P. A., 1798, was approved as cantonment site May 21, 1917. The 30th Division trained here from August 28, 1917 to May 1, 1918; the 81st, from May 18, 1918 to July 16, 1918; the 20th, from August 12, 1918 to February 28, 1919. *Erected by the American Legion of South Carolina, 11 November 1938*
GPS Coordinates: 34° 53.986' N, 82° 20.245' W

23–3 Battle of Great Cane Brake

Fork Shoals Rd., S of One Hundred Rd. (S.C. Sec. Rd. 23-565), Simpsonville

Here along the south side of the creek to Reedy River was fought, Dec. 22, 1775, the Battle of Great Cane Brake between a force of South Carolinians under Colonel William Thomson and a band of Tories under Patrick Cuningham. The Tories were completely routed, and Cuningham himself narrowly escaped. *Erected by Behethland Butler Chapter, D. A. R., 10 May 1941*
GPS Coordinates: 34° 39.367' N, 82° 18.983' W

23–4 Indian Boundary Line

N. Line St. at Greer City Park, Greer

This marks the eastern boundary (present Greenville-Spartanburg county line) between the Cherokee Nation and the Province of South Carolina from the end of the Cherokee War (1759–61) until 1777. In that year the treaty of DeWitt's Corner extended the western boundary of South Carolina to the Savannah River. *Erected by the City of Greer, S.C. Dept. of Highways and Public Transportation, and Greenville County, 1979, replacing a marker erected in 1952 by the Joyce Scott Chapter, Daughters of the American Revolution*
GPS Coordinates: 34° 56.266' N, 82° 13.346' W

23–5 General Store Alexander McBeth & Co.

U.S. Hwy. 25 (White Horse Rd.), just S of S.C. Hwy. 253, N of Greenville

One of the first stores in this section of the state stood near this spot. Its day book shows that it was in operation in 1794, three years before the founding of the town of Greenville. *Erected by Behethland Butler Chapter, Daughters of the American Revolution, 1956*
GPS Coordinates: 34° 51.071' N, 82° 27.022' W

23–6 Old Fountain Inn

S.C. Hwy. 14, just N of Fountain Inn

According to tradition an antebellum inn with a gushing fountain in the front yard stood near here on the old stage road between Greenville and Columbia and served as a meeting place for men in the area in those stirring days. The present town chartered in 1886 is named for the old inn. *Erected by Oliver Thompson Chapter, United Daughters of the Confederacy, 1960*
GPS Coordinates: 34° 42.082' N, 82° 12.973' W

23–7 Ordinance of Secession

North Main St., Greenville, in park just outside Springwood Cemetery

Dedicated in reverence and admiration for their courage and integrity to the five signers of the Ordinance of Secession from Greenville County, December 20, 1860/William Hans Campbell/1823–1901/Perry Emory Duncan /1800–1867/William King Easley/1825–1872/ James Clement Furman/1809–1891/James Perry Harrison/1813–1871. *Erected by Greenville County Confederate Centennial Commission, 1961*
GPS Coordinates: 34° 51.32' N, 82° 23.816' W

23–8 Whitehall

310 W. Earle St., Greenville

Built by Henry Middleton on land bought from Elias Earle in 1813, Whitehall served as Middleton's summer home until 1820 when it was sold to George W. Earle, whose descendants have occupied it ever since. Henry

Middleton was son of Arthur Middleton, Signer of the Declaration of Independence. He served as Governor of South Carolina from 1810 to 1812. *Erected by Behethland Butler Chapter, D. A. R., 1964*
GPS Coordinates: 34° 51.808' N, 82° 24.098' W

23–9 "The Poplars"/Elias Earle

Intersection of Rutherford & Buncombe Rds., Greenville

"The Poplars" (FRONT)
This was approximately the center of the many-acred estate and "seat of hospitality" of Elias Earle, pioneer Greenville settler who began acquiring property here as early as 1787. His home, "The Poplars," stood at the NE corner of Rutherford and Buist streets.
Elias Earle (REVERSE)
June 19, 1762-May 19, 1823/Builder of the "Great Wagon Road" across the western mountains from South Carolina to Tennessee in 1797. Elias Earle served as State Legislator 1794–1798, State Senator 1798–1804, and U.S. Congressman 1805–1807, 1811–1815, and 1817–1821. Of distinguished Virginia ancestry, his family served South Carolina well. *Erected by Behethland Butler Chapter, Daughters of the American Revolution, 1967*
GPS Coordinates: 34° 52.051' N, 82° 24.255' W

23–10 Christ Church (Episcopal)

10 N. Church St., Greenville

Started in 1820 as St. James' Mission, the first church built here in 1825 on land given by Vardry McBee, was consecrated in 1828 by Bishop Nathaniel Bowen as Christ Church. The present church was built 1852–54 with Rev. John D. McCollough as architect, using plans drawn by Joel R. Poinsett, and consecrated in 1854 by Bishop Thomas Davis. *Erected by Christ Church Guild, 1967*
GPS Coordinates: 34° 51.06' N, 82° 23.686' W

23–11 Joel Roberts Poinsett

Poinsett Hotel, S. Main St., Greenville

(FRONT) 1779–1851/Born in Charleston, S. C., educated in this country and Great Britain,

he travelled widely in Europe and Asia before returning to a distinguished career. He served South Carolina in the state legislature, 1816–1820; 1830–1832; and as Chairman of the Board of Public Works 1818–1820. He represented S.C. in Congress 1821–1825, was first American Minister to Mexico 1825–1829, and Secretary of War, 1837–1841.
(REVERSE) Planter, Writer, Botanist/Diplomat, Statesman./Joel R. Poinsett had a summer home near here dividing his time in later life between it and his plantation on the Peedee River. He brought the lovely poinsettia to this country from Mexico. His cultural interests and scientific pursuits with this political career earned him the title "Versatile American." He died December 12, 1851, at Stateburg, S.C., and was buried there at the Church of the Holy Cross. *Erected by Greenville County Historical Society, 1968*
GPS Coordinates: 34° 50.933' N, 82° 23.997' W

23–12 Old Greenville Graveyard

Old Buncombe Rd. at Hammett St., near Poe Mills, Greenville

(FRONT) About 150 feet east of this point are buried some of Greenville's earliest settlers, including Elias Earle (1762–1823), State Representative and Senator and United States Congressman; George Washington Earle (1777–1821), wealthy planter and early Greenville Clerk of Court; and their immediate families.
(REVERSE) Among the Earle descendants buried about 150 feet east of this point is George Earle Yancey, infant son of William Lowndes Yancey, known as the "father of secession," and Sarah Caroline Earle Yancey. In an unmarked grave is buried Elias Drayton Earle, South Carolina Superintendent of Public Works, 1847. *Erected by Behethland Butler Chapter, Daughters of the American Revolution, 1980, replacing a marker erected by the Behethland Butler Chapter in 1971*
GPS Coordinates: 34° 52.49' N, 82° 24.95' W

23–13 Chick Springs

[Reported missing in June 2009.]

S.C. Sec. Rd. 23-38, ½ mi. SE of U.S. Hwy. 29, at entrance to Chick Springs Park, Greer vicinity

(FRONT) Dr. Burwell Chick opened a resort at these mineral springs in 1840. A spacious hotel and cottages accommodated a large number of summer guests. After Dr. Chick's death, the springs were operated by his sons Pettus and Reuben, and after 1857 by Franklin Talbird and John T. Henery, lowcountry developers. In the 1860s, the war ended the heyday of the resort.

(REVERSE) After 1885, George Westmoreland began to reestablish the springs as a resort. In 1903, the Chick Springs Company was formed to sell water and maintain a hotel. From this time, J. A. Bull was principal developer. A military academy was located here 1916–17, and Steedly Clinic and Sanitarium 1919–32. An amusement park has been operated at Chick Springs since 1927. *Erected by Taylors Garden Club, 1972*

GPS Coordinates: 34° 55.733' N, 82° 17.283' W

23–14 Furman University

Court Square, between Church St. & Howe St., Greenville

Established in 1825 by the S.C. Baptist Convention, the Furman Academy and Theological Institution opened at Edgefield, 1826, moved to Sumter District, 1829–34, and to Fairfield, 1837–50. Chartered in 1850 as Furman University, it opened in Greenville, 1851, and for over a century, 1852–1958, occupied this site purchased from Vardry McBee. In the summer of 1958, Furman moved to a new campus six miles north of town. *Erected by Furman University, 1975*

GPS Coordinates: 34° 50.408' N, 82° 24.202' W

23–15 Greenville Woman's College

Heritage Green, College St., Greenville

Established in 1854 by the S.C. Baptist Convention, this institution opened as Greenville Baptist Female College in February 1856, on this site originally donated by Vardry McBee to the Greenville Academies. Its name was changed

to Greenville Woman's College in 1914. It was coordinated with Furman University in 1933, merged with Furman in 1938, and moved in 1961 to the consolidated campus six miles north of town. *Erected by Furman University, 1975*

GPS Coordinates: 34° 51.33' N, 82° 24.079' W

23–16 Lebanon Church

Intersection of Dunklin Bridge Rd. (S.C. Sec. Rd. 23-68) & Latimer Mill Rd. (S.C. Sec. Rd. 23-69), just S of the Reedy River, Fork Shoals vicinity

This United Methodist Church was originally located about 1¼ miles east and named the Grove. It was visited by Bishop Francis Asbury in 1790 and 1800. Relocated about ¼ mile SW of here after the land was obtained in 1832. Present house of worship was erected in 1850's and name changed to Lebanon. Sunday School annex completed 1951 and steeple and portico in 1955. *Erected by the Congregation, 1975*

GPS Coordinates: 34° 33.724' N, 82° 15.913' W

23–17 Sullivan (Grove) Cemetery

Latimer Mill Rd. (S.C. Sec. Rd. 23-69), just S of the Reedy River, near the Greenville County-Laurens County line, Fork Shoals vicinity

The cemetery located about ½ mile north, marks the site of Grove Church, established prior to 1790, one of the first Methodist churches in Greenville County. The present church, renamed Lebanon, is located about 1¼ miles W. of here. A number of Revolutionary War soldiers and church founders are buried in this cemetery, now maintained by the church and the Sullivan family. *Erected by Lebanon United Methodist Church, 1982*

GPS Coordinates: 34° 33.567' N, 82° 15.055' W

23–18 John Broadus Watson

Renfrew Baptist Church Cemetery, 951 Greer Hwy. (U.S. Hwy. 276), about ½ mi. N of Travelers Rest

Born in 1878 about ½ mile SW, Watson was a pioneer in behavioral psychology. He graduated from Furman University, earned his Ph. D. from the University of Chicago, served as president of the American Psychological Association, and professor and director of

the psychological laboratory at Johns Hopkins University for 12 years. Scientist, author, editor, teacher, he died in 1958. *Erected by Furman University and The S.C. Hall of Science and Technology, 1984*
GPS Coordinates: 34° 58.807' N, 82° 27.628' W

23–19 Fairview Church/Fairview Cemetery

126 Fairview Church Rd. (S.C. Sec. Rd. 23–451), just S. of its intersection with Fairview Rd. (S.C. Sec. Rd. 23–55), NE of Fork Shoals

Fairview Church (FRONT)
Settlers from the Nazareth area of Spartanburg County founded this Presbyterian church in 1786 on land ceded by the Cherokee Indians in the Treaty of Dewitt's Corner, 1777. It is said that three buildings, two of logs and one of brick, preceded this 1858 building. The Sunday School annex was built in 1949 and the office-historical building in 1986.
Fairview Cemetery (REVERSE)
The oldest graves in this cemetery are those of Margaret Alexander, d.1791, and Elizabeth Alexander, d. 1797. Soldiers of the American Revolution, War of 1812, Civil War, and World Wars I and II are buried here. A special marker denotes the area where blacks were interred. *Erected by the Congregation, 1986*
GPS Coordinates: 34° 38.685' N, 82° 15.112' W

23–20 Site of First Baptist Church/ Baptist Seminary

Corner of Irvine St. & McBee Ave., Greenville
Site of First Baptist Church (FRONT)
In 1825, Wm. Bullein Johnson opened a subscription for a Baptist meetinghouse, which was soon built here. The 120 foot-square lot, which extended well into present McBee Ave., was given by Vardry McBee. After its organization in 1831, First Baptist Church occupied the building here until it moved to West McBee Ave. in 1857. The church moved to its present location on Cleveland Street in 1974.
Baptist Seminary (REVERSE)
When Southern Baptist Theological Seminary was organized in 1859, the old Baptist church building once located here was divided into

two classrooms and library for the school's use. First faculty was James Petigru Boyce, John A. Broadus, Basil Manly, Jr., and William Williams. Crawford H. Toy and William H. Whitsitt joined before the seminary moved to Louisville, Ky. in 1877. *Erected by First Baptist Church and the South Carolina Baptist Historical Society, 1987*
GPS Coordinates: 34° 50.931' N, 82° 23.818' W

23–21 Cotton Mills

S.C. Hwy. 14 at the Enoree River, Pelham-Batesville vicinity

By 1820 one of the first cotton mills in Greenville County was located at these river shoals. Pelham Manufacturing Co. purchased a mill here sixty years later. *Erected by Greenville County Recreation District, 1992*
GPS Coordinates: 34° 51.4' N, 82° 13.55' W

23–21 Tullyton

[Double numbered, 23–22 was never assigned.]
Fairfield Rd. (S.C. Sec. Rd. 23–55), 5 mi. S of S.C. Hwy. 418, Fountain Inn vicinity

This house was built by T. C. Bolling ca. 1840 near the old Indian boundary. C. B. Stewart minister of nearby Fairview Presbyterian Church lived here 1859–1890. *Erected by the Greenville County Historic Preservation Commission, 1993*
GPS Coordinates: 34° 36.467' N, 82° 13.967' W

23–23 William Preston Few 1867–1940

Jackson Grove Rd., near Jackson Grove Methodist Church, 1401 Jackson Grove Rd., Travelers Rest vicinity

(FRONT) William Preston Few, prominent Southern educator, was born 1.6 mi. NE in 1867. Few received his Ph.D. from Harvard in 1896 and joined the faculty of Trinity College, Durham, N.C., that same year. He became Trinity's fifth president in 1910 and was instrumental in transforming the small Methodist college into a major university by cultivating the financial support of industrialist James Buchanan Duke (1856–1925).

(REVERSE) Few persuaded Duke to establish the Duke Endowment in 1924, a trust which created Duke University and which still supports it and other institutions and charities in the Carolinas, including children's homes, hospitals, Davidson College and Johnson C. Smith University in N.C., and Furman University in S.C. William Preston Few was the first president of Duke University, serving from 1924 until his death. *Erected by Furman University, 1997*
GPS Coordinates: 34° 58.468' N, 82° 21.382' W

23–24 Fountain Fox Beattie House/ Greenville Woman's Club

8 Bennett St., corner of Bennett and N. Church Sts., Greenville

Fountain Fox Beattie House (FRONT)
This house, built in 1834, first stood a few blocks south on East North St. It was built by Fountain Fox Beattie (1807‑1863), a textile merchant, for his new bride Emily Edgeworth Hamlin. Their son Hamlin Beattie (1835‑1914), who founded the National Bank of Greenville in 1872, added wings and elaborate Italianate ornamentation. The house was listed in the National Register of Historic Places in 1974.
Greenville Woman's Club (REVERSE)
The house remained in the Beattie family until 1946, when the city bought the property to widen Church St. When the house was moved to Beattie Place in 1948 it was leased to the women's organizations of Greenville. The Greenville Woman's Club officially opened in 1949. The house was moved a second time in 1983 to make room for downtown expansion. Member clubs maintain the house and gardens. *Erected by the Greenville Woman's Club, 1998*
GPS Coordinates: 34° 51.427' N, 82° 23.38' W

23–25 Campbell's Covered Bridge

Campbell Bridge Rd., just SW of the intersection of Pleasant Hill Rd. (S.C. Sec Rd. 23–114) and S.C. Hwy. 414, SW of Gowensville

This bridge, built in 1909, is the last extant covered bridge in S.C. Built by Charles Irwin Willis (1878–1966), it was named for Alexander Lafayette Campbell (1836–1920), who owned and operated a grist mill here for many years. Measuring 35 feet long and 12 feet wide, it is an excellent example of a four-span Howe truss, featuring diagonal timbers and vertical iron rods. *Erected by the Cherokee Foothills National Scenic Byway Association, 2002*
GPS Coordinates: 35° 5.159' N, 82° 15.845' W

23–26 Donaldson Air Force Base /Captain John O. Donaldson

Marker 1: Just off Exchange St., at the Donaldson Center, Greenville

Marker 2: Kodak Rd., near its intersection with Perimeter Rd., at the Donaldson Center, Greenville

Donaldson Air Force Base (FRONT)
Greenville Army Air Base opened on this site in 1942 and trained B-25 bomber crews during World War II. Emphasizing air transport after 1945 and renamed Donaldson Air Force Base in 1951, it was home to C-124 transports and called "The Airlift Capital of the World" for its role in the Berlin airlift, Korean War, and Cold War. Closed in 1962, it has been an industrial park since 1963.
Captain John O. Donaldson (REVERSE)
John Owen Donaldson (1897–1930), for whom the base was named, grew up in Greenville and attended Furman University and Cornell University before joining the British Royal Air Force in World War I. He became an ace, shooting down eight enemy planes, and was decorated by the United States, Great Britain, and Belgium. Davidson was killed in a plane crash at an air show in 1930. *Erected by the Donaldson Development Commission, 2002*
GPS Coordinates: 34° 45.13' N, 82° 21.447' W

23–27 Working Benevolent Society Hospital

Corner of Green Ave. and Jenkins St., Greenville

(FRONT) The Working Benevolent Society Hospital, first known as St. Luke Colored Hospital, was a two-story frame building standing here at the corner of Green Avenue and Jenkins Street. Founded in 1920, it served blacks in Greenville for twenty-eight years. The Working Benevolent Grand Lodge of S.C., at Broad and Fall Streets in Greenville, operated the hospital from 1928 until it closed in 1948.

(REVERSE) The hospital, described at its opening as "one of the most modern institutions in the South for colored people," had three wards and twenty-two beds in semi-private and private rooms. Mrs. M. H. Bright was the first superintendent. A registered nurse and a graduate of the Tuskegee Institute, she had been superintendent of the Institute hospital. Most of the superintendents after her were nurses as well. *Erected by the Green Avenue Area Civic Association, 2003*
GPS Coordinates: 34° 50.233' N, 82° 24.739' W

23–28 Cooley's Bridge

Cooley Bridge Rd. (S.C. Hwy. 247) just NE of the Saluda River, Possum Kingdown community, NE of Belton

(FRONT) The original Cooley's Bridge, built across the Saluda River in 1835–36 to replace a ferry, stood about 150 yds. above the present bridge over S.C. Hwy. 247. It was built for Hiram Cooley (ca. 1796–1864), a cotton planter who owned more than 1600 acres and operated a cotton gin and grist mill nearby. His house, built about 1830, was just NE of the present bridge; it burned in 1983.

(REVERSE) This part of southwestern Greenville County was officially Dunklin Township in the late 19th century but has long been called "Possum Kingdom." Several bridges over the river here have been washed away by floods and replaced. A steel through truss bridge was built on the site of the original Cooley's Bridge in 1896–97. The present concrete highway bridge was built here in 2000. *Erected by the Belton Chapter # 1843, United Daughters of the Confederacy, 2005*
GPS Coordinates: 34° 33.403' N, 82° 25.003' W

23–29 Stone's Mill/Jones Mill

Jones Mill Rd. (S.C. Sec. Rd. 23–191) at Durbin Creek, N of Fountain Inn

Stone's Mill (FRONT)

The first grist mill on Big Durbin Creek was built about 1813 for John Bruce (d. 1818), a veteran of the American Revolution, who also ran a sawmill and woolen mill here. The present mill, built by slave labor before 1860, is made of heart pine, with a granite foundation. It was built for Jesse K. Stone (1825–1899), and the mill was known as Stone's Mill until his death.

Jones Mill (REVERSE)

The mill complex was sold to R. B. Holland in 1899, then to the Jones family soon afterward. Walter T. Jones ground corn and wheat, ran a cotton gin, and operated a small grocery store here for many years. The grist mill, along with the shoals, rocks, and a nearby covered bridge, was a "favorite gathering place" in the vicinity until the mill shut down in the 1950s. *Erected by the Oliver Thompson Chapter # 1850, United Daughters of the Confederacy, 2005*
GPS Coordinates: 34° 43.784' N, 82° 12.02' W

23–30 Cherokee Boundary 1767

#1: Woodruff Rd. (S.C. Hwy. 296), just E of its intersection with Scuffletown Rd., Mauldin vicinity

#2: Milacron Dr. (S.C. Sec. Rd. 418), just SW of its intersection with the I-385 ramp, Fountain Inn

(FRONT) In 1766–67 S.C. & N.C. negotiated with the Cherokee to establish a boundary between Indian land to the west and new settlement to the east. This north-south line ran past this point to N.C. and on to Va. In S.C. it ran north from near present-day Honea Path, crossed the Reedy River near present-day Princeton, and ended at the S.C.-N.C. line.

(REVERSE) The Cherokee ceded all land east of the 1767 line to the colonies of S.C. and N.C. In 1786, when S.C. created its first counties, the line from the Reedy River to the S.C.–N.C. line south of Tryon, N.C. was the boundary for Greenville County between both Spartanburg and Laurens Counties. In 1793 the Greenville boundary shifted east to accommodate new settlers south of the Enoree River. *Erected by the Greenville County Historic Preservation Commission, 2005*
GPS Coordinates: 34° 51.248' N, 82° 13.683' W

23–31 Textile Hall

W. Washington St. near its intersection with N. Academy St., Greenville

(FRONT) Textile Hall, built in 1917 to host the annual Southern Textile Exposition, stood on this side until 1992. The first exposition of the Southern Textile Association had been held in Greenville in 1915. Textile Hall, designed by J. E. Sirrine & Co. at a cost of $130,000, was a five-story Renaissance Revival building; its façade featured a limestone tablet bearing the initials "STE" for "Southern Textile Exposition" and the words "Textile Hall."
(REVERSE) When built, Textile Hall was described as "a fitting monument to . . . the proper cooperative spirit." It hosted the Southern Textile Exposition from 1917 to 1962 and gave Greenville the title "Textile Center of the South." It also hosted many other meetings and special events, such as the annual Southern Textile Basketball Tournament, with teams representing mills across the South. Listed in the National Register of Historic Places in 1980, it was demolished in 1992. *Erected by the City of Greenville and the Hampton-Pinckney Neighborhood Association, 2006*
GPS Coordinates: 34° 51.132' N, 82° 24.181' W

23–32 Sterling High School

Corner of Calhoun & Pendleton Sts., Greenville

(FRONT) Sterling High School stood ¾ mi. southeast of here and served generations of African Americans in Greenville. Founded in 1896 by Rev. D. M. Minus and called Greenville Academy, it was first located in West Greenville. It moved into a new two-story brick school nearby in 1902 and was then renamed Sterling Industrial College after Mrs. E. R. Sterling, who had financed Rev. Minus's education at Claflin University.
(REVERSE) The school closed briefly but reopened in 1915 as Enoree High School, owned by the Enoree Baptist Assn. The Greenville Co. School District bought the school in 1929, made it the first black public high school in the county, and restored the name Sterling. After it burned in Sept. 1967, classes moved to Greenville Jr. High, renamed Sterling Jr.-Sr. High. It closed after the 1969–70 school year.

Erected by the Greenville County Historical Commission and the Sterling High School Association, 2007
GPS Coordinates: 34° 50.589' N, 82° 24.956' W

23–33 Early White Settlement/The Massacre of Jacob Hite

Woodland Elementary School, 1730 Gibbs Shoals Rd., Greer

Early White Settlement (FRONT)
By 1768 Indian traders and land speculators Richard Pearis (d. 1794) and Jacob Hite of Virginia acquired large tracts from the Cherokees in present-day Greenville County. Though royal authorities disputed the validity of these titles, Pearis and Hite moved their families to this area between 1768 and 1775.
The Massacre of Jacob Hite (REVERSE)
Jacob Hite settled nearby with his wife Frances Madison Hite and their family in 1775. He continued his trade with the Cherokees. In June 1776, Cherokees killed his son James. On July 1, 1776, Cherokees killed Jacob Hite and kidnapped his wife and two daughters. Frances Hite's body was recovered, but the Hite daughters were never found. *Erected by the Hite Family Association, 2009*
GPS Coordinates: 34° 53.868' N, 82° 14.682' W

23–34 Hopkins Farm

3717 Fork Shoals Rd., Simpsonville vicinity

(FRONT) This farm has been owned by the Hopkins family since 1834, when John Hopkins (1793–1837) purchased it from William Toney. The Greek Revival main house was built ca. 1840, with later additions ca. 1890 and ca. 1925. Hopkins' Widow Lucinda (1800–1876) managed the farm after his death, growing cotton and corn as cash crops, supplemented by subsistence crops and livestock.
(REVERSE) John and Lucinda Hopkins are buried in the family cemetery nearby. The farm complex includes a cook's house, smoke house, and corn crib built ca. 1850 as well as other outbuildings from the 1870s to the present. John Drayton Hopkins (b. 1913) took over the farm in 1939, making it a model of modern soil conservation techniques such

as terracing and crop rotation. *Erected by the Greenville County Historical Commission, 2007* GPS Coordinates: 34° 39.355' N, 82° 18.995' W

23–35 Toney's Store/Militia Muster Ground

3717 Fork Shoals Rd., Simpsonville vicinity

Toney's Store (FRONT)
William Toney, prominent in business and civic affairs in early Greenville and Greenville County, ran a store here 1816–1829. The store was near the boundary established in 1767 between Cherokee land to the west and new settlement to the east. John Hopkins (1793–1837) acquired this property in 1834. His family lived in the old store while building their house, completed ca. 1840.
Militia Muster Ground (REVERSE)
The field adjacent to Toney's Store, called "Toney's Old Field," was a militia muster ground from 1818 to the Civil War. The 15th Regiment was organized in 1794 in the lower part of Greenville County. "The Lower Regiment" was redesignated the 3rd Regiment in 1819. "The Butler Guards," an independent company from Greenville organized in 1855, also mustered here 1855–1861. *Erected by the Greenville County Historical Commission, 2008*
GPS Coordinates: 34° 39.355' N, 82° 18.995' W

23–36 Lickville Presbyterian Church

[Reported missing in January 2010.]

10020 Augusta Rd., Pelzer

(FRONT) This church, which takes its name from a nearby salt lick, was founded in 1882. Mrs. Ellen C. Woodside (1838–1906) worked with Rev. C. L. Stewart to organize services on her farm in 1880–81. A commission from the Enoree Presbytery, including Rev. Stewart, formally established the church with 20 charter members.
(REVERSE) Rev. C. L. Stewart, the first and longest-serving minister here, served this congregation 1882–1895 and 1905–1921. This church, a frame building, was constructed in 1882 and remodeled in 1943–44 and 1968. The

church cemetery includes the plots of many prominent families of Lickville and Possum Kingdom. *Erected by the Greenville County Historical Commission, 2008*
GPS Coordinates: 34° 36.25' N, 82° 21.8' W

23–37 Sans Souci

W. Blue Ridge Dr. (S.C. Hwy. 253), Sans Souci community, Greenville

(FRONT) This early twentieth century suburb takes its name from Sans Souci, the nearby house and estate of Gov. Benjamin F. Perry (1805–1886). Perry, a prominent Unionist before the Civil War, was appointed provisional governor of S.C. by President Andrew Johnson in June 1865 and served until December 1865. In 1876–77 he built an ornate Second Empire house N of this location.
(REVERSE) After B. F. Perry's death in 1886, the house was briefly a girls' school. His heirs sold the property in 1902 and it became the Sans Souci Country Club in 1905. The club moved to Byrd Blvd. and became the Greenville Country Club in 1924. The house burned in 1927. Residential and commercial development in this area from 1911 through World War II featured the name Sans Souci. *Erected by the Greenville County Historical Commission, 2008*
GPS Coordinates: 34° 53.376' N, 82° 24.973' W

23–38 Brutontown

Rutherford Rd., Greenville

(FRONT) Brutontown, an historic African-American community, grew up around the intersection of Paris Mountain Rd. and Rutherford Rd. Benjamin Bruton, a mulatto freedman, bought 1.75 acres here in 1874. He built a house and blacksmith shop, labeled "Bruton's Shop" on Kyzer's 1882 map of Greenville County. Other blacks, a few of them tradesmen like Bruton but most tenant farmers, soon moved to this area. By 1880 sixty African-American families lived here.
(REVERSE) The community, on both sides of Rutherford Rd., was known as "Brutontown" by about 1900. In 1921 farm land was subdivided into town lots, in an area 2 blocks deep

and 6 blocks wide. Bruton Temple Baptist Church, the first church here, was founded in 1921. By 1930 Brutontown numbered about 300 residents. The three-acre "Society Burial Ground" on Leo Lewis St., dating from before the Civil War, includes many graves of slaves, free blacks, and freedmen. *Erected by the Greenville County Redevelopment Authority, 2009*
GPS Coordinates: 34° 52.317' N, 82° 24.067' W

23–39 Tigerville

NE corner of N. Tigerville Rd. (S.C. Hwy. 253) & S.C. Hwy. 414, Tigerville

(FRONT) Tigerville got its name from early settlers who settled here shortly after the Revolution. They called bobcats they saw here "tygers," and named the nearby Tyger River. The Head of Tyger Baptist Church, later Tyger Baptist Church, was founded about 1800. A community grew up here centered at the intersection of the State Road, built in 1820, and the Tugaloo Path, an old Indian trail.
(REVERSE) The first post office here opened in Lemuel Jennings' general store in 1881, with Jennings as postmaster. Tigerville, described as "charming and romantic" in 1883, boasted several large houses, a cotton gin, a blacksmith shop, and an academy. Jennings' store, later operated as Wood General Store for almost 90 years, still stands nearby, as does J. H. Roe & Co., built in 1904. *Erected by the Greenville County Historic Preservation Commission, 2009*
GPS Coordinates: 35° 4.086' N, 82° 22.115' W

23–40 Pepper School

Augusta Rd. (U.S. Hwy. 25), Sandy Springs vicinity, next to Greenville Memorial Gardens

Pepper School, established in 1914–15, was built on land donated "for the children of my community" by William A. Pepper (1829–1914). The school, with three teachers and about 75–100 students in grades 1–7 for much of its history, closed after the 1952–53 school year. The Augusta Road Ruritan Club bought the building in 1964, preserved it for the community, and meets there now. *Erected*

by the Augusta Road Ruritan Club, 2010
GPS Coordinates: 34° 42.217' N, 82° 23.583' W

23–41 The Lynching of Willie Earle

[Torn down shortly after initial dedication in 2010. New marker with same text approved in 2018.]

Old Easley Rd. (S.C. Hwy. 124) & Bramlett Rd., Greenville

(FRONT) The Willie Earle lynching was the last recorded in S.C. and the one of the last in the South. On the night of February 15, 1947, white cabdriver Thomas W. Brown was found mortally wounded beside his cab in Pickens County. Earle, a young black man, was thought to be Brown's last passenger. He was arrested near Liberty on February 16, accused of assault and robbery, and held in the Pickens County Jail.
(REVERSE) Early on February 17, 1947, a white mob forced the Pickens Co. jailer to give Earle up. They drove Earle back to Greenville, lynched him, and left his body on Bramlett Rd. Brown died later that day. The May 12–21 trial of 31 men drew national attention. Though 26 men admitted being part of the mob, an all-white jury acquitted all defendants. Outrage led to new federal civil rights policies. *Erected by the Willie Earle Commemorative Trail Committee, 2010. Restored by Wofford College Campus Union, 2018*
GPS Coordinates: 34° 50.692' N, 82° 27.837' W

23–42 Greenville County Courthouse/The Willie Earle Lynching Trial

35 W. Court St., behind the old Greenville County Courthouse, Greenville

Greenville County Courthouse (FRONT)
This Beaux Arts building, built in 1916–18, was the fourth Greenville County Courthouse, from 1918 to 1950. It was listed in the National Register of Historic Places in 1994. The largest lynching trial in U.S. history was held here May 12–21, 1947. Willie Earle, a young black man accused of assaulting white cabdriver Thomas W. Brown, had been lynched by a white mob on Bramlett Road in Greenville.

The Willie Earle Lynching Trial (REVERSE)
The trial of 31 whites, 28 of them cabdrivers,
was rare at the time and drew national attention. Though 26 defendants admitted being
part of the mob, all defendants were acquitted
by an all-white jury. Rebecca West's "Opera
in Greenville," published in *The New Yorker*
on June 14, 1947, interpreted the trial and
its aftermath. Widespread outrage over the
lynching and the verdict spurred new federal
civil rights policies. *Erected by the Willie Earle
Commemorative Trail Committee, 2010*
GPS Coordinates: 34° 50.939' N, 82° 24.045' W

23–43 "Shoeless Joe" Jackson House

356 Field St., Greenville

(FRONT) This house, built in 1940, was originally 3 mi. SW at 119 E. Wilburn Ave. It was
the last home of Joseph Jefferson Wofford
"Shoeless Joe" Jackson (1888–1951), one of the
greatest natural hitters in the history of baseball. Jackson, born in Pickens Co., moved to
Greenville as a boy. He worked at the Brandon
Mill, joined the mill baseball team as a teen-
ager, and was a star long before he made the
major leagues in 1908.
(REVERSE) In 1911, his first full season, Jackson
batted .408. He played for the Philadelphia A's
1908–10, the Cleveland Naps 1910–15, and the
Chicago White Sox 1915–20, with a lifetime
average of .356. He helped the White Sox win
the 1917 World Series, but he and 7 teammates
were banned from baseball for fixing the 1919
Series. This house, where Jackson died in 1951,
was moved here in 2006 and opened as a museum in 2008. *Erected by the Shoeless Joe Jackson Museum and Baseball Library, Greenville*
GPS Coordinates: 34° 50.483' N, 82° 24.433' W

23–44 Oakland Plantation

259 Adams Mill Rd., Simpsonville

(FRONT) This house was built in 1823 by Dr.
Thomas Collins Austin (1790–1883), physician
and planter. Austin attended the Medical University of Pennsylvania in Philadelphia, and
practiced medicine here for sixty years. His
office, just north of the house, was demolished
in 1953. Austin and his wife Mary Turner

James (1805–1889) raised eleven children here.
(REVERSE) In 1897 the Austin family sold
the house and 550 acres to Thomas Martin
Vaughan (1865–1939). Vaughan, a farmer,
married Ida Tyson Vaughan (1875–1952) the
next year. They raised eleven children here,
just as the Austins had. Their daughter Lucille
Jessie Vaughan Rice (1912–2006), the last fam-
ily member to live here, sold the house to the
YMCA of Greenville in 2004. *Erected by the
YMCA of Greenville and the Greenville County
Historic Preservation Commission, 2011*
GPS Coordinates: 34° 46.933' N, 82° 14.75' W

23–45 Fountain Inn Rosenwald School

Mt. Zion Dr., near Mt. Zion Baptist Church,
Fountain Inn

(FRONT) The Fountain Inn Rosenwald School,
also known as the Fountain Inn Colored
School, was a complex of several buildings
built here from 1928 to 1942. The first school,
a frame seven-room elementary school for
grades 1–7, was a Rosenwald school, one of
500 rural schools in S.C. funded in part by
the Julius Rosenwald Fund from 1917 to 1932.
It was built in 1928–29 at a cost of $7,200.
(REVERSE) The Fountain Inn Colored High
School, a frame three-room high school for
grades 8–11, was built in 1930. A frame teacherage was built in 1935 for principal Gerard A.
Anderson, and by 1942 this complex included
a library, gymnasium, and three new classrooms. The high school closed in 1954, and
the elementary school closed in 1960. The 1935
teacherage is the only building standing; the
rest were demolished in 2000. *Erected by the
City of Fountain Inn and the Greenville County
Historic Preservation Commission, 2011*
GPS Coordinates: 34° 41.8' N, 82° 11.55' W

23–46 Mauldin

City Center Dr., Mauldin

(FRONT) This area was settled soon after the
Revolution, and a community grew up here
on the road from Greenville to Laurens. It was
later known as Butler's Crossroads for Willis W.
Butler, who acquired a tract including the

intersection of the Laurens and Reedy River roads in 1853. This community became a town after the Greenville & Laurens Railroad completed its line here in 1885 and built a frame passenger and freight depot ¼ mi. N on Jenkins Street in 1886.

(REVERSE) The new town was named for Lt. Gov. William L. Mauldin (1845–1912), president of the Greenville & Laurens Railroad 1881–85, state representative and senator, and lt. governor 1886–1890. Mauldin was first chartered in 1890, with its limits a half-mile radius from the depot. The depot was torn down in 1953. Two historic stores of note are the John S. Hill Store (ca. 1906), ¼ mi. E on Main Street, and Massey's General Store (1931), at Main Street and White Drive. *Erected by the City of Mauldin and the Greenville County Historical Commission, 2011*
GPS Coordinates: 34° 46.8' N, 82° 18.317' W

23-47 Mush Creek Baptist Church

940 Mush Creek Rd., Travelers Rest

(FRONT) This church, established in 1882, grew out of services held by itinerant Baptist ministers in a nearby log school, encouraged by Ann Pool Neves (1809–1898) and her husband Alsey A. Neves (1814–1888). In 1884 Mrs. Neves and her son W. P. Z. F. Neves (1835–1917) deeded three acres for a church. A frame sanctuary was dedicated in 1886, with Rev. J. G. Fowler as pastor.

(REVERSE) This church was covered in brick veneer in 1967. The cemetery, with early burials dating to the 1820s, includes several generations of the Neves family, including William Neves (1789–1844) and his wife, Anah Mitchell Neves (1787–1877), the first members of the family to settle in this area. Mush Creek Baptist Church was renamed Living Grace Baptist Church in 2010. *Erected by the Travelers Rest Historical Society, 2011*
GPS Coordinates: 35° 2.815' N, 82° 22.975' W

23-48 Simpsonville

In front of City Hall, 118 NE Main St., Simpsonville

(FRONT) This town grew up around a stagecoach stop on the Old Stage Road from Laurens to Greenville. For many years the community was known as "Plain," the name given to the first post office, opened in 1838 with Jesse T. Cook as postmaster. It was later named for Peter Simpson (d. 1847), who had come here from Laurens District in 1836. Silas Gilbert opened a general store here about the same time. Gilbert was postmaster in 1839–44, followed by Simpson in 1844–47.

(REVERSE) Sidney J. Wilson (1854–1919) came here from N.C. about 1875 and opened a general store. In 1885–86 the Greenville & Laurens Railroad completed its line from Laurens to Greenville. Wilson had the town surveyed and city lots laid out on Main St., and soon built the first brick store here. The post office was renamed Simpsonville in 1885, and the city was incorporated in 1901. Simpsonville Cotton Mill, later a branch of Woodside Mills, operated here from 1908 to 1989. *Erected by the City of Simpsonville and the Rotary Club of Simpsonville, 2011*
GPS Coordinates: 34° 44.3' N, 82° 15.333' W

23-49 Old Stage Road/Railroads in Simpsonville

City Common, SE Main St., Simpsonville

Old Stage Road (FRONT)
The town of Simpsonville grew up around a stagecoach stop nearby operated by Thomas Goldsmith (1788–1868). Goldsmith's house, on the Old Stage Road from Laurens to Greenville, was near a crossroads where the Old Stage Road met an old Cherokee trail, later known as the Georgia Road. The road was the main route through this area ca. 1820-ca. 1870. The railroad arrived in 1885–86 when the Greenville & Laurens Railroad completed its line through the town.

Railroads in Simpsonville (REVERSE)
Main Street was laid out parallel to the tracks, and the railroad ushered in a period of rapid growth and prosperity. The G&L RR and its successor the Port Royal & Western Carolina Railway were absorbed by the Charleston & Western Carolina Railway in 1896. The Atlantic Coast Line RR took control of the C&WC in 1897 and operated it until 1959. The first passenger and freight depot here was

demolished in the 1970s. *Erected by the Ralph and Virginia Hendricks Foundation, 2011*
GPS Coordinates: 34° 44.2' N, 82° 15.317' W

23–50 Simpsonville Cotton Mill/ Woodside Mill

Corner of South St. & W. Curtis St., Simpsonville

Simpsonville Cotton Mill (FRONT)
This mill, opened in 1908, was built after several leading men of Simpsonville asked Edward F. Woodside of the Pelzer Manufacturing Co. to help them establish a textile mill. The Simpsonville Cotton Mill, with Woodside as president and his brother John T. as secretary, opened with 8,000 spindles and 200 looms, making several kinds of cotton cloth. By 1911 it boasted 25,000 spindles and 600 looms.
Woodside Mill (REVERSE)
In 1911 this mill was merged with Fountain Inn Cotton Mill and Woodside Cotton Mill in Greenville to create Woodside Cotton Mills. This branch was Simpsonville's largest employer until after World War II, with as many as 650 employees in the 1950s and 1960s. The mill village, with four streets of mill houses, included a company store, recreation building, and baseball field. The Woodside Gym, built in 1947, is now part of the Simpsonville Senior Center. *Erected by The Cotton Mill Place and Para Chem, Inc., 2011*
GPS Coordinates: 34° 44.167' N, 82° 15.483' W

23–51 City Hospital/Greenville General Hospital

East side of S. Memminger St. & Hamilton Ave. intersection, Greenville

City Hospital (FRONT)
City Hospital, founded here in 1912 and later renamed Greenville General Hospital, occupied most of the block bounded by Memminger, Mallard, and Dunbar Sts. and Arlington Ave. by the early 1950s. The Ladies Hospital Board and the Greenville Hospital Association, founded in 1896, acquired a building on this site, previously a sanitorium, in 1911. It opened as City Hospital in January 1912.
Greenville General Hospital (REVERSE)
The hospital was sold to the City of Greenville

in 1917. Expansions from 1921 to 1953 increased capacity to more than 600 beds. Renamed Greenville General Hospital in 1935, it became a city-county hospital in 1948 and flagship of the Greenville Hospital System by the 1960s. Most services moved to the new Greenville Memorial Medical Campus on Grove Road by 1983, and the historic buildings here were demolished in 1998. *Erected by Greenville Hospital System Employees, Physicians, and Volunteers, 2012*
GPS Coordinates: 34° 40.420' N, 82° 24.919' W

23–52 Dunean Mill

Corner of Stevens and Emery Sts., Dunean Mill Village, Greenville

(FRONT) Dunean Mill, chartered in 1911 and opened in 1912, was one of several textile mills owned by Capt. Ellison Adger Smyth (1847–1942), a national leader in the textile industry for more than 60 years. Dunean was named for the Irish village where Smyth's Adger ancestors lived. The mill, called "the Million Dollar Mill" while it was being built by J. E. Sirrine & Company, was an all-electric mill with 50,000 spindles and 1,200 looms when it opened, making fine cotton goods.
(REVERSE) The light gray brick and black mortar of this mill gives it a distinctive look unlike almost any other textile mill of its era. The Dunean Mill village included 585 houses, an elementary school, three churches, a company store, a community building, a gymnasium, and a baseball field. Its Y.W.C.A. was the first in any mill village in S.C. In 1935 the mill switched to rayon and other synthetic fibers. It was for many years a division of J. P. Stevens & Company. *Sponsored by the Dunean Historical Society, 2011*
GPS Coordinates: 34° 49.525' N, 82° 25.321' W

23–53 Cedar Grove Baptist Church /Simpsonville Rosenwald School

206 Moore St., Simpsonville

Cedar Grove Baptist Church (FRONT)
According to tradition, this African-American church was organized by Rev. Tom Jones shortly after the Civil War. It held its first

services in a brush arbor, then built its first permanent church here. The congregation, with a membership of about 250, built a second frame sanctuary in 1938 at a cost of $3,000. It was covered in brick veneer in 1962. The present brick church was dedicated in 1986.

Simpsonville Rosenwald School (REVERSE)
The Reedy River Baptist Association built a school for the African-American children of Simpsonville and other area communities here in 1891–92, on the present site of the church. In 1923–24 the Simpsonville Rosenwald School, an eight-room elementary and high school, was built nearby. One of about 500 schools in S.C. funded in part by the Julius Rosenwald Foundation 1917–1932, it closed after the 1953–54 school year. *Sponsored by the Greenville County Council and the Greenville Hospital System, 2012*
GPS Coordinates: 34° 44.104' N, 82° 15.095' W

23–54 Suber's Mill

2002 Suber Mill Rd., Greer

(FRONT) Four generations of the Suber family have owned and operated a water-powered grist mill on Princess Creek, a branch of the Enoree River, since shortly after the Civil War. James A. Suber (1826–1923) ran a sawmill and whiskey still a short distance upstream before serving in the Confederate army, and added a grist mill at that site soon after he returned to Greenville County.
(REVERSE) Suber's Mill is one of the only water-powered mills still grinding corn and selling corn meal in S.C. James Suber's son Walter Hillary Suber (1860–1952) built this mill between 1908 and 1912; it has been in almost continuous operation since. Though occasionally run by renters, it has been run by the family since 1955, beginning with Walter H. Suber, Jr. (1915–2010). *Sponsored by Mitsubishi Polyester Film and the Greenville County Historic Preservation Commission, 2012*
GPS Coordinates: 34° 55.909' N, 82° 15.852' W

23–55 Fountain Inn Cotton Mill /Woodside Mill and Village

Woodside Ave. & 1st St., Fountain Inn

Fountain Inn Cotton Mill (FRONT)
Fountain Inn Cotton Mill, which stood here from 1898 to 2002, was first owned and operated by brothers A. J., C. E., R. L., and W. J. Graham. Built with 5,000 spindles, it expanded to 10,000 spindles and later to 17,000 spindles, making cotton yarns and cloth. In 1906 textile mill entrepreneur John T. Woodside bought the mill from the Grahams. A few years later it was described as "among the best mills in the South."
Woodside Mill and Village (REVERSE)
This mill had 250 employees in 1907, with a population of 450 in a mill village of eighty houses that included a company store, recreation building, baseball field, and two churches. The two-room school operated until 1924. In 1911 this mill was merged with mills in Greenville and Simpsonville to create Woodside Cotton Mills. Sold to Dan River Mills in 1956, this mill was closed in 1983 and was demolished in 2002. *Sponsored by Brown's Mill LLC and Palmetto Pride, 2013*
GPS Coordinates: 34° 41.543' N, 82° 12.223' W

23–56 Old Pilgrim Baptist Church /Old Pilgrim Rosenwald School

3540 Woodruff Rd., Simpsonville

Old Pilgrim Baptist Church (FRONT)
This church was founded in 1868 by black members of nearby Clear Spring Baptist Church who named their new church Pilgrim Baptist Church. Rev. John Abraham, their first pastor, held services in a brush arbor until a log church was built here. It was renamed Old Pilgrim Baptist Church in 1894. A frame church built here in 1907 was covered in brick veneer in 1962. The present brick church was built in 1983.
Old Pilgrim Rosenwald School (REVERSE)
Old Pilgrim Rosenwald School, named for the church, was built in 1930. It was one of almost 500 schools in S.C. funded in part by the Julius Rosenwald Foundation from 1917 to 1932. Built at a cost of $3,800 with local funds

raised by Henry Locke and trustees of Old Pilgrim Baptist Church, it operated 1930–1954 with three teachers, teaching as many as 83 elementary school students in grades 1–7. *Sponsored by Old Pilgrim Baptist Church, 2013*
GPS Coordinates: 34° 47.578' N, 82° 11.812' W

23–57 Woodside Mill

301 Woodside Ave., Greenville

Woodside Cotton Mill was the first and largest textile mill owned by brothers John T. (1864–1946), J. David (1871–1945), and Edward F. Woodside (1875–1943). Built in 1902 with 11,000 spindles and 300 looms, it expanded in 1912 to 112,000 spindles and was claimed to be "the largest cotton mill under one roof" in America. The Woodside brothers also owned mills in Fountain Inn and Simpsonville, as well as Easley and Liberty in Pickens County. By 1929 the 220-acre mill village housed more than 2,400 workers and their families in 442 houses. It featured gently-curving oak-lined streets, a company store, two schools, a Baptist church (1910) and Methodist church (1921), a baseball field, and a YMCA building. The mill sold 10 acres for Parker High School, built in 1924 to serve several area mill villages. Woodside Mill and its village were listed in the National Register of Historic Places in 1987. *Sponsored by the Friends of Woodside, 2013*
GPS Coordinates: 34° 51.235' N, 82° 25.758' W

23–58 Springfield Baptist Church

600 E. McBee Ave., Greenville

(FRONT) This is the oldest black Baptist congregation in downtown Greenville. It was founded in 1867 by members of Greenville Baptist Church (now First Baptist Church), which had been a combined congregation of whites and blacks before the Civil War. Rev. Gabriel Poole, known as "Father Poole," was its first pastor. The new church worshipped in First Baptist Church until it built its own church here in 1872.
(REVERSE) The congregation purchased this site from the estate of Vardry McBee in

1871 and completed its first church, a frame building later covered in brick veneer, in 1872. That church was replaced by a brick Gothic Revival church in 1959. Springfield Baptist Church hosted many significant meetings during the Civil Rights Movement. The 1959 church burned in 1972 and was replaced by the present church in 1976. *Sponsored by the Congregation, 2013*
GPS Coordinates: 34° 50.838' N, 82° 23.520' W

23–59 McBee Chapel/McBee Methodist Church

Main St., just SW of 5th Ave., Conestee

McBee Chapel (FRONT)
This church is notable for its unusual octagonal form. It was built by John Adams for workers at the nearby McBee's Factory, a complex owned by Vardry McBee (1775–1864), the industrialist often called "the father of Greenville." Workers were required to attend services here, in a chapel McBee organized in 1841 for them and their families.
McBee Methodist Church (REVERSE)
McBee hired Adams, a mechanic and carpenter, to build his factories and other buildings. This church, first served by Methodist circuit riders, was one of several which McBee built or gave land or money to build. With a capacity of about 150, its octagonal form seated more worshippers in a smaller space. The church was listed in the National Register of Historic Places in 1972. *Sponsored by McBee Chapel United Methodist Church, 2013*
GPS Coordinates: 34° 45.966' N, 82° 21.195' W

23–60 Simpsonville Library

Corner at Academy St. and E. Curtis St. at 102 Academy St., Simpsonville

(FRONT) This Classical Revival building, constructed in 1940, was the Simpsonville Branch of the Greenville County Library until 1997. The first town library started ca. 1915 when Miss Nannie Cox, a literature teacher, placed books in the window of R. D. Jones's furniture store on South Main Street. A more formal library was later on the second floor of the Simpsonville City Hall on East Curtis Street.

(REVERSE) This building, the first separate library in the town, was built by the Work Projects Administration at a cost of $7,400, with significant local donations as well. It features two reading rooms, one often serving as a community center. The library was renovated and expanded in 1968. It closed in 1997 with the opening of the Hendricks Branch of the Greenville County Library on Northeast Main Street. *Sponsored by the City of Simpsonville, 2014*

GPS Coordinates: 34° 44.361' N, 82° 15.118' W

23–61　Fountain Inn High School

315 North Main St., Fountain Inn

(FRONT) Fountain Inn High School was built in 1939 and was the town high school until 1957. It remained in use as Fountain Inn Elementary School until 1997. The City of Fountain Inn purchased the property in 1999 and at that time the original 800 seat auditorium became the Fountain Inn Center for the Performing Arts. The school was listed in the National Register of Historic Places in 2009 for its architectural significance.

(REVERSE) Construction of the school was funded in part by a grant from the Public Works Administration (PWA). The firm of Beacham and LeGrand of Greenville designed the building, which exemplifies the Classical Moderne style. Also referred to as PWA Moderne, this style blended Neoclassical and Art Deco forms, and was intended to celebrate "modern" life while also conveying a sense of permanency and stability to the community. *Sponsored by the City of Fountain Inn, 2014*

GPS Coordinates: 34° 41.795' N, 82° 12.219' W

23–62　Fountain Inn Cemetery

Gulliver St., in front of Fountain Inn Municipal Cemetery, Fountain Inn

(FRONT) Fountain Inn Cemetery was established ca. 1890. Most of the land was deeded to the town by Lafayette Martin, and his son, D. R. Martin, sold an adjoining parcel in 1924 to expand the cemetery. An earlier graveyard had been located adjacent to First Baptist Church, but as the town expanded the

decision was made to establish a new cemetery at this spot and transfer the previous burials to this location.

(REVERSE) The various grave markers found here illustrate how burial practices evolved through time. The monuments and obelisks offer witness to Victorian sentimentality while the more uniform granite headstones that became popular by the mid-20th century show that the cemetery has remained in use over multiple generations. Through those years it has served as the final resting place for many Fountain Inn residents. *Sponsored by City of Fountain Inn and Fountain Inn History Museum, 2014*

GPS Coordinates: 34° 41.537' N, 82° 11.599' W

23–63　Dunean School

Centennial Park, corner of Smith and Duke Streets, Greenville

Dunean School, later Dunean Elementary, opened in 1928 with J. H. Anderson as its first principal. Located at the corner of Smith and Blake Streets, on land donated by Dunean Mill, the school served students from the surrounding Dunean Mill village. Before Dunean School opened students from both the Mills and Dunean Mill villages had attended the consolidated Mills-Dunean School. Dunean Elementary School closed in 1980 and was torn down shortly thereafter. *Sponsored by the Dunean Mills Community Alliance, 2014*

GPS Coordinates: 34° 49.268' N, 82° 25.245' W

23–64　Union Bleachery

Corner of Old Buncombe Road and Bud Street, Greenville

(FRONT) The Union Bleaching and Finishing Company began operations in 1903 with an initial capacity of 500,000 yards of cloth per week. It was the second custom finishing company in S.C. and was one of four original plants worldwide licensed to use the Sandfordizing Process, which reduced shrinkage of cotton cloth. In 1922 it was rechartered as Union Bleachery and by that time had a capacity of 2 million yards per week, making it the largest finishing plant in the South.

(REVERSE) John White Arrington, who became company president in 1906, was key to the growth of both the plant and the surrounding mill village. The first homes were built along Arrington and Stephenson Avenues and in 1923 mill owners added a community building with a gymnasium. Employees played in the Textile Baseball League and the mill also maintained a nine-hole golf course. The mill, which was then operating as U.S. Finishing, burned in 2003. *Sponsored by the Union Bleachery Historical Society, 2014*
GPS Coordinates: 34° 53.187' N, 82° 25.802' W

23–65 Taylors First Baptist Church

200 West Main St., Taylors

(FRONT) Taylors First Baptist Church traces its origins to the years of the American Civil War. The church organized as Chick Springs Church on August 28, 1864 at the conclusion of a week of camp meetings. The congregation first met near the Chick Springs area. Alfred Taylor was the first clerk. Dr. James C. Furman, first president of Furman University, was pastor 1867–1870.
(REVERSE) In 1873 the Atlanta & Richmond Air-Line Railway completed its new line, which included a depot on land owned by Alfred Taylor. In 1884 the congregation voted to move their church to a new location nearer the depot. The original building was deconstructed and rebuilt at the new location in 1885, and the church was renamed Taylors Church. The oldest extant building on the current campus was built in 1922. *Sponsored by Taylors First Baptist Church, 2014*
GPS Coordinates: 34° 55.182' N, 82° 18.170' W

23–66 Simpsonville Elementary School/Simpsonville High School

110 Academy St., near intersection of E. College St., Simpsonville

Simpsonville Elementary School (FRONT)
This school was built in 1939 with local funds and with federal funds from the Public Works Administration and the Works Projects Administration. It was the forth school, and the third public school, in Simpsonville. A two-story brick school built here in 1907 was a combined elementary and high school until a separate high school opened here in 1921. Simpsonville Elementary School closed in 2002.
Simpsonville High School (REVERSE)
In 1917 Simpsonville became the first Greenville County school to offer grade 11 and award high school diplomas. The high school built here in 1920–21 was the first separate high school in Simpsonville. Grade 12 was added in 1948. Both schools shared the auditorium and gymnasium 1939–57. Simpsonville High School closed in 1957 and was torn down after the new Hillcrest High School opened that fall. *Sponsored by Simpsonville Area Chamber of Commerce Foundation and Simpsonville Arts Foundation Inc., 2014*
GPS Coordinates: 34° 44.421' N, 82° 15.130' W

23–67 Greenville High School

South side of Vardry St., 350 ft. east of Green Ave., Greenville

(FRONT) The cornerstone for this building, the third to house Greenville High School, was laid July 27, 1937 and it was first opened to students in 1938. Construction was paid for in part by the Works Progress Administration at a total cost of nearly one million dollars. The WPA also funded construction of nearby Sirrine Stadium, the home venue for Greenville High School football games since 1936.
(REVERSE) The three-story, yellow brick building was designed by J. E. Sirrine & Co. of Greenville and is built in the Classical Moderne style typical of New Deal architecture. The stylized and simplified interpretation of Neoclassical forms was meant both to inspire confidence in the future and to convey a sense of stability in the midst of the economic uncertainty of the 1930s. *Sponsored by Troop 19, Boy Scouts of America and Friends of Greenville High School, 2014*
GPS Coordinates: 34° 50.450' N, 82° 24.503' W

23–68 John L. Plyler Home

302 Main St., Traveler's Rest

(FRONT) This house was the boyhood home and birthplace of John L. Plyler (1894–1966), a Furman University alumnus and Harvard Law School graduate who served as an attorney, judge, and dean of the Furman University Law School before becoming the seventh president of Furman University in 1939. Plyler was Furman's longest serving president, remaining in that post until his retirement in 1964.
(REVERSE) During Plyler's tenure as president he supported the first written campus statement on academic freedom, aligning Furman with the Statement on the Principles of Academic Freedom and Tenure of 1940. Plyler also oversaw the development of a new university campus north of Greenville, where classes began in 1958, and the physical unification of Furman University and the Greenville Woman's College on that new campus several years later. *Sponsored by Furman University, 2015*
GPS Coordinates: 34° 58.244' N, 82° 26.745' W

23–69 Monaghan Mill

Corners of Hellams St., McBeth St., and Smyth St., Greenville

(FRONT) Lewis Wardlaw Parker (1865–1916) and Thomas Fleming Parker (1860–1926) established Monaghan Mill in 1900 and named it in memory of their grandfather's native county in Ireland. Located along the Reedy River, the mill was designed by the firm of Lockwood, Greene & Co. When it opened in 1901 it contained 25,000 spindles. By the end of the decade it had expanded to 60,000 spindles and employed 700 workers, many of whom lived in the nearby mill village.
(REVERSE) In 1904 Thomas Parker built a Young Men's Christian Association (Y.M.C.A.) at Monaghan. L. P. Hollis (1883–1978), a long-time director of the Monaghan Y.M.C.A., introduced basketball at Monaghan and founded the Southern Textile Basketball Tournament, hosted annually in Greenville from 1921–1996. After operating for 100 years, Monaghan Mill closed in 2001. It was listed in the National Register of Historic Places in 2005. *Sponsored by Monaghan Textile Heritage Society, 2015*
GPS Coordinates: 34° 52.067' N, 82° 25.462' W

23–70 Simpsonville Municipal Cemetery

100 Park Dr., Simpsonville

(FRONT) Established in the 1840s as a family cemetery, the two and one-half acre parcel was donated to Simpsonville First Baptist Church by J. H. Todd in 1890. The church deeded the property to the Town of Simpsonville in 1929. The stone wall that surrounds the cemetery was constructed from native field stone collected from the surrounding countryside. The distinctive arches that mark the entry gates were added in the early 2000s.
(REVERSE) The cemetery serves as the final resting place for many of the founding families in Simpsonville, as well as veterans from many of the nation's wars. The earliest grave sites are located at the center of the cemetery and include Capt. Banister Stone (1777–1844), his wife Elizabeth Kilgore Stone (1788–1855), and his mother Anne Moon Stone Lynch (1754–1842). Stone was a member of the S.C. Assembly for 16 years. *Sponsored by Simpsonville Area Chamber of Commerce Foundation and Education Committee, and Richard C. Moore Attorney at Law, P.C., 2015*
GPS Coordinates: 34° 44.435' N, 82° 15.134' W

23–71 Simpsonville Methodist Church

215 S.E. Main St., Simpsonville

(FRONT) Simpsonville UMC was organized in April 1916 as Simpsonville Methodist Episcopal Church, South. The congregation originally met in the Forum, the community building of the Woodside Mill. The first pastor was J. L. Singleton. In 1917, members pledged to build their own sanctuary and by the end of that year had built a church at the corner of S.E. Main and Crisp Streets on property donated by H. H. Griffin.
(REVERSE) A recreational building and Sunday School were added in 1943 and a new parsonage, replacing the original built in 1926, was added in 1959. In 1965 a four-phase project

began to expand the campus and build a new sanctuary. This project included educational buildings and a modern A-frame church, completed in 1986. The new sanctuary, the third on the site, replaced both the 1917 building and a 250-seat sanctuary built in 1967. *Sponsored by Simpsonville United Methodist Church, 2015*
GPS Coordinates: 34° 44.039' N, 82° 15.262' W

23–72 Buncombe Street Methodist Church

Buncombe St. & Richardson St. intersection., Greenville

(FRONT) As early as 1800 Bishop Francis Asbury, founder of American Methodism, rode circuit in the S.C. upcountry, spreading the message of Methodism. In 1832 Vardry McBee deeded land to the trustees of the Methodist Episcopal Church. The Greenville Methodist Church, mother church of Buncombe Street Methodist, was organized in 1834 in the home of Maria Turpin. A frame building was built on Coffee Street in 1836.
(FRONT) The current sanctuary, the second to house the congregation, was dedicated in 1873. Built in the Greek Revival style, it has undergone renovations but retains its form. The congregation has operated a Sunday School since 1836. Troop 9, Boy Scouts of America has met here since 1929. As the church expanded an education building was added in 1927 and a new children's building was dedicated in 1962. *Sponsored by Buncombe Street United Methodist Church, 2015*
GPS Coordinates: 34° 51.190' N, 82° 24.000' W

23–73 Fork Shoals School

916 McKelvey Rd., Pelzer

(FRONT) Originally associated with Fork Shoals Baptist Church, Fork Shoals School was in operation by 1877. A private Fork Shoals H.S. was built on the eastern side of the Reedy River in 1908. A two-story frame building was then built near this spot in 1916, replacing the church school, and housed a graded school. Expansion of this building allowed the H.S. to move here in 1922.

(REVERSE) By 1922 the H.S. had become an accredited public school. In 1938 WPA funds were used to build a new school complex. One of these buildings still stands north of the current school. Further consolidation led to the closure of Fork Shoals H.S. in 1952, after which the buildings were used as an elementary school. Two of three 1930s buildings were razed in 1998 when the current school was built. *Sponsored by the Fork Shoals Historical Society, 2016*
GPS Coordinates: 34° 37.174' N, 82° 18.811' W

23–74 Claussen Bakery

400 Augusta St., Greenville

(FRONT) This two-story trapezoidal plan industrial building is one of two surviving Claussen bakeries in S.C. Built in 1930, the bakery initially employed forty workers who produced 45,000 loaves of bread a day. In February 1967 twenty-two African American employees, including organizer and spokesman Horace Butler Sr., who would later serve as the first African American foreman at the bakery, went on strike to protest discrimination in hiring and promotion practices.
(REVERSE) The Greenville branch of the NAACP, led by Rev. D. C. Francis, called for a boycott of Claussen baked goods in protest. Jesse Jackson, then working as director of SCLC's Operation Breadbasket, helped bring Rev. Martin Luther King Jr. to Greenville. On April 30, 1967 King spoke to a crowd of 3,500 at Greenville Memorial Auditorium. King preached economic justice and support for the Clausen workers who "had been called boys . . . then they stood up like men." *Sponsored by Afro-American Historical and Genealogical Society, the Greater Sullivan Neighborhood, and the Greenville Branch of the NAACP, 2016*
GPS Coordinates: 34° 50.301' N, 82° 24.388' W

23–75 Rose Hill Cemetery

Corner of Greenville St., Lee St., and Piedmont Hwy. (S.C.-20), Piedmont

(FRONT) Rose Hill cemetery was established in 1876 by the Piedmont Manufacturing Co.,

an early textile mill that began production in that same year. Originally known as Piedmont Cemetery, the earliest known burial dates to 1877. The cemetery served as final resting place for mill workers and their families, as well as members of the broader community, from 1876 until the mill's closure in 1977. (REVERSE) The cemetery expanded in 1922 when G. W. McAbee donated three-and-a-half acres of land for burials. Oral tradition holds that the cemetery was named "Rose Hill" in honor of McAbee's daughter, Rose May McAbee Norris, who died in 1922 and is buried here. Other notable burials include local newspaper editor and mill supervisor Albert Smith Rowell. In 1995 title transferred to the Rose Hill Cemetery Association, which continues to maintain the cemetery. *Sponsored by the Bonnes Amies Club of Piedmont S.C., 2016*
GPS Coordinates: 34° 42.524' N, 82° 27.217' W

23–76 Little Texas

Near intersection of E. North St. and N. Academy St., just south of Bon Secours Wellness Arena, Greenville

(FRONT) William E. Earle acquired much of the land now bounded by Beattie Pl., N. Church, Academy, and E. North Sts. at a foreclosure sale in 1869. He subdivided the land and sold the parcels. Much of the land was purchased by African Americans, including Milton Brooks, a 30-year-old laborer who bought the first lot in 1872. The community grew from about a dozen families in 1876 to become a neighborhood of more than 75 houses by the 1920s. Little Texas developed just south of Allen School.
(REVERSE) Allen School, which had its origins as a Freedmen's school in the 1860s, was a fixture of the neighborhood until a new Allen School was built on Stone Ave. in 1936. Memorial Auditorium was built adjacent to Little Texas in 1958. As the city continued to expand, Little Texas would succumb to the pressures of urban development. In 1971 the city condemned 65 homes in order to use the land for future development, effectively marking the end of Little Texas. *Sponsored by*

Greenville Arena District Board of Directors, 2016
GPS Coordinates: 34° 51.130' N, 82° 23.446' W

23–77 Congregation Beth Israel

425 Summit Drive, Greenville

(FRONT) Around 1910 a group of Jewish families began to meet for Orthodox services in their homes and rented halls around Greenville. Within two years these recent Eastern European immigrants hired Charles Zaglin as their rabbi and kosher butcher. Congregation Beth Israel was incorporated in 1916 and was Greenville's earliest chartered Jewish organization. The first synagogue was built on Townes Street in 1929.
(REVERSE) In 1957 Beth Israel, which affiliated with the Conservative movement in 1954, began construction of its second synagogue. The campus was built in two stages, with the Davis Social Hall, classrooms, and offices built in the first stage. By 1970 the second stage, including a chapel donated by the Heller family, was completed. Max Heller was a past president of Beth Israel and mayor of Greenville, 1971 to 1979. *Sponsored by Congregation Beth Israel, Greenville and the Jewish Historical Society of South Carolina, 2016*
GPS Coordinates: 34° 52.488' N, 82° 23.025' W

23–78 Fork Shoals Baptist Church

110 Fork Shoals Church Rd., Pelzer

(FRONT) Fork Shoals Baptist Church traces its origins to at least 1789, when Horse Creek Church was organized as a member of the Bethel Association. Local tradition, however, places the date earlier, between 1777–1780. Fork Shoals first appears in the Bethel Association minutes in 1799, when the Big Branch Enoree and Horse Creek Churches merged with Fork Shoals Baptist Church.
(REVERSE) By 1857 church membership had grown to 510 and in 1860 Fork Shoals was a founding member of the Greenville Baptist Association. Also in that year, Micajah Berry deeded the land on which the current church is built. The first sanctuary on this site was completed in 1888. While the current

sanctuary dates to 1961, components of the 1888 structure were retained. Seven area churches began as the result of the ministry of Fork Shoals Baptist Church. *Sponsored by Fork Shoals Historical Society, 2016*
GPS Coordinates: 34° 37.235' N, 82° 18.790' W

23–79 Poinsett Mill

10 Gates St., Greenville

(FRONT) Originally established as the Gates Desk Company in 1893, the mill was renovated and re-chartered as Carolina Cotton Mills in 1900. Mill ownership built 123 homes to house supervisors and workers, as well as a church and later a school. In 1916 the mill was reorganized as Poinsett Mill, named for S.C. statesman Joel Poinsett, who was an early advocate of southern industry. In 1928 Brandon, Woodruff, Renfrew, and Poinsett Mills merged to become Brandon Corporation. (REVERSE) In the spring of 1929 mill hands at Poinsett joined workers from Brandon Mill in an 8-week strike to protest what they called "the stretchout," an attempt by management to increase workloads in the face of declining wages. The strike ended when the mill agreed to minimal reforms. Abney Mills gained control of Poinsett in 1949 and owned it until the mill closed in 1981. The Reynolds Co., a producer of adhesives and coatings, acquired the former textile mill in 1983. *Sponsored by the Reynolds Company and the Poinsett Historic Society, 2017*
GPS Coordinates: 34° 51.117' N, 82° 25.159' W

23–80 Bryson High School

Bryson Drive, Fountain Inn

(FRONT) Bryson H.S. opened in 1954, serving African American students in lower Greenville Co. It was one of the many schools constructed in the 1950s as part of the school equalization program in S.C. The school consolidated the populations from five high schools, all that had inadequate facilities. The new Bryson H.S. featured a gym, auditorium, industrial and agricultural shops, home economics laboratories, and library. First serving grades 7–12, in 1958 they began serving grades 8–12.

(REVERSE) Dr. A. M. Anderson was the first and only principal. More than 1,000 students graduated from Bryson under his watch. The school mascot was the Hurricane and the newspaper was the Hurricane Times. The class of 1970 was the last to graduate. After the Civil Rights Act of 1964 the U.S. government put more pressure on the states to finally implement school desegregation. In 1970 S.C. schools complied. Bryson students moved to the all white Woodmont, Hillcrest and J. L. Mann High Schools. *Sponsored by the Bryson High School Alumni Association, 2017*
GPS Coordinates: 34° 42.801' N, 82° 13.102' W

23–81 Garrison Cemetery

500 Old Pelzer Road, Piedmont

(FRONT) Garrison Cemetery is named for the Garrison family, who were among the first European settlers in the area that became Piedmont, S.C. The patriarch of the family, David Garrison, settled here in the 1780s and operated a grist mill on the Saluda River along what became known as Garrison Shoals. A marker for Garrison is located here, though the actual site of his burial is unknown. (REVERSE) The first known burial occurred in 1853, when Barksdale Dunham Garrison, a veteran of the War of 1812 who achieved the rank of Brig. Gen., was buried here. In addition, there are veterans from every major American War from the Civil War to Vietnam. In total, more than 100 interments have been recorded here. *Sponsored by Piedmont Historic Preservation Society, 2017*
GPS Coordinates: 34° 43.441' N, 82° 26.656' W

23–82 Wilkins House

105 Mills Ave., Greenville

(FRONT) The Wilkins House was built in 1878 by Greenville builder Jacob Cagle for William Wilkins and his wife Harriett Cleveland Wilkins. The home, which originally fronted Augusta St., was designed in the Italianate style, but also incorporated Gothic and Moorish elements. The interior finishes, including complex millwork and Lincrusta wall coverings, matched the high style of the exterior.

An 1898 article declared it "the finest home of any man in northern South Carolina." (REVERSE) William Wilkins died in 1895 but Harriett lived here until her death in 1930. In 1933 the house was leased by the Wilkins family to R. D. Jones, who used it as both a residence and funeral home. When the home was threatened with demolition in 2014 a public fundraising campaign, along with the efforts of a new owner, combined to raise enough money to move the 750-ton building to its current site. At the time, it was believed to be the heaviest building ever moved in S.C. *Sponsored by the City of Greenville, 2017*
GPS Coordinates: 34° 49.837' N, 82° 24.365' W

23–83 National Highway

Intersection of East Poinsett St. and Depot St., Greer

(FRONT) The Bankhead National Hwy. Association was formed in 1916 with the goal of creating a transcontinental highway that would run from Washington, D.C., to San Diego, CA. When completed in 1920, it became the second transcontinental highway in the U.S. The National Hwy., also known as the Bankhead Hwy., connected towns across the S.C. Upstate. It crossed into S.C. near Blacksburg and passed through Gaffney, Spartanburg, Greer, Greenville, and Anderson. (REVERSE) John Hollis Bankhead (1842–1920), A U.S. Senator from Alabama and advocate of the Good Roads Movement, sponsored the Federal Road Aid Act of 1916, which authorized $75 million for road improvement and was the first federal highway funding law. The National Hwy. passed through Greer, following what is now Poinsett St. Later, the Super Hwy. (now Wade Hampton Blvd.) and Interstate 85 would replace the National Hwy. as the main route from Charlotte to Atlanta. *Sponsored by the Citizens Building and Loan Charitable Foundation, 2017*
GPS Coordinates: 34° 56.273' N, 82° 13.509' W

23–84 Standing Springs Baptist Church

1111 W. Georgia Rd., Simpsonville

(FRONT) Standing Springs Baptist Church was organized in 1818 as an arm of Fork Shoals Baptist Church. There were ten charter members and Rev. Nathan Berry was the first pastor. Early meetings were held in the home of James Cox and the first meeting house was constructed ca. 1836 on land donated by Mr. Cox. (REVERSE) The congregation derives its name from a nearby spring that originates underground and appears as standing water. Like many Baptist churches, the congregation here included enslaved people before the Civil War. A second sanctuary was built in 1917 and expanded in 1959. The current sanctuary was dedicated in 1970. *Sponsored by Standing Springs Baptist Church, 2018*
GPS Coordinates: 34° 43.635' N, 82° 17.370' W

23–85 Berea First Baptist Church

529 Farr's Bridge Rd., Greenville

(FRONT) Berea Baptist Church was officially founded in Dec. 1843, but local tradition holds that the earliest meetings were held under a brush arbor in the yard of Isham J. Ward. The name "Berea" derives from Acts 17: 10–11, which was said to have been part of the first sermon, delivered by Rev. Samuel Gibson. The church would later lend its name to the surrounding area. (REVERSE) Dr. James C. Furman, first president of Furman University, became pastor in 1862 and would serve three separate terms as pastor from then until his death in 1891. A second sanctuary was built in 1892. In 1965 the name of the church was changed to Berea First Baptist Church to differentiate it from other Baptist congregations. The current church building dates to 1976. *Sponsored by Berea Historic Society, 2018*
GPS Coordinates: 34° 53.573' N, 82° 28.208' W

23–86 Berea School

104 Farrs Bridge Rd., Greenville

(FRONT) The first Berea School built at this location opened in 1916. It was a two-story building with an auditorium on the second floor. In 1924 a basketball team was formed and in 1930 a new auditorium and gymnasium were added. In 1939 the original school was replaced by a new brick building funded by the Work Projects Administration (WPA). The WPA also funded a cannery and potato house, both meant to serve the community. The school housed students from elementary to high school.

(REVERSE) In 1961 the high school students were moved to a new campus, leaving grades 1–6 at this location. In 1970 sixth-grade students were transferred as part of the county's plans for racial integration. Kindergarten was added in 1973. It continued to operate as an elementary school until a new Berea Elementary was opened in 1998. Berea was among the last remaining WPA-funded school campuses in Greenville Co. when it was razed in 2017. *Sponsored by the Berea Historic Society, 2018*
GPS Coordinates: 34° 53.573' N, 82° 28.208' W

23–87 Col. John and Jane Thomas

Hwy. 101 near O'Neal Church Rd., Greer

(FRONT) John Jane Black Thomas emigrated to S.C. ca. 1755 from Chester Co., PA. John was a local magistrate and militia captain. As the Revolutionary War began, he was elected Colonel of the Spartan Regiment. Captured in 1779, he was held in Ninety Six and Charleston up to the end of the war. Returning to the upstate, John farmed here till death, October 2, 1811.

(REVERSE) Jane Black Thomas was also a staunch whig. Learning of British plans to attack patriots at Cedar Spring, she rushed the intelligence to American forces. As a result, the patriots were able to spring an ambush. She boldly defended a cache of weapons stored on their place. Both John and Jane Thomas are buried here, in sight of their home, later owned by S.C. Chief Justice John Belton O'Neall. *Sponsored by Greenville*

County Historical Preservation Commission and Mark III Properties, 2019
GPS Coordinates: 34° 59.802' N, 82° 16.672' W

23–88 Poe Mill

A St. between Hammett St. Ext. and Buncombe Rd., Greenville

(FRONT) Francis Winslow Poe (1853–1926) established the Poe Mill in 1896. The mill was built adjacent to the main line of the Southern R.R. and the White Oak branch of the Reedy River. The mill and the surrounding village were designed by Joseph E. Sirrine, who was then in the employ of Lockwood, Greene & Co. Sirrine's unique design included two smoke stacks and also 238 mill houses. Construction was handled by local contractor Jacob O. Cagle. Production began in March 1896.

(REVERSE) The mill was steam-powered and opened with 10,000 spindles and 300 looms. Within a decade, equipment had increased to more than 70,000 spindles and 1,700 looms. They employed 800 workers. A graded school was built in 1902 and the village supported both Baptist and Methodist Churches. During WWII the mill produced duck cloth that was used for tents and women replaced men on the factory floor. The mill closed in 1977 and was destroyed by fire in 2003. *Sponsored by the F. W. Poe Textile Heritage Society, 2019*
GPS Coordinates: 34° 52.245' N, 82° 24.734' W

23–89 Gap Creek Baptist Church

381 Gap Creek rd., Marietta

(FRONT) Gap Creek Baptist Church was established in 1840 and meetings were held in a log building that stood nearby to Gap Creek. In 1850 the church was a founding member of the Enoree River Association. A second church was built ca. 1859 on land donated by Champion Osborn. This church would remain in use until it burned in 1868 and was promptly replaced by a new building.

(REVERSE) In 1887 Gap Creek became a founding member of the North Greenville Association, of which it is still a member. The frame building with octagonal-roofed bell tower became the fifth sanctuary to serve the

congregation when it was built in 1928. The stained glass windows were imported from France. It served the community until 2008, when the current sanctuary was completed. *Sponsored by Descendants of Posey D. & Marie P. Tankersley, 2019*
GPS Coordinates: 35° 7.557' N, 82° 31.437' W

23–90 Post 3 American Legion

430 N. Main St., Greenville

(FRONT) In 1919, fifteen World War I veterans from Greenville established Post 3 of The American Legion. This was the Post's first dedicated lodge. It was built 1933–34 on municipal land using locally quarried granite. Labor was provided by the Reconstruction Finance Corporation. Costs were paid through membership dues and findraisers. Post members began meeting here in Oct. 1933, and the lodge was dedicated June 18, 1934.

(REVERSE) In 1960, Post 3 was renamed in honor of James F. Daniel, Jr. (ca. 1899–1959), the first Post Commander at this location and later National Executive Chairman for The American Legion. Among the Post's civic projects in the mid-century Greenville area were the Goodfellows Club and Greenville County Fair. The Women's Auxiliary was est. 1920. Members helped raise funds for the lodge's construction and used it for events and meetings. *Erected by James F. Daniel, Jr., Post 3, The American Legion, 2019*
GPS Coordinates: 34° 51.404' N, 82° 23.751' W

Greenwood County

24–1 Long Canes Massacre

[Replaced a marker erected in 1937 by American Legion Post No. 20 of Greenwood. This was the first marker erected after the formal establishment of the South Carolina Historical Marker Program.]

Intersection of Main St. W. (S.C. Sec. Rd. 24–24) and Twigg St. (S.C. Hwy. 10), Troy

Three miles west is site of an attack by Cherokee Indians upon settlers of Long Canes in the Cherokee War of 1759–1761. There on February 1, 1760, about 150 settlers, refugeeing to Augusta, were overtaken by 100 Cherokee warriors. Twenty-three victims left on the scene of action are there buried in one grave. *Erected by Abbeville District Historical Association, Town of Troy, McCormick County Historical Commission, 1976*
GPS Coordinates: 33° 59.261' N, 82° 17.864' W

24–2 Long Cane Associate Reformed Presbyterian Church

Intersection of Main St. W. (S.C. Sec. Rd. 24–24) and Twigg St. (S.C. Hwy. 10), Troy

4.5 miles northwest is Long Cane Church, organized in 1771 as Associate Presbyterian, with the Rev. William Ronaldson as first stated supply. It united with Cedar Spring, March 7, 1786, under Dr. Thos. Clark; withdrew September 15, 1803; part of congregation under the Presbyterian Church, 1813–1819; all reunited with Cedar Spring, Feb. 28, 1828; withdrew, Jan. 13, 1892. The present building was dedicated July 10, 1856. *Erected by Members and Friends of the Church, 1940*
GPS Coordinates: 33° 59.261' N, 82° 17.864' W

24–3 Old Ninety Six

(2 miles south) at the Ninety Six Visitors' Center, 97 E. Main St., Ninety Six

Even before 1730 the fork in the Cherokee Path, 96 miles south of Keowee, was called Ninety Six. Here a trading post was operated, a fort was built, and a courthouse town was established. Here the first land battle of the Revolutionary War in the South was fought, Nov. 19–20, 1775; and here Gen. Nathanael Greene besieged the British in Star Fort, May 22–June 20, 1781. *Erected by Ninety Six Chamber of Commerce, 1959*
GPS Coordinates: 34° 10.509' N, 82° 1.438' W

24–4 Preston Brooks Dinner

Intersection of Main St. W. (S.C. Hwy 34) and S.C. Hwy 248, Ninety Six

National attention was focused here on Oct. 3, 1856, when some 10,000 people honored Preston S. Brooks, Congressman from this district, with a public dinner in vindication of his assault on Charles Sumner of Massachusetts on the Senate floor for a speech insulting to this state. The Preston Brooks home was five miles south on Highway 246. *Erected by Ninety-Six Chamber of Commerce, 1959*
GPS Coordinates: 34° 10.492' N, 82° 1.438' W

24–5 Tabernacle Cemetery

Marker 1: S.C. Hwy. 254, SE of Cokesbury

1000 feet east is Tabernacle Cemetery on the site of Tabernacle Methodist Church and Tabernacle Academy. Buried here are Generals M. W. Gary & N. G. Evans and other Confederate veterans. From Tabernacle Academy organized in 1820 by Stephen Olin developed Mount Ariel and Cokesbury Conference School. *Erected in 1961 by the Robert A. Waller and John McKellar Reynolds Chapters, United Daughters of the Confederacy*

Marker 2: At the cemetery gate, approximately 1000 ft. E of Marker 1

Site of Old Tabernacle Methodist Church. Buried here are Confederate Generals Martin Witherspoon Gary, Nathan George Evans and other Confederate officers and soldiers. *Erected in 1961 by the Robert A. Waller and John McKellar Reynolds Chapters, United Daughters of the Confederacy*
GPS Coordinates: 34° 15.98' N, 82° 11.252' W

24–6 John Henry Logan December 7, 1821–March 29, 1885

S.C. Sec. Rd. 24-236, .7 mi. E of U.S. Hwy. 25 Bypass, E of Greenwood

Teacher, Historian, Physician/Born and reared in this house/John Henry Logan/first practiced medicine and taught school in this region before publishing in 1859 his History of Upper South Carolina. He served as a Confederate Army Surgeon and afterwards

taught at Atlanta Medical College. *Erected by Greenwood County Historical Society, 1962*
GPS Coordinates: 34° 12.499' N, 82° 7.07' W

24–7 John Perkins Barratt May 11, 1795–September 29, 1859

Callison Hwy. (S.C. Hwy. 67), 1.1 mi. S of U.S. Hwy. 25, S of Greenwood

Physician, naturalist, versatile intellect, agricultural leader. President of Abbeville District Medical Society, 1835. Friend of Agassiz, Audubon and other major scientists; by his own advanced thinking, he outlined a theory of serial evolution and foretold airplanes and lunar trips. His home was across this road. *Erected by Greenwood County Historical Society, 1962*
GPS Coordinates: 34° 6.492' N, 82° 7.81' W

24–8 Londonborough Settlement

W side of Callison Rd. (S.C. Sec. Rd. 24-48), 4.1 mi. S of U.S. Hwy. 221, S of Bradley

Two miles west is Powder Spring, traditional site of the town laid out for the Londonborough settlers in 1765. Abandoned by their promoter in London, some 300 German settlers were brought to South Carolina, given aid and bounty, and granted land in Londonborough Township. They settled in this area along Hard Labor and Cuffytown Creeks. *Erected by Edgefield and Greenwood County Historical Societies, 1964*
GPS Coordinates: 34° 0.532' N, 82° 11.781' W

24–9 Patrick H. Bradley 1813–1887

N of U.S. Hwy. 221 at its intersection with Callison Rd. (S.C. Sec. Rd. 24-48), Bradley

His efforts brought R.R. through this town which bears his name. He was Brig. Gen. State Militia, Captain in Confederate War, Member of S.C. Legislature, Trustee of Erskine College and First President of the Augusta-Knoxville Railroad. He lived nearby and is buried in Cedar Springs Church Yard. *Erected by Bradley Community Association, 1966*
GPS Coordinates: 34° 2.944' N, 82° 14.676' W

24-10 John Waller 1741-1802

E. Scotch Cross Rd. (S.C. Sec. Rd. 24-131), 3.1 mi. E of U.S. Hwy. 25, SE of Greenwood

One half mile south is the grave of John Waller, early minister of the Baptist faith in Virginia, where he is credited with founding eighteen churches. He was persecuted and imprisoned by the established church and civil authorities. In 1793, he moved to South Carolina, where he founded Bethabara and Siloam Churches. *Erected by South Carolina Baptist Historical Society, 1971*
GPS Coordinates: 34° 8.576' N, 82° 4.584' W

24-11 Francis Salvador 1747-1776

Laurens Hwy. (S.C. Hwy. 221), Coronaca vicinity, about 3.6 mi. NE of Greenwood

This young English Jew settled near Coronaca in 1774, represented Ninety Six District in the provincial congresses of 1775-1776, and died in defense of his adopted home on Aug. 1, 1776. He was the first South Carolinian of his faith to hold an elective public office and the first to die for American independence. *Erected by the Jewish Citizens of Greenwood, 1960*
GPS Coordinates: 34° 14.397' N, 82° 6.106' W

24-12 Dr. Wesley C. Norwood

[Reported missing in January 2010]

U.S. Hwy. 25, about .6 mi. NW of Cokesbury

Dr. Wesley C. Norwood (1806-1884), whose home was located near here, raised a storm of medical controversy in the 1850s by promoting the use of "Norwood's Tincture" as a cure for pneumonia, yellow fever, and a wide variety of other diseases. The medicine, derived from the poisonous plant *veratrum viride,* was a familiar sight in pharmacies until ca. 1890. *Erected by Greenwood County Historical Society, 1985*
GPS Coordinates: 34° 17.696' N, 82° 13.559' W

24-13 Dr. Benjamin E. Mays

U.S. Hwy. 178, about 3.7 mi. SE of Epworth and 1/10 mi. NW of Mays Crossroads

The spiritual mentor of Martin Luther King, Jr. Born here in 1894. Served as president of Morehouse College 1940-67 and as presidential advisor. Died in 1984. *Erected by Greenwood County, 1995*
GPS Coordinates: 34° 3.789' N, 82° 1.036' W

24-14 Louis Booker Wright

Intersection of Maxwell Ave. (S.C. Hwy. 10) and S.C. Hwy. 225 ByPass, in front of the Connie Maxwell Children's Home, Greenwood

Louis Booker Wright (18991984), scholar of American colonial history and Elizabethan culture, was born in the Phoenix community and spent his early years at Maxwellton near this site. A prolific author, he was educated at Wofford College and received the M.A. and Ph.D. from the University of N.C. He was director of the Folger Shakespeare Library in Washington D.C. 194868. *Erected by the Greenwood County Heritage Corridor Committee, 1998*
GPS Coordinates: 34° 10.867' N, 82° 11.033' W

24-15 Siloam Baptist Church

2409 Siloam Church Rd. (S.C. Sec. Rd. 24-29), Ninety Six vicinity

This church was organized in 1799 by Rev. John Waller, Rev. David Lilly, William Chiles, and Meshec Overby, with 32 charter members. Waller, its first minister, served until his death in 1802. Other notable pastors included Revs. John Broadus, Basil Manley, and W. H. Biers. The first sanctuary on this site, built in 1836, was demolished in 1984. The present sanctuary was built in 1977. *Erected by the Congregation, 2000*
GPS Coordinates: 34° 12.546' N, 82° 2.379' W

24-16 Rock Presbyterian Church

122 NW Rock Church Rd., just off U.S. Hwy. 221, Greenwood vicinity

(FRONT) This church, originally known as Rocky Creek Presbyterian Church, was founded in 1770 by ministers sent to upper S.C. from the Synods of New York and Philadelphia. The first church here, a frame sanctuary, was replaced in 1815 by a larger frame church built by John and Adam Blake.

The church, incorporated in 1844, was re-named Rock Presbyterian Church by the S.C. Presbytery in 1845.

(REVERSE) Rev. John McLees (d. 1882) was minister here 1847–1882 and father of Green-wood First Presbyterian Church, which had its origins as a chapel in the 1850s and was formally organized from this congregation in 1883. Rock Presbyterian Church, inactive in 1892, reorganized in 1956. This stone sanctu-ary, built in 1959–60, replaced the 1815 church, which had burned in 1959. *Erected by the Congregation, 2003*

GPS Coordinates: 34° 13.678' N, 82° 6.657' W

24–17 Good Hope Baptist Church

U.S. Hwy. 25, just S of its intersection with N. Riley Rd., Hodges

(FRONT) This church, founded about 1870, has its origins in Walnut Grove Baptist Church, founded in 1820. Walnut Grove included both white and black members before the Civil War, but after the war black members asked for letters of dismissal to organize a new church. Good Hope was founded by David Agnew, Doc McIntosh, Henry Moon, Wesley Posey, and others, with Rev. W. L. Evans as its first pastor.

(REVERSE) Good Hope Baptist Church grew to more than 250 members by 1900 under its first two ministers, Revs. W. L. Evans and H. Donaldson. The first church here was a frame building constructed soon after 1870; it was destroyed by arson in 1966. The present church, a brick building, was constructed in 1967–68 during the pastorate of Rev. M. B. Norman. *Erected by the Congregation, 2006*

GPS Coordinates: 34° 20.717' N, 82° 13.232' W

24–18 Cedar Springs A.R.P. Church

S.C. Sec. Rd. 24-112 at its intersection with Cedar Springs Rd., Bradley vicinity, Greenwood County

(FRONT) This church was organized 1779–1780 by Dr. Thomas Clark (d. 1791), who had emi-grated from Ireland to N.Y. in 1764. Clark moved to this area permanently about 1786, preaching here, at Long Cane (now Lower Long Cane), and at Little Run. He is the father of the Associate Reformed Presbyterian Church in the South.

(REVERSE) The first church, then called Cedar Creek, was a log building 2 mi. SE. The con-gregation was renamed Cedar Springs in 1790. It moved here and built a frame church in 1791. The cemetery includes graves of several ministers, including Thomas Clark, and many early members. The present brick church was built in 1853. *Erected by the Members and Friends of the Church, 2006, replacing a marker erected in 1947*

GPS Coordinates: 34° 4.807' N, 82° 18.119' W

24–19 Benjamin E. Mays Birthplace

At the Mays House Museum, 237 N. Hospital St., Greenwood

(FRONT) This house, originally 14 mi. SE on U.S. Hwy. 178 in the Epworth community, was the birthplace of Dr. Benjamin E. Mays (1894–1984), Baptist minister, college presi-dent, author, and civil rights pioneer. Mays was the eighth child of Hezekiah and Louve-nia Mays, both born into slavery. In 1911 he left the tenant farm where this house stood to attend high school at S.C. State College in Orangeburg.

(REVERSE) Mays, a graduate of Bates College and the University of Chicago, was an early and forceful opponent of segregation. Best known as president of Morehouse College, in Atlanta, 1940–1967, Mays was described by Dr. Martin Luther King, Jr. as his "spiritual men-tor." Mays's inspiring memoir Born To Rebel (1971) is a civil rights classic. This house was moved here, renovated, and dedicated as a museum in 2011. *Sponsored by the Mays House Museum, 2012*

GPS Coordinates: 34° 11.962' N, 82° 8.589' W

24–20 Southern Railway Depot

99 S.C. Hwy. 34, Ninety Six

(FRONT) This depot, built for the Southern Railway in 1915, is an outstanding example of an early-20th century combination passenger and freight depot. A settlement called Ninety Six predates the Revolution, but the mod-ern town grew up around a stop on the

Greenwood & Columbia RR, completed in 1853. Its population grew even more dramatically after 1890 with a boom in the textile industry in Greenwood County.

(REVERSE) The Ninety Six Cotton Mill opened in 1902. By 1906 400 of the town's 600 residents worked there. That year the Southern Railway, led by the town's rapid growth and the need to carry people and ship goods to and from Greenwood County, promised Ninety Six a new depot. Built in 1915, it closed in 1978 and has been a community center since 1982. It was listed in the National Register of Historic Places in 2011. *Sponsored by the Historic 96 Development Association, 2014*
GPS Coordinates: 34° 10.506' N, 82° 1.423' W

24–21 Ninety Six Colored School

N. Main St., ½ mi. E of the town limits of Ninety Six

(FRONT) The Ninety Six Colored School, built nearby between 1927 and 1932, was a combined elementary and high school through the 1951–52 school year and an elementary school through the 1955–56 school year. It was a six-room frame building, with a small frame lunchroom nearby. Six to eight teachers taught grades 1–7 and 8–11 until grade 12 was added in 1947–48. The school closed in 1956. (REVERSE) Rev. Elliott F. Johnson, the first principal here, was succeeded by Rev. W. T. Boggs in 1943. Ninety Six Colored School averaged about 200 elementary and about 60 high school students for most of its history. After county districts consolidated in 1951, its high school students went to Brewer High School until a new Edgewood School for elementary and high school students opened in 1956. *Sponsored by the Historic 96 Development Association, 2014*
GPS Coordinates: 34° 10.586' N, 82° 0.920' W

24–22 Ware Shoals School

56 S. Greenwood Ave., Ware Shoals

Ware Shoals School (FRONT)
This school, built in 1926 as Ware Shoals School, was a grammar and high school until 1991 and has been a high school since. A 1951 grammar school on the campus has been a middle school since 1991. The first school in the town opened in 1905. After Ware Shoals Manufacturing Company opened its textile mill in 1906, it sponsored the school. Marion B. Camak (1888–1962) came to Ware Shoals in 1924 and was school superintendent here until he retired in 1955.
Ware Shoals High School (REVERSE)
This school designed by J. E. Sirrine & Co. of Greenville, was built at a cost of $160,000. It was dedicated in 1926 by Gov. Thomas G. McLeod and State Superintendent James H. Hope, and had 23 teachers and 750 students when it opened. Riegel Stadium, built in 1935 with federal funds from the Emergency Relief Administration, has hosted many high school, college, and other baseball and football games. *Sponsored by Ware Shoals School District No. 51, 2014*
GPS Coordinates: 34° 23.692' N, 82° 14.310' W

24–22 Bradley CCC Camp F-7

Adjacent to S.C. Hwy. 221/10, south of intersection with Callison Rd. (State Rd. S-24-48), Bradley

(FRONT) Bradley Civilian Conservation Corps Camp F-7, opened in Nov. 1934, was the first CCC Camp on the Long Cane Ranger District. CCC Company 1449, which was stationed here, worked for the USDA Forest Service on conservation projects from 1934–1942. The U.S. Forest Service Bradley Work Center, built in 1936, is the only structure that remains of what was once Camp Bradley. (REVERSE) The Civilian Conservation Corps (CCC) was established in 1933 as a New Deal program. In S.C. there were 29 CCC Camps that employed nearly 50,000 men during the life of the program. Conservation work on the Long Cane District included tree planting, erosion control, road construction, building five fire lookout towers, and construction of the Parsons Mountain Recreation Area. *Sponsored by USDA Forest Service, 2017*
GPS Coordinates: 34° 2.842' N, 82° 14.793' W

Hampton County

25-1 Hampton County

Hampton County Courthouse, near the intersection of Elm St. E (U.S. Hwy. 278) & 1st St. E (S.C. Hwy. 68), Hampton

Established February 18, 1878, once a part of Beaufort District. Named in honor of WADE HAMPTON, Lieutenant General, C.S.A., Governor of South Carolina, 1876–79, United States Senator, 1879–91. Corner stone of courthouse laid by Gen. Hampton, Oct. 12, 1878. *Erected by Hampton County and James Moore Chapter, U.D.C., 1957*
GPS Coordinates: 32° 51.981' N, 81° 6.519' W

25-2 Town of Brunson

N side of U.S. Hwy. 278 between Morris & Broad Sts., Brunson

On November 7, 1872, a post office was established in this community, named for William E. Brunson, Sr., who donated the site. Brunson was chartered in 1874. The Town Hall, built in 1906, originally stood on stilts and covered the town's artesian well. Brunson's school system traces its origin to the 1800s, to Pineville Academy and Brunson Graded & Military School. *Erected by Brunson Civic Council, 1971*
GPS Coordinates: 32° 55.651' N, 81° 11.475' W

25-3 Miles McSweeney Home Site

403 First St., E., Hampton

On this site stood the home of Miles Benjamin McSweeney (1854–1909), first governor of South Carolina from Hampton County. He was founder of the *Hampton County Guardian,* S.C. Representative 1894–96, Lieutenant Governor 1897–99, and Governor 1899–1903. His grave is in Hampton Cemetery. *Erected by Hampton County Historical Society, 1973*
GPS Coordinates: 32° 51.933' N, 81° 6.498' W

25-4 Lawtonville Church [First Marker]

Corner of Lawton Ave. & 4th St., Estill

This Baptist Church, constituted in March 1775, was first situated on Pipe Creek in upper St. Peter's Parish near the Savannah River. Prior to 1836 it was moved to Lawtonville, where its building was used as a hospital by Union Forces in 1865. Pipe Creek Church became Lawtonville Church in 1884. The Church moved here in 1911 when the present building was erected. *Erected by The Board of Deacons of Lawtonville Baptist Church, 1975*
GPS Coordinates: 32° 45.302' N, 81° 14.298' W

25-5 Prince Williams Baptist Church

S.C. Sec. Rd. 25-512 just E of its intersection with S.C. Sec. Rd. 25-315, about 3 mi. E of Brunson

Previously a branch of nearby Coosawhatchie Baptist Church (now Beech Branch), this church was constituted as a separate church in 1813 and takes its name from the parish in which it was located. Espousing Primitive Baptist principles, the church broke with the Savannah River Association in 1840. The present structure was erected prior to 1859. *Erected by The Congregation, 1979*
GPS Coordinates: 32° 55.054' N, 81° 7.97' W

25-6 Hampton Colored School

Hampton Colored School Museum and Resource Center, 608 First St. W., Hampton

Constructed for black students, this elementary school was built shortly after Hampton County School District purchased the land in the late 1920s. Two of the school's alumni of the 1930s and 1940s, brothers James F. and Julius C. Fields, achieved national stature as actors, dancers, and choreographers in stage, television, and motion picture productions.

Erected by Hampton County Historical Society, 1989
GPS Coordinates: 32° 52.111' N, 81° 7.212' W

25–7 Morrison Academy

S.C. Sec. Rd. 25–19 at Lawtonville Cemetery, just S of its intersection with S.C. Sec. Rd. 25–39, Lawtonville, just W of Estill

In old Lawtonville Community, across from this site, was the first Morrison Academy, a one-room elementary and college preparatory school. It was later moved 3.4 miles north of here on Orangeburg Road to be near the home of Rev. John Timothy Morrison, headmaster from 1865 to 1905, minister, legislator, Lt. C.S.A. *Erected by Hampton County Tricentennial Commission, 1969*
GPS Coordinates: 32° 45.092' N, 81° 16.297' W

25–8 Old Pocotaligo Road, March from the Sea

Intersection of 1st St. W (U.S. Hwy. 601) & Old Pocotaligo Rd. (S.C. Sec. Rd. 25–68), about 1 mi. S of Hampton

(FRONT) This was a major road in the northern part of old Beaufort District for many years, appearing in Mills' Atlas of 1825. Gen. Wm. T. Sherman used this route from Savannah, Georgia, to North Carolina in February of 1865 with much of his invasion force, including 15,000 troops of the 15th Corps. These and [. . .]
(REVERSE) [. . .] other Union soldiers fought their way through the present Hampton County countryside, against Confederates under generals Joe Wheeler and Lafayette McLaws and Colonel Charles J. Colcock. Engagements in the county occurred at Lawtonville, Hickory Hill (2.9 miles SE), Whippy Swamp, and Broxton's Bridge. *Erected by Hampton County Historical Society, 1990*
GPS Coordinates: 32° 50.553' N, 81° 7.487' W

25–9 Lawtonville Church [Second Marker]

Augusta Rd. (S.C. Sec. Rd. 25–20), about 1 mi. N of its junction with S.C. Sec. Rd. 25–62, Lawtonville

This Baptist congregation, originally known as Savannah River, Carolina Church, was constituted near here March 1, 1775, mainly by members of Coosawhatchie (Beech Branch) Church. Rev. Joshua Lewis was its first known minister. In 1786, the church changed its name to Pipe Creek and by 1836 had moved to Lawtonville. Renamed Lawtonville in 1884, the church moved to Estill, 1911. *Erected 1991 by Lawtonville Baptist Church, Estill, S.C.*
GPS Coordinates: 32° 42.923' N, 81° 21.4' W

25–10 Hermitage Plantation

On the grounds of the Estill Correctional Institution, Federal Bureau of Prisons, just off S.C. Sec. Rd. 25–35, about 1.5 mi. S of its intersection with S.C. Sec. Rd. 25–208 Estill vicinity

This plantation was owned by large land owner Geo. Rhodes (1802–1881) who signed Ordinance of Secession in 1860. Tradition holds house was burned in 1865 during Civil War. *Erected by Hampton County Historical Society, 1993*
GPS Coordinates: 32° 43.059' N, 81° 15.062' W

25–11 Hickory Grove Baptist Church and Cemetery

125 Hickory Grove Rd., Brunson vicinity

(FRONT) This church, founded by 1869 with Rev. G. D. Kinard as its first pastor and 22 charter members, was admitted to the Barnwell Association that year. The congregation first met in a brush arbor, then built a log church near this site. That building also housed the Hickory Grove School for many years.
(REVERSE) Hickory Grove became a member of the Savannah River Association in 1904 and helped form the Allendale-Hampton Association in 1958. The present frame church, built in 1885, was moved across the road in 1953, with renovations completed in 1954. The cemetery nearby includes the plots of many early church families. *Erected by the Congregation, 2005*
GPS Coordinates: 32° 58.737' N, 81° 6.646' W

25–12 James Washington Moore House

503 Oak St., W, Hampton

(FRONT) This house, built between 1878 and 1885, was the home of James Washington Moore (1837–1912), lawyer, Confederate officer, state legislator, and militia officer. Moore, a native of Gillisonville, was educated at the University of Ga. and returned to S.C. in 1859 to practice law. He was a sergeant in the Hampton Legion Cavalry, then 1st lt. and adjutant of the 2nd S.C. Cavalry, and was wounded in 1863.

(REVERSE) Moore represented Beaufort District in the S.C. House 1866–67 and moved to Hampton when Hampton County was created in 1878. He was Hampton County's first state senator, serving 1878–1894 and 1901–02. Moore was also chairman of the senate military committee and an officer in the militia, retiring as a major general in 1891. He is buried at Gillisonville Baptist Church, in what is now Jasper County. *Erected by the Rivers Bridge Camp #842, Sons of Confederate Veterans, 2008*

GPS Coordinates: 32° 52.111' N, 81° 6.832' W

25–13 Cherry Grove Christian Church

1895 Cherry Grove Rd., Brunson

This African-American church, a congregation of the Disciples of Christ, was founded in 1855 by members of Three Mile Creek Christian Church. A Rev. Ervin was its first pastor, and it met in a brush arbor before building its first sanctuary here. The present brick church was built in 2002. *Erected by the Congregation, 2009*

GPS Coordinates: 33° 0.104' N, 81° 4.63' W

25–14 World War II POW Camp

Corner of S. Hoover St. & Jackson Ave., Hampton

(FRONT) German prisoners of war were held in a camp on this site from September 1943 to the spring of 1946. This camp, one of 21 in S.C., was a sub-camp of Fort Jackson, in Columbia. 250 prisoners captured in North Africa were the first held here; later arrivals were captured in Italy and France. The camp averaged about 250 prisoners at any time. POWs lived in tents with wooden floors or in wooden barracks.

(REVERSE) The Hampton Armory across Hoover Street was headquarters for the U.S. Army officers in charge. POWs worked 8–10 hours a day, harvesting peanuts, cutting pulpwood or lumber, or at the Plywoods-Plastics Corporation. They were paid 25 to 80 cents a day in scrip, which they spent at the camp store. When not working prisoners often tended small flower or vegetable gardens, or put on Sunday concerts. *Erected by the Hampton Museum & Visitors' Center, 2010*

GPS Coordinates: 32° 52.25' N, 81° 7.109' W

25–15 Bank of Hampton

15 Elm St. E., Hampton

(FRONT) The Bank of Hampton, built in 1892, was the first bank organized in Hampton and an important part of the rapid growth and development of the county seat from the 1890s to the mid-1920s. It was designed by Vincent Joseph Fontaine, a French-born architect who moved to S.C. after the Civil War. This two-story building, with its raised brickwork, segmental arches, and stepped parapet, is a good example of the Italianate influence in commercial buildings of the period.

(REVERSE) This building housed the Bank of Hampton on the first floor and law offices on the second floor for more than thirty years. Though the bank closed in 1926, the second floor housed law offices into the 1960s. The building was donated to the Town of Hampton in 1987, and a town museum opened here in 1989. Now home of the Hampton Museum & Visitors' Center, it was listed in the National Register of Historic Places in 2001. *Erected by the Hampton Museum & Visitors' Center, 2010*

GPS Coordinates: 32° 51.991' N, 81° 6.486' W

25–16 American Legion Hut

Jackson Ave. W & Hoover St. S, Hampton

(FRONT) This 1933 cypress-log hut is the headquarters of American Legion Post #108. Legionnaires and other local citizens cut cypress

trees for it, designed it, and built it, with funding from the Reconstruction Finance Corporation, a Depression-era federal program. State Senator George Warren donated this one-acre site to the Town of Hampton, which deeded it to American Legion Post #108 in 1940.
(REVERSE) This building, described at its opening as "one of the most beautiful in the state," hosted Friday night dances for many years. During World War II it was a dining hall for German prisoners of war held nearby. The hut, a fine example of vernacular log construction and long a center of social and cultural events in Hampton County, was listed in the National Register of Historic Places in 2000. *Erected by the American Legion Post #108, 2010*
GPS Coordinates: 32° 52.334' N, 81° 7.07' W

25–17 Whippy Swamp Muster Ground

At Harmony Presbyterian Church, Bamberg Rd. (U.S. Hwy. 601), Crocketville

(FRONT) This area, called Whippy Swamp Cross Roads, was in Beaufort District before Hampton County was created in 1878. In 1840 the Whippy Swamp Guards of the 12th S.C. Militia built their "militia house" nearby. It hosted inspections, drills, picnics, and political speeches. Two Confederate companies formed in 1861–62 were made up of men of the antebellum Guards: Co. D, 11th S.C. Infantry, and Co. D, 24th S.C. Infantry.
(REVERSE) Other members of the antebellum Whippy Swamp Guards served in several Confederate units from this area. On October 22, 1862, at the Battle of Pocotaligo, the silk flag of the Whippy Swamp Guards was captured by the 48th N.Y. Infantry. Maj. John J. Harrison of the 11th S.C., former captain of the Guards, was killed. The militia house was torn down shortly after the Civil War. *Erected by the Hampton Museum and Visitors' Center, 2011*
GPS Coordinates: 32° 55.023' N, 81° 4.695' W

25–18 Plywoods-Plastics Corporation/Westinghouse Micarta Division

U.S. Hwy. 601 N, Hampton

Plywoods-Plastics Corporation (FRONT)
This complex, opened in 1942 as Plywoods-Plastics Corporation, has been significant in the industry and economy of Hampton and the lowcountry ever since. In 1941 Plywood Products Corporation bought this site from the town and the Hampton & Branchville RR. It moved its operations here from Michigan to make plywood and laminated plastics for building construction and various household applications.
Westinghouse Micarta Division (REVERSE)
Westinghouse bought this plant in 1951 as a branch of its Micarta Division. Until 1995 the Decorative Division made countertops and furniture while the Industrial Division made components for the U.S. Navy and NASA, among other clients. The plant, which employed 1200 at its peak, was sold to International Paper in 1995, then to Kohlberg & Co. in 2002, making laminates under the brand name Nevamar. *Sponsored by the Hampton Museum & Visitors Center, 2012*
GPS Coordinates: 32° 52.623' N, 81° 6.862' W

25–19 Estill Presbyterian Church

343 Clarke Ave., Estill

(FRONT) This church was founded in 1898 by residents of Estill and Lawtonville who were members of distant Presbyterian churches and desired to organize a congregation here. It held its first services in a school on Fourth St. The first permanent church, a frame building, was built here in 1909 on land donated by Sumpter Mills Clarke, Sr.
(REVERSE) Temporary, or stated supply, pastors served here 1898–1955. Among the most notable was Dr. Paul Frederick Brown, who served here 1912–1923. Dr. Frank B. Estes became the first full-time minister in 1955. The church burned during services in 1934. This Classical Revival church, built 1934–37, opened in 1937 and was completed after World War II. *Sponsored by the Congregation, 2014*
GPS Coordinates: 32° 45.120' N, 81° 14.390' W

25–20 Estill Methodist Church

287 Keene Ave., Estill

(FRONT) Members of distant Lebanon Methodist Church held regular prayer meetings in Janie Boyd Rhodes's Estill home from 1902 until this church was built in 1908. Dr. W. M. O'Neal and his daughter Laura O'Neal Johnston donated the land here for a new church. Janie Rhodes's husband Julian, though a Baptist, milled the lumber at his sawmill, was appointed to the building committee, and became a charter member.

(REVERSE) This Carpenter Gothic church was built in 1908 with Rev, W. W. Williams as its pastor and dedicated a few years during the pastorate of Rev. J. R. Copeland. In 1938 the entrance in the north tower was replaced by a window like the one in the south tower and the Gothic arched window between the towers was replaced by a central entrance. The church still retains its essentially Carpenter Gothic style. *Sponsored by the Congregation, 2014*
GPS Coordinates: 32° 45.485' N, 81° 14.633' W

25–21 Gifford Rosenwald School

Columbia Hwy. (U.S. Hwy. 321), near its northern junction with Nunn St., Gifford

(FRONT) Gifford Rosenwald School, sometimes called Gifford Colored School, was built here in 1920–21. It was one of 500 rural schools built for African-American students in S.C., founded in part by the Julius Rosenwald Foundation from 1917 to 1932. The first of four Rosenwald schools in Hampton County, it was a two-room frame building constructed at a cost of $3,225.

(FRONT) Gifford Rosenwald School had two to five teachers for an average of almost 200 students a year in grades 1–9 until it closed in 1958. That year a new school serving Gifford and Luray, built by an equalization program seeking to preserve school segregation, replaced the 1921 school. The old school has been used for church services and Sunday school classes since 1958. *Sponsored by the Arnold Fields Community Endowment, the Faith Temple Deliverance Ministry, and the Town of Gifford Council, 2014*
GPS Coordinates: 32° 51.837' N, 81° 14.268' W

25–22 Steep Bottom Baptist Church

Steep Bottom Church, Steep Bottom Road, Estill vicinity

(FRONT) Steep Bottom Baptist Church was constituted in 1814 through the efforts of Rev. Hezekiah A. Boyd and Rev. James Sweat. Steep Bottom, along with Prince William and Cypress Creek Churches, was admitted into the Savannah River Baptist Association in that same year. Across the road is a pond referred to as the "Punch Bowl," which was long used as a baptismal pool.

(REVERSE) During the Civil War the XX Corps of the Union Army camped near the church in early February 1865. Union forces fired the nearby town of Lawtonville, which never recovered, and tradition holds they also burned Steep Bottom Church. A new church was built in 1872 and served as the sanctuary until the present church was built in 1982. The 1872 church remains and is now the social hall. *Sponsored by Steep Bottom Baptist Church, 2014*
GPS Coordinates: 32° 41.962' N, 81° 12.985' W

25–23 Huspah Baptist Church and School

729 Magnolia St. W., Hampton

(FRONT) Huspah Baptist Church was organized ca. 1873. The congregation first met in the homes of church members before erecting a permanent sanctuary. A two-room school was added to the property ca. 1890 and was operated as a school for African American students. In 1898 the congregation purchased the "Old Baptist Church" lot, a one-acre plot of land that included the former church building of a white congregation.

(REVERSE) The first school was burned in 1895, a victim of suspected arson. It re-opened the following year in a new building. Elizabeth Evelyn Wright and Jessie Dorsey were the first teachers at the new school. Wright would go on to found Voorhees College in 1897. The school at Huspah remained in service until the county built a new school for African American students on Holly St. in 1927. *Sponsored by Huspah Baptist Church, 2015*
GPS Coordinates: 32° 52.412' N, 81° 6.828' W

25–24 Davis Swimming Pool and Airstrip

SE side of county road S-25-25 near 1395 Shirley Rd.

(FRONT) Built by Wilbur Davis on an artesian well in 1916, this private swimming pool was a popular picnic and party venue for Georgia and South Carolina residents for much of the twentieth century. In 1925, Davis jacked the dance pavilion onto piers, creating the shaded picnic area underneath. When Davis died in 1926, his son Emory carried on the business until his death in 1971.

(REVERSE) In 1945, Emory Davis put in an airstrip in the field across the road to attract private pilots flying past the venue. Thereafter, the South Carolina Breakfast Club, a group of pilots, stopped here for brunches and annual meetings. Often a stop on the stump speech circuit, the pool was host to U.S. Sen. Strom Thurmond in 1966 for the pool's 50th anniversary celebration. *Sponsored by the Hampton County Historical Society, 2018*
GPS Coordinates: 32° 40.061' N, 81° 18.540' W

25–25 Yemassee Rosenwald School/ Fennell Elementary School

131 Yemassee Hwy., Yemassee

Yemassee Rosenwald School (FRONT)
In 1929 Elvira Jackson sold 4 acres of land to Yemassee School District #26 for $500. The land was to be used to build an African American school and Yemassee Rosenwald School (Yemassee Colored School), a five-teacher school funded in part by the Rosenwald Foundation helped to fund four schools in Hampton Co.
Fennell Elementary School (REVERSE)
Yemassee Rosenwald School served the African American community 1929–1954. In 1954 it was replaced by Fennell Elementary School. Fennell, which remains today, was built with funds from the S.C. Equalization Program. It was named for Clarence Fennell, an African American farmer, preacher, and community leader from Hampton Co. it remained a segregated African American school until 1970. *Sponsored by Pilgrim Ford Church*

and the Arnold Fields Community Endowment, 2018
GPS Coordinates: 32° 41.582' N, 80° 51.337' W

25–26 Brunson Rosenwald School/ Allen Elementary School

N. Broad St. near intersection with Preacher St., Brunson

Brunson Rosenwald School (FRONT)
The Brunson Rosenwald School, also known as the Brunson Colored School, was built on this site in 1925–26. The two-teacher schoolhouse was one of four in Hampton County that was funded in part by the Julius Rosenwald Foundation (1917–1932). The school was constructed at a total cost of $2,700 and served the African American community here from 1926 until 1954. Brunson Rosenwald School was replaced by Allen Elementary School in 1954.
Allen Elementary School (FRONT)
Allen Elementary was one of many schools in S.C. built as part of the state's "school equalization program." It remained a segregated school for African American students until the county desegregated schools in 1969–70. It was given to the Committee for the Betterment of Poor People and then the Town of Brunson. *Sponsored by the Town of Brunson, the Committee for the Betterment of Poor People, and the Arnold Fields Community Endowment, 2018*
GPS Coordinates: 32° 55.914' N, 81° 11.126' W

25–27 Estill Rosenwald School /Estill Training School

555 3rd St., Estill

Estill Rosenwald School (FRONT)
The Estill Rosenwald School (Estill Colored School), was built on this site in 1925–26. Funded in part by the Julius Rosenwald Foundation (1917–1932), it was one of four Rosenwald Schools in Hampton Co. The Estill School was originally a five-teacher school and was constructed at a cost of $7,200. The Foundation gave $1,300, the local African American community gave $2,900, and the balance was from public funds.

Estill Training School (FRONT)
Estill Rosenwald School served the African American community 1926–1954. In 1954 a new school, Estill Training School, was built on this site. Funded by the S.C. equalization program, Estill Training also served African American students. Estill Training became

Estill Middle School in 1970 when federal court rulings required all S.C. school districts to finally implement plans to racially integrate their schools. *Sponsored by the Estill Community and the Arnold Fields Community Endowment, 2018*
GPS Coordinates: 32° 45.250' N, 81° 14.210' W

Horry County

26–1 Washington's Southern Tour

Kings Rd. (S.C. Sec. Rd. 26–559), Myrtle Beach

On April 27, 1791, President George Washington spent the night nearby at the indigo plantation of Jeremiah Vereen. He wrote in his diary that he was "entertained (& very kindly) without being able to make compensation." The next day Vereen guided Washington across Lewis Swash (now Singleton Swash) and onto the strand at Long Bay (now Myrtle Beach). *Erected by Horry County, 2008, replacing a marker erected by the Horry County Historical Society in 1941*
GPS Coordinates: 33° 46.722' N, 78° 46.336' W

26–2 Rev. George Whitefield

U.S. Hwy. 17, about 1 mi. N of the Intracoastal Waterway Bridge and N of Cedar Creek Cemetery, North Myrtle Beach vicinity

(FRONT) On Jan. 1, 1740 George Whitefield (1714–1770), Anglican evangelist, stopped at a tavern nearby on his way to Savannah. Whitefield, the most famous revivalist of the Great Awakening in colonial America, wrote in his diary that since it was New Year's Day and the crowd at the tavern was "dancing country dances," he believed they "wished I had not come to be their guest."
(REVERSE) Whitefield, who believed dancing was a sin, tried to convince a woman dancing a jig "how well-pleased the devil was with every step she took." Although she kept dancing and the fiddler kept fiddling, they soon stopped and allowed Whitefield to preach and baptize a child. Once he retired for the night, however, the New Year's

spirit prevailed, and the music and dancing resumed. *Erected by the Horry County Board of Architectural Review and Historic Preservation, 2009, replacing a marker erected by the Horry County Historic Preservation Commission in 1976*
GPS Coordinates: 33° 51.873' N, 78° 39.14' W

26–3 Boundary House

U.S. Hwy. 17 near South Carolina-North Carolina state line, Little River vicinity

During the colonial era the Boundary House, on the S.C.-N.C. line 1.3 mi. SE, was both a private residence and "public house." In 1775 Isaac Marion (d. 1781), eldest brother of future partisan leader Gen. Francis Marion, lived there. On May 9, 1775, when Isaac Marion received news of the Battle of Lexington, Mass., he forwarded the dispatch on to the Committee of Safety in Little River. *Erected in 2005 by the Horry County Historic Preservation Commission, replacing a marker erected by the commission in 1976*
GPS Coordinates: 33° 53.2' N, 78° 35.856' W

26–4 Fort Randall

Intersection of N. Myrtle Point Blvd. & U.S. Hwy. 17, North Myrtle Beach

Located about 5 miles E. of here, this Confederate fort included a blockhouse pierced for musketry and earthworks surrounded by a ditch about 10 ft. broad and 5 ft. deep. The fort was captured Jan. 1863 by U.S. Navy Lt. Wm. B. Cushing and twenty-five men while looking for blockade-runner pilots. Cushing held the fort briefly until his supply of ammunition

was exhausted. *Erected by The Horry County Historic Preservation Commission, 1976*
GPS Coordinates: 33° 50.7' N, 78° 39.283' W

26–5 Robert Conway/Kingston-Conway

Conway City Hall, 1001 Third Ave., Conway

Robert Conway (FRONT)
Robert Conway came to this area from Charleston before 1790. He became a large landholder and public official, serving six terms in the South Carolina General Assembly. He was a veteran of the American Revolution, and in 1806 succeeded Peter Horry as brigadier of the Sixth South Carolina Brigade. Conway died in Georgetown in 1823, at age seventy.
Kingston-Conway (REVERSE)
By 1733, Kingston Township had been "marked out" in this area, and by 1737 the town of Kingston was in existence. Since many landowners were nonresidents, the township did not flourish. In 1801, the town was renamed Conwayborough. Robert Conway had acquired large landholdings in the area, and in 1805 he conveyed some 223 acres to the town. In 1883, the town name was changed to Conway. *Erected by City of Conway and Horry County Historic Preservation Commission, 1976*
GPS Coordinates: 33° 50.103' N, 79° 2.759' W

26–6 First Methodist Church

Corner of Main St. and 5th Ave., Conway

Methodist Bishop Francis Asbury's many visits to Kingston (Conway) between 1785 and 1815 preceded the organization of a Methodist congregation here. Land was obtained in 1842 and the first church building was constructed here in 1844. Still standing are the 1898 gothic-style and the 1910 mission-style buildings. The church was renamed First Methodist in 1958 and the current Georgian sanctuary was completed in 1961. *Erected by The Congregation, 1985*
GPS Coordinates: 33° 50.244' N, 79° 2.861' W

26–7 Kingston Church

Kingston St. and 3rd Ave., Conway

A Presbyterian congregation existed here in the village of Kingston by 1756. Its meeting-house was on this site but by 1795 the congregation had apparently disbanded. In 1855 a proposal to reestablish a Presbyterian church in the town was favorably received, and in 1857 an "Association" for that purpose was formed. In 1858 the present house of worship was erected, and Kingston Church was officially organized. *Erected by The Congregation, 1986*
GPS Coordinates: 33° 50.151' N, 79° 2.69' W

26–8 Horry County/Peter Horry

Horry County Courthouse, 1201 Third Ave., Conway

Horry County (FRONT)
Originally part of colonial Craven County, Horry County has also been part of Prince George Winyah (1722), Prince Frederick (1734), and All Saints (1767) parishes, which served as early religious and civic jurisdictions. This area, which became part of newly-formed Georgetown District in 1769, was given its present boundaries and named Kingston County in 1785. In 1801, it was renamed Horry District, and, in 1868, Horry County.
Peter Horry (REVERSE)
A planter of French Huguenot descent, Peter Horry (O-ree) was born in S.C. ca.1747. A lieutenant colonel in the Revolution and later brigadier general in the S.C. Militia, he represented Prince George Winyah and All Saints parishes in the S.C. House and Senate. In 1801, Kingston County was renamed Horry District for Peter Horry. He died in 1815 and is buried at Trinity Episcopal Church in Columbia, S.C. *Erected by Horry County Historical Society, 1989*
GPS Coordinates: 33° 50.031' N, 79° 2.932' W

26–9 True Vine Missionary Baptist Church

3765 S.C. Hwy. 90, E of Conway, Grahamville vicinity

(FRONT) This church was organized in 1894 by founders Antey Graham, Beney Graham, Samuel Graham, Will Hill, and Ben Wilson, and became a member of the Kingston Lake Association. The first sanctuary, a frame building, was built about 1913 and located near what is now S.C. Hwy. 90; it was later on Burroughs Road.

(REVERSE) Rev. Patrick Dewitt, Rev. Solomon Chestnut, Rev. A. T. Graham, and Rev. H. H. Wilson were among the earliest pastors serving True Vine Missionary Baptist Church. In 1943 the old sanctuary was moved to this site by a team of mules. The present brick sanctuary, the second serving this congregation, was built in 1971. *Erected by the Congregation, 1999*
GPS Coordinates: 33° 49.317' N, 78° 54.367' W

26–10 Green Sea Baptist Church

1241 Green Sea Rd., Green Sea

(FRONT) This church, known as Honey Camp Baptist Church until 1924, was founded in 1807. It is the mother church to several Baptist churches in eastern S.C., including Spring Branch (1830), Pleasant View (1875), Mt. Zion (1887), Mt. Olive (1890), Dogwood (1896), Carolina (1902), and Grassy Bay (1905). It was first located a few miles southwest, near Honey Camp Swamp.

(REVERSE) Admitted to the Cape Fear (N.C.) Association in 1822, then to the Waccamaw Association in 1876, this congregation worshipped near Honey Camp Swamp until 1869, when J. H. Derham donated this site. The first sanctuary here, a frame building, was replaced by a larger one in 1886. It burned in 1931 and was replaced by the present brick sanctuary, completed in 1932. *Erected by the Congregation, 2003*
GPS Coordinates: 34° 7.737' N, 78° 58.525' W

26–11 Galivants Ferry

U.S. Hwy. 501, Galivants Ferry

(FRONT) In 1792 Galivants Ferry was named for Richard Gallevan, owner of ferry rights for Elirsee's Landing on the Little Pee Dee River. The ferry was an important crossing on the road to Conwayborough, the county seat, later renamed Conway. "Evans Store" appears here in Robert Mills's Atlas of S.C. (1825). In 1869

Joseph William Holliday (1827–1904) opened a general store here.

(REVERSE) By 1900 J. W. Holliday was one of the leading tobacco farmers in the region and Galivants Ferry was the center of a large community of tenant farmers who grew tobacco on Holliday's land. The Galivants Ferry Historic District, including houses, barns, and other agricultural buildings, was listed in the National Register of Historic Places in 2001. *Erected by Horry County, 2004*
GPS Coordinates: 34° 3.309' N, 79° 14.694' W

26-12 Galivants Ferry Stump Meeting, Horry Co.
IMAGE COURTESY OF SCDAH

26–12 Galivants Ferry Stump Meeting

U.S. Hwy. 501, Galivants Ferry

(FRONT) The Galivants Ferry Stump Meeting, a Democratic Party tradition, has been held here in the spring every two years since 1880. Sponsored by the Holliday family, its origins are associated with Wade Hampton's 1876 appearance. Hampton, a former Confederate general, was elected governor later that year.

(REVERSE) Joseph William Holliday (1827–1904), prominent local merchant and tobacco farmer, invited local Democratic candidates to speak at his store in 1880. The public meeting soon became a statewide event, featuring national candidates as well, and has been carried on by succeeding generations of the Holliday family. *Erected by Horry County, 2004*
GPS Coordinates: 34° 3.377' N, 79° 14.745' W

26–13 Socastee

S.C. Hwy. 544 at its intersection with Peachtree Rd., Socastee

(FRONT) Socastee is a Native American name referred to as "Sawkastee" in a 1711 land grant to Percival Pawley. A skirmish between small forces of American and British troops occurred near Socastee Creek in 1781. By the 1870s, the Socastee community was a significant center for the production and distribution of naval stores such as turpentine and tar. (REVERSE) This area included a saw mill, turpentine distilleries, cotton gin, grist mill, cooper shop, and general store, and was also a gateway to the coast. The Socastee Historic District, including the S. S. Sarvis House (1881), T. B. Cooper Store (1905), T. B. Cooper House (1908), and the Intracoastal Waterway Bridge (1936), was listed in the National Register of Historic Places in 2002. *Erected by Horry County, 2004*
GPS Coordinates: 33° 41.333' N, 79° 0.35' W

26–14 Socastee Methodist Church

Dick Pond Rd., just E of the Atlantic Intercoastal Waterway, Socastee

(FRONT) This church, originating with services held in a brush arbor, was formally organized by 1818. Its first sanctuary, a log building, was built here soon afterwards on land donated by Philip Elkes. The cemetery, dating from the 19th century, includes the plots of the Clardy, Cooper, Elkes, Hucks, Macklen, Outlaw, Sarvis, Stalvey, and other early church families. (REVERSE) The second sanctuary, a frame building featuring a large portico and square columns, was built in 1875 by W. T. Goldfinch of Conway. Sunday school rooms were added in 1933 and the church was extensively remodeled and enlarged in the 1950s, with work completed in 1957. The present sanctuary was built in 1987. *Erected by Horry County, 2004*
GPS Coordinates: 33° 41.009' N, 79° 0.098' W

26–15 St. James Rosenwald School

S.C. Hwy. 707, Burgess community

(FRONT) St. James Rosenwald School, which stood here from the late 1920s until the early 1970s, was one of several African-American schools in Horry County funded in part by the Julius Rosenwald Foundation. Rev. Smart Small, Sr. (1891–1961), assisted by Eugene Beaty (1889–1958), Dave Carr (1886–1992), Henry Small (1897–1999), and Richard Small, Sr. (1893–1950) led fundraising efforts. (REVERSE) The school, built in 1928 or 1929, was a five-room frame schoolhouse typical of the larger rural schools built by the Rosenwald Foundation between 1917 and 1932. It educated about 150 students a year in grades 1–10, with five or six teachers. St. James Rosenwald School had two principals: Eula G. Owens (d. 1971), succeeded by her husband, Boyd Williams Owens (d. 1981). It closed in 1970 after desegregation. *Erected by the Burgess Organization for the Advancement of Young People, Inc., 2005*
GPS Coordinates: 33° 37.273' N, 79° 2.513' W

26–16 Atlantic Beach

Atlantic Beach Town Hall, 30th Ave. & Atlantic Ave., Atlantic Beach

(FRONT) Atlantic Beach, nicknamed "The Black Pearl," was established about 1934 as an oceanfront community for blacks denied access to other area beaches by segregation. Many became year-round residents, but most spent their vacations here. From the 1930s to the 1970s "The Black Pearl" was one of the most popular beach resorts on the East Coast for blacks from Va. to Fla. Its hotels, nightclubs, restaurants, shops, and pavilion were packed every May to September. (REVERSE) George Tyson was the first to develop this area, from 1934 to 1943. In 1943 the Atlantic Beach Co. – J. W. Seabrook, R. K. Gordon, and P. C. Kelly III – bought the tracts and continued to develop them. As other area beaches began desegregating in the 1970s the beach saw fewer visitors. The town of Atlantic Beach, chartered in 1966 with Emery Gore and Millard Rucker as its first two mayors, is one of a few black-owned and governed oceanfront communities in the United States. *Erected by the Atlantic Beach Historical Society, 2005*
GPS Coordinates: 33° 48.323' N, 78° 43.101' W

26–17 Myrtle Beach Colored School

Mr. Joe White Avenue, Myrtle Beach

(FRONT) Myrtle Beach Colored School stood
here from the early 1930s to 2001. The first
public school for African-American students in
Myrtle Beach, it was a six-room frame building similar to the schools funded in part by
the Julius Rosenwald Foundation 1917–1932.
The school opened as early as 1932, with three
teachers and 113 students in grades 1–7 for a
four-month academic year from October to
February.
(REVERSE) During the 1930s and 1940s the
school's academic year expanded to eight
months, with as many as six teachers and 186
students in grades 1–7 before World War II.
It added grades 8–12 after 1945 and reached
a peak of eight teachers and 241 students in
its last year. The school, replaced by Carver
Training School in 1953, was torn down in
2001 but was reconstructed nearby at Dunbar
St. and Mr. Joe White Ave. in 2006. *Erected by
the City of Myrtle Beach and the Myrtle Beach
Colored School Committee, 2006*
GPS Coordinates: 33° 41.866' N, 78° 53' W

26–18 Roberts Pavilion 1936–1954 /Ocean Drive Pavilion

**At the intersection of Main St. & Ocean Blvd. at the
Ocean Drive Pavilion, North Myrtle Beach**

Roberts Pavilion 1936–1954 (FRONT)
The Roberts Pavilion, built in 1936 by William
Roberts, was an early open-air oceanfront
pavilion on the Grand Strand. The rhythm
& blues of the post-World War II era—later
called beach music-was played on jukeboxes
here and at other popular pavilions on the
beach. At these pavilions, dancers perfected
the Shag, named the state dance in 1984.
Beach music was named the state popular
music in 2001.
Ocean Drive Pavilion (REVERSE)
Roberts Pavilion was one of several local
pavilions destroyed by Hurricane Hazel on
October 15, 1954. Ocean Drive Pavilion was
built here 1955–57 with salvaged timbers and
the same foundation. This area is still called
Ocean Drive or "O.D." although it was consolidated into North Myrtle Beach in 1968. O.D.

is home to the Shaggers' Hall of Fame, and
the pavilion hosts shag events from April to
November. *Erected by the O.D. Pavilion Social
and Shag Club, 2007*
GPS Coordinates: 33° 49.122' N, 78° 40.35' W

26–19 Myrtle Beach Army Air Field /Myrtle Beach Air Force Base

U.S. Hwy. 17 & U.S. Hwy. 17 Bypass, Myrtle Beach

Myrtle Beach Army Air Field (FRONT)
Myrtle Beach Army Air Field operated here
1940–47 and grew out of city plans to expand
the municipal airport from two grass landing
strips to a more permanent facility. In 1940
–41 the U.S. Army Air Corps trained civilian pilots for the Civil Air Service; the War
Department acquired the airport in late 1941.
Observation squadrons, an aviation squadron,
and a fighter squadron trained here during
World War II.
Myrtle Beach Air Force Base (REVERSE)
Deactivated in 1947, the field became a mu-
nicipal airport again but was donated by the
city to the U.S. Air Force as an active air base
in 1954. The 354th Fighter Day Wing/Tactical
Fighter Wing, based here 1956–1993, deployed
squadrons in Europe, Southeast Asia, and the
Middle East, with major service in Lebanon,
Germany, Cuba, the Dominican Republic,
Vietnam, and the Persian Gulf. The base
closed in 1993. *Erected by the Myrtle Beach
Air Base Redevelopment Authority and the
City of Myrtle Beach, 2008*
GPS Coordinates: 33° 39.629' N, 78° 55.691' W

26–20 Loris Training School

3416 Cedar St., Loris

(FRONT) Loris Training School, which stood
here from 1928 to 1955, was the first school
for black students in Loris and other nearby
communities. Built at a cost of $4,700, it
was one of more than 5000 schools in the
South funded in part by the Julius Rosenwald
Foundation between 1917 and 1932. William
P. Johnson, Sr. (1910–2007), the first principal once it became a public school, led Loris
Training School 1931–1941.
(REVERSE) The Loris Training School opened
in 1928 with grades 1–7 and a six-month term,

but William P. Johnson eventually won approval for a nine-month term and for adding grades 8–11. George C. Cooper (1915–1991) was principal here from 1941 until the school closed in 1955. Its students were transferred to the Finklea Consolidated High School, with Cooper as principal there until it closed with desegregation in 1970. *Erected by the Finklea High/Loris Training Schools Alumni Association, 2008*
GPS Coordinates: 34° 3.903' N, 78° 53.44' W

26–21 Sonny's Pavilion

Intersection of N. Ocean Blvd. & Sea Mountain Hwy., Cherry Grove, North Myrtle Beach

(FRONT) Sonny's Pavilion, built in 1949 by N.F. "Sonny" Nixon, was an open-air pavilion on the Grand Strand. The rhythm & blues of the post-World War II era—later called beach music—was played on jukeboxes at area pavilions where dancers perfected the Shag, named the state dance in 1984. Beach music was named the state popular music in 2001. Nixon bought a small gazebo here and added a jukebox in 1947, then built a large pavilion here in 1949.

(REVERSE) Ocean Drive had a strict midnight curfew for its clubs, but Cherry Grove did not, and Sonny's became a favorite of late-night shaggers from midnight to dawn. Sonny's was one of several area pavilions destroyed by Hurricane Hazel in 1954, but Nixon rebuilt it the next year. It remained popular with shaggers and other fans of beach music until it became a family arcade in the 1970s. Sonny's was destroyed by Hurricane Hugo in 1989. *Erected by the O.D. Pavilion Social and Shag Club, 2009*
GPS Coordinates: 33° 49.667' N, 78° 38.589' W

26–22 Myrtle Beach Pavilions

N. Ocean Blvd. & 9th Ave. N., Myrtle Beach

(FRONT) A succession of four beach pavilions stood here or nearby from 1902 to 2006, all built by the Burroughs & Chapin Co. or the Myrtle Beach Farms Co. The first, built in 1902, was a simple oceanfront shelter. The second, built in 1907, was a frame building 1 ½ blocks from the beach. The third pavilion,

a two-story frame building, was built here in 1923. An amusement park added in the 1930s grew to more than 11 acres.

(REVERSE) The 1923 pavilion burned in 1944 and was replaced by a two-story concrete pavilion in 1949. Dancing at these and other pavilions evolved into the Shag, named the state dance in 1984. The 1949 pavilion's "Magic Attic" hosted bands and other acts; its jukebox, on the promenade's dance floor, played the rhythm & blues of the post-World War II era, later called Beach Music. The pavilion closed and was demolished in 2006. *Erected by the O.D. Pavilion Social and Shag Club, 2009*
GPS Coordinates: 33° 41.502' N, 78° 52.755' W

26–23 Coastal Carolina University

At the Edward M. Singleton Building, Coastal Carolina University, Conway

(FRONT) Coastal Carolina University was founded in 1954 as Coastal Carolina Junior College, holding evening classes in Conway High School 1954–1963. Its first enrollment numbered 53 students. Originally sponsored by the College of Charleston 1954–1958, the junior college became a branch of the University of S.C. in 1960.

(REVERSE) Coastal Carolina Junior College moved here in 1963 on the completion of its first building, later named for Edward M. Singleton, chancellor 1963–1983. As Coastal Carolina College, it began offering four-year degrees in 1974. In 1993 Coastal Carolina University became an independent state university. *Erected by Coastal Carolina University, 2009*
GPS Coordinates: 33° 47.607' N, 79° 0.662' W

26–24 Conway High School

1001 Laurel St., Conway

Conway High School was located here from 1929 to 1979. A two-story brick Classical Revival building, its cornerstone was laid in 1928 and the building was completed in 1929. Classes began that fall. Coastal Carolina Junior College (now Coastal Carolina University), founded in 1954, held evening classes in Conway High School from 1954 to

1963. The Conway High Class of 1979 was the last to graduate from the 1929 building, which was demolished in 1988. *Erected by Coastal Carolina University, 2009*
GPS Coordinates: 33° 50.613' N, 79° 3.19' W

26–25 Levister Elementary School

100 11th Ave., Aynor

(FRONT) This school, built in 1953, was one of many African-American schools built by the equalization program of Gov. James F. Byrnes, intended to preserve school segregation by building new schools for black children. Students in grades 1–7, who had previously attended the Allen, Cool Springs, Pleasant Hill, and Union Chapel schools, began the 1953–54 school year here. The last graduating class was the Class of 1969. (REVERSE) This school became the Aynor Elementary School Annex in 1973; it closed in 1997. It was named for Nellie Burke Levister (1884–1968), the first Jeanes teacher in Horry County, who held that post from 1922 until 1958. The Jeanes Fund, established in 1908, was also called the Negro Rural School Fund. Its supervising teachers were consultants for the rural teachers and schools in their counties. *Erected by the Levister Development Activity Center, 2010*
GPS Coordinates: 33° 59.6' N, 79° 11.867' W

26–26 Whittemore School

1808 Rhue Street, Conway

Whittemore School (FRONT)
Whittemore School, one of the first African-American schools in Horry County, educated elementary and high school students on this site from 1936 to 1970. Founded in 1870, it was named for Benjamin F. Whittemore (1824–1894), former Union Army chaplain, Freedmen's Bureau educator 1865–67, and later a state senator and U.S. Congressman. The first school was just E on Race Path Ave. After it burned, classes moved to the Conwayborough Academy on 5th Ave.
Whittemore High School (REVERSE)
A new Whittemore Training School was built at Race Path Ave. and Thompson St. in 1911,

with students in grades 1–9 until 1929, 1–10 until 1933, and 1–11 afterwards. A new school built here in 1936 burned in 1944 and occupied temporary buildings until separate new elementary and high schools were completed in 1954. Grade 12 was added in 1949. The schools closed when Horry County schools desegregated in 1970. *Erected by the Whittemore High School Historical Marker Commission, 2011*
GPS Coordinates: 33° 50.295' N, 79° 4.202' W

26–27 Chestnut Consolidated School

At North Myrtle Beach Middle School, 11240 Hwy. 90, Little River

Chestnut Consolidated School (FRONT)
Chestnut Consolidated School, which was located here 1954–1970, was built under the equalization program of Gov. James F. Byrnes, intended to preserve segregation by building new schools for blacks. Named to honor Horry County educator J. T. Chestnut (1885–1967), it educated African-American students in grades 1–12.
Chestnut Consolidated High School (REVERSE)
This school, consolidating schools in several northeastern Horry County communities, was a one-story brick building with two wings. After county schools desegregated in 1970, it became North Myrtle Beach High School and was later North Myrtle Beach Middle School. The 1954 building was demolished in 1995. *Erected by the Chestnut Consolidated High School Alumni Association, 2011*
GPS Coordinates: 33° 51.191' N, 78° 40.765' W

26–28 Ark Cemetery

S. Hollywood Dr. and Juniper Dr., Surfside Beach

(FRONT) This marker stands adjacent to the burial ground of the former Ark Plantation, which dates back to the 1700s. Although the names of most of those buried here are now unknown, records indicate that it was primarily a cemetery for African Americans who lived at the Ark. In 1860, 63 slaves were recorded as living here. Descendants of those buried here continued to utilize the cemetery until 1952.

(REVERSE) Sabe Rutledge, who was born in the 1860s at the Ark, requested to be buried here and was so in 1952. Although town maps reserved two blocks as Ark Cemetery, in 1980 a circuit court judge ruled against those who claimed that the property was a cemetery and decreed the property free and clear of any claims by the defendants. Development of the property soon followed that court ruling. Documented evidence of the site now exists. *Sponsored by the Town of Surfside Beach, 2019*
GPS Coordinates: 33° 36.356' N, 78° 58.852' W

26–29 Ark Plantation

3rd Ave. S. and S. Willow Dr., Surfside Beach

(FRONT) In colonial and antebellum days, at this site stood the planter's residence of the Ark, a large indigo plantation. On July 18, 1765 John Bartram recorded he lodged here, at Peak's, "on ye west end of long bay." A property re-survey for John M. Tillman in 1838 records that the property consisted of 3,194 acres at that time. It also shows several dwellings north of the main house.

(REVERSE) This plantation was located at the southwestern end of the Long Bay Road, an alternate route for those going north or south who wished to travel along the ocean shore instead of on the Broad Road, located in the area of present-day U.S. Hwy. 17. The home was used as an "inn" for travelers heading

north and who wanted to time their journey along the shore road at low tide. *Sponsored by the Town of Surfside Beach, 2019*
GPS Coordinates: 33° 36.323' N, 78° 58.570' W

26–30 Charlie's Place

1420 Carver St., Myrtle Beach

(FRONT) Charlie and Sarah Fitzgerald opened Charlie's Place as a supper club in 1937. It was a stop on the "Chitlin' Circuit," nightclubs where black entertainers such as Billie Holiday, the Mills Brothers, Little Richard, Ruth Brown, Otis Redding, and the Drifters performed during the era of racial segregation. While the club is gone, the Fitzgerald Motel, built in 1948, remains. The motel served black entertainers and travelers who could not stay in whites-only hotels.

(REVERSE) Oral tradition holds that "the Shag," a form of southern swing dancing, originated here. Both white and black customers gathered here to listen to music and dance. In 1950 the Ku Klux Klan led a parade through "The Hill," the African American neighborhood where Charlie's Place was located. The Klan returned later and shots were fired into the club, injuring many. Charlie was severely beaten but survived. Some Klansmen were charged, but no one was prosecuted. *Sponsored by the Horry County Board of Architectural Review and Historic Preservation, 2018*
GPS Coordinates: 33° 42.280' N, 78° 52.629' W

Jasper County

27–1 Robertville

Robertville Baptist Church, U.S. Hwy. 321 & S.C. Sec. Rd. 27-26, Robertville, Garnett vicinity

Named for descendents of Huguenot minister Pierre Robert, it was the birthplace of Henry Martyn Robert, author of Robert's Rules of Order, and of Alexander Robert Lawton, Confederate Quartermaster General. The town was burned by Sherman's army in 1865. The present church was built in Gillisonville in 1848 as an Episcopal church, moved here

by Black Swamp Baptists in 1871. *Erected by The Board of Deacons of Robertville Baptist Church, 1971*
GPS Coordinates: 32° 35.199' N, 81° 11.955' W

27–2 Battle of Honey Hill

U.S. Hwy. 278/S.C. Hwy. 336, just NW of its intersection with S.C. Hwy. 462, about 1.8 mi. E of Grahamville

(FRONT) During this battle of Nov. 30, 1864, Confederate commander Charles J. Colcock, by ordering that a nearby field of grass be set ablaze, delayed approaching Federal troops and gave the Confederates time to collect additional forces. When the Confederate position could not be taken, Union troops retreated. The site is located about 1 mile north. (REVERSE) On Nov. 30, 1864, Union troops under Brig. Gen. John P. Hatch were marching to Grahamville to cut the nearby Charleston-to-Savannah rail line when they met Col. Charles J. Colcock's smaller Confederate force posted in a redoubt located about 1 mi. N. of here. In the ensuing battle, Union troops were repelled, owing to their lack of ammunition and strong Confederate positions. *Erected by Jasper County Bicentennial Committee, 1978* GPS Coordinates: 32° 28.818' N, 80° 56.388' W

27–3 Purrysburg Township

Intersection of Purrysburg Rd. (S.C. Sec. Rd. 27–34) & Honey Hill Rd. (S.C. Sec. Rd. 27–203) at Purrysburg Landing on the Savannah River

(FRONT) In 1730, the British Crown instructed S.C. Governor Robert Johnson to lay out eleven townships to populate and protect the interior of the province. Purrysburg Township, laid out in 1731, stimulated the settlement of this area; but the growth of Savannah caused the town of Purrysburg to be unsuccessful.
(REVERSE) By 1732, Swiss Protestants led by entrepreneur Jean Pierre Purry had begun to arrive here, and by August of the next year, 260 Swiss had settled at Purrysburg Township. Each settler was provided with a specific amount of land, tools, livestock, and provisions by the Royal Assembly. *Erected by Jasper County Bicentennial Committee, 1980* GPS Coordinates: 32° 18.344' N, 81° 7.209' W

27–4 Church of the Holy Trinity

Intersection of S.C. Sec. Rd. 27–13 & S.C. Sec. Rd. 27–29, Grahamville

(FRONT) This Episcopal church was a chapel of ease in the Parish of St. Luke for a number of years before it became a separate congregation in 1835. It is said that William Heyward gave the church land on which the present

building, donated by James Bolan and completed by 1858, is built.
(REVERSE) This Episcopal church, listed in the National Register of Historic Places, is an outstanding example of Carpenter Gothic church architecture. The wheel window, board and batten sheathing, and buttressed tower are typical features of this style. A pipe organ is located in the gallery where slaves once worshipped. *Erected by The Congregation, 1983* GPS Coordinates: 32° 28.258' N, 80° 57.896' W

27–5 Tillman

Intersection of U.S. Hwy. 321 & S.C. Hwy. 336, Tillman

By 1820, the road to Two Sisters Ferry intersected the Purrysburg road at this spot, which had become known as Hennis Crossroads by 1848. A post office established here in 1880 was given the name Tillman. According to tradition, this was to honor U.S. Congressman George D. Tillman, brother of Benjamin Ryan ("Pitchfork Ben") Tillman, Governor of S.C. from 1890 to 1894. *Erected by Citizens of Jasper County and Jasper County Historical Society, 1984* GPS Coordinates: 32° 27.808' N, 81° 6.432' W

27–6 Gillisonville

Main St. (U.S. Hwy. 278), Gillisonville

Shown on the 1820 Beaufort District map by Vignoles and Ravenel, Gillisonville had a free school by 1831, and a post office in 1840. The seat of Beaufort District from 1840 to 1868, Gillisonville was burned by General William T. Sherman's army on its march through South Carolina in early 1865. *Erected by Citizens of Gillisonville and Jasper County Bicentennial Committee, 1984* GPS Coordinates: 32° 36.552' N, 80° 59.988' W

27–7 Tomb of Thomas Heyward, Jr. 1746–1809

Just SW of the intersection of Old House Rd. (U.S. Hwy. 278/S.C. Hwy. 336) & S.C. Hwy. 462, 5 mi. E of Ridgeland

Member of South Carolina Provincial Congress and Council of Safety and of Continental Congress. Signer of Declaration of Independence and Articles of Confederation and captain of militia at Battle of Port Royal and Siege of Charleston. Prisoner of war 1780–81. Circuit Court judge 1778–89. *Erected by the Beaufort County Historical Society, 1955*
GPS Coordinates: 32° 27.485' N, 80° 53.863' W

27–8 Fighting Near Coosawhatchie /General Robert E. Lee

Point South Dr., near I-95 Exit 33 & U.S. Hwy. 17, Point South

Fighting Near Coosawhatchie (FRONT)
On October 22, 1862, in running encounters near Coosawhatchie, Frampton's Plantation, and Pocotaligo, Confederate troops successfully defended the Charleston-Savannah railroad and the interior of South Carolina against a Union attack force of 4,448 men from Hilton Head.
General Robert E. Lee (REVERSE)
Following the capture of Hilton Head, Beaufort, and the nearby sea islands in the fall of 1861, General Robert E. Lee was given command of the coastal military department of South Carolina, Georgia, and East Florida. From his headquarters at Coosawhatchie, about 4 miles SW, he planned the strategy and defenses that successfully contained the enemy until the end of the war. *Erected by Point South Merchants Association, 1991*
GPS Coordinates: 32° 37.875' N, 80° 52.657' W

27–9 Narrow Gauge Locomotive No. 7

In park at the intersection of Main & Charles Sts., Hardeeville

This woodburning steam locomotive with balloon smoke stack, was built by the H. K. Porter Company about 1910. It was used by Argent Lumber Company, a leading area employer established in 1916, to haul timber from forest to mill. In 1960 the locomotive was donated to the Town of Hardeeville for public display as a logging and lumbering relic of this area. *Erected by Town of Hardeeville, 1991*
GPS Coordinates: 32° 17.14' N, 81° 4.759' W

27–10 Jasper County/Jasper County Courthouse

Jasper County Courthouse, Russell St. between 2nd & 3rd Aves., Ridgeland

Jasper County (FRONT)
This county was established in 1912 from portions of Beaufort and Hampton counties and named, it is said, for Sergeant William Jasper, hero of the American Revolution. The same act establishing the new county also designated Ridgeland (incorporated 1894) as the county seat. Charles E. Perry, John M. Langford, J. H. Woods, J. P. Wise and Rodger Pinckney were first county commissioners.
Jasper County Courthouse (REVERSE)
Land for this courthouse was given to Jasper County in 1912 by Charles E. Perry, a local farmer, lumberman, and merchant. The courthouse was completed in 1915 with William A. Edwards, a native South Carolinian as architect; and C. V. York as contractor. The Georgian Revival style building was entered in the National Register of Historic Places in 1981. *Erected by the Ivy Garden Club, 1993*
GPS Coordinates: 32° 29.046' N, 80° 59.103' W

27–11 Gillisonville Baptist Church

Grays Hwy. (S.C. Hwy. 462), Gillisonville

(FRONT) The Euhaw congregation constituted this ecclesiastical group 24 March 1832, naming it Coosawhatchie Baptist Church. The South Carolina Baptist Convention met at the church in December 1845 and unanimously voted to join the recently formed Southern Baptist Convention. In February 1865, General William Tecumseh Sherman's troops visited the church and etched "War of 1861 & 62 & 63 & 64 Feb. [. . .]
(REVERSE) [. . .] 7th 1865 this is done by a Yankee Soldier," on the communion silver. The congregation became Gillisonville Baptist Church 19 November 1885. The 1845 church building, placed on the National Register of Historic Places in 1971, is a local interpretation of Greek Revival style of architecture; notable features include the slave gallery and box pews. *Erected by The Congregation, 1994*
GPS Coordinates: 32° 36.448' N, 80° 59.92' W

27–12 Euhaw Baptist Church

S.C. Sec. Rd. 27-13, 1 mi. E of Ridgeland

(FRONT) Established on Edisto Island about 1686 by Scotch dissenters, this is the second oldest Baptist organization in the South. For many years a branch of First Baptist Church in Charleston, Euhaw declared itself a separate church in 1745 after relocating to this vicinity from Edisto Island. A sanctuary was built 6 mi. NE [. . .]

(REVERSE) [. . .] in 1751; it burned in 1857. The first sanctuary on this site was built in 1860. It burned in 1904 and was replaced by this sanctuary in 1906, which is still used for occasional services. The present sanctuary nearby was built in 1982. *Erected by Members and Friends, 1995*

GPS Coordinates: 32° 28.105' N, 80° 57.991' W

27–13 Great Swamp Baptist Church

Intersection of S.C. Sec. Rd. 27-22 and S.C. Sec. Rd. 27-39, Ridgeland

(FRONT) This church, organized October 12, 1845, was the result of a clash in doctrines at nearby Sardis Baptist Church. Some in the congregation favored the primitive Baptist movement, but others, including Rev. John N. Youmans, favored a ministry based on missions. Seventeen members then left Sardis to form a new, more missionary church, with Rev. Youmans as their minister.

(REVERSE) A brush arbor served as the first meeting place until a small one room frame sanctuary was built. A larger sanctuary was completed in 1909, and Sunday school rooms were added in 1925. Baptisms took place at "Old Dam" on the nearby stream until the 1950s. Great Swamp Baptist Church called its first full-time minister in 1956. Church membership in 1998 exceeds 600. *Erected by Members of the Church, 1998*

GPS Coordinates: 32° 29.672' N, 81° 1.221' W

27–14 Pine Level Baptist Church

Grays Hwy. (U.S. Hwy. 278), just S. of Pine Level Church Rd., Grays vicinity

(FRONT) This church, organized on January 6, 1872 with Rev. M. H. Shuman as its first

minister, held services in members' homes until a sanctuary was built on this site between 1876 and 1881. A second sanctuary, built in 1906, served the congregation until a new sanctuary was built .4 mi. N. in 1995. Revs. J. J. Nix (1900–1929) and Frank Fisher (1945–1966) were the longest-serving ministers here.

(REVERSE) Charter members of Pine Level Baptist Church were Mary Cleland, Rebecca Dewitt, Oscar Ellis, J. J. Gooding, Deborah Gooding, Rosa C. Grimes, Rachel Mew, Mary Phillips, Alexander Smith, Cecelia R. Smith, Deliah W. Smith, George H. Smith, James R. Smith, Lucretia Smith, Mary Smith, Harriet Tindal, W. F. Wheeler, and Sarah J. Wheeler. *Erected by Members and Friends of Pine Level Baptist Church, 1998*

GPS Coordinates: 32° 42.067' N, 81° 1.733' W

27–15 Tillman Baptist Church

Cotton Hill Rd., Tillman

(FRONT) This church, formally established in 1883 as Savin Grove Baptist Church, had its origins in a congregation active before the Civil War just south of present-day Tillman. When Revs. J. F. Morrall and Jonas Trowell reestablished the church it took the old name of Savin Grove. Rev. W. H. Dowling served as its first minister and Rev. J. M. Bostick as its second minister.

(REVERSE) This church moved to Tillman in 1897 after the congregation acquired property for a new sanctuary; work began that year and was completed in 1901. Renamed Edon Baptist Church (also spelled Eden), it was known by that name until the 1930s, when it was renamed Tillman Baptist Church. The congregation has been a member of the Savannah River Assn. of Baptist Churches since 1883. *Erected by the Congregation and the Jasper County Historical Society, 2000*

GPS Coordinates: 32° 27.869' N, 81° 6.463' W

27–16 Grahamville

Intersection of S.C. Hwys. 13 and 29, Grahamville

(FRONT) This summer village, established about 1800 by the rice planters of St. Luke's Parish, was a thriving settlement in what

was Beaufort District until the creation of Jasper County in 1912. Named for Capt. John Graham (1784–1833), its prominent residents included members of the Bull, Fripp, Glover, Hasell, Hazzard, Heyward, Jenkins, Screven, and Seabrook families, among others. (REVERSE) The village boasted several stores, three churches, a post office, a tavern, and the Grahamville Academy. When the Charleston & Savannah RR was constructed in 1860, villagers objected to locating a station here so one was built 1 mi. W and Ridgeland grew around it. Grahamville was burned by Union troops in 1864, and Holy Trinity Church is all that survives of the old village. *Erected by the Jasper County Historical Society, 2000*
GPS Coordinates: 32° 28.251' N, 80° 57.894' W

27–17 Ridgeland Baptist Church

1448 Grays Hwy. (U.S. Hwy 278), Ridgeland

(FRONT) This church was organized February 28, 1892, by Revs. W. H. Dowling and J. T. Morrison with nine charter members. It was admitted to the Savannah River Baptist Association with Rev. Dowling as its first minister. The congregation held services in the Masonic hall until 1894, when it built its first sanctuary, a frame building, on Main St. in Ridgeland. (REVERSE) Ridgeland Baptist Church, originally on Main St. in Ridgeland, moved to a brick sanctuary on the corner of Third Ave. and U.S. Hwy. 17 in 1925. A third sanctuary, built there in 1950, was enlarged and remodeled in 1963 and 1992. The church and all buildings except the fellowship hall burned in 1995. The congregation then moved to this site, dedicating this new sanctuary in 1998. *Erected by the Congregation, 2001*
GPS Coordinates: 32° 29.651' N, 80° 59.24' W

27–18 Coosawhatchie

S.C. Hwy. 462, Coosawhatchie

(FRONT) Coosawhatchie, dating to the 1740s, was named for the Coosaw tribe. At first it was little more than a store and inn built on the King's Highway by Henry DeSaussure, a Huguenot settler from Purrysburg. By the 1760s, it was a regional trading post and

crossroads. During the Revolution British troops burned most of the buildings and the nearby bridge in a 1779 raid. (REVERSE) Coosawhatchie served as the capital of Beaufort District from 1789 to 1836, when a new courthouse was built in Gillisonville. In 1861–62 Gen. Robert E. Lee, commanding the Confederate Dept. of S.C. and Ga., had his headquarters here. In 1864, during the last months of the Civil War, several skirmishes were fought nearby. This has been a village of farmers and merchants ever since. *Erected by Citizens and Friends of Coosawhatchie, 2001*
GPS Coordinates: 32° 35.317' N, 80° 55.65' W

27–19 The Frampton Lines/John Edward Frampton House

Frampton House, Lowcountry & Resort Islands Visitors Center, I-95 Exit 33 and U.S. Hwy. 17 Point South

The Frampton Lines (FRONT)
Remnants of a large earthwork originally more than 100 yards long are still visible south, west, and northwest of the Frampton House. This battery, constructed in 1861–62 by Confederate troops in the Department of S.C. and Ga., was part of an extensive system of lines intended to defend the Charleston & Savannah Railroad, a vital route through the Lowcountry.
John Edward Frampton House (REVERSE)
This was the site of "The Hill" Plantation, owned by John Edward Frampton (1810–1896), cotton planter, state senator 1842–45, and delegate from Prince William Parish to the Secession Convention. The main houses here and at Frampton's other plantations in what was then Beaufort District were burned by Federal troops in early 1865. This house was built in 1868. *Erected by the Lowcountry and Resort Islands Tourism Commission, 2002*
GPS Coordinates: 32° 38.237' N, 80° 51.794' W

27–20 St. Matthew Baptist Church

S.C. Hwy. 336 between Tillman and Ridgeland

(FRONT) This church was founded in 1870 with Rev. Plenty Pinckney as its first minister and worshipped in a "bush tent" nearby until a

log church was built a few years later. A new frame church was built on this site in the 1890s during the pastorate of Rev. C. L. Lawton. The present sanctuary was built in 1960 during the tenure of Rev. R. M. Youmans, who served here for more than 35 years. *Erected by the Congregation, 2002*
GPS Coordinates: 32° 27.751′ N, 81° 5.407′ W

27–21 Oak Grove Baptist Church

Rivers Mill Rd., Grays vicinity

(FRONT) This church was organized in 1870 by Revs. John D. Nix, W. H. Shuman, and Jonas Trowell. F.J. Bryan and A. W. Crosby were its first deacons; Rev. Trowell became its first minister. This sanctuary, dedicated in 1871, was built on land later donated by John D. Rivers. The congregation, which grew to as many as 66 members by 1913, held services the second Sunday of each month.
(REVERSE) Oak Grove, long affiliated with the Savannah River Baptist Association, saw its membership decline over the years and eventually discontinued regular services in 1942. In 1989 descendants of charter members and other former members began restoring the original frame sanctuary. Oak Grove Baptist Church was formally reorganized and resumed services once more in 2000. *Erected by the Congregation in Memory of George and Elise Malphrus Roberts, 2003*
GPS Coordinates: 32° 40.254′ N, 81° 4.321′ W

27–22 Battle of Pocotaligo

Point South Dr., I-95 Exit 33 and U.S. Hwy. 17, Pocotaligo

(FRONT) The Battle of Pocotaligo, the largest action of a three-day expedition intended to disrupt the Charleston & Savannah Railroad, took place nearby on October 22, 1862. With 2000 Confederates under Col. W. S. Walker defending the area between Charleston and Savannah, 4500 Federals under Brig. Gens. J. M. Brannan and A. M. Terry landed at Mackays Point, seven miles south.
(REVERSE) The Confederates, with only 475 men in the immediate vicinity when the day began, delayed the Federals in engagements

at Caston's Plantation and Frampton's Plantation until 200 reinforcements arrived by train. Most of the fighting centered around Pocotaligo Bridge, and by dusk the Federals withdrew toward Port Royal having done only minimal damage to the Charleston & Savannah Railroad. *Erected by the S.C. Society of the Military Order of the Stars and Bars, 2002*
GPS Coordinates: 32° 37.919′ N, 80° 52.553′ W

27–23 St. Paul's Methodist Church

506 West Main St., Ridgeland

(FRONT) This church, organized in 1890, is the oldest in Ridgeland, with its origins in several area Methodist congregations before the Civil War. When Julius G. Sipple of Grahamville encouraged Methodists in Ridgeland to organize a separate congregation, Rev. J. R. Buchanan led the formal organization of the new church. Its first sanctuary, a frame building, was built nearby in 1891.
(REVERSE) In 1927 the Gillisonville Methodist Church, organized in 1886, merged with St. Paul's. This sanctuary, across the street from the original church site, was built in 1949 as a gift from Mr. and Mrs. William J. Ellis and was renovated in 1990. Six members of St. Paul's later became Methodist ministers: Revs. Robert Drew, Leroy Dyches, Elton Hendricks, Carolyn Malphrus, James Thompson, and Robert Way. *Erected by Members and Friends of St. Paul's United Methodist Church, 2003*
GPS Coordinates: 32° 28.925′ N, 80° 59.107′ W

27–24 Ridgeland

Intersection of the CSX Railroad & W. Main St., Ridgeland

(FRONT) Ridgeland, named for its location on the ridge between Charleston and Savannah, has been the seat of Jasper County since the county was created in 1912. It was first named Gopher Hill and grew up around a depot built on the Charleston & Savannah RR in 1860. The tracks were the boundary line between Beaufort and Hampton counties, and Ridgeland belonged to two counties until 1912.
(REVERSE) Chartered and incorporated in 1894, Ridgeland had a population of about 500

when it became the new seat of Jasper County in 1912. The Georgian Revival courthouse was designed by William Augustus Edwards and built in 1915. U.S. Hwy. 17, constructed through Ridgeland in the 1920s, has long brought many visitors through the town on their trips to and through the lowcountry. *Erected by the Town of Ridgeland, 2004*
GPS Coordinates: 32° 28.89' N, 80° 58.963' W

27–25 Grays Consolidated High School

U.S. Hwy. 278, Grays

(FRONT) This school, built in 1927 and rebuilt in 1931, was one of many constructed in the late 1920s, as small rural one- or two-room schools were consolidated into elementary or high schools in towns and cities. Built on land donated by Robert L. Robinson, it included grades 1–11 until grade 12 was added in 1948–49.
(REVERSE) This school, designed by Columbia architect James Hagood Sams (1872–1935), was burned by an arsonist in 1929. It was rebuilt according to Sams's plans in 1931, at a cost of $14,000. The Grays Consolidated High School closed in the early 1970s. It was listed in the National Register of Historic Places in 2007. *Erected by the Grays School Preservation Committee, Alumni, and Friends of the School, 2008*
GPS Coordinates: 32° 40.453' N, 81° 1.269'

27–26 Cummingsville Cemetery

State Rd S-27-193 near Pilgrim Church, Hardeeville

Cummingsville Cemetery dates to the 1870s when a group of freedmen formed the

Cummingsville Society and purchased 10 acres for a cemetery. Oral tradition holds that James (John) Cummings, a former slave, was namesake of both the Cummingsville community and burial society. The Cummings, Crawford, German, Hamilton, Latson, Scott, and West families are among those buried here. *Sponsored by Cummingsville Society, 2018*
GPS Coordinates: 32° 8.479' N, 80° 59.390' W

27–27 Clementa Carlos Pinckney

2740 Tillman Rd., Ridgeland

(FRONT) Clementa Carlos Pinckney (1973–2015) answered the call to preach at the age of 13 here at St. John A.M.E. Church and received his first appointment to pastor at the age of 18. As a pastor, he served innumerable parishioners in many S.C. churches, including Youngs Chapel A.M.E., Mt. Horr A.M.E., and Campbell Chapel A.M.E. His last appointment was as pastor at Mother Emanuel A.M.E. Church in Charleston.
(REVERSE) Pinckney was elected to the S.C. House of Representatives in 1996 at the age of 23, becoming the youngest African American elected to the S.C. legislature. In 2000 he was elected to the S.C. Senate. Sen. Pinckney was killed on June 17, 2015 along with 8 of his parishioners at Emanuel A.M.E. A public viewing was held here at St. John A.M.E. President Barack Obama delivered the eulogy at his funeral. *Sponsored by the Jasper County Historical Society and Those He Loved and Served, 2019*
GPS Coordinates: 32° 27.651' N, 81° 3.632' W

Kershaw County

28–1 Battle of Camden/British Troops Engaged – American Troops Engaged

S.C. Sec. Rd. 28-58 (Flat Rock Rd.), about 6 mi. N of Camden and 5.6 mi. N of the intersection of U.S. Hwy. 521 & U.S. Hwy. 1

Battle of Camden (FRONT)
Near here on August 16, 1780, an American army under General Gates was defeated by British forces commanded by Lord Cornwallis. Major General Baron deKalb was mortally wounded in this battle.

(REVERSE)
British Troops Engaged
Tarleton's Legion, Twenty-third, Thirty-third and Seventy-first Regiments, Volunteers of Ireland, Royal Artillery, four light infantry companies, Royal North Carolina Militia, volunteer militia, and pioneers.
American Troops Engaged
Armand's Legion, First and Second Maryland Brigades, Delaware Regiment, First Artillery Regiment, Porterfield's Light Infantry, North Carolina Militia, and Virginia Militia. *Erected by The Kershaw County Historical Society, 1974, replacing a marker erected in 1954*
GPS Coordinates: 34° 21.515' N, 80° 36.675' W

28–2 Battle of Hobkirk Hill

Marker # 1: Broad St. (U.S. Hwy. 521/601 N), Camden

Marker # 2: Lyttleton St., Camden

Battle of Hobkirk Hill in the Revolutionary War took place on this ridge April 25, 1781. The British Army was commanded by General Lord Rawdon, the Continental Army by General Nathanael Greene. *Erected by the Kershaw County Historical Society, 1956*
GPS Coordinates: 34° 15.827' N, 80° 36.538' W

28–3 General Greene's Headquarters

Broad St. (U.S. Hwy. 521/601 N), Camden

150 yards to the east is where Gen. Nathanael Greene had the headquarters of the American Army during the Battle of Hobkirk Hill April 25, 1781. *Erected by the Kershaw County Historical Society, 1956*
GPS Coordinates: 34° 15.824' N, 80° 36.529' W

28–4 Camden

Marker # 1: Monument Square, N. Broad St., across from the Camden Archives & Museum, Camden

Marker # 2: Hampton Park, Broad St., Camden

This area, first held by Wateree and Catawba Indians, was laid out as Fredericksburg Township in 1733. Here on the Catawba Path the trading town of Pine Tree Hill was settled. In

1769 courts were set up and the town named Camden in honor of Lord Camden, friend of the colonies. During the Revolution, Camden was the center of British activity in this region. It was incorporated in 1791. *Erected by Kershaw County Historical Society and the City of Camden, 1958*
GPS Coordinates: 34° 15.069' N, 80° 36.461' W

28–5 Gaol

Corner of King & Broad Sts., Camden

On this corner stood the gaol, built in 1771 and burned in 1812. During the Revolution the British imprisoned in it many American soldiers and civilians. Among them, after his capture near the Waxhaws, was the boy Andrew Jackson, later seventh President. He is said to have watched the battle of Hobkirk Hill through a hole he cut in the wall of the gaol's second story. *Erected by Kershaw County Historical Society and the City of Camden, 1958*
GPS Coordinates: 34° 14.364' N, 80° 36.378' W

28–6 Battle of Boykin's Mill

S.C. Hwy. 261, Boykin's Mill

Gen. Edward E. Potter commanding 2700 white and negro Union troops left Georgetown April 5, 1865, to destroy the railroad between Sumter and Camden. Here on April 18, in one of the last engagements of the war, a small force of Confederate regulars and local Home Guard fought a defensive action which delayed their advance for a day. *Erected by United Daughters of the Confederacy, Central District, 1967*
GPS Coordinates: 34° 7.844' N, 80° 34.854' W

28–7 Pleasant Hill Baptist Church

2602 Mecklenburg Rd. (S.C. Sec. Rd. 28–531), Bethune

(FRONT) The first Baptist Church in this area of Kershaw County was founded in a wooded area on Mecklenburg Road, two miles south of Lynchwood, now the town of Bethune. The church was founded in 1852 by Ellie Copeland and established on land owned by the Copeland family, who deeded most of the 1.68 acre lot in 1895.

(REVERSE) Five buildings have been used for worship services: a log and plank church about 1852–1897; a one room white frame building 1897–1951, sold at auction in 1951; a 1 ½ story brick sanctuary, burned in 1953; the John M. Catoe store building; and this sanctuary, educational building and pastorium dedicated on January 30, 1955. *Erected by Lynches River Historical Society, 1973*
GPS Coordinates: 34° 23.892' N, 80° 19.71' W

28–8 Baruch Home

Broad St. between Walnut & Lafayette Sts., Camden

On this site stood the birthplace and boyhood home of Bernard M. Baruch (1870–1965), financier, philanthropist, and advisor to presidents. He was instrumental in establishing the Camden Hospital, which opened in 1913, as a tribute to his father, Dr. Simon Baruch, surgeon in the Confederate Army and later a pioneer in medicine in New York. *Erected by The City of Camden, 1977*
GPS Coordinates: 34° 14.917' N, 80° 36.445' W

28–9 Midway High School

At the site of the school, U.S. Hwy. 1, Cassatt vicinity

(FRONT) Midway School, established on this site in 1923 with grades 1–11, served Cassatt and other rural areas in Kershaw County near U.S. Hwy. 1 from Little Lynches River to the Shepard community. The high school later added grade 12, then closed in 1966, after forty-three years of service to the area.
(REVERSE) Midway Elementary School continues to operate at this site. The original Midway School building, constructed in 1923, was demolished in 1976 to make way for a new building at Midway Elementary; only its cornerstone survives. A separate gymnasium, built after World War II, still stands. *Erected by Midway School Reunion, 1998*
GPS Coordinates: 34° 20.999' N, 80° 29.741' W

28–10 John C. West Boyhood Home

Cleveland School Rd., just S of I-20, Camden vicinity

This farm was the boyhood home of John Carl West (b. 1922), governor of South Carolina 1971–75. West, a graduate of the Citadel and the University of S.C., served as an intelligence officer in World War II, as state senator 1955–66, and as lieutenant governor 1967–71 before his term as governor. He was later U.S. ambassador to Saudi Arabia 1977–81. *Erected by the Kershaw County Historical Society, 1999*
GPS Coordinates: 34° 12.521' N, 80° 32.141' W

28–11 Mather Academy

Corner of South Campbell and West Dekalb Sts., Camden

(FRONT) Mather Academy was founded in 1887 by the New England Southern Conference of the Women's Home Missionary Society of the Methodist Church. It succeeded a freedmen's school opened during Reconstruction by Sarah Babcock, who returned to Massachusetts, married Rev. James Mather, and became the corresponding secretary of the Southern Conference when it organized in 1883. The Methodists opened a "Model Home and Industrial School" on this site in 1887.
(REVERSE) Mather Academy educated girls, and later boys, in grades 1–11 until grade 12 was added in 1928. The Southern Assn. of Secondary Schools and Colleges gave it an "A" rating in 1937. A new main building, library, chapel, dormitories, and gym were all built between 1900 and 1964. In 1959 Mather merged with the Boylan-Haven School of Jacksonville, Fla., to become Boylan-Haven-Mather Academy. It closed here in 1983; the last building was demolished in 1995. *Erected by the Boylan-Haven-Mather Academy National Alumni Association, 2000*
GPS Coordinates: 34° 14.759' N, 80° 36.691' W

28–12 West's Crossroads/Donald H. Holland House

Intersection of Porter and Holland Rds., Cassatt vicinity

West's Crossroads (FRONT)

This crossroads, long owned by the West family, is the junction of the Georgetown and Porter Bridge Roads, both of which appear on Robert Mills's 1825 *Atlas of S.C.* In early 1865 opposing forces camped nearby as Gen. M. C. Butler's Confederates attempted to slow the advance of Gen. W. T. Sherman's Federals toward N.C., and fought a brief skirmish here on February 25th.

Donald H. Holland House (REVERSE)
The boyhood home of Donald H. Holland (b. 1928), Kershaw County lawyer and legislator, once stood 300 yds. E. Holland, a graduate of the University of South Carolina law school, served as a state representative 1951–54 and 1957–64, as a state highway commissioner 1964–68, and as a state senator 1969-present, serving as chair of the Senate Judiciary Committee 1995-present. *Erected by the Kershaw County Historical Society, 2000*
GPS Coordinates: 34° 23.13′ N, 80° 28.464′ W

28–13 E.H. Dibble Store/Eugene H. Dibble

Corner of Broad and DeKalb Sts., Camden

E. H. Dibble Store (FRONT)
This store, constructed in 1891 on what was then the corner of 6th Avenue (now Broad Street) and DeKalb Streets, was the second home of E. H. Dibble and Brothers Grocery, which sold "general merchandise" as well as "heavy and fancy groceries" and operated in downtown Camden for more than fifty years. "The family is known all over the state," historian Asa Gordon wrote in 1929, "and its achievement in the mercantile business is of historic importance."
Eugene H. Dibble (REVERSE)
Eugene Heriot Dibble (1855–1934), prominent Camden merchant, was the son of Andrew H. and Ellie Naudin Dibble. He also served in the S.C. House 1876–78. The first Dibble store in Camden, founded by Eugene's brothers John Moreau Dibble (1848–1877), was on lower Main Street; after his death Ellie Naudin Dibble and her sons operated it. After E. H. Dibble's death in 1934 an obituary recalled, "he always lent his influence for the good of the community." *Erected by the*

Naudin-Dibble Heritage Foundation, 2001
GPS Coordinates: 34° 14.773′ N, 80° 36.433′ W

28–14 Warrenton Muster Ground

S.C. Hwy. 522, about .02 mi. S of the Lancaster County-Kershaw County line, between Stoneboro and Liberty Hill

(FRONT) The Warrenton Muster Ground, originally known as Gardner's Old Field, was a nineteenth and early-twentieth century meeting place for local militia companies. The area was named Warrenton after thirty families from Warrenton, N.C. settled here shortly after the American Revolution. The Beaver Creek Militia and Liberty Hill Rifles met here for many years.
(REVERSE) The Beaver Creek Militia, made up of men from southern Lancaster and northern Kershaw counties, met here between the Revolution and the Civil War. The Liberty Hill Rifles, made up of men from the same area and Fairfield County as well, met here between the Civil War and about 1910. Both companies mustered for inspections, drills, mock battles, picnics, and political speeches. *Erected by the Kershaw County Historical Society, 2005*
GPS Coordinates: 34° 31.22′ N, 80° 46.279′ W

28–15 Peay's Ferry/Peay's Ferry Road

S.C. Hwy. 97 near its intersection with Peay's Ferry Rd., Liberty Hill

Peay's Ferry (FRONT)
A ferry was operated on the Wateree Point, at a point about 4 mi. W, as early as 1775. In 1808 ferry rights were granted to Thomas Starke, Jr. and Austin Ford Peay (d. 1841), planters with property in Fairfield and Kershaw Districts. Peay received ferry rights for another 7 years in 1825. Peay served in the S.C. House between 1812 and 1831 and in the S.C. Senate between 1832 and 1839.
Peay's Ferry Road (REVERSE)
The road from the Wateree River E to Liberty Hill was known as Peay's Ferry Road by 1820. In 1865, elements of Gen. W. T. Sherman's Federal army crossed the ferry on their way to Camden and Cheraw. In 1919, when the

Wateree Power Co. completed a dam across the Wateree River, the ferry site and most of the road were flooded. This is the only extant portion of the old road. *Erected by the Kershaw County Historical Society, 2005*
GPS Coordinates: 34° 28.347' N, 80° 48.257' W

28–16 Tiller's Ferry

S.C. Hwy. 341 & S.C. Sec. Rd. 28-15, Bethune vicinity

(FRONT) In 1760 Joseph Tiller received a grant for 100 acres on Lynches River, including this crossroads. James Tiller operated a ferry across the river 1 mi. N before 1806. He operated a toll bridge near the ferry, on the Stagecoach or Camden Road, beginning in 1830. A post office opened at Tiller's Ferry in 1838, with James Tiller as its first postmaster; it closed in 1903.
(REVERSE) In 1865, as Gen. W. T. Sherman's Federal army advanced NE, Gen. John A. Logan's XV Corps found its way blocked by a flooded Lynches River. Logan camped and foraged nearby February 25–March 2 before crossing into Darlington County. A skirmish on the other side of the river on February 26 cost Logan's infantry and Gen. M. C. Butler's Confederate cavalry a few minor casualties each. *Erected by the Kershaw County Historical Society, 2011*
GPS Coordinates: 34° 21.784' N, 80° 18.394' W

28–17 Monroe Boykin Park

Campbell St., Camden

(FRONT) In the 1798 city plan, this five-acre park was laid out as a public square. In 1900 the Seaboard Air Line Railway built a passenger depot next to it, on the SW corner of Chesnut & Gordon Sts. The city beautified the square to welcome visitors and named it Seaboard Park. After the depot moved in 1937, the area near it was named Seaboard Park. The present name, first given to an African-American suburb absorbed into Kirkwood, honors Rev. Monroe Boykin.
(REVERSE) Rev. Monroe Boykin (d. 1904), born into slavery, became a community leader after the Civil War. After emancipation he

was given two tracts of land nearby by the heirs of his former owner. In 1866 Boykin and other freedmen withdrew from Camden (First) Baptist Church to form Mount Moriah Baptist Church on Broad St. Boykin, its first pastor, served there for 34 years. He helped found many churches in Kershaw, Clarendon, Sumter, and Lancaster Counties. *Erected by the City of Camden, 2011*
GPS Coordinates: 34° 15.349' N, 80° 36.742' W

28–18 Samuel Mathis House

1409 Broad St., Camden

(FRONT) The Samuel Mathis House, known as "Aberdeen," was built ca. 1805 and is among the oldest extant houses in Camden. It was home to prominent Camden residents Samuel and Margaret Mathis. Samuel (1760–1823) was reportedly the first white male child born in Camden and enjoyed a long career as a soldier, merchant, lawyer, politician, and preacher. He and Margaret Miller (1776–1845) were married in 1793. They had two daughters who survived to adulthood.
(REVERSE) Despite being raised as a Quaker, Mathis enlisted in Kershaw's Battalion of S.C. Militia in 1776. He was captured and paroled in 1780, but broke parole and fought with Francis Marion in 1781. After the war, Mathis operated a mercantile business with his brother-in-law Joseph Kershaw. He was admitted to the S.C. Bar in 1790 and served in numerous public offices, including the S.C. House, Intendant (Mayor) of Camden, and two terms as Ordinary for Kershaw District. *Sponsored by the Camden Archives and Museum, 2018*
GPS Coordinates: 34° 15.161' N, 80° 36.471' W

28–19 The Price House

802 Broad St., Camden

(FRONT) The Price House dates to 1829–30 and was built shortly after the Camden fire of 1829 burned many of the homes and businesses on Broad St. The Greek Revival home is representative of other buildings that once stood nearby, with the lower floor devoted to commercial use and the upper floor to residential. Today it is a unique example of this form in

Camden. For much of its history the lower floor served as a dry goods store, known locally as the "Old Brick Corner" by the 1870s. (REVERSE) In 1902 Susan S. Price purchased the building. She and her husband, Richard Price, ran a grocery out of the ground floor and lived above. Susan conveyed the store to her daughter, Fannie, in 1913 and she continued

to run the business until her death in 1954. The building, which stands as a symbol of the African American business community in Camden, was acquired by Richard Lloyd and donated to the city in 1961. It is part of the City of Camden Historic District. *Sponsored by the City of Camden, 2018*
GPS Coordinates: 34° 14.461' N, 80° 36.388' W

Lancaster County

29–00 Birthplace of Dr. James Marion Sims

U.S. Hwy. 521, just N of Salem Cemetery, near its intersection with S.C. Sec. Rd. 29–34, Heath Springs vicinity

About 1 ¾ miles west of this spot stood the house in which Dr. James Marion Sims was born on January 25, 1818. Father of modern gynecology, Dr. Sims was honored by the American and by European governments for his service to suffering women, empress and slave alike. Dr. Sims died in the city of New York on November 13, 1883. *Erected by Lancaster County, 1949; Sponsored by the Waxhaws Chapter, Daughters of the American Revolution*
GPS Coordinates: 34° 36.096' N, 80° 41.016' W

29–1 Battle of Hanging Rock

Intersection of Flat Rock Rd. & U.S. Hwy. 521, Heath Springs

About 2.5 miles south is Hanging Rock, where Maj. Davie surprised a British force, Aug. 1, 1780, and killed or wounded most of them. There also, Aug. 6, 1780, Col. Hill, Col. Irwin, and Maj. Davie, all under Gen. Sumter, successfully attacked the Prince of Wales's American Regiment and detachments of the 63rd and of the 71st Infantries, under Maj. Carden. *Erected by Lancaster County, 1941*
GPS Coordinates: 34° 35.378' N, 80° 40.476' W

29–2 Buford's Bloody Battleground

Lancaster County Park, S.C. Hwy. 522 just S of intersection of S.C. Hwy. 522 & S.C. Hwy. 9, between Lancaster and Tradesville

Col. Buford's 11th Virginia Regiment and a detachment of Washington's Cavalry, retreating after the fall of Charles Town, were attacked by Col. Tarleton, May 29, 1780, at the site of the monument 955 feet southwest. The American loss was 113 killed, 150 wounded, 53 made prisoners; the British, 5 killed, 14 wounded. In that grave lie many of Col. Buford's men. *Erected by Lancaster County, 1941*
GPS Coordinates: 34° 44.648' N, 80° 37.566' W

29–3 Waxhaw Presbyterian Church

Marker # 1: U.S. Hwy. 521 & S.C. Sec. Rd. 29–775, N of Lancaster

Marker # 2: S.C. Hwy. 9 at the S.C. Hwy. 9 Bypass, W of Lancaster

About 3 miles W. is Waxhaw Presbyterian Church, organized 1755, first church in upper South Carolina. President Andrew Jackson, born nearby, was baptized there. His father lies in the churchyard with other early settlers of the Waxhaws and many veterans of various wars, including: Gen. Wm. R. Davie, Maj. Robt. Crawford, Major John Barkley, Col. J. H. Witherspoon, Isaac Donnom. *Erected by Lancaster County, 1948*
GPS Coordinates: 34° 48.786' N, 80° 48.096' W

29–4 The Courthouse Lancaster County/John Simpson

Lancaster County Courthouse, Main St., Lancaster

The Courthouse Lancaster County (FRONT)
Built in 1825–1828. Designed by Robert Mills of Charleston, South Carolina, America's first native born, professionally trained architect, State Civil and Military Engineer and designer of the Washington Monument.
John Simpson (REVERSE)
in 1792 gave a courthouse site to the people of the region known as Lancaster County (1785–1798), Lancaster District (1798–1868), and Lancaster County since 1868. Three courthouses have occupied the site: a log house (1795–1800), a frame building (1800–1828), and the present structure. *Erected by the Waxhaws Chapter, Daughters of the American Revolution, 1957*
GPS Coordinates: 34° 43.218' N, 80° 46.251' W

29–5 The Jail/Robert Mills

208 W. Gray St., Lancaster

The Jail (FRONT)
Lancaster County. Built, 1823. This is the "gaol" that Willis W. Alsobrook contracted to build for LANCASTER DISTRICT ". . . agreeable to the plans and specifications signed by Robert Mills . . ." In 1868 Lancaster District became Lancaster County and this structure became the Lancaster County Jail.
Robert Mills (REVERSE)
Robert Mills of Charleston, South Carolina, Civil and Military Engineer of his state, was America's first native born, professionally-trained architect. He is best known as the designer of the Washington Monument. *Erected by the Waxhaws Chapter, Daughters of the American Revolution, 1958*
GPS Coordinates: 34° 43.092' N, 80° 46.32' W

29–6 Lancaster Normal and Industrial Institute

East Barr St., Lancaster

(FRONT) Located on this site, Lancaster Normal and Industrial Institute for black students was incorporated in 1905; M. D. Lee was president and J. G. McIlwain chairman of the board.

By 1912, the school was offering both elementary and advanced education to a number of students, many of whom trained for industrial employment or as teachers.
(REVERSE) This school, incorporated in 1905, was operated by the General Conference of the African Methodist Episcopal Zion Church. By 1908 the campus included the Springs Industrial Building, named in honor of Colonel Leroy Springs (a benefactor of the institute), and the Clinton Young Men's Building, named for African Methodist Episcopal Zion Bishop I. C. Clinton. *Erected by Lancaster County Historical Commission, 1977*
GPS Coordinates: 34° 43.446' N, 80° 46.056' W

29–7 King Hagler's Murder

Rock Hill Hwy. (S.C. Hwy. 5), 2 mi. W of Charlotte Hwy. (U.S. Hwy. 521), Van Wyck vicinity

On the Catawba Path near here/King Hagler,/ Chief of the Catawba Nation/(1750–1763),/was slain on August 30, 1763, by a raiding band of northern Indian braves as he journeyed from the Waxhaws Settlement on Cane Creek to a Catawba town on Twelve Mile Creek. *Erected by the Waxhaws Chapter, Daughters of the American Revolution, 1965*
GPS Coordinates: 34° 50.802' N, 80° 51.048' W

29–8 Franklin Academy/Oldest Continuous Public School Site in Lancaster County

Central Elementary School, Dunlap St., Lancaster

Franklin Academy (FRONT)
Organized in 1825, was the most widely-known of the four schools that occupied this site. Henry Connelly was its first principal. J. Marion Sims who later achieved world fame as a surgeon was one of its pupils. The building of brick was said by Robert Mills to be a fine structure, two stories high.
Oldest Continuous Public School Site in Lancaster County (REVERSE)
This land has been dedicated to the cause of education since 1799 when Rev. John Brown, Dr. Samuel C. Dunlap, Wm. Nisbet, John Ingram, and John Montgomery were named trustees for a school, known in 1802 as Lancaster Academy. It grew into Franklin

Academy, 1825, the Graded School, 1893, and Central School, 1915. *Erected by Waxhaws Chapter, Daughters of the American Revolution, 1967*

GPS Coordinates: 34° 43.14' N, 80° 46.416' W

29–9 Birthplace of Andrew Jackson

U.S. Hwy. 521, S of Andrew Jackson State Park, Van Wyck vicinity

Seventh President of the United States. Near this site on South Carolina soil, Andrew Jackson was born on March 15, 1767, at the plantation whereon James Crawford lived and where Jackson himself said he was born. *Erected by the Waxhaws Chapter, Daughters of the American Revolution, 1967*

GPS Coordinates: 34° 50.568' N, 80° 48.618' W

29–10 James Ingram Home

Flat Rock Rd. (S.C. Sec. Rd. 29-15) at its intersection with Hanging Rock Rd. (S.C. Sec. Rd. 29-467), about 2.5 mi. S of Heath Springs

While on his Southern tour, President George Washington spent the night of May 26, 1791, at the James Ingram house, near here. According to Washington's diary, he left Ingram's at four o'clock the next morning and continued his journey northward, traveling eighteen miles before breakfast. Sherman's Army is said to have destroyed the house in 1865. *Erected by Waxhaws Chapter, Daughters of the American Revolution, 1970*

GPS Coordinates: 34° 33.972' N, 80° 40.356' W

29–11 Barr's Tavern Site

E of U.S. Hwy. 521 at N city limits of Lancaster

On the morning of May 27, 1791, President George Washington had breakfast near here at Nathan Barr's Tavern, which was located about a mile and a half north of the present Lancaster Courthouse. According to local tradition, Washington paid for his meal by giving Barr's young daughter half of a Spanish dollar he had cut with his sword. *Erected by Waxhaws Chapter, Daughters of the American Revolution, 1970*

GPS Coordinates: 34° 44.514' N, 80° 46.674' W

29–12 Major Crawford's Home

Rock Hill Hwy. (S.C. Hwy. 5), ¼ mi. W of its intersection with Charlotte Hwy. (U.S. Hwy. 521), Van Wyck vicinity

Near this site was the home of Major Robert Crawford, where President George Washington spent his last night in South Carolina on his Southern tour, May 27, 1791. Here Washington was met by a delegation of the Chiefs of the Catawba Nation, who set forth their apprehensions that attempts would be made to deprive them of their land. *Erected by Waxhaws Chapter, Daughters of the American Revolution, 1970*

GPS Coordinates: 34° 50.118' N, 80° 48.798' W

29–13 Mt. Carmel Campground

Mt. Carmel Rd. (S.C. Sec. Rd. 29-19), just S of its intersection with S.C. Sec. Rd. 29-620, S of Cauthen's Crossroads

(FRONT) According to local tradition, this African Methodist Episcopal Zion Campground was established ca. 1870. Instrumental in organizing the campground was former slave Isom Caleb Clinton, who was ordained Bishop of the church in 1892. Through the years the campground has flourished; hundreds now participate in the annual ecumenical encampment.

(REVERSE) Mt. Carmel A.M.E.Z. Campground was entered in the National Register of Historic Places in 1979. Frederick A. Clinton (1834–1890), organizer and lifetime trustee of Mt. Carmel, brother of Bishop I. C. Clinton and the first Lancaster County black elected to the S.C. Senate (1870–1877), is buried here. *Erected by Mt. Carmel A.M.E. Zion Church, 1981*

GPS Coordinates: 34° 35.814' N, 80° 46.671' W

29–14 Boundary Line

Andrew Jackson State Park, Charlotte Hwy. (U.S. Hwy. 521), Van Wyck vicinity

One of the last refinements in the N.C.–S.C. boundary was marked with a stone inscribed "1813" and located about ½ mile SE of here. This adjustment was made because of uncertainty in location of the Salisbury Road which

had served as north-south boundary from the western terminus of the state line, surveyed in 1764, to the Catawba Indian lands of 1763. *Erected by Lancaster County Historical Commission, 1983*
GPS Coordinates: 34° 49.656' N, 80° 48.21' W

29–15 Lancasterville Presbyterian Church

W. Gay St. between S. French St. & Plyler St., Lancaster

This congregation was organized May 5, 1835. Its first minister was James H. Thornwell, who later headed S.C. College in Columbia. The Gothic Revival building was dedicated 1862 and entered in the National Register of Historic Places in 1977. The congregation, now First Presbyterian Church, moved in 1926 and this building, purchased in 1961 by Dr. Ben F. Emanuel, was presented to the community in 1976. *Erected by Lancaster County Historical Commission, 1985*
GPS Coordinates: 34° 43.05' N, 80° 46.398' W

29–16 Kilburnie

1824 Craig Farm Rd, Lancaster

This late Federal-style house blending elements of the Greek-revival style with Victorian-era modifications was built by local dentist Joseph Lee between 1826 and 1834. Thought to be the oldest residence in the town of Lancaster, Kilburnie was owned by the Crawford family for a number of years and was entered in the National Register of Historic Places in 1979. *Erected by the Lancaster County Historical Commission, 1984*
GPS Coordinates: 34° 45.411' N, 80° 46.044' W

29–17 Leroy Springs House

Corner of Gay & Catawba Sts., Lancaster

The original part of this house was built by Robert W. Gill soon after he purchased the lot in 1828. About thirty years later, it was enlarged by Samuel B. Massey. Local textile manufacturer and banker Col. Leroy Springs remodeled the house 1906–1907. Springs' son Elliott, noted author and World War I flying

ace, was born here, 1896. The house became city hall after a 1957 lease-purchase agreement with the city of Lancaster. *Erected by Lancaster County Historical Commission, 1988*
GPS Coordinates: 34° 43.104' N, 80° 46.266' W

29–18 Stephen Decatur Miller

Intersection of Charlotte Hwy. (U.S. Hwy. 521) & W. Rebound Rd. (S.C. Hwy. 75), Van Wyck vicinity

(FRONT) Governor of South Carolina from 1828 until 1830, Miller was born near here May 8, 1787, the son of Charles and Margaret White Miller. He served in the U.S. House of Representatives (1822–1828), S.C. Senate (1822–1828) and U.S. Senate (1831–1833). He died March 8, 1838 in Raymond, Mississippi and is buried there.

(REVERSE) After his graduation from South Carolina College in 1808 and his admission to the bar in 1811, Miller practiced law for many years. He was one of South Carolina's foremost leaders of the states' rights movement, which culminated in the ordinance of nullification, 1832. A Diary From Dixie is based upon diaries kept by his daughter, Mary Boykin Chesnut. *Erected by Lancaster County Historical Commission, 1989*
GPS Coordinates: 34° 51.909' N, 80° 48.318' W

29–19 Beaver Creek Skirmish/ Capture of Provisions at Flat Rock

Intersection of Flat Rock Rd. (S.C. Sec. Rd. 29-15) and Kershaw Country Club Rd. (S.C. Sec. Rd. 29-13), S of Heath Springs, near the Lancaster County-Kershaw County line

Beaver Creek Skirmish (FRONT)
American forces under Major William R. Davie had captured a British convoy July 21, 1780, and were retreating with prisoners mounted two to the horse when ambushed by British several miles west of here on Beaver Creek. Nearly all the British prisoners were killed or wounded. One American was killed and two were wounded.
Capture of Provisions at Flat Rock (REVERSE)
Near here on July 21, 1780, an American expedition commanded by Major William R.

Davie captured a convoy of provisions, spirits, and clothing destined for British troops at Hanging Rock. Davie withdrew at dusk with the British captives and their horses. *Erected by Flat Rock Chapter, National Society of The Daughters of the American Revolution, 1977*
GPS Coordinates: 34° 31.248' N, 80° 38.691' W

29–20 Flat Creek Baptist Church

3737 Victory Rd., just S of Old Jefferson Rd. (S.C. Hwy. 265), Midway community, Kershaw vicinity

This church, organized July 4, 1776 by Rev. George Pope, a native of Virginia, held its first meetings in a brush arbor on this site and was known as the Upper Fork of Lynches Creek until it was renamed Flat Creek Baptist Church in 1881. The first permanent sanctuary, a log building, was replaced by a frame sanctuary which burned in 1912; the present sanctuary was built in 1913. *Erected by the Lancaster County Historical Commission, 1997*
GPS Coordinates: 34° 37.734' N, 80° 27.984' W

29–21 Camp Creek Methodist Church

4721 Great Falls Hwy., Lancaster vicinity

(FRONT) This church, organized in 1798 by Bishop Francis Asbury, held its first services in a log meeting house. On July 10, 1798, Middleton McDonald donated the meeting house and ten acres to church trustees Gideon Glaze, John Graham, George Hicklin, Thomas Howze, and William Marlowe.
(REVERSE) Rev. William Capers was one of the first and most renowned ministers of Camp Creek. In 1809 he was assigned to the Wateree Circuit, including this and 23 other churches. This sanctuary, the third here, was built of hand-hewn timbers about 1834–35. It was moved about 140 feet closer to the road and renovated in 1952. *Erected by the Congregation, 2000*
GPS Coordinates: 34° 37.152' N, 80° 51.24' W

29–22 Clinton Memorial Cemetery /Isom C. Clinton

Clinton School Rd., Lancaster

Clinton Memorial Cemetery (FRONT)
More than 300 members of Lancaster's black community are buried here, with the first grave dating to 1864. Originally the Clinton family cemetery, it was donated to Mt. Zion A.M.E. Church in 1960 by Dr. John J. Clinton (1889–1974). Prominent citizens buried here include clergymen, educators, businessmen, and politicians, and many veterans of American wars from World War I through Vietnam.
Isom C. Clinton (REVERSE)
This cemetery is named for Isom Caleb Clinton (1830–1904), buried here with his family. Born a slave, Clinton organized Mt. Carmel A.M.E. Zion Church in 1866 and served as an elder for many years until he became a bishop in the A.M.E. Zion Church in 1892. He also founded one of the first black public schools in Lancaster County and served as county treasurer both during and after Reconstruction. An obituary called Clinton's influence "manifest in this community and throughout the county." *Erected by the Lancaster County History Commission, 2001*
GPS Coordinates: 34° 43.47' N, 80° 46.008' W

29–23 Kershaw

Intersection of N. Hampton St. (U.S. Hwy. 521) and E. Hilton St. (U.S. Hwy. 601), Kershaw

(FRONT) Kershaw, originally Welsh's Station, was founded in 1888 when Capt. James V. Welsh (1845–1906) persuaded the Charleston, Cincinnati, & Chicago Railroad to build a depot halfway between Camden and Lancaster, on what was then the county line between Kershaw and Lancaster Counties. The town was incorporated later that year and renamed in honor of Maj. Gen. Joseph B. Kershaw (1822–1894), prominent Confederate general and state senator from Camden.
(REVERSE) Kershaw, with a population of 500 by 1890, grew even more dramatically after an 1897 fire which destroyed most of the downtown. By 1900 a guide to Lancaster County called it "a pretty and prosperous town of about fifteen hundred inhabitants." Among

the most significant early businesses here were the Kershaw Oil Mill (1902) and the Kershaw Cotton Mill (1912). The Benton Hotel on S. Cleveland St. was well known and frequently hosted tourists visiting the nearby Haile Gold Mine. *Erected by the King Alfred Garden Club and the Kershaw Centennial Commission, 2002*
GPS Coordinates: 34° 33.696' N, 80° 35.256' W

29-24 Kershaw's First Library

N. Cleveland St., Kershaw

This building, originally just south of Kershaw on what is now U.S. Hwy. 521, was built in 1900 for Capt. James V. Welsh (1845–1906) as the office for J. V. Welsh & Sons, a lumber mill. It later housed Kershaw's first circulating library, founded by the McDowell Music Club, from its creation in 1934 until a new library was built in 1949. The building, moved to this site in 2001, serves as the office for the Stevens Foundation. *Erected by the Stevens Foundation and the Kershaw Centennial Commission, 2002*
GPS Coordinates: 34° 32.844' N, 80° 34.986' W

29-25 Welsh's Station/Kershaw Depot

At the Kershaw Depot, N. Cleveland St., Kershaw

Welsh's Station (FRONT)
Welsh's Station, a depot on the Charleston, Cincinnati, & Chicago Railroad built in 1888, stood at or near this site. The town of Kershaw was first named for Capt. James V. Welsh, who donated 63 acres on which to establish a town and promised the railroad title to every other lot laid out in it. When it was incorporated in 1888 the town limits of Kershaw extended one-half mile in every direction from the depot.
Kershaw Depot (REVERSE)
This depot, built in 1926 by the Southern Railway, replaced a late 19th-early 20th century passenger and freight depot/cotton platform which burned that year. It is typical of 20th-century depots built throughout the Southeast. Primarily a passenger station, it also handled cotton and textile products from nearby farms and textile or cotton oil mills. The Kershaw Depot was listed in the National

Register of Historic Places in 1990. *Erected by the Lancaster County History Commission, 2002*
GPS Coordinates: 34° 32.877' N, 80° 34.986' W

29-26 Lancaster

In the park at the corner of S. Main and Arch Sts., Lancaster

(FRONT) Lancaster, founded in 1798, was first called Lancaster Court House and later known as Lancasterville. The seat of Lancaster District from 1800 to 1868, it has been the seat of Lancaster County since then. The town and county were named for Lancaster, Pennsylvania, the home of the Scots-Irish families who moved to this part of the South Carolina backcountry by the 1750s. Lancaster was the only incorporated town in the county until after the Civil War.
(REVERSE) The town grew rapidly as upcountry cotton production increased between 1800 and 1830, but grew more slowly for the next fifty years. Lancaster, revitalized by the arrival of the railroad in the 1880s and the rise of the textile industry in the 1890s, was described as "delightful and flourishing" in 1900. The Lancaster Downtown Historic District, a collection of significant public and commercial buildings, was listed in the National Register of Historic Places in 1984. *Erected by the Lancaster County Historical Commission, 2004*
GPS Coordinates: 34° 43.065' N, 80° 46.17' W

29-27 Haile Gold Mine

Haile Gold Mine Rd., Kershaw vicinity

(FRONT) In 1827 Benjamin Haile (1768–1842) found gold here while panning in the streams on his plantation. After he found gold ore as well, Haile set up a mining operation. By 1837 the Haile Gold Mine included a 5-stamp mill, with steel stamps or pestles that crushed ore into dust from which gold was extracted. Haile leased small plots to entrepreneurs who used slave labor to mine gold.
(REVERSE) The mine was not successful until the 1880s, when its owners hired Adolf Thies (1832–1917), a German mining engineer

who perfected a new extraction process. A 60-stamp mill processed 100 tons a day, producing more gold than any mine east of the Mississippi. After a deadly boiler explosion in 1908, the mine closed in 1912. It operated briefly during World Wars I and II and the 1990s. *Erected by the Lancaster County Historical Commission, 2004*
GPS Coordinates: 34° 34.51' N, 80° 33.309' W

29–28 The Revolution in the Backcountry/Sumter's Camp at Clems Branch

Harrisburg Rd. (S.C. Sec. Rd. 64), between Hancock and Fort Mill

The Revolution in the Backcountry (FRONT)
After British forces took Charleston in May 1780, they set up outposts in the backcountry and attempted to control the state by encouraging Loyalists. Backcountry Patriots organized a resistance in response, with an important camp ½ mi. E at Clems Branch of Sugar Creek, on the wagon road from Camden to Charlotte.
Sumter's Camp at Clems Branch (REVERSE)
In June 1780 Col. Thomas Sumter's troops were among the few organized Patriot units in S.C. The camp at Clems Branch gave him a strategic location, water, and forage while reinforcements joined him in late June and early July. Sumter's troops would play a major role in several Patriot victories in 1780 and 1781. *Erected by the Lancaster County Historical Commission, 2006*
GPS Coordinates: 35° 1.566' N, 80° 52.248' W

29–29 Lancaster & Chester Railway

512 S. Main St., Lancaster

(FRONT) The Lancaster & Chester Railway, founded in 1896, was originally the Cheraw & Chester Railroad, chartered in 1873. The C&C, which never finished its route, was sold to Col. Leroy Springs (1861–1931) for $25,000 and renamed the Lancaster & Chester Railway. A narrow gauge line, running only 29 miles from Chester to Lancaster, it was later converted to standard gauge track in 1902 at a cost of $125,000.

(REVERSE) The L&C carried freight and passengers 1896–1913 but only freight after a 1913 accident. Springs's son Elliott White Springs (1896–1959) succeeded him as President. He named 29 Vice Presidents, one for each mile of the road. This depot, built in 1951 and designed by Joe Croxton, included the L&C offices. From 1902 to 1994 Springs Mills was the L&C's largest customer, hauling coal and cotton to its plants. *Erected by the Lancaster County Historical Commission, 2008*
GPS Coordinates: 34° 42.87' N, 80° 46.023' W

29–30 Thomas L. Clyburn House

5082 Gold Mine Hwy., Kershaw

Thomas Lorenzo Clyburn (1809–1869), prominent planter of Lancaster District and the first postmaster of Butler, 1853–56, lived here and is buried in the family cemetery nearby. He and his first wife Katherine Blue Clyburn had two sons, Benjamin Rutledge (1840–1877) and Thomas Franklin (1843–1896), who were Confederate officers and in the S.C. General Assembly after the war. Benjamin, major of the 2nd S.C. Infantry, was wounded and captured, then served in the S.C. House 1865–66. Frank, lieutenant colonel of the 12th S.C. Infantry, was also wounded, then served in the S.C. House 1868–70 and the S.C. Senate 1882–85. William Uriah (1857–1917), son of T. L. Clyburn and his second wife Martha Williams Clyburn, served in the S.C. House 1884–85. *Sponsored by the Town of Kershaw Historical Society, 2012*
GPS Coordinates: 34° 35.174' N, 80° 32.990' W

29–31 Ashe's Ferry

S.C. Hwy. 5 (Rock Hill Hwy.), just E of the Catawba River, Van Wyck

(FRONT) A ferry nearby crossed the Catawba River between Lancaster County and York County for more than 30 years and was the last state-run ferry in S.C. It was built in 1927–28 by William N. Ashe (1862–1932), owner of the nearby Ashe Brick Company, to transport bricks and crops. As a private ferry it charged 25¢ for buggies and 35¢ for cars but was free after it became a public ferry.

(REVERSE) The ferry was taken over by the S.C. Highway Department in 1944. It was operated for many years by Early Morgan Brown (1891–1963), a Catawba Indian who lived on the York County side of the river. The ferry, pushed by poles until a small motor was installed in 1955, closed in 1959 after the construction of a bridge on S.C. Hwy. 5 that spanned the river. *Sponsored by the Lancaster County Historical Commission, 2014*
GPS Coordinates: 34° 51.240' N, 80° 52.031' W

29–32 Lancaster County Home and Cemetery

Pageland Hwy (S.C. Hwy 9) and Old Dixie School Rd (State Rd S-29-70), Lancaster

(FRONT) The Lancaster Commissioners of the Poor were established in 1791 to provide support for the orphaned, aged, and indigent. In 1867 Dr. J. Marion Sims donated $1,000 in gold to the Commission. They used the funds to improve and expand the county poor house, renaming it the Sims Home. A new, 16-room home was completed in 1914 and replaced the old complex, which had consisted of a number of smaller buildings.
(REVERSE) The Lancaster County Home continued to serve the local population, including both white and black, until the 1940s. Today, however, all that remains of the old county home is the cemetery. The earliest known

burials date to 1818 and the last dates to 1954. Because most buried here died as paupers it is likely that there are additional burials that remain unmarked. *Sponsored by the Lancaster County Historical Commission, 2017*
GPS Coordinates: 34° 43.436' N, 80° 43.590' W

29–33 Old Six Mile Cemetery

Adjacent to 8175 Henry Harris Rd., Fort Mill, S.C.

(FRONT) Congregants of Six Mile Spring Presbyterian Church, later known as Six Mile Creek Church, established this cemetery ca. 1790. The original church's exact location is unknown, but it is said to have burned down ca. 1804. By 1835, the congregation had left the immediate vicinity and built a new church approx. 1.5 miles southwest of here. Congregants began another cemetery at the new site. (REVERSE) Burials continued at Old Six Mile Cemetery as late as the mid-1800s. Among those interred here are the Morrow, Hagins, Coffey, and Patton families. The buried include several veterans of the Revolutionary War and War of 1812. The oldest known grave belongs to William Hagins (ca. 1727–1790), an Irish immigrant and officer in the Mecklenburg County (N.C.) Regiment of Militia. *Sponsored by Friends of Old Six Mile Cemetery and Faith Presbyterian Church (USA), 2019*
GPS Coordinates: 34° 56.900' N, 80° 49.311' W

Laurens County

30–1 Jefferson Davis' Flight

Intersection of S.C. Hwy. 56 & Jefferson Davis Rd. (S.C. Sec. Rd. 29-38), about 2 ½ mi. SW of Joanna

Jefferson Davis/President of the Confederacy/ on his flight from Richmond, Va./with his Cabinet and other/high ranking officers/spent the night of April 30, 1865/at the house 1 ½ miles west/then the home of Lafayette Young./ Arriving there from Union/Davis left early next morning/for Cokesbury and Abbeville. *Erected by Stephen D. Lee Chapter No. 1066,*

United Daughters of the Confederacy, Clinton, South Carolina, 1961
GPS Coordinates: 34° 22.917' N, 81° 51.517' W

30–2 Rosemont

Intersection of U.S. Hwy. 221 & Dillard Rd. (S.C. Sec. Rd. 30-149), Waterloo vicinity

About 2 ½ miles southwest, a granite monument stands on the site of Rosemont, birthplace and home of Ann Pamela Cunningham, founder and first regent of the Mount Vernon

Ladies' Association of the Union. Through her efforts Mount Vernon was purchased by the association in 1858, and Washington's home was restored and maintained for posterity. *Erected by Ann Pamela Cunningham Chapter, Daughters of the American Revolution, 1974*
GPS Coordinates: 34° 19.05' N, 82° 3.722' W

30–3 Providence Associate Reformed Presbyterian Church–First Marker

W. Carolina Ave. (U.S. Hwy. 76), near Copeland Plaza, 1 mi. W of Clinton

The cemetery, located about ½ mile SW, marks the original site of this church, founded Sept. 10, 1836. Buried here is William Blakely, Sr., survivor of Hayes Station Massacre, 1781, who with Samuel Blakely donated the land for the church and cemetery. The congregation moved to Clinton about 1902. *Erected by the Congregation, 1977*
GPS Coordinates: 34° 28.167' N, 81° 54.433' W

30–4 Providence Associate Reformed Presbyterian Church–Second Marker

350 yds. N of S.C. Sec. Rd. 30–43, about 1.2 mi. W of Clinton

This cemetery marks the original site of Providence Associate Reformed Presbyterian Church, founded Sept. 10, 1836. Buried here is William Blakely, Sr., survivor of Hayes Station Massacre, 1781, who with Samuel Blakely donated the land for the church and cemetery. The congregation moved to Clinton about 1902. *Erected by the Congregation, 1977*
GPS Coordinates: 34° 28.167' N, 81° 54.433' W

30–5 Young's School

Intersection of Young's Schoolhouse Rd. (S.C. Sec. Rd. 30–399) & Harris Bridge Rd. (S.C. Sec. Rd. 30–263), Youngs community, about 6 mi. N of Gray Court

Here at Young's School in 1915 Dr. Wil Lou Gray (1883–1984) initiated for her native county of Laurens a seven-school program of night education for adults, which led to

the adoption of a state-wide system and her national recognition as a tireless and effective opponent of illiteracy. *Erected by Young's Community Association and Laurens County Historical Society, 1984*
GPS Coordinates: 34° 40.532' N, 82° 3.843' W

30–6 Laurens County/Laurens Historic District

Laurens County Courthouse, Courthouse Square, Laurens

Laurens County (FRONT)
Laurens County was one of the six counties created from Ninety-Six District March 12, 1785. The courthouse here, built in 1838 by Dr. John W. Simpson, and remodeled and enlarged in 1858, 1911, 1940, and 1973, was entered in the National Register of Historic Places in 1972. Three Laurens women, Ann Pamela Cunningham, Dr. Wil Lou Gray, and Dr. Anne A. Young are in the S.C. Hall of Fame.

Laurens Historic District (REVERSE)
This historic district, part of a Royal landgrant to John Rodgers in 1774, was entered in the National Register of Historic Places in 1980. It includes the courthouse square and surrounding commercial buildings and extends north and west into residential areas. In the 1820s Andrew Johnson, 17th president of the U.S., worked as a tailor here. S.C. governors Wm. D. Simpson & Robert A. Cooper were natives of Laurens. *Erected by Laurens County Historical Society and Laurens County, 1985*
GPS Coordinates: 34° 29.972' N, 82° 0.862' W

30–7 Masonic Lodge #19/Samuel Saxon

Corner of East Main & Harper Sts., Laurens

Masonic Lodge (FRONT)
The first recorded meeting of this organization, known as Palmetto Lodge #19, took place Aug. 7, 1794, at the Samuel Saxon home, which stood nearby. Officers present were: Master, Joseph Downs; Deputy Master, Nathaniel McCoy; Senior Warden, Wm. Holiday; Junior Warden, John Wolff; and Secretary, Ezekiel Roland. Still in existence, this is the

oldest known masonic lodge in Laurens County; its minutes date from 1794.

Samuel Saxon (REVERSE)
In 1792, this local attorney, merchant and Palmetto Lodge member conveyed the present court house land to Laurens County for the sum of two guineas. Saxon also cleared a number of surrounding acres. He served in the S.C. House 1789–91; was elected sheriff of Ninety Six District 1791. His home was located on the south side of present East Main St., about 150 feet east of here. *Erected by Palmetto Lodge #19 and Laurens County Historical Society, 1985*
GPS Coordinates: 34° 29.933' N, 82° 0.801' W

30–8 Lindley's Fort/Jonathon Downs

S.C. Sec. Rd. 30-398, about 2 mi. S of its intersection with S.C. Hwy. 252, W of Laurens

Lindley's Fort (FRONT)
On July 15, 1776, a number of Indians and Tories attacked this frontier fort where area settlers had gathered for protection. Major Jonathan Downs, with a company of men, had arrived the previous evening & helped repulse the attack. This victory gave encouragement to the American cause locally. The site is located about 600 yds. south.

Jonathan Downs (REVERSE)
One of the Justices of the Peace to select a courthouse site for Laurens County, Jonathan Downs was a member of the 1st & 2nd Provincial Congresses and served in the South Carolina General Assembly. His Revolutionary War service included the Laurens County battles of Lindley's Fort (1776), where he was commander & Hayes' Station (1781). He died in 1818. *Erected by Laurens County Council and Laurens County Historical Society, 1990*
GPS Coordinates: 34° 27.667' N, 82° 7.004' W

30–9 Watts-Todd-Dunklin House

544 W. Main St., Laurens

(FRONT) The Watts-Todd-Dunklin House, built about 1818, is an excellent example of a Federal-era upcountry farmhouse. According to family tradition, it was built for

Washington Williams (1777–1829), who gave it to his daughter Nancy (1799–1845) when she married James Watts, Jr. (1795–1833). In 1845 Nancy Watts sold the house and 30 acres to Samuel R. Todd (1809–1891). It remained in the Todd family until 1938.

(REVERSE) The Todd family owned this house from 1845 to 1938. It then passed through a succession of owners until 1950, when James Gray Dunklin (1911–1973), an antiques collector and historic preservationist, acquired it. Dunklin, who restored the house, donated it to the Laurens County Landmarks Foundation as a house museum upon his death in 1973. It was listed in the National Register of Historic Places in 1974. *Erected by the Laurens County Landmarks Foundation, 2001*
GPS Coordinates: 34° 29.783' N, 82° 1.34' W

30–10 Laurens County Training School

Just off West Mill St., Gray Court

(FRONT) The Laurens County Training School, located here 1924–1954, had its origins in Gray Court School, a one-room school founded ca. 1890 on the grounds of Pleasant View Baptist Church. The training school, opened in 1924 in a building constructed with assistance from the Rosenwald Fund, taught grades 8–11 until 1948.

(REVERSE) This school, at first emphasizing farming and homemaking skills, later expanded its curriculum to include more academic courses and became an accredited high school in 1948–49 with the addition of grade 12. The school closed and was later demolished when Laurens County schools were consolidated in 1954. *Erected by the Laurens County Training School Alumni Committee, 2001*
GPS Coordinates: 34° 36.317' N, 82° 7.134' W

30–11 Martin's Store

Indian Mound Rd. (S.C. Sec. Rd. 30-6), Mt. Gallagher community, Ware Shoals vicinity

(FRONT) This store, first known as Daniel's store or the "Beehive," was built before the Civil War by James Wright Daniel (1814–1904) and several business partners. In 1878 James

Martin (1815–1879) bought the store from the other partners and became sole owner until his death early the next year. Martin's son J. C. Martin (1861–1949) and his grandsons ran this general store for the next 119 years.
(REVERSE) The grandsons, J. Y. Martin (1906–1969) and J. H. Martin (1907–2000) continued to operate the store until it closed in 1997. It sold groceries, dry goods, automotive and farm supplies; was a polling place; housed a doctor's office and was the site of many community gatherings. The Masons, the Grange, and the Woodmen of the World held meetings on the second floor for many years. *Erected by the Laurens County Historical Society, 2004*
GPS Coordinates: 34° 23.95' N, 82° 11.817' W

30–12 Rich Hill

Corner of E. Hampton and Silver Sts., Laurens
(FRONT) This African-American neighborhood, roughly bounded by N. Caroline St., E. Hampton St., Laurel St., and E. Laurens St., was an uncleared forest owned by James H. Irby and then N. B. Dial before the Civil War. After 1865 so many freedmen and women bought lots and built homes here that by the 1880s the area was called "Rich Hill." The historic houses here, most from the first half of the 20th century, reflect such architectural styles as Queen Anne and Craftsman.
(REVERSE) Bethel A.M.E. Church, founded in 1868, and St. Paul First Baptist Church, founded in 1877, anchor this neighborhood. The present Bethel A.M.E. Church was built in 1910 and the present St. Paul First Baptist Church was built in 1912. Both are brick Romanesque Revival churches designed and built by local contractor Columbus White. St. Paul First Baptist Church also housed the first black public school in Laurens County until 1937. *Erected by the Piedmont Rural Telephone Cooperative, 2006*
GPS Coordinates: 34° 30.104' N, 82° 0.887' W

30–13 Francis Rapley Owings House/Owings

4706 N. Old Laurens Rd., Owings
Francis Rapley Owings House (FRONT)
Owings is named for Francis Rapley Owings

(1840–1920), who lived in this house after the Civil War. His ancestor Richard Owings III had settled 2 mi. W in 1757. Francis R. Owings, a farmer and merchant, built the general store across the road in 1873. It also housed the town's first post office.
Owings (REVERSE)
The town was originally named Rapley since there was already one in S.C. named Owings. After Francis Rapley Owings donated the land and lumber for a depot here, it was renamed Owings Station. Owings also helped found the Bank of Owings and served as its vice president. The bank, built in 1914, is one of several commercial buildings here built with locally-made bricks. *Erected by the Gray Court-Owings Historical Society, 2009*
GPS Coordinates: 34° 37.833' N, 82° 8.04' W

30–14 Friendship A.M.E. Church & Cemetery/Bell Street Schools

At Friendship Cemetery, N. Bell St. at Friendship Dr., Clinton
Friendship A.M.E. Church (FRONT)
This church held its first services in a nearby brush arbor shortly after the Civil War and was formally organized in 1880. Trustees purchased this 3-acre lot, and members and friends built a frame church here, naming their congregation Friendship A.M.E. Church. The present brick church on South Bell Street was built in 1937. The cemetery here includes graves of veterans of American wars from World War I to Vietnam.
Bell Street Schools (REVERSE)
Friendship School, founded in 1883 by Friendship A.M.E. Church, eventually grew to include grades 1–11. In 1926 it became a public school, moved into a new building, and was renamed Bell Street School. It was the first accredited black high school in the county. The 1950 school nearby became an elementary school in 1956, renamed Martha Dendy School in 1960. Later a middle school, it closed in 2008. *Erected by Friendship A.M.E. Church, 2010*
GPS Coordinates: 34° 28.582' N, 81° 53.621' W

30–15 Dials Methodist Church

11828 S.C. Hwy. 101 South (Saluda Gap Rd.),
Gray Court vicinity

(FRONT) This is one of the oldest Methodist congregations in Laurens County. Its earliest records have been lost, but tradition holds that Martin Dial (1744–1843), a veteran of the Revolution, organized a "Methodist Society" about 1808. It met for years in his log cabin nearby. After a camp meeting in 1835 his family donated an acre here for the first permanent church, a log building.
(REVERSE) The present frame sanctuary was built about 1860. Dials Male and Female Academy, later Dials School, opened nearby before the Civil War and closed in the1930s. The church cemetery, dating from 1832, includes graves of veterans of American wars since the War of 1812. Dials Methodist Church is the mother of Gray Court Methodist Church (1890) and Owings Methodist Church (1920).
Erected by the Congregation, 2010
GPS Coordinates: 34° 35.65' N, 82° 9.506' W

30–16 Belfast Plantation

9830 S.C. Hwy. 56 South, Kinards vicinity

(FRONT) This Federal plantation house was built between 1786 and 1815 for John Simpson (1751–1815), merchant and planter. Simpson came to S.C. from England in 1786 and named Belfast after his birthplace in Ireland. A post office here was called Belfast by 1804. Simpson was the first of four generations representing Laurens County in the S.C. House of Representatives from 1797 to 1886.
(REVERSE) John Simpson's grandson William Dunlap Simpson (1823–1890), born here, was a state representative and senator 1854–1863, and a Confederate officer and Congressman 1861–65. Simpson was lt. governor 1878–79, then governor 1879–1880, and was chief justice of the S.C. Supreme Court at his death. Belfast was acquired by the S.C. Department of Natural Resources in 2008. *Erected by the Kenelm Winslow Chapter, S.C. Society of the Colonial Dames XVII Century, 2011*
GPS Coordinates: 34° 19.583' N, 81° 50.983' W

30–17 Bell Street School/Martha Dendy School

301 N. Bell St., Clinton

Bell Street School (FRONT)
This school, built in 1950, was the third African-American school on Bell Street. Friendship School, founded in 1883 by nearby Friendship A.M.E. Church, was a combined elementary and high school. The frame school was replaced in 1926 by a brick school, named Bell Street School, with students in grades 1–11 until grade 12 was added in 1948–49. In 1937 it became the first black high school in Laurens County to be fully accredited by the state.
Martha Dendy School (REVERSE)
Bell Street School burned in 1949, and this school opened in 1950. It became Bell Street Elementary in 1956 when a new high school was built. In 1960 it was renamed Martha Dendy Elementary School in memory of principal David Dendy's mother. It became a junior high school when county schools desegregated in 1970, then a middle school in 1972, and a 6th grade center in 1997. The school closed in 2008. *Sponsored by the City of Clinton and Concerned Citizens for the Preservation of Bell Street / Martha Dendy School, 2012*
GPS Coordinates: 34° 28.436' N, 81° 53.569' W

30–18 Broad Street Methodist Church

310 N. Broad St., Clinton

(FRONT) This congregation can trace its roots to Zion Church, est. in 1826 in Laurens County. Its founding took place during the expansion associated with the Second Great Awakening. In 1854, this Methodist congregation moved to W Main St. in Clinton, one of the first to locate in town. The original structure was destroyed by fire in 1880. As it grew in numbers, the church rebuilt twice on that site.
(REVERSE) By 1914, additional growth required larger facilities and property was purchased on N Broad St. A brick neoclassical church, designed by architect J. H. Casey, was built and the congregation was renamed Broad St. In 1917, this church was host to the bishop and delegates of the Upper S.C. Methodist

Conference. After 54 years of useful service, this old church was replaced by a new sanctuary in 1970. *Sponsored by Broad Street United Methodist Church, 2014*
GPS Coordinates: 34° 28.615' N, 81° 52.857' W

30–19 Mt. Carmel A.M.E. Church

209 Mt. Carmel Rd., Gray Court

(FRONT) Mt. Carmel A.M.E. Church was founded in 1878. The congregation first met in the home of Mack and Caroline Saxon, freed slaves who had acquired substantial land holdings in Laurens County by 1877. The congregation later expanded and moved to a brush arbor before constructing a wood frame building on a three-acre tract donated by the Saxons. The current brick church was completed in 1922.
(REVERSE) During Reconstruction the A.M.E. Church sent missionaries to the South in order to cultivate new members. Rev. B. F. Martin was one of these individuals. Martin worked in Laurens County during the 1870s and in 1880 reported he had, "procured three acres and built and paid for a nice little structure in size 28 by 37," referring to the first church built on this site. *Sponsored by Mt. Carmel A.M.E. Church, 2014*
GPS Coordinates: 34° 39.048' N, 82° 9.131' W

30–20 Laurens City Cemetery

Laurens City Cemetery, 400 Block of N. Harper St., Laurens

(FRONT) Laurens City Cemetery began as the Porter family cemetery and the earliest grave is that of two-year old Laura Adelaide Porter, who died in 1817. The cemetery expanded in the early 20th century when J. W. Ferguson, R. C. Watts, and W. A. Watts deeded land along North Harper St. A gift from William

Mills allowed the property to extend to the Little River. It has also been known as "New Cemetery" and "Riverside Cemetery."
(REVERSE) Among those interred here are William Simpson (1823–1890) and Robert Archer Cooper (1874–1953), both of whom served as governor of S.C., as well as Nathaniel B. Dial (1862–1940), the only person from Laurens to serve in the U.S. Senate. Wil Lou Gray (1883–1984), a Laurens native who was a pioneer in adult education and devoted her career to eradicating illiteracy, is also buried here. *Sponsored by the Laurens Cemetery Association, 2016*
GPS Coordinates: 34° 30.107' N, 82° 0.708' W

30–21 First United Methodist Church

244 W. Main St., Laurens

(FRONT) First Methodist Church began as the "Methodist Society of Friends," a group of 15 men and women who organized in 1819. Early services were held in homes and in the Old Rock Church. In 1825 the members moved to a permanent structure .2 mile west of this site. In 1852 a second church, which still stands next to the Main St. bridge, was constructed. In 1894 the S.C. Annual Conference of Methodism was hosted in Laurens for the first time.
(REVERSE) It was this Conference that approved establishment of the Epworth Orphanage in Columbia. By 1898 membership growth led to construction of the present sanctuary. Built in Romanesque Revival style, it features a four-story bell tower. In 1936 an educational building was added and in 1961 the Fellowship Hall was built. The Annual Conference was hosted three times in the present sanctuary in 1908, 1924, and 1938. *Sponsored by First United Methodist Church, 2019*
GPS Coordinates: 34° 29.918' N, 82° 1.050' W

Lee County

31–1 Cash-Shannon Duel

Hartsville Hwy. (U.S. Hwy. 15), just W of entrance to Lee State Park at Lee State Park Rd., Bishopville vicinity

This was the site of the last fatal duel fought in S.C., in which Col. E. B. C. Cash of Cash's Depot killed Col. Wm. M. Shannon of Camden on July 5, 1880. This tragedy influenced the S.C. legislature to enact a law in December, 1880, making dueling a crime and requiring public officers, until 1954, to swear they had not been in a duel. *Erected by the Lee County Historical Commission, 1963*
GPS Coordinates: 34° 15.09' N, 80° 12.198' W

31–2 Battle of Ratcliff's Bridge

Near corner of N. Main St. (U.S. Hwy. 15) & E. Church St. (S.C. Hwy. 341), Bishopville

On March 6, 1781 General Thomas Sumter with a force of 250 men was attacked by a British detachment commanded by Major Fraser about 3 miles northeast at the head of Stirrup Branch. In a running fight, the Gamecock retreated along a road near here to Ratcliff's Bridge on Lynches River, 3 miles southeast. *Erected by Lee County Historical Commission, 1963*
GPS Coordinates: 34° 13.072' N, 80° 14.893' W

31–3 Rev. John Leighton Wilson, D.D. March 25, 1809-July 13, 1886

S.C. Sec. Rd. 31-154 (Nancy Branch Rd.), about 1.8 mi. S of its intersection with U.S. Hwy. 401, S of St. Charles

His home stood on this site. With his wife, Jane Bayard Wilson, he served as a Presbyterian missionary on the western coast of Africa 1833–1852. He advocated ending the slave trade and by 1844 had freed all his own slaves. Foreign Mission Secretary in the Presbyterian Church for 33 years, he served as a chaplain,

C.S.A. *Erected by Lee County Historical Commission, 1963*
GPS Coordinates: 34° 3.145' N, 80° 11.78' W

31–4 Skirmish at Spring Hill

Spring Hill Rd. (S.C. Sec. Rd. 31-7), 6.4 mi. W of Manville at Spring Hill

Gen. Edward E. Potter commanding 2700 Federal troops left Georgetown on April 5, 1865, to destroy the railroad between Sumter and Camden. On April 16 after a skirmish with militia under Col. James F. Pressley he camped at Spring Hill nearby. The McKinley Barfield home which stood on this site bore scars of the skirmishing on its walls. *Erected by Lee County Historical Commission, 1963*
GPS Coordinates: 34° 8.696' N, 80° 25.687' W

31–5 Bishopville

Lee County Courthouse, S. Main St. (U.S. Hwy. 15), Bishopville

A trading center and polling place for Upper Salem in old Claremont County in the early 1800's, Bishopville was laid out on land acquired by Dr. Jacques Bishop. In 1824 a post office was established here. The town was chartered in 1888. When Lee County was organized in 1902, commemorating Gen. Robert E. Lee, it became the county seat. *Erected by Lee County Historical Commission, 1963*
GPS Coordinates: 34° 13.046' N, 80° 14.976' W

31–6 Battle of Mount Elon

Sandy Grove Church Rd., .1 mi. W of S.C. Sec. Rd. 31-39 (Cypress Rd.), Cypress Crossroads, E of Bishopville

Three miles south of Mount Elon on the night of Feb. 27, 1865, a mounted Union detachment led by Captain William Duncan encountered a superior force of Confederate cavalry commanded by Colonel Hugh K. Aiken. After a sharp hand to hand fight Captain Duncan was

forced to fall back across Lynches River. Colonel Aiken was killed. *Erected by Lee County Historical Commission, 1963*
GPS Coordinates: 34° 12.832' N, 80° 8.115' W

31–7 Rev. Thomas Reese English 1806–1869

Intersection of St. Charles Rd. (S.C. Hwy. 154) & English Ln. (S.C. Sec. Rd. 31-228) at English Crossroads, about 7.5 mi. S of Bishopville

One mile east stood the home of T. R. English, Presbyterian minister, statesman, delegate to the Secession Convention. After attending S.C. College, he was admitted to the Bar and served as a legislator, 1830–1832. Ordained in 1833, as the evangelist of Harmony Presbytery he founded many churches in the Pee Dee area. *Erected by Lee County Historical Commission, 1963*
GPS Coordinates: 34° 6.914' N, 80° 13.329' W

31–8 Ellison Durant Smith August 1, 1864–November 17, 1944

Intersection of Church St. (S.C. Hwy. 341) & Potts St. (U.S. Hwy. 76), Lynchburg

Known nationally as "Cotton Ed" and active in 1905 in forming the Southern Cotton Association, Ellison DuRant Smith was elected to the U.S. Senate in 1908 and served until his death in 1944, having been Committee Chairman of Agriculture and of Interstate Commerce. His home, Tanglewood, is 3 miles east on Highway 341. *Erected by Lee County Historical Commission, 1964*
GPS Coordinates: 34° 3.6' N, 80° 4.275' W

31–9 Thomas Gordon McLeod

W. Church St. (S.C. Hwy. 34 W), Bishopville, .4 mi. from its intersection with Main St. (U.S. Hwy. 15)

This house is the birthplace of Thomas Gordon McLeod (Dec. 17, 1868-Dec. 11, 1932). He was the first State Senator from Lee County, 1903–1907, then Lieutenant Governor 1907–1911, and Governor of South Carolina from 1923 to 1927. His grave and that of his wife, the former Elizabeth Alford, are in Bethlehem Cemetery, 1 mi. N.W. *Erected by Lee County*

Historical Commission, 16 July 1965
GPS Coordinates: 34° 13.377' N, 80° 15.285' W

31–10 Captain Peter DuBose 1755–1846

N side of Hartsville Hwy. (U.S. Hwy. 15) at Lynches River, 4 mi. NE of Bishopville

After serving in the militia under General Francis Marion during the Revolutionary War, this planter and patriot lived near here and operated a ferry, known as DuBose's Crossing, close by the present bridge over Lynches River. His grave is in the family cemetery 100 yards north. *Erected by Lee County Historical Commission, 1966*
GPS Coordinates: 34° 14.959' N, 80° 13.002' W

31–11 Henry Durant

[Reported missing in April 2010.]

Lynchburg Hwy. N (S.C. Hwy. 341), .7 mi. NW of its intersection with Darlington Hwy. E (U.S. Hwy. 401), Elliott vicinity

Near this site stood the house of Henry Durant, soldier in the American Revolution. He served under General Francis Marion against British forces who had overrun this area of South Carolina. Durant later became a substantial landholder from whom many people in this area trace descent. *Erected by Lee County Historical Commission/Sponsored by Henry Durant Chapter, Daughters of the American Revolution, 1968*
GPS Coordinates: 34° 7.547' N, 80° 9.113' W

31–12 James Jenkins 1764–1847 /James Jenkins

Sumter Hwy. (U.S. Hwy. 15), 1½ mi. SW of Bishopville

James Jenkins 1764–1847 (FRONT)
The Reverend James Jenkins served in the Methodist ministry for 55 years. He was born in Britton's Neck, the son of Samuel and Elizabeth Britton Jenkins. His mother was a Revolutionary War heroine. In 1805 he married Elizabeth Ann Gwyn and from 1814 to 1836 he lived near here. He died and was buried in Camden.

James Jenkins (REVERSE)

The Reverend James Jenkins was a pioneer circuit-riding Methodist minister. He began his ministry in 1792 among the settlers and Indians of the Cherokee Circuit. In 1801 he was presiding elder of the S.C. District. He organized many churches, including Bethlehem Methodist Church in Bishopville. In later years, he supervised and disciplined younger preachers. *Erected by Dr. Henry Woodward Chapter, S.C. Society, Daughters of the American Colonists, 1972*
GPS Coordinates: 34° 12.151' N, 80° 16.401' W

31–13 Rembert Church

Rembert Branch Church Rd. (S.C. Sec. Rd. 31–37), Woodrow vicinity, about 1 mi. N of Lee County-Sumter County line

Site of camp meetings where Bishop Francis Asbury preached. First service held about 1786. In 1834 Caleb Rembert deeded eight acres to nine trustees for the use of the Methodist Church. John A. Colclough gave an adjacent tract of 2 ½ acres, and soon after the present church was erected. Successors of the original trustees maintain both church and cemetery. *Erected by Rembert's Church Cemetery Association, 1958*
GPS Coordinates: 34° 5.873' N, 80° 21.142' W

31–14 William Apollos James House

208 North Dennis Ave., Bishopville

(FRONT) William Apollos James (1857–1930), prominent local businessman and public servant, lived here from 1904 until his death. James founded the Farmers Loan and Trust Company and was its president for more than 20 years. When Lee County was created in 1902 James was one of the commissioners who laid out county boundaries and built a new courthouse. He later represented the county in the S.C. House in 1913–14.
(REVERSE) This house, built as a one-story cottage in 1903, became a large Classical Revival house in 1911 with the addition of a large second story and wraparound porch. The garden here, laid out by a daughter, Sara B. "Tallie" James, is also notable for its 136 varieties of

camellias. The house, donated to the Lee County Historical Society in 1995, was listed in the National Register of Historic Places in 1999. *Erected by the Lee County Historical Society, 2002*
GPS Coordinates: 34° 13.223' N, 80° 14.893' W

31–15 Hall's Mill

S.C. Sec. Rd. 31–21 at Scape Ore Creek, 1.1 mi. W of its intersection with S.C. Sec. Rd. 31–41, Lucknow

(FRONT) A water-powered grist mill stood here as early as 1824, on land owned by William W. Hall, who had acquired the property from John Hall in 1809. William Hall operated the mill until he sold it to Harrison Hall shortly before the Civil War. Hall's Mill, which appears in Robert Mills's 1824 Atlas of South Carolina, was destroyed by a flood in 1928. The present mill was built by C. M. Stokes in 1929.
(REVERSE) This mill, built in 1929, was operated by Hall descendant Archie Hopkins when it closed in 1965. The first floor included a general store which served as the center of the Lucknow community for many years, while the second floor was reserved for the Masonic lodge. Hall's Mill, with its original equipment intact, is an excellent early twentieth-century grist mill. *Erected by the Lee County Historical Society, 2000*
GPS Coordinates: 34° 16.623' N, 80° 22.32' W

31–16 Mt. Zion Presbyterian Church

S.C. Hwy. 154, approximately 2 mi. N of St. Charles

(FRONT) This church was established in 1809. Its first building, a frame church, was built 1.5 mi. N on Broad Branch. The congregation moved to this site in 1829 and built a second church, also a frame building, in the 1830s. Mt. Zion's longest serving minister, Rev. William M. Reid, was the pastor here from 1833 to 1872.
(REVERSE) The cemetery here dates from 1830, and the session house was built in 1851. A third frame church, built in 1855, burned in 1910. The present Neo-Classical Revival brick church, designed by the firm of Wilson & Sompayrac, was built in 1911. Mt. Zion was listed in the National Register of Historic

Places in 2003. *Erected by the Congregation, 2005*
GPS Coordinates: 34° 6.026' N, 80° 13.637' W

31–17 Lynchburg Presbyterian Church and Cemetery

S.C. Hwy. 341, South Lynchburg

(FRONT) This church was organized in 1855 by 21 charter members who met in the nearby Methodist church. This Greek Revival church, built of hand-hewn pine and featuring galleries on either side, was built that year with the help of their neighbors. Rev. W. W. Wilson, a native of Ireland, served as its first pastor. (REVERSE) This church is one of the few buildings still standing from the original town of Lynchburg. When the railroad was built one mile north in 1854 and that area was renamed Lynchburg, this community became South Lynchburg. The church and cemetery were listed in the National Register of Historic Places in 2004. *Erected by the Lynchburg Cemetery Association, Inc., 2005*
GPS Coordinates: 34° 3.289' N, 80° 3.844' W

31–18 Dennis High School

410 West Cedar Ln., Bishopville

(FRONT) Dennis High School, built in 1936, was the first high school for African-American students in Lee County. Built on land donated by philanthropist Rebecca Dennis, it was named in her honor. This school was originally intended as an elementary school, but when the old elementary school burned shortly before this school opened it became both an elementary school and high school. It was the only black high school in Lee County for several years.

(REVERSE) The auditorium here was a significant social center for blacks throughout Lee County. In 1948, when a new Dennis High School opened, this became Dennis Elementary School. In 1954, a state program to equalize funding for black and white schools built a new Dennis High and Elementary School. The original Dennis High School was renovated and served as Dennis Primary School until it closed in 1970. It was listed in the National Register of Historic Places in 2005. *Erected by the Dennis Community Development Corporation of Lee County, 2007*
GPS Coordinates: 34° 13.451' N, 80° 14.926' W

31–19 Bishopville High School

600 N. Main St., Bishopville

(FRONT) This high school, built in 1936, is an excellent example of a Colonial Revival school built by the Public Works Administration (PWA), a New Deal program of Franklin D. Roosevelt's administration. Designed by architect Henry Dudley Harrall (1878–1959) of Bennettsville, it was built and furnished for $71,000 and was described as "one of the most modern school plants in the state" when it was completed.
(REVERSE) The high school featured sixteen large classrooms and a combination gymnasium and auditorium. Its first graduating class was in 1937. The school included grades 8–11 until 1947, when it added grade 12. It was expanded in 1956, 1965, and 1986 before closing in 2000 when a new high school was built south of town. This school was listed in the National Register of Historic Places in 2004. *Erected by Alumni, Former Employees, and Friends of Bishopville High School, 2009*
GPS Coordinates: 34° 13.435' N, 80° 14.47' W

Lexington County

32–1 Congaree Fort

U.S. Hwy. 21 near Congaree Creek and I-26, West Columbia vicinity

In 1718, at a site 2.7 miles east, near the place where the Cherokee Path crossed Congaree Creek, the first frontier outpost in central South Carolina was established under the command of Captain Charles Russell. The fort was abandoned in 1722, but the trading factory was soon revived as a private venture

by Thomas Brown, an Indian trader. *Erected 1993 by the Saxe Gotha Museum, replacing a marker erected by South Carolina Society Daughters of the American Colonists, 1958*
GPS Coordinates: 33° 56.226' N, 81° 4.632' W

32–2 Lexington Courthouses

Lexington County Courthouse, E. Main St. (U.S. Hwy. 1), Lexington

On this site or close by have stood five courthouses of Lexington District or County. In 1820 Barbara Corley deeded land in the present town for a centrally located courthouse. A later antebellum building was burned Feb. 17, 1865, by Sherman. Two successive buildings were in use before the present one was dedicated on Jan. 15, 1940. *Erected by Lexington County Historical Society, 1961*
GPS Coordinates: 33° 58.867' N, 81° 14.167' W

32–3 Saluda Factory
[Marker no longer extant.]

Sunset Blvd. (U.S. Hwy. 378) at Botanical Pkwy., West Columbia

One mile east on the Saluda River stood a 4-story granite building erected by the Saluda Manufacturing Company, incorporated in 1834. Operated by slave labor, it was, at one time, the largest cotton factory in the State. Burned by Sherman Feb. 17, 1865, it was rebuilt and operated for some time after the war. *Erected by Lexington County Historical Society, 1962*
GPS Coordinates: 33° 59.949' N, 81° 5.479' W

32–4 Battle of Cloud's Creek
[Marker no longer extant.]

Summerland Ave. (S.C. Hwy. 391) N of Leesville, near Lexington County-Saluda County line

On November 17, 1781, in a house near Cloud's Creek one mile east Captain Sterling Turner's Patriot militia were surrounded and massacred by Tory militia under Major William Cunningham. Among the more than twenty dead were Captain James Butler and his son, James, who were buried with the others at the site, and whose graves have been marked

there. *Erected by Lexington County Historical Society, 1964*
GPS Coordinates: 33° 57.820' N, 81° 31.797' W

32–5 Shelling of Columbia

Sunset Blvd. (U.S. Hwy. 378), at its intersection with N. Lucas St., West Columbia

Prior to the capture of Columbia by Gen. William T. Sherman, Federal artillery shelled the city on February 16, 1865, from batteries on this hill and in the road at this end of the Congaree River bridge. Shots were fired at the Arsenal (site of the Governor's Mansion) and the State House, which still bears scars of the bombardment. *Erected by Lexington County Historical Society, 1964*
GPS Coordinates: 33° 59.8' N, 81° 3.789' W

32–6 Old State Road

Brookland-Cayce High School, 1300 State St., Cayce

This route follows an old Indian trail, which became a trading path and later in 1747 a public road from Charleston to Granby and points west. The State Road laid out by the newly established Board of Public Works in 1820 from Charleston to Columbia and on to the mountains perpetuated one of the oldest and most traveled routes in the development of the South Carolina back country. *Erected by West Columbia-Cayce Junior Woman's Club, 1965*
GPS Coordinates: 33° 58.9' N, 81° 3.316' W

32–7 The Cherokee Path

Intersection of Augusta Rd. (U.S. Hwy 1) & Hook Ave., West Columbia

Before the Revolution, two major trading routes came together near here. Branching to the west was the road to New Windsor Township on the Savannah. The Cherokee Path extended north to Ninety Six and south through Saxe Gotha Township on the Congaree. George Washington passed here in 1791 on his way from Augusta to Columbia via Friday's Ferry. *Erected by Lexington County Historical Society, 1970*
GPS Coordinates: 33° 59.061' N, 81° 5.538' W

32–8 Lutheran Classical and Theological Seminary

[No longer extant. Replaced by marker 32-38.]

U.S. Hwy. 378, Lexington

The Seminary of the Evangelical Lutheran Synod of S.C. and Adjacent States was located here from 1834 to 1859, on a tract of 124 acres. E. L. Hazelius was presiding official and Professor of Theology. The dormitory became the Lexington County Museum in 1969. Two other Seminary associated buildings are nearby. *Erected by Lexington County Historical Society, 1970*

32–9 Lee's Tavern Site

E. Columbia Ave. (U.S. Hwy. 1), Leesville

Mills' Atlas of 1820 shows this site on the Augusta-Columbia road as the location of John W. Lee's Stage Tavern. According to local tradition, this vicinity was the probable site of President George Washington's breakfast stop on May 22, 1791. The Town of Leesville derives its name from the family of John W. Lee, who were early settlers of this area. *Erected by Lexington County Historical Society, 1970*
GPS Coordinates: 33° 54.65' N, 81° 31.65' W

32–10 Hartley House

305 E. Columbia Ave. (U.S. Hwy. 1), Batesburg

This house was built before 1800 for John Pearson Bond, according to local tradition. It later came into the possession of John Bates, of the family from whom Batesburg derives its name, and has been owned for over a century by Lodwick Hartley and his family. It was the first meeting place of the Batesville Masonic Lodge and was a stagecoach mail stop. *Erected by Lexington County Historical Society, 1970*
GPS Coordinates: 33° 54.85' N, 81° 31.05' W

32–11 The Sycamore Tree

(Old Two Notch Rd.) U.S. Hwy. 1, 4 mi. E of Lexington

This tree was planted from a cutting of the old sycamore tree that stood several hundred feet west of here on the historic Two Notch Road. Local tradition holds that a succession of sycamore trees had been at that site and used as a landmark or point of reference since the road was an Indian path and also that George Washington rested there in 1791. *Erected by Lexington County Historical Society, 1973*
GPS Coordinates: 33° 58.502' N, 81° 9.992' W

32–12 Tomb of Dr. E.L. Hazelius

St. Stephen's Lutheran Church, 119 N. Church St., Lexington

At this site is the grave of the Reverend Ernest L. Hazelius, 1777–1853, Lutheran clergyman, Doctor of Divinity, teacher, and author of several books on church history and theology. From 1834 to 1853, he was professor of theology in the Lutheran Classical and Theological Seminary, and resided in a house near the campus, ¼ mile north. *Erected by Lexington County Historical Society, 1973*
GPS Coordinates: 33° 59.017' N, 81° 14.217' W

32–13 Columbia Army Air Base/The Doolittle Raiders

Off S.C. Sec. Rd. 378 (Columbia Metropolitan Airport Dr.) near the airport terminal, West Columbia vicinity

Columbia Army Air Base (FRONT)
Built during 1941 as the Lexington County Airport, this airfield became the Columbia Army Air Base shortly after the U.S. entered World War II in December, 1941. The base was used to train crews for medium bombardment groups flying B-25s and A-26s. Reaching a military population of 7,800 in February of 1945, the base reverted to a standby status after the war.
The Doolittle Raiders (REVERSE)
In February 1942, twenty-four B-25 bomber crews of the 17th Bombardment Group at Columbia Army Air Base volunteered to take part in a secret project headed by Lt. Col. James H. Doolittle. This group was the nucleus of the Doolittle Raiders who, taking off from the aircraft carrier "Hornet," bombed Tokyo on April 18, 1942. *Erected by South Carolina Department, Council on Abandoned Military Posts, 1979*
GPS Coordinates: 33° 56.873' N, 81° 7.675' W

32–14 St. Andrew's Lutheran Church

St. Andrews Rd., about 1 mi. W of I-26, Irmo vicinity

These four acres were conveyed to St. Andrew's Lutheran Church in 1835, and by November of that year, the congregation had built and dedicated a building. It is believed that the community of St. Andrews derived its name from this church. In 1949, the church moved to its present location on Broad River Road. *Erected by The Congregation, 1985*
GPS Coordinates: 34° 2.682' N, 81° 8.098' W

32–15 Mt. Hebron United Methodist Church/Temperance Hall

3041 Leaphart Rd., West Columbia

Mt. Hebron United (FRONT)
This congregation, organized ca.1800 in the home of Martin Hook, built its first house of worship at the Half Way Ground, near here. In 1837 a new church was erected at this site on land donated by John and Elizabeth Roof. Another structure was built here in 1907 and was replaced in 1963 by the present sanctuary. *Erected by The Congregation, 1982*
Temperance Hall (REVERSE)
The frame building behind the church was built 1862 by Saludaville Sons of Temperance, a society chartered in 1858 that reflected the nationwide movement to combat intemperate use of alcohol. In 1871 the society was rechartered as Mt. Hebron Sons of Temperance and probably continued until the State Dispensary was established 1893. This building was restored in 1979. *Erected by the Pineview Ruritan Club, 1982*
GPS Coordinates: 33° 59.883' N, 81° 7.495' W

32–16 Zion Lutheran Church/ Dreher's Fort

226 Corley Mill Rd. (S.C. Sec. Rd. 32–68), ½ mi. from I-20, Lexington vicinity

Zion Lutheran Church (FRONT)
This congregation, the oldest continuing church in Lexington County, originated with pioneers who settled in this area in the 1740s. Organized at Zion in 1787 was the "Corpus

Evangelicum," consisting of fifteen congregations to supervise the German churches in the state's interior. The church was located at two previous sites near the river before moving here in 1922. *Erected by the Congregation, 1986*
Dreher's Fort (REVERSE)
An early FRONTier fort was built near here by Godfrey Dreher on land that he received in the 1740s. During the Cherokee War in 1760, the fort provided protection from hostile Indians for 121 men, women, and children. Near the fort on Twelve Mile Creek was the first location of Zion Church. *Erected by the Pineview Ruritan Club, 1986*
GPS Coordinates: 34° 1.259' N, 81° 9.257' W

32–17 319th Bombardment Group

Off S.C. Sec. Rd. 378 (Columbia Metropolitan Airport Dr.) near the airport terminal, West Columbia vicinity

Activated in 1942 and stationed here at Columbia Army Air Base February through April of 1945, the 319th participated in many World War II campaigns in Europe and the Pacific. The group has received numerous honors, including two Presidential Unit Citations and France's Croix de Guerre from General Charles de Gaulle. *Erected by the 319th Bomb Group Reunion Association, 1986*
GPS Coordinates: 33° 56.873' N, 81° 7.675' W

32–18 Revolutionary Skirmish Near Juniper Springs

Gilbert High School, Main St., Gilbert

A party of Sumter's soldiers, harassing a rear guard of British foragers under Lord Rawdon (en route to relieve besieged Ninety Six), was ambushed several miles north of here on June 18, 1781. The state troops, under Col. Charles S. Myddelton, were dispersed and the British continued unimpeded to Ninety Six. *Erected by Lexington County Historical Society, 1980*
GPS Coordinates: 33° 55.067' N, 81° 23.617' W

32–19 Town of Irmo

Corner of Woodrow St & Columbia Ave., Irmo

(FRONT) The Town of Irmo was established in a small farming community when the

Columbia, Newberry and Laurens Railroad constructed its line here in February of 1890. The town was incorporated by the S.C. General Assembly in December of 1890. The original town limits extended ½ mile north, south, east, and west from the depot, which was located near here.

(REVERSE) Irmo was incorporated in 1890 and, according to tradition, took its name from the last names of C. J. Iredell and H. C. Moseley, officers of the Columbia, Newberry and Laurens Railroad, who were involved in planning and developing the town. A number of the town's streets were named for early railroad officials. *Erected by the Town of Irmo, 1989*
GPS Coordinates: 34° 5.038' N, 81° 10.9' W

32–20 Providence Church

Old Chapin Rd. (S.C. Sec. Rd. 32–52), about 3 mi. N of Lexington

Lutheran church said est. 1862. Admitted to synod 1866. Present remodeled building, built by 1869, is on land deeded church by Jacob Rauch family. *Erected by Providence Evangelical Lutheran Church, 1991*
GPS Coordinates: 34° 1.158' N, 81° 15.817' W

32–21 Bombardment Groups

Off S.C. Sec. Rd. 378 (Columbia Metropolitan Airport Dr.) near the airport terminal, West Columbia vicinity

In 1942 the 310th, 321st, 340th groups trained here at Columbia Army Air Base for World War II. All participated in 9 campaigns, and each received 2 Distinguished Unit Citations. *Erected by 57th Bomb Wing Association, 1992*
GPS Coordinates: 33° 56.873' N, 81° 7.675' W

32–22 Lexington Baptist Church

Corner of E. Main St. (U.S. Hwy. 1) & Creps St., Lexington

This church was constituted May 21, 1893, with ten charter members. The original one-room frame building, dedicated 1894 and located on land given by James C. Fort, was across Main Street about 600 feet east of here. The congregation of about 150 with

W. C. Wallace as pastor, moved here June 6, 1926, upon completing this house of worship. *Erected by The Congregation, 1993*
GPS Coordinates: 33° 58.767' N, 81° 13.983' W

32–23 Christian Theus

I-26 & Charleston Hwy. (U.S. Hwy 21), Silver Lake vicinity, near Lexington County-Calhoun County line

One mile east was the original grave of the Reverend Christian Theus. A native of Switzerland, Theus ministered to Reformed and Lutheran groups in Saxe-Gotha Township, 1739–1789, and was teacher of the local school. His grave was moved to Sandy Run Lutheran Church Cemetery in 1932. *Erected by S.C. Daughters of American Colonists in 1993, replacing a Marker Erected by the S.C. Daughters of American Colonists in 1941*
GPS Coordinates: 33° 52.805' N, 81° 2.110' W

32–24 St. Stephen's Church

119 N. Church St., corner of N. Church & Butler Sts., Lexington

This Lutheran Church, founded by 1830, and the earliest church in Lexington, dedicated its first-known house of worship on this site in 1831. In 1865 Union troops under Wm. T. Sherman burned the structure. The congregation's second building, dedicated 1870, was destroyed by fire in 1898. The third church, built by 1901 on the present site, was replaced by the current edifice, dedicated in 1958. *Erected by the Congregation, 1994*
GPS Coordinates: 33° 59' N, 81° 14.2' W

32–25 Camp Moore

Fish Hatchery Rd. (S.C. Sec. Rd. 32–73), 100 yds. from its intersection with Pine Ridge Rd. (S.C. Sec. Rd. 32–103), Pine Ridge, E of South Congaree

The military began this post, also known as Camp Styx, in 1913 as a National Guard training center. The post sent men to a Mexican border disturbance after Pres. Woodrow Wilson mobilized the guard in 1916, and its 1st Infantry Regiment, later the 118th, played a significant role in World War I, breaking the purportedly impregnable Hindenburg line of

defense. The camp closed in the early 1920s. *Erected by Pine Ridge Woman's Club, 1994*
GPS Coordinates: 33° 54.755' N, 81° 6.178' W

32–26 St. Peter Church

900 Dreher Island Rd. (S.C. Sec. Rd. 32-231), SW of Chapin

S.C. Gen. Assembly incorp. this Lutheran Church 17 Dec. 1794. Frederick Josephus Wallern served as 1st pastor. Today's church, dedicated 1936, is the 3rd building. *Erected by St. Peter Lutheran Church Bicentennial Committee, 1995*
GPS Coordinates: 34° 8.539' N, 81° 24.383' W

32–27 Skirmish at Red Bank Creek /Site of Federal Encampment

S.C. Hwy. 6 near Red Bank Creek, Lexington vicinity

Skirmish at Red Bank Creek (FRONT)
On February 15, 1865 Gen. Henry W. Slocum's Army of Georgia, the left wing of the Federal advance toward Columbia, marched along this route toward Lexington. The Federals, led by skirmishers of the 28th Pennsylvania at the head of the 1st Brig., 2nd Div., XX Corps, were delayed by elements of Gen. Joseph Wheeler's Confederate cavalry, which clashed with them briefly at Congaree Creek and then here along Red Bank Creek.
Site of Federal Encampment (REVERSE)
After the Confederates withdrew toward Lexington, two miles north, elements of the XX Corps occupied the town. The XIV and XX Corps camped ½ mi. N. at the junction of Old Orangeburg and Old Barnwell Rds. on the night of Feb. 15th. Elements of Gen. Judson Kilpatrick's cavalry division burned much of Lexington before the left wing advanced to Winnsboro; one observer described the town as "a blackened ruin." *Erected by Company D, 7th South Carolina Infantry (Reenactors), 1997*
GPS Coordinates: 33° 55.714' N, 81° 14.314' W

32–28 Laurance Corley House

[Reported missing in 2004.]

Lexington County Museum, 122 Berly St., Lexington

(FRONT) This log house was built ca. 1771 by Laurance Corley (1742–1815), whose plantation of over 1700 acres occupied much of present-day Lexington. Corley later served in Capt. Gabriel Friday's militia company during the Revolution. The house stood on two previous locations near Twelve Mile Creek, approximately 1 mile east, and was moved here on part of the original tract in 1974, then restored by the Lexington Co. Museum.
(REVERSE) Laurance Corley was the father of sixteen children, founding a prominent and well-known Lexington County family. His first wife Christena died in 1806, and he later married a widow, Barbara Derrick Drafts (1770–1858), later known as "Granny Corley." In 1820, five years after Corley's death, Mrs. Corley deeded two acres to the state for the establishment of a new county seat, which became the town of Lexington. *Erected by Lexington County Museum, 1997*
GPS Coordinates: 33° 59.217' N, 81° 14.45' W

32–29 St. Peter's (Meetze's) Lutheran Church

1130 St. Peter's Church Rd., Lexington vicinity

This church, organized in 1780, held services in German and English until 1874. In 1835 it aligned with the Tennessee Synod and remained in it until 1922, when St. Peter's reunited with the South Carolina Synod. This 1953 sanctuary is the fourth house of worship. Among St. Peter's most prominent ministers were Revs. John Yost Meetze, who served 1810–33, and J. A. Cromer, who served 1883–1921. *Erected by the Congregation, 1998*
GPS Coordinates: 34° 0.294' N, 81° 18.216' W

32–30 Battle of Congaree Creek

Old State Rd., just S of its intersection with New State Rd., Cayce vicinity

(FRONT) On February 15, 1865, as Gen. W. T. Sherman's Federal army advanced to Columbia, Gen. O. O. Howard's Army of the Tennessee found its way blocked by Confederates entrenched behind Congaree Creek and defending the Old State Rd. bridge. Gen. George G. Dibrell's dismounted cavalry brigade, supported by infantry and artillery, manned the nearby earthworks, portions of which survive.

(REVERSE) Gen. Charles R. Woods' 1st Div. of Gen. John A. Logan's XV Corps pushed Federal skirmishers ahead while one of Woods' brigades crossed upstream and turned the Confederate right flank. Dibrell's force withdrew from Congaree Creek and then from its earthworks, retreating to Columbia. Though the Confederates set fire to the bridge the Federals saved it and made their camp nearby that night. *Erected by the 15th Regt. S.C. Vols., Sons of Confederate Veterans, 1998*
GPS Coordinates: 33° 57.634' N, 81° 2.284' W

32–31 Lewie Chapel (Old Gilbert Methodist Church)/The Lewie Family

Lewie St., Gilbert

Lewie Chapel (Old Gilbert Methodist Church) (FRONT)
Lewie Chapel, a Methodist church founded on this site in the 1870s by Solomon R. Lewie (1835–1878) and others, was later known as Lewiedale Methodist Church and after 1910 as Gilbert Methodist Church. The original sanctuary, replaced in 1960 by a new sanctuary about 1 mi. W, burned in the early 1970s.
The Lewie Family (REVERSE)
The town of Gilbert, also known as Gilbert Hollow, was called Lewiedale from 1886 to 1899 after the family of Samuel (1802–1865) and Nancy Hendrix Lewie (1807–1865). Four of six Lewie sons saw Confederate service in the 15th S.C. Infantry, with Frederick S. (1831–1873) as its lieutenant colonel and James H. (1838–1889) as a captain. Several family members are buried here. *Erected by the 15th Reg. S.C. Vols., Sons of Confederate Veterans, 2000*
GPS Coordinates: 33° 55.413' N, 81° 23.317' W

32–32 Saluda Factory Cemetery

Botanical Ln., West Columbia

This cemetery, thought to contain graves of supervisors and workers in the post-Civil War community of Saludaville, includes 31 marked graves and between 525 and 900 total burials.

The Saluda Factory was a modest success before the war and was burned by Union troops in 1865. Rebuilt as the Saluda Manufacturing Company in 1974, it employed about 100 workers before it burned in 1884. *Erected by the South Carolina Electric & Gas Company and the Mungo Company, 2004*
GPS Coordinates: 34° 0.457' N, 81° 5.154' W

32–33 Pinarea/Quattlebaum Sawmill, Flour Mill, And Rifle Factory

Intersection of U.S. Hwy. 178 and Bagpipe Rd., Leesville vicinity

Pinarea (FRONT)
Pinarea, the plantation owned by soldier, statesman, and manufacturer Paul Quattlebaum (1812–1890), was a mile E. Quattlebaum was a captain in the Seminole War and a brig. gen. in the S.C. militia by 1843. He was a state representative 1840–43, state senator 1848–52, and delegate to the Secession Convention and signer of the Ordinance of Secession. He is buried in the cemetery at Pinarea.
Quattlebaum Sawmill, Flour Mill, and Rifle Factory (REVERSE)
The Quattlebaums operated a sawmill, flour mill, and rifle factory near here. The mills were both powered by Lightwood Knot Creek. The sawmill had a turbine wheel and circular saw. The rifle factory, founded by Paul's father John (1774–1853), was leased to the Confederate government to make percussion rifles. *Erected by the Lexington County Camps (# 22, 51, and 412), Sons of Confederate Veterans, 2006*
GPS Coordinates: 33° 50.1' N, 81° 28.383' W

32–34 Site of the "Swamp Rabbit" Bridge/"The Swamp Rabbit"

Columbia Ave. (U.S. Highway 1), Batesburg

Site of the "Swamp Rabbit" Bridge (FRONT)
A concrete highway bridge, built in 1928–29 when U.S. Highway 1 was paved through Batesburg, stood here until 2003. The 111-foot-long bridge, featuring graceful arches, spanned the track of the Sievern & Knoxville Railroad. It was built at a cost of $13,000 by Cohen Dick Fulmer (1890–1972) a contractor who built

many bridges for the S.C. Highway Department from the 1920s until World War II. "The Swamp Rabbit" (REVERSE)

The Sievern & Knoxville RR was completed from Perry to Batesburg in 1898. The S&K train, known as "The Swamp Rabbit," ran until 1933 on a passenger and freight line that linked to the Southern Railway at Batesburg. For 35 years "The Swamp Rabbit" shipped lumber, turpentine, produce, and kaolin to Batesburg and to points beyond via the Southern Railway. *Erected by the Batesburg-Leesville Community Committee, 2007*
GPS Coordinates: 33° 54.258' N, 81° 32.746' W

32–35 Springdale

Corner of Platt Springs Rd. & Springdale Rd., Springdale

This community, which was incorporated as Springdale in 1955, was known as Long Branch for many years and named for a nearby branch of the Congaree River. At the turn of the twentieth century it was a farming community along both sides of Platt Springs Road. In 1955 residents who opposed plans to annex Long Branch into West Columbia voted to incorporate as a town, named for the many springs in the area. Job B. Roof was elected the town's first intendant, or mayor. *Erected by the Town of Springdale, 2008*
GPS Coordinates: 33° 57.542' N, 81° 6.566' W

32–36 World War II Bombing Ranges

S.C. Hwy. 6, on the N (Irmo) side of the Lake Murray Dam, Irmo vicinity

(FRONT) Lake Murray islands, most notably Lunch Island (since 1945 also called Bomb Island or Doolittle Island), Shull Island, and Dreher Island, were used as bombing ranges during World War II. B-25 crews from the Columbia Army Air Base (now Columbia Metropolitan Airport) flew thousands of training missions here 1942–45.
(REVERSE) These islands were used for many types of practice runs, in which crews dropped flare, incendiary, and demolition bombs. Five B-25s ditched or crashed into Lake Murray

while training here. Four were salvaged during the war, and the last aircraft, a rare B-25C, was salvaged from the lake in 2005. *Erected by the Lake Murray B-25 Rescue Project, Inc., 2008*
GPS Coordinates: 34° 3.756' N, 81° 13.267' W

32–37 Batesburg Institute

Corner of Academy and Peachtree Sts., Batesburg

(FRONT) The Batesburg Institute opened here in 1893. Also called the Batesburg Collegiate Institute, it was created by the merger of the town's Methodist and Baptist schools, founded in the 1880s. The Institute moved into the Baptist school, a one-story frame building later enlarged with a second story. W. J. Helms, its first principal, served here from 1893 to 1896, when the institute had more than 100 students.
(REVERSE) Principals of the Institute from 1896 to 1911 inclueed D. W. Daniel, L. C. Perry, J. R. T. Major, and W. C. Martin. John Broadus Watson (1878–1958), who taught at the Batesburg Institute 1899–1900, was later a renowned psychologist and a pioneer in the field of behaviorism. The Batesburg Institute burned in 1911 and was replaced by the Batesburg Graded and High School, a new brick school on U.S. Highway 1, in 1912. *Erected by the Batesburg-Leesville Community Committee, 2008*
GPS Coordinates: 33° 54.084' N, 81° 32.942' W

32–38 Lutheran Classical and Theological Seminary

421 Columbia Ave., Lexington

(FRONT) The Lutheran Classical and Theological Seminary was located here from 1834 to 1855. The Synod of S.C. established a new seminary in 1831 in an effort to promote the education of Lutheran ministers in the southeast. It opened in Pomaria, Newberry County, but plans were soon made to move to this site, then ½ mi. from the town of Lexington Court House.
(REVERSE) The seminary opened here in 1834, with Dr. Ernest L. Hazelius (1777–1853), a native of Prussia who had come to America

in 1800, as headmaster until 1851. The seminary, headmaster's house (1833), and academic building (ca. 1830) are listed in the National Register of Historic Places. The seminary moved to Newberry in 1855 and became Newberry College in 1856. *Sponsored by the Lutheran Theological Southern Seminary and the Lexington County Historical Society, 2014*
GPS Coordinates: 33° 59.291' N, 81° 14.389' W

32–39 345th Bombardment Group

Columbia Metropolitan Airport, Airport Blvd., West Columbia

(FRONT) The 345th Bombardment Group of the 5th Air Force, "the Air Apaches," served in the Southwest Pacific during World War II. Four squadrons (the 498th, 499th, 500th, and 501st) trained here at Columbia Army Air Base November 1942–April 1943, with bombing runs over Lake Murray, aerial gunnery practice at Myrtle Beach, and maneuvers at Aiken before transferring to Walterboro.
(REVERSE) The 345th left Walterboro in April 1943 for California, Australia, and the front, flying its first combat missions over New Guinea in June. The group flew B-25 Mitchell bombers in 8 campaigns from New Guinea to Japan June 1943-August 1945, sinking 260 vessels and shooting down 107 planes. It won 4 Distinguished Unit Citations and a Philippine Presidential Unit Citation. *Sponsored by the 345th Bomb Group Association, 2012*
GPS Coordinates: 33° 56.697' N, 81° 6.879' W

32–40 Congaree Creek Earthworks

Timmerman Trail, 12,000 Year History Park, Cayce

(FRONT) These earthworks were constructed in early 1865 and were the site of brisk fighting between the Union XV Corps and Confederate forces on Feb. 15, 1865. Approximately 750 enslaved and free African Americans who were responsible for building much of the defensive line, which ran from Congaree Creek to the Saluda Factory four miles north.
(REVERSE) The Confederate Congress approved legislation authorizing impressment of black laborers in March 1863 because slaveholders were reluctant to provide slaves for service. Still, labor shortages persisted. Maj. John R.

Niernsee, S.C. Militia Chief Engineer, complained that he had to begin work at Congaree Creek with only 12 black workers and his request for 2,000 laborers was never met. *Sponsored by S.C. Civil War Sesquicentennial Advisory Board and S.C. African American Heritage Commission, 2015*
GPS Coordinates: 33° 56.350' N, 81° 2.144' W

32–41 Tarrar Springs

U.S. Hwy. 1 at Tarrar Springs Rd., Lexington

(FRONT) At this location on Nov. 16, 1781 Patriot militia under Capt. Sterling Turner met Tories under Col. Hezekia Williams as part of Maj. William Cunningham's "Bloody Scout" raid. The Tories had stolen a herd of cattle in the Mt. Willing area of Ninety Six District (now Saluda Co.) and were taking them toward Charleston. After exchanging gunfire, both sides negotiated a settlement allowing for a return of the cattle and for Williams' command to leave the field.
(REVERSE) The next day much of Turner's force was killed by Cunningham and Williams during an engagement called the Clouds Creek Massacre near current-day Batesburg-Leesville. These battles were among roughly a dozen Revolutionary War engagements that occurred in what is now Lexington Co. In the early 20th Century the area served as a granite quarry operated first by Dr. Crawford Long and then by Caspari's Stone Company. A pond remains at the quarry site. *Sponsored by the Godfrey Dreher Chapter SAR and Granby Chapter DAR, 2016*
GPS Coordinates: 33° 58.582' N, 81° 12.615' W

32–42 Old Lexington Baptist Church

800 Old Lexington Rd., Leesville

(FRONT) Old Lexington Baptist Church, known originally as Saluda Baptist Church, was established in 1813. Worship here began, however, as early as the late 1700s when camp meetings were held nearby. Early services were held under a brush arbor and the first sanctuary was of log construction. Rev. Joseph King was the first pastor.
(REVERSE) A second church was constructed in 1852 and it was renamed Lexington Baptist

Church. The congregation was dismissed from the Edgefield Baptist Association in 1877 to become a founding member of the Lexington Baptist Association. It remains the oldest church in that association. The current church was built in 1953. *Sponsored by Old Lexington Baptist Church, 2016*
GPS Coordinates: 34° 3.079' N, 81° 27.382' W

32–43 Blinding of Isaac Woodard

West Church St. near Fulmer St., Batesburg-Leesville

(FRONT) Sgt. Isaac Woodard, a black soldier, was removed from a bus in Batesburg and arrested on Feb. 12, 1946, after a dispute with the bus driver. Woodard was beaten and blinded by a town police officer and the next day convicted in town court for "drunk and

disorderly." The incident led Harry Truman to form a Council on Civil Rights and issue Executive Order 9981, which desegregated the U.S. Armed Forces in 1948.
(REVERSE) The police officer was charged with violating Woodard's civil rights but was acquitted by an all-white jury. The result troubled the presiding judge, J. Waties Waring, who would go on to issue landmark civil rights rulings, including a dissent in *Briggs v. Elliott* (1952), which became a model for *Brown v. Board of Education* (1954). In 2018 a judge, on the town's motion, expunged Woodard's conviction. *Sponsored by the Sgt. Isaac Woodard Historical Marker Association, 2019* [Dedicated to the memory of Isaac Woodard, 2019] (bracketed text written in Braille)
GPS Coordinates: 33° 54.417' N, 81° 32.963' W

Marion County

34–1 Battle of Blue Savannah

Hwy. 41, just south of intersection with Hwy. 501, Ariel Crossroad

(FRONT) On Sept. 3, 1780, Lt. Col. Francis Marion led his men to Port's Ferry, south of here, where they crossed the Pee Dee River. Before dawn on Sept. 4, Marion's mounted command of about 53 men marched and attacked an advance part of loyalist militia volunteers in Maj. Micajah Ganey's force, led by Capt. Jesse Barfield.
(REVERSE) During a second skirmish, occurring roughly three miles north, in the vicinity of a Carolina Bay known as Blue Savannah, Marion again attacked and dispersed a larger detachment of approximately 200 loyalists. Marion's victory here encouraged new recruits to join his force. Reinforcements to the local Tory militia, however, soon forced the Patriot militia leaders to withdraw from here into N.C. *Erected by Blue Savannah-Swamp Fox Chapter, D.A.R., 2016* [Replaced two previous markers erected by the Blue Savannah Chapter, D.A.R. in 1955 and 1967.]
GPS Coordinates: 34° 4.202' N, 79° 18.421' W

34–2 Confederate Navy Yard
[Reported missing in 2004.]

U.S. Hwy. 76/301, about 8 mi. W of Marion at the Pee Dee River, Pee Dee vicinity

The Confederacy established a navy yard ¼ mile NW about 1863 on the banks of the Great Pee Dee River. Here, under the command of Lt. Van Renssalaer Morgan, a wooden gunboat, the C.S.S. Pee Dee, was built. Launched by November 1864, it was burned to prevent its capture by Federal Forces in March 1865. *Erected by U.D.C., Pee Dee District, 1968*
GPS Coordinates: 34° 12.265' N, 79° 32.413' W

34–3 Britton's Neck/Britton's Ferry

U.S. Hwy. 378, .3 mi. SE of its intersection with S.C. Hwy. 908, at Britton's Neck

Britton's Neck (FRONT)
One of the oldest settlements in Marion County, Britton's Neck lay between Great and Little Pee Dee Rivers extending northward from the mouth of the Little Pee Dee. It was named for Francis, Timothy, Daniel, Moses, Joseph and Philip Britton, who settled in the

neck about 1735–36. They were the sons of Francis Britton, who was in Carolina by 1697. Britton's Ferry (REVERSE)

Six miles south of here was the site of Britton's Ferry, on Great Pee Dee River at the junction of Williamsburg, Georgetown, and Marion County lines. The ferry was established by Francis Britton and two other commissioners under an Act of 1747. Britton's Neck was the center of patriot sympathy during the American Revolution, making the ferry important to both sides. *Erected by Dr. Henry Woodward Chapter, S.C. Society Daughters of the American Colonists, 1971*

GPS Coordinates: 33° 51.977' N, 79° 20.097' W

34–4 Snow's Island

[Replaced by marker 34-16.]

U.S. Hwy. 378 at its intersection with Dunham's Bluff Rd., Britton's Neck vicinity

During the winter of 1780–1781, General Francis Marion established his camp 1 ½ miles south of here on Snow's Island. Named for early settlers James and William Snow, the island forms the southeast corner of present Florence County and is bounded by Pee Dee River, Lynch's River, and Clark's Creek. Snow's Island was the site of a battle fought in March 1781. *Erected by Snow's Island Chapter, Children of the American Revolution, Mullins, S.C., 1972*

GPS Coordinates: 33° 51.967' N, 79° 20.085' W

34–5 Marion County/Marion Courthouse

Marion County Courthouse, corner of N. Main & W. Dozier Sts., Marion

Marion County (FRONT)

Originally part of colonial Craven County and Georgetown District of 1769, Marion was created as Liberty County by an Act of the General Assembly in 1785. The name was changed to Marion District in 1798 and to Marion County in 1868. The present lines were established by the withdrawal of Florence County in 1888 and Dillon County in 1910. The area is 480 square miles.

Marion Courthouse (REVERSE)

Erected in 1853 at a cost of twelve thousand five hundred dollars, this is the third structure built on this site to house the court. Restored in 1970, the original ironwork remains and each step bears the name and address of the metal worker, "Hayward Bartlett, Baltimore." *Erected by Marion County Historical Society, 1972*

GPS Coordinates: 34° 10.726' N, 79° 24.027' W

34–6 Moody Cemetery

U.S. Hwy. 501, just N of Spring Branch and S. of E. Pines Rd., Spring Branch vicinity N of Marion

Named for the Moody family, members of whom were buried here 1883 to 1903. Among others interred here are John Smith Sr., Revolutionary War veteran who owned an adjacent plantation, and Enos Tart Jr., who served Marion District as Sheriff, S.C. Representative and Senator, Clerk of Court, and contractor for the district's 1823 courthouse. *Erected by Blue Savannah Chapter, Daughters of the American Revolution, 1976*

GPS Coordinates: 34° 15.307' N, 79° 24.948' W

34–7 Marion Presbyterian Church

208 S. Main St., corner of S. Main & Presbyterian Sts., Marion

(FRONT) David E. Frierson of Harmony Presbytery first preached here at Marion Courthouse in 1841. The church was organized in Feb. 1852 with six charter members: Archibald and Margaret Carmichael of Little Pee Dee Church, Rebecca E. Frierson of Great Pee Dee Church, Sophia E. McIntyre of Hopewell Church, Duncan J. McDonald from Smyrna, N.C., and David Gibson from Dalry, Scotland. (REVERSE) This house of worship, dedicated in February 1852, stands on land given by Archibald McIntyre. In 1913 Sunday School rooms were added on the west end of the original structure and new pews were purchased. The bell dates from 1911 and the organ from 1919. During the early 1970s, the church was renovated to include an enlarged sanctuary, new choir room and rear entrance. It was rededicated in April 1975. *Erected by the Congregation, 1977*

GPS Coordinates: 34° 10.579' N, 79° 24.042' W

34–8 Bowling Green

U.S. Hwy. 501, just N. of Bowling Green Rd., Spring Branch vicinity, N of Marion

On this site, located about ½ mile northeast, at least 500 Loyalists under the command of Major Micajah Ganey laid down their arms in accordance with a previous agreement made between Francis Marion and Ganey. This treaty signed June 8, 1782 at Burch's Mill on the Pee Dee River, ended the partisan warfare in the area. *Erected by Marion County Historical Society, 1978*
GPS Coordinates: 34° 14.793' N, 79° 24.456' W

34–9 Mullins Depot/Mullins

1 Main St., between N. & S. Front Sts., Mullins

Mullins Depot (FRONT)
The town of Mullins, first known as Mullins Depot, grew up as a result of the opening of the Wilmington and Manchester Railroad in 1854. Land for the railroad's buildings and for right-of-way was given here by Wm. S. Mullins (1824–1878) who was elected Wilmington and Manchester president in 1857. A frame railroad depot, constructed here in 1901, was remodeled in 1931 as it is today.
Mullins (REVERSE)
The town of Mullins was incorporated March 4, 1872 by an act of the S.C. General Assembly which set town limits "half a mile north, one-quarter of a mile east and west, and one-third of a mile south" from a stake near here. Dr. Rudolph Vampill was elected first intendant and A. E. Gilchrist, D. W. Ketchum, James Norton, and Stephen Smith, wardens. Smith was also the community's first postmaster, appointed in 1855. *Erected by Marion County Historical Society, 1981*
GPS Coordinates: 34° 12.33' N, 79° 15.264' W

34–10 Old Town Hall and Opera House

Corner of W. Court St. & W. Godbold St., Marion

(FRONT) This brick building is a fine vernacular interpretation of the Classic Revival style. Completed in 1892, the construction was financed through a $10,000 bond issue; this included an artesian well nearby. The lower floor contained a council room, market, guard rooms and, after 1910, sleeping rooms for the fire department. The council room also provided the setting for many social occasions. (REVERSE) The second floor of this building contained a 525-seat auditorium that was used for traveling road shows, graduations, and other Marion events for many years. In 1920 the property was sold and converted to commercial use. The city of Marion purchased the historic building in 1980, and with guidance from Mayor T. C. Atkinson, Jr., renovated it for civic use. *Erected by Marion County Historical Society, 1983*
GPS Coordinates: 34° 10.684' N, 79° 24.06' W

34–11 Ebenezer Church

Intersection of Old Ebenezer Rd. (S.C. Sec. Rd. 34–197) & Dudley Rd. (S.C. Sec. Rd. 34–22), Temperance Hill vicinity, near Marion County-Dillon County line

According to local tradition three Methodist meeting houses of this area united ca. 1835 to form Ebenezer. An early church building burned in 1855 and was replaced in 1856 by this present building, which is listed in the National Register of Historic Places. William Haselden Ellerbe, Governor of S.C. from 1897–1899, was once a member of Ebenezer. *Erected by Ebenezer Memorial and Historical Association, 1982*
GPS Coordinates: 34° 17.167' N, 79° 24.65' W

34–12 Marion Academy

Marion County Museum, 101 Willcox Ave., Marion

This building, the first public school in Marion County, was built in 1886 by the Marion Academy Society, chartered in 1811. The Society, which had operated a private school here for almost seventy-five years, then turned the school over to the Marion School District as the new public school. The Marion Graded School, which closed in 1976 after ninety years' continuous service to the community, now houses the Museum of Marion County. *Erected by the Marion County Historical Society and the Pee Dee Committee, Colonial Dames of America, South Carolina, 1996*
GPS Coordinates: 34° 10.74' N, 79° 24.174' W

34-13 Mt. Olive Baptist Church

Corner of E. Church and N. Mullins Sts., Mullins

This church was founded in 1882 by 16 charter members, all former slaves or the children of former slaves. It held services in a brush arbor and a cotton gin before building its first sanctuary in 1886 at Main and Marion Streets. The present sanctuary, designed by Negro architect Wade Alston Ford and built by members of the congregation in 1922–26, was listed in the National Register of Historic Places in 2000. *Erected by the Congregation, 2002*
GPS Coordinates: 34° 12.618' N, 79° 14.989' W

34-14 Bluefields

1203 N. Main St., Marion

(FRONT) "Bluefields," named for the Blue family, was built by 1870. Annie Evans Blue (d. 1912) was given this land in 1872 by her father William Evans (1804–1876), Marion District planter, militia general, and state representative. Annie Blue and her husband, John Gilchrist Blue (1829–1889) raised their family here. John Gilchrist Blue, born in N.C., was an attorney and Confederate officer who served as a S.C. state representative 1876–80 and 1884–85.
(REVERSE) Two of the Blues's sons were nationally prominent. Victor (1865–1928), a graduate of the U.S. Naval Academy, was promoted for heroism during the Spanish-American War and commanded a battleship during World War I; he retired as a rear-admiral. Rupert (1867–1948), a graduate of the University of Maryland medical school, was surgeon general of the U.S. Public Health Service; he led in eradicating the bubonic plague in San Francisco and Los Angeles. *Erected by the Marion County Historical Society, 2004*
GPS Coordinates: 34° 11.467' N, 79° 23.883' W

34-15 Marion Depot

Marion Chamber of Commerce, 209 E. Bobby Gerald Pkwy., Marion

This one-story brick passenger depot, typical of the period, was built in 1908 for the Atlantic Coast Line Railroad. The first railroad through Marion was the Wilmington &

Manchester Railroad, completed here in 1854 and later incorporated into the Atlantic Coast Line when that railroad was created in 1900. This depot replaced an earlier frame passenger station and closed in 1966. The City of Marion renovated the building in 2004–05. *Erected by the Marion Chamber of Commerce, 2009*
GPS Coordinates: 34° 11.008' N, 79° 23.883' W

34-16 Marion's Camp at Snow's Island

U.S. Hwy. 378, just SE of Dunham Bluff Rd., Britton's Neck vicinity

(FRONT) During the American Revolution Gen. Francis Marion (ca. 1732–1795), the most successful of the Patriot partisan leaders, made his camp and headquarters about 1.8 mi. SSW on Snow's Island. The island, named for settlers James and William Snow, is bounded by the Pee Dee River, Lynch's River, and Clark's Creek.
(REVERSE) Marion, called "the Swamp Fox," led a S.C. militia brigade that camped on the island in the winter of 1780–81. In March 1781, with Marion and his men absent, Loyalists under Col. Welborn Doyle raided and destroyed the camp. Marion continued to frustrate British and Loyalist commanders until the end of the war. *Sponsored by the Blue Savannah-Swamp Fox Chapter, Daughters of the American Revolution, 2012*
GPS Coordinates: 33° 51.966' N, 79° 20.05' W

34-17 Centenary Rosenwald School /Terrell's Bay High School

Johnny Odom Dr., Centenary

Centenary Rosenwald School (FRONT)
Centenary Rosenwald School was built here in 1924–25. It was one of 500 rural schools in S.C. for blacks, constructed with partial funding from the Julius Rosenwald Foundation from 1917 to 1932. A two-room frame school, it was built at a cost of $2,100. An average of 125 students a year attended, at first in grades 1–7 but later adding grades 8–12. Centenary School closed in 1954.
Terrell's Bay High School (REVERSE)

Terrell's Bay High School was built in 1954 by the equalization program intended to preserve segregation by building new schools for blacks. It, a new Terrell's Bay Elementary, and a new Pleasant Grove Elementary replaced Centenary Rosenwald School and Rains Colored School. Terrell's Bay High was desegregated in 1970. It closed in 2003 when two county school districts were consolidated. *Sponsored by the Marion County Performing Arts & Science Academy, 2014*
GPS Coordinates: 34° 1.717' N, 79° 21.574' W

34–18 Palmetto High School

305 O'Neal St., Mullins

(FRONT) Palmetto High School, completed in 1953, was built as a school for African American students. It replaced the previous Palmetto High School, which was a Rosenwald School completed in 1924. The new school was one of the equalization schools built in the early 1950s as part of an effort to equalize African American educational facilities. It opened in the spring of 1954 with James T. McCain as principal.
(REVERSE) When completed, the new high school was described as "modern in every detail and constructed entirely of concrete, masonry, and steel." The class of 1970 was the last to graduate from Palmetto High School. Court rulings finally implemented public school integration in 1970–71 and the white and black high schools were combined. The building then became Palmetto Middle School. *Sponsored by the Pee Dee Museum of African-American Culture, 2014*
GPS Coordinates: 34° 12.507' N, 79° 16.008' W

34–19 St. James A.M.E. Church

5333 South Highway 41, Ariel Crossroads

(FRONT) The congregation of St. James A.M.E. Church first worshiped under a bush arbor in the vicinity of what is now Ariel Crossroads. Mattie Munnerlyn White sold one-half acre of land, including the original church, to the Trustees of St. James A.M.E. in 1891. The cornerstone of the current church was laid in 1914 under the leadership of Rev. A. J. Starks,

Pastor, and Rev. W. P. Carolina, Presiding Elder.
(REVERSE) In 1919 Zack R. Leonard sold land to the church for what is now St. James Cemetery, located 3/4 of a mile north. St. James School, built in 1925, once stood nearby and was among 500 schools built for African American students in S.C. that was funded in part by the Rosenwald Foundation (1917–1932). It remained the principal school for local black students until 1954. *Sponsored by St. James A.M.E. Church, 2014*
GPS Coordinates: 34° 3.880' N, 79° 18.646' W

34–20 Antioch Baptist Church

Antioch Church Rd. (S.C. State Rd. S-34-83) west of intersection with James Johnson Rd. (S.C. State Rd. S-34-83), Sellers vic.

(FRONT) Antioch Baptist Church was organized in 1829. The original membership was composed of 36 members dismissed from Catfish Baptist Church. In the first year 31 baptisms were recorded and membership rose to 83. Antioch was a member of the Charleston Baptist Association until 1832. In that year 17 churches, including Antioch, organized the Welsh Neck Baptist Association.
(REVERSE) In 1876 Antioch helped form the Pee Dee Baptist Association. The current building is the third church on this site and was built in 1882. The original baptistry was added the next year. It burned in 1991 and was rebuilt in 1998. A Sunday School was in operation by at least 1891. The church remained in active use until 1935, when Antioch's last members left for other congregations. *Sponsored by the Isham and Mary Watson Descendants Association, 2017*
GPS Coordinates: 34° 17.002' N, 79° 26.889' W

34–21 Tobacco Culture

104 NE Front St., Mullins

(FRONT) In 1892 Dr. C. T. Ford became the first tobacco grower in Mullins when he planted a small patch of Bright Leaf behind his home. Two years later, merchant William H. Daniel proved the viability of the crop by planting 8 acres, which he sold for a good price at

the market in Danville, VA. Daniel would persuade his customers, many of whom were frustrated by depressed cotton prices, to plant tobacco. By 1895, many of the fields around Mullins were planted in the new boom crop. (REVERSE) Construction of the Planters' Warehouse began in late 1894 and in August 1895 Mullins hosted its first tobacco market. By 1902, Mullins had two banks, three tobacco warehouses, four tobacco re-drying plants, and had become the leading tobacco market in the state. The early 20th century commercial buildings on N. Main St. and large homes on E. Wine St. remain as reminders of the prosperity that tobacco once brought to the town. *Sponsored by Marion County, 2018*
GPS Coordinates: 34° 12.333' N, 79° 15.262' W

Marlboro County

35–1 Bennettsville

Marlboro County Courthouse, 105 Main St., Bennettsville

In 1819 the court house of Marlborough District was transferred from Carlisle, a village on the Pee Dee River, to this more central location. Bennettsville developed around the new court house in the heart of a rich farm land area. On March 6, 1863, it was occupied by the 17th Army Corps, United States Army, commanded by Gen. W. T. Sherman. *Erected by the Marlboro County Historic Preservation Commission, 1980*
GPS Coordinates: 34° 37.008' N, 79° 41.059' W

35–1 Bennettsville

Bennettsville City Hall, 501 E. Main St., Bennettsville

In 1819 the court house of Marlborough District was transferred from Carlisle, a village on the Pee Dee River, to this more central location. Bennettsville developed around the new court house in the heart of a rich farm land area. On March 6, 1863, it was occupied by the 17th Army Corps, United States Army, commanded by Gen. W. T. Sherman. *Erected by Bennettsville Jaycees, 1962*
GPS Coordinates: 34° 37.167' N, 79° 40.689' W

35–2 Marlborough County Courthouse

Marlboro County Courthouse, 105 Main St., Bennettsville

Four court houses for Marlborough District or County have stood on this square since Apr. 4, 1820, when it was deeded by John S. Thomas for that purpose. The first court house, completed before 1824, was replaced by a new building in 1852. It was occupied by Union troops in 1865. A third building was finished in 1885. The present court house was built in 1951–1952. *Erected by the Bennettsville Jaycees, 1962*
GPS Coordinates: 34° 36.999' N, 79° 41.076' W

35–3 Edward Crosland House

204 Parsonage St., Bennettsville

This marks the oldest house in Bennettsville, built in 1800 by Edward Crosland, who was born in England and later married Ann Snead. He died in Bennettsville in 1821. He was a Patriot, American Revolutionary Soldier and Plantation Owner. His youngest son, William Crosland, was born in this house on April 23, 1800. *Erected by Marlborough Chapter, Colonial Dames of XVII Century, 1967*
GPS Coordinates: 34° 36.852' N, 79° 40.772' W

35–4 Old Female Academy

121 S. Marlboro St., Bennettsville

The oldest part of this building served as Bennettsville Female Academy 1833–1881. It originally stood opposite First Methodist

Church on East Main Street, was purchased in 1967 by Marlborough Historical Society, moved to its present location, and restored by public donations. Bennettsville Academ- ical Society, organized about 1828, built the Academy. *Erected by Marlborough Historical Society, 1968*
GPS Coordinates: 34° 36.962' N, 79° 40.981' W

35–5 Welsh Neck Settlement

NW side of U.S. Hwy. 15–401, on the Marlboro County-Darlington County line at the Pee Dee River, Society Hill vicinity

Welsh Baptists from Pennsylvania and Dela- ware settled on the east bank of the Pee Dee as early as 1737. Most of the lands in the Welsh Neck, from Crooked Creek to Hunt's Bluff, had been granted by 1746. A Baptist congre- gation was organized in 1738. The first church, predecessor of the Welsh Neck Baptist Church in Society Hill, stood one mile upstream. *Erected by Marlboro County Historic Preser- vation Commission, 1970*
GPS Coordinates: 34° 31.652' N, 79° 49.72' W

35–6 Albert M. Shipp

Near Gillespie Cemetery, U.S. Hwy. 1, 1 mi. N of Wallace

In Gillespie Cemetery, west of here, is buried Albert M. Shipp, Methodist minister, Pro- fessor of History at the University of North Carolina 1849–59, second President of Wof- ford College 1859–75, Vanderbilt University Professor and Dean 1875–85, and author of "Methodism in South Carolina." Dr. Shipp's last home, "Rose Hill" Plantation, is two miles NE. *Erected by Wofford College Alumni Association of Chesterfield-Dillon-Marlboro Counties, 1970*
GPS Coordinates: 34° 43.318' N, 79° 51.801' W

35–7 Bennettsville Methodist Church

311 E. Main St., Bennettsville

The first Methodist house of worship in Marl- boro County was at Beauty Spot, two miles north of here, where, in 1788, Bishop Asbury attended a meeting. By 1834, the first church

in town had been built here on 1 ½ acres of land donated by W. J. Cook. A second build- ing was erected about 1871. The present church dates from 1900 and was extensively reno- vated and improved during 1955 and 1956. *Erected by the Congregation, 1971*
GPS Coordinates: 34° 37.115' N, 79° 40.8' W

35–8 John Lyde Wilson

Intersection of S.C. Hwy. 9 & Old Wire Rd. (S.C. Sec. Rd. 35–165), Wallace vicinity

Near this site stood Stony Hill, boyhood home of John Lyde Wilson, State Senator and Rep- resentative, Governor of South Carolina from 1822 to 1824, and author of *The Code of Honor* (1838), widely used by antebellum duellists. His parents, John Wilson and Mary Lide, are buried in nearby Wilson family cemetery. In 1957, a tornado destroyed the home. *Erected by the Marlboro County Historic Preservation Commission, 1980* [Replaced a marker erected by the same commission in 1971.]
GPS Coordinates: 34° 42.976' N, 79° 50.425' W

35–9 General John McQueen

On the side of the McColl Building, corner of S. Marlboro & E. Main Sts., Bennettsville

This U.S. congressman was born on Febru- ary 9, 1804, at Queensdale, N.C. After being admitted to the bar in 1828, he established a law office on this corner in Bennettsville. Mc- Queen served in the U.S. House of Represen- tatives from 1849 to 1860, resigning on South Carolina's secession from the Union. He was a General of S.C. Militia, a prominent seces- sionist, and a member of the First Confed- erate Congress. *Erected by Marlboro County Historic Preservation Commission, 1972*
GPS Coordinates: 34° 37.007' N, 79° 41.02' W

35–10 Robert Blair Campbell/John Campbell

Intersection of S. Main St. (S.C. Hwy. 38) & E. High St. (S.C. Hwy. 381), Blenheim

Robert Blair Campbell (FRONT)
This U.S. Congressman and diplomat was born at Woodstock (Argyle) Plantation, 3 ½ miles southwest. He was a Brigadier General

in the State Militia and served in the S.C. Senate 1822–23, 1830–34. He represented this district in the U.S. Congress 1823–25, 1834–37. He was U.S. Consul to Cuba 1842–50 and to England 1854–61. In 1862 he died and was buried in London.

John Campbell (REVERSE)

This U.S. congressman, the younger brother of Robert Blair Campbell, was born 3 ½ miles southwest of here. He graduated from the South Carolina College in 1819 and practiced law in Brownsville and Parnassus. He served in Congress as a States Rights Whig 1829–31 and as a States Rights Democrat 1837–45. He died in 1845 and was buried in the family cemetery. *Erected by Marlboro County Historic Preservation Commission, 1972*
GPS Coordinates: 34° 30.622' N, 79° 39.173' W

35–11 Daniel Calhoun Roper 1867–1943

Intersection of U.S. Hwy. 15-401 & S. Stanton St. (S.C. Sec. Rd. 35-22), Tatum

This cabinet member and diplomat was born two miles south of here. He graduated from Trinity College in 1888 and later became head of Marlboro High School, near here. He was Franklin D. Roosevelt's first secretary of commerce from 1933 to 1938 and U.S. minister to Canada, 1939. He was author of *Fifty Years of Public Life*. *Erected by Marlboro County Historic Preservation Commission, 1972*
GPS Coordinates: 34° 38.63' N, 79° 35.194' W

35–12 John Lowndes McLaurin 1860–1934

Intersection of S.C. Hwy. 9 & S.C. Hwy. 79, NW of Bennettsville

One mile west is the last home of John Lowndes McLaurin, Marlboro County native, U.S. Congressman and Senator. He served as S.C. Representative 1890–91, S.C. Attorney General 1891–92, U.S. Congressman 1892–97, U.S. Senator 1897–1903, and State Warehouse Commissioner 1915–17. The mill pond west of here bears his name. *Erected by Marlboro County Historic Preservation Commission, 1972*
GPS Coordinates: 34° 40.679' N, 79° 44.755' W

35–13 Bennettsville Presbyterian Church

130 Broad St., corner of Broad St. (S.C. Hwy. 38) and McColl St., Bennettsville

(FRONT) This church was founded in 1855 by nine members of the Great Pee Dee Presbyterian Church, 5 mi. SE. Rev. Pierpont E. Bishop was its first permanent minister. The first church, a frame building, was dedicated in 1855. Elder J. Beatty Jennings was a delegate to the First General Assembly of the Confederate States, in 1861. The second church here, a brick building, was completed in 1907.
(REVERSE) The second church burned Aug. 24, 1907, before any worship service could be held in it. The present church, described as "almost a duplicate of the burned church," was dedicated in 1911. The chapel and educational building were constructed in 1946. The sanctuary, chapel, and educational building were completely renovated in 2003–05 in honor of the church's 150th anniversary. *Erected by the Congregation, 2007, replacing a marker erected in 1972*
GPS Coordinates: 34° 36.921' N, 79° 41.026' W

35–14 Battle of Hunt's Bluff/Old River Road

W side of Hunts Bluff Rd. (S.C. Sec. Rd. 35-57) near the Great Pee Dee River, SW of Blenheim

Battle of Hunt's Bluff (FRONT)

On July 25, 1780, a convoy of British boats en route from Cheraw to Georgetown was captured here by local Patriots. Wooden logs resembling cannon were mounted on this bluff. When boats appeared, Captain Tristram Thomas demanded unconditional surrender. At this signal, the Loyalist escort joined forces with the Patriots, making prisoners of the British troops.

Old River Road (REVERSE)

This "River Road" was in existence before the Revolution and was a principal trading route from the upper Pee Dee basin and N. C. Piedmont to Georgetown and Charleston on the coast. The road follows the course of the Great Pee Dee River and was traveled extensively by Patriot forces during the Revolution. Early plantations lay along the road. *Erected*

by Marlboro County Historic Preservation Commission, 1973
GPS Coordinates: 34° 29.196' N, 79° 43.129' W

35-15 Pegues Place/Revolutionary Cartel

W side of U.S. Hwy. 1, less than 1 mi. S of South Carolina-North Carolina state line, NW of Wallace

Pegues Place (FRONT)
About 1760, French Huguenot immigrant Claudius Pegues settled in this area. His home, Pegues Place, is located one mile west of here. A founder and early officer of St. David's Episcopal Church in Cheraw, he was elected in 1768 as parish representative to the Commons House of Assembly and in 1785 was named a justice of the county. He died in 1790.
Revolutionary Cartel (REVERSE)
On May 3, 1781, a cartel for the exchange of prisoners of war taken during the American Revolution was signed one mile west of here at the home of Claudius Pegues. Lt. Col. Edward Carrington acted for Maj. Gen. Nathanael Greene of the Continental Army. Capt. Frederick Cornwallis, acting for his cousin, Lieut. Gen. Earl Cornwallis, signed for the British. *Erected by Marlboro County Historic Preservation Commission, 1973*
GPS Coordinates: 34° 48' N, 79° 53.357' W

35-16 Blenheim

Intersection of S. Main St. (S.C. Hwy. 38) & E. High St. (S.C. Hwy. 381), Blenheim

This community was named for Blenheim Palace in England, home of the Duke of Marlborough, for whom Marlboro County is said to have been named. Formerly called Mineral Spring or Spring Hill for the mineral springs ½ mile east, Blenheim traces its origin to wealthy planters who built summer homes in this healthy locality during the antebellum period. *Erected by Marlboro County Historic Preservation Commission, 1973*
GPS Coordinates: 34° 30.618' N, 79° 39.174' W

35-17 Abel Kolb's Murder/Welsh Neck Cemetery, Welsh Neck. IMAGE COURTESY OF SCDAH

35-17 Abel Kolb's Murder/Welsh Neck Cemetery

Intersection of U.S. Hwy. 15-401 & S.C. Sec. Rd. 35-167 just E of the Great Pee Dee River near the Marlboro County-Chesterfield County line, Welsh Neck

Abel Kolb's Murder (FRONT)
Colonel Abel Kolb was a prominent Revolutionary War Patriot of this area. A band of Tory raiders, on the night of April 27–28, 1781, surrounded the home of Colonel Kolb and his family. He was shot while surrendering himself as a prisoner of war and his home was burned. His grave is in old Welsh Neck cemetery, one mile north, a short distance from his home site.
Welsh Neck Cemetery (REVERSE)
One mile north on the east bank of Pee Dee River is the site of Old Welsh Neck Baptist Church and its cemetery, where early Welsh settlers and their descendants are buried. Two stone monuments and several river rocks mark the few remaining graves of members of the Marshall, Kolb, and Wilds families. When the church moved to Society Hill, the cemetery was abandoned. *Erected by Marlboro County Historic Preservation Commission, 1973*
GPS Coordinates: 34° 31.678' N, 79° 49.687' W

35–18 Grave of General Tristam Thomas/Saw Mill Baptist Church

S.C. Sec. Rd. 35-209 at its junction with Willamette Rd (S.C. Hwy. 912), W of Bennettsville

Grave of Tristam Thomas (FRONT)
In Saw Mill Church cemetery is the grave of Tristram Thomas, major of militia during the Revolution. At Hunt's Bluff, ten miles south, a band of Patriots under his command seized a British flotilla in 1780. He served as legislator, as first Brigadier General of the Cheraw Militia, and as commissioner for locating the county seat.
Saw Mill Baptist Church (REVERSE)
In 1785 Philip Pledger donated to the Cheraw Hill Baptist Church a tract of land here adjoining his saw mill. Pledger's Saw Mill Church was eventually constituted in 1820 as a separate church. The original congregation relocated in 1832 as Bennettsville Church. Sawmill Church today is a member of the S.C. Baptist Educational and Missionary Convention. *Erected by Marlboro County Historic Preservation Commission, 1974*
GPS Coordinates: 34° 37.732' N, 79° 46.301' W

35–19 Barnabas Kelet Henegan Home Site

100 yds. S of intersection of S.C. Hwy. 38 & Screw Pin Rd. (S.C. Sec. Rd. 35-18), Bristow

Governor Henagan (1798–1855), son of Drusilla and Darby Henagan, planter and physician, lived about one mile northwest of this site. Senator, Marlboro District 1834–38; Lieut. Governor of S.C. 1838–40; Governor of South Carolina 1840; moved to Marion District 1843; Senator, Marion District 1844–46; S.C. Secretary of State 1846–50. *Erected by Marlboro County Historic Preservation Commission, 1974*
GPS Coordinates: 34° 25.178' N, 79° 37.108' W

35–20 Old Beauty Spot

Intersection of Beauty Spot Rd. E. (S.C. Sec. Rd. 35-47) & Wallace Rd. (S.C. Sec. Rd. 35-17), Breeden vicinity

Here stood the first Methodist church of Marlboro County, a single log cabin built in 1783. Here Bishop Francis Asbury presided over and preached at an early Quarterly Conference, held on February 23, 1788. Camp meetings were held here 1810–1842. In 1883, the church was moved to another site, also called Beauty Spot, two miles eastward. *Erected by Marlboro County Historic Preservation Commission, 1974*
GPS Coordinates: 34° 38.79' N, 79° 40.018' W

35–21 Grave of Mason Lee/Will of Mason Lee

200 yds. S of intersection of S.C. Hwy. 38 & Gray Rd. (S.C. Sec. Rd. 35-465), Bristow

Mason Lee (FRONT)
Mason Lee (1770–1821), a wealthy Pee Dee planter known for his eccentricities, is buried in old Brownsville graveyard two miles south of here. He believed all women were witches and that his kinsmen wished him dead to inherit his property. He felt they used supernatural agents to bewitch him and went to great extremes to avoid these supposed powers.
Will of Mason Lee (REVERSE)
This will, which named S.C. and Tenn. as heirs, was the subject of suits in the 1820's charging Lee was of unsound mind when making his will. An 1827 appellate verdict exonerated Lee and established *Heirs at Law of Mason Lee vs. Executor of Mason Lee* as the leading case in South Carolina regarding mental capacity in the execution of a will. *Erected by Marlboro County Historic Preservation Commission, 1975*
GPS Coordinates: 34° 25.415' N, 79° 37.34' W

35–22 Frederick Charles Hans Bruno Poellnitz/Ragtown

Near the intersection of S.C. Hwy. 38 & Screw Pin Rd. (S.C. Sec. Rd. 35-18), Bristow vicinity

Frederick Charles Hans Bruno Poellnitz (FRONT)
Born 1754 [1734] in Gotha, Germany, this former chamberlain to King Frederick the Great of Prussia came to America in 1782. Known as Baron Poellnitz, he lived in New York City nearly 8 years before moving 4 mi. W of here on the Pee Dee River. He and George Washington exchanged ideas about farming projects and equipment.

Ragtown (REVERSE)

Located four miles west, this plantation of 2,991 acres was acquired by Baron Poellnitz in 1790 in exchange for some 22 acres in Manhattan, N.Y. Tradition says that deeds for the transaction were drawn in Alexander Hamilton's law office. Poellnitz continued his agricultural experiments at Ragtown. He died in 1801 and was buried on the plantation. *Erected by the Marlboro County Historic Preservation Commission, 2004* [Replaced a marker erected in 1976.]
GPS Coordinates: 34° 25.304' N, 79° 37.227' W

35–23 Jennings-Brown House

121 S. Marlboro St., Bennettsville

In 1826 Dr. Edward W. Jones bought a lot at S. Marlboro and present E. Main and built this house thereon shortly after. Owned by Dr. J. Beatty Jennings when Union forces occupied Bennettsville 1865, the house is said to have served as their headquarters. Moved here ca. 1905, purchased by Lura G. Brown 1930, and opened by Marlboro County Preservation Commission as a house museum 1976. *Erected by Marlboro County Historic Preservation Commission, 1976*
GPS Coordinates: 34° 36.969' N, 79° 40.986' W

35–24 Greene's Encampment /Sherman's March

Just N of intersection of U.S. Hwy. 1 & S.C. Hwy. 9, Wallace

Greene's Encampment (FRONT)
During December 1780, Major General Nathanael Greene, commander of the Southern Army, brought a number of troops to a "camp of repose" near this spot. Here he hoped for abundant food and improvement of strength, discipline, and spirit of his men. Greene departed camp on January 28, 1781 to resume active campaigning against the British.
Sherman's March (REVERSE)
Units of the Union Army under Maj. Gen. Wm. T. Sherman crossed the Pee Dee River near here during March, 1865, leaving Cheraw for N.C. The 17th Corps advanced to and occupied Bennettsville; the 15th Corps marched about 4 miles and camped at Harrington's

Plantation; the 14th and 20th Corps crossed the river several miles north of here at Pegues' Crossing. *Erected by the Marlboro County Historic Preservation Commission, 1976*
GPS Coordinates: 34° 43.204' N, 79° 51.692' W

35–25 Magnolia

508 E. Main St., Bennettsville

Constructed in 1853, this house was the home of William D. Johnson, a Bennettsville attorney and one of three Marlboro County signers of South Carolina's Ordinance of Secession. He served in the state Senate 1862–1865 and was elected chancellor of the Equity Court in 1865. According to tradition, Magnolia was occupied by Union troops on March 6, 1865. The house is listed in the National Register of Historic Places. *Erected by Marlboro County Historic Preservation Commission, 1978*
GPS Coordinates: 34° 37.17' N, 79° 40.632' W

35–26 Marlborough Court House /Old River Road

U.S. Hwy. 401/15 at its intersection with Willamette Rd. (S.C. Hwy. 912), Welsh Neck

Marlborough Court House (FRONT)
Located about one mile N. of here was the original county seat of Marlborough County, established in 1785. Tristram Thomas conveyed two acres of land to the county for the erection of public buildings in 1787, and the court house and jail were built there shortly afterward. The county seat was removed to a more central location in 1819. No trace of the original town remains.
Old River Road (REVERSE)
This river road follows the course of the Great Pee Dee River and crosses U.S. 15 here. It was in existence before the Revolution and was a principal trade route from North Carolina and the Upper Pee Dee to Georgetown and Charleston. Early plantations lay along the road and it was traveled extensively by Patriot forces during the American Revolution. *Erected by Marlboro County Historic Preservation Commission, 1978*
GPS Coordinates: 34° 34.969' N, 79° 45.676' W

35–27 Early Cotton Mill

S.C. Hwy. 385 at its intersection with Burnt Factory Rd. (S.C. Sec. Rd. 35–372), Breeden vicinity

About 1836 William T. Ellerbe, John Mc-Queen, and John N. Williams built a cotton mill approximately one mile northwest. Power for operation of the mill came from the waters of nearby Crooked Creek. Ellerbe and Williams sold their stock in the mill to Meekin Townsend in 1844. The mill was destroyed by fire in 1851, but Burnt Factory Pond remains today. *Erected by Marlboro County Historic Preservation Commission, 1978*
GPS Coordinates: 34° 39.9' N, 79° 39.434' W

35–28 Clio

Corner of Main St. (S.C. Hwy. 9) & Society St. (S.C. Hwy. 381), Clio

McLaurin's Muster Ground, located at this crossroads, became a polling place in 1825. According to local tradition, the community was later called Ivy's Crossroads. A post office named Clio was established here in 1836 and the town was incorporated in 1882. The Florence Railroad Company extended its Latta branch line into Clio in 1895. *Erected by Marlboro County Historic Preservation Commission, 1979*
GPS Coordinates: 34° 34.773' N, 79° 32.78' W

35–29 Brownsville Church

Screw Pin Rd. (S.C. Sec. Rd. 35–18), about 2.1 mi. NW of S.C. Hwy. 38, at the intersection of Screw Pin Rd. with River Rd. (S.C. Sec. Rd. 35–44), Bristow vicinity

In 1788, this Baptist congregation, while still a branch of Cashaway Church (1756), purchased this land from the Rev. John Brown. The branch became an independently constituted church in 1789 named Muddy Creek and by 1829 was known as Brownsville. Welsh Neck Baptist Association was organized here in 1832. The church moved 2 miles NE in 1860. *Erected by The Congregation, 1989*
GPS Coordinates: 34° 25.594' N, 79° 39.075' W

35–30 Brownsville Baptist Church

100 yds. S of intersection of Old S.C. Hwy. 38 & S.C. Sec. Rd. 35–99, 5 mi. SE of Blenheim

(FRONT) In 1788, this Baptist congregation, a branch of Cashaway Church (1756) founded by Welsh Neck Church (1738), purchased land 2 miles SW of here from the Rev. John Brown. The congregation was independently constituted in 1789 and named Muddy Creek. The church, which was known as Brownsville by 1829, moved here in 1860.
(REVERSE) Completed in 1979 to resemble the 1860 church which burned in 1977, this building contains the original pine pews & pulpit furniture from the 1860 building. Both the Welsh Neck & Pee Dee Baptist Associations were organized in Brownsville Church in 1832 and 1876, respectively. Prior to 1832, Brownsville belonged to the Charleston Association. *Erected by The Congregation, 1989*
GPS Coordinates: 34° 26.52' N, 79° 37.649' W

35–31 Shiness

100 Fayetteville Ave., Bennettsville

(FRONT) According to a plaque placed on its western wall at time of construction, Shiness was built in 1903 by Alexander James Matheson and named for his paternal grandmother's home in Sutherlandshire, Scotland. Matheson was born in Marlboro County in 1848, became a successful businessman and large landowner, married Sarah Ellen Jarnigan in 1870 and became the father of nine [. . .]
(REVERSE) [. . .] children. He died in 1918 and is buried in McCall Cemetery in Bennettsville. Shiness was sold in 1939 to J. L. Powers, who converted it into apartments. A key structure in Bennettsville's 1978 National Register District, Shiness was purchased by William Light Kinney, Jr., in 1984 for adaptive use as business offices and retail shops. *Erected by Marlboro County Historic Preservation Commission, 1991*
GPS Coordinates: 34° 36.86' N, 79° 40.923' W

35–32 D. D. McColl House 1826/D. D. McColl House 1884

Bennettsville Visitors Center and Chamber of Commerce, 304 West Main St., Bennettsville

D. D. McColl House 1826 (FRONT)
This house, built in 1826 on Darlington St. (now Main St.), was first owned by H. H. Covington. It was sold in 1871 to Duncan Donald McColl (1842–1911), prominent Marlboro County lawyer and businessman; the McColls lived in this house until 1884. Later moved to S. Liberty St., then McColl St., and finally to its present location by Hugh L. McColl, Jr., the house was donated to the county by McColl in 1991.

D. D. McColl House 1884 (REVERSE)
This Queen Anne house, built in 1884 for D. D. McColl, features local brick made from yellow clay and stained to simulate red brick. McColl organized the S.C. & Pacific Railway in 1884, served as its first president, and brought the railroad to Bennettsville and nearby areas. He also helped organize the Bank of Marlboro in 1886 and the Bennettsville Cotton Mill in 1897, and the town of McColl was named after him. *Erected by Pee Dee Committee of the Colonial Dames of America in the State of South Carolina, 1998*
GPS Coordinates: 34° 36.928' N, 79° 41.207' W

35–33 Clio Passenger Depot

Corner of Calhoun and Society Sts., Clio

(FRONT) This depot was built in 1915 by the Atlantic Coast Line Railway. The first railroad line in Clio was a branch of the Florence Railroad, extended here from Latta in 1895, with a freight depot on S. Main St. After the Atlantic Coast Line Railway absorbed the Florence Railroad it built this depot. A cotton boom spurred the dramatic growth of Clio between 1900 and 1920 but did not survive the Depression.
(REVERSE) The Atlantic Coast Line Railway ended rail service to Clio in 1941 and removed the tracks along Calhoun Street. The Clio Woman's Club persuaded the town to buy the depot, which has been a community center and has also housed the Woman's Club, Clio Library, and Clio Fire Department. The depot,

renovated in 2002, was listed in the National Register of Historic Places in 1979 as part of the Clio Historic District. *Erected by the Town of Clio, 2003*
GPS Coordinates: 34° 34.724' N, 79° 32.862' W

35–34 J. F. Kinney House/P. M. Kinney House

123 S. Marlboro St., Bennettsville

J. F. Kinney House (FRONT)
This house was built as a one-story residence in 1902 for Dr. John Frank Kinney (1870–1928) and his wife Florence McLeod Kinney (1874–1936). They added a second story and wraparound porch in 1907 and raised their five children here. Kinney was educated at Wofford College and the Medical College of S.C. He was county physician for 28 years, served on the Bennettsville Board of Health, and was also president of the Pee Dee Medical Association.

P. M. Kinney House (REVERSE)
In 1929 J. F. Kinney's son, Dr. Prentiss McLeod Kinney (1899–1977), bought this house; he lived here with his wife Adelaide Smith Kinney (1899–1984). Kinney, educated at Wofford, the U. of Ga., and the Medical College of S.C., practiced medicine in Marlboro County for more than 50 years. During World War II he commanded a company and a battalion in the U.S. Army in Europe. He willed this house to the county, and it became the Marlboro County Historical Museum in 1997. *Erected by the Marlborough Historical Society, 2007*
GPS Coordinates: 34° 36.949' N, 79° 40.973' W

35–35 Murchison School

Fayetteville Ave. & S. Marlboro St., Bennettsville

(FRONT) The Murchison School, built in 1902, was named for John D. Murchison (1826–1892), a merchant and the first mayor of Bennettsville. It was given to the city in his memory by his widow, former teacher Harriet Murchison Beckwith (1855–1927). This Romanesque Revival school features a central bell tower with a terra cotta tablet over its ornate arched entrance. It was designed by Denver architect John J. Huddart and built by contractor W. T. Wilkins of Florence.

(REVERSE) Murchison School was an elementary and high school from 1902 to 1918, when Bennettsville High School was built next to it, and an elementary school from 1918 until it closed in 1989. The auditorium has hosted many civic events, club meetings, and theater productions. During World War II its balcony was renovated to house a dual library for this school and Bennettsville High after the high school burned. The balcony was later restored to its original appearance. *Erected by the Marlborough Historical Society, 2008*
GPS Coordinates: 34° 36.87' N, 79° 40.923' W

35–36 Ammons Family Cemetery

U.S. Hwy. 15–401E, between Bennettsville & Tatum, Bennettsville vicinity

(FRONT) The family cemetery of Joshua Ammons (1756–1833), veteran of the American Revolution, is all that remains of his 500-acre plantation near the Three Creeks. Ammons, a native of Virginia, moved to S.C. by 1775, when he enlisted in the 3rd S.C. Militia. Ammons reenlisted in 1777 and was in the battles of Savannah and Stono Ferry and the Siege of Savannah in 1777–1779.
(REVERSE) Ammons, captured by the British at the fall of Charleston in 1780, was exchanged in time for the siege of Yorktown and the British surrender there in 1781. An early history of Marlboro County praised him for his "great firmness of character and solid worth." Ammons, a longtime member of Beauty Spot Baptist Church, received a veteran's pension shortly before his death in 1833. *Erected by the Marlborough Historical Society, 2011*
GPS Coordinates: 34° 37.455' N, 79° 37.626' W

35–37 Palmer Field/Capt. William White Palmer

S.C. Hwy. 9 West near its intersection with Beauty Spot Rd. West (S.C. Sec. Rd. 35–47, Bennettsville
Palmer Field (FRONT)
Palmer Field, originally Marlboro Aviation School, operated here from Oct. 1941 to Nov. 1944 as a primary training facility for the U.S. Army Air Corps during World War II. Civilian flight instructors led cadets through a 9-week course in PT-17 Stearman biplanes.

The 55th Army Air Corps Flying Training Detachment trained 6,410 pilots here; 4,769, or 73%, graduated.
Capt. William White Palmer (REVERSE)
Flight training ended here in late 1944, but the field briefly housed German POWs in 1945. In 1943 the field had been renamed for Capt. William White Palmer (1895–1934), Bennettsville native and World War I pilot. Palmer, in Capt. Eddie Rickenbacker's 94th Aero Squadron, was awarded the Distinguished Service Cross and Croix de Guerre for gallantry in aerial combat. *Erected by the Marlborough Historical Society, 2011*
GPS Coordinates: 34° 39.542' N, 79° 42.981' W

35–38 "The Gulf"

SW Corner of W. Market St. and N. Liberty St., Bennettsville

(FRONT) This area has been the center of the African-American business district and a popular gathering place since the late 19th century. It has been called "the Gulf" since about 1925. Its most prominent early figure was E. J. Sawyer, Jr. (1854–1929), who was born a slave in N.C. and came here about 1869. Sawyer, postmaster 1883–85 and 1892–93, was also principal of the Colored Graded School 1878–1893, and editor of the Pee Dee Educator 1890–1900.
(REVERSE) The block of Market St. going W from Liberty St. to Cheraw St. got its name from the large Gulf Oil Company sign at Everybody's Service Station. That station, on the corner of N. Liberty and W. Market Sts., was long owned by J. D. "Bud" McLeod. Heber E. Covington (1887–1952) ran a popular cafe next door for many years, as well as a taxi service. The street was often blocked off at night on the weekends for dancers enjoying the latest recorded or live music. *Sponsored by the Marlborough Historical Society, 2012*
GPS Coordinates: 34° 37.016' N, 79° 41.139' W

35–39 Marlboro Training High School

612 King St., Bennettsville

(FRONT) This school, built in 1928 and founded by the Marlboro Educational Society, was the first high school for black students in the county. It was accredited by the state as a four-year high school by 1939. An elementary and high school 1928–1956, it included students in grades 1–11 until 1948 and added grade 12 in 1949. It was an elementary school 1956–1972, then was a child development center for the school district until 1987.

(REVERSE) The Colonial Revival school was designed by Bennettsville architect Henry Dudley Harrall (1878–1959). It was also called Marlboro County Training High School. Charles D. Wright, Sr., principal here from 1929 to his death in 1949, was its longest-serving principal, responsible for many advances in its curriculum. This building has housed a local non-profit community center since 1988. *Sponsored by the Marlborough Historical Society, 2012*

GPS Coordinates: 34° 36.545' N, 79° 41.548' W

35–40 Great Pee Dee Presbyterian Church/Pee Dee Missionary Baptist Church

Just S of the intersection of S.C. Hwy. 38 S and Coxe Rd. W, Monroe Crossroads

Great Pee Dee Presbyterian Church (FRONT) This church, built in 1834, was organized by Rev. Archibald McQueen and is the oldest church building in Marlboro County. Notable features include its cupola and the fanlights over the entrance. It was the mother church for Bennettsville (1855) and Blenheim Presbyterian (1888), and was replaced by those churches.

Pee Dee Missionary Baptist Church (REVERSE) In 1891 the church was sold to black Baptists who renamed it Pee Dee Union Baptist Church. It was later renamed Pee Dee Missionary Baptist Church. Rev. Furman D. Peterkin, its first pastor, served here to 1927. This church, remodeled in 1945, was replaced by New Pee Dee Missionary Baptist Church, built in 2008. *Sponsored by the Marlborough Historical Society, 2014*

GPS Coordinates: 34° 32.540' N, 79° 39.263' W

35–41 Adamsville School

Intersection of Adamsville Rd. N (S.C. State Rd 28) and Bradley Rd. (S.C. State Rd 122)

(FRONT) Adamsville School opened in 1954 as part of S.C.'s equalization program, an attempt to forestall racial integration by improving facilities for African American students. The Black elementary school in the McColl area, it consolidated students from local one- and two-room schools.These were Boykin, Brightsville, Fletcher Grove, Lester, Reedy Branch, Saint Paul, and Tatum Schools.

(REVERSE) The high school building was finished in 1955 and students from McColl Industrial and Marlboro Training Schools moved to Adamsville High School. The last graduating class was 1969. The next year S.C.'s dual school system finally ended. Adamsville became a middle school and remained open until 1989. It was later destroyed by fire. *Sponsored by the Adamsville School Reunion, 2018*

GPS Coordinates: 34° 42.171' N, 79° 36.412' W

35–42 Playhouse Theater

106 Clyde St., Bennettsville

(FRONT) Built in 1917 as an opera house and theater, "The Playhouse" was considered among the finest theaters in the Pee Dee. It hosted traveling Broadway productions, musical theater, and vaudeville shows on the New York to Miami circuit. Seating capacity was 1,000 on two levels, including a balcony. The theater also featured a large stage and orchestra pit, as well as a full time orchestra, that all served to attract shows to the venue.

(REVERSE) By the 1930s motion pictures had eclipsed live theater as popular entertainment and the Playhouse was converted to a movie theater. It continued as the Carolina Theatre or Cinema until the 1980s. In 1987, Carmike Cinemas donated this building to the Marlboro Area Arts Council. In 1995, the newly renovated theater reopened as a performing arts center, now known as the Marlboro Civic Center. The building was listed in the National Register of Historic Places in 1993. *Sponsored by the Marlboro Civic Center Foundation, 2018*

GPS Coordinates: 34° 37.070' N, 79° 40.968' W

35–43 Miller-Turner House

117 S. Parsonage St., Bennettsville

(FRONT) The Miller-Turner House is situated on a 450-acre land grant issued in 1772. The oldest sections of the house may date to ca. 1837, when the property was owned by local builder Alexander J. Miller (b. c.1797). Originally one-story, the house's second floor was completed in 1896 by owner and businessman Samuel C. Turner (1864–1896). The house remained in the Turner family until 1989.

(REVERSE) Among the house's owners were Charles A. Thornwell (1820–1855), who may have lived here while serving in the S.C. legislature. Merchant John D. Murchison (1826–1862) lived here 1877–1882. The house is said to have boarded teachers for the Bennettsville Female Academy in the early 1900s, as well as Army Air Corps instructors during World War II. It was included in the Bennettsville Historic District, established 1978. *Sponsored by Christian Fellowship Church, 2019*
GPS Coordinates: 34° 36.925' N, 79° 40.807' W

McCormick County

33–1 Fort Charlotte

Intersection of Savannah River Scenic Byway (S.C. Hwy. 81) & S.C. Sec. Rd. 33-91, Mt. Carmel

6.6 miles southwest are the ruins of Fort Charlotte, built of local stone, 1765–1767, to protect the French, British, and German settlements near Long Canes. Maj. James Mayson's seizure of it, defended by Capt. George Whitefield and Lieut. St. Pierre, July 12, 1775, in the name of the Council of Safety, was the first overt act of the Revolutionary War in South Carolina. *Sponsored by The American Legion of South Carolina 1941*
GPS Coordinates: 34° 0.353' N, 82° 30.432' W

33–2 Willington Academy

Savannah River Scenic Byway (S.C. Hwy. 81), Willington

Two miles southwest is the site of this famous classical academy which was established in 1804 by Rev. Moses Waddel, D.D., one of the greatest educators of his day. Here from 1804 to 1819 he taught hundreds of ambitious boys of great potentiality who became some of the South's most notable men. Their record is his greatest monument. *Erected by McCormick Lions Club, 1962*
GPS Coordinates: 33° 58.304' N, 82° 28.037' W

33–3 Bethany Church

U.S. Hwy. 378 just E of S.C. Sec. Rd. 33-138, E of McCormick

The first Bethany Meeting House was erected by 1809 on the old Edgefield-Abbeville Stagecoach Road midway between Hard Labor and Cuffey Town Creeks. Bethany Baptist Church was constituted in December 1809, with Amos Dubose as pastor. The present church is said to have been built in 1850 at Shinburg Muster Grounds, about two miles south of the original site. *Erected by McCormick County Historical Society, 1970*
GPS Coordinates: 33° 55.479' N, 82° 11.205' W

33–5 Guillebeau Home and Family Cemetery

[Marker number 33-4 was never assigned.]

Intersection of Savannah River Scenic Byway (S.C. Hwy. 81) & S.C. Sec. Rd. 33-196, Willington vicinity

(FRONT) One half mile west is the pioneer home of Andre Guillebeau, a member of the original Huguenot group, which settled in New Bordeaux in 1764, having fled from persecution in France under the leadership of the Reverend Jean Louis Gibert. The house is constructed of logs and according to family tradition was built sometime before 1800.
(REVERSE) Among eighteen members of the Guillebeau family buried in the cemetery one half mile west are Andre Guillebeau,

French Huguenot and soldier of the American Revolution, his wife, Mary Jane Roquemore, their son Pierre Guillebeau, who was for many years a ruling elder of Willington Presbyterian Church, and his wife, Mary Jane Bellot. *Erected by The Huguenot Society of South Carolina, McCormick County Historical Society, and Long Cane Chapter, Daughters of the American Revolution, 1972*
GPS Coordinates: 33° 57.079' N, 82° 26.491' W

33–6 Badwell/Badwell Cemetery

Intersection of Savannah River Scenic Byway (S.C. Hwy. 28) & Barksdale Ferry Rd. (S.C. Sec. Rd. 33–61), about 1½ mi. NW of McCormick

Badwell (FRONT)
Three miles west is the site of "Badwell," home of James Louis Petigru (1789–1863), leader of opposition to secession in South Carolina, outstanding Charleston lawyer, and S.C. Attorney General. He studied at Willington Academy under Moses Waddel and at South Carolina College. The Petigru Law School at the University of South Carolina is named in his honor.
Badwell Cemetery (REVERSE)
Located four miles west is Badwell Cemetery. Among the graves are those of Rev. Jean Louis Gibert (1722–1773), leader of the the 1764 French Huguenot settlement at New Bordeaux and grandfather of James L. Petigru, his son John Joseph Gibert, William and Louise Petigru, parents of James L. Petigru, and Louise Gibert Allston, daughter of Governor R. F. W. Allston. *Erected by McCormick County Historical Commission, 1973*
GPS Coordinates: 33° 55.775' N, 82° 19.836' W

33–7 Battle of Long Cane

Intersection of S.C. Hwy. 28 & S.C. Sec. Rd. 33–38, near McCormick County-Abbeville County line, NE of Willington

About four miles southeast is the site of the American Revolutionary Battle of Long Cane. On December 12, 1780, Lieutenant Colonel Isaac Allen and a British force of 400–500 men defeated Colonel Elijah Clarke and 100 Americans, an advance detachment of a Patriot force commanded by Colonel Benjamin

Few. *Erected by McCormick County Historical Commission, 1977*
GPS Coordinates: 34° 1.934' N, 82° 23.647' W

33–8 Fort Boone

Mt. Carmel Rd. (S.C. Hwy. 823) near McCormick-County-Abbeville County line, NE of Mt. Carmel

Driven from the area at the start of the Cherokee War, settlers from Long Canes returned in the fall of 1760 and, under the protection of a party of Chickasaw Indians, reclaimed the land by building Fort Boone near here. *Erected by McCormick County Historical Commission, 1980*
GPS Coordinates: 34° 3.554' N, 82° 27.017' W

33–9 Dorn's Mill/Dorn Gold Mine

Cedar St. between N. Main St. and W. Gold St., McCormick

Dorn's Mill (FRONT)
Built ca. 1899, this steam-powered mill employed a milling process pioneered earlier by inventor Oliver Evans which virtually eliminated manual labor. First known as the McCormick Enterprise Ginnery, the mill became Dorn-Finley Co. in 1917, its purpose "to operate, conduct and carry on an oil mill, cotton gin and grist mill." Dorn's Mill closed in the 1940s.
Dorn Gold Mine (REVERSE)
Area resident William B. Dorn discovered gold here and developed this mine which produced a yield of $72,000 from 1857 to 1859. The mine was later owned by Cyrus Hall McCormick, inventor of the reaper, for whom the town of McCormick is named. The mine operated at intervals until as late as the 1930s. *Erected by McCormick County Historical Commission, 1983*
GPS Coordinates: 33° 54.767' N, 82° 17.833' W

33–10 Calhoun Mill

Intersection of S.C. Hwy. 823 & S.C. Sec. Rd. 33–40, Calhoun Mills, NE of Mt. Carmel

Built ca. 1854 on a mill site in use since the 1770s, this large brick building on Little River was used for grinding corn, wheat, and other grains. A post office and various commercial

enterprises operated near the mill during the 1800s. The mill yard was a popular place for political rallies and social gatherings well into the 20th century. *Erected by McCormick County Historical Society and McCormick County Historical Commission, 1986*
GPS Coordinates: 34° 1.955' N, 82° 28.55' W

33–11 Cherry Hill/Noble Cemetery

Savannah River Scenic Byway (S.C. Hwy. 81), Willington

Cherry Hill (FRONT)
Three miles southwest is "Cherry Hill," site of the home of George McDuffie (1790–1851), orator of nullification, member of the U.S. House of Representatives and the U.S. Senate, Major General of the State Militia, and Governor of South Carolina. He studied at Willington Academy under Moses Waddel. "Cherry Hill" was his home during most of his adult life.
Noble Cemetery (REVERSE)
Five miles southwest is the Noble Cemetery. Among the members of the Noble family buried there is Patrick Noble (1787–1840). He was a member of the S.C. House of Representatives and Senate and was Governor of South Carolina from 1838 until his death. The cemetery is located on a high knoll overlooking the Savannah River. *Erected by McCormick County Historical Commission, 1974*
GPS Coordinates: 33° 58.301' N, 82° 28.035' W

33–12 John De La Howe (ca. 1710–1797)/John De La Howe School

At the entrance to the John De La Howe School campus, Savannah River Scenic Byway (S.C. Hwy. 81), N of McCormick

John De La Howe (ca. 1710–1797) (FRONT)
Dr. John De La Howe, a French physician, came to South Carolina in 1764 and settled in the New Bordeaux community by the 1780s. His will left most of his estate, including Lethe Plantation, to the Agricultural Society of

South Carolina to establish a home and school for underprivileged children. The Lethe Agricultural Seminary was founded here after De La Howe's death in 1797. Initially restricted [. . .]
John De La Howe School (REVERSE)
[. . .] to 24 boys and girls from what was then Abbeville County, with preference given to orphans, the school emphasized manual training, or instruction in operating a self-sufficient farm. In 1918 it was turned over to the State of South Carolina, opened to children from every county in the state, and renamed John De La Howe School; it is now a group child care agency serving over 200 students a year. *Erected by McCormick County Historical Commission, 1997*
GPS Coordinates: 33° 57.455' N, 82° 25.344' W

33–14 New Bordeaux 1764
[Marker number 33–13 was never assigned.]

Intersection of S.C. Sec. Rd. 33-7 and Huguenot Pkwy., Bordeaux

(FRONT) The town of New Bordeaux, the last of seven French Huguenot colonies founded in colonial S.C. and the only one in the upcountry, was established 1 mi. E in 1764. After Protestants fleeing religious persecution in France petitioned the British crown for land to create a permanent settlement in S.C., they received a 28,000-acre grant in the newly-formed Hillsborough Township.
(REVERSE) Almost 200 French Huguenots led by Rev. Jean Louis Gibert (1721–1773) landed at Charleston in April 1764 and began settling here in August. Others followed, including a group led by Jean Louis Dumesnil De St. Pierre (d. 1776), which arrived in 1768. The colony, which produced silk and wine on a modest scale, later furnished a militia company during the American Revolution. *Erected by the McCormick County Historical Commission and the Huguenot Society of South Carolina, 2000*
GPS Coordinates: 33° 55.317' N, 82° 24.8' W

Newberry County

36–1 Lutheran Theological Southern Seminary

Columbia Hwy. (U.S. Hwy. 176), just N of Pomaria

Here in 1830, in the house of Colonel John Eigleberger, the Evangelical Lutheran Synod of South Carolina and Adjacent States opened a seminary which grew into the Lutheran Theological Southern Seminary now located in Columbia, S.C. *Erected by Southern Lutheran Seminary Auxiliary, 1955*
GPS Coordinates: 34° 16.367' N, 81° 25.55' W

36–2 Bush River Quaker Meeting

Dennis Dairy Rd. (S.C. Sec. Rd. 36-66), 1.2 mi. SW of its intersection with Mendenhall Rd. (S.C. Sec. Rd. 36-273), S of Newberry

This old cemetery marks the site of the Bush River Meeting House. Settled by Quakers in the 1760's, it was a Monthly Meeting 1770–1822 and a Quarterly Meeting with jurisdiction over all meetings in South Carolina and Georgia from 1791 to 1808. Opposing slavery, the members moved west and settled Quaker meetings in Illinois, Indiana, and Ohio. *Erected by Hartford Grange No. 460, 1966*
GPS Coordinates: 34° 13.717' N, 81° 38.267' W

36–3 Newberry College

At the entrance to the Newberry College Campus, 2100 College St., Newberry

This fully accredited Lutheran controlled college was chartered by the General Assembly of South Carolina on December 20, 1856. Dr. John Bachman, noted divine and naturalist, was the first President of the Board of Trustees. The college was used as a Confederate hospital and a U.S. garrison. It removed to Walhalla in 1868 but returned to Newberry in 1877. *Erected by Newberry County Historical Society, 1970*
GPS Coordinates: 34° 17' N, 81° 37.35' W

36–4 Old Court House

On the wall of the Old Newberry County Courthouse, Town Square between Main St. and Boyce St., Newberry

Designed by Jacob Graves and built by John Damron, Newberry County's fourth court house was erected in 1852. It replaced an earlier building on this site which was probably designed by Robert Mills. The Old Court House is now used as a community hall. The bas-relief, added by Osborne Wells, is said to depict the Prostrate State held by the Federal eagle, the gamecock defiantly representing the Spirit of South Carolina. *Erected by Newberry Civic League, 1970*
GPS Coordinates: 34° 16.469' N, 81° 37.199' W

36–5 The Opera House

Corner of Boyce St. & Nance St. (S.C. Hwy. 395), Newberry

This building was erected by the Town of Newberry, and dedicated in February of 1882. An outstanding example of Victorian civic architecture of eclectic design, it was placed on the National Register of Historic Places in 1969. Now housing city offices, the Opera House was for over half a century the center of entertainment for this community. Plays, college commencements, and balls were held in the auditorium upstairs. *Erected by Newberry County Historical Society, 1970*
GPS Coordinates: 34° 16.471' N, 81° 37.245' W

36–6 Bush River Church

Intersection of Garys Ln. (S.C. Sec. Rd. 36-64) & Reeder Rd. (S.C. Sec. Rd. 36-56), SW of Gary

Constituted by Daniel Marshall and Philip Mulkey in June, 1771, Bush River Church is one of the oldest Baptist churches in the up country. The original meeting house stood in the old grave yard, on a tract of two acres willed to the congregation by Samuel

Newman, its first minister. Bush River was the mother church of several antebellum churches. *Erected by the Congregation, 1970*
GPS Coordinates: 34° 19.25' N, 81° 45.583' W

36–7 St. John's Church

Hope Station Rd. (S.C. Sec. Rd. 36-170), .5 mile N of its intersection with Columbia Hwy.(U.S. Hwy. 176), between Pomaria and Peak

This Lutheran church stands on a royal grant of 100 acres made in 1763 to John Adam Epting and Peter Dickert, elders of the Dissenting congregation on Crim's Creek. The origins of St. John's date as early as 1754, when the Reverend John Gasser settled near here. The church was incorporated in 1794 as "the German Lutheran Congregation of St. John."
Erected by the Congregation, 1970
GPS Coordinates: 34° 15.133' N, 81° 22.233' W

36–8 The Rock House

St. Luke's Church Rd. (S.C. Sec. Rd. 36-42), just N of Kinard Creek, S of Newberry

On December 7, 1756, the Council of the Colony recorded a petition of Jacob Hoffman for 200 acres of bounty land. He was granted this acreage on Palmetto Branch in 1758. The building on this tract, which has long been known as "The Rock House," exhibits details of construction which support the local tradition that it was built before the American Revolution. *Erected by Newberry County Historical Society, 1970*
GPS Coordinates: 34° 13.367' N, 81° 36.05' W

36–9 Newberry College Historic District

Newberry College Campus, in front of Smeltzer Hall, College St., Newberry

Listed in the National Register of Historic Places are Smeltzer Hall (1877–78), dormitory for women and campus reception area, renovated and re-dedicated in 1978; Keller Hall (1894), used as chapel, museum, library, laboratory, and now for student activities; Holland Hall (1904), administrative offices for the college; and Derrick Hall (1924), women's

dormitory. *Erected by Newberry College, 1978*
GPS Coordinates: 34° 17.017' N, 81° 37.35' W

36–10 Pomaria

Main St. & Columbia Hwy. (U.S. Hwy. 176), Pomaria

Originally named Countsville, this post office was established in 1823. In 1840, it was renamed Pomaria, probably for William Summer's nearby Pomaria Nursery. By 1851 the Columbia and Newberry Railroad had completed a line through here, and six years later a free school had opened. The town of Pomaria was incorporated in 1903. *Erected by Bicentennial Commission, 1981*
GPS Coordinates: 34° 15.75' N, 81° 24.9' W

36–11 Mount Bethel Academy

U.S. Hwy. 176, about .7 mi. NW of Browns Crossroads, NE of Newberry

(FRONT) Located about one mile northeast on land conveyed by Edward Finch, this school, the first Methodist educational venture in the state, was established by Bishop Francis Asbury and opened by him, 1795. A number of Mt. Bethel students became the first S.C. College graduates. The first Methodist conference in S.C. outside Charleston met here at Finch's house in 1793.
(REVERSE) Among the leading citizens who attended this school, opened 1795 and closed ca.1820, was William Harper, United States Senator and Judge. William Harper was the son of John Harper, who in 1803 founded Washington Street United Methodist Church in Columbia and is buried in the cemetery near the Mount Bethel school site. *Erected by Washington Street United Methodist Church, Columbia, 1987*
GPS Coordinates: 34° 22.5' N, 81° 32.233' W

36–12 New Chapel Church

Deadfall Rd. (S.C. Sec. Rd. 36-83), about 3.5 mi. SE of Silverstreet

Once housing a school for area students, this United Methodist church was located closer to the Saluda River around 1820. The

congregation moved to this site after Isaac Herbert, a member of the S.C. House of Representatives (1844–45), donated the land in 1833. The present building was constructed in 1879. *Erected by Newberry County Historical Society, 1988*
GPS Coordinates: 34° 10.917' N, 81° 39.917' W

36–13 Calvin Crozier Murder Site

Nance St. (S.C. Hwy. 395), between Burton St. and the railroad tracks, Newberry

(FRONT) Col. Charles Trowbridge of the 33rd U.S. Colored Troops ordered the execution of Calvin Crozier, former private 3rd KY Cavalry, on Sept. 8, 1865. Crozier, while en route to his Texas home, cut a troop member on the back of the neck during a quarrel concerning two ladies traveling with Crozier. Soldiers of the 33rd arrested an innocent man for the assault, but Crozier identified himself as the assailant. He was [. . .]
(REVERSE) [. . .] taken to 33rd headquarters, shot, and buried in a shallow grave about 100 yards south. The same day residents of Newberry exhumed the body, placed it in a coffin, and reburied it. In 1891 citizens moved Crozier's remains to Rosemont Cemetery about 1.4 miles west and erected a monument to his memory. The army court-martialed Trowbridge for Crozier's execution. *Erected by John M. Kinard Camp #35, Sons of Confederate Veterans, 1994*
GPS Coordinates: 34° 16.167' N, 81° 37.017' W

36–14 Newberry Cotton Mills

Corner of Main & Tarrant Sts., Newberry

Newberry Cotton Mills, incorporated in 1882, began operation in 1885. The mill was designed by prominent textile mill architects Lockwood, Greene, & Co. and was one of the first cotton mills in the United States operated by steam power. Z. F. Wright, who served as president 1905–1947, was responsible for several expansions. Newberry Cotton Mills, which also sponsored the Newberry Concert Band 1906–1968, closed in 1982. *Erected by the Newberry Co. Historical Society, 1997*
GPS Coordinates: 34° 16.369' N, 81° 37.402' W

36–15 Peak

In Town Park, Peak

This town, founded in 1853 as Peak's Station on the Greenville & Columbia Railroad, was named for railroad superintendent H. T. Peake. In 1865 Federal troops destroyed the tracks here and over the Broad River. Peak, incorporated in 1880, prospered as a railroad town and local center of farming, business, and medical care, in spite of fires in its commercial district in 1909, 1953, and 1978. *Erected by the Town of Peak, 1999*
GPS Coordinates: 34° 14.474' N, 81° 19.35' W

36–16 Mollohon Mill and Village

Glenn St., Newberry, adjacent to the original Mollohon Mill office

This mill was built and operated by the Mollohon Manufacturing Co. from 1901 to 1926, when it was sold to the Kendall Co.; the mill closed in 1976 and was razed in 1980. Original mill village housing was built 1901–02; new mill village was built 1924. The village also included the Mollohon School for grades 1–4 (1921–73), Mollohon Park, pavilion, bandstand and adjacent baseball park, all opened in 1921–22. *Erected by the Newberry County Historical Society, 1999*
GPS Coordinates: 34° 16.15' N, 81° 36.4' W

36–17 Folk-Holloway House

Intersection of Holloway & Folk Sts., Pomaria

This house, built ca. 1820 for John Adam Folk (1799–1855) is an excellent example of a 19th-century two-story farmhouse. Folk, a farmer and merchant, was also postmaster at Tanner's Hill (now Pomaria) 1829–40. Later the home of Folk's daughter Martha and her husband Thomas W. Holloway (1829–1903), who chartered the town of Pomaria in 1903, it was listed in the National Register of Historic Places in 1992. *Erected by the Newberry County Historical Society, 2001*
GPS Coordinates: 34° 16.074' N, 81° 25.177' W

36–18 Bethlehem Lutheran Church

209 New Hope Rd., Pomaria

(FRONT) This church, with its origins in services held in the 1780s at nearby Wicker's Camp Ground, was formally organized in 1816 with Rev. Godfrey Dreher as its first pastor. A log meeting house was built on this site soon afterwards. In 1830 its third pastor, Rev. John G. Schwartz, founded the first Lutheran seminary in the South here in Pomaria, at the home of Col. John Eichelberger.
(REVERSE) In 1855 the S.C. Synod met here and voted to establish a Lutheran college at Newberry. Among the notables buried in the churchyard are Col. John Eichelberger, veteran of the American Revolution; Rev. John G. Schwartz; and Rev. Thaddeus Boinest, who encouraged the German settlement of the Dutch Fork region. The present church, built in 1881–82, was remodeled in 1942 and 1966. *Erected by the Congregation, 2001*
GPS Coordinates: 34° 17.051' N, 81° 25.975' W

36–19 Miller Chapel A.M.E. Church

500 Caldwell St., Newberry

(FRONT) This church, founded in 1867, was one of the first A.M.E. churches north of Columbia. It was organized when black Methodists in Newberry sent Carolina Brown and Winnie Simmons to Columbia for the third annual meeting of the South Carolina Conference of the A.M.E. Church. They asked Rev. Simeon Miller to serve their new church and later named it for him. Rev. Hiram Young was the first presiding elder.
(REVERSE) The congregation first held its services in a cotton warehouse, but acquired this lot and built a church of their own in 1869–70. In 1870, when Miller Chapel A.M.E. Church hosted the first meeting of the Columbia Conference, conference delegates voted to found Payne Institute (now Allen University). This church, later enlarged several times, was covered in brick veneer in the 1970s. *Erected by the Newberry County African American Heritage Committee, 2006*
GPS Coordinates: 34° 16.101' N, 81° 36.883' W

36–20 Hope Rosenwald School

1917 Hope Station Rd., Pomaria vicinity

(FRONT) This school, built in 1925–26 at a cost of $2,900, was one of more than 500 rural African-American schools in S.C. funded in part by the Julius Rosenwald Foundation between 1917 and 1932. The original two-acre lot for the school was donated by James H. Hope, Mary Hope Hipp, and John J. Hope. James H. Hope, then S.C. Superintendent of Education, was its longest-serving head, 1922–1947.
(REVERSE) This two-room school, with grades 1–8 taught by two teachers, closed in 1954. In 1958 it was sold to the Jackson Community Center and Cemetery Association, comprised of nine members of the adjacent St. Paul A.M.E. Church. That group maintained the school for many years. It became the Hope Community Center in 2006 and was listed in the National Register of Historic Places in 2007. *Erected by the Hope School Community Center, 2010*
GPS Coordinates: 34° 16.203' N, 81° 21.869' W

36–21 St. Paul Lutheran Church

2496 S.C. Hwy. 773, Pomaria

(FRONT) This church, founded ca. 1761 by the Rev. Joachim Bulow, is one of the earliest Lutheran congregations in what is now Newberry County. A log church built nearby before the Revolution was replaced by a frame church. A larger frame sanctuary, built ca. 1830 during the pastorate of the Rev. Michael Rauch, would serve the congregation of St. Paul for 108 years.
(REVERSE) The Rev. J. A. Sligh (1835–1917), the longest-serving pastor here, served St. Paul from 1865 to 1912 and is buried in the church cemetery. This Gothic Revival sanctuary, built in 1936–38, was constructed of granite quarried near Pomaria and designed by Willie Koon, brother of the Rev. S. P. Koon, pastor here 1916–1934. The first service here was in 1938; the church was dedicated in 1941. *Erected by the Congregation, 2011*
GPS Coordinates: 34° 14.56' N, 81° 27.296' W

36–22 Newberry Village Cemetery

Coates St., just S of the Boundary Street School, Newberry

This cemetery dates from 1809, 23 years before Newberry's incorporation in 1832. George McCreless donated an acre here for a village cemetery, and his brother Lewis was the first person buried in it. The Town Council bought another acre from John Caldwell in 1847. After Rosemont Cemetery was established 1 mi. N in 1863, this early cemetery was neglected. The last known burial was that of Dr. P. B. Ruff, in 1890. *Erected by the Newberry County Historical and Museum Society, 2011*
GPS Coordinates: 34° 16.286' N, 81° 36.937'

36–23 Oakland Mill

2802 Fair Ave., Newberry

(FRONT) This textile mill, which began operation in 1912, was the third mill built in Newberry, after Newberry Cotton Mills (1885) and Mollohon Mill (1901). It was chartered in 1910 and built in 1911 with 20,000 spindles and 500 looms. The mill was designed by prominent textile mill architects Lockwood, Greene and Co. The Oakland Mill village began with the construction of 75 houses and grew to almost twice that number, with a school and three churches.
(REVERSE) By 1925, when the mill was sold to the Kendall Co., there were 200 employees. The next year the mill village was called "one of the best and prettiest mill sites in the state." By 1930 Oakland Mill had expanded to 30,000 spindles and 600 looms. Other major expansions followed in the 1950s and 1960s. The mill closed in 2008. Listed in the National Register of Historic Places in 2011, it has since been renovated for Newberry College student housing. *Sponsored by the Oakland Mill Development Group and the Newberry County Historical and Museum Society, 2012*
GPS Coordinates: 34° 17.738' N, 81° 37.676' W

36–24 Newberry

1209 Caldwell St. Newberry

(FRONT) Newberry County was one of six counties created from Ninety Six District in 1785. In 1789 John Coate donated two acres for a courthouse and public square. When additional land was surveyed the town was laid out in 25 one-acre squares of four lots each. Originally called Newberry Village and later Newberry Court House, the town was first incorporated in1832. Its population grew dramatically after the Greenville & Columbia RR reached here in 1851.
(REVERSE) Newberry College, founded in1856, opened in 1859. The population almost doubled between 1860 and 1890 after the arrival of the Newberry & Chester RR and Newberry & Augusta RR. It grew still more during the boom generated by three textile mills, Newberry (1885), Mollohon (1901), and Oakland (1912). The Newberry Opera House, built in 1881–82 and restored in 1995–98, is a vibrant community theater hosting a wide range of concerts and other events. *Sponsored by the City of Newberry, 2014*
GPS Coordinates: 34° 16.471' N, 81° 37.196' W

36–25 Rosemont Cemetery

At the cemetery entrance, College Street between Smith Rd. and Cemetery St., Newberry

(FRONT) This cemetery, chartered and established in 1863, was the second major cemetery in Newberry. It replaced the Village Cemetery 1 mi. S on Coates St., which had been established in 1809. Laid out on an 8–2-acre tract between Newberry College and the Calmes Family Cemetery, Rosemont Cemetery was later expanded to its present 40 acres. Some Newberry families moved the graves of loved ones from the Village Cemetery to Rosemont Cemetery.
(REVERSE) In 1890 John A. Chapman called Rosemont "the Silent City adjoining our town," commenting, "Eternal peace broods over it." The granite piers flanking the original entrance were donated by the Newberry Civic League, founded in 1905. Among the notables buried here are a governor who was later a U.S. Senator, state senators and representatives, judges, ministers, doctors, and soldiers of wars from the American Revolution to the present. *Sponsored by the City of Newberry, 2014*
GPS Coordinates: 34° 17.405' N, 81° 37.357' W

36–26 Peoples Hospital

Vincent Street Park, Vincent St. at Cline St., Newberry

(FRONT) Peoples Hospital, the first and only hospital for African Americans in the county from 1937 until Newberry County Memorial Hospital was desegregated in 1952, stood here until 1970. It was founded by Dr. Julian Edward Grant (1900–1997), who practiced medicine in Newberry County for more than fifty years. Grant, a native of Marlboro County, was educated at Claflin University and Meharry Medical College in Nashville, Tenn., before moving to Newberry in 1930.
(REVERSE) Grant, recognizing the need for a hospital for blacks in Newberry, organized a board of trustees from the community. By 1935 the board acquired this site, with a two-story, seven-room frame house on a two-acre lot, for $1,500. The house, renovated and fitted with medical equipment, opened as Peoples Hospital in 1937. The building, later the Vincent Street Community Center after the hospital closed in 1952, was demolished in 1970 to build Vincent Street Park. *Sponsored by the City of Newberry, 2014*
GPS Coordinates: 34° 16.583' N, 81° 37.726' W

36–27 Frederick Nance House-Oak Grove

921 Jessica Ave., Newberry

(FRONT) The Frederick Nance House-Oak Grove, is an early nineteenth-century Classical Revival home, distinct from other early architecture in Newberry for its scale and masonry construction. The home was built on land owned by Frederick Nance (1770–1840), a businessman, planter, and well-respected public official. Appointed Newberry's Clerk of Court in 1794, Nance also served as S.C. Lt. Governor 1808–10 and State Senator 1812–19.
(REVERSE) Although the house now sits on just under two acres, it was once the center of a substantial plantation that was carved from a 785-acre land grant secured by Nance in 1813. The design of the home has been attributed to Robert Mills, who was born in Charleston in 1781 and was preeminent among the first generation of native-born American architects. The property was listed in the National Register of Historic Places in 2014. *Sponsored by the Newberry County Historical and Museum Society, 2014*
GPS Coordinates: 34° 16.061' N, 81° 37.492' W

Oconee County

37–1 First Soil Conservation District Plan

Corner of West South 4th St., Seneca, .4 mi. W from intersection with S. Oak St. (S.C. Hwy. 59) & Quincey Road, Seneca

On February 4, 1938, Mrs. Ploma M. Adams, owner of this farm, assisted by the Upper Savannah Soil Conservation District, initiated the first Farm-Conservation Plan of any district in America. *Erected by Oconee, Pickens and Anderson Soil Conservation Districts, 1963*
GPS Coordinates: 34° 40.583' N, 82° 58.083' W

37–2 St. John's Lutheran Church

301 W. Main St., Walhalla

(FRONT) On November 20, 1853, St. John's was organized by members of the German Colonization Society of Charleston, S.C. who founded the town of Walhalla in 1850. Services were originally held in a house in West Union which was purchased from Col. Joseph Gresham and belonged to Jacob Schroder. The present structure was begun in 1859 and dedicated on March 17, 1861.
(REVERSE) John Kaufmann designed and directed the building of St. John's with the assistance of August Brennecke and members of the congregation. Most of the heart pine timbers were cut from the site on which the church stands. Many of the architectural

features are distinctive and unique to St. John's. Except for the stained glass windows, placed in 1910, the church has changed little since 1861. *Erected by Oconee County Historical Society, 1972*
GPS Coordinates: 34° 45.933' N, 83° 4.161' W

37–3 The Cherokee Path

Intersection of N. S.C. Hwy. 11 & N. Little River Rd., .7 mi. from the intersection of S.C. Hwys. 11 & 130, Salem vicinity

(FRONT) The main trading path to the Cherokee Nation paralleled the route of Highway 11 for several miles at this point. This section of the path was used by travelers going from Keowee, the main Lower Town of the Cherokees, across the mountains to the Middle and Overhill Towns. The botanist William Bartram left a written account of his journey in 1776.
(REVERSE) In addition to its importance in the Indian trade, the path played a military role in the Cherokee War and the Revolution. It linked Fort Prince George (1753) on the Keowee River with Fort Loudoun (1756) on the Little Tennessee. Expeditions against the Cherokees were led by Archibald Montgomery in 1760, James Grant in 1761, and Andrew Williamson in 1776. *Erected by S.C. Society, Daughters of the American Colonists, 1973*
GPS Coordinates: 34° 53.833' N, 82° 59.817' W

37–4 Seneca

N. Fairplay St., just above its junction with Railroad St., Seneca

Founded August 14, 1873, as "Seneca City," and chartered on March 14, 1874, the town of Seneca was named for an Indian village on the Seneca River. Its location was determined by the junction of the Blue Ridge Railroad and the Atlanta and Richmond Air Line Railway. 1880 population: 382/1970 population: 6382. *Erected by Seneca Centennial and Historical Commission, Inc., 1973*
GPS Coordinates: 34° 41.067' N, 82° 57.283' W

37–5 Keowee Town

[Replaced by Marker 37–11, erected by the Wizard of Tamassee Chapter, Daughters of the American Revolution, and the Oconee County Arts and Historical Commission, 2006]

S.C. Sec. Rd. 37-128, 1.6 mi. N of S.C. Hwy. 130, SE of Salem

37–6 Capt. Samuel Earle

Tucker Farm Rd., Fair Play vicinity

(FRONT) Capt. Samuel Earle (1760–1833), an officer during the American Revolution, state representative, and U.S. representative, lived at nearby Beaverdam Plantation. He also furnished land for the town of Andersonville, once 12 mi. SE, at the fork of the Tugaloo and Seneca Rivers. A native of Va., Earle came to S.C. in 1773–74, when his father settled in Spartanburg District.
(REVERSE) During the Revolution Earle was an officer in the 5th S.C. Regiment, then the militia, and then the captain of a ranger company. He served in the S.C. House 1784–88; as delegate to the state convention ratifying the U.S. Constitution in 1788; as delegate to the state constitutional convention of 1790; and in the U.S. House 1795–97. He is buried in the Earle family cemetery nearby. *Erected by the Pendleton District Historical, Recreational, and Tourism Commission, and the Col. Robert Anderson Chapter, National Society of the Sons of the American Revolution, 2005*
GPS Coordinates: 34° 33.967' N, 82° 59.5' W

37–7 Oconee County Training School

South 2nd St., Seneca

(FRONT) Oconee County Training School, which educated the African American children of this county from 1925 to 1955, was the successor to the Seneca Colored Graded School. This school, also known as OCTS, was founded in 1925 with Rev. B. F. Stewart as its first principal. Funded by local taxes and the Peabody Fund, it was built with 8 classrooms and later expanded to 26 classrooms, for students in grades 1–10 until 1931, grades 1–11 1931–1947, and grades 1–12 1947–1955.
(REVERSE) Oconee County Training School taught both academic classes and the trades, and added teachers and offered new classes as

it grew during the 1930s and 40s and especially after World War II. More than 700 students attended OCTS between 1925 and 1955, and its last graduating class was its largest. The main building here later housed East End Elementary School 1955–1970 and the Seneca Preschool 1972–1992. *Erected by the Oconee County African American Heritage Committee, 2006*
GPS Coordinates: 34° 40.967' N, 82° 56.65' W

37–8 Seneca Institute/Seneca Junior College

South 3rd St. and Poplar St., Seneca

Seneca Institute (FRONT)
The Seneca Institute (later Seneca Junior College) educated African American children of this region from 1899 to 1939. It was founded and sponsored by the Seneca River Baptist Association, which in 1898 acquired eight acres here. The first home of Seneca Institute, a frame three-room building, was built in 1899. Its first principal, Dr. John Jacob Starks (d. 1944), served here 1899–1912 before serving as president of Morris College and then Benedict College.
Seneca Junior College (REVERSE)
Seneca Institute taught academic courses to primary and secondary students and industrial courses as well to secondary students. Its campus featured a two-story frame classroom building, a two-story frame boys' dormitory, and a two-story brick girls' dormitory and chapel. Though it expanded its curriculum to become Seneca Junior College in 1930, it struggled through the Depression and finally closed in 1939. *Erected by the Oconee County African American Heritage Committee, 2006*
GPS Coordinates: 34° 40.838' N, 82° 57.571' W

37–9 Newberry College 1868–1877

Corner of North College and North Broad Sts., Walhalla

(FRONT) Newberry College, founded in 1856, moved here from Newberry in 1868 and remained in Walhalla until 1877, returning to Newberry for the opening of the 1877–78 academic year. The Lutheran college struggled during the Civil War and its aftermath as enrollment dropped and debts mounted. In 1869 it sold its main building and other property in Newberry at auction to pay its significant debts.
(REVERSE) Walhalla, with a large community of Germans who were primarily Lutherans, was chosen as a suitable home for the college, which retained the name Newberry. Under Josiah P. Smeltzer (1818–1887), president 1861–77, the college first occupied a building at Main and College Streets and then one at College and North Broad Streets. In 1877 the Synod of S.C. and Adjacent States voted to move it back to Newberry. *Erected by the Oconee County Arts and Historical Commission, 2006*
GPS Coordinates: 34° 46' N, 83° 3.905' W

37–10 Stumphouse Tunnel

Walhalla vicinity

(FRONT) The unfinished railroad tunnel cut into the SE face of Stumphouse Mtn. is the largest of three begun before the Civil War by the Blue Ridge Rail Road, for a line from Anderson, S.C., to Knoxville, Tenn. Work began in late 1853. About 1,500 Irish miners, who lived in the Tunnel Hill village atop the mountain, cut through blue granite with hand drills, hammers and chisels, and black powder. Four shafts meant miners could cut through ten rock faces at one time.
(REVERSE) Stumphouse Tunnel was the westernmost tunnel of the three; Middle Tunnel was ½ mi. SE and Saddle Tunnel was 1 ¾ mi. NE. The longest section of this tunnel is 1,600' long, 25' high, and 17' wide. Work ceased in 1859 when the S.C. legislature refused to fund more construction. Clemson University acquired the tunnel in 1951 and cured blue cheese here for several years. Stumphouse Tunnel, long a tourist attraction, is managed by the City of Walhalla. *Erected by Oconee Forever and Save Stumphouse Donors, 2010*
GPS Coordinates: 34° 48.621' N, 83° 7.414' W

37–11 Keowee Town

S.C. Sec. Rd. 37-128, 1.6 mi. N of S.C. Hwy. 130, Salem vicinity

(FRONT) Keowee Town, which means "mulberry grove place," was the largest and most

important of the Cherokee "Lower Towns" in what is now S.C. It was 1 mi. E on the Keowee River, and was already considered a significant Cherokee town when the British took a census of the Lower Towns in 1721. Keowee was also a major town on the main trading path between the British and the Cherokees. (REVERSE) Most Cherokees left Keowee by 1752 amid conflict with the Creeks but asked the British to build Fort Prince George across the river in 1753–54. Keowee was abandoned in 1760, during the Cherokee War, but later resettled. In 1776, during the Revolution, Maj. Andrew Williamson's S.C. militia burned it and other Lower Towns. The town and fort sites were covered by Lake Keowee in 1971. *Erected by the Wizard of Tamassee Chapter, Daughters of the American Revolution, and the Oconee County Arts and Historical Commission, 2006*
GPS Coordinates: 34° 51.774' N, 82° 55.182' W

37–12 Oconee Town

Oconee Station State Historic Site, 500 Oconee Station Rd., Walhalla vicinity

Oconee, also spelled "Aconnee," was one of the Cherokee "Lower Towns" in what is now S.C. At the base of Oconee Mountain and on the main trading path between the British and Cherokees, it was abandoned in 1752. Oconee Station was built in 1792 as an outpost where the path crossed the Cherokee boundary. This county, created from Pickens District in 1868, was named for Oconee Town. *Erected by the Oconee County Arts and Historical Commission and the South Carolina Heritage Corridor, 2006*
GPS Coordinates: 34° 50.428' N, 83° 3.976' W

37–13 Cherokee Boundary (1777)

Marker 1: Oconee State Park, Mountain Rest vicinity

Marker 2: S.C. Hwy. 130 at its intersection with Gunns Way, NW of Salem

Marker 3: S.C. Hwy. 28 at its intersection with Ham Dr., SE of Mountain Rest

Marker 4: U.S. Hwy. 76 just S of its intersection with Brasstown Church Rd., SE of Long Creek

(FRONT) The Cherokees sided with the British during the American Revolution, and in 1776 Maj. Andrew Williamson's S.C. militia destroyed their "Lower Towns" in what is now S.C. He then cooperated with the N.C. militia in expeditions against the Cherokees in N.C. and Ga. The Cherokees, seeking peace, soon negotiated with the Patriots to give up most of their lands in S.C.
(REVERSE) On May 20, 1777, at Dewit's Corner, the Cherokees signed a treaty with S.C., moving the frontier boundary line westward into what is now Oconee County. The boundary line crossed the top of Oconee Mountain near here. The remaining Cherokee land in present-day S.C. was ceded in the Treaty of 1816, extending the S.C. frontier to the present state boundary on the Chattooga River. *Erected by the Oconee Arts and Historical Commission and the South Carolina Heritage Corridor, 2006*
GPS Coordinates: 34° 51.917' N, 83° 6.286' W

37–14 Jocassee Town

Devils Fork State Park, Seneca vicinity

Jocassee was one of several Cherokee "Lower Towns" in what is now S.C. It was located about 2 mi. E on the Jocassee River and in the Vale of Jocassee, near the modern Jocassee Dam. The town, like other Cherokee Lower Towns, was abandoned and resettled several times during the period 1750–1800. The town site and valley were covered by Lake Jocassee in 1973. *Erected by the Oconee Arts and Historical Commission and the South Carolina Heritage Corridor, 2006*
GPS Coordinates: 34° 57.198' N, 82° 56.94' W

37–15 The English School

Corner of S. Church and Short Sts., Walhalla

(FRONT) Walhalla, in what was Pickens District until Oconee County was created in 1868, was founded by the German Colonization Society of Charleston in 1850 and boasted as many as 500 German settlers by 1855. The first school offering instruction in English opened in a frame building on Church Street between mid-1850 and late 1852. It was described in January 1853 as "a good English school on the square attended by twenty German children."

(REVERSE) Prof. G. H. D. Cramer was the first teacher at this elementary school for younger German children. In late 1853, St. John's Evangelical Lutheran Church was formally organized with Rev. Carl F. Bansemer as its first pastor and as professor at the English school. Bansemer was also professor of a classical academy founded in 1857. When he left Walhalla in 1860, Prof. Cramer resumed teaching at the English school and remained until his death in 1874. *Erected by the Oconee County Arts and Historical Commission, 2007*
GPS Coordinates: 34° 45.905' N, 83° 4.148' W

37–16   Chattooga Town

S.C. Hwy. 28 near the Russell Farm Site, Sumter National Forest, Mountain Rest vicinity

(FRONT) Chattooga was one of the Cherokee "Lower Towns" in what is now S.C. during the 17th and early 18th centuries and was a short distance north in the Chattooga River bottom. Chattooga Town, in a remote location in the backcountry, was the smallest of the Lower Towns in 1721 when it appeared as "Chattoogie," with only 90 inhabitants, in that year's British census of Cherokee towns.
(REVERSE) Chattooga Town was on a main trading path that crossed the Chattooga River and connected Lower Towns in what is now S.C. to those in what are now Ga. and N.C. Historical and archaeological research shows that the town was largely abandoned by 1740; accounts of expeditions to this area in 1760–61 do not mention it. Walter Adair, the last Cherokee to live here, sold his land in 1816. *Erected by the USDA Forest Service, Sumter National Forest, 2007*
GPS Coordinates: 34° 53.795' N, 83° 10.324' W

37–17   Cross Roads Baptist Church /Cross Roads School

Intersection of Dr. Johns Rd. and Dales Dr., Westminster

Cross Roads Baptist Church (FRONT)
This church was founded between 1860 and 1880 by Forch Allen (1823–1911) and members of the Allen and Oglesby families, including other descendants of Cherokees who lived in early Lower Towns such as Tugaloo and Seneca. Its first building, completed about 1884, was a log church. The present frame church, built in 1900, was rebuilt in 1973.

Cross Roads School (REVERSE)
Longtime members of the congregation include the Adair, Allen, Jones, Martin, Oglesby, Poole, Ross, Sizemore, Thompson, Walker, and other families. The Cross Roads School, one of several separate Indian schools in S.C. during the early-to-mid 19th century, stood behind the church. It opened in 1921, closed in 1962, and was torn down by the church in 1979. *Erected by the Eastern Cherokee, Southern Iroquois, and United Tribes of South Carolina, Inc., 2008*
GPS Coordinates: 34° 37.204' N, 83° 7.295' W

37–18   West Union Grammar School /West Union Elementary School

Intersection of Cherokee Foothills Scenic Hwy. (S.C. Hwy. 11) and Neville St., West Union

West Union Grammar School (FRONT)
West Union Graded School, also known as West Union Grammar School or West Union Elementary School, was built here in 1923–24. In 1922 trustees purchased 4 acres from Marvin Phinney for a new school to replace an earlier frame building. This two-story brick school was ready for the opening of the 1924–25 school year with Jerome Douglass as its principal and 5 teachers for about 100–150 students in grades 1–6.

West Union Elementary School (REVERSE)
Miss Clara Smith taught here for more than 40 years, from the mid-1920s until the school closed in 1969. She usually taught two or more grades a year and was also West Union's last principal from 1949 to 1969. The town of West Union purchased the school from the Oconee County School District in 1969, leasing it back to the school district for office space 1970–1981. *Erected by the West Union School Preservation Association, 2008*
GPS Coordinates: 34° 45.733' N, 83° 2.347' W

37–19 Tamassee DAR School

Bumgardner Dr. & S.C. Hwy. 11, near the north entrance to Tamassee DAR School, Tamassee

(FRONT) Tamassee DAR School, founded by the S.C. Society of the Daughters of the American Revolution (DAR) in 1919, was established in an area described as "remote but accessible where the need was greatest." It has long met the needs of children and families in crisis from the southern Appalachian Mountains. The S.C. Cottage, the first building on campus, was built by volunteers.
(REVERSE) At first a boarding school for girls and a day school for boys, Tamassee offers academic, vocational, and citizenship training. As a partner with the Oconee County School District, it served as an elementary and high school until 1965 and has since been an elementary school. The National Society of the DAR began funding the school in 1921 and continues to support its programs. *Erected by Tamassee DAR School, 2009*
GPS Coordinates: 34° 53.204' N, 83° 1.001' W

37–20 Retreat Rosenwald School

150 Pleasant Hill Circle, Westminster vicinity

(FRONT) This school, often called Retreat Colored School, was built in 1923 for the African-American students in and near Westminster. A two-room, two-teacher, elementary school, it was built by local builder William Walker Bearden of Oakway at a cost of $2,300. It was one of more than 500 schools in S.C. funded in part by the Julius Rosenwald Foundation between 1917 and 1932.
(REVERSE) This public school replaced a one-room private school established by Pleasant Hill Baptist Church about 1870. About 50–60 students a year, in grades 1–7, attended Retreat Colored School from 1923 until it closed after the 1949–50 school year. The school was sold to Pleasant Hill Baptist Church in 1950. It was listed in the National Register of Historic Places in 2011. *Erected by Pleasant Hill Baptist Church, 2011*
GPS Coordinates: 34° 38.483' N, 83° 3.852' W

37–21 Cheowee Town

Off Jumping Branch Rd. near Lake Cherokee, Tamassee vicinity

(FRONT) Cheowee Town, sometimes spelled "Chehohee," and meaning "otter place," was one of several Cherokee "Lower Towns" in what is now S.C. Located on the headwaters of Little River, it predated European contact and was considered a significant town when the British took a census of the Lower Towns in 1721. Leaders representing Cheowee signed treaties with S.C. in 1734 and again in 1751.
(REVERSE) Conflict with the Creeks, and the threat of an attack on Cheowee, led most residents to abandon the town in 1751. A band of Creeks looted it the next year. The Cherokees later returned and resettled the town. In 1776, after the Cherokees sided with the British during the American Revolution, Maj. Andrew Williamson's S.C. militia burned Cheowee and the other Lower Towns in S.C. *Sponsored by Oconee County Arts and Historical Commission, 2014*
GPS Coordinates: 34° 54.848' N, 83° 3.628' W

37–22 Chauga Town

Intersection of Taylor Rd. and S.C. Hwy. 28, 1 mi. S of Mountain Rest

Chauga, one of the Cherokee "Lower Towns" in what is now S.C., was near the headwaters of the Chauga River. It, like many other Lower Towns, was abandoned and resettled several times and likely abandoned before the Revolution. In 1797 U.S. Indian agent Benjamin Hawkins described the town site as in "a healthy position and neighbourhood . . . . convenient for a trading establishment." *Sponsored by Oconee County Arts and Historical Commission, 2014*
GPS Coordinates: 34° 51.320' N, 83° 9.253' W

37–23 Beaverdam Baptist Church

328 Beaverdam Church Rd., Fair Play

(FRONT) Beaverdam Baptist Church was first organized in 1803 as an offshoot of Hepsibah Baptist Church. Rev. George Vandiver was the first pastor. Beaverdam was formally organized as an independent church in 1816.

Like many churches in the South, Beaverdam counted enslaved men and women among its members. After emancipation, the portion used by enslaved people was converted for use as a Sunday School.

(REVERSE) Originally a member of the Tugaloo Association, Beaverdam Baptist became a founding member of the Beaverdam Baptist Association in 1887. A new church, replacing the original log structure, was built in 1859. A bell tower and steeple were built in 1893, with additional wings added in 1927. After years of faithful service the 1859 building was replaced by the current church in 1971. *Sponsored by Oconee County Arts and Historical Commission, 2016*

GPS Coordinates: 34° 30.728' N, 82° 58.699' W

37–24 Mountain Rest School /Hillbilly Day

S. Side of Verner Mill Rd., W. of S.C. Hwy. 28, Mountain Rest

Mountain Rest School (FRONT)

The building across the road was constructed in 1948 to house the Mountain Rest School. Initially staffed by four teachers, the school served local white children in grades 1–6. In 1964, the Oconee County School District closed the school and transferred students to Walhalla. In 1967, the Mountain Rest Community Club acquired the building and made it their headquarters.

Hillbilly Day (REVERSE)

On July 4, 1961, around 75 people attended a barbecue and bluegrass jam at the grounds of the Mountain Rest School. Sponsored by the Mountain Rest Community Club, it grew into an annual event known as "Hillbilly Day" that featured music, games, and contests that paid homage to the region's agrarian heritage. By the 1980s, as many as 14,000 people attended the event each year. *Sponsored by Oconee County Arts and Historical Commission, 2019*

GPS Coordinates: 34° 50.552' N, 83° 8.046' W

Orangeburg County

38–1 Eutaw Springs Battlefield

S.C. Hwy. 6, Eutaw Springs, about 2½ mi. E of Eutawville

Last major battle in S.C. of the War for American Independence September 8, 1781.

GPS Coordinates: 33° 24.433' N, 80° 17.905' W

38–2 Albergotti Playground

Edisto Memorial Gardens, 200 Riverside Dr., just off U.S. Hwy. 301, Orangeburg

Named in honor of Mr. and Mrs. J. M. Albergotti, Sr., For Their Sustaining Interest in Public Recreation for Children. Their Generous Financial Contribution Made Possible the Establishment of the First City Playground near This Site, 1922. Dedicated to the Youth of Orangeburg. *Erected by the Orangeburg Garden Club, 1955*

GPS Coordinates: 33° 29.43' N, 80° 52.515' W

38–1 Eutaw Springs Battlefield, Eutawville.
PHOTO CA. 1963, COURTESY OF SC FORESTRY COMMISSION

38-3 South Carolina Canal & Rail Road Company Original Track Location

At the Branchville Depot, 110 N. Main St. (U.S. Hwy. 21), Branchville

Began first successful scheduled steam railroad service in America on December 25, 1830, and by 1833 its 136 miles from Charleston to Hamburg made it the world's longest railroad. Now part of Southern Railway System. *Erected by the American Society of Civil Engineers, 1970*
GPS Coordinates: 33° 15.067' N, 80° 48.95' W

38-4 Old Dixie Club Library

Corner of Bull & Middleton Sts., Orangeburg

This antebellum structure once stood on Orangeburg's Public Square. In 1865 it was occupied by Federal troops. From 1924 to 1955 it housed the first public library in Orangeburg County, organized by the Dixie Club (1896). Given to the Orangeburg County Historical Society, it was moved in 1955 to its present site—the Pioneer Graveyard (1749). *Erected by the Dixie Club, 1958*
GPS Coordinates: 33° 29.555' N, 80° 52.074' W

38-5 Defense of Edisto Bridge

Edisto Memorial Gardens, 200 Riverside Dr., just off U.S. Hwy. 301, Orangeburg

Occupying Rifle Pits and manning a small battery in defense of the Edisto River Bridge, at this point less than six hundred Confederates temporarily halted the advance of the right wing of the Federal Army commanded by Gen. W. T. Sherman. On Feb. 12, 1865, the defenders were outflanked by a much larger force and compelled to withdraw and entrain for Columbia, South Carolina. *Erected by the Orangeburg County Historical Society, Inc., 1962*
GPS Coordinates: 33° 29.392' N, 80° 52.541' W

38-6 The Santee Limestone /Limestone and Marl Formations

[Replaced by Marker 38-29, erected by the Carolinas Geological Society, 2004.]

S.C. Hwy. 6, Eutaw Springs, about 2 ½ mi. E of Eutawville

The Santee Limestone (FRONT)
Sir Charles Lyell, famous British geologist, visited this locality in January, 1842, and gave the name Santee Limestone to the geological

formation underlying this area, pronouncing its age to be Eocene. Solution of this rock has formed sinks and subsurface caves. Eutaw Springs, now flooded by Lake Marion, flowed from such underground channels.
Limestone and Marl Formations (REVERSE) Santee Limestone, the bedrock formation underlying this area, is locally used as a source of lime. Embedded in it are many kinds of fossil marine animals. A few miles to the south it is overlain by an impure limestone called Cooper Marl. This marl together with the limestone are basic materials used in Portland cement manufactured nearby. *Erected by the S.C. State Commission of Forestry, 1964*
GPS Coordinates: 33° 24.485' N, 80° 17.901' W

38–7 Grave of Major Majoribanks /Northampton

S.C. Hwy. 6, Eutaw Springs, about 2 ½ mi. E of Eutawville

Grave of Major Majoribanks (FRONT) The British army encamped at Wantoot Plantation, home of Daniel Ravenel, after the Battle of Eutaw Springs. Now under Lake Moultrie, it was about 25 miles southeast in St. John's Parish, five miles west of Bonneau. Major John Majoribanks died and was buried there on October 22, 1781. His grave and marker were moved here in 1941 by the South Carolina Public Service Authority.
Northampton (REVERSE)
Northampton Plantation, residence of General William Moultrie, is now under the waters of Lake Moultrie. It was in St. John's Parish near Black Oak Church about five miles west of the present town of Bonneau. Before inundation, the "Northampton Plantation" marker was moved to its present location by the South Carolina Public Service Authority. *Erected by the S.C. State Commission of Forestry, 1965*
GPS Coordinates: 33° 24.485' N, 80° 17.901' W

38–8 Eutawville

Intersection of S.C. Hwy. 6 & Eutaw Hwy. (S.C. Hwy. 45), Eutawville

(FRONT) Settled in the 1840s on higher ground in the healthy pines of upper St. John's Parish,

the town of Eutawville was founded by Santee River plantation owners as a summer refuge for their families. In 1886 the railroad was established. The town was chartered December 24, 1888, in Berkeley County and annexed to Orangeburg County in 1910.
(REVERSE) Long before the founding of the village of Eutawville, the area immediately to the north and east was an important avenue of trade, using Nelson's Ferry Road, the Cherokee Path, and the Santee River. At Eutaw Springs, a strategic point guarding the British supply line from Charleston, a major battle of the American Revolution took place. *Erected by The Eutawville Civic League, 1970*
GPS Coordinates: 33° 23.887' N, 80° 20.467' W

38–9 Old Charleston Road

Charleston Hwy. (U.S. Hwy. 178) near its intersection with U.S. Hwy. 21 (Rowesville Rd.), S of Orangeburg

This was the first public road connecting Orangeburg with Charleston and was authorized by an Act of the General Assembly passed March 16, 1737. It was laid out from Izard's Cowpen, about ten miles north of Old Dorchester, and spanned two wide swamps. The early settlers of the area constructed the road and provided for maintenance. *Erected by Moultrie Chapter Daughters of the American Revolution, 1970* [Replaced a marker erected in 1916.]
GPS Coordinates: 33° 28.252' N, 80° 50.764' W

38–10 Court House Square

Orangeburg County Courthouse, Courthouse Square, Russell St., Orangeburg

The third court house for Orangeburg County was erected on this site in 1826. It was designed by Robert Mills, who was state architect at that time. This structure was destroyed by Union forces during their occupation of February 12–13, 1865. The fourth court house was constructed in 1875 and served the county until 1928, when it was razed and the site converted into a park. *Erected by The City of Orangeburg, 1970*
GPS Coordinates: 33° 29.428' N, 80° 51.811' W

38–11 Pioneer Graveyard

Bull St. between N. Broughton (U.S. Hwy. 178) and Middleton Sts., Orangeburg

From the time of the first settlement of Orangeburg Township in 1735 until the founding of various denominational cemeteries, this plot of ground was the final resting place for the early inhabitants. The first church in the Orangeburg area was erected here about 1750 by the Swiss and German settlers of the Reverend John Giessendanner's congregation. *Erected by the City of Orangeburg, 1970*
GPS Coordinates: 33° 29.538' N, 80° 52.08' W

38–12 The Town of North

North Rd. (U.S. Hwy. 178), North

In the year 1891, John F. North, Samson A. Livingston, and George W. Pou gave jointly and equally one hundred acres of land to establish a town and railway depot. The separate tracts joined near this spot. The town was named in honor of John F. North, a Confederate veteran and the oldest of the three men, who was elected first mayor. *Erected by The Citizens of North; Sponsored by the Tricentennial Committee of North, 1970*
GPS Coordinates: 33° 36.928' N, 81° 6.209' W

38–13 Judge Glover's Home

525 Whitman St., Orangeburg

This house, used as headquarters by General William T. Sherman on February 12, 1865, was built in 1846 by Thomas Worth Glover (1798–1884), Teacher, Lawyer, Legislator, Circuit Judge, and Signer of the Ordinance of Secession. The house has been remodeled several times. It fronted originally on Russell Street. *Erected by Orangeburg County Historical Society, 1970*
GPS Coordinates: 33° 29.475' N, 80° 51.438' W

38–14 Alexander S. Salley
1871–1961

Belleville Rd., about 65 yds. from its intersection with King's Rd. NE, Orangeburg

Here was the birthplace of Alexander Samuel Salley, who devoted fifty years to the collection, preservation, and publication of the historical records of the state as Secretary of the South Carolina Historical Society, Secretary of the South Carolina Historical Commission, and State Historian. *Erected by Orangeburg County Historical Society, 1970*
GPS Coordinates: 33° 30.564' N, 80° 49.813' W

38–15 Church of the Redeemer

606 Russell St., Orangeburg

The first Anglican church in Orangeburg Township was established about 1750 by John Giessendanner, and a chapel at Orangeburg was later provided by the Act of 1768 that created St. Matthew's Parish. Following a long dormant period, the Episcopal Church of the Redeemer was organized. The church building was erected in 1854–55 and was moved to its present site, improved and renovated in 1895. *Erected by the Congregation, 1970*
GPS Coordinates: 33° 29.538' N, 80° 51.477' W

38–16 Miller Cemetery

S.C. Sec. Rd. 38–141, .5 mile E of its intersection with U.S. Hwy. 601, Jamison

This cemetery was the burial site of the Miller family from the early 1800s. The remaining stones were erected in 1836 to John Miller (1750–1814), soldier of the Revolution; his wife, Margaret Ott Miller; and their son, John Miller, Jr. Their genealogical connections with many of Orangeburgh District's oldest families make them historically significant to this area. *Erected by Calhoun County Historical Commission, 1978* [Replaced a marker erected in 1971 by the same commission.]
GPS Coordinates: 33° 34.784' N, 80° 48.54' W

38–17 Holly Hill

State St. (U.S. Hwy. 176) near its intersection with Eutaw Rd., Holly Hill

(FRONT) This community had come into existence by 1848 near the Camden fork of the Old State Road. It was chartered in 1887 in Berkeley County, following the coming of the railroad in 1886. The town was annexed to Orangeburg County in 1910. The post office was established in 1848. The public school dates from the 1880s, and the oldest church from 1890.

(REVERSE) Near this site grew the grove of holly trees around which the town of Holly Hill was built. The last tree from the original grove was removed in January 1957. Its age was estimated at 98 years by the State Forestry Department. In April, 1970, a replacement for this tree was planted during South Carolina's Tricentennial celebration. *Erected by Ivy Garden Club and the Holly Hill Garden Club, 1972*
GPS Coordinates: 33° 19.35' N, 80° 24.803' W

38–18 White House Church

Five Chop Rd. (U.S. Hwy. 301), 1 mi. E of its intersection with I-26 at Exit 154B, 10 mi. E of Orangeburg

This four acre tract of land with an earlier structure known as the "White Meeting House" was given to the Methodist Episcopal Church on October 1, 1790, by a deed which is said to be the earliest documented record of Methodism in Orangeburg County. In 1801 and 1803 the Society was visited by Francis Asbury, pioneer Bishop of American Methodism. *Erected by Historic White House Commission, 1972*
GPS Coordinates: 33° 27.573' N, 80° 43.268' W

38–19 Zion Church

Bamberg Rd. (U.S. Hwy. 301/601), near Zion Church Rd. (S.C. Sec. Rd. 38–751), SW of Orangeburg and NW of Cordova

Evidence indicates that it was one of the earliest Methodist churches in the Orangeburg area. The original building, built before the Civil War, was replaced in the 1880s. Appointed ministers replaced circuit riders about 1843. Zion was abandoned as a full-time church in the early 1930s when its members moved to nearby Cope and Orangeburg. *Erected by The Committee for Restoration and Preservation of Zion Church and Cemetery, 1974*
GPS Coordinates: 33° 27.773' N, 80° 56.145' W

38–20 Walnut Grove Church

Landsdowne Rd. (S.C. Sec. Rd. 38–92), 4 mi. S of U.S. Hwy. 301 and just N of S.C. Sec. Rd. 38–692, NE of Bowman

This Baptist Church, a branch of Four Holes Baptist Church in present Orangeburg County from 1840 to 1869, was admitted to the Charleston Association in 1869 and joined the Orangeburg Association in 1913. The present building was constructed ca. 1883. Foundation sills are pegged together, and the seats and backs of pews are solid wide boards that were hand planed. *Erected by the Congregation, 1976*
GPS Coordinates: 33° 24.52' N, 80° 37.598' W

38–21 Hawthorne School of Aeronautics

Rowesville Rd. (U.S. Hwy. 21) at its intersection with Live Oaks Dr. SW (S.C. Sec. Rd. 38–57), at the entrance to The Methodist Oaks Retirement Home, about 2.6 mi. S of Orangeburg

From 1941 to 1945, 5924 American & French pilots were trained here, totaling almost 330,000 flight hours. Site is 1 mi. NW. *Erected by the World War II Hawthorne Pilot Training Association and the Association Du Personnel Navigant Francais Forme Aux USA, 1991*
GPS Coordinates: 33° 25.899' N, 80° 50.258' W

38–22 Episcopal Church of the Redeemer and Graveyard

Boulevard St. NE between Amelia St. NE & Peasley St. NE, Orangeburg

(FRONT) Anglicanism was established in Orangeburg Township about 1750. After a period of no recorded activity, efforts were made to rekindle the Anglican tradition resulting in establishment of Episcopal Church of The Redeemer, circa 1850. Catharine C. Palmer donated this land to the congregation where they built a house of worship and consecrated it [. . .]

(REVERSE) [. . .] in 1857. The frame building, moved on logs to Russell Street in 1895, was later enlarged and brick veneered; it is the oldest church building in Orangeburg. Stiles Mellichamp, rector during the 1860s and

1870s, is buried in the cemetery along with a number of Confederate soldiers and many communicants of Episcopal Church of The Redeemer. *Erected by the St. Agnes Chapter Episcopal Church Women, the Episcopal Church of the Redeemer, 1993*
GPS Coordinates: 33° 29.854' N, 80° 51.357' W

38–23 The Rocks Plantation

S.C. Hwy. 6 at its intersection with Rocks Pond Rd. (S.C. Sec. Rd. 38-139), about 2 mi. E of Eutaw Springs

House built 1803–05 by Capt. Peter Gaillard (1757–1833), pioneer cotton planter, S.C. Assemblyman 1796-7 & 1812–15. House was moved in 1942 to site .6 mi. N. Burned 1992. *Erected by Orangeburg County Historical Society, 1993*
GPS Coordinates: 33° 23.196' N, 80° 15.086' W

38–24 Trinity United Methodist Church

185 Boulevard St. NE, Orangeburg

This African-American church, established in 1866, built its first sanctuary 4 blocks SE in 1870. Construction began on this sanctuary in 1928 and was completed in 1944. Trinity, headquarters for the Orangeburg Movement during the 1960s, hosted many civil rights meetings and rallies attended by leaders such as Martin Luther King, Jr., Roy Wilkins, and Thurgood Marshall. *Erected by the Congregation, 1995*
GPS Coordinates: 33° 29.749' N, 80° 51.369' W

38–25 South Carolina State University

At the entrance to the South Carolina State University campus, Boulevard St. NE, Orangeburg

(FRONT) S.C. State University was founded in 1896 as the Colored Normal, Industrial, Agricultural & Mechanical College of S.C., with its origins in the Morrill Land Grant Acts of 1862 and 1890 providing for land-grant colleges. Intended "for the best education of the hand, head and heart of South Carolina's young manhood and womanhood of the Negro

race," it became S.C. State College in 1954 and S.C. State University in 1992.
(REVERSE) South Carolina State has been called "at least symbolically, the most important educational institution in black Carolina since its founding." Students were also active in the Civil Rights Movement of the 1950s and 60s, taking part in sit-ins, the Orangeburg Movement of 1963–64 seeking desegregation of downtown businesses, and the Orangeburg Massacre in 1968. *Erected by South Carolina State University, 1997*
GPS Coordinates: 33° 29.728' N, 80° 51.318' W

38–26 Claflin College

At the entrance to the Claflin University campus, 400 Magnolia St., Orangeburg

(FRONT) Claflin College, founded in 1869 as Claflin University, is the oldest historically black college in S.C. and was established to "advance the cause of education, and maintain a first-class institution . . . open to all without distinction of race or color." It was named for two generations of the Claflin family of Mass., Lee Claflin (1791–1871), a prominent Methodist layman, and his son Gov. William Claflin (1818–1903), who supported and helped fund the new institution.
(REVERSE) The S.C. Agricultural and Mechanical Institute opened at Clafin in 1872 and was the predecessor of S.C. State University, founded in 1896. Claflin, associated with and supported by the Methodist Church, featured in its early years industrial, manual, and agricultural training; primary and secondary education; and college-prep and college courses, including architecture, law, teacher education, and theology. *It was renamed Claflin College in 1979. Erected by Claflin College, 1998*
GPS Coordinates: 33° 29.83' N, 80° 51.277' W

38–27 The Orangeburg Massacre

Watson St., near the entrance to the campus of South Carolina State University, Orangeburg

On February 8, 1968, after three nights of escalating racial tension over efforts by S.C. State College students and others to desegregate the All Star Bowling Lanes, 3 students

died and 27 others were wounded on this campus. S.C. Highway Patrolmen fired on a crowd here, killing Samuel Hammond Jr., Delano Middleton, and Henry Smith. This tragedy was the first of its kind on any American college campus. *Erected by South Carolina State University, 2000*
GPS Coordinates: 33° 29.701' N, 80° 51.308' W

38–28 Shiloh A.M.E. Church

2902 Cleveland St., Elloree

(FRONT) This church, founded in 1886, was organized by Revs. D. A. Christie and C. Heyward with Sol Ellerbe and Mordecai Williams as trustees and Galas Culay, Walter Montgomery, and Henry Tilley as stewards. Its first services were in a brush arbor, and its first sanctuary was built nearby in 1887. This sanctuary, a frame building later covered in brick veneer, was built in 1892.
(REVERSE) Member Robert Lee Williams (1862–1949) was a community leader and progressive farmer. When he died at the age of 87 Elloree businesses closed in his memory and the New York Times called him "generally and sincerely mourned." The church also hosted numerous meetings during the Civil Rights Movement of the 1950s and 60s seeking to desegregate local schools and businesses. *Erected by the Williams-Waymer-Carrion-Murray Family Reunion, 2003*
GPS Coordinates: 33° 31.622' N, 80° 34.671' W

38–29 Santee Limestone/Limestone and Marl Formations

S.C. Hwy. 6, about 2.5 mi. E of Eutawville at Eutaw Springs

Santee Limestone (FRONT)
Sir Charles Lyell (1797–1875), noted British geologist, visited S.C. in 1842 and described its geology in his Travels in North America . . . , published in several editions. He named the bedrock limestone underlying this area "Santee Limestone." Lyell estimated Santee Limestone to date from the Eocene epoch, more than 40 million years ago.
Limestone and Marl Formations (REVERSE)
Many kinds of fossil marine animals are found embedded in Santee Limestone. This

limestone, in solution, forms sinks and subsurface caves. Eutaw Springs, now flooded by Lake Marion, flowed from such channels. An impure limestone-based clay known as "Cooper Marl" overlies Santee Limestone throughout the lowcountry. Both are primary raw materials in portland cement produced nearby. *Erected by the Carolinas Geological Society, 2004* [Replaced a marker erected by the Division of State Parks, South Carolina State Forestry Commission, in 1964.]
GPS Coordinates: 33° 24.485' N, 80° 17.901' W

38–30 Williams Chapel A.M.E. Church

1198 Glover St., Orangeburg

(FRONT) This church was founded in 1873 with Rev. Dave Christie as its first pastor. In 1877 trustees Emily A. Williams, Richard Howard, and Irwin Mintz purchased a small lot here, on what was then Market Street before Glover Street was laid out. They soon built a frame church, which stood for almost thirty years. Additional acreage purchased in 1909 allowed the congregation to build an addition and parsonage.
(REVERSE) This Gothic Revival church was designed by Miller F. Whittaker (1892–1949), a professor at S.C. State Agricultural & Mechanical College (now S.C. State University), one of the first black architects in S.C., and a member of this congregation. The cornerstone was laid in 1919, and the church was completed about 1925. Williams Chapel A.M.E. Church was listed in the National Register of Historic Places in 1985. *Erected by the Congregation, 2006*
GPS Coordinates: 33° 29.191' N, 80° 51.626' W

38–31 Great Branch School and Teacherage

2890 S.C. Hwy. 4 (Neeses Highway), Orangeburg vicinity

(FRONT) The Great Branch School, which stood here from 1918 to the early 1960s, was one of the first Rosenwald schools in S.C. A two-room frame school built in 1917–18, it was typical of the rural black schools funded in part by the Julius Rosenwald Foundation between 1917 and 1932.

(reverse) A three-room addition and three-room teacherage were built in 1922–23; Principal W. M. Jennings lived here until 1933. The school closed about 1954 and was later burned by arsonists. The teacherage, one of only eight Rosenwald teacherages in S.C., was listed in the National Register of Historic Places in 2007. *Erected by The Orangeburg Chapter of The Links, Incorporated, 2008*
GPS Coordinates: 33° 31.253' N, 81° 2.151' W

38–32 Trinity Lutheran Church

390 Hampton St., Elloree

(front) Trinity Lutheran Church was founded in 1849 by German-Swiss Lutherans who came to Orangeburg District from Charleston. The first church, a cypress-log building, was built 2 mi. S on the old Moncks Corner Rd., now S.C. Hwy. 6. By 1880 the center of the community shifted, and the Lutherans and Methodists traded churches. The Lutherans moved to a frame church 2 mi. N, establishing their cemetery there.
(reverse) Elloree was incorporated in 1886, and the Lutherans built a frame church on this site in 1889. It was struck by lightning and burned in 1913. The present blue granite church, a Late Gothic Revival design by architect J. Carroll Johnson (1882–1967) of the Columbia firm Urquhart & Johnson, was built in 1914 and dedicated on Palm Sunday 1915. It was listed in the National Register of Historic Places in 2008. *Erected by the Congregation, 2009*
GPS Coordinates: 33° 31.976' N, 80° 34.3' W

38–33 Target Methodist Church

705 Target Rd., Holly Hill

(front) This church, founded about 1800, is one of the oldest Methodist congregations in this part of the state. It takes its name from Target Branch, a nearby tributary of Four Holes Swamp. The name "Target" is thought to be a corruption of the "tar gates" along the edges of the swamp, where tar, turpentine, and timber were harvested. It held its first services in a brush arbor, with a sycamore stump for a pulpit.

(reverse) Target Methodist Church was one of several area congregations long served by circuit riders, on the Cypress Circuit 1810–1855, then on the Providence Circuit 1855–1916. Its first permanent church, a log building, was rebuilt as a frame sanctuary in 1830. A second frame church built in 1873 was replaced by the present sanctuary in 1920. The cemetery here includes graves dating as early as 1820. *Erected by the Congregation, 2010*
GPS Coordinates: 33° 20.239' N, 80° 27.017' W

38–34 Bowman Rosenwald School

The corner of Adam & Center Sts., Bowman

(front) Bowman Rosenwald School, which stood here from 1927 to 1952, was one of several African-American schools in Orangeburg County funded in part by the Julius Rosenwald Foundation. The school, built in 1926–27 at a cost of $6,000, was a five-room frame building typical of the larger rural schools built by the Rosenwald Foundation between 1917 and 1932. The school burned in 1952.
(reverse) Bowman Rosenwald School educated about 250 students a year for most of its history, at first in grades 1–8 with five teachers and a five-month session, but by 1948–49 in grades 1–12 with nine teachers and an eight-month session. Its enrollment grew dramatically after World War II, reaching a peak of 576 students in 1951–52, its last full school year. *Erected by the Bowman-Rosenwald Historical Marker Committee, and the Orangeburg Chapter of The Links, Incorporated, 2011*
GPS Coordinates: 33° 20.574' N, 80° 41.224' W

38–35 Providence Methodist Church

4833 Old State Rd., Holly Hill

(front) This church grew out of services held in the area by circuit riders as early as 1806. Its first church, a log building, was built on what is now Vance Rd., ½ mi. SW. About 1810 Timothy Shuler donated 4 acres here for a frame sanctuary, built soon afterwards. It was renovated in the 1850s and again in the 1890s.
(reverse) The present Neo-Classical Revival Church, built in 1919–1920, was designed by Charles Coker Wilson. The cemetery here

dates back to 1856 and numbers more than 400 graves, including veterans of most American wars since. The church was listed in the National Register of Historic Places in 2009. *Erected by the Congregation, 2011*
GPS Coordinates: 33° 23.525' N, 80° 32.457' W

38–36 Bushy Pond Baptist Church

1396 Wire Rd., Norway

(FRONT) This church was organized during or just after the Civil War by black members of Willow Swamp Baptist Church, a combined congregation of whites and blacks before the war. In 1869–70 members received formal letters of dismissal to organize their own church. They named it Bushy Pond for the bush arbor they built nearby for their first services, and the pond close to it.
(REVERSE) Rev. John Fitzsimmons was the first pastor. By 1871 Bushy Pond Baptist Church had 103 members. In 1905, during the pastorate of Rev. W. O. Carmichael, the congregation built its first permanent church, a frame Gothic Revival sanctuary, on this site. The church also sponsored the Bushy Pond School, built nearby. The present brick church was dedicated in 1974. *Sponsored by the Congregation, 2013*
GPS Coordinates: 33° 27.510' N, 81° 9.703' W

38–37 Rocky Swamp Rosenwald School

Norway Rd. (S.C. Sec. Rd. 38–36), E of Levi Pond Rd., Neeses vicinity

(FRONT) This is the site of Rocky Swamp Rosenwald School, a frame three-room school built here in 1920–21 for African-American students in Neeses and vicinity. An elementary school with two to three teachers in grades 1–9, it was one of more than 500 schools in S.C. funded in part by the Julius Rosenwald Foundation.
(REVERSE) This school was built at a total cost of $4,100, with contributions from the black community, the white community, Orangeburg County, and the Rosenwald Fund. It opened for the 1921–22 school year with 199 students, averaging 145 students until 1942. Rocky Swamp closed after the 1950–51 school

year. *Sponsored by the Rocky Swamp Rosenwald School Historical Marker Committee and the Orangeburg Chapter of The Links, Incorporated, 2013*
GPS Coordinates: 33° 28.443' N, 81° 11.253' W

38–38 John Benjamin Taylor House

Boulevard & Oak St., Orangeburg

(FRONT) This Craftsman house, built by 1903, was the home of Rev. John Benjamin Taylor (1867–1936) until his death. Taylor, a minister and administrator in the Methodist Episcopal Church 1892–1936, was also a longtime trustee of Claflin University, 1908–1928. Educated at Claflin, he was a teacher and principal in Orangeburg before being appointed a minister in the Methodist Episcopal Church in 1892.
(REVERSE) Taylor was superintendent of the Charleston District of the Methodist Episcopal Church 1907–1913, then superintendent of the Orangeburg District 1924–1929. He purchased this lot in 1900 and built this house for his first wife Harriet Catherine Dibble Taylor (1873–1918) and four children. He added a half-story in 1927. His second wife Daisy McLain Buckley Taylor lived here until her death in 1965. *Sponsored by the Naudin-Dibble Heritage Foundation, 2014*
GPS Coordinates: 33° 29.947' N, 80° 51.321' W

38–39 Holly Hill Rosenwald School

Corner of Unity Road and Gardener Blvd., Holly Hill

(FRONT) The Holly Hill Rosenwald School once stood near this location. Built 1926–27, the Holly Hill School was the third school for African American students built in the area and one of almost 500 S.C. schools funded in part by the Julius Rosenwald Foundation (1917–32). Local African American residents matched the $1,500 Rosenwald grant and the remainder of the funding for the six-teacher schoolhouse came from public sources.
(REVERSE) Separate lunch room, home economics, and library buildings were later added. In 1946 the main school building was lost to fire. It was replaced by a new building in 1948 and in 1954 a modern high school was constructed on Pratt St. with funds from S.C.'s school equalization program. Both of the new

schools were named in honor of James S. Roberts (1891–1955) who served as principal from 1929–1955. *Sponsored by Holly Hill Rosenwald Alumni and Community, 2014*
GPS Coordinates: 33° 19.457' N, 80° 24.365' W

38–40 Felton Training School & Teacherage

S.C. State University Campus between Duke's Gym and the Student Services Building, Orangeburg

(FRONT) Felton Training School was completed in 1925 and was financed in part by the Rosenwald Fund (1917–1948). It was a four-teacher school for African American students built according to Rosenwald floor plan no. 400. Felton was a practice school constructed to support Normal School instruction at S.C. State A&M (now S.C. State U.). A Rosenwald supported teacherage was built in 1927 to complete the teacher training center. (REVERSE) Felton Training School was named for J. B. Felton, S.C. Supervisor of African American Schools 1919–1948 and advocate for Rosenwald School construction. The school drew students from Orangeburg public schools. For those families who could afford the small attendance fees, the selective program offered here was viewed as the best option for educating their children. In 1964 the original school was replaced by a new facility. *Sponsored by Orangeburg Chapter of The Links, Incorporated, 2015*
GPS Coordinates: 33° 29.870' N, 80° 51.064' W

38–41 Jewish Merchants/Jewish Life

Russell St. (S.C. Rte. 33), midway between Broughton (U.S. Rte. 178 Bus.) and Middleton (Sec. Rte. 211) Sts., Orangeburg

Jewish Merchants (FRONT) Russell St., historic hub of Orangeburg's commercial life, was home to Jewish merchants for over 160 years. German Jews began settling in Orangeburg in the 1830s, followed in the next century by Eastern European Jews. Deopold Louis was likely the first Jewish merchant in town. Theodore Kohn, known as father of Orangeburg's graded schools, co-founded Ezekial & Kohn in 1868. By the mid-1900s as many as 15 stores downtown were Jewish owned. In 1996

Barshay & Marcus was the last to close. Jewish Life (REVERSE) Temple Sinai, built in 1955 on Ellis Ave., became the center of religious life for Jews who lived in Orangeburg and surrounding towns. As in many small towns in S.C., in the second half of the 20th century descendants of Jewish merchants moved to larger cities in the state and beyond. Noted past residents of Jewish descent include Robert F. Furchgott, a Nobel Prize-winning biochemist, and Evelyn Marcus, the first woman from Orangeburg County admitted to the S.C. Bar. *Sponsored by the Jewish Historical Society of South Carolina, 2015*
GPS Coordinates: 33° 29.354' N, 80° 51.898' W

38–42 St. Paul's Episcopal Church

1170 State Rd S-38-226, Orangeburg

(FRONT) St. Paul's Episcopal Church was established in 1912. It was founded by Dr. Robert Shaw Wilkinson (1865–1932) and his wife, Marion Birnie Wilkinson (1870–1956), as St. Paul's Episcopal Mission. Services were held in the Wilkinson's home for the first decade. Beginning in 1922 the YWCA Hut on the S.C. State campus became home to the congregation. They would remain there until the current sanctuary was consecrated Nov. 4, 1951. (REVERSE) Robert Shaw Wilkinson came to S.C. State in 1896 as professor of mathematics. In 1911 he became the college's second president, serving until his death in 1932. Wilkinson High School in Orangeburg is named in his honor. Marion Wilkinson was an active community leader and founder of the S.C. Federation of Colored Women's Clubs. St. Paul's remains the only African American Episcopal Church in Orangeburg. *Sponsored by St. Paul's Episcopal Church, 2016*
GPS Coordinates: 33° 29.663' N, 80° 51.300' W

38–43 Rocky Swamp Methodist Church and Cemetery

7387 Neeses Hwy (Hwy 4), Springfield vic.

(FRONT) Rocky Swamp Methodist Episcopal Church was among the first Methodist congregations in this part of S.C. A meeting house on one acre was here by 1809. A Methodist campground may have predated the

construction of the first meeting house. (REVERSE) Another 20 acres were purchased in 1828. A second church was thought to have been built around that time. It burned in 1859. The current meeting house was built ca. 1860. The modest structure and its nearby cemetery, with more than 300 interments, are visible reminders of the families and individuals who once lived here. *Sponsored by Orangeburg Co. Historical Society, 2017*
GPS Coordinates: 33° 30.580' N, 81° 11.410' W

38–44 Wilkinson High School

822 Goff Ave., Orangeburg

(FRONT) In 1938, Orangeburg's first black high school opened in this building, constructed by the Works Progress Administration. It was named for Dr. Robert Shaw Wilkinson (1865–1932), pres. of S.C. State A&M College. The school's mascot was the Wolverines, and its colors were maroon and gray. Its motto was "Strive to excel, not to equal." Throughout Wilkinson's history, it was the only black high school in the city of Orangeburg. (REVERSE) In 1953, Wilkinson moved to a new campus on Belleville Rd., built to help the state preserve segregation by equalizing black and white schools. Wilkinson students were active in the 1960s in the civil rights movement. After Swann v. Mecklenburg (1971), Wilkinson integrated with the white high school to form Orangeburg-Wilkinson High. Grades 9–10 attended the Wilkinson campus

until 1973, when it became Belleville Junior High. *Sponsored by Wilkinson High School Alumni, 2019* [Pair of markers to be located at each of the school's two historical sites.]
GPS Coordinates: 33° 30.040' N, 80° 51.103' W

38–45 Wilkinson High School

1255 Belleville Rd., Orangeburg

(FRONT) In 1938, Orangeburg's first black high school opened on Goff Ave. at a campus built by the Works Progress Administration. It was named for Dr. Robert Shaw Wilkinson (1865–1932), pres. of S.C. State A&M College. The school's mascot was the Wolverines, and its colors were maroon and gray. Its motto was "Strive to excel, not to equal." Throughout Wilkinson's history, it was the only black high school in the city of Orangeburg. (REVERSE) In 1953, Wilkinson moved to a new campus at this site, built to help the state preserve segregation by equalizing black and white schools. Wilkinson students were active in the 1960s in the civil rights movement. After Swann v. Mecklenburg (1971), Wilkinson integrated with the white high school to form Orangeburg-Wilkinson High. Grades 9–10 attended the Wilkinson campus here until 1973, when it became Belleville Junior High. *Sponsored by Wilkinson High School Alumni, 2019* [Pair of markers to be located at each of the school's two historical sites.]
GPS Coordinates: 33° 30.009' N, 80° 50.332' W

Pickens County

39–1 Pickensville

½ mi. S of S.C. Hwy. 123 at the junction of Pelzer Hwy. (S.C. Hwy. 8) & Cherish Dr. (S.C. Hwy. 135), S of Easley

A town laid out at this site in 1791 called Rockville was officially named Pickensville the next year in honor of Gen. Andrew Pickens. It served as the court house town of Washington District (today's Pickens, Greenville, Anderson, and Oconee counties) from 1791 to 1800 when the district was divided

into Greenville and Pendleton. *Erected by Fort Prince George Chapter, Daughters of the American Revolution, 1954*
GPS Coordinates: 34° 48.694' N, 82° 36.154' W

39–2 Fort Hill

In front of Fort Hill, at Fort Hill St. and Daniel Dr., Clemson University Campus, Clemson

Home of/JOHN C. CALHOUN/1825–1850/United States Congressman 1811–1817/Secretary of

War 1817–1825/Vice President of the United States 1825–1832/United States Senator 1832–1843/ Secretary of State 1844–1845/United States Senator 1845–1850./Home of/Thomas G. Clemson 1872–1888/Son-in-law of/John C. Calhoun.
GPS Coordinates: 34° 40.715' N, 82° 50.331' W

39–3 Old Stone Church/Old Stone Church Graveyard

Intersection of Anderson Hwy. (U.S. Hwy. 76) and Old Stone Church Rd., 2 mi. SW of Clemson

Old Stone Church (FRONT)
This church was built in 1797 for Hopewell (Keowee) Presbyterian congregation by John Rusk on land given by John Miller. Andrew Pickens and Robert Anderson of Revoltuonary war fame were elders at its organization. The Reverend Thomas Reese, D.D., eminent Presbyterian clergyman, was the first minister. He died in 1796 and was buried here.
Old Stone Church Graveyard (FRONT)
Among the graves here are those of John Miller, London printer and publisher of the Pendleton Messenger, Andrew Pickens and Robert Anderson, Revolutionary War heroes, and other veterans of the Revolutionary War, Creek War, War of 1812, Mexican War, Civil War and World Wars I and II. Gen. Anderson's remains were moved here in 1958 from his plantation. *Erected by the Old Stone Church Commission, 1965*
GPS Coordinates: 34° 39.775' N, 82° 48.868' W

39–4 Hopewell/Hopewell Indian Treaties

Old Cherry Rd. (S.C. Sec. Rd. 39–149) at the Seneca River, just W of its junction with Fants Grove Rd., 3.5 mi. S of Clemson

Hopewell (FRONT)
Hopewell was the family home of General Andrew Pickens, Revolutionary War hero and Indian Commissioner, and his wife, Rebecca Calhoun Pickens. The son, Andrew Pickens, S.C. Governor, 1816–1818, later owned Hopewell, and it was the childhood home of his son, Francis Wilkinson Pickens, S.C. Governor, 1860–1862.
Hopewell Indian Treaties (REVERSE)

300 yds. NW on November 28, 1785, U.S. Treaty Commissioners, Benjamin Hawkins, Andrew Pickens, Joseph Martin & Lachlan McIntosh, met with 918 Cherokees and signed the first treaty between the United States of America and the Cherokee Nation. Similar treaties were signed here with the Choctaws and Chickasaws on January 3 and 10, 1786. *Erected by Foundation for Historic Restoration in the Pendleton Area, 1966*
GPS Coordinates: 34° 39.327' N, 82° 50.209' W

39–5 Keowee/John Ewing Colhoun

Six Mile Hwy. (S.C. Hwy. 133), 1.7 mi. N of its intersection with U.S. Hwy. 123, N of Clemson

Keowee (FRONT)
2 ¼ miles west is the site of Keowee built by John Ewing Colhoun as his upcountry seat in 1792. His sister, Mrs. Andrew Pickens, lived nearby at Hopewell. His daughter, Floride, married her cousin, John C. Calhoun, and lived at Fort Hill, 2 ½ miles south. This estate was inherited by his son, John Ewing, who lived here and made lavish improvements.
John Ewing Colhoun (REVERSE)
Lawyer, Planter, Privy Councillor, State Legislator and U.S. Senator. Born in 1751 in Virginia, he moved to the Long Canes in 1756. He studied and practiced law in Charleston. He served in the militia during the Revolution and was appointed in 1782 as a Commissioner of Forfeited Estates. He died on October 26, 1802, at Keowee and was buried there. *Erected by Foundation for Historic Restoration in the Pendleton Area, 1966*
GPS Coordinates: 34° 42.899' N, 82° 49.851' W

39–6 Asbury F. Lever (1875–1940)

At the entrance to Cemetery Hill, Clemson University Campus, Clemson

Asbury Francis Lever served in Congress, 1901–1919. On May 8, 1914, the Smith-Lever Act, introduced in the U.S. House of Representatives by Lever, was signed into law, providing for cooperative agricultural extension services to be administered by land-grant colleges. Clemson, founded in 1889, has such a service. Rep. Lever is buried here on Cemetery Hill. *Erected by Clemson University*

Cooperative Extension Service, 1989
GPS Coordinates: 34° 40.564' N, 82° 50.58' W

39–7 Oolenoy Baptist Church

201 Miracle Hill Rd., just N of S.C. Hwy. 135, Pumpkintown vicinity

(FRONT) This church, named for the Cherokee chief, Woolenoy—the spelling was changed to Oolenoy in 1827—was organized in 1795 by Rev. John Chastain, who became its first minister. By 1797, with 50 members, it was admitted to the Bethel Baptist Association; it has since been a member of the Saluda, Twelve Mile River, Pickens, and Pickens-Twelve Mile Baptist Associations.
(REVERSE) Rev. Tyre L. Roper, the longest-serving minister here, preached at Oolenoy from 1840 until his death in 1876. The first sanctuary, a log building, was replaced about 1830 by a frame church, later enlarged in 1876 and 1899. The present brick sanctuary was built in 1952. The cemetery includes the graves of many veterans of American wars from the Revolution through World War II. *Erected by the Oolenoy Baptist Church Bicentennial Project, 2001*
GPS Coordinates: 34° 59.683' N, 82° 38.467' W

39–8 Pumpkintown

Pumpkintown Rd. (S.C. Hwy. 8), near its intersection with Table Rock Rd. (S.C. Hwy. 288), Pumpkintown

This community, settled before 1800, was named "Pumpkin Town" by an anonymous early traveler awed by the sight of the Oolenoy Valley covered with huge yellow pumpkins. It and Pickens Court House (Old Pickens) were the only two towns in present-day Pickens County in 1791. The many tourists who visited nearby Table Rock Mtn. often stayed at William Sutherland's inn at Pumpkintown. *Erected by the Pumpkintown Heritage Corridor Group, 2000*
GPS Coordinates: 35° 0.143' N, 82° 39.083' W

39–9 Integration with Dignity, 1963

At Tillman Hill on the Clemson University campus, Clemson

(FRONT) Clemson University became the first white college or university in the state to integrate on January 28, 1963. Harvey B. Gantt, a Charleston native wanting to study architecture, had applied for admission in 1961. When Clemson delayed admitting him, he sued in federal court in the summer of 1962. President Robert C. Edwards, meanwhile, worked behind the scenes to make plans for Gantt's eventual enrollment.
(REVERSE) Edwards and several leading businessmen, politicians, and others drew up an elaborate plan, described as "a conspiracy for peace," designed to ensure that Gantt would enter Clemson without the protests and violence that marked the integration of other Southern universities. After a federal court ruled that Clemson should admit him, Gantt enrolled without incident. He graduated with honors in 1965. *Erected by Clemson University, 2003*
GPS Coordinates: 34° 40.793' N, 82° 50.216' W

39–10 Clemson University

Marker 1: at the main entrance to the Clemson University campus, Walter T. Cox Blvd. (S.C. Hwy. 93), Clemson

Marker 2: Pendleton Rd. (S.C. Hwy. 93) near YMCA Circle, Clemson University campus, Clemson

(FRONT) Clemson University was founded in 1889 as the Clemson Agricultural College of S.C., with its origins in the Morrill Land Grant Act of 1862 creating public land-grant colleges. It was established by a bequest from Thomas Green Clemson (1807–1888), noted scientist, agriculturist, and son-in-law of John C. Calhoun, whose plantation at Fort Hill formed the core of the new college campus.
(REVERSE) Clemson, intended to be "a high seminary of learning" to advance scientific agriculture and the mechanical arts, opened in 1893 as a military school and was sometimes improperly known as Clemson A&M College. It became a civilian co-educational institution in 1955, then became Clemson University, reflecting its modern and expanded

mission, in 1964. *Erected by Clemson University, 2003*

GPS Coordinates: 34° 40.789' N, 82° 49.556' W

39–11 Bowen's Mill

Near intersection of Saluda Dam Rd (S.C. Hwy. 36) and Old Saluda Dam Rd., Easley vicinity

(FRONT) This mill was built about 1880 by Colonel Robert E. Bowen (1830–1909), Confederate officer, state representative, state senator, and Pickens County businessman. Bowen, a prominent advocate for progressive farming, was also active in the railroad and timber industries. In addition to this mill, the complex here included a store, blacksmith's shop, saw mill, and cotton gin.

(REVERSE) The mill passed through several owners in the first quarter of the twentieth century, from Bowen's son James O. Bowen to Albert B. Kay and Kay's widow Tallulah, and then successively to R. T. Waddell, Ida S. Johnson, and a Mrs. Shembosky, who sold it to Hovey A. Lark (1890–1968) during the Depression. Lark ground corn here from the early 1930s until about 1965. *Erected by the Society for the Preservation of Old Mills, Pickens Chapter, 2004*

GPS Coordinates: 34° 51.235' N, 82° 31.183' W

39–12 Hanover House

In the South Carolina Botanical Garden, intersection of U.S. Hwy. 76 and Pearman Blvd., Clemson University campus, Clemson

(FRONT) Hanover House, built 1714–16 in what is now Berkeley County and moved to the Clemson College campus in 1941, is a fine example of Dutch Colonial architecture. It was built for French Huguenot planter Paul de St. Julien (d. 1741). St. Julien's grandfather Pierre Julien de St. Julien had been granted 3,000 acres on the Cooper River in 1688 by the Lords Proprietors.

(REVERSE) When the Public Works Administration (PWA) built the Santee-Cooper Dam, Lake Marion, and Lake Moultrie in 1938–1942 Hanover Plantation was in the area inundated by Lake Moultrie. The house was disassembled, moved to Clemson, and reassembled in 1941, then restored 1954–62. Listed in the

National Register of Historic Places in 1970, the house was moved to the S.C. Botanical Garden in 1994. *Erected by the City of Clemson and Clemson University, 2007*

GPS Coordinates: 34° 40.483' N, 82° 49.083' W

39–13 The Battle of Seneca Town /Fort Rutledge

On the banks of the Seneca River near the Madren Conference Center, 100 Madren Ctr. Dr., Clemson University campus

The Battle of Seneca Town (FRONT) Seneca Town, on the Seneca River E of present-day Seneca, was one of several Cherokee "Lower Towns." On August 1, 1776, Maj. Andrew Williamson's S.C. militia, on a raid against these towns, was ambushed by Loyalists and Cherokees nearby. The eventual Patriot victory was also notable for the death of Francis Salvador, the first Jewish Patriot killed during the Revolution.

Fort Rutledge (REVERSE) In September 1776, soon after the Battle of Temassee in present-day Oconee County, Williamson returned to build a log fort nearby which he named Fort Rutledge in honor of John Rutledge, President of S.C. The fort and its 300-man garrison surrendered to Loyalists in 1780. The concrete block monument was built in 1908 by Clemson College for the Daughters of the American Revolution. *Erected by the City of Clemson and Clemson University, 2007*

GPS Coordinates: 34° 40' N, 82° 50.7' W

39–14 Central

Corner of S.C. Hwy. 93 and Banks St., Central

(FRONT) The town of Central, chartered in 1875, grew up along what is now Gaines Street. The post office was called Five Mile from 1851 to 1871. In the 1870s the Atlanta & Richmond Airline Railway built its depot, hotel, offices, and railroad shops at Central. The railroad, later the Atlanta & Charlotte, was acquired by the Southern Railway in 1894. Also called "Centre" and "Central Station," the town was halfway between Atlanta and Charlotte, 133 miles each way.

39-16 Hagood Mill
/Prehistoric Rock
Carvings, Pickens Co.
IMAGE COURTESY OF SCDAH

(REVERSE) Issaqueena Cotton Mill, founded by D. K. Norris in 1903, was later operated by Central Mills, Cannon Mills, and Central Textiles. Wesleyan Methodist Bible Institute was founded in 1906 as an elementary and Bible school. It became a junior college in 1928, Central Wesleyan College in 1959, and Southern Wesleyan University in 1994. S.C. Hwy. 93 was once U.S. Hwy. 123, a main route from Atlanta to Charlotte. *Erected by the Central Heritage Society and the Town of Central, 2009*
GPS Coordinates: 34° 43.433' N, 82° 46.967' W

39–15　Hagood-Mauldin House

104 N. Lewis St., Pickens

(FRONT) This house, built ca. 1856, originally sat 14 mi. W in the town of Pickens Court House, then the seat of Pickens District. It was the home of James Earle Hagood (1826–1904), Pickens District clerk of court, state representative during Reconstruction, and U.S. District clerk of court. In 1868, when the district was divided to create Pickens and Oconee Counties, he helped select the site for the "new" town of Pickens.
(REVERSE) Hagood moved this house here in 1868. His daughter Frances (1870–1954) and son-in-law Judge Thomas J. Mauldin (1870–1931) later remodeled the house in the Classical Revival style. Mrs. Mauldin, nationally prominent in several historical organizations,

hosted an annual picnic for Confederate veterans. This house has been a museum since 1988 and was listed in the National Register of Historic Places in 1997. *Erected by the Pickens County Historical Society, 2010*
GPS Coordinates: 34° 53.101' N, 82° 42.341' W

39–16　Hagood Mill/Prehistoric Rock Carvings

U.S. Hwy. 178, 3.5 mi. NNW of Pickens

Hagood Mill (FRONT)
This grist mill was rebuilt in 1845 by James Earle Hagood (1826–1904), son of Benjamin Hagood (1788–1865), who had bought it in 1825. James E. Hagood, a planter and merchant, served in the S.C. House and was longtime Pickens District and U.S. district clerk of court. Hagood Mill, commercially operated until 1966, features a 20-ft. waterwheel, one of the largest in S.C.
Prehistoric Rock Carvings (REVERSE)
Hagood Mill was listed in the National Register of Historic Places in 1972. In 2003 prehistoric Native American rock carvings, called petroglyphs and long buried under a 19th century road, were discovered here and preserved in place. They feature 17 human figures and other carvings, and are among the most significant of their kind in S.C. *Sponsored by the Pickens County Cultural Commission, 2013*
GPS Coordinates: 34° 55.580' N, 82° 43.307' W

39-17 Fort Prince George

Near the entrance to Mile Creek Park, 757 Keowee Baptist Church Rd., Six Mile

(FRONT) Fort Prince George, covered by Lake Keowee since 1968, was built nearby in 1753, near the unofficial boundary between Cherokee lands and white settlements. Across the Keowee River from the Cherokee Lower Town of Keowee, it was built to protect whites and Cherokees from the Creeks or other enemies and had been promised to the Cherokee "headmen" by Gov. James Glen since 1748.

(REVERSE) The fort, a palisaded earthwork with bastions on the corners, was manned by about 25 men. Conflict between its officers and Cherokees helped bring on the Cherokee War of 1760–61. Fort Prince George was abandoned in 1768 as relations between Great Britain and the colonies worsened. Archaeologists excavated the fort site in 1966–68 before Duke Power Company flooded the valley in 1968. *Sponsored by the Piedmont Chapter, South Carolina Society, Daughters of the American Colonists, 2014*
GPS Coordinates: 34° 51.433' N, 82° 52.913' W

39-18 Fort Hill Slave and Convict Cemetery/Woodland Cemetery Clemson University

Woodland Cemetery, Clemson University Campus, Clemson

Fort Hill Slave and Convict Cemetery (FRONT) African Americans enslaved at Fort Hill were buried along the hillside below the Calhoun family plot in graves marked only by field stones. The exact number of burials is unknown. Beginning in 1890, Clemson College leased prisoners, primarily African Americans, from the state to construct campus buildings. Until 1915, those who died during their incarceration were buried adjacent to the slave cemetery.

Woodland Cemetery Clemson University (REVERSE)
Clemson University's Woodland Cemetery began as statesman John C. Calhoun's Fort Hill Plantation graveyard. Early maps show the hillside had been an orchard. The first known burial was a child, also named John C.

Calhoun, who died in 1837. Clemson College laid out the present cemetery in 1924 as a graveyard for faculty and staff. Many prominent Clemson University leaders are buried here. *Sponsored by Clemson University, 2016*
GPS Coordinates: 34° 40.594' N, 82° 50.498' W

39-19 Fort Hill Slave Quarters /Clemson College Convict Stockade

Lee Hall vicinity, Clemson University Campus, Clemson

Fort Hill Slave Quarters (FRONT)
Located one-eighth mile from the main house, the Fort Hill slave quarters were described in 1849 as being "built of stone and joined together like barracks, with gardens attached." Some 70–80 enslaved African Americans then lived at Fort Hill. In 1854, Andrew P. Calhoun moved to Fort Hill from Alabama with his property, including slaves. At his death in 1865, the estate included 139 enslaved African Americans.

Clemson College Convict Stockade (REVERSE)
In 1890, convicted laborers, mostly African Americans with sentences ranging from two months to life, were jailed in a prison stockade nearby. They cleared land, and made and laid bricks. They also dismantled the stone slave quarters to use as foundations for Clemson College's earliest buildings, including the Chemistry Building, Main Administration Building, and faculty residences. *Sponsored by Clemson University, 2016*
GPS Coordinates: 34° 40.470' N, 82° 50.338' W

39-20 Cherokee Village of Esseneca /Fort Hill Plantation of John C. Calhoun

Calhoun Bottoms, Clemson University Campus, Clemson

Cherokee Village of Esseneca (FRONT)
Native Americans inhabited this site prior to the American Revolution. In 1775 naturalist William Bartram described the Cherokee village of Esseneca as "situated on the east bank of Keowee," later the Seneca River, with a council-house and chief's house on the west shore. The Cherokee presence ended when

Maj. Andrew Williamson ordered the town and food stores burned during the Cherokee War of 1776.

Fort Hill Plantation of John C. Calhoun (REVERSE)

Fort Hill Plantation covered some 1,100 acres. Enslaved African Americans cleared fields, terraced hillsides, and herded livestock. They also planted and harvested crops. The enslaved labor force included blacksmiths, carpenters, millers, and gardeners, along with domestics and field hands. The gristmill stream called Sawney's Branch for enslaved laborer Sawney Calhoun was the Mill Creek, later renamed Hunnicutt Creek. *Sponsored by Clemson University, 2016*
GPS Coordinates: 34° 40.677' N, 82° 50.333' W

39–21 Old Pickens Gaol

Corner of Johnson and Pendleton Sts., Pickens

Designed by H. D. Breeding, B. E. Grandy built Pickens County gaol (jail) in 1902. For years it housed not only prisoners but also local sheriffs and their families. In the first year three members of Sheriff J. H. G. McDaniel's family died here of typhoid fever. In 1976 the building became home of the Pickens County Museum of Art & History. It was expanded to include a cultural center in 2006. Listed in the National Register of Historic Places in 1979. *Sponsored by the Pickens County Museum, 2016*
GPS Coordinates: 34° 52.871' N, 82° 42.362' W

39–22 Pickens Railroad

Near intersection of Railroad St. and E. Cedar Rock St., Pickens

(FRONT) The Easley-Pickens line was chartered in 1890 by the S.C. General Assembly. Construction of the line, which ran from Pickens to Easley, was completed in 1898. At Easley the Pickens Railroad joined the Southern Railway. Ex-governor John Gary Evans was a prominent booster for the Pickens Railroad and also one of its first passengers. The line was known as the "Pickens Doodle" because there was no turning track and the train would run backward to Easley and forward to Pickens.

(REVERSE) Passenger service was discontinued in 1928 and the primary users of the Pickens Railroad became Singer Manufacturing and Poinsett Lumber and Manufacturing Co. Singer built a sewing machine cabinet plant next to the line in the 1920s and in 1939 acquired both the Pickens Railroad and Poinsett Lumber, which they used to supply wood veneer. After more than a century of service, the last run from Pickens to Easley took place in April 2013. *Sponsored by City of Pickens, 2017*
GPS Coordinates: 34° 53.005' N, 82° 42.181' W

39–23 Cherokee Path

N. Main St. near the intersection with Mt. Olivet Rd., Six Mile

(FRONT) The Cherokee Path was once part of an important trade network that connected the Upper, Middle, and Lower Cherokee towns in the west with English settlements at Charles Town and, later, inland outposts like Fort Congaree, in the east. In 1715 there were at least 60 Cherokee villages, totaling roughly 11,000 people, that were connected to the coast via this travel and trade corridor. The trade in deer hides was particularly important to the early Carolina economy.
(REVERSE) The Cherokee Path once passed through Six Mile, roughly approximating the current route of Main St. The town of Six Mile derived its name from its location along the Path, which was six miles east of the Cherokee town of Keowee and later the trading post at Fort Prince George, both of which are now submerged under the waters of Lake Keowee. During the Anglo-Cherokee Wars (1759–61, 1776–77) the Path was used as a supply line by British and colonial forces. *Sponsored by the Town of Six Mile, 2018*
GPS Coordinates: 34° 48.468' N, 82° 49.223' W

39–24 Eastatoee Valley

Intersection of Shooting Tree Ridge Rd. and Cleo Chapman Hwy., Sunset

(FRONT) Human settlement in this valley dates to the Clovis people, present as early as 13,000 years ago. By the early 1700s, the valley was part of a cluster of Cherokee Lower Towns.

Near here was the town of Eastatoee, which had more than 200 houses ca. 1760. Valley residents included Cherokee leader Seroweh and European trader James Beamer, who interpreted and mediated with the Cherokee. (REVERSE) Conflicts with Europeans and other tribes weaked Eastatoee, which was destroyed in 1760 and rebuilt. The Cherokee abandoned the town in 1776, when it was burned by Patriot forces. Sustained white settlement in the valley began in 1784, when the state first issued land grants in former Cherokee territory. Descendants of some of those 18th c. settlers still live in the valley. *Sponsored by Pickens County Historical Society, 2019*
GPS Coordinates: 34° 58.342' N, 82° 51.607' W

Richland County

40–1 Trinity Episcopal Church

1100 Sumter St., across from the South Carolina State House, Columbia

Parish organized 1812. Original church dedicated 1814; present church dedicated 1846. In the churchyard lie buried the three Wade Hamptons; Thomas Cooper, educator; Henry Timrod, poet; W. C. Preston, U. S. senator; five governors of S. C.: three Mannings, Hampton, and Thompson; soldiers of the Revolutionary and later American wars, including Colonel Peter Horry, Generals Ellison Capers, John S. Preston, and States Rights Gist. *Erected 1938 by the Columbia Sesquicentennial Commission of 1936*
GPS Coordinates: 34° 0.064' N, 81° 1.895' W

40–2 Site of Parade Ground

1322 Greene St., in front of Thomas Cooper Library, University of South Carolna, Columbia

During Federal military occupation of South Carolina 1865–1877, this square was part of the parade ground used by United States troops. The barracks were located on this and adjacent squares. *Erected in 1938 by the Columbia Sesquicentennial Commission of 1936*
GPS Coordinates: 33° 59.788' N, 81° 1.713' W

40–3 "Commissioners' Oak"

University of South Carolina Law Center Plaza, Greene St. and S. Main St., Columbia

In April 1786, Alexander Gillon, Henry Pendleton, Richard Winn, Richard Hampton, and Thomas Taylor, Commissioners appointed to lay out Columbia, are said to have met under an oak which grew near here. According to tradition the first court and jury in Richland County also met here. *Erected by the University of South Carolina, 1974* [Replaced a marker erected in 1938 by the Columbia Sesquicentennial Commission of 1936.]
GPS Coordinates: 33° 59.706' N, 81° 1.872' W

40–4 "Chestnut Cottage"

1718 Hampton St., Columbia

Temporary wartime home of Gen. and Mrs. James Chesnut. Here they entertained Jefferson Davis, president, C. S. A., and his staff, October 5, 1864. President Davis addressed the citizens of Columbia from the front steps of this cottage. *Erected 1938 by the Columbia Sesquicentennial Commission of 1936*
GPS Coordinates: 34° 0.48' N, 81° 1.578' W

40–5 Original Site of Winthrop College

At the Carriage House, Robert Mills House and Park, Henderson St., between Taylor & Blanding Sts., Columbia

In 1886, chiefly through the efforts of D. B. Johnson, first superintendent of Columbia public schools, Winthrop Training School, later Winthrop College, was started here in a small brick building which had been the chapel of Columbia Theological Seminary. In 1936 this building was moved to the campus of Winthrop College, Rock Hill, S.C. *Erected 1938 by the Columbia Sesquicentennial Commission of 1936*
GPS Coordinates: 34° 0.587' N, 81° 1.697' W

40–6 Former Site of Columbia Theological Seminary

Robert Mills House and Park, 1616 Blanding St., Columbia

Founded 1828 by Presbyterian Synod of South Carolina and Georgia. Located here 1831. Moved to Decatur, Georgia 1925. Woodrow Wilson's father and uncle were among faculty members. Central building, erected 1823, was designed by Robert Mills as home for Ainsley Hall (1783–1823), Columbia merchant. *Erected 1938 by the Columbia Sesquicentennial Commission of 1936*
GPS Coordinates: 34° 0.612' N, 81° 1.755' W

40–7 Hampton-Preston House

1600 Blanding St., Columbia

Built about 1818 by Ainsley Hall. Purchased 1823 by Wade Hampton, I. Inherited by his daughter, Mrs. John S. Preston, 1863. Headquarters of Union Gen. J. A. Logan, 1865; residence of Gov. F. J. Moses 1872–74; Ursuline Convent 1887–90; College for Women 1890–1915; Chicora College for Women 1915–30. The gardens, developed during Hampton-Preston ownership, were adorned with work of Hiram Powers, sculptor. *Erected 1938 by the Columbia Sesquicentennial Commission of 1936*
GPS Coordinates: 34° 0.619' N, 81° 1.764' W

40–8 Site of Columbia Male Academy

Corner of Pickens & Laurel Sts., Columbia

Trustees appointed by legislature 1792 were incorporated 1795 and served as trustees for male and female academies. School located here 1827 on land given by Gov. John Taylor. Though publicly endowed, the school was conducted as a private academy until 1883 when it was merged with public school system. Hugh S. Thompson, Governor of S.C. 1882–86, was principal of male academy 1865–80. *Erected 1938 by the Columbia Sesquicentennial Commission of 1936*
GPS Coordinates: 34° 0.681' N, 81° 1.84' W

40–9 Ebenezer Lutheran Church

Corner of Richland & Sumter Sts., Columbia

First Lutheran congregation in Columbia. Church dedicated in this square in 1830 was burned by Union troops in 1865. It was rebuilt 1870, partly through aid of northern Lutherans, and used for Sunday School after present church was completed in 1931. *Erected 1938 by the Columbia Sesquicentennial Commission of 1936*
GPS Coordinates: 34° 0.686' N, 81° 2.131' W

40–10 State Fairgrounds

Elmwood Ave. at Logan School, Columbia

(FRONT) This block was part of the fairgrounds where the S.C. State Fair was held 1856–1861 and 1869–1903. The fair, sponsored by the State Agricultural Society, featured agricultural, mechanical, household, and art exhibits. During the Civil War a Confederate "camp of instruction" and hospital were here 1861–63, then a lab for making medicines and a branch of the Nitre & Mining Bureau, 1863–65. All the buildings were burned by Federal troops in February 1865.

(REVERSE) In 1869 the State Fair was revived by the State Agricultural & Mechanical Society, which hoped to "beautify Carolina homes and enliven Carolina hearths." The new fair added carnival attractions and rides as it grew in size and attendance over the next 34 years. The 1903 State Fair was the last here, as the site was too small and the buildings too old to accommodate it. The State Fair moved to its present location south of downtown Columbia in 1904. *Sponsored by the Elmwood Park Neighborhood Association, 2013, replacing a marker erected in 1938 by the Columbia Sesquicentennial Commission of 1936*
GPS Coordinates: 34° 0.707' N, 81° 2.691' W

40–11 Cemetery of the Columbia Hebrew Benevolent Society

Corner of Gadsden & Richland Sts., Columbia

In this cemetery, 2 ½ blocks south on Gadsden Street, are buried many distinguished Jewish citizens, including two mayors of Columbia: Mordecai Hendricks DeLeon

(1791–1849) and Henry Lyons (1805–1858). The Benevolent Society was organized in 1822; chartered 1834. *Erected 1938 by the Columbia Sesquicentennial Commission of 1936*
GPS Coordinates: 34° 0.501' N, 81° 2.673' W

40–12 Governor's Mansion

Corner of Richland & Lincoln Sts., Columbia

Arsenal Academy, converted from a state arsenal, occupied this square from 1842 to 1865 when Union troops burned all the academy buildings except officers' quarters, erected 1855. Since 1868 this building has been the Governor's Mansion. *Erected 1938 by the Columbia Sesquicentennial Commission of 1936*
GPS Coordinates: 34° 0.573' N, 81° 2.568' W

40–13 Site of Palmetto Iron Works

In front of the South Carolina Governor's Mansion, 800 Richland St., Columbia

On the SW corner of this square was located the Palmetto Armory, later called Palmetto Iron Works, originally built for converting flint and steel muskets into percussion guns. Arms and munitions were manufactured here during the Confederate War, 1861–1865. *Erected by the City of Columbia, 1966, replacing a marker erected in 1938 by the Columbia Sesquicentennial Commission of 1936*
GPS Coordinates: 34° 0.541' N, 81° 2.534' W

40–14 Ladson Presbyterian Church

1720 Sumter St., Columbia

Congregation originated in the Sabbath School for colored people organized by the First Presbyterian Church 1838, later conducted by the Rev. G. W. Ladson. A chapel for the Negro members of that church was built here 1868. Rebuilt 1896. The title was transferred to Ladson Church trustees in 1895. *Erected 1938 by the Columbia Sesquicentennial Commission of 1936*
GPS Coordinates: 34° 0.555' N, 81° 2.107' W

40–15 Debruhl-Marshall House

1401 Laurel St., Columbia

A fine example of the classic style in Southern domestic architecture. Built in 1820, probably after a design of Robert Mills. For almost one hundred years the home of the DeBruhl and Marshall families. *Erected 1977, replacing a marker erected 1938 by the Columbia Sesquicentennial Commission of 1936*
GPS Coordinates: 34° 0.624' N, 81° 2.029' W

40–16 Site of Blanding House

Corner of Marion & Blanding Sts., Columbia

In this square stood the home of Colonel Abram Blanding (1776–1839) for whom this street was named. He was first principal, Columbia Male Academy 1798, a noted lawyer and philanthropist, ably served the state on Board of Public Works 1819–28. Financed and built city's first water works, 1820. *Erected 1938 by the Columbia Sesquicentennial Commission of 1936*
GPS Coordinates: 34° 0.538' N, 81° 2.013' W

40–17 First Baptist Church

1306 Hampton St., Columbia

Congregation organized 1809. Original church, built 1811 on Sumter Street corner, was burned Feb. 17, 1865 by Union troops who mistook it for the present church, built 1859, where the Secession Convention had met Dec. 17, 1860. Because of reported smallpox in Columbia, the convention adjourned to Charleston. *Erected 1938 by the Columbia Sesquicentennial Commission of 1936*
GPS Coordinates: 34° 0.349' N, 81° 1.996' W

40–18 Site of Gibbes House

Corner of Sumter & Hampton Sts., Columbia

On this corner stood the home of Dr. Robert W. Gibbes (1809–66) distinguished physician, scientist, historian, editor, antiquarian; Surgeon General of South Carolina 1861–65. The house with his notable library, art treasures and scientific collections was burned by Union troops February 17, 1865. *Erected 1938 by the Columbia Sesquicentennial Commission of 1936*
GPS Coordinates: 34° 0.361' N, 81° 1.986' W

40–19 Site of Carolina Hall

[No longer extant.]

Sumter St., between Hampton & Washington Sts., Columbia

After Red Shirt campaign of 1876 Wade Hampton was inaugurated governor of South Carolina at Carolina Hall which stood in center of this square. During the dual government that followed, the Democratic House of Representatives (Wallace House) met here until the Hampton administration gained possession of the State House. *Erected 1938 by the Columbia Sesquicentennial Commission of 1936*

40–20 Site of Columbia Female Academy

Corner of Washington & Marion Sts., Columbia

Authorized by legislature 1792, the Columbia Female Academy was located here from about 1820 to 1883, when this property was leased to Columbia Public School Commissioners, two of whom still represent the Academy Board. The remodeled academy became the first Columbia High School, in use until 1915. *Erected 1938 by the Columbia Sesquicentennial Commission of 1936*
GPS Coordinates: 34° 0.297' N, 81° 1.919' W

40–21 Washington Street Methodist Church

1401 Washington St., Columbia

A church was built here between 1803 and 1805; another church, erected 1832, was burned by Union troops in 1865 and reconstructed in 1866 of salvaged brick and clay mortar. Present church dedicated 1875. Bishop Wm. Capers (1790–1855), founder of missions to slaves in S. C., was pastor and is buried here. *Erected 1938 by the Columbia Sesquicentennial Commission of 1936*
GPS Coordinates: 34° 0.318' N, 81° 1.9' W

40–22 First Presbyterian Church

1324 Marion St., at the corner of Marion & Lady Sts., Columbia

First congregation organized in Columbia (1795). The churchyard, allotted as a public burying ground in 1798, was granted to this church 1813. Here are buried: D. E. Dunlap, first pastor; Chancellor H. W. DeSaussure; Jonathan Maxcy, first President of S.C. College; Ann Pamela Cuningham, founder of Mt. Vernon Ladies' Association; U. S. Senators F. H. Elmore and Wm. F. DeSaussure, and the parents of Woodrow Wilson. *Erected 1938 by the Columbia Sesquicentennial Commission of 1936*
GPS Coordinates: 34° 0.237' N, 81° 1.862' W

40–23 Last Home of Wade Hampton

Corner of Senate & Barnwell Sts., Columbia

Wade Hampton, III, born March 28, 1818, was commander of Hampton Legion, 1861, with rank of Colonel; Lieutenant General, C. S. A., 1865; Governor of S.C. 1876–79; U.S. Senator 1879–91. He died April 11, 1902 in this house, given to him in 1899 by a grateful people. *Erected 1938 by the Columbia Sesquicentennial Commission of 1936*
GPS Coordinates: 34° 0.17' N, 81° 1.381' W

40–24 Horry-Guignard House

1527 Senate St., Columbia

One of the oldest houses in Columbia; built before 1813, probably by Peter Horry (1747–1815), Colonel in Revolution, Brigadier General of S.C. militia. Later home of John Gabriel Guignard (1751–1822), Surveyor General of S.C., 1798–1802. *Erected 1938 by the Columbia Sesquicentennial Commission of 1936*
GPS Coordinates: 34° 0.114' N, 81° 1.617' W

40–25 Birthplace of General Maxcy Gregg

Senate St., between Sumter & Marion Sts., Columbia

Maxcy Gregg, Confederate general and leader in Southern rights movement, was born Aug. 1, 1815 in a house on this site. Member of committee which framed the Ordinance of Secession, Dec. 1860, Colonel 1st Regiment South Carolina Volunteers; Brigadier General in 1861. Mortally wounded at Fredericksburg Dec. 13, 1862; died two days later. *Erected 1938*

by the Columbia Sesquicentennial Commission of 1936
GPS Coordinates: 34° 0.026' N, 81° 1.836' W

40–26 Entrance to Cemetery of the Columbia Hebrew Benevolent Society

Corner of Taylor & Gadsden Sts., Columbia

The society has been in continuous existence since its organization in 1822. It was chartered 1834. Its charities are administered to the needs of the community without regard to creed or race. *Erected 1938 by the Columbia Sesquicentennial Commission of 1936*
GPS Coordinates: 34° 0.294' N, 81° 2.571' W

40–27 University of South Carolina

Marker #1: Sumter St. Entrance to the Horseshoe, University of South Carolina Campus, Columbia

Marker #2: Bull St. Entrance to the Horseshoe, University of South Carolina Campus, Columbia

Marker #3: Greene St, in front of the Thomas Cooper Library, University of South Carolina Campus, Columbia

Chartered 1801 as the S.C. College, opened January 10, 1805. Entire student body volunteered for Confederate service 1861. Soldiers' hospital 1862–65. Rechartered as U. of S.C. 1865. Radical control 1873–77. Closed 1877–80. College of Agriculture and Mechanic Arts 1880–82. S.C. College 1882–87. U. of S.C. 1887–90. S.C. College 1890–1905. U. of S.C. 1906. Faithful index to the ambitions and fortunes of the state. *Erected 1938 by the Columbia Sesquicentennial Commission of 1936*
GPS Coordinates: 33° 59.857' N, 81° 1.798' W

40–28 South Carolina State Hospital

At the entrance to the South Carolina State Hospital Grounds, Bull St. at the end of Elmwood Ave., Columbia

Institution authorized 1821 by General Assembly, mainly through the work of two members, Samuel Farrow and William Crafts, Jr. The original building, on right, designed by Robert Mills, shows a pioneer grasp of the ideas of humanitarian treatment. *Erected 1938*

by the Columbia Sesquicentennial Commission of 1936
GPS Coordinates: 34° 0.896' N, 81° 2.037' W

40–29 Horrell Hill

Garner's Ferry Rd. (U.S. Hwy. 76/378) near its junction with Congaree Rd. (S.C. Hwy. 769), Horrell Hill

300 yards north is the site of the Richland County Court House built about 1794; abandoned when county courts were abolished 1798. Corn was ground in 1781 for Sumter's army at John Marshall's Mill, on Cedar Creek, ¾ mi. east. There has been a mill on this creek since the Revolution. *Erected by Lower Richland Ruritan Club, 1975* [Replaced a marker erected in 1938 by the Columbia Sesquicentennial Commission of 1936.]
GPS Coordinates: 33° 57.092' N, 80° 50.535' W

40–30 Hopkins

Hopkins Post Office, Lower Richland Blvd. (S.C. Hwy. 37), Hopkins

Land granted to Jno. Hopkins 1765. Minerva Academy located here 1802–34. Old plantations nearby: CABIN BRANCH (Hopkins, Chappell); ELM-SAVANNAH (Adams); LIVE OAK (Gov. J. H. Adams); GREENFIELD (Goodwyn, Howell); WAVERING PLACE (Tucker, Hopkins, Hayne); GROVEWOOD (Weston). *Erected in 1938 by the Columbia Sesquicentennial Commission of 1936*
GPS Coordinates: 33° 54.070' N, 80° 52.609' W

40–31 Gadsden

Bluff Rd. (S.C. Hwy. 48), Gadsden

Named in honor of James Gadsden President of the Louisville, Cincinnati and Charleston Railroad. Station built here 1840 was the first railroad station in Richland County. A stage line ran to Columbia until 1842 and to Camden until 1848. *Erected 1938 by the Columbia Sesquicentennial Commission of 1936*
GPS Coordinates: 33° 50.76' N, 80° 46.137' W

40–32 Early Summer Resorts

[No longer extant.]

Two Notch Rd. (U.S. Hwy. 1), Dentsville community, Columbia

Lightwood Knot Springs, situated about two miles north, a popular summer resort during the first half of the nineteenth century, was later Confederate training camp for recruits. A few miles east was Rice Creek Springs, another early summer resort and the site of Richland Polytechnic Institute, 1830–1845. *Erected 1938 by the Columbia Sesquicentennial Commission of 1936*

40–33 South Carolina Female Collegiate Institute

Two Notch Rd. (U.S. Hwy. 1), near Covenant Rd., Dentsville community, Columbia

At Barhamville, about ½ mi. west of this point, a famous girls' school, founded by Dr. Elias Marks (1790–1886), was located 1828–65. Among the students were Anna Maria, daughter of John C. Calhoun; Ann Pamela Cuningham, founder of Mt. Vernon Ladies' Association; Martha Bulloch, mother of President Theodore Roosevelt. *Erected in 1938 by the Columbia Sesquicentennial Commission of 1936*

GPS Coordinates: 34° 1.676' N, 81° 0.586' W

40–34 St. Peter's Church and Ursuline Convent

1529 Assembly St., Columbia

First church built 1824; present church 1906. In the churchyard is buried John R. Niernsee (1823–85), Major C. S. A.; architect of the State House. Ursuline convent located SE corner Main and Blanding streets 1858–65; VALLE CRUCIS 1865–87; Hampton-Preston House 1887–90; erected here 1889. *Erected in 1938 by the Columbia Sesquicentennial Commission of 1936*

GPS Coordinates: 34° 0.316' N, 81° 2.258' W

40–35 Site of Wayside Hospital

700 block of Gervais St., Columbia

Established March 10, 1862 by a group of Columbia women to care for sick and wounded Confederate soldiers. Supported by voluntary contributions. About 75,000 men were cared for before the hospital was closed February 15, 1865. "From this little nucleus spread the grand system of wayside hospitals." *Erected 1938 by the Columbia Sesquicentennial Commission of 1936*

GPS Coordinates: 33° 59.944' N, 81° 2.438' W

40–36 Historic Printing Plant and Warehouse

[No longer extant. Replaced by Marker 40-124, erected by the United Daughters of the Confederacy, 2002.]

Corner of Gervais & Pulaski Sts., Columbia

Erected 1938 by the Columbia Sesquicentennial Commission of 1936

40–37 Columbia Canal

Gervais St. (U.S. Hwy. 1) on the Congaree River Bridge, Columbia

Completed 1824. Important link in the system of waterways transporting freight between the up country and Charleston. Supplanted by railroads for transportation after 1850. Leased to Confederate government to run powder works. Enlarged 1880–95 and since sold to successive power companies. *Erected 1938 by the Columbia Sesquicentennial Commission of 1936*

GPS Coordinates: 33° 59.794' N, 81° 2.913' W

40–38 Congaree River Bridges

Gervais St. (U.S. Hwy. 1) on the Columbia side of the Congaree River Bridge, Columbia

This river took its name from the Congaree Indians, a Siouan tribe which occupied the valley until the Yemassee War in 1715. The first wooden bridge here was completed in 1827. It was burned to delay the advance of Sherman's Army in 1865, and rebuilt in 1870. A concrete bridge was completed in 1927. *Erected by the City of Columbia 1966, replacing marker erected 1938 by the Columbia Sesquicentennial Commission of 1936*

GPS Coordinates: 33° 59.783' N, 81° 2.947' W

40-39 Early Country Homes

Corner of Forest Dr. (S.C. Hwy. 12) & N. Beltline Blvd. (S.C. Hwy. 16), Columbia

In this malaria-free sandhill section were the antebellum summer homes of many Columbians: QUININE HILL (Dr. J. M. Taylor, Dr. James Davis); HILLTOP (W. J. Taylor); EDGEHILL (B. F. Taylor); LAUREL HILL (D. J. McCord); COOPER'S HILL (Thos. Cooper); WINDY HILL (Langdon Cheves); ROSE HILL (Arthur Middleton); DIAMOND HILL (Singleton, McDuffie, Hampton). *Erected 1938 by the Columbia Sesquicentennial Commission of 1936*
GPS Coordinates: 34° 1.158' N, 80° 59.379' W

40-40 Fisher's Mill on Gill Creek

Forest Dr. (S.C. Hwy. 12), about 100 yds. E of its intersection with Trenholm Rd. and just E of Trenholm Plaza, Columbia

About 1800, Col. Thomas Taylor erected the small building, ¼ mile upstream, where cotton goods were woven for his plantation needs. Here John and Edward Fisher later established one of the earliest spinning mills in Richland County, using slave labor and manufacturing cotton yarn. *Erected 1938 by the Columbia Sesquicentennial Commission of 1936*
GPS Coordinates: 34° 1.113' N, 80° 57.834' W

40-41 Friday's Ferry

[Reported missing in 2004.]

Bluff Road (S.C. Hwy. 48), just SE of its intersection with Rosewood Dr., Columbia

1 mi. west was East Granby Landing of Friday's Ferry (licensed 1754) across Congaree River. Floods destroyed two bridges built 1791 and 1796 by Wade Hampton I. President Washington crossed here May 22, 1791 on his southern tour. MT. TACITUS, 3 mi. south, was a plantation of Charles Pinckney (1757–1824), four times governor of South Carolina. *Erected 1938 by the Columbia Sesquicentennial Commission of 1936*
GPS Coordinates: 33° 58.238' N, 81° 2.520' W

40-42 Early Richland County Settlements

[Reported missing in 2005.]

Bluff Rd. (S.C. Hwy. 48) at Mill Creek, S of Columbia

First settlements made about 1740 on this creek, originally called Raiford's, now Mill Creek. Howell's Ferry across Congaree River below creek's mouth was used 1756 through the Revolution. John Pearson (1743–1819) born near here was first known white child born in bounds of present county. *Erected 1938 by the Columbia Sesquicentennial Commission of 1936*
GPS Coordinates: 33° 58.984' N, 81° 1.895' W

40-43 Wateree River Ferries

Garner's Ferry Rd. (U.S. Hwy. 378/76) at Richland County-Sumter County line, Eastover vicinity

River took its name from Wateree Indians, a Siouan tribe which occupied the valley until about 1715. Near this site was Simmons' Upper Ferry, used during the Revolution; later called Brisbanes, then Garner's Ferry. Used until bridge completed 1922. *Erected in 1938 by the Columbia Sesquicentennial Commission of 1936*
GPS Coordinates: 33° 56.817' N, 80° 37.681' W

40-44 Antebellum Plantations

Intersection of Garner's Ferry Rd. (U.S. Hwy. 378/76) & Old Eastover Rd. (S.C. Hwy. 764), Eastover vicinity

Among the early Richland County plantations between the Wateree River and Columbia were: DEER POND and KENSINGTON (Singleton); GOODWILL (Huger, Heyward); NUT SHELL (Bynum, Heyward); THE RAFT and MIDDLEBURG (Clarkson). *Erected 1938 by the Columbia Sesquicentennial Commission of 1936*
GPS Coordinates: 33° 56.553' N, 80° 46.324' W

40-45 Congaree Baptist Church

Garner's Ferry Rd. (U.S. Hwy. 378/76), Horrell Hill

A few miles south was the site of original Congaree Baptist Church, organized 1766 with the Rev. Joseph Reese as pastor. Probably

first church in bounds of present Richland County. Since 1800 located on Tom's Creek 22 miles south of Columbia. *Erected 1938 by the Columbia Sesquicentennial Commission of 1936*
GPS Coordinates: 33° 57.095' N, 80° 50.468' W

40–46 Woodlands and Millwood

100 Hampton Place, Garner's Ferry Rd. (U.S. Hwy. 378/76), Columbia

1 ½ mi. south was WOODLANDS, built before 1800 by Wade Hampton, I (1752–1835), Colonel in Revolution, Major General in War of 1812. ¼ mi. north was MILLWOOD, built before 1820 by Wade Hampton II (1791–1858), aide to Gen. Jackson, War of 1812. Boyhood home of Wade Hampton, III (1818–1902), Lieutenant General, C. S. A.; Governor of South Carolina 1876–79. Union troops burned both houses 1865. *Erected 1938 by the Columbia Sesquicentennial Commission of 1936*
GPS Coordinates: 33° 59.035' N, 80° 58.056' W

40–47 Camp Jackson

Corner of Garner's Ferry Rd. (U.S. Hwy. 378/76) and Wildcat Rd., Columbia

Named in honor of Gen. Andrew Jackson. This cantonment site 1 ½ mi. north was approved by the War Dept. June 2, 1917. Maximum strength was recorded in June 1918: 3,302 officers; 45,402 men. 81st Division was trained here Aug. 29, 1917-May 18, 1918; the 5th Division stationed here Oct. 20, 1920–Oct. 4, 1921.Made a training camp for National Guard 1925. *Erected 1938 by the Columbia Sesquicentennial Commission of 1936*
GPS Coordinates: 33° 59.035' N, 80° 58.056' W

40–48 Early Columbia Racetrack

Corner of Devine St. (U.S. Hwy. 76/21) & Sims St., Columbia

From early days horse racing was a favorite sport in Columbia and many famous horses were bred on neighboring plantations. Columbia Jockey Club was organized by Col. Wade Hampton II and Col. Richard Singleton in 1828. Congaree Race Course was located 300 yards north on present Epworth Orphanage

property. *Erected 1938 by the Columbia Sesquicentennial Commission of 1936*
GPS Coordinates: 33° 59.874' N, 80° 59.946' W

40–49 Sherman's Headquarters

On the wall of the Clarion Town House Hotel, 1615 Gervais St., Columbia

During the Federal occupation of Columbia February 17–19, 1865 commanding General William T. Sherman had his headquarters here. *Erected 1938 by the Columbia Sesquicentennial Commission of 1936*
GPS Coordinates: 34° 0.234' N, 81° 1.585' W

40–50 Broad River

River Dr. (U.S. Hwy. 176) at the Broad River Bridge, Columbia

Early boundary between Cherokee and Catawba Indians. Name first applied about 1745. Faust's Ford, 2 mi. above, used in Revolution. First bridge opened 1829, burned 1865 to delay Sherman's army which crossed on pontoon bridges downstream. Bridge rebuilt 1867, burned 1925. Concrete bridge completed 1930. *Erected 1938 by the Columbia Sesquicentennial Commission of 1936*
GPS Coordinates: 34° 1.561' N, 81° 4.113' W

40–51 Thomas Taylor 1743–1833 /Taylor Cemetery

Corner of Richland & Barnwell Sts., Columbia

Thomas Taylor 1743–1833(FRONT)
Member of Provincial Congresses 1775 and 1776; Colonel of militia under General Thomas Sumter in the American Revolution; Senator in the Jacksonborough Assembly; member of S.C. Convention which ratified the United States Constitution; member S.C. Legislature; commissioner who helped plan the city of Columbia and one of the founders and first elders of the First Presbyterian Church.
Taylor Cemetery (REVERSE)
In 1786 the State of S.C. bought as part of the site of Columbia the plantation of Colonel Thomas Taylor, Revolutionary soldier, and elected him one of the commissioners to lay out the capital city. The home was situated near the southeast corner of Richland and

Barnwell streets. On the northwest corner lie buried Colonel Taylor, his son Governor John Taylor and members of the family. *Erected by the William Capers Chapter, Daughters of the American Revolution, 1968*
GPS Coordinates: 34° 0.81' N, 81° 1.714' W

40–52 Original Site of Columbia College

Hampton St., between Pickens and Henderson Sts., Columbia

This land was purchased in 1854 by the South Carolina Conference of the Methodist Episcopal Church as the site of Columbia Female College, Chartered by S.C. General Assembly Dec. 21, 1854. Classes were held from 1859 to 1865. The college survived the burning of Columbia and was reopened in 1873. In 1905, the school was moved to its present site as the Columbia College. *Erected 1979 by Columbia College Alumnae Association, replacing a marker erected by the same association in 1969*
GPS Coordinates: 34° 0.445' N, 81° 1.701' W

40–53 Court House Square

Affixed to the Carolina National Bank, corner of Main & Washington Sts., Columbia

Richland County's second court house was built in 1803–04 on the northeast corner of Richardson (Main) and Washington Streets. In the 1850s, it was razed and a new court house erected on the same site. On the southeast corner was located the Athenaeum, incorporated in 1856, which contained a lecture and exhibit hall and a library. The Athenaeum and the new court house were both burned by Union troops in 1865. *Erected by Columbia Chapter, Daughters of the American Revolution, 1970*
GPS Coordinates: 34° 0.235' N, 81° 2.073' W

40–54 100th Inf Division

Between Jackson Blvd. & Magnolia Ave., Fort Jackson, Columbia

At this site on 15 November 1942, Maj. Gen. W. A. Burress received the 100th Infantry Division colors, marking the official activation of the "Century Division." After a

distinguished World War II record in southern France and Germany, the 100th was reorganized in the Army Reserve. It was the only USAR training division recalled during the 1961 Berlin crisis. *Erected by 100th Division (Tng), USAR, 1982, replacing a marker placed by the division in 1971*
GPS Coordinates: 34° 0.086' N, 80° 57.076' W

40–55 30th Inf Division

Jackson Blvd., Fort Jackson, Columbia

(FRONT) After a brilliant combat record in World War I and 14 years of dedicated National Guard service, the "Old Hickory" Division was mobilized at Fort Jackson, S.C. on 16 September 1940. During World War II, the 30th Division distinguished itself in combat in the campaigns through Normandy, Northern France, the Ardennes, the Rhineland, and Central Europe.

(REVERSE) For its illustrious combat record throughout World War II, this "Work Horse of the Western Front" was selected as the outstanding infantry division of the European Theater of Operations. It was awarded two Belgian Fourrageres and the French Croix de Guerre with Palm. On 25 Nov. 1945, it was inactivated at Fort Jackson, resuming its National Guard role. *Erected by 30th Infantry Division Association, 1972*
GPS Coordinates: 34° 0.626' N, 80° 56.738' W

40–56 87th Inf Division

Jackson Blvd., Fort Jackson, Columbia

Activated at Camp McCain, Miss. in 1942, the "Golden Acorn" Division trained at this site in 1944. The division distinguished itself in the Ardennes, the Rhineland, and Central Europe during the Battle of the Bulge, the assault of the Sauer, Moselle, and Rhine rivers, capture of Coblenz, the cracking of the Siegfried Line, and the final assault into Czechoslovakia. *Erected by 87th Division Association, 1972*
GPS Coordinates: 34° 1.551' N, 80° 56.262' W

40–57 106th Inf Division

Jackson Blvd., Fort Jackson, Columbia

Near this site on 15 March 1943 the 106th Infantry Division was officially activated and became known as the "Golden Lion Division." Although badly mauled in the "Battle of the Bulge," the division stubbornly continued to fight on. The 106th saw action in the Ardennes, the Rhineland, and Central Europe. *Erected by 106th Infantry Division Association, 1974*
GPS Coordinates: 34° 1.263' N, 80° 56.289' W

40–58 Grave of Joseph Reese

Garner's Ferry Rd. (U.S. Hwy. 378/76) at Trotter Rd. (S.C. Sec. Rd. 40–222), Horrell Hill vicinity

Joseph Reese, pioneer Baptist minister and Revolutionary patriot who died in 1795, is buried 2 mi. SW of here. Born in Pennsylvania, he came to the Congarees in 1745, became a Baptist as a result of Philip Mulkey's preaching and was ordained by Oliver Hart and Evan Pugh. Reese won Richard Furman to the Baptists and was the first pastor of Congaree Baptist Church. *Erected by S.C. Baptist Historical Society, 1976*
GPS Coordinates: 33° 56.678' N, 80° 54.231' W

40–59 Richardson Street/The North-South Streets in the City of Columbia

South Carolina State House Grounds at Main St., Columbia

Richardson Street (FRONT)
Columbia's chief business street, Main, was first named Richardson Street, for Richard Richardson (1704–1780). This Virginia native settled in present Clarendon County; served in the "Snow Campaign" of 1775; was commissioned Brigadier General in 1778; was a member of the Commons House of Assembly, the First and Second Provincial Congresses, and the First General Assembly. Six S.C. Governors are among his descendants.
The North-South Streets in the City of Columbia (REVERSE)
The north-south streets, laid out in the two-mile square of the original city of Columbia in 1786, were named (except for Assembly)

for generals and officers who fought in the American Revolution. Most of these were native Americans, but one was the Polish Count Pulaski. *Erected by Columbia Committee, National Society Colonial Dames of America in the State of S.C. A Richland County Bicentennial Project, 1976*
GPS Coordinates: 34° 0.075' N, 81° 2.005' W

40–60 Gervais Street/The East-West Streets in the City of Columbia

South Carolina State House Grounds at Gervais St., Columbia

Gervais Street (FRONT)
Named for John Lewis Gervais (ca. 1742–1798) who was educated in Germany, emigrated first to England, arrived in Charleston in 1764 with a letter of introduction to Henry Laurens. He served in the American Revolution, took part in the defense of Charleston, was a member of the Continental Congress. S.C. Senate member from Ninety Six, he introduced the bill that resulted in the selection of the site of Columbia as Capital of S.C.
The East/West Streets in the City of Columbia (REVERSE)
The streets of Columbia running from east to west (with a few exceptions) were named for products in the State's economy, for the two Taylor plantations on which the new Capital was located, and for prominent individuals such as Gervais, author of the bill establishing Columbia as Capital. *Erected by The Lions Club of Columbia, a Richland County Bicentennial Project, 1976*
GPS Coordinates: 34° 0.07' N, 81° 2.022' W

40–61 Pickens Street

Corner of Pickens & Gervais Sts., Columbia

This street was named for Andrew Pickens (1739–1817). One of three S.C. Partisan Generals in the Revolution, he fought in the battles of Cowpens and Eutaw Springs both in 1781. Pickens served fourteen years in the S.C. House of Representatives, four in the S.C. Senate and two in Congress. From 1785 to 1791, he was appointed several times by Congress to treat with the Indians. He is

buried at Old Stone Church near Pendleton. *Erected by Richland County Bicentennial Commission; Sponsored by Richland County Historical Society, 1977*
GPS Coordinates: 34° 0.177' N, 81° 1.639' W

40–62 Williams Street/Gist Street

Gervais St. between Gist & Williams Sts., Columbia

Williams Street (FRONT)
This street was named for Otho H. Williams, Brig. Gen. of the Continental Army during the American Revolution. Williams served as Adjutant General under Southern Army commanders Gates and Greene and saw military action in the battles of Camden, Guilford Courthouse, Hobkirk Hill, and Eutaw Springs. He commanded the light corps which protected Greene during a portion of his retreat across N.C. in 1781. *Erected by Richland County Bicentennial Commission; Sponsored by Columbia Mills, 1977*
Gist Street (REVERSE)
This street was named for Mordecai Gist, Brigadier General of the Continental Army. During the American Revolution, Gist participated in the Battle of Camden in 1780, and commanded a light corps in an engagement on the Combahee River August 27, 1782, in which Colonel John Laurens was killed. After the Revolution, Gist settled in Charleston, where he died in 1792. *Erected by Richland County Bicentennial Commission; Sponsored by S.C. Federal Savings and Loan Association, 1977*
GPS Coordinates: 33° 59.824' N, 81° 2.813' W

40–63 Bull Street

Corner of Bull & Gervais Sts., Columbia

This street was named for Brigadier General Stephen Bull (ca. 1733–1800). Grandson of Lt. Gov. William Bull I, Stephen was a member of the Commons House of Assembly, the First Provincial Congress, the First General Assembly. He saw military action in the Battle of Beaufort and the Savannah campaign and later served in the S.C. Senate and House of Representatives. He is buried at Sheldon Church, Beaufort County. *Erected by Richland*

County Bicentennial Commission; Sponsored by WIS-TV, 1977
GPS Coordinates: 34° 0.142' N, 81° 1.726' W

40–64 Huger Street

Corner of Huger & Gervais Sts., Columbia

This street was named for Brig. Gen. Isaac Huger, who fought in the Cherokee War of 1760 and during the American Revolution at Stono, Savannah, Siege of Charlestown, Guilford Court House, Hobkirk Hill. Born 1743 at Limerick Plantation in the parish of St. John's Berkeley, Huger was in the Commons House of Assembly and the First Provincial Congress, and later in the S.C. Senate and House of Representatives. He died in 1797. *Erected by Richland County Bicentennial Commission; Sponsored by W. O. Blackstone and Co., Inc., 1977*
GPS Coordinates: 33° 59.851' N, 81° 2.707' W

40–65 Roberts Street/Pinckney Street

[Marker removed due to damage.]

E side of Gervais St. (U.S. Hwy. 1) at the Congaree River Bridge, Columbia

Roberts Street (FRONT)
This street, which is located five blocks north and is the westernmost in Columbia's original plan of 1786, was named for Owen Roberts. He was a member of the First Provincial Congress from the parishes of St. Philip and St. Michael, and was commissioned colonel of the S.C. Continental Regiment of Artillery during the Revolution. Roberts was killed at the Battle of Stono, June 20, 1779.
Pinckney Street (REVERSE)
This street, located several blocks to the north and south, was named for Charles Cotesworth Pinckney. He fought in the American Revolution, became a Brevet Brig. Gen. in 1783, and served in both houses of the legislature. A framer of the U.S. Constitution and a delegate to the 1790 S.C. Constitutional Convention, he was appointed minister to France in 1796 and was also three times Federalist candidate for president. Pinckney died in 1825. *Erected by Richland County Bicentennial Commission; Sponsored by Kline Iron and Steel Co., 1977*
GPS Coordinates: 33° 59.786' N, 81° 2.934' W

40–66 Blanding Street

Corner of Main & Blanding Sts., Columbia

Originally named Walnut Street, Blanding Street was by 1869 renamed for Abram Blanding, a Massachusetts native who came to Columbia in 1797 to take charge of Columbia Male Academy. Blanding was admitted to the bar in 1802 and served two terms in the legislature. He built the city's first water works, was a Trustee of South Carolina College, and S.C. Superintendent of Public Works. His house was located on the NW corner of Blanding and Marion streets. Blanding died in 1839. *Erected by Richland County Bicentennial Commission, 1978*
GPS Coordinates: 34° 0.467' N, 81° 2.167' W

40–67 College Street

Corner of College & Main Sts., Columbia

This street, originally named Medium Street and part of the original 1786 Columbia plan, bisected the area which was to be the campus of South Carolina College. The college, established in 1801 by an act of the General Assembly, later became the University of South Carolina. Medium Street was renamed College Street shortly after 1891. *Erected by Richland County Bicentennial Commission, 1978*
GPS Coordinates: 33° 59.821' N, 81° 1.885' W

40–68 Elmwood Avenue

Corner of Elmwood & Main Sts., Columbia

This street, originally named Upper Street, was the northernmost street in the original 1786 Columbia plan. The plan of the city depicted an area two miles square divided into lots of one-half acre, eight acres were reserved for erecting public buildings. Upper Street was renamed Elmwood Avenue shortly after 1872 for adjacent Elmwood Cemetery, which was incorporated in 1854. *Erected by Richland County Bicentennial Commission; Sponsored by the Keenan Company, Realtors, 1978*
GPS Coordinates: 34° 0.787' N, 81° 2.312' W

40–69 Wilson House

1705 Hampton St., Columbia

Built by 1872, this house was the boyhood home of Woodrow Wilson (1856–1924), twenty-eighth President of the United States (1913–21). It was constructed by his parents, the Reverend Joseph Ruggles Wilson and Jessie Woodrow Wilson, when they lived in Columbia. The Reverend Wilson was a professor at Columbia Theological Seminary from 1870 to 1874 and was minister of Columbia's First Presbyterian Church from 1871 to 1873. *Erected by Historic Columbia Foundation, 1978*
GPS Coordinates: 34° 0.481' N, 81° 1.621' W

40–70 Laurens Street
[No longer extant.]

Gervais St., just east of Gregg St., Columbia

(FRONT) Laurens Street, located one block south, is named for Lt. Col. John Laurens of South Carolina whose father, Henry, was president of the Continental Congress. Young Laurens studied in London several years and in 1777, while still in his early twenties, returned to America and was named aide-de-camp to General George Washington. After distinguishing himself at Germantown and Monmouth, he joined the troops fighting the British in the South.

(REVERSE) Lt. Col. John Laurens of South Carolina, for whom Laurens Street is named, was made prisoner at the fall of Charlestown in May 1780. He was quickly exchanged and was named special envoy to France by Congress. With Benjamin Franklin and the French he planned the 1781 campaign, which led to the surrender of Cornwallis. Six months later he rejoined Washington and fought at Yorktown. Laurens was killed in South Carolina in 1782 in a Combahee River skirmish. *Erected by Richland County Bicentennial Commission; Sponsored by Gibbes Machinery Company, 1978*

40–71 Washington Street

Corner of Washington & Main Sts., Columbia

This street is named for George Washington, commander of the Continental Army

throughout the Revolution, first President of the United States, and president of the 1787 Constitutional Convention. Early in his presidency, Washington toured the southern states. He visited South Carolina in 1791 and spent May 22–24 in the new capital city, Columbia. While here, he attended a public dinner in the new State House. *Erected by Richland County Bicentennial Commission; Sponsored by Rotary Club of Columbia, 1978*
GPS Coordinates: 34° 0.237' N, 81° 2.082' W

40–72 Calhoun Street

[No longer extant.]

Corner of Main & Calhoun Sts., Columbia

Named Lumber Street by 1793, this street was renamed Calhoun shortly after 1911 for S.C. statesman John C. Calhoun (1782–1850). Calhoun was admitted to the S.C. bar in 1807, was United States Secretary of War 1812–25, Vice President 1825–1832, and Secretary of State 1844–45; he also served many years in Congress. Calhoun is buried in St. Philip's churchyard in Charleston. *Erected by Richland County Bicentennial Commission; Sponsored by Columbia Office Supply, 1978*

40–73 Laurel Street

Corner of Main & Laurel Sts., Columbia

This street probably takes its name from the cherry laurel (laurocerasus caroliniana) and the mountain laurel (Kalmia latifolia), both of which are indigenous to South Carolina. Laurel Street is one of the original streets in the 1786 plan of Columbia. *Erected by Richland County Bicentennial Commission; Sponsored by Colonial Life and Accident Insurance Company, 1978*
GPS Coordinates: 34° 0.549' N, 81° 2.202' W

40–74 Richland Street

Corner of Richland & Main Sts., Columbia

One of the original streets in the 1786 Columbia plan, Richland Street was probably named after Richland County, which had been so designated by an act of the General Assembly in 1785. By November 1786, two town commissioners, Alexander Gillon and

Thomas Taylor, owned lots on this street. The Governor's Mansion is located on Richland Street. *Erected by Richland County Bicentennial Commission; Sponsored by Capital Electric Supply, 1978*
GPS Coordinates: 34° 0.63' N, 81° 2.239' W

40–75 Hampton Street

[Marker removed due to damage.]

Corner of Hampton & Main Sts., Columbia

Part of the 1786 plan of Columbia, this street was first named Plain. It is thought to have been named after the plain of Taylor's Hill, on part of which the city of Columbia was built. Plain Street was renamed ca. 1907 for Wade Hampton, III (1818–1902), Confederate general, South Carolina Governor (1876–1879), and United States Senator (1879–1891). Hampton is buried in the churchyard of Trinity Cathedral in Columbia. *Erected by Richland County Bicentennial Commission; Sponsored by Belk of Columbia, 1978*

40–76 Lincoln Street

Corner of Gervais & Lincoln Sts., Columbia

Gen. Benjamin Lincoln, for whom this street is named, was a division commander in the Saratoga Campaign. In 1778, he became commander of the Southern Department of the American Army and was in command at Charleston when the city surrendered to the British in 1780. After his exchange, Lincoln fought at Yorktown and was present at the British surrender. He served as Secretary of War (1781–83) and returned to his native Massachusetts where he died in 1810. *Erected by Richland County Bicentennial Commission; Sponsored by Wallace Concrete Pipe Company, Inc., 1978*
GPS Coordinates: 33° 59.976' N, 81° 2.325' W

40–77 Senate Street

Corner of Senate & Gervais Sts., Columbia

The South Carolina General Assembly created Columbia as the state's capital city in 1786, and Senate Street was named for the upper house of that legislative body. In 1790, the General Assembly, which designated that the

town be located on the Congaree River near Friday's Ferry, first met in Columbia in the new State House, designed by James Hoban, who later designed the White House. *Erected by Richland County Bicentennial Commission; Sponsored by Standard Savings and Loan Association, 1978*
GPS Coordinates: 34° 0.024' N, 81° 1.893' W

40–78 Blossom Street
Corner of Blossom & Main Sts., Columbia

This street is thought to take its name from the cotton blossom. Cotton became an important commercial crop in South Carolina after the cotton gin was patented by Eli Whitney in 1794. A variety of cotton, known as Sea Island cotton and grown along coastal South Carolina, was especially prized for its long staple. *Erected by the Richland County Bicentennial Commission; Sponsored by Owen Steel Company, 1978*
GPS Coordinates: 33° 59.57' N, 81° 1.776' W

40–79 Lady Street
Corner of Lady & Main Sts., Columbia

One of the original streets in the 1786 Columbia plan, Lady Street is thought to have been named for Martha Custis Washington, the new nation's first lady whom South Carolina wished to honor. Lady Washington presided over the president's home, Mount Vernon, a national landmark which was saved from destruction in 1859 by South Carolinian Ann Pamela Cunningham, organizer and first regent of the Mount Vernon Ladies' Association of the Union. *Erected by Richland County Bicentennial Commission; Sponsored by Allen Brothers Milling Company, 1978*
GPS Coordinates: 34° 0.146' N, 81° 2.024' W

40–80 Gregg Street
Corner of Gregg & Gervais Sts., Columbia

(FRONT) Richard Winn, for whom this street was first named, was born in Virginia in 1750 and came to South Carolina as a young man. He fought throughout the Revolution (including the battles of Hanging Rock, Fish Dam Ford, Blackstock's) and became brigadier

general in 1783. One of Columbia's original commissioners, he later was lieutenant governor and also served in the General Assembly and Congress. He died in Tennessee in 1818. (REVERSE) Maxcy Gregg, native Columbian for whom this street was named ca.1893, was a leader in the States Rights party, a delegate to the Secession Convention, and a distinguished Confederate General. A colonel in the First Regiment of S.C. Volunteers, Gregg was appointed brigadier general, CSA, in 1861. He died in 1862 from wounds received at the battle of Fredericksburg and is buried in the churchyard of First Presbyterian Church in Columbia. *Erected by the Richland County Bicentennial Commission, 1978*
GPS Coordinates: 34° 0.265' N, 81° 1.347' W

40–81 Taylor Street
Corner of Taylor & Main Sts., Columbia

(FRONT) Named for the Taylor family, this street is one of the original streets in the 1786 Columbia plan. Thomas Taylor was a member of the first and second Provincial Congresses, the General Assembly and was a trustee of S.C. College. In 1791 he escorted President Washington into Columbia. Taylor died in 1833. His son, John, was a planter, lawyer, Governor (1826–28), first intendant of Columbia, and a member of Congress (1807–16). He died in 1832.
(REVERSE) This street is named for the Taylor family, whose plantations were selected in 1786 as part of the site of the city of Columbia. Thomas Taylor, appointed by the state as one of the commissioners to plan the new town, served in the Revolution as captain and colonel in the militia under brigadier generals Sumter and Henderson. Captured at Fishing Creek, Taylor escaped, and took part in the defeat of Tarleton at Blackstock's. *Erected by the Richland County Bicentennial Commission; Sponsored by IBM, 1978*
GPS Coordinates: 34° 0.386' N, 81° 2.133' W

40–82 Henderson Street
Corner of Henderson & Gervais Sts., Columbia

This street is named for Brig. Gen. William Henderson, who was in the Third S.C.

Regiment at the fall of Charlestown in 1780. He was captured, imprisoned, and later exchanged. In 1781, he was wounded while commanding a brigade at the Battle of Eutaw Springs. When General Sumter resigned in 1782, Henderson was named brigadier general of State Troops, a post he held until 1783. He served in the Second Provincial Congress (1775–76) and in the S.C. House. He died in 1788. *Erected by the Richland County Bicentennial Commission; Sponsored by First National Bank, 1978*
GPS Coordinates: 34° 0.205' N, 81° 1.538' W

40–83 Sumter Street

Corner of Sumter & Gervais Sts., Columbia

(FRONT) A Virginia native who came to South Carolina ca. 1765, General Thomas Sumter was a leader in civil as well as military affairs. He served in the First and the Second Provincial Congresses, in the S.C. General Assembly, as U.S. Congressman and U.S. Senator. South Carolina's last Revolutionary War general, he died in 1832 at his Sumter District home in Stateburg, where he was a large land-owner and planter. His tomb there notes him as a founder of the Republic.
(REVERSE) This street is named for one of the great Partisan generals of the American Revolution, Thomas Sumter, the fighting "Gamecock." After Charlestown fell in May 1780, Sumter rallied the up country against the British with major victories at Hanging Rock, Fishdam Ford, and Blackstock's. In 1781, Congress cited Sumter for his gallant leadership and military conduct and for the conspicuous courage, perseverance, and patriotism of his volunteer militia. *Erected by the Richland County Bicentennial Commission; Sponsored by the Columbia Sertoma Club, 1978*
GPS Coordinates: 34° 0.205' N, 81° 1.538' W

40–84 Park Street
[No longer extant.]

Corner of Park & Gervais Sts., Columbia

This street was originally named Gates for Gen. Horatio Gates. He was commander of the victorious Northern Army in 1777 in the Saratoga campaign which helped bring France into the war. Named commander of the Southern Army, Gates suffered disastrous defeat at Camden in 1780 by Cornwallis. Replaced by Gen. Nathanael Greene, Gates retired to Virginia. He died, 1806, in New York. This street was renamed Park Street shortly after 1940 for adjacent Sydney, later Seaboard Park. *Erected by the Richland County Bicentennial Commission, 1978*

40–85 81st Inf Division

Jackson Blvd., Fort Jackson, Columbia

The 81st was organized at Camp Jackson, Aug. 25, 1917, where the training area included Wildcat Creek. Soon dubbed the Wildcat Division, the 81st designed and wore a wild-cat insignia on one sleeve of their uniforms, thereby becoming the first division of the U.S. Army to originate and wear a divisional patch, now a widespread custom. *Erected by 81st Division, Wildcat Veterans Association, Inc., 1979*
GPS Coordinates: 34° 1.056' N, 80° 56.335' W

40–86 Columbia Bible College

1600 Hampton St., Columbia

Columbia Bible School classes began in 1923 in the towered building which once stood on this site (originally as Columbia Female College, later as the Colonia Hotel). Under the leadership of its first president, Robert C. McQuilkin, the school grew into Columbia Bible College and, in 1960, moved to its present campus NW of Columbia. Its alumni now serve in church-related ministries around the world. *Erected by Columbia Bible College Alumni Association, 1979*
GPS Coordinates: 34° 0.443' N, 81° 1.708' W

40–87 Richland Presbyterian Church

Fork Church Rd. (S.C. Sec. Rd. 40-1314), just W of its junction with Poultry Ln. (S.C. Sec. Rd. 40-56), Gadsden vicinity

(FRONT) This church building was dedicated in May 1884 by Dr. John L. Girardeau. The congregation of 11 members, including 2 elders and 1 deacon, was organized on the Sabbath

Day, November 16, 1883 by the Charleston Presbytery. In 1914, the church became a charter member of Congaree Presbytery, moving to Eastover in August 1922.
(REVERSE) The eleven charter members of this church were Thomas and Lula B. Auld, Augusta H. Bates, Joseph and Clair H. Bates, Elise M. Dwight, Peter and Isabel H. Garick, Glenn and Hattie H. Kaminer, and Belton A. Williams. *Erected by the Congregation, 1980*
GPS Coordinates: 33° 50.639' N, 80° 42.039' W

40–88 Church of the Good Shepherd

1512 Blanding St., Columbia

Beginning in 1883 with services held in nearby private homes by Trinity Church, this Episcopal church then constructed a building on Barnwell Street, was organized into a mission, and became a separate parish in 1886. Rt. Rev. Albert S. Thomas, 9th Bishop of S.C., was lay reader of Good Shepherd, 1893–1900. The church moved to this site after the present building was completed in 1901. *Erected by the Women of the Church, 1980*
GPS Coordinates: 34° 0.576' N, 81° 1.865' W

40–89 Marion Street

Corner of Marion & Gervais Sts., Columbia

(FRONT) Brigadier General Francis Marion was born in South Carolina about 1732 of French Huguenot descent. Marion was a member of the First Provincial Congress, served eight years in the S.C. Senate, and was a member of the Constitutional Convention of 1790. He died Feb. 27, 1795, and is buried in Berkeley County at Belle Isle Plantation, home of his brother, Gabriel.
(REVERSE) This street was named for Francis Marion, one of the three S.C. Partisan Generals during the American Revolution. The guerilla tactics against the British by Marion and his Partisan band earned for him the name of "Swamp Fox." Congress voted its thanks to Marion for distinguished service in the battles of Parker's Ferry and Eutaw Springs, bouth fought in 1781. *Erected by the Richland County*

Bicentennial Commission; Sponsored by Southeastern Freight Lines, 1977
GPS Coordinates: 34° 0.115' N, 81° 1.827' W

40–90 Assembly Street

Corner of Assembly & Gervais Sts., Columbia

In 1786, when Columbia was established as the state capital, the General Assembly decided that two principal thoroughfares should run perpendicular to each other through the center of the town. One of these, Assembly Street, was named for the General Assembly, which first met in Columbia in 1790 in South Carolina's new State House, a building designed by James Hoban, who later designed the White House. *Erected by the Richland County Bicentennial Commission; Sponsored by Cromer's P-Nuts, 1977*
GPS Coordinates: 34° 0.038' N, 81° 2.131' W

40–91 Harden Street

Corner of Gervais & Harden Sts., Columbia

This street was named for William Harden, a native South Carolinian. In 1776 he was given command of Ft. Lyttleton near Beaufort by the Second Provincial Congress of which he was a member. In 1781, serving as colonel under Francis Marion, he commanded patriot forces who captured British troops both at Four Holes and Ft. Balfour at Pocotaligo. He died in 1785 while senator from Prince William's Parish, Beaufort District. *Erected by the Richland County Bicentennial Commission; Sponsored by Sears, Roebuck and Company, 1978*
GPS Coordinates: 34° 0.327' N, 81° 1.152' W

40–92 Gibbes Green

Near W side of Pickens St. Pedestrian Bridge, between Pendleton & Greene Sts., University of South Carolina campus, Columbia

Named for Maj. Wade Hampton Gibbes (1837–1903) prominent Columbian who owned much of the land to the east, Gibbes Green consisted of an area of land bounded by Pendleton, Bull, Pickens, and Greene Streets. Acquired by S.C. College by 1838,

the land was kept for many years as open space, serving as a playground, ball field, and park for several generations of Columbians. Davis College, which opened in 1910, was the first building in Gibbes Green. *Erected by Historic Columbia Foundation, 1980*
GPS Coordinates: 33° 59.915' N, 81° 1.596' W

40–93 77th Inf Division

Jackson Blvd., Fort Jackson, Columbia

The "Statue of Liberty Division" was reviewed by England's Winston Churchill and President Franklin D. Roosevelt after it was reactivated here in 1942. The 77th fought in World War II Pacific campaigns of Guam, Leyte, Kerama Retto Islands, and Okinawa. It was inactivated after occupying Hokkaido, Japan, in 1946. War correspondent Ernie Pyle was killed in action with the 77th. *Erected by 77th Infantry Division Association, Inc., 1982*
GPS Coordinates: 34° 1.686' N, 80° 56.228' W

40–94 Paul R. Redfern

Entrance of Dreher High School, Millwood Ave. at Adger Rd., Columbia

Born in 1902, Paul Redfern at an early age showed a marked mechanical aptitude and excitement for aviation. Shortly after graduating from old Columbia High School in 1923, he built his own airplane and established the city's first commercial aviation company and flying field on this site. Later, Redfern attempted a non-stop flight to Brazil, leaving from Brunswick, Georgia, August 25, 1927. He has never been heard from again. *Erected by Shandon Neighborhood Council, 1982*
GPS Coordinates: 33° 59.902' N, 80° 59.624' W

40–95 St. Paul Church/Oak Grove

Intersection of Broad River Rd. (U.S. Hwy. 176) & Kennerly Rd., Irmo

St. Paul Church (FRONT)
One of the first black churches after the Civil War, St. Paul A.M.E. began as Oak Grove African Methodist Episcopal Church. Local tradition says that the original small congregation worshiped in the 1850s in the "Bush

Arbor;" later in the 1880s building a church on present Kennerly Rd. In the 1930s this was moved to its present site 3/10 mi. N.
Oak Grove (REVERSE)
By 1870 a substantial black settlement had developed in this area of the Dutch Fork Township known as Oak Grove. Prominent in its history have been the families of Octavius Bookman, Miles Bowman, Henry Corley, Moses Geiger, and John Richardson. A number of their descendants still live in the area. *Erected by The Irmo-St. Andrews Women's Society, 1985*
GPS Coordinates: 34° 5.812' N, 81° 9.618' W

40–96 4th Infantry Division

Jackson Blvd., Ft. Jackson, Columbia

Organized in 1917, the 4th Infantry Division was stationed in this area at Ft. Jackson during World War II and received its final training here for the June 6, 1944 D-Day invasion of Normandy. The division was one of the first on the beaches. The 4th was also in other campaigns, including the Siegfried Line, Hurtgen Forest, and Battle of the Bulge. *Erected by the Raymond O. Barton Chapter of the National 4th Association, 1986*
GPS Coordinates: 34° 0.475' N, 80° 56.818' W

40–97 Site of Columbia High School

Washington St. between Sumter & Marion Sts., Columbia

Described as "Collegiate Italian Renaissance" in style, this school was designed by J. Carroll Johnson, of Urquhart and Johnson, in Columbia. The cornerstone was laid in 1915 with Gov. Richard I. Manning as a featured speaker. Final classes were held here in December 1975, when Columbia High moved into a new building. Thus came the end of an institution of education and culture that meant so much to so many. *Erected 1986 by the Columbia High School Class of 1925*
GPS Coordinates: 34° 0.293' N, 81° 1.915' W

40–98 8th Infantry Division

Jackson Blvd., Ft. Jackson, Columbia

Activated in 1918 and inspected by Gen. Dwight D. Eisenhower and Lt. Gen. George S.

Patton during World War II, the 8th landed in France 28 days after D-Day (the invasion of Normandy) and participated in three other campaigns during the war. The division occupied this area at Ft. Jackson after being reactivated in 1940; they were also here 1950–54. *Erected by all units who served with the 8th Infantry Division in World War II, 1986*
GPS Coordinates: 34° 1.186' N, 80° 56.298' W

40–99 Gladden Home Site

Wheat St., just W of its intersection with Pickens St., Columbia

States-rights advocate Adley Hogan Gladden, who lived here before the Civil War, served Columbia as postmaster 1841–45 and was later bursar of S.C. College, captain of the Governor's Guard, and intendant of Columbia 1851–52. In 1847 he assumed command of the Palmetto Regiment during the Mexican War and later rose to the rank of brigadier general during the Civil War. Gladden was killed in Tennessee at the Battle of Shiloh, 1862. *Erected by the University of S.C. Chapter, National Society, Daughters of the American Revolution, 1987*
GPS Coordinates: 33° 59.59' N, 81° 1.48' W

40–100 City Hall
[Marker removed due to damage.]

Corner of Main & Laurel Sts., Columbia

Completed in 1874, this superb example of renaissance revival architecture was built of local and Fairfield County granite. The building was designed by Alfred B. Mullett, supervising architect of the U. S. Treasury Dept. and designer of such buildings as the Old Executive Office Building in Washington. Originally built as a U. S. courthouse and post office, this building has been Columbia's city hall since 1937. *Erected by the City of Columbia, 1987*

40–101 The Big Apple
Corner of Park & Hampton Sts., Columbia

Originally built 1907–1910 as the House of Peace Synagogue and located 100 yards south, this building was sold in 1936 and shortly thereafter became a black nightclub known as the Big Apple. A dance by this name originated here and soon swept the country, inspiring the song, "The Big Apple," which was recorded by Tommy Dorsey's orchestra. "The Big Apple" became a best-selling hit in September of 1937. *Erected by the City of Columbia, 1987*
GPS Coordinates: 34° 0.252' N, 81° 2.295' W

40–102 Shandon
Devine St., near its intersection with Maple St., Columbia

(FRONT) In 1890 the Columbia Land and Investment Co. purchased farm land in this area for development, laying out streets and sidewalks in 1893. In 1894 the Columbia Electric Street Railway provided streetcars to the vicinity and built a public pavilion and park near Harden Street. By 1900 the area generally bounded by Woodrow, Wheat, Harden, College, and Greene streets, and Millwood Ave., was known as Shandon, for the Rev. Peter J. Shand.
(REVERSE) The town of Shandon, incorporated in 1904, was annexed in 1913 to the city of Columbia. Development of streetcar lines encouraged suburban growth in the Shandon area: Shandon Annex (1906), South Shandon (1910), and Shandon Terrace (1919). By 1906 Shandon School existed, and by 1914 a business district had been developed on Devine Street. Shandon's architectural styles date from about 1895 to the present. *Erected by Shandon Neighborhood Council, 1986*
GPS Coordinates: 33° 59.898' N, 81° 0.234' W

40–103 Greene Street
[No longer extant.]

Corner of Main & Greene Sts., Columbia

Why this street was named "Green" on the original 1786 plan of Columbia is not certain; but in keeping with presumed original intentions and as a deserved Bicentennial tribute, Columbia City Council added an "e" in 1979, honoring the Rhode Island general, Nathanael Greene. As commander of the Southern Army, Greene masterminded the campaign of 1780–1781, which finally drove the British

out of South Carolina. *Erected by the Richland County Bicentennial Commission; Sponsored by Southern Bank and Trust Company, 1979*
GPS Coordinates: 33° 59.756' N, 81° 1.866' W

40–104 Pendleton Street
[Marker removed due to damage.]

Corner of Pendleton & S. Main Sts., Columbia

This street is named for Judge Henry Pendleton, one of the Town of Columbia's original commissioners. He was elected assistant state judge by the Provincial Congress in 1776 and to the South Carolina House of Representatives in 1780. In 1782 Judge Pendleton was captured by the British while riding the circuit. One of the authors of the 1785 County Court Act, he died in Charleston in 1788. Pendleton County was named to honor him in 1789. *Erected by the Richland County Bicentennial Commission; Sponsored by Anchor Continental, Inc., 1977*
GPS Coordinates: 33° 59.911' N, 81° 1.946' W

40–105 Barnwell Street
Corner of Barnwell & Gervais Sts., Columbia

This street is named for General John Barnwell, St. Helena's Parish. He was elected to the Provincial Congress of 1775–76 and to the 1776 General Assembly. A captain in the First Provincial Regiment, he was major, colonel, and brigadier general in the militia, 1779–81. Barnwell was captured in Charlestown in 1780 and later imprisoned on the schooner Pack-Horse. From 1778 until his death in 1800, he served several terms in the S.C. Senate. *Erected by the Richland County Bicentennial Commission; Sponsored by South Carolina National Bank, 1977*
GPS Coordinates: 34° 0.233' N, 81° 1.44' W

40–106 Gadsden Street
Corner of Gadsden & Gervais Sts., Columbia

This street was named for Charlestonian Christopher Gadsden, member of the 1759 Cherokee expedition, the Commons House of Assembly, and the two Continental and Provincial congresses. He also served in several General Assemblies. During the Revolution

he became a brigadier general and later served S.C. both as Vice-President and Lieut. Governor. He died in 1805 and is buried in St. Philip's churchyard in Charleston. *Erected by the Richland County Bicentennial Commission; Sponsored by R. L. Bryan Company, 1977*
GPS Coordinates: 33° 59.95' N, 81° 2.416' W

40–107 Pulaski Street
[Marker removed due to damage.]

Corner of Pulaski & Gervais Sts., Columbia

This street was named for Casimir Pulaski, a Polish count who came to America in 1777 to aid the Patriot cause. In 1777, Pulaski was appointed brigadier general by the Continental Congress and was placed in command of a Troop of Horse. He participated in the defense of Charlestown against Prevost's raid in May of 1779 and in the siege of Savannah where he was mortally wounded on October 9, 1779. *Erected by the Richland County Bicentennial Commission, 1977*
GPS Coordinates: 33° 59.888' N, 81° 2.586' W

40–108 Wayne Street
[No longer extant.]

Corner of Wayne & Gervais Sts., Columbia

This street was named for Anthony Wayne (1745-1796) of Pennsylvania. Appointed brigadier general in 1777, he fought at Brandywine, Germantown, and Monmouth. In 1779 Congress awarded him a gold medal for his victory at Stoney Point, New York. Wayne led patriot forces into Savannah and Charlestown after the 1782 British evacuation and, in 1794, was commander of troops victorious over the Indians of the Northwest at the Battle of Fallen Timbers. *Erected by the Richland County Bicentennial Commission, 1977*
GPS Coordinates: 33° 59.918' N, 81° 2.489' W

40–109 Bethlehem Church—First Marker
10000 Broad River Rd., Columbia

The organization date of this Lutheran church is unknown. In 1788, however, Bethlehem and fourteen other churches signed the articles of the "Corpus Evangelicum," an early church

supervising body. By 1815, Bethlehem's first known building had been built about ca. 5 mi. N. of here. The church moved near Hollinshead Creek, it is said, in 1847, and by 1897 the congregation was located here. *Erected by Bethlehem's Bicentennial Committee, 1988*
GPS Coordinates: 34° 6.588' N, 81° 11.473' W

40–110 Bethlehem Church–Second Marker

Intersection of Kennerly Rd. and Pink Daily Rd., Columbia

Bethlehem Lutheran Church erected its first known building about 350 feet north of here on a 17-acre tract purchased from George Metz in 1817. According to tradition, the church was first called Ellisor Church after people of this name living nearby. In 1847, Bethlehem sold this site to Alexander Daily and moved near Hollinshead Creek, about 3 miles south of here. *Erected by Bethlehem's Bicentennial Committee, 1989*
GPS Coordinates: 34° 10.359' N, 81° 12.066' W

40–111 Howard School Site

Laurel St., just W of its intersection with Huger St., Columbia

Established after the Civil War, this public school for blacks was located at the NW corner of Hampton & Lincoln streets by 1869 and was partially supported by the Freedmen's Bureau. It is said the school was named for Oliver O. Howard, commissioner of Refugees, Freedmen, and Abandoned Lands during Reconstruction. Moved here in 1924, Howard School was for many years the only public school for blacks in Columbia. *Erected by the Howard School Community Club and the Arsenal Hill Concerned Citizens Club, 1988*
GPS Coordinates: 34° 0.31' N, 81° 3' W

40–112 Early Howard School Site

Corner of Lincoln & Hampton Sts., Columbia

On this site stood Howard School, a public school for blacks established after the Civil War. By 1869 there was a two-story frame building large enough for 800 pupils. Partially funded by the Freedmen's Bureau, the school reportedly was named for Oliver O. Howard, first commissioner, Bureau of Refugees, Freedmen, and Abandoned Lands. For years the only public school for blacks in Columbia, Howard was moved 5 blocks NW, 1924. *Erected by the Howard School Community Club, 1990*
GPS Coordinates: 34° 0.226' N, 81° 2.44' W

40–113 Richlex School Site

Dutch Fork Elementary School, 7900 Broad River Rd. (U.S. Hwy. 176), Irmo

Julius Rosenwald, Chicago philanthropist and president of Sears, Roebuck & Co., (1910–1925), helped fund this black school, built 1918. The original two-room structure was named in

40-113 Richlex School Site, Irmo. IMAGE COURTESY OF SCDAH

Rosenwald's honor and the school's curriculum eventually included grades 1–12. It was renamed Richlex in the 1950s, but closed in 1968; Robert Lee Floyd served as principal during this time. *Erected July 1, 1990 by Class of 1970*
GPS Coordinates: 34° 6.313' N, 81° 11.186' W

40–114 James H. Adams

Congaree Rd. (S.C. Hwy. 769), 0.4 mi. NW of Congaree

Gov. of S.C. 1854–56, lived near here in his home named Live Oak, which burned ca. 1910. Adams is buried nearby at St. John's Church. *Erected by the Richland County Historic Preservation Commission, 1993*
GPS Coordinates: 33° 54.575' N, 80° 48.262' W

40–115 Seibels House

Corner of Pickens & Richland Sts., Columbia

(FRONT) This house, listed in the National Register of Historic Places and probably built during the last decade of the 18th century, is one of the few remaining houses from this era in Columbia. It was purchased prior to 1860 by the Seibels family, pioneers in the insurance field, and remained in the family until 1984 when Seibels descendant George R. P. Walker donated it to Historic Columbia Foundation.
(REVERSE) This house stands on plantation lands of Thomas Taylor, one of Columbia's founding fathers, who is buried two blocks east of here in the old family cemetery. The date 1796, seen on a hand-hewn basement beam by a local historian about 1935, indicates the house was built shortly after the new city's founding in 1786. An early separate kitchen built of hand-made brick stands behind the house. Erected 1991 by the Columbia Committee of the National Society of the Colonial Dames of America in the State of South Carolina
GPS Coordinates: 34° 0.77' N, 81° 1.845' W

40–116 Camp Johnson

Richland County Adult Activity Center, 7494 Parklane Rd., Dentsville community

This Confederate camp of instruction was once located about 1 mi. NW at Lightwood Knot Springs, site of a popular resort prior to the War Between the States. *Erected by the General Wade Hampton Camp #273, Sons of Confederate Veterans and the 20th S.C. Volunteers, 1993*
GPS Coordinates: 34° 4.644' N, 80° 57.459' W

40–117 26th Inf Division

Jackson Blvd., Fort Jackson, Columbia

The "Yankee" Division, which saw extensive combat in World War I, was mobilized for active duty in World War II in January 1941. It trained here in 1942–43 and again in 1944, leaving 16 August 1944 for Europe. As part of 3rd Army the division was credited with 210 days of combat in France, the Ardennes, the Rhineland, and Central Europe, and was particularly distinguished for its role in the Battle of the Bulge. *Erected by the Yankee Division Veterans Association, 1996*
GPS Coordinates: 34° 0.317' N, 80° 56.916' W

40–118 Calvary Baptist Church 1865–1945

Richland St., Columbia

Site of an African-American church organized in 1865 with Samuel Johnson as its first pastor. It met under a brush arbor and in the basement of the Mann-Simons Cottage until its first sanctuary was built in 1875. Calvary helped found Present Zion (1865), First Nazareth (1879), and Second Calvary (1889). After the first church burned in 1945 the congregation built a new sanctuary at Pine and Washington Sts. in 1950. *Sponsored by the Congregation, 1996*

40–119 31st Inf Division

Jackson Blvd., Fort Jackson, Columbia

The "Dixie" Division, created in 1917, spent most of World War II as a training division, with some units training at Ft. Jackson, but later saw combat in the Philippines 1944–45. The postwar "Dixie" Division, composed of National Guard units from Alabama and Mississippi, was mobilized for active service

in 1951 and served here as a training division during the Korean War. *Erected by the 31st Infantry ("Dixie") Division Society, 1997*
GPS Coordinates: 34° 0.676' N, 80° 56.686' W

40–120 Spring Hill

11733 Broad River Rd. (U.S. Hwy. 176) at Mt. Olivet Lutheran Church, Spring Hill community

This community, named by 1791 for the springs at the foot of the Stone Hill, included Eleazer's Tavern, a post office, schools, grist mills, and Spring Hill Baptist Church before the Civil War. In February 1865, as the war ended in S.C., Federal troops camped nearby looted and burned several homes. Mt. Olivet Lutheran Church was founded in 1873; the town was incorporated in 1889. *Erected by Mt. Olivet Lutheran Church, 1998*
GPS Coordinates: 34° 10.387' N, 81° 17.079'

40–121 St. Phillip A. M. E. Church

4351 McCords Ferry Rd. (U.S. Hwy. 601), Congaree community, Eastover vicinity

This church, organized by 1835, met first in a brush arbor 1 ½ mi. N., then constructed a sanctuary on this site shortly thereafter. Its first pastor was Rev. Anderson Burns, and its original trustees were Joseph and Robert Collins, Barnes Flowers, Saylor Pope, Harkness Smith, and Red Stroy. A later sanctuary, built in 1952; burned in 1981; the present sanctuary was dedicated that year. *Erected by the St. Phillip A.M.E. Church Anniversary Committee, 1999*
GPS Coordinates: 33° 50.973' N, 80° 39.012' W

40–122 The State House

On the grounds of the South Carolina State House, Gervais St., Columbia

(FRONT) Columbia was founded in 1786, replacing Charleston as the state capital. The first State House here, built in 1789, was a small wooden building just W. of this site. Construction on this State House, designed by John R. Niernsee, began in 1855; exterior walls were almost complete when work was suspended in 1863 during the Civil War. In

February 1865 Union troops burned the old State House, shelled this unfinished building, and raised the United States flag over it. (REVERSE) Niernsee supervised postwar repairs and new work until his death in 1885. His partner J. Crawford Nielson succeeded him, followed by Niernsee's son Frank. In 1901 the General Assembly hired Frank P. Milburn, but often clashed with him over workmanship and his design for the present dome, a radical departure from J. R. Niernsee's original design. He was replaced by Charles C. Wilson in 1903. A major renovation by the firm of Stevens and Wilkinson was completed in August 1998. *Erected by The Columbia Committee of The National Society of The Colonial Dames of America in the State of South Carolina, 1999*
GPS Coordinates: 34° 0.037' N, 81° 1.964' W

40-___ 102nd Cavalry

[Marker not assigned number. Proposed location. Location information is approximate.]

Jackson Blvd., Fort Jackson, Columbia

Formed 1890 as the Essex Troop of Lt. Cavalry; mustered into the N.J. National Guard in 1893. After World War I service, became 102nd Cav. in 1921. Reorganized 1940 as 102nd Cav. (Horse- Mechanized); mobilized for active duty in World War II and trained here 1941–42. Saw more than 300 days of combat in France, North Africa, Italy, the Ardennes, the Rhineland, and Central Europe. *Erected by the Essex Troop, 2001*
GPS Coordinates: 34° 1.056' N, 80° 56.335' W

40–123 Bethel Methodist Church

4600 Daniel Dr., Forest Acres, Columbia

This church was organized in 1835 in what was then rural Richland District. The first sanctuary here, built soon afterwards, burned in a forest fire in 1867; the cemetery dates from as early as 1862. The second sanctuary, built in 1868, was remodeled about 1890. As Forest Acres grew after World War II, the church expanded and built its first brick sanctuary in 1948; the present church was built in 1964. *Erected by the Congregation, 2002*
GPS Coordinates: 34° 1.483' N, 80° 58.255' W

40–124   Confederate Printing Plant

Intersection of Gervais and Huger Sts., Columbia

(FRONT) From April 1864 to February 1865 Confederate bonds and currency were printed and processed in this building, constructed in 1863–64 for the printing and stationery firm of Evans & Cogswell. That firm, founded in Charleston, produced bonds and currency for the Confederacy throughout the war and moved to Columbia in 1863. The Confederate Treasury Note Bureau moved its headquarters here as well in the spring of 1864.

(REVERSE) After 1864 Evans and Cogswell printed almost all bonds and currency for the Confederate Treasury. Many young women were employed here to sign and cut sheets as they came off the press. When Federal troops burned part of the building in February 1865 they carried off the printing plates and "an immense quantity" of currency. The building served as a warehouse for the state liquor dispensary system from 1895 to 1907. *Erected by the Mary Boykin Chesnut Chapter No. 2517, United Daughters of the Confederacy, 2002, replacing a marker erected by the City of Columbia in 1966*

GPS Coordinates: 33° 59.881' N, 81° 2.658' W

40–__   108th Division

[Marker not assigned number. Proposed location. Location information is approximate.]

Jackson Blvd., Fort Jackson, Columbia

The "Golden Griffon" Division was created in 1946 as the 108th Airborne Division of the Army Reserve. It was reorganized as an infantry division in 1952, as a training division in 1956, and as an institutional training division in 1993. It has trained Fort Jackson soldiers since the early 1950s and mobilized units here for active service in 1991 and 2001. *Erected by the 108th Division (Institutional Training), 2003*

GPS Coordinates: 34° 1.056' N, 80° 56.335' W

40–125   Seaboard Air Line Passenger Depot

Marker 1: 1200 Lincoln St. at Gervais St., Columbia

Marker 2: Lincoln St. at Lady St., Columbia

(FRONT) This depot, built by the Seaboard Air Line Railway in 1904, was the third passenger depot built in Columbia, following the South Carolina Railroad Depot on Gervais St., built about 1850, and the Union Station on Main St., built in 1902. This depot and its adjacent baggage room was an alternative to Union Station, which served passengers on the Atlantic Coast Line Railroad and the Southern Railway.

(REVERSE) This depot and baggage room were listed in the National Register of Historic Places in 1983 as part of the West Gervais Street Historic District. They served passengers on the Seaboard Air Line Railway (later the Seaboard Coast Line Railroad) until 1991. The relocation of the tracks across Gervais Street was an important step in the revitalization of the Congaree Vista in the 1980s and 1990s. *Erected by the Columbia Development Corporation, 2003*

GPS Coordinates: 34° 0.007' N, 81° 2.533' W

40–126   Mann-Simons Site

1403 Richland St., Columbia

(FRONT) This property once featured homes, businesses and rental properties that belonged to the same African American family for more than 125 years. The remaining house, built between 1872 and 1883, replaced the earlier home of midwife Celia Mann (1799–1867) and her husband, boatman Ben Delane (1800–1890). Enslaved at birth, both achieved freedom and became members of antebellum Columbia's small community of free people of color.

(REVERSE) Three Baptist churches (First Calvary, Second Calvary, and Zion) trace their origins to services held on this site. After Mann's death, her daughter, Agnes Jackson Simons (1831–1907), inherited the property. Descendants remained here until 1970. It was listed in the National Register of Historic Places in 1973 and has been a museum since 1977. *Erected by First Calvary Baptist Church, Second Calvary Baptist Church, and Zion Baptist Church, 2003* [Marker text revised in 2016. Original sponsor line and date retained.]

GPS Coordinates: 34° 0.704' N, 81° 2.059' W

40–127 Skirmish at Killian's Mill

Killian Rd., near its intersection with Farrow Rd.
(S.C. Hwy. 555), Killian, Blythewood vicinity

On February 18, 1865, the day after Federals
under Gen. W. T. Sherman occupied Columbia, Gen. Frank Blair ordered units of his
XVII Corps to destroy railroad tracks north of
the city. Portions of Gen. M. C. Butler's Confederate cavalry division, including the 4th,
5th, & 6th S.C. Cavalry, fought a rear-guard
action with Blair at nearby Killian's Mill, then
withdrew toward Winnsboro. *Erected by the
Hampton's Iron Scouts Camp # 1945, Sons of
Confederate Veterans, 2003*
GPS Coordinates: 34° 8.14' N, 80° 56.742' W

40–128 R.L. Bryan Co. Warehouse

1310 Gadsden St., Columbia

(FRONT) This warehouse was built in 1913 as
the schoolbook depository for the R. L. Bryan
Company. The company, founded in 1844 by
R. L. Bryan (1823–1900) and his brother-in-
law James J. McCarter (d. 1872), was originally
a bookstore and stationery shop on Main St.
known as Bryan & McCarter. In 1900 R. L.
Bryan & Company merged with the Bryan
Printing Company, founded in 1889, to become the R. L. Bryan Company.
(REVERSE) In 1901 the S.C. General Assembly,
in an effort to improve public education,
adopted standardized texts. The R. L. Bryan
Company, selected as the statewide distributor, used this building as its depository
and warehouse from 1913 to 1973. In 1976
the building was renovated and opened as
a restaurant, in one of the first examples of
the adaptive reuse of historic buildings in
this part of Columbia. *Erected by the Historic
Columbia Foundation, 2003*
GPS Coordinates: 34° 0.048' N, 81° 2.426' W

40–129 Kensington

Intersection of McCords Ferry Rd. (U.S. Hwy.
601) & S.C. Hwy. 764 (Old Eastover Rd.), at the
entrance of Kensington, Eastover vicinity

(FRONT) This plantation on the Wateree River
features a remarkable Italianate Revival house
built in 1852–54. Designed by Charleston

architects Edward C. Jones and Francis D.
Lee, it was built for Matthew Richard Singleton (1817–1854) and Martha Kinloch Singleton
(1818–1892). Jacob Stroyer described life as a
slave here in his memoir, first published in 1879.
(REVERSE) Kensington was owned by members
of the Singleton, Hamer, and Lanham families
until the late twentieth century, and though
the house fell into disrepair the land was
farmed for many years. Kensington was listed
in the National Register of Historic Places in
1971. It was sold to Union Camp (later International Paper) in 1981, restored in 1983–84,
and opened for educational programs. *Erected
by the Scarborough-Hamer Foundation, 2005*
GPS Coordinates: 33° 52.139' N, 80° 39.503' W

40–130 Jefferson Hotel

Corner of Main and Laurel Sts., Columbia

(FRONT) The Jefferson Hotel, designed and
built by Columbia entrepreneur and contractor John Jefferson Cain (1869–1929), stood
here at the corner of Main and Laurel Streets
from 1914 until 1968. The hotel (also sometimes called the Hotel Jefferson) was built in
1912–13 at a cost of $250,000. Notable features
included Indiana limestone on the 1st and 6th
story exteriors and mahogany, marble, and
terra cotta tile throughout the lobby, dining
room, and ballroom.
(REVERSE) For 55 years the Jefferson was Columbia's premier hotel, hosting conventions
as well as more informal meetings among
legislators. It was demolished in 1968. In 1938,
during the 48th reunion of the United Confederate Veterans, former officers and their
descendants met here to organize the Order
of the Stars and Bars. Now the Military Order
of the Stars and Bars, this genealogical society
is for descendants of Confederate officers and
civil officials. *Erected by the Military Order of
the Stars and Bars, 2004*
GPS Coordinates: 34° 0.59' N, 81° 2.256' W

40–131 State Dispensary Warehouse

Corner of Pulaski and Gervais Sts., Columbia

(FRONT) This building, built in 1863–64 and
burned by Federal troops in 1865, was rebuilt in 1872 as a cotton batting factory and

warehouse. It burned again in 1897, leaving only the outer walls. In 1898 the S.C. State Dispensary, created by Gov. Benjamin R. Tillman to ensure state control over the production and sale of alcohol, rebuilt it as a two-story building to serve as the State Dispensary Warehouse.

(REVERSE) Though the State Dispensary system generated impressive revenue, it also allowed corruption and violence to flourish, and was finally abolished in 1907. Vacant from 1907 until the 1920s, this building served as a warehouse for a succession of businesses for the next fifty years. It was vacant again from the late 1970s until 2004, when it was rehabilitated for a neighborhood grocery store. *Sponsored by Holmes Smith Developments, Inc.*
GPS Coordinates: 33° 59.942' N, 81° 2.62' W

40-132 Cain-Matthews-Tompkins House

1619 Pendleton St., Columbia

(FRONT) This house, built ca. 1910 for Columbia businessman John Jefferson Cain (1869–1929), was designed by William Augustus Edwards (1866–1939), a prominent regional architect. Cain, who moved to Columbia in 1899, became one of the state's leading contractors and built such Columbia landmarks as the Arcade (1912) and the Palmetto Building (1913). He also financed, built, and owned the Jefferson Hotel (1913).

(REVERSE) J. Pope Matthews, president of the Palmetto National Bank, lived here from ca. 1913 to 1931, when Arthur S. Tompkins bought the house. It remained in the Tompkins family until 1974, when the University of South Carolina acquired it. The house, threatened by demolition for several years, was designated a local historic landmark in 2002. It was renovated and opened as The Inn at USC in 2005. *Erected by the Historic Columbia Foundation, 2006*
GPS Coordinates: 34° 0.044' N, 81° 1.512' W

40-133 Randolph Cemetery

At the W terminus of Elmwood Ave., Columbia

(FRONT) Randolph Cemetery, founded in 1871, was one of the first black cemeteries in Columbia. It was named for Benjamin Franklin Randolph (1837–1868), a black state senator assassinated in 1868 near Hodges, in Abbeville County. Randolph, a native of Kentucky and a free black before the Civil War, had been a chaplain in the Union Army, an agent of the Freedmen's Bureau, and a newspaper publisher before he was elected to represent Orangeburg County in the S.C. Senate in 1868.

(REVERSE) Eight other black lawmakers from the Reconstruction era are buried here: Henry Cardozo (1830–1886), William Fabriel Myers (1850–1917), William Beverly Nash (1822–1888), Robert John Palmer (1849–1928), William M. Simons (1810–1878), Samuel Benjamin Thompson (1837–1909), Charles McDuffie Wilder (1835–1902), and Lucius W. Wimbush (1839–1872). Randolph Cemetery was listed in the National Register of Historic Places in 1995. *Erected by the Downtown Columbia Task Force and the Committee for the Restoration and Beautification of Randolph Cemetery, 2006*
GPS Coordinates: 34° 0.578' N, 81° 3.126' W

40-134 Visanska-Starks House

2214 Hampton St., Columbia

(FRONT) This house, built after 1900, was originally a two-story frame residence with a projecting bay and wraparound porch; a fire in 1989 destroyed the second story. Barrett Visanska (1849–1932), a jeweler, bought the house in 1913. Visanska, a native of Poland, was a leader in Columbia's Jewish community and a founder of the Tree of Life Congregation. In 1938 Dr. John J. Starks, president of Benedict College, bought the house.

(REVERSE) Dr. John Jacob Starks (1876–1944), the first black president of Benedict College, lived here from 1938 until his death. Starks was president of Seneca Institute 1899–1912; Morris College 1912–1930; and Benedict College 1930–1944. After World War II this house served as the nurses' home for Good Samaritan-Waverly Hospital, created by merger in 1939. It was later a private residence once more. *Erected by the Richland County Conservation Commission, 2007*
GPS Coordinates: 34° 0.633' N, 81° 1.105' W

40–135 George P. Hoffman House

Off S.C. Sec. Rd. 40-54, Blythewood

(FRONT) This house was built ca. 1855 for George P. Hoffman (1829–1902), a native of N.C. Hoffman ran a nearby sawmill and became the first postmaster of Doko (as Blythewood was first known) in 1856. This area was part of Fairfield County until 1913, when it was annexed into Richland County. Capt. John L. Kennedy owned the house during the Civil War; his widow Judith owned it afterwards.
(REVERSE) This house was one of several ransacked by Gen. W. T. Sherman's Federals as they advanced through this area in February 1865. Hoffman, a section master on the Charlotte & South Carolina Railroad, owned the house again by 1875. It later housed an antique shop and was listed in the National Register of Historic Places in 1986. It became the Blythewood Town Hall in 2000. *Erected by Blythewood Middle School, 2007*
GPS Coordinates: 34° 12.899' N, 80° 58.314' W

40–136 Killian School

Killian Elementary School, 2621 Clemson Rd., Columbia

(FRONT) This one-room primary school, built about 1925, stood about 1 mi. E, at the intersection of Killian and Longtown Roads, until 2001. There was a school at Killian (also called Killian's) as early as 1905. From 1913 to 1948 Killian School had two teachers and an enrollment of 30 to 80 students in grades 1–7, with an average attendance of 30 to 40 and an eight- to nine-month school year.
(REVERSE) Killian School closed in 1948, and its students and one teacher went to Blythewood Grammar School. In 1954 Richland County sold the school to the citizens of Killian for $100.00 as a community center. The Killian School was deeded to Richland County School District Two in 2000 and moved here in 2001 to be renovated as a museum of 20th century rural education and a conference center. *Erected by the Richland County Conservation Commission, 2007*
GPS Coordinates: 34° 8.308' N, 80° 55.857' W

40–137 Sandfield Baptist Church/ Sandfield Cemetery

Russ Brown Rd., near the intersection of N. Melton Rd. & Sandfield Rd., Blythewood

Sandfield Baptist Church (FRONT)
Twenty-Five Mile Creek Church, a Primitive Baptist congregation, was organized in this area before 1772. It was renamed Sandfield Church by ca. 1830 and the mother church for Cedar Creek, Harmony, Jackson Creek, and Sawney's Creek. After some members left in 1840 to organize a new church this congregation became Sandy Level Baptist Church in 1843.
Sandfield Cemetery (REVERSE)
In 1856 Sandy Level Baptist Church built a new church 3 mi. W on Blythewood Rd. The congregation gave this site and the old church to the community provided any organization using it would be Baptist. A second Sandfield Baptist Church, organized here ca. 1870, was disbanded ca. 1938. The cemetery here dates to the second church and is now maintained by Sandy Level Baptist Church. *Erected by Sandy Level Baptist Church, 2007*
GPS Coordinates: 34° 13.261' N, 80° 56.339' W

40–138 Sandy Level Baptist Church

408 Blythewood Rd., Blythewood

(FRONT) Twenty-Five Mile Creek Church, a Primitive Baptist congregation, was organized in this area before 1772. The mother church for several area Baptist churches, it was renamed Sandfield ca. 1830 and stood about 3 mi. E. Sandfield Baptist Church was renamed Sandy Level Baptist Church in 1843 and the congregation moved to this site in 1856.
(REVERSE) This frame sanctuary, built in 1856 during the pastorate of Rev. A. K. Durham, was described at its dedication as being the result of "the liberal contributions and unfaltering zeal of this community." Notable features include its large inset portico and interior gallery. The rear addition was built in 1950 to house the Sunday School and baptistry. *Erected by Sandy Level Baptist Church, 2007*
GPS Coordinates: 34° 12.85' N, 80° 59.381' W

40–139 Columbia Bible College, 1937–1960/Westervelt Home, 1930–1937

At the Robert Mills House & Park, 1616 Blanding St., Columbia

Columbia Bible College, 1937–1960 (FRONT)
In 1937 Columbia Bible College (now Columbia International University) acquired the Ainsley Hall House, designed by Robert Mills. The students housed here were trained for Christian service around the world. In 1960 CBC moved to its present campus in north Columbia. The Robert Mills House has been operated as a house museum since 1967 by the Historic Columbia Foundation.
Westervelt Home, 1930–1937 (REVERSE)
The Westervelt Home, for children of Christian missionaries, was founded in Indiana in 1926 and moved to Columbia in 1929. Associated with Columbia Bible College, it was in the Hampton-Preston Mansion 1930–34 and the Robert Mills House 1934–37, then moved to Batesburg in 1937. The Hampton-Preston Mansion has been a house museum since 1970 and operated by Historic Columbia Foundation since 1972. *Erected by the Columbia International University Alumni Association, 2007*
GPS Coordinates: 34° 0.609' N, 81° 1.764' W

40–140 Carver Theatre

1519 Harden St., Columbia

Carver Theatre, built about 1941, was one of Columbia's two exclusively African-American theatres during the segregation era of the mid-20th century. It was run by black operators but owned by the white-owned Dixie Amusement Company for most of its history. Carver Theatre also hosted weekly talent shows based on the popular "Amateur Hour" in Harlem. The theatre, which closed in 1971, was listed in the National Register of Historic Places in 2003. *Erected by the Historic Columbia Foundation, the City of Columbia, and the S.C. Department of Transportation, 2011*
GPS Coordinates: 34° 0.633' N, 81° 1.291' W

40–141 Matthew J. Perry House

2216 Washington St., Columbia

(FRONT) Matthew J. Perry, Jr. (b. 1921), lawyer, civil rights pioneer, and jurist, lived in a house on this site as a youth; the house was torn down in 1997. He served in the U.S. Army during World War II, then graduated from S.C. State College (now S.C. State University) in 1948. After graduating in the first class of the S.C. State Law School in 1951 Perry practiced law in Spartanburg, specializing in civil rights cases.
(REVERSE) Perry returned to Columbia in 1961 as chief counsel of the S.C. State Conference of the National Association for the Advancement of Colored People (NAACP). For fifteen years he tried numerous pivotal civil rights cases before the U.S. Supreme Court. In 1976 Perry was appointed to the U.S. Military Court of Appeals, and in 1979 he became the first black U.S. district court judge in S.C. *Erected by the Historic Columbia Foundation, the City of Columbia, and the S.C. Department of Transportation, 2008*
GPS Coordinates: 34° 0.556' N, 81° 1.081' W

40–142 James M. Hinton House

1222 Heidt St., Columbia

(FRONT) This is the site of the home of James Miles Hinton (1891–1970), businessman, civil rights pioneer, and minister. Hinton moved to Columbia in 1939 and was elected president of the Columbia branch of the National Association for the Advancement of Colored People (NAACP) that year. He was president of the S.C. State Conference of the NAACP from 1941 through 1958, as it grew from 13 chapters to 80 chapters.
(REVERSE) Hinton helped overthrow the all-white Democratic primary in S.C. and helped plan strategy for *Briggs v. Elliott*, the S.C. case of those that led to *Brown v. the Board of Education* and school desegregation. He was often threatened, was kidnapped from Augusta in 1949, and had shots fired at his house here in 1956. Hinton was later pastor of Second Calvary Baptist Church in Columbia and died in Augusta in 1970. *Erected by the Historic Columbia Foundation, the City of Columbia, and*

the *S.C. Department of Transportation,*
2008
GPS Coordinates: 34° 0.502' N, 81° 0.894' W

40–143 Heidt-Russell House/Edwin R. Russell

1240 Heidt St., Columbia

Heidt-Russell House (FRONT)
This house, with Greek Revival and Italianate architectural influences, was built about 1879 by William J. Heidt, builder and contractor who managed Heidlinger's Steam Bakery. The Heidts lived here until 1912. Mary E. Russell, whose husband Nathaniel was a postman for the U.S. Post Office, bought the house in 1919.
Edwin R. Russell (REVERSE)
Edwin Roberts Russell (1913–1996) spent his early years here. A research scientist, he was one of the few blacks directly involved in the Manhattan Project to develop the atomic bomb. Educated at Benedict College and Howard University, in 1942–45 Russell helped separate plutonium from uranium at the University of Chicago. He returned to Columbia to teach at Allen University, then was a research chemist at the Savannah River Plant form 1957 to 1976. *Erected by the Historic Columbia Foundation, the City of Columbia, and the S.C. Department of Transportation, 2008*
GPS Coordinates: 34° 0.523' N, 81° 0.906' W

40–144 The Lighthouse & Informer/John H. McCray

1507 Harden St., Columbia

The Lighthouse & Informer (FRONT)
The Lighthouse & Informer, long the leading black newspaper in S.C., was a weekly published here from 1941 to 1954 by journalist and civil rights advocate John Henry McCray (1910–1997). McCray, who founded and paper "so our people can have a voice and some means of getting along together," published articles covering every aspect of black life and columns and editorials advocating equal rights.
John H. McCray (REVERSE)
In 1944, after the S.C. General Assembly repealed laws regulating primaries and the S.C. Democratic Party excluded blacks from voting in them, John H. McCray helped

found the Progressive Democratic Party, the first black Democratic party in the South. He was an editor for other leading black newspapers in the 1950s and 1960s, then spent many years as an administrator at his alma mater, Talladega College. McCray died in Alabama in 1987. *Erected by the Historic Columbia Foundation, the City of Columbia, and the S.C. Department of Transportation, 2008*
GPS Coordinates: 34° 0.614' N, 81° 1.278' W

40–145 Waverly Five and Dime /George Elmore and *Elmore v. Rice*

2317 Gervais St., Columbia

Waverly Five and Dime (FRONT)
The Waverly Five & Dime, located here until about 1957, was managed 1945–48 by George A. Elmore (1905–1959), the African American plaintiff in a landmark voting rights case soon after World War II. Elmore ran this store and two liquor stores, and also worked as a photographer and cab driver. In 1946, when he tried to vote in the all-white Democratic primary in Richland County, he was denied a ballot.
George Elmore and Elmore v. Rice (REVERSE)
In 1947 the National Association for the Advancement of Colored People (NAACP) sued to end the all-white primary in S.C. Judge J. Waties Waring (1880–1948) ruled in U.S. district court that it was "time for S.C. to rejoin the Union." Blacks voted in the next S.C. primary, in 1948. As a result of the case, George Elmore endured numerous personal threats and economic reprisals that ruined his business. *Erected by the Historic Columbia Foundation, the City of Columbia, and the S.C. Department of Transportation, 2008*
GPS Coordinates: 34° 0.434' N, 81° 0.895' W

40–146 Wesley Methodist Church

1727 Gervais St., Columbia

(FRONT) Wesley Methodist Church is the oldest African American Methodist congregation in Columbia. It was founded in 1869 by Rev. J. C. Emerson and was a separate black congregation instead of forming from an established white church. First called the Columbia

Mission, it met upstairs in a Main St. building and later built its own chapel. About 1910 the Columbia Mission bought this lot and was renamed Wesley Methodist Episcopal Church. (REVERSE) This Gothic Revival church, built in 1910–11, was designed by noted Columbia architect Arthur W. Hamby, who designed other churches in Columbia as well as in Winnsboro, Bishopville, and St. Matthews. Its high-style Late Gothic design is relatively unusual for an African-American church of its period, and is notable for its two asymmetrical towers, decorative brickwork, and pointed-arch stained glass windows. *Erected by the Historic Columbia Foundation, the City of Columbia, and the S.C. Department of Transportation, 2008*
GPS Coordinates: 34° 0.264' N, 81° 1.452' W

40–147 Benedict College

At the entrance to the campus, Harden St. at the end of Blanding St., Columbia

(FRONT) Benedict College, founded in 1870 by the American Baptist Home Mission Society to educate freedmen and their descendants, was originally called Benedict Institute. It was named for Stephen and Bathsheba Benedict of Rhode Island, whose bequest created the school. Mrs. Benedict donated money to buy land in Columbia for it. The institute was chartered as Benedict College in 1894. Its early presidents were all white Baptist ministers from the North.
(REVERSE) By the time Dr. J. J. Starks became Benedict College's first black president in 1930, its curriculum included primary and secondary courses, college-level liberal arts courses, and courses in theology, nursing, and teaching. This curriculum was streamlined in the 1930s to emphasize the liberal arts and theology. Benedict College was also a significant center for civil rights activities in Columbia from the 1930s through the 1960s. *Erected by the Historic Columbia Foundation, the City of Columbia, and the S.C. Department of Transportation, 2011*
GPS Coordinates: 34° 0.756' N, 81° 1.312' W

40–148 Modjeska Simkins House

2025 Marion St., Columbia

(FRONT) This house was for sixty years the home of Modjeska Monteith Simkins (1899–1992), social reformer and civil rights activist. A Columbia native, she was educated at Benedict College, then taught high school. Director of Negro Work for the S.C. Anti-tuberculosis Association 1931–1942, Simkins was the first black in S.C. to hold a full-time, statewide, public health position.
(REVERSE) Simkins was a founder of the S.C. Conference of the National Asssociation for the Advancement of Colored People (NAACP). As the secretary of the conference 1941–1957, Simkins hosted many meetings and planning sessions here, for cases such as *Brown v. Board of Education*. In 1997 the house was acquired by the Collaborative for Community Trust; it was transferred to the Historic Columbia Foundation in 2007. *Erected by the Historic Columbia Foundation, the City of Columbia, and the S.C. Department of Transportation, 2008*
GPS Coordinates: 34° 0.842' N, 81° 2.139' W

40–149 Blossom Street School/Celia Dial Saxon School

At the Strom Thurmond Fitness and Wellness Center, Blossom St. just E of its intersection with Park St., Columbia

Blossom Street School (FRONT)
Blossom Street School, at the corner of what was then Blossom & Gates (now Park) Streets, was built in 1898 as the first public school in Columbia south of Senate Street. A frame building, it was originally a school for white children. After it burned in 1915, a brick school was built here the next year. Blossom Street became a school for black children in Ward One in 1929 and was renamed Celia Dial Saxon School in 1930.
Celia Dial Saxon School (REVERSE)
Blossom Street School was renamed to honor Celia Dial Saxon (1857–1935). Saxon was educated at the Normal School at the University of S.C. 1875–77, during Reconstruction. She taught in Columbia schools for 57 years and was a founder of the Wilkinson Orphanage,

Wheatley YWCA, and Fairwold Industrial School. Saxon School closed in 1968 and was demolished in 1974 as a result of campus expansion by the University of S.C. *Erected by the Ward One Families Reunion Organization and the Historic Columbia Foundation, 2008*
GPS Coordinates: 33° 59.526' N, 81° 1.966' W

40–150 Bethel A.M.E. Church

1528 Sumter St., Columbia

(FRONT) This church, founded in 1866, was one of the first separate African-American congregations established in Columbia after the Civil War. It met in buildings on Wayne St., at Lincoln & Hampton Sts., and at Sumter & Hampton Sts. before acquiring this site. This sanctuary, a Romanesque Revival design, was built in 1921 and as designed by noted black architect John Anderson Lankford (1874–1946).
(REVERSE) John Anderson Lankford, one of the first registered black architects in the U.S., was later supervising architect of the A.M.E. Church. Bethel was listed in the National Register of Historic Places in 1982. In 1995 its congregation moved to the former Shandon Baptist Church on Woodrow St. In 2008 the Renaissance Foundation began restoring the historic church as a cultural arts center. *Erected by the Historic Columbia Foundation, the City of Columbia, and the S.C. Department of Transportation, 2008*
GPS Coordinates: 34° 0.413' N, 81° 2.046' W

40–151 Israelite Sunday School/ Columbia's First Synagogue

Assembly St., between Taylor and Hampton Sts., Columbia

Israelite Sunday School (FRONT)
The Israelite Sunday School, the first Jewish religious school in Columbia, met in a building on this site until 1865. It had been founded in 1843 to give Jewish children of the city "an intimate . . . and full exposition of our faith." Supported by the Columbia Hebrew Benevolent Society, the school had 20–30 students when it was organized in a nearby building, in space donated by a member of the society.

Columbia's First Synagogue (REVERSE)
In 1846 the Columbia Hebrew Benevolent Society built a frame building on this site for the Israelite Sunday School, which met on the first floor. The society also organized the first formal congregation in Columbia, which they named Shearith Israel (Remnant of Israel), with its synagogue on the second floor. The building burned when Gen. William T. Sherman's Federals captured the city in February 1865. *Erected by the Beth Shalom Synagogue, the Tree of Life Temple, and the Jewish Historical Society of S.C., 2008*
GPS Coordinates: 34° 0.239' N, 81° 2.192' W

40–152 Allen University

1530 Harden St., Columbia

(FRONT) Allen University, chartered in 1880, was founded by the African Methodist Episcopal (A.M.E.) Church. It had its origin in Payne Institute, founded in 1870 in Cokesbury, in Greenwood County. In 1880 the S.C. Conference of the A.M.E. Church voted to move Payne Institute to Columbia. It opened in Columbia in 1881 and was renamed in honor of Bishop Richard Allen (1760–1831), founder of the A.M.E. Church. The first university building on this site was in use by 1888.
(REVERSE) Allen University, founded to educate ministers for the A.M.E. Church, also had primary and secondary courses, and college-level liberal arts courses. It also offered courses in the arts and had one of the few black law schools in the South before 1900. Its primary and secondary programs ended in the 1920s and 1930s. Allen was also a significant center for civil rights activities in Columbia from the 1930s through the 1960s. *Erected by the Historic Columbia Foundation, the City of Columbia, and the S.C. Department of Transportation, 2011*
GPS Coordinates: 34° 0.63' N, 81° 1.252' W

40–153 North Carolina Mutual Building

1001-1003 Washington St., corner of Washington & Park Sts., Columbia

(FRONT) The North Carolina Mutual Building was built in 1909 by the N.C. Mutual and

40–155 Matilda A. Evans House, Columbia.
IMAGE COURTESY OF SCDAH.

Provident Association, a black-owned insurance company with an office here until the mid-1930s. Built as a two-story commercial building, with a third story added after 1927, it was part of the Washington Street business district, an important part of Columbia's African-American community for most of the 20th century.

(REVERSE) This building had stores on the first floor and offices on the upper floors. First-floor tenants included barbers and beauticians, tailors and dressmakers, and restaurants. Second and third floor tenants included insurance agents, doctors, and lawyers. The Palmetto Grand Lodge owned the building from 1927 to the early 1940s. The N.C. Mutual Building was listed in the National Register of Historic Places in 1995. *Erected by the Historic Columbia Foundation, the City of Columbia, and the S.C. Department of Transportation, 2011*
GPS Coordinates: 34° 0.197' N, 81° 2.231' W

40–154 Good Samaritan-Waverly Hospital

2204 Hampton St., Columbia

(FRONT) Good Samaritan-Waverly Hospital, created in 1938 by the merger of two older hospitals, served the black community of Columbia for 35 years. It merged Good Samaritan Hospital, founded in 1910 by Dr. William

S. Rhodes and his wife Lillian, and Waverly Hospital, founded in 1924 by Dr. Norman A. Jenkins and his four brothers. The hospitals competed for the same doctors, nurses, and patients for several years.

(REVERSE) By the mid-1930s the Duke Endowment and the Rosenwald Fund recommended a merger of the two hospitals to improve the quality of health care for blacks in Columbia and surrounding counties. This building, the first in Columbia built specifically as a hospital for blacks, opened in 1952. After the new integrated Richland Memorial Hospital opened in 1972, Good Samaritan-Waverly Hospital closed the next year. *Sponsored by the Richland County Conservation Commission, 2014*
GPS Coordinates: 34° 0.626' N, 81° 1.121' W

40–155 Matilda A. Evans House

2027 Taylor St., Columbia

(FRONT) Dr. Matilda A. Evans (1872–1935), an African American physician, as well as a public health and civil rights advocate, lived here 1928–1935. A graduate of the Schofield School in Aiken and Oberlin College, Evans received her M.D. from the Woman's Medical College of Pennsylvania in 1897. She moved to Columbia that year and in 1901 founded the first African American hospital in the city.

(REVERSE) Taylor Lane Hospital & Training School for Nurses, described in 1910 as

"a monument to her industry and energy," burned in 1914. Evans soon opened St. Luke's Hospital & Training School for Nurses, which closed in 1918. She served in the U.S. Army Sanitary Corps during World War I and later founded the S.C. Good Health Association. In 1922, Evans became the first female president of the all-black Palmetto Medical Association. *Sponsored by the Richland County Conservation Commission, 2014*
GPS Coordinates: 34° 0.660' N, 81° 1.327' W

40–156 Alston House

1811 Gervais St., Columbia

This Greek Revival cottage, built ca. 1872, was the residence and business of Caroline Alston, a black businesswoman who lived and ran a dry goods store here as early as 1873. She purchased the house in 1888, becoming one of the few black business owners in Columbia during the period. Alston, known for the "esteem and confidence" of her black and white customers, sold the house in 1906. It was listed in the National Register of Historic Places in 1979. *Sponsored by the Richland County Conservation Commission, 2014*
GPS Coordinates: 34° 0.278' N, 81° 1.406' W

40–157 Waverly

1400 block of Harden St., Columbia

(FRONT) Waverly has been one of Columbia's most significant black communities since the 1930s. The city's first residential suburb, it grew out of a 60-acre parcel bought by Robert Latta in 1855. Latta's widow and children sold the first lots here in 1863. Shortly after the Civil War banker and textile manufacturer Lysander D. Childs bought several blocks here for development. Waverly grew for the next 50 years as railroad and streetcar lines influenced expansion.
(REVERSE) The City of Columbia annexed Waverly in 1913. Two black colleges, Benedict College and Allen University, drew many African Americans to this area as whites moved to other city suburbs. By the 1930s this community was almost entirely black. The Waverly Historic District, bounded by Gervais, Harden, and Taylor Streets and Millwood

Avenue, was listed in the National Register of Historic Places in 1989. *Erected by the Historic Columbia Foundation, the City of Columbia, and the S.C. Department of Transportation, 2011*
GPS Coordinates: 34° 0.585' N, 81° 1.238' W

40–158 Fair-Rutherford House /Rutherford House

1326 Gregg St., Columbia

Fair-Rutherford House (FRONT)
The Fair-Rutherford House, a Greek Revival cottage, stood here from ca. 1850 until it was demolished in 2004. Built for Dr. Samuel Fair, it passed through several owners before 1905, when William H. Rutherford (1852–1910) bought and enlarged it. Rutherford, an African-American businessman born a slave, taught school, then made lodge regalia and supplies and briefly co-owned a local cigar factory.
Rutherford House (REVERSE)
The Rutherford House was built in 1924–25 for Carrie Rutherford, daughter-in-law of W. H. Rutherford. Her son Dr. Harry B. Rutherford, Jr. (1911–1980) and his wife Dr. Evaretta Sims Rutherford (1910–1978) were prominent educators, he as a teacher and principal and later a dean at Benedict College, and she as a professor and department chair at Benedict College and Howard University. The house was listed in the National Register of Historic Places in 1984. *Erected by the Historic Columbia Foundation, the City of Columbia, and the S.C. Department of Transportation, 2011*
GPS Coordinates: 34° 0.443' N, 81° 1.398' W

40–159 Sidney Park C.M.E. Church

1114 Blanding St., Columbia

(FRONT) Sidney Park C.M.E. Church was founded in 1886 and has been at this site since 1889. It grew out of a dispute among members of Bethel A.M.E. Church, who left that congregation and applied to join the Colored Methodist Episcopal (now Christian Methodist Episcopal) Church. The congregation acquired this site in 1886 and built its first sanctuary, a frame building, in 1889. That church burned by 1892.

(REVERSE) This Gothic Revival brick church, built in 1893, was constructed by members who provided materials and labor. In the 1930s many members joined the National Association for the Advancement of Colored People (NAACP), and the church later hosted many meetings during the Civil Rights Movement. Sidney Park was listed in the National Register of Historic Places in 1996. *Erected by the Historic Columbia Foundation, the City of Columbia, and the S.C. Department of Transportation, 2011*
GPS Coordinates: 34° 0.47' N, 81° 2.221' W

40–160 Richard Samuel Roberts House

1717 Wayne St., Columbia

(FRONT) Richard Samuel Roberts (1880–1936), a photographer who documented individuals, families, and institutions in Columbia's black community and across S.C., lived here from 1920 until his death. Roberts, a self-taught photographer, moved his family from Florida to Columbia and bought this house at 1717 Wayne Street for $3,000. Roberts and his wife Wilhelmina Williams Roberts (1881–1977) raised their children here.
(REVERSE) Roberts, who was a full-time custodian at the main Columbia post office, first used an outbuilding here for his photography studio. From 1922 to 1936 his studio was downtown at 1119 Washington Street. Roberts often advertised in the Palmetto Leader, the leading black newspaper in S.C. Some of Roberts' best photographs were published in 1986 in A True Likeness: The Black South of Richard Samuel Roberts. *Erected by the Historic Columbia Foundation, the City of Columbia, and the S.C. Department of Transportation, 2011*
GPS Coordinates: 34° 0.371' N, 81° 2.707' W

40–161 Nathaniel J. Frederick House

1416 Park St., Columbia

(FRONT) Nathaniel J. Frederick (1877–1938), educator, lawyer, newspaper editor, and civil rights activist, lived here from 1904 until his death. This house was built in 1903 by Cap J. Carroll, a prominent businessman and city official whose daughter Corrine married Frederick in 1904. Frederick, who was educated at Claflin College and the University of Wisconsin, was admitted to the S.C. bar in 1913.
(REVERSE) Frederick argued more cases before the Supreme Court of S.C. than any black lawyer of his day. He won national attention for defending clients accused of murdering a sheriff in State v. Lowman (1926), but his clients were later lynched. Frederick was principal of the Howard School 1902–18 and president of the State Negro Teachers Association. He edited the Palmetto Leader, the major black newspaper in S.C., 1925–38. *Erected by the Historic Columbia Foundation, the City of Columbia, and the S.C. Department of Transportation, 2011*
GPS Coordinates: 34° 0.208' N, 81° 2.291' W

40–162 Bethel Baptist Church

McNulty Rd., Blythewood

Bethel Baptist Church was founded in 1884 by black members of nearby Sandy Level Baptist Church seeking to organize a separate congregation. They met at first in a brush arbor, then built a frame sanctuary here in 1892. It was covered in granite veneer in 1952. The church also sponsored the Bethel School, which stood behind the church. The present sanctuary was built in 2003. *Erected by Bethel Baptist Church and Blythewood Middle School, 2009*
GPS Coordinates: 34° 12.948' N, 80° 58.676' W

40–163 Monteith School

6505 Main St., Columbia

(FRONT) This African-American school, built nearby before 1900, was originally New Hope School, a white school affiliated with Union Church. It closed about 1914. In 1921 Rachel Hull Monteith (d. 1958) opened Nelson School as a black public school in the Hyatt Park School District. With about 100 students in grades 1–5, it later became a 3-teacher school with Monteith as its principal and added grades 6 and 7.
(REVERSE) Nelson School was renamed Monteith School in 1932 to honor Rachel Monteith. A civil rights activist, she was the mother of prominent civil rights activist Modjeska

Monteith Simkins (1899–1992). By 1936 her daughter Rebecca (1911–1967) also taught here; she became principal when her mother retired in 1942. The Hyatt Park School District was annexed into the city in 1947, and the school closed in 1949. Moved here in 2003, it now serves as a community center. *Erected by the Historic Columbia Foundation, the City of Columbia, and the S.C. Department of Transportation, 2009*

GPS Coordinates: 34° 4.143' N, 81° 0.226' W

40–164   Booker T. Washington School/Booker T. Washington High

1400 Wheat St., Columbia

Booker T. Washington School (FRONT)
The two-story main building at Booker T. Washington School, built in 1916, stood here until 1975. At first an elementary school with grades 1–10, it became Booker T. Washington High School with grades 9–10 in 1918, added grade 11 in 1924, and added grade 12 in 1947. Columbia's only black high school from 1917 to 1948 and for many years the largest black high school in the state, it closed in 1974.
Booker T. Washington High (REVERSE)
Booker T. Washington High, one of the first black high schools accredited by the S.C. Dept. of Education, was also one of the most significant institutions in Columbia's black community for more than fifty years. Notable principals included C. A. Johnson, 1916–1931; J. Andrew Simmons, 1932–1945; and Harry B. Rutherford, 1950–1965. The University of S.C. bought the property in 1974 and demolished the main building in 1975. *Erected by the Historic Columbia Foundation, the City of Columbia, and the S.C. Department of Transportation, 2009*

GPS Coordinates: 33° 59.586' N, 81° 1.533' W

40–__   Fort Jackson Elementary School/Hood Street Elementary School

[Marker never assigned a number. Proposed location. Location information is approximate.]

In front of the Hood Street Elementary School, Hood St., Fort Jackson, Columbia

Fort Jackson Elementary School (FRONT)
Fort Jackson Elementary School was one of the first public schools in S.C. to desegregate when classes began on September 3, 1963. The first school on post and one of the first permanent buildings at Fort Jackson, it was built in only three months. A new federal policy required all schools on military bases to admit African-American students instead of sending them to separate schools off-base.
Hood Street Elementary School (REVERSE)
This school opened under Principal Thomas Silvester with nine civilian teachers and 245 students in Grades 1–6. A newspaper article described it as "operated without regard to race, creed or color." Fort Jackson Elementary School, later renamed Hood Street Elementary School after additional schools opened on post, has served the families of Fort Jackson servicemen and servicewomen for more than 45 years. *Erected by Fort Jackson, United States Army, 2009*

GPS Coordinates: 34° 0.662' N, 80° 56.073' W

40–165   South Carolina Memorial Garden

1919 Lincoln St., Columbia

(FRONT) This garden was established in 1944 by the Garden Club of South Carolina. It was the first memorial garden in the U.S. created by a state garden club in honor and in memory of those who served in World War II. Sarah P. Boylston donated part of her own garden for it and noted landscape architect Loutrel W. Briggs (1893–1977) donated his landscape design. It opened in 1946 and was dedicated at its completion in 1957.
(REVERSE) This garden was described in a 1946 award citation from the National Council of State Garden Clubs as "expressed in terms of beauty, a place apart." It has long hosted events on Memorial Day and other occasions. The Garden Club of South Carolina, founded in 1930, was incorporated in 1945. It and its member clubs and leaders promote education, beautification, and environmental awareness. *Erected by The Garden Club of South Carolina, Inc., 2010*

GPS Coordinates: 34° 0.624' N, 81° 2.597' W

40–166 Kingville

Bluff Rd. & Kingville Rd., Kingville (Gadsden vicinity)

(FRONT) Kingville, a rural community, was established in 1840 as a station on the Louisville, Cincinnati, and Charleston Railroad, on the line from Charleston to Columbia. In 1848 the S.C. Railroad extended its line northeast from here to Camden, making Kingville a significant railroad town. By 1860 it boasted a hotel, post office, shops, offices, and several residences.

(REVERSE) Kingville is thought to be named for its status as "king" of the railroad line between Charleston and Columbia and between Columbia and Camden. In February 1865 Gen. William T. Sherman's Federals burned the depot, hotel, and sheds and destroyed 3,000 ft. of track. The railroad line was rebuilt in the 1880s and a sawmill was built about 1900, but the area declined by the mid-20th century. *Erected by South East Rural Community Outreach, 2010*
GPS Coordinates: 33° 48.333' N, 80° 41.971' W

40–167 Minervaville

Intersection of Cabin Creek Rd. & Minervaville Rd., Minervaville (Hopkins vicinity)

Minervaville, between Cabin Branch and Cedar Creek, was an early 19th-century community. Named after the Minerva Academy, founded in 1802 with William J. Bingham as its headmaster, Minervaville appears on Robert Mills's *Atlas of S.C.* (1825). It was later a station on the S.C. Railroad, with a post office 1831–1835. The area declined after the Minerva Academy closed in 1834. *Erected by South East Rural Community Outreach, 2010*
GPS Coordinates: 33° 53.992' N, 80° 50.01' W

40–168 Harriet Barber House

Intersection of Lower Richland Blvd. (S.C. Sec. Rd. 40–37) & Barberville Loop Rd., Hopkins vicinity

(FRONT) In 1872 Samuel Barber (d. 1891) and his wife Harriet (d. 1899), both former slaves, bought 42 1/2 acres here from the S.C. Land Commission, established in 1869 to give freedmen and freedwomen the opportunity to own land. Barber, a well-digger as a slave, was a farmer and minister after the Civil War. The Barber family has owned a major portion of this tract since Samuel and Harriet Barber purchased it in 1872.

(REVERSE) Samuel Barber's wife Harriet (d. 1899) received title to this land in 1879. This one-story frame house was built ca. 1880. The Barbers' son Rev. John B. Barber (1872–1957) inherited the property in 1899. He was a schoolteacher and pastor of St. Mark and New Light Beulah Baptist churches. This house was listed in the National Register of Historic Places in 1986. *Erected by South East Rural Community Outreach, 2010*
GPS Coordinates: 33° 53.718' N, 80° 52.647' W

40–169 Hopkins

Intersection of Back Swamp Rd. & Lower Richland Blvd. (S.C. Sec. Rd. 40–37), Hopkins

(FRONT) This rural community grew up around the plantation of John Hopkins (1739–1775). Hopkins, a native of Virginia, settled here in 1764. A surveyor and planter, he was later a delegate to the First Provincial Congress of 1775. Between 1836 and 1842, when the South Carolina RR line from Kingville to Columbia was completed, a turntable was named "Hopkins' Turnout" for the family.

(REVERSE) The Hopkins' Turnout post office opened in 1849. After the Civil War many freedmen, freedwomen, and their families settled in the area, some farming land they had purchased during Reconstruction from the S.C. Land Commission. The completion of the Wilmington, Columbia, & Augusta RR in 1871 expanded area markets, until the agricultural depression of the 1920s weakened the local economy. *Erected by South East Rural Community Outreach, 2010*
GPS Coordinates: 33° 54.325' N, 80° 52.612' W

40–170 Eastover

Intersection of Main St. & Weston St., Eastover

(FRONT) Eastover, so named for being "east and over" from Columbia, was a small rural community of the mid-19th century that grew into a town after the Wilmington, Columbia, & Augusta RR completed its line through this area in 1871. The town, chartered in 1880, was incorporated in 1907 with its limits designated as one-half mile in each direction from the tracks through the center of town.

(REVERSE) Railroad lines to and through Lower Richland County allowed local markets to expand and farmers and merchants to prosper. By 1910 Eastover, then the only incorporated town in the county outside of Columbia, boasted a post office, a bank, several stores, and a cotton gin. In 1984 Union Camp, later International Paper, opened a pulp and paper plant near the town. *Erected by South East Rural Community Outreach, 2010*
GPS Coordinates: 33° 52.657' N, 80° 41.717' W

40–171 Robert Weston Mance House

Corner of Pine & Hampton Sts., Columbia

(FRONT) The Robert Weston Mance House, built in 1903, stood here at the corner of Pine and Hampton Streets until 2008. A two-story American Foursquare frame house, it was later clad in brick veneer. It was built for grocers Thomas J. and Ida Roberts, whose store was next door. Rev. Robert W. Mance (1876–1930) acquired the house in 1922. After his death Dr. Robert W. Mance, Jr. (1903–1968) lived here until 1957.

(REVERSE) Rev. Robert W. Mance, an African Methodist Episcopal minister, lived here while he was president of Allen University 1916–1924. Dr. Robert W. Mance, Jr. was a physician, superintendent of Waverly Hospital, and civil rights activist. Three Allen University presidents lived here from the 1950s to the 1980s. A new dormitory project here resulted in the relocation of the house two blocks E to Heidt Street in 2008. *Erected by the Historic Columbia Foundation, the City of Columbia, and the S.C. Department of Transportation, 2011*
GPS Coordinates: 34° 0.613' N, 81° 1.156' W

40–172 Pine Grove Rosenwald School

937 Piney Woods Rd., Columbia

(FRONT) This school, built in 1923 at a cost of $2,500, is one of 500 African-American schools in S.C. funded in part by the Julius

Rosenwald Foundation from 1917 to 1932. It is a two-room school typical of smaller Rosenwald schools. From 1923 to 1950 an average of 40–50 students a year attended this school, in grades 1–7.

(REVERSE) This school closed after the 1949–50 school year, when many districts were consolidated. It was sold to the Pine Grove Community Development Club in 1968, then to the Richland County Recreation Commission in 2002. Pine Grove Rosenwald School was listed in the National Register of Historic Places in 2009. *Erected by the Richland County Recreation Commission, 2011*
GPS Coordinates: 34° 3.74' N, 81° 7.464' W

40–173 Curtiss-Wright Hangar

At Jim Hamilton / L.B. Owens Airport, Jim Hamilton Blvd. near its intersection with Airport Blvd., Columbia

(FRONT) This hangar, built in 1929 by the Curtiss-Wright Flying Service, was the first building at Owens Field, a municipal airport then 3 mi. S of the city limits. Curtiss-Wright built and operated numerous airports across America for the next two decades, also offering flight training. The airport, named for Mayor Lawrence B. Owens (1869–1941), was dedicated in 1930 with an airshow seen by 15,000 spectators.

(REVERSE) Regularly scheduled flights began in 1932, and civilian flight training began in 1939. Observation flights of the U.S. Army Air Corps began in 1940, and military training by the U.S. Army Air Force continued through World War II and beyond. In 1962 the city transferred the airport to Richland County, which has owned and operated it since. This hangar was listed in the National Register of Historic Places in 1998. *Erected by the Richland County Airport Commission, 2011*
GPS Coordinates: 33° 58.614' N, 81° 0.096' W

40–174 Maxcy Gregg Park

1800 block of Blossom St., Columbia

(FRONT) This city park, established in 1911, was named for Confederate general Maxcy Gregg (1814–1862). It was one of several parks in

Columbia proposed by landscape architect Harlan P. Kelsey of Boston, whose 1905 plan was commissioned by the Civic Improvement League. The park, donated to the city by George R. Rembert (1875–1913), was the central portion of a tract originally bounded by Bull, Wheat, and Greene Streets and the Southern Railway.

(REVERSE) The park was later divided by Pickens Street in the late 1930s and by the extension of Blossom Street in 1939. The Woman's Club of Columbia (1941), across Blossom Street, was built in what was then still part of the park. The Memorial Youth Center, dedicated in 1948, was demolished in 1987. A swimming pool and bathhouse were dedicated in 1949. Recent additions include the Capital Senior Center (1995) and Richard and Annette Bloch Cancer Survivors Garden (2003). *Erected by the Maxcy Gregg Park Centennial Committee and the City of Columbia, 2011*

GPS Coordinates: 33° 59.853' N, 81° 1.245' W

40–175 I. DeQuincey Newman House

2210 Chappelle Street, Columbia

(FRONT) Isaiah DeQuincey Newman (1911–1985), Methodist minister, civil rights leader, and state senator, lived here from 1960 until his death. Born in Darlington County, he attended Claflin College and was a graduate of Clark College and Gammon Theological Seminary. Newman, a long-time pastor, was also a major figure in the Civil Rights Movement in S.C. for more than forty years, beginning in the 1940s.

(REVERSE) In 1943 Newman helped found the Orangeburg branch of the National Association for the Advancement of Colored People. State field director of the S.C. NAACP 1960–69, he later advised governors and Congressmen on poverty and on improving housing and medical care in S.C. In 1983 Newman became the first black member of the S.C. Senate since 1888. He resigned in 1985 because of ill health and died a few months later. *Sponsored by the South Carolina United Methodist Advocate, 2012*

GPS Coordinates: 34° 2.184' N, 81° 1.679' W

40–176 Redfern Field/Paul R. Redfern

Dreher High School, 3319 Millwood Ave., Columbia

Redfern Field (FRONT)

This is the site of Redfern Field, established in 1923 as the first commercial airfield in Columbia. Paul Rinaldo Redfern (1902–1927?) had shown an early interest in and aptitude for aviation, building his first full-scale airplane in 1916, while still a student at Columbia High School. Though he soon left high school to gain experience working on and flying planes, Redfern returned in 1919 and graduated in 1923.

Paul R. Redfern (REVERSE)

Redfern built his own plane, opened his airfield here, and flew passengers all over S.C. before barnstorming across the Southeast for a few years. In 1927 businessmen in Brunswick, Ga., financed Redfern's attempt to make the first solo flight from North America to South America. On August 25, he took off in the monoplane *Port of Brunswick* from that city, bound for Rio de Janeiro. Redfern, last seen over Venezuela, was never heard from again. *Sponsored by the Paul Rinaldo Redfern Aviation Society, 2012*

GPS Coordinates: 33° 59.871' N, 80° 59.583' W

40–177 Bethel Lutheran Church

2081 Dutch Fork Rd., White Rock

(FRONT) This church, organized in 1762 by German colonists, is one of the first Lutheran congregations in the Dutch Fork region. Incorporated in 1788 as "the German Lutheran Church of Bethel on High Hill Creek," it first met in a log church 3.5 mi. S, near the juncture of that creek and the Saluda River. It built later churches ca. 1800, in 1843, and in 1881 further up High Hill Creek.

(REVERSE) An original member of the South Carolina Lutheran Synod when the synod was organized in 1824, Bethel was forced to move when Lake Murray was constructed. In 1929 it merged with Mt. Vernon Lutheran Church, organized in 1893 at White Rock, to form a "new" Bethel Evangelical Lutheran Church. This Gothic Revival church, designed by J. B.

Urquhart of Columbia, was dedicated in 1930. *Sponsored by the Congregation, 2012* GPS Coordinates: 34° 8.663' N, 81° 16.440' W

40–178 Zion Chapel Baptist Church No. 1

130 Walter Hills Rd., Columbia

(FRONT) This African-American church was organized ca. 1865 when four men left Sandy Level Baptist Church, founded before the Revolution with both white and black members, to form their own congregation. They elected Rev. Joe Taylor as their first pastor and held early services in a brush arbor nearby. (REVERSE) The first permanent church here, a log building, was replaced by a frame church 1907–1922, during the pastorate of Rev. T. H. McNeal. It was covered in brick veneer in 1941, then extensively renovated 1964–1978, during the pastorate of Rev. A. J. Grove, Sr. The historic church cemetery dates to the 1880s. *Sponsored by the Richland County Conservation Commission and the Congregation, 2013* GPS Coordinates: 34° 5.588' N, 81° 1.68' W

40–179 State Fairgrounds

Inside Fairgrounds, Approx. 100 Ft. SE of Rosewood Ave. entrance, Columbia

(FRONT) The S.C. State Fair was founded in 1856 by the State Agricultural Society. The fair was held at the fairgrounds on Elmwood Ave. near downtown Columbia 1856–1861, then suspended by the Civil War. The State Agricultural & Mechanical Society revived the fair in 1869; it stayed on Elmwood Ave. until 1903, when the society acquired 100 acres here for its "thoroughly modern" fairgrounds. The first State Fair held at this location opened in October 1904. (REVERSE) The S.C. State Fair, with exhibits and competitions, attractions and rides, and musical and other acts, has been held here every fall since 1904 except during World War I in 1918. Other events are held year-round. A highlight from 1904 to 1959 was "Big Thursday," the football game between the University of S.C. and Clemson University. The "rocket" near the North Gate, a U.S. Air Force missile

given to the City of Columbia, has been an icon here since 1969. *Sponsored by the South Carolina State Fair, 2013* GPS Coordinates: 33° 58.622' N, 81° 1.412' W

40–180 Victory Savings Bank

919 Washington St., Columbia

(FRONT) Victory Savings Bank, founded in 1921, was the first, and for many years the only, black-owned bank in S.C. It was chartered by I. S. Joseph as president and I. S. Leevy and C. E. Stephenson as vice presidents, and opened at 1107 Washington St. in the heart of Columbia's black business district. It was in this building 1955–1985, then moved to Sumter St., where it became S.C. Community Bank in 1999. (REVERSE) Dr. Henry D. Monteith, who became president in 1948, led the bank for many years. His sister Modjeska Monteith Simkins, notable civil rights leader, held several positions here. This bank offered loans to blacks after widespread economic reprisals, many related to the Clarendon County school desegregation case *Briggs v. Elliott,* later included in the landmark *Brown v. Board of Education* case (1954). *Sponsored by the City of Columbia, 2014* GPS Coordinates: 34° 0.166' N, 81° 2.329' W

40–181 Hopkins Family Cemetery

Just off Back Swamp Rd., Hopkins vicinity

(FRONT) This cemetery was established about 1775 when John Hopkins (1739–1775) was buried here, in what was the garden of his Back Swamp Plantation. Hopkins, a native of Va., arrived in S.C. in 1762. He received a grant of 250 acres here in 1764, built his house on this site, and increased his holdings to 2,950 acres. He was a delegate to the First Provincial Congress in 1775 but died that fall. (REVERSE) Other prominent members of the family buried here include Hopkins's son John (1765–1832), lt. governor of S.C. 1806–08, and grandson William (1805–1863), delegate to the Secession Convention. The cemetery is also notable for its ca. 1836–37 stile, or stone steps over a wall, a feature which is quite rare in S.C. It was listed in the National Register

of Historic Places in 2010. *Sponsored by the Hopkins Family Cemetery Trust, 2014*
GPS Coordinates: 33° 54.518' N, 80° 53.264' W

40–182 Bible Way Church of Atlas Road

2440 Atlas Rd., Columbia

(FRONT) This church, founded in 1963, was originally about 3 mi. NW on Bluff Road. It was organized by Elizabeth Simmons (1900–1965), known as "Mother Simmons," Andrew C. Jackson (1927–2006), and eleven other adults and their children. The first church, a modest building, was called "the Little Red Church." Jackson, its first pastor and later a bishop, served this church from 1963 until he retired in 1996.
(REVERSE) After the first church burned in 1966, services were held in Atlas Road Elementary School across the street until a new church was built here. That church, chartered as Bible Way Church of Arthurtown but later renamed Bible Way Church of Atlas Road, was dedicated in 1967. Over the next forty years it grew from a few faithful members to more than 10,000, building new sanctuaries here in 1981 and 2001. *Sponsored by the Congregation, 2013*
GPS Coordinates: 33° 56.486' N, 80° 58.503' W

40–183 A.S. Salley House

901 Laurens St., Columbia

(FRONT) Alexander Samuel Salley (1871–1961), the historian described as "a walking encyclopedia" of S.C. history, lived here from 1910 until his death. Salley, born in Orangeburg County, was secretary of the S.C. Historical Society in Charleston 1899–1905 and founding editor of the S.C. Historical & Genealogical Magazine. He was secretary of the Historical Commission of S.C. 1905–1949, preserving and publishing many state historical records.
(REVERSE) Salley directed the Historical Commission (now the S.C. Department of Archives and History) until his reluctant retirement in 1949. In 1910 he built this Classical Revival house, designed by Wilson, Sompayrac, & Urquhart. Salley later converted a small

house he had built nearby in 1908 (now at 1917 College Street) as his office and library. Connected to this house by a breezeway, it housed his extensive collection of S.C. history. *Sponsored by the Orangeburg County Historical Society, 2014*
GPS Coordinates: 34° 0.075' N, 81° 1.166' W

40–184 Harriett Cornwell Tourist Home

1713 Wayne St., Columbia

(FRONT) This home's first owner was John R. Cornwell, an African American business man and civic leader who owned a successful barber shop on Main St. After his death, Cornwell's wife Hattie and daughters Geneva Scott and Harriett Cornwell lived here. From the 1940s until after the Civil Rights Act of 1964 they ran the house as a "tourist home" for black travelers. Harriett also taught at Waverly Elementary School.
(REVERSE) During the Jim Crow era, segregation gave African American travelers very few choices for restaurants or lodging. Many chose to stay in a network of private houses located across the South and nation. These tourist homes often relied on word-of-mouth, but many were also listed in guides such as The Negro Travelers' Green Book. This house was listed in the National Register of Historic Places in 2007. *Sponsored by the Richland County Conservation Commission, 2014*
GPS Coordinates: 34° 0.355' N, 81° 2.702' W

40–185 Congaree River Ferries

U.S. Hwy. 601, near crossing of Bates Old River, Lower Richland

(FRONT) Joseph Joyner owned a private ferry on the Congaree River near this site by 1749. John McCord's private ferry succeeded Joyner's by 1757, becoming public in 1766 by statute. A route from Charleston to Camden crossed the river at McCord's Ferry. Due to its strategic location, the ferry figured in actions on the south side of the river during the Revolutionary War.
(REVERSE) As the river cut a new channel, isolating the oxbow lake now called Bates Old

River, a second ferry was chartered in 1845. This ferry was operated by the Bates family from the Civil War until bridges replaced both crossings in the 1920s. U.S. Hwy. 601 crosses the old river west of the McCord's Ferry site and the Congaree River two miles downriver from the former Bates Ferry site. *Sponsored by Richland County Conservation Commission, 2014*
GPS Coordinates: 33° 45.781' N, 80° 38.533' W

40–186 Zion Baptist Church

801 Washington St., Columbia

(FRONT) Zion Baptist Church first organized in 1865 and met in a humble dwelling on Gadsden St. The congregation moved to this site in 1871. The current sanctuary, the second on this spot, was built in 1916. Zion Baptist has long served as a center for community organization. Both the Women's Baptist Educational and Missionary Convention of S.C. (1888) and the Women's Auxiliary to the Gethsemane Baptist Association (1919) were founded here, as were other important missions.
(REVERSE) In 1930 Dr. Matilda Evans, the first African American woman to have a practice in the state, started a free clinic in the basement of the church. It served 700 patients on its first day. On March 2, 1961 over 200 African American students met at Zion Baptist before beginning their march to the State House to protest racial segregation. The U.S. Supreme Court later overturned the convictions of those students arrested during the march in the case Edwards v. S.C. (1963). *Sponsored by Zion Baptist Church, 2014*
GPS Coordinates: 34° 0.124' N, 81° 2.468' W

40–187 S.C. Confederate Soldiers' Home

Confederate Ave., near intersection with Bull St., Columbia

(FRONT) The Confederate Infirmary opened here in 1909. S.C. was the last southern state to create a residence for indigent Civil War veterans. Legislation authorized space for two veterans from each county. The United Daughters of the Confederacy played a key role at the facility, which was renamed the Soldiers' Home in 1915. The UDC prompted investigations that led to renovation of the Greek Revival building and nearby hospital in 1921.
(REVERSE) Women's influence at the Soldiers' Home continued and in 1921 the state authorized the UDC to name four women to the Home's nine-person commission. In 1925 the state opened the Home to veterans' Widows, and later extended eligibility to sisters, daughters, and nieces. The last veteran living in the Home died in 1944 and it closed in 1957. The state demolished the building in 1963. *Sponsored by Richland County Conservation Commission and S.C. Civil War Sesquicentennial Advisory Board, 2014*
GPS Coordinates: 34° 1.240' N, 81° 2.241' W

40–188 Burning of Columbia

1200 Block of Main St., Columbia

(FRONT) Due to Columbia's strategic value, capture of the city was an objective of the Union Army during the Carolinas Campaign of 1865. By Feb. 15 Union forces had moved to within 4 miles of the city and met opposition from Confederate skirmishers and artillery batteries. After offering a cursory defense of the city, C.S.A. commanders P. G. T. Beauregard and Wade Hampton ordered a final evacuation of Columbia on the morning of Feb. 17, 1865 and by the afternoon Union forces occupied the town.
(REVERSE) By 1865 Columbia had become a central store of cotton in the Confederacy and as Union forces entered the city cotton bales lined much of Richardson (now Main) St. Several cotton fires were reported on the night of Feb. 16–17 and others were burning on the afternoon of Feb. 17. On the night of Feb. 17–18—aided by high winds, burning cotton, and Union soldiers—destroyed much of Columbia's main commercial district and more than 450 buildings in all, a large portion of the city. *Sponsored by S.C. Civil War Sesquicentennial Advisory Board, 2015*
GPS Coordinates: 34° 0.090' N, 81° 2.012' W

40–189 DuPre Building

807 Gervais St., Columbia

(FRONT) The DuPre Building was built in 1919 and was designed by prominent S.C. architect James B. Urquhart. It served as showroom for DuPre Auto Co., a local distributor of Ford cars and Fordson tractors. The first commercially successful small tractor, the Fordson was produced by Ford Motor Co. from 1917–1928. During the first year of sales, DuPre Auto Co. placed over 700 Fordson tractors on S.C. farms, an important advance in pre-harvest mechanization in the state. (REVERSE) By 1933 DuPre Auto Co. no longer operated from this location. The property housed engravers, equipment suppliers and manufacturers during the Depression. From 1943–1945, the Associated Press service bureau and Columbia Record newspaper occupied the building. Listed in the National Register of Historic Places in 1983, rehabilitation of the building in 1998 was part of the movement to preserve and redevelop Columbia's Congaree Vista that began in the 1980s. *Sponsored by Historic Columbia, 2016*
GPS Coordinates: 33° 59.974' N, 81° 2.370' W

40–190 First Calvary Baptist Church

Corner of Pine St. and Washington St., Columbia

(FRONT) First Calvary Baptist Church descended from African American congregants who left First Baptist Church following the Civil War. These founding members, like many African Americans at the time, sought greater autonomy by breaking from white-controlled churches. The congregation of First Calvary first organized under a brush arbor and later met in the home of Celia Mann, now the Mann-Simons Cottage. (REVERSE) The congregation built a permanent home, a frame structure, on Richland St. ca. 1870. They remained at that location until building a new stone sanctuary at Pine and Washington Sts., which was completed in 1950. After more than fifty years of useful service that church was replaced by a modern brick sanctuary, built on the same site as the 1950 building, which was dedicated in 2005.

Sponsored by First Calvary Baptist Church, 2016
GPS Coordinates: 34° 0.557' N, 81° 1.133' W

40–191 Beth Shalom Cemetery

1300 Block of Whaley St., Columbia

(FRONT) In 1883 members of Columbia's Jewish community founded the Hebrew Cemetery Society of Columbia as an alternative to the Hebrew Benevolent Society's cemetery, which had been established in 1822. The organization purchased a 4-acre tract bounded by Indigo (Whaley), Lower (Heyward), Marion, and Sumter streets as a free cemetery for Hebrew burials. In 1896 the Society sold 3 acres to W. B. Smith Whaley for textile mill development. (REVERSE) By 1911 the Society deeded cemetery oversight to the Beth Shalom (House of Peace) synagogue. Early burials included Orthodox Jews from Columbia and elsewhere. This site later became identified as a place specifically for synagogue members. As the Univ. of S.C. expanded in the 1960s it grew around the cemetery. Jewish migration into Forest Acres and fewer available plots here led to the creation of Arcadia Lakes Cemetery in 1995. *Sponsored by Historic Columbia, Columbia Jewish Heritage Initiative, and Jewish Historical Society of South Carolina, 2016*
GPS Coordinates: 33° 59.316' N, 81° 1.463' W

40–192 Tree of Life Synagogue

100 Woodrow St., Columbia

(FRONT) In 1896 members of 18 Jewish families assembled to worship at the Independent Fire Company's station overlooking Sidney Park. Organized as Etz Chayim (Tree of Life), this group's members embraced Judaism's Reform branch or liberal movement. In 1907, members moved into the first temple built in Columbia since the Civil War. Located at 1320 Lady St., the synagogue was paid for by funds raised by local Jewish citizens. (REVERSE) To meet the needs of their growing congregation, Tree of Life members began making plans for a new synagogue in 1950. Following a design by Columbia firm LBC&W,

M. B. Kahn Construction erected a modern temple in 1952. The highly-touted, contemporary building was a unique addition to the Shandon neighborhood. The Reform congregation worshipped here until 1986, when members relocated to a new synagogue in Forest Acres. *Sponsored by Historic Columbia, Columbia Jewish Heritage Initiative, and Jewish Historical Society of South Carolina, 2016*
GPS Coordinates: 33° 59.460' N, 81° 0.371' W

40–193 Beth Shalom Synagogue

1719 Marion St., Columbia

(FRONT) In 1905 disagreements over religious practices divided members of Columbia's Tree of Life Synagogue. Jews embracing Orthodoxy formed a new synagogue, which they named Beth Shalom (House of Peace). Meetings were held in a private home on the corner of Park and Lady Sts. until a sanctuary was completed in 1907. Destroyed by fire in 1915, it was rebuilt eight months later. Growth of the congregation led to a new temple in 1928.
(REVERSE) Designed by noted Columbia firm Lafaye & Lafaye and built by M. B. Kahn, a member of the congregation, the new House of Peace was dedicated Sept. 8, 1935. In 1955, its members shifted from Orthodoxy to embrace the Conservative movement. For more than three decades the Marion St. landmark met the spiritual, cultural, and social needs of its members. In 1973 the congregation built a new synagogue on Trenholm Rd. in Forest Acres. *Sponsored by Historic Columbia, Columbia Jewish Heritage Initiative, and Jewish Historical Society of South Carolina, 2016*
GPS Coordinates: 34° 0.546' N, 81° 1.994' W

40–194 Shandon Presbyterian Church

607 Woodrow St., Columbia

(FRONT) Shandon Presbyterian Church began as Shandon Mission, which first met in Oct. 1913. By 1915, the Church had acquired title to a lot at the S.E. corner of Wheat and Maple Sts. and was incorporated the next year. The first sanctuary was completed in Nov. 1916. The Rev. William Sumner Harden was the first minister. By the late 1920s the church

had outgrown this building and construction began on a second sanctuary.
(REVERSE) Columbia firm Lafaye and Lafaye designed the second sanctuary, located at the present site on Woodrow St. It was completed in April 1929. The church building expanded in the 1950s, 1960s and 1990s, evidence of the growth of the congregation. In the 1950s, led by Rev. Dr. Fred V. Poag, the church actively supported racial desegregation. The congregation is still recognized for its local and global outreach. *Sponsored by Shandon Presbyterian Church, PCUSA, 2016*
GPS Coordinates: 33° 59.843' N, 81° 0.345' W

40–195 Canal Dime Savings Bank / *Bouie v. City of Columbia* (1964)

1530 Main St., Columbia

Canal Dime Savings Bank (FRONT)
This three-story building was designed by the noted Columbia architectural firm of W. B. Smith Whaley and Co. Completed in 1895 and featuring a granite façade and red barrel tile roof, the building is a rare example of Romanesque-style architecture in Columbia. Originally built to house the Canal Dime Savings Bank, the building was acquired by Eckerd's Pharmacy in 1936 and continued to operate as a drugstore until the 1980s.
Bouie v. City of Columbia (1964) (REVERSE)
On March 14, 1960, African American college students Simon Bouie and Talmadge Neal led a protest march to the Eckerd's luncheonette. The pair were jailed and convicted for refusing to leave their seats after being denied service due to their race. In *Bouie v. Columbia* (1964), the U.S. Supreme Court overturned their convictions. The sit-in demonstration was part of broader protest movements against racial segregation in Columbia and the nation. *Sponsored by Columbia S.C. 63, 2017*
GPS Coordinates: 34° 0.361' N, 81° 2.131' W

40–196 Columbia Civil Rights Sit-Ins/*Barr v. City of Columbia* (1964)

1520 Taylor St., Columbia

Columbia Civil Rights Sit-Ins (FRONT)

On March 15, 1960 five African American students from Benedict College—Charles Barr, David Carter, Richard Counts, Milton Greene, and Johnny Clark—were arrested after refusing to leave the lunch counter at the Taylor Street Pharmacy, which once occupied this building. Their actions followed similar sit-ins at S. H. Kress and Eckerd's Pharmacy, both located on nearby Main Street. *Barr v. City of Columbia* (1964) (REVERSE) In *Barr v. City of Columbia* the U.S. Supreme Court held that lower courts had denied the students due process, as guaranteed by the 14th Amendment. Columbia attorney Matthew J. Perry served as lead counsel and delivered oral arguments to the Court. The Civil Rights Act of 1964, enacted ten days after the decision in *Barr*, finally prohibited racial segregation of public accommodations such as hotels and restaurants. *Sponsored by Columbia S.C. 63, 2017*
GPS Coordinates: 34° 0.507' N, 81° 1.776' W

40–197 New Light Beulah Baptist Church

1330 Congaree Rd., Hopkins

(FRONT) New Light Beulah Baptist Church was organized in 1867 when 565 African American members withdrew from Beulah Baptist Church. Before the Civil War enslaved people composed the majority of the Beulah congregation. After emancipation they left to form an independent congregation, with Rev. William W. Williams the first pastor.
(REVERSE) New Light Beulah shared the sanctuary with the white members, but in 1871 they were forcibly expelled and moved to a brush arbor until a new church was built. The congregation persisted and the year 1876 saw a record number of conversions. New Light Beulah has been mother church to many other congregations in its first 150 years. *Sponsored by New Light Beulah Baptist Church, 2017*
GPS Coordinates: 33° 56.087' N, 80° 49.570' W

40–197 Veterans Hospital
[The markers for New Light Beulah Baptist Church and Veterans Hospital were mistakenly assigned the same number.]

Dorn Dr., William Jennings Bryan Dorn VA Hospital, Columbia

(FRONT) The Columbia Veterans Hospital opened to patients in 1932 and was among a set of VA Hospitals built throughout the nation. The campus is similar in design to other VA Hospitals of the period. Originally built with large day-rooms and open wards, the design was modified to include smaller patient rooms and private spaces as health care philosophy evolved. The siting of the hospital just outside the city helped to generate growth in the surrounding area.
(REVERSE) The VA attempted to reflect local history and local architecture in the design of its facilities. While the Colonial Revival style was similar to other VA hospitals, the Recreational Building (Bldg 5), with its raised basement, sweeping stairs, and monumental portico, may have taken inspiration from the Mills Building on the campus of the S.C. State Hospital. The facilities here were segregated by race until 1954, when the VA officially ended the practice. *Sponsored by the Department of Veterans Affairs, 2017*
GPS Coordinates: 33° 58.578' N, 80° 57.590' W

40–198 Dentsville School

Near intersection of Decker Blvd. and Trenholm Rd., Dentsville

(FRONT) Dentsville Consolidated School opened at this site in 1926. The brick building was the first school in the newly created Richland Two school district and served students who had previously attended numerous, smaller schools in the area. The school was named for the Dent family, who donated the land for the school and also lent their name to the surrounding Dentsville community.
(REVERSE) The 1926 schoolhouse served as Dentsville School, 1926–57; Dentsville H.S., 1957–70; Dent Jr. H.S., 1970–78; and Dent Middle School, 1978–2007. Dentsville School remained racially segregated and for whites only until 1964 when the first two African American students were admitted. The original building was replaced by the current Dent Middle School in 2007. *Sponsored by Richland County Conservation Commission*

*and Dentsville High School Class of 1965,
2017*
GPS Coordinates: 34° 3.701' N, 80° 57.208' W

40–199 Olympia Cemetery

Granby Lane, SW of Bluff Rd., Columbia vic.

(FRONT) The Olympia Cemetery was established ca. 1904 and served the families of mill workers from Capital City, Richland, Granby, and Olympia Mills. The land was set aside by W. B. Smith Whaley & Co. When a death occurred the company would provide a burial plot. In 1944, Pacific Mills, which had purchased the Whaley Mills in 1915, deeded ownership to the Olympia Cemetery Association. The Association drew its members from the eight Olympia community churches.
(REVERSE) The oldest portion of the cemetery is the SW section, with more recent burials proceeding to the NE. Oral tradition holds that when a child in the community died, mill workers would build a wooden coffin, line it with material from the company store, and carry it to the gravesite. It is believed that, in addition to the many gravesites marked by headstones, there are also many unmarked burials in Olympia Cemetery. *Sponsored by the Olympia Cemetery Association, 2017*
GPS Coordinates: 33° 58.283' N, 81° 1.945' W

40–200 Sylvan Building

1500 Main St., Columbia

(FRONT) The Sylvan Building, built ca. 1871, is attributed to prominent Philadelphia architect Samuel Sloan. Distinguished by its slate Mansard roof, it is today the lone remaining example of French Second Empire architecture on Columbia's Main Street. It was originally built to house the Central National Bank, which was chartered in 1871. In its original configuration the banking floor was on the basement level, with entrance via a monumental staircase.
(REVERSE) The Sylvan Brothers, Gustaf and Johannes, emigrated from Sweden and began operating Sylvan Brothers Jewelers in 1897. In 1905 they acquired the former Central National Bank building and moved their business here. In 1908 the Sylvan Brothers

added the street clock at the corner of Main and Hampton. Likely produced by the Seth Thomas Co., it was one of a set of five. One other is in Columbia. Others are in Boston, New Orleans, and San Francisco. *Sponsored by Great Southern Corporation, 2017*
GPS Coordinates: 34° 0.331' N, 81° 2.101' W

40–201 Little Zion Baptist Church

8229 Winnsboro Rd., Blythewood

(FRONT) The congregation at Little Zion dates to ca. 1832, when enslaved individuals worshipped in white-controlled churches. After emancipation, these former slaves founded independent congregations like this one. A group led by Doctor Entzminger purchased the land where the church now stands ca. 1886. In earlier years services were held under a brush arbor. Later, a frame sanctuary was built.
(REVERSE) In the past 130 years, Little Zion has had only five pastors. The longest pastorate was Rev. Abraham Chandler, who served for fifty years from 1887–1937. Under the leadership of Pastor Eddie W. Davis, the newest edifice was built in 1995 and added land was purchased. In 2016, a part of Winnsboro Hwy. was named for him in honor of all his accomplishments and service as pastor since 1983. *Sponsored by Little Zion Baptist Church, 2017*
GPS Coordinates: 34° 10.278' N, 81° 2.502' W

40–202 Town Theatre

1012 Sumter St., Columbia

(FRONT) The Town Theatre was founded in 1919 by public-spirited Columbians who yearned for a community theatre. Daniel A. Reed, the first director, was an actor and director stationed at Camp Jackson during WWI. The first home for the theatre was the Sloan House at 1012 Sumter St. The present building, designed by Arthur W. Hamby, was completed in 1924 and is listed in the National Register of Historic Places. Renovations over the years have added dressing rooms, a fly loft, and scene shop.
(REVERSE) On this stage Carl Sandburg recited poetry; Academy Award winners Delbert Mann directed and Stanley Donen acted;

Martha Graham danced; DuBose Heyward lectured; and famed artist Jasper Johns painted sets. Town Theatre initiated the Junior Stage Society program in 1921, becoming one of the pioneers of youth theatre in the U.S. By virtue of its 100 year legacy to the arts, Town Theatre has contributed significantly to the cultural life of the city of Columbia and state of S.C. GPS Coordinates: 33° 59.979' N, 81° 1.849' W

40–203 S.C. Education Association

1510 Gervais St., Columbia

(FRONT) Formally organized in 1881 as the S.C. Association of Teachers, the S.C. Education Association established its first permanent headquarters here at 1218 Senate St. in 1928. A temporary move to Drayton Hall on the Univ. of S.C. campus facilitated the renovation of a new headquarters building nearby, at 1510 Gervais St. The Gervais St. location remained home to the Association from 1940 until they moved again in 1968.
(REVERSE) The S.C. Education Association remained dedicated to improving the quality of public schools and student curricula, as well as improving salaries and benefits, professional development, and working conditions for its members. SCEA membership was limited to white teachers until 1967, when SCEA integrated and merged with the Palmetto Education Association. The headquarters was moved to Zimalcrest Dr. in 1968. *Sponsored by the South Carolina Education Association, 2018*
GPS Coordinates: 34° 0.181' N, 81° 1.701' W

40–204 Palmetto Education Association

1719 Taylor St., Columbia

(FRONT) Founded in 1900 as the S.C. State Teachers Association, and known from 1918–1953 as the Palmetto State Teachers Association, the Palmetto Education Association (PEA) was a state-wide professional association for African American teachers and public school employees. In 1947 the PEA purchased a house at this site to serve as their first permanent headquarters. The building was razed in 1957 and a new headquarters was built here.

(REVERSE) The Palmetto Education Association pressured for equitable salaries, working conditions, and professional development for African American teachers. They also worked to improve schools and curricula for African American students. In 1968 the PEA merged with the formerly all-white S.C. Education Association and moved from this location. The building that stands here today was PEA headquarters from 1957–68. *Sponsored by the South Carolina Education Association, 2018*
GPS Coordinates: 34° 0.578' N, 81° 1.585' W

40–205 Gonzales Gardens

Forest Dr. and Lyon St., Columbia

(FRONT) Opened in September 1940, Gonzales Gardens was named for N. G., Ambrose, and William Gonzales, founders of The State newspaper and early public housing advocates. James B. Urquhart designed the 18-acre complex, which included an administrative building and 24 residential structures. Six apartment buildings were added in 1942, bringing the total number of housing units to 280. A preschool and open play areas were part of the original design.
(REVERSE) The project was overseen by the Columbia Housing Authority, created in 1934, and planning was initiated by the New Deal-era Public Works Administration (PWA). The goal was to provide affordable housing to low-income residents. Gonzales Gardens was originally racially segregated for whites only. Nearby Allen-Benedict Court was designated for African American residents. Both were integrated in the 1970s. Gonzales Gardens was razed in 2017. *Sponsored by the Columbia Housing Authority, 2018*
GPS Coordinates: 34° 0.759' N, 81° 0.918' W

40–206 McCord House

1431 Pendleton St., Columbia

(FRONT) This Greek Revival house was built in 1849 for David and Louisa McCord by slaves from her plantation, Lang Syne, in Fort Motte, S.C., David McCord (1797–1855) was a lawyer, editor, planter, banker, and legislator. Louisa McCord (1810–79) was a noted author of essays, poetry, and drama. Among the enslaved

carpenters who built the home were John Spann and Anderson Keitt. The house was later owned by the Oxner-Adams family, who were also connected to Lang Syne plantation. (REVERSE) During the Civil War the house was a central depot for food intended for patients at the Confederate hospital located on the South Carolina College campus. In 1865, Maj. Gen. O. O. Howard, who later headed the Freedmen's Bureau and was namesake of Howard University, used the house as his headquarters when the U.S. Army captured the city. Though a large part of the city was burned on the night of Feb. 17–18, 1865, the McCord House survived. *Sponsored by the Richland County Conservation Commission and the United Family Reunion, 2018*
GPS Coordinates: 33° 59.998' N, 81° 1.670' W

40–207 Benjamin Mack House

5248 Ridgeway St., Columbia

(FRONT) Educator and civil rights leader Benjamin Mack (1916–1970) lived in this house from the late 1950s until his death in 1970. Mack was a graduate of Booker T. Washington H.S. and S.C. State Univ. He taught at Lower Richland H.S. in the 1940s, where he was known as "Professor B. J. Mack." He married Gladys Hendrix of Batesburg, who operated a daycare center here. They raised two children. Mack also served as a Deacon at Ridgewood Baptist Church.
(REVERSE) In the 1960s Mack served as the State Field Secretary for the Southern Christian Leadership Conference (SCLC) in S.C. As part of his work with SCLC he taught courses in African American history for the Citizenship Education Program (CEP). With SCLC and CEP Mack worked with Martin Luther King Jr., Andrew Young, and Septima Clark. He remained committed to SCLC's mission of non-violent direct action and helped plan both the 1963 March on Washington and 1968 Poor People's Campaign. *Sponsored by Richland County Conservation Commission, Ridgewood Foundation, and Ridgewood Baptist Church, 2018*
GPS Coordinates: 34° 3.216' N, 81° 2.615' W

40–208 Minton Family Home/ Henry McKee Minton

1012 Marion St., Columbia

(FRONT) This Italianate-style home was built ca. 1872 for Theophilus and Virginia McKee Minton. The Mintons were prominent African American residents of Columbia during the era of Reconstruction. They were married in 1870. Their son, Henry McKee Minton (1871–1946), was born the next year. Theophilus Minton graduated from the Univ. of S.C. Law School in 1876.
(REVERSE) The Mintons lived in this home, which was originally located near the corner of Marion and Gervais, until they left Columbia in 1877. Henry Minton later pursued a career in pharmacy and medicine. On May 15, 1904, Dr. Minton and a distinguished group of physicians in Philadelphia, PA founded Sigma Pi Phi Fraternity, the oldest African American Greek-letter organization in the nation. *Sponsored by Alpha Iota Member Boule, Sigma Pi Phi Fraternity, 2018*
GPS Coordinates: 34° 0.006' N, 81° 1.753' W

40–209 St. Timothy's Episcopal Church

900 Calhoun St., Columbia

(FRONT) St. Timothy's Episcopal Church dates to 1892 and is the third oldest Episcopal parish in Columbia. It began as a mission to provide Sunday School for the children of Arsenal Hill. As the congregation grew the church moved, first to a house on Lincoln St. in 1893 and then to a chapel on Calhoun St., which was completed in 1895. In 1912 the church was admitted into union with the diocese of S.C.
(REVERSE) After the first chapel burned, the congregation began construction of the present sanctuary, completed in 1914. The Gothic Revival church is built of granite and includes 15 stained glass windows constructed by Mayer Studios in Germany. The church's Wicks organ was installed in 1963. St. Timothy's also has two gardens, including Beckham Garden, which was designated an official Affiliate Quiet Garden in 2006. *Sponsored by St. Timothy's Episcopal Church, 2018*
GPS Coordinates: 34° 0.565' N, 81° 2.515' W

40–210 Blythewood School

501 Main St., Blythewood

(FRONT) The first school here built ca. 1890 was a one-room frame building. In 1921 a two-story brick schoolhouse and auditorium replaced the original school. The New Deal-era Works Progress Administration (WPA) helped fund several projects here including the construction of a new gymnasium in 1938. The two-story school was razed in 1958 and replaced by the one-story building that remains today. The 1921 auditorium and the 1938 gymnasium also survive.

(REVERSE) When Richland Co. decided to consolidate their school districts in 1951 Blythewood was one of four schools in the new Richland School District 2. For much of its history Blythewood School remained segregated and only open to white students. That ended in 1969 when Richland District 2, along with school districts throughout S.C., implemented desegregation plans. From 1970–1991 the building housed Blythewood Elementary, and then in 1994 became Blythewood Academy. *Sponsored by Richland County Conservation Commission and Blythewood Historical Society and Museum, 2019.*
GPS Coordinates: 34° 13.172' N, 80° 58.329' W

40–211 Cyril O. Spann Medical Office

2226 Hampton St., Columbia

(FRONT) From 1963 to 1979, this was the office of Dr. Cyril O. Spann (1916–1979), one of the first fully trained African American surgeons in S.C. Born in Chester, Spann fought in World War II and attended nearby Benedict College. After graduating from Meharry Medical College, he traveled to different S.C. towns to perform surgery and train other black doctors. He built this office after acquiring the site in 1962.

(REVERSE) A local civil rights leader, Spann helped desegregate public accommodations and once performed life-saving surgery on a student stabbed during a sit-in. While Spann saw patients at this office, he conducted surgery at Good Samaritan-Waverly Hospital, where he worked as early as 1957 and later served as chief of staff. After Spann's death, other black doctors continued practicing at his office into the 1990s. *Sponsored by Tnovsa Global Commons and Richland County Conservation Commission, 2019.*
GPS Coordinates: 34° 0.634' N, 81° 1.091' W

40–212 1900 Block of Henderson Street/William J. Sumter

1931 Henderson St., Columbia

1900 Block of Hernderson Street (FRONT)
This block features a dense collection of late 19th and early 20th c. houses historically associated with and home to African Americans. Residing here through the mid-1900s were many middle- and working-class African Americans, including barbers, teachers, nurses, carpenters, cooks, porters, maids, a butcher, a pastor, and a blacksmith. By the 1940s, several properties here were owned by barber William J. Sumter.

William J. Sumter (REVERSE)
The house at 1931 Henderson St. was the home of William J. Sumter (1881–1967), an African American entrepreneur who owned and operated a well-known barber shop on Main St. from 1905–1954, said to have been the oldest in Columbia when it closed. Sumter purchased this house in 1909 from African American carpenter John W. Bailey. Sumter and his wife Daisy A. Robinson, lived here with their children. He later owned 1921 and 1921 Henderson St., which he rented to tenants. *Sponsored by Richland County Conservation Commision, 2019*
GPS Coordinates: 34° 0.844' N, 81° 1.814' W

40–213 Columbia Hospital "Negro Unit"/Columbia Hospital "Negro Nurses"

SW Corner of Harden St. and Washington St. intersection, Columbia

Columbia Hospital "Negro Unit" (FRONT)
Columbia Hospital, est. 1892, opened a segregated wing for African Americans in 1934 at its Hampton St. location. In 1943, it built an expanded "Negro Unit" at this site, then 1301 Harden St. This 4-story facility was designed by architects Lafaye, Lafaye, & Fair and cost

$333,000. When opened, it was equipped for 165 patients plus 30 infants. In 1972, Columbia Hospital was replaced by Richland Memorial Hospital.

Columbia Hospital "Negro Nurses" (REVERSE)
In 1935, Columbia Hospital opened a segregated School of Nursing for African Americans. A first class of ten graduated in 1938. In 1941, a 3-story dormitory for African American nurses was built at the corner of Laurens and Washington Sts. It included classrooms, an auditorium, and a library. By the time the school closed in 1965, more than 400 nurses had graduated. The school was accredited by the state of S.C. *Sponsored by the Columbia Hospital School of Nursing Alumnae Association Black Nurses, 2019*
GPS Coordinates: 34° 0.500' N, 81° 01.229' W

Saluda County

41–1 Pierce M. Butler/The Palmetto Regiment

Saluda County Courthouse, 115 W. Church St. (U.S. Hwy. 378), Saluda

Pierce M. Butler (FRONT)
Six miles NE, in a family cemetery at Butler Church, is the grave of Colonel Pierce M. Butler, Governor of South Carolina from 1836 to 1838. During his military career, he was a Captain in the U.S. Army, a Lt. Colonel in the Seminole War, and was Commander of the Palmetto Regiment in the Mexican War, when he was killed in battle on August 20, 1847.
The Palmetto Regiment (REVERSE)
The S.C. Volunteer Regiment in the Mexican War entered service in Dec. 1846 and was part of Winfield Scott's army. At the Battle of Churubusco, its Commander, Pierce M. Butler, was killed leading a charge in the face of devastating fire. The unit was in the vanguard of the final assault on Mexico City and first to plant its flag on the city walls. *Erected by Saluda County Historical Commission, 1970*
GPS Coordinates: 34° 0.082' N, 81° 46.3' W

41–2 Red Bank Church

309 E. Church St. (U.S. Hwy. 378), Saluda
Red Bank Baptist Church antedates the Town of Saluda by about a century. The congregation, which is said to have been founded in 1784, was incorporated by the State on December 18, 1802. According to tradition, the first church building was a log house. In 1856, a frame structure was erected, which was replaced by the present brick church in 1911.

Erected by Saluda County Historical Commission, 1970
GPS Coordinates: 34° 0.134' N, 81° 45.983' W

41–3 Jacob Odom House

Batesburg Hwy. (S.C. Hwy. 23/39), near Double Branch Church, between Ridge Spring & Monetta
This site, approximately halfway between Augusta and Columbia, was the location of Jacob Odom's house, where George Washington spent the night of May 21, 1791, on his trip northward through South Carolina. His escort at this time consisted of Colonels Wade Hampton and Thomas Taylor, and Mr. Robert Lythgoe. This stop is noted in Washington's diary. *Erected by Saluda County Historical Commission, 1970*
GPS Coordinates: 33° 51.07' N, 81° 37.086' W

41–4 Luther Rice 1783–1836
[Reported missing in August 2009.]

Newberry Hwy. (S.C. Hwy. 121) near Hollywood School Rd. (S.C. Sec. Rd. 41–44), NW of Coleman's Crossroads
In Pine Pleasant Cemetery, west of here, is the grave of Luther Rice, prominent Baptist clergyman and orator who organized American Baptists on a national scale for support of foreign missions and education. He traveled into all parts of the nation in his work, and his personal influence helped shape Baptist history. *Erected by Saluda County Historical Commission, 1970*
GPS Coordinates: 34° 7.635' N, 81° 44.867' W

41–5 Lucinda Horn

Just off S.C. Hwy. 39 at Chestnut Hill Baptist Church, Chapman vicinity

At Chestnut Hill Baptist Church is the grave of Lucinda Horn, Confederate War heroine, wife of Cornelius Horn and mother of William Horn, both members of Company K, 14th S.C. Volunteers. She accompanied her husband and son to the front and remained with McGowan's Brigade during the hardest fighting of the war, nursing the wounded and dying. *Erected by Saluda County Historical Commission, 1970*
GPS Coordinates: 34° 7.241' N, 81° 50.2' W

41–6 Butler Family Graves

S.C. Hwy. 194, Denny's Crossroads, NW of Saluda

At Butler Church, about one mile west, is the burial plot of the Butler family. Among the graves are those of William Butler, Captain in the American Revolution, United States Congressman, and Major General of S.C. Militia; Andrew Pickens Butler, United States Senator; Pierce M. Butler, Governor of South Carolina who was killed in the Mexican War. *Erected by Saluda County Historical Commission, 1970*
GPS Coordinates: 34° 3.918' N, 81° 42.85' W

41–7 Faith Cabin Library Site

[Reported missing in March 2010.]

Intersection of McCormick Hwy. (U.S. Hwy. 378) & S.C. Sec. Rd. 41-65, Limp community, between Owdoms and Saluda

Built in 1932 about ½ mi. NE and stocked with donated books, this library was the first of over 110 libraries founded by W. L. Buffington for rural blacks. *Erected by Saluda County Historical Society, 1994*
GPS Coordinates: 33° 59.283' N, 81° 51.14' W

41–8 Delmar School

Old Delmar School Rd. and S.C. Hwy. 391, Delmar community

This school, established in 1896 as both a grammar and high school, was built as a 1-room building and was expanded to 3 rooms by 1900. With as many as 4 teachers and well over 100 students in its best years, Delmar School taught over 600 students in its 56-year history. Though the high school (grades 8–10) closed in the mid-1930s the grammar school (grades 1–7) continued to serve the Delmar community until it closed in 1952. *Erected by Students and Friends of Delmar School, 1996*
GPS Coordinates: 34° 1.257' N, 81° 31.4' W

41–9 Spann Methodist Church /Captain Clinton Ward

150 Church St. (S.C. Hwy. 23), Ward

Spann Methodist Church (FRONT)
This church was founded ca. 1805 at the plantation of John Spann, Jr., about 1 mi. N. Bishop Francis Asbury preached there in 1807 and 1811. The first church on this site was built and the cemetery was established ca. 1840. The present Greek Revival sanctuary, built in 1873, is almost unchanged. The church and cemetery were listed in the National Register of Historic Places in 2003.
Captain Clinton Ward (REVERSE)
Clinton Ward (1828–1905), a member of this church, was a prominent landowner and a state representative 1880–83. The Charlotte, Columbia, & Augusta RR ran its tracks through Ward's property about 1870. He laid out and planned the town first named Ward's Depot, then Clintonward, then Wards, and finally Ward. Clinton Ward, his wife Martha, and their daughter Josephine are buried here. *Erected by the Ridge Heritage Association, 2005*
GPS Coordinates: 33° 51.433' N, 81° 43.678' W

41–10 Hare's Mill

Spann Rd., at Cloud's Creek between U.S. Hwy. 378 and S.C. Hwy. 391, between Saluda and the traffic circle, Saluda vicinity

(FRONT) Hare's Mill, which stood here on Cloud's Creek, was a large grist mill owned by James Hare (1838–1929). Hare bought the mill from the Rinehart family in 1885 and moved it here. The two-story mill ground both corn and wheat, using water power to grind corn and steam power to grind wheat. It was also an important meeting place for this community over many years.

(REVERSE) James and Elizabeth Black Hare had nine sons: John Allen, Samuel Jacob, Noah Ephram, Butler Black, Joseph William, Henry Benjamin, Jemmie Lee, George Tillman, and Sidney Bowles. They helped their father run Hare's Mill until it closed in 1928, when S.C. Electric and Gas Company bought land on Cloud's Creek before building Lake Murray. The mill was demolished soon afterwards. *Erected by the Saluda County Historical Society, 2006*
GPS Coordinates: 34° 2.381' N, 81° 34.073' W

41–11   Jones Cemetery/General James Jones

S.C. Hwy. 23, just W of the Ridge Spring town limits

Jones Cemetery (FRONT)
This is the family cemetery of Mathias Jones (1779–1829), planter, merchant, and state representative 1814–17. Jones moved from Virginia to Ridge Spring, in what was then Edgefield District, about 1800. He, his wife Clara Perry Jones (1786–1841), and 4 of their 12 children are buried here. The 1887 will of daughter Elizabeth Watson set up an endowment for perpetual maintenance.
General James Jones (REVERSE)
Gen. James Jones (1805–1865), the son of Mathias & Clara Jones, is buried here. A partner in textile mills at Graniteville and Vaucluse, he was chairman of commissioners to build the State House 1855–61. Jones also served as adjutant & inspector general 1836–41, chairman of the board of visitors of the Citadel and the Arsenal Academy 1842–65, and state quartermaster general 1863–65. *Erected by the Ridge Heritage Association, 2006*
GPS Coordinates: 33° 50.978' N, 81° 40.674' W

41–12   Ridge Spring Cemetery/W.H. Scarborough

E. Main St./Batesburg Hwy. (S.C. Hwy. 23), just E of Trojan Dr., just E of the Ridge Spring town limits

Ridge Spring Cemetery (FRONT)
This cemetery, dating to the early 19th century, was originally the Watson and Boatwright family cemetery before it was enlarged to become the town cemetery. Many descendants of Capt. Michael Watson (1726–1782)

are buried in the walled section, built ca. 1850 by Chloe Wimberly Watson. They include Sarah Pressley Watson (1885–1959), who directed the Foyer International des Etudiantes in Paris 1920–1959.
W. H. Scarborough (REVERSE)
William H. Scarborough (1812–1871), the leading portrait painter in 19th-century S.C., is buried here. A Tennessee native, he came to S.C. in 1836 and settled in Columbia in 1846. His portraits of prominent politicians and others are in collections such as the State House, State Museum, Columbia Museum of Art, and Gibbes Museum of Art. At first buried in Columbia, his remains were moved here by his widow Miranda when she lived in Ridge Spring. *Erected by the Ridge Heritage Association, 2009*
GPS Coordinates: 33° 50.791' N, 81° 38.744' W

41–13   Ridge Hill School/Faith Cabin Library

At the Ridge Spring Star Community Center, 206 Ridge Hill Dr., Ridge Spring

Ridge Hill School (FRONT)
This school, built in 1934, replaced the Ridge Hill Rosenwald School, a six-classroom frame school built in 1923–24. That school was funded in part by the Julius Rosenwald Foundation, building more than 500 African-American schools in S.C. 1917–1932. It burned in 1934, but the new school was built on the same plan, at a cost of about $8000. Grades 1–11 attended this school until grade 12 was added in 1947. Ridge Hill School closed in 1957.
Faith Cabin Library (REVERSE)
This building has been the Ridge Spring Star Community Center since 1978. The chimney nearby is all that remains of a Faith Cabin Library, part of a program founded in 1932 by Willie Lee Buffington (1908–1988) to help give small-town and rural African-Americans better access to books. The library built here in 1934 was the second Faith Cabin Library in the state. More than 100 were built in S.C. and Ga. from 1932 to 1960. *Erected by the Ridge Spring Star Community Center, 2009*
GPS Coordinates: 33° 51.167' N, 81° 39.55' W

41–14 Ambush at Mine Creek

Intersection of Old Charleston Rd. (S.C. Sec. Rd. 41-177) and S.C. Hwy. 121, Saluda vicinity

(FRONT) On November 3, 1775, Loyalists ambushed a supply wagon nearby, in a prelude to the first land battle of the Revolution in S.C. The Council of Safety sent gunpowder and lead to the Cherokees in an effort to prevent their siding with the Crown. Capt. Patrick Cunningham, with 150 men, overtook the wagon about 1 ¾ mi. SW, where the Old Charleston Rd. crosses Mine Creek.

(REVERSE) After Cunningham captured the wagon and escort, Loyalists claimed that the Patriots wanted the Cherokees to wage war on them. Loyalist forces soon outnumbered Patriots in the area by more than three to one. The First Battle of Ninety Six, on November 19, saw the first bloodshed in the Revolution in S.C. The brief truce that followed did little to ease tensions in the backcountry. *Erected by the Gen. James Williams Chapter, Sons of the American Revolution, in Memory of Joseph C. M. Goldsmith, 2010*
GPS Coordinates: 33° 57.053' N, 81° 47.344' W

Spartanburg County

42–1 Reidville Public School

Corner of Reidville Rd. (S.C. Hwy. 296) and College St., Reidville

built in 1948 on the site of Reidville Female College (operated 1871 to 1901), one of two private schools founded in 1857 by Rev. Robert Harden Reid and located on lands given by James N. Gaston, James Wakefield, and Anthony Wakefield. Reidville Male Academy (1857–1905) occupied building ½ mile east. The schools were combined in 1905. *Erected in 1958 by Centennial Committee* [The first word ("built") appears in lowercase on the marker. Sponsor was the Reidville Centennial Committee.]
GPS Coordinates: 34° 51.646' N, 82° 6.864' W

42–2 Converse College

Entrance to Converse College Campus, E Main St., Spartanburg

Founded by citizens of Spartanburg in 1889 for the liberal education of women. Named for Dexter Edgar Converse, pioneer textile manufacturer. Opened in 1890 on this site, the grounds of which have been used for educational purposes since 1849. [Erected in 1957.]
GPS Coordinates: 34° 57.263' N, 81° 55.006' W

42–3 Wofford College

[No longer extant. Replaced by Marker 42-18, erected by Wofford College, 1998.]

Entrance to Wofford College Campus, N Church St., Spartanburg

Erected by the Class of 1960

42–4 "Kate Barry"

S.C. Sec. Rd. 42-196 (Stillhouse Rd.), near I-26 & U.S. Hwy. 221 interchange, Moore vicinity

1½ SE is Walnut Grove, home of Margaret Catherine Moore Barry (1752–1823). Local tradition says she was known as "Kate Barry" and acted as scout for the Patriots before the Battle of Cowpens, Jan. 17, 1781. With her parents, Charles and Mary Moore, and her husband, Captain Andrew Barry, she lies buried in the plantation cemetery. *Erected by Descendants of Charles and Mary Moore and the Battle of Cowpens Chapter, Daughters of the American Revolution, 1968*
GPS Coordinates: 34° 50.423' N, 81° 58.123' W

42–5 Camp Wadsworth

At the head of the Willis Road Pedestrian Path, Westside Club, 501 Willis Rd., Spartanburg

This camp, named in honor of Brigadier General James Samuel Wadsworth, U.S.V., was approved June 1917 as a cantonment site. The 27th division trained here from September 1,

1917 to May 4, 1918; the 6th, from May 10, 1918 to June 23, 1918; the 96th, from October 20, 1918 to January 7, 1919. *Erected by the National 27th Division Association, 1969* [Replaced a marker erected by the American Legion of South Carolina in 1938.]
GPS Coordinates: 34° 55.873' N, 82° 0.653' W

42–6　First Erosion Control Work in the Southeast

Intersection of Bethany Church Rd. (S.C. Sec. Rd. 42-121) & S.C. Hwy. 417, Poplar Springs

On Dec. 18, 1933, work began on the J. L. Berry Gully, 1.5 miles S.E., as part of the South Tyger River Erosion Control Demonstration Project by the USDI Soil Erosion Service, Dr. T. S. Buie, Project Director. This project was a forerunner of the USDA Soil Conservation Service and the Soil and Water Conservation Districts. *Erected by the South Carolina Association of Conservation Districts, 1974*
GPS Coordinates: 34° 51.967' N, 82° 3.135' W

42–7　Grave of William Walker /Magnolia Cemetery

Magnolia Cemetery, Magnolia St., Spartanburg

Grave of William Walker (FRONT)
William "Singin' Billy" Walker (1809–1875) was the author of Southern Harmony, a collection of religious music employing shaped musical notes to aid those who could not read standard musical notation. He later published the more elaborate Christian Harmony and taught "singing schools" throughout the middle, southern and western states. He is buried in Magnolia Cemetery.
Magnolia Cemetery (REVERSE)
In 1838, Jesse Cleveland deeded 2 ½ acres of this land, including the village cemetery, to the town of Spartanburg for a graveyard. It was enlarged in 1868 by the purchase of 1 ⅛ acres from Robert E. Cleveland. The earliest legible inscription is found on the marker to Robert Walker, who died in 1810. Many of Spartanburg's early civic, educational, and political leaders are buried here. *Erected by the Spartanburg Garden Club Council, 1976*
GPS Coordinates: 34° 57.302' N, 81° 56.264' W

42–8　Fort Prince

[Marker removed for relocation of I-85 and never replaced.]

S.C. Hwy. 129, about ½ mi. W of I-85, Spartanburg

Located nearby, this fort protected early settlers from the Indians and served as camp for a detachment of militia en route to join the 1776 expedition against the Cherokees. The fort was headquarters in 1780 for a British garrison commanded by Colonel Alexander Innes. *Erected by Wellford Bicentennial Committee, 1977*
GPS Coordinates: 34° 57.75' N, 82° 3.317' W

42–9　Site of Fredonia

U.S. Hwy. 221, about ½ mi. NE of Moore

Believed built in 1786 by Thomas Moore, Revolutionary soldier, brigadier general in the War of 1812 and a member of Congress, Fredonia was later owned by Andrew B. Moore, earliest known doctor in this region, and Thomas J. Moore, Confederate soldier and state legislator. On the National Register of Historic Places. The house burned in 1977. *Erected by Spartanburg County Historical Society, 1979*
GPS Coordinates: 34° 50.066' N, 81° 58.903' W

42–10　Early Iron Works

Intersection of Clifton-Glendale Rd. & Glendale Ave., Glendale

Near here on Lawson's Fork, during the American Revolution, the S.C. government as part of the war effort supported Joseph Buffington, William Wofford, and others in the construction of an iron works. It became a well-known landmark and the scene of several skirmishes, notably the "Battle of Wofford's Iron Works" on August 8, 1780. *Erected by the Spartanburg County Historical Association, 1979*
GPS Coordinates: 34° 56.632' N, 81° 50.397' W

42–11　Calvary Church/Glenn Springs

Glenn Springs Rd. (S.C. Hwy. 150), 1 mi. E of the center of town, Glenn Springs

Calvary Church (FRONT)

The Reverend John D. McCullough was the first rector of this Episcopal Church, which was established in 1848. The original building, consecrated in 1850, stood at the cemetery about ½ mile to the north. The congregation's present house of worship was consecrated in 1897 by Bishop Ellison Capers.

Glenn Springs (REVERSE)

Early recognized by the Indians for the healing qualities of its mineral waters, nearby Glenn Springs became a popular summer resort when the Glenn Springs Co. bought the land from John B. Glenn in 1838 and built a large hotel. This stood until it burned in 1941. In the spa's heyday, its bottled waters were shipped far and wide. *Erected by the Congregation, 1982*
GPS Coordinates: 34° 48.965' N, 81° 49.84' W

42–12 Hampton Heights Historic District

Intersection of South Church St. and Marion Ave., Spartanburg

Located one block west, this historic district was entered in the National Register of Historic Places in 1983 because of its historical and architectural significance as an example of an intact early-twentieth-century neighborhood. A number of popular architectural styles of the period are represented in the district. *Erected by Spartanburg County Historical Foundation, 1984*
GPS Coordinates: 34° 56.425' N, 81° 55.686' W

42–13 Elvins-Bivings House

563 North Church St., Spartanburg

According to family tradition, this house was built in 1854 by the Bivings family, local textile pioneers. In 1869, the house was purchased by John H. Evins (1830 to 1884), Confederate Lieutenant-Colonel, state legislator, mayor of Spartanburg, and U.S. Congressman (1877–1884). The house was placed in the National Register of Historic Places in 1970. *Erected by the Spartanburg Historical Association, 1986*
GPS Coordinates: 34° 57.575' N, 81° 56.414' W

42–14 Nazareth Church

680 Nazareth Church Rd., Fairmont vicinity

This Presbyterian Church, located about .4 mile SE, was organized soon after 1766 by Scotch-Irish who settled the area. From Revolutionary War days the congregation has been influential in religious, educational, and civic affairs of Spartanburg County. A number of new congregations have been formed from Nazareth whose present building was erected in 1832. *Erected by the Congregation, 1980*
GPS Coordinates: 34° 54.014' N, 82° 2.159' W

42–15 Spartanburg Methodist College

Duncan Memorial United Methodist Church, 570 Brawley St., Spartanburg

While minister of Duncan Memorial Methodist Church, the Rev. David E. Camak established the Textile Industrial Institute in the dwelling across the street to educate cotton mill workers. The institute opened Sept. 5, 1911, and its operation was soon assumed by the Methodist Church; it became a junior college in 1927. In 1974, the school was renamed Spartanburg Methodist College. *Erected by David E. Camak Society, 1988*
GPS Coordinates: 34° 54.014' N, 82° 2.159' W

42–16 Old City Cemetery

Cemetery St., just N. of Duncan St., Spartanburg

(FRONT) This cemetery, established on this site about 1900 as the Spartanburg Colored Cemetery, includes many graves moved here from the first black cemetery in the city, established in 1849 1 mi. W. and closed by the expansion of the Charleston & Western Carolina RR. Also known as the New Colored Cemetery until 1928 and later known as Freeman's Cemetery, it has been known as the Old City Cemetery since 1959.

(REVERSE) Prominent persons buried here include educator Mary Honor Farrow Wright (1862–1946), for whom Mary Wright School was named; midwife Phyllis Goins (1860–1945) and policeman Tobe Hartwell (d. 1932), for whom city housing developments were named; city councilman Thomas Bomar

(1864–1904), and educator Annie Wright McWhirter (1885–1976), first woman to teach at the South Carolina School for the Deaf and Blind. *Erected by the Spartanburg Community Memorial Committee and the African American Heritage Committee, 1997*
GPS Coordinates: 34° 56.32' N, 81° 55.112' W

42–17 Cowpens Depot

120 Palmetto St., Cowpens

This passenger and freight depot was built in 1896 by the Southern Railway and was originally 1 block N. at Brown & Church Sts. It replaced an 1873 depot on the Atlanta & Charlotte Air Line Railway, later merged into the Southern. This depot served passengers into the 1950s and handled freight until 1967. It was moved in 1982, renovated and opened as the Cowpens Museum & Civic Center in 1985, and was listed in the National Register of Historic Places in 1997. *Erected by the Cowpens Museum Committee, 1998*
GPS Coordinates: 35° 0.886' N, 81° 48.162' W

42–18 Wofford College

Church St., on the Wofford College campus, Spartanburg

Wofford College, chartered in 1851, was established by a $100,000 bequest from the Rev. Benjamin Wofford of Spartanburg, who envisioned a college for "literary, classical and scientific education" affiliated with the Methodist Church. The college opened in the fall of 1854 and still occupies its historic campus, listed in the National Register of Historic Places in 1974. Wofford's Phi Beta Kappa chapter, chartered in 1941, was the first at a private college in South Carolina. *Erected by Wofford College, 1998* [Replaced a marker erected by the Wofford College Class of 1960.]
GPS Coordinates: 34° 57.514' N, 81° 56.338' W

42–19 Old Rutherford Road

Campobello-Gramling Elementary School, 250 Fagan Ave., Campobello

This old roadbed is the last extant portion of the Rutherford Road, which appears in Robert Mills's 1825 *Atlas of the State of S.C.* and was one of at least three historic roads in northern Spartanburg Co. named for Rutherfordton, county seat of Rutherford Co., N.C., 20 mi. NE. The road was a significant route for travel, mail, and commerce until well into the twentieth century. *Erected by Campobello-Gramling Elementary School, 2000*
GPS Coordinates: 35° 6.186' N, 82° 8.58' W

42–20 Shiloh Methodist Church

Between Blackstock Rd. and W. Clark Rd., Inman vicinity

(FRONT) This church, organized late in the eighteenth century, held its first services in a brush arbor and later constructed a log meeting house. This frame sanctuary, built between 1825 and 1830, was the second building to serve Shiloh. In 1836 Adam Gramling, Jr., donated it and three acres to church trustees William Brooks, Adam Gramling, Sr., John Gramling, and Ruben Gramling.
(REVERSE) Shiloh Methodist Church was the mother church of many Spartanburg County Methodist churches and some affiliated with other denominations. It was active until about 1915, when its last 14 members transferred to Inman Methodist Church. The old sanctuary, still an important part of the community, has been the site of an annual homecoming service since 1915. *Erected by the Friends of Shiloh, 2000*
GPS Coordinates: 35° 1.561' N, 82° 5.07' W

42–21 New Hope Baptist Church

154 Burnt Factory Rd., Cross Anchor

(FRONT) This church, established in 1804, grew out of Padgett's Creek Baptist Church, mother to several area Baptist congregations. Rev. Spencer Bobo (d. 1816), a member there, was given permission to take "as many members as he thinks fit" and organize a new church. Bobo chose a site W of present-day Cross Anchor, near his home, deeding 7 acres for a sanctuary and cemetery.
(REVERSE) The first church was a log building known as "Bobo's Meeting House." Bobo and Rev. Nathan Langston (1762–1834) preached there until Bobo's death in 1816 and Langston preached there until 1832. The congregation,

renamed New Hope Baptist Church in 1809, built a frame church by 1834. New Hope moved here and built this frame sanctuary in 1924–26. It was covered in brick veneer in 1961. *Erected by the Congregation, 2010*
GPS Coordinates: 34° 38.66' N, 81° 51.515' W

42–22 Mount Zion Baptist Church Cemetery

842 Mt. Zion Rd., Spartanburg vicinity

(FRONT) Mount Zion Baptist Church, founded as early as 1804 as an affiliated branch of Bethlehem Baptist Church, was formally established in 1827. The cemetery here, dating from 1832, includes the graves of many early church families and of several veterans of the American Revolution and the Civil War. (REVERSE) Rev. John Gill Landrum (1810–1882), pastor here 1831–1852 and 1863–1882, also served for many years at First Baptist Church in Spartanburg and at Bethlehem, New Prospect, and Wolf Creek as well. He is buried here, as is his son J. B. O. Landrum (1844–1901), physician and author of an early history of Spartanburg County. *Erected by the Mt. Zion Cemetery Association, 2002*
GPS Coordinates: 34° 58.633' N, 82° 3.404' W

42–23 Battle of Earle's Ford

Landrum Rd. (S.C. Sec. Rd. 42-128), just N of the N. Pacolet River, Landrum vicinity

(FRONT) After British forces took Charleston in May 1780, they set up outposts in the backcountry and attempted to control the state by encouraging Loyalists. Patriot militia from Ga. and N.C. operated with S.C. militia as opportunities arose. On the night of July 14–15, 1780, one of a series of engagements in the vicinity took place nearby, just E of Earle's Ford over the North Pacolet River. (REVERSE) Col. Charles McDowell, with 300 N.C. militia, and Col. John Jones, with 35 Ga. militia, camped near the ford on the night of July 14. Maj. James Dunlap, with 70 British dragoons and Loyalists, surprised the Patriots sleeping in their camp but retreated when he saw he was outnumbered. The Americans lost 8 men killed and 24 men wounded; the British and Loyalists lost a single man wounded.

Sponsored by the South Carolina Department of Transportation, 2014
GPS Coordinates: 35° 11.414' N, 82° 8.582' W

42–24 Central Methodist Church

233 North Church St., Spartanburg

Organized in 1837 as the first congregation of any denomination in Spartanburg, when this site was deeded to nine trustees. Services began in early 1838. Original frame meeting house with belfry was replaced in 1854 by a larger brick church. The present Gothic Revival sanctuary, built in 1886 and described as "an ornament to our town," was enlarged in 1897 & 1910. *Erected by the Congregation, 2005*
GPS Coordinates: 34° 57.146' N, 81° 55.994' W

42–25 15th N.Y. Infantry/"Harlem Hell Fighters"

Corner of W.O. Ezell Blvd. (U.S. Hwy. 29) & Westgate Mall Dr., just E of I-26 Exit 21-B, Spartanburg

15th N.Y. Infantry (FRONT)
The 15th N.Y. Infantry, a volunteer National Guard unit of African American soldiers, arrived here Oct. 10, 1917, to train at Camp Wadsworth. Race riots that summer in East St. Louis and Houston raised the fears of Spartanburg's whites about the potential for racial violence if Northern black soldiers trained here. Though the 15th N.Y. was ordered not to respond to any insults or physical abuse by local whites, tensions rose for the next two weeks.
"Harlem Hell Fighters" (REVERSE)
The War Dept., fearing that minor incidents would soon escalate, ordered the unit back to N.Y. on Oct. 24 and on to France. As the 369th U.S. Infantry, it joined the 4th French Army and its band won acclaim all over France for its concerts. It was the first American unit in combat, and was soon nicknamed "the Harlem Hell Fighters." It was at the front for 191 days, longest of any American unit in World War I. *Erected by ReGenesis and the Spartanburg County Historical Association, 2004*
GPS Coordinates: 34° 56.178' N, 81° 59.442' W

42–26 Camp Croft

Corner of Southport Rd. (S.C. Hwy. 295) and Patch Dr., Spartanburg vicinity

(FRONT) Camp Croft, constructed in 1940–41, was named for Greenville native Maj. Gen. Edward Croft (1875–1938). The pillars from the main gate stand nearby. Camp Croft was one of nine U.S. Army Infantry Replacement Training Centers during World War II. More than 250,000 soldiers took basic and specialty training courses here. Camp Croft contained more than 600 buildings, almost half of them barracks, on a 19,000-acre site between S.C. Hwys. 56 and 176.

(REVERSE) Units at Camp Croft were designated as the 6th, 7th, 8th, 9th, and 10th Infantry Training Regiments. The camp also housed as many as 900 German prisoners of war between 1944 and 1946, who were hired out to work on local farms and forests. Camp Croft was deactivated and sold to the Spartanburg County Foundation in April 1947. 7000 acres of it became Croft State Park (now Croft State Natural Area), while the rest was developed for industries and homes. *Erected by the Spartanburg County Historical Association, 2004*
GPS Coordinates: 34° 55.122' N, 81° 50.928' W

42–27 Clifton Baptist Church/First Baptist Church

551 Hawk Hill Rd., Clifton

Clifton Baptist Church (FRONT)
This church, originally called Clifton Baptist Church, was founded in 1881 with ten charter members and Rev. T. J. Taylor as its organizing minister. Rev. W. T. Tate was its first permanent minister. Admitted into the Broad River Association later that year, it was originally a union church, also serving other denominations in the village at Clifton Mill (later Clifton No. 1).
First Baptist Church (REVERSE)
This church, the mother of new congregations at Converse and Second Baptist, bought its building from the mill company in 1896; it was demolished in 1904–05 and the present church was built in 1905. It became the First Baptist Church in 1937. About 1945 the 1905

bell tower was replaced in memory of the seven citizens of the community who died in World War II. *Erected by the Congregation, 2005*
GPS Coordinates: 34° 59.25' N, 81° 49.254' W

42–28 Converse Heights

At the intersection of Mills Ave. & E. Main St., Spartanburg

(FRONT) Converse Heights is one of Spartanburg's earliest suburbs, with most of the houses built between 1906 and 1950. This area was originally the antebellum plantation of Govan Mills (1805–1862). In 1906 Mills' heirs sold the property to Spartanburg Realty Company for development. Mills Avenue is named for Govan Mills. Converse Heights is named for Converse College, the private women's college across East Main Street, which was founded in 1889.

(REVERSE) A mix of modest and larger houses, this area includes examples of the Queen Anne, Colonial Revival, and Craftsman architectural styles. Governors John Gary Evans (1863–1942), James F. Byrnes (1882–1972), and Donald F. Russell (1906–1998) lived here. Happy Hollow Park, one of the city's oldest playgrounds, is in the heart of the neighborhood. The Converse Heights Historic District was listed in the National Register of Historic Places in 2007. *Erected by the Converse Heights Neighborhood Association, 2008*
GPS Coordinates: 34° 57.246' N, 81° 54.996' W

42–29 National Ass. of Soil Conservation Districts

Montgomery Building, 187 N. Church St., Spartanburg

(FRONT) The first office of the National Association of Soil Conservation Districts (NASCD) was located in the Montgomery Building on N. Church St. from 1946 to 1947. Soil conservation, with its focus on reducing erosion and flooding, became a nationwide effort during the Depression and gained additional funding and resources after World War II.

(REVERSE) The NASCD, organized in Chicago in 1946, elected E. C. McArthur of Gaffney, S.C., its first president. McArthur was instru-

mental in creating the NASCD as a national voice for soil conservation districts. T. S. Buie, director of the Southeast Office of the Soil Conservation Service of the U.S. Department of Agriculture, provided space here for the NASCD office. *Sponsored by the S.C. Conservation Districts Foundation, 2013*
GPS Coordinates: 34° 57.128' N, 81° 55.940' W

42–30 Apalache Mill

2200 Racing Road, Greer vicinity

(FRONT) This site was the location of active mill operations from 1837–2007. The core of the current mill building was completed in 1888, with subsequent additions enlarging the complex as operations expanded. The most notable of these came in 1903, just after Lewis Parker acquired the mill. The 1903 addition was designed by J. E. Sirrine and added 400 looms and 17,000 spindles. By 1907 Apalache Mill employed 300 workers who ran 500 looms and 20,000 spindles.
(REVERSE) The adjacent dam and mill pond were completed in 1904 and represented an important shift in how the mill was powered. The energy generated by the falling water as it dropped 40 feet from the mill pond to the South Tyger River below was harnessed by a 2,300 volt water wheel-driven generator and 75 H.P. induction motor. These, in turn, drove a series of belts and pulleys that powered mill equipment. Apalache Mill was listed in the National Register of Historic Places in 2015. *Sponsored by Upstate Developers, LLC, 2016*
GPS Coordinates: 34° 57.715' N, 82° 12.528' W

42–31 Tucapau Mill

Intersection of Tucapau Rd. (State Rd. S-42-63) and Spartanburg Rd.

(FRONT) Tucapau Mill opened in 1896 on the Middle Tyger River at Penney Shoals by investors including John Montgomery. The mill made cotton cloth using a water wheel powered by the Middle Tyger River. In 1902 a dam and power plant were built at Berry Shoals. A village built by the mill at first included a store, a school, and 33 houses. Later, 350 houses filled the village. A Baptist, Methodist, and Church of God all were built. An

elementary school was constructed in 1900. (REVERSE) The mill village was self-sufficient, with a mill store, post office, movie theater, café, churches, and three-story community building. Organizations included a Textile League baseball team, Masonic Lodge, and Scouts. Following the Depression and labor strikes of the 1930s, Walter Montgomery bought the mill in 1936 and changed the name to Startex. At its height in the 1960s the mill employed 1,100 workers. Demand for U.S. textiles declined and the mill closed in 1997. *Sponsored by Startex-Tucapau Preservation Foundation, 2016*
GPS Coordinates: 34° 56.185' N, 82° 5.661' W

42–32 The "Hub City"/Spartanburg Union Station

298 Magnolia St., Spartanburg

The "Hub City" (FRONT)
The first rail line to serve the Hub City, the Spartanburg & Union R.R., was completed in 1859. In 1873, the Atlanta & Charlotte Air Line R.R., later Southern Railway, linked Spartanburg to cities along the East Coast, resulting in major growth for the city and the local textile industry. Later, Spartanburg emerged as a major rail junction with 7 lines serving the city. The lines radiated outward like spokes on a wheel, leading to the moniker "Hub City." Spartanburg Union Station (REVERSE) Spartanburg Union Station, sometimes called Southern Station, was designed by architect Frank Pierce Milburn. Southern Railway built Spartanburg Union Station here in 1905 to serve their passenger trains. The main station was razed in 1973. The remaining section, which now houses the Hub City Railroad Museum, was built in 1915 to serve Southeastern Express, a railroad-owned parcel shipping company. *Sponsored by the Hub City Railroad Museum, 2018*
GPS Coordinates: 34° 57.221' N, 81° 56.242' W

42–33 The Church of the Advent

141 Advent St., Spartanburg

(FRONT) The Church of the Advent dates from the 1840s, when Episcopal services were held in Glenn Springs, Limestone Springs, and

Spartanburg. In 1848, the congregation was admitted into the Diocese of S.C. The Rev. L. Clements Johnson served as the first rector. The Gothic-style granite church was designed by second rector, the Rev. John DeWitt Mc-Collough, and consecrated to the glory of God in 1864.

(REVERSE) The church was enlarged in 1897 with transepts and a chancel designed by noted church architect Silas McBee. He also designed Pendleton Hall, which was completed in 1913. The Cleveland Memorial Bell Tower was added in 1915. In 1927, the scout hut was erected for Boy Scout Troop No. 1, founded in 1914 as the first troop in S.C. The church was listed in the National Register of Historic Places in 2000. *Sponsored by the Church of the Advent Archives Committee, 2018*

GPS Coordinates: 34° 56.983' N, 81° 55.482' W

42–34 Montgomery Building

187 N. Church St, Spartanburg

(FRONT) The Montgomery Building was completed in 1924. The 10-story Chicago skeletal frame construction skyscraper was designed by the firm of Lockwood, Greene & Co., who also designed many upstate textile mills. The home of Capt. John H. Montgomery, founder of Spartan Mills, once stood here and it was Montgomery's sons who developed the property as high-rise office space. Many companies associated with Spartanburg's textile industry once maintained offices here.

(REVERSE) In addition to office space the Montgomery Building also housed a theater and radio station. The theater, first known as The Montgomery and later as The Carolina, was used for live performances and later for motion pictures. In 1956 Elvis Presley performed here. The theater closed in the 1970s. The building was also home to Spartanburg's first commercial radio station. WSPA began broadcasting as an AM station in 1930 with studios on the top floor of the building. *Sponsored by BF Spartanburg, LLC, 2018*

GPS Coordinates: 34° 57.103' N, 81° 55.958' W

42–35 Little Africa

Intersection of Little Africa Rd. and S.C. Hwy. 9, Chesnee

(FRONT) Little Africa was one of a number of independent African American communities formed across the South after the Civil War. Founded ca. 1880 by former slaves Simpson Foster and Emanuel Waddell, it was originally just a few acres set aside for their relatives. It grew to several hundred residents as other families settled nearby seeking economic opportunity and refuge from white supremacy.

(REVERSE) Many early residents were farmers, and agriculture remained central to life in Little Africa for decades. By 1910, community leaders had built the two-room Africa School to teach local children. One of S.C.'s first Rosenwald Fund schools later opened there. Near the school, community members built Fairview C.M.E. ca. 1912, .5 miles east of here. Congregants first organized themselves ca. 1902. *Sponsored by Little Africa Community Members and Friends, 2019*

GPS Coordinates: 35° 10.124' N, 82° 1.661' W

42–36 Episcopal Church of the Epiphany

121 Ernest L. Collins Ave., Spartanburg

(FRONT) The Episcopal Church of the Epiphany was est. 1893 as a mission to Spartanburg's African American residents. Rev. Theodore D. Bratton (1862–1944) organized the church as an affiliate of historically white Church of the Advent. The earliest members of Epiphany met downtown in a building on Wall St. The church founded a school in 1904. Its first settled pastor Rev. Samuel Whittemore Grice (1881–1940) began service in 1905.

(REVERSE) The Church of the Epiphany moved to this site by 1912, when the current chapel was completed. S.C.'s bishop at the time called it "one of the most attractive and churchly buildings in the Diocese." Its new location along what was then South Liberty Street was a common settling place for freed blacks after the Civil War. After urban renewal in the 1970s, this was one of the few historic

structures left in the neighborhood. *Sponsored by the Church of the Epiphany, 2019*
GPS Coordinates: 34° 56.520' N, 80° 55.563' W

42–37 New Prospect Baptist Church

South of intersection of S.C. Hwy. 9 and S.C. Hwy. 11, Inman

(FRONT) The congregation of New Prospect Baptist Church formally organized on June 3, 1820, with a membership of twenty-six. They met at a simple log cabin meeting house near this site before erecting a larger building in 1837. Before 1820, congregants are thought to have met at leaders' homes as Mount Vernon Baptist Church.

(REVERSE) New Prospect was initially part of the Broad River Association of Baptists, later joining the Tyger River Association in 1844. Worshippers included local families and some of the people they held as slaves. Fires destroyed the church in 1922 and 1983. The current church building was finished in 1984. *Sponsored by New Prospect Baptist Church, 2019*
GPS Coordinates: 35° 7.889' N, 82° 2.669' W

Sumter County

43–1 Site of Manchester

N. King's Hwy. (S.C. Hwy. 261), about 3 mi. S of Wedgefield Post Office between Wedgefield and Pinewood

A flourishing town once stood here; settled before 1799; stage-coach relay; shipping center for cotton traffic by boat to Charleston; a busy point on Wilmington & Manchester Railroad, 1852–1872, (station was 1 mile southeast); noted for its taverns, horse-racing, games of ball-alley, and cock-fighting; raided by Union troops, 1865; and abandoned by railroad, 1872, in favor of Wedgefield. *Erected by Sumter County Historical Commission, 1949*
GPS Coordinates: 33° 50.377' N, 80° 30.998' W

43–2 Green Swamp Methodist Church

W. Liberty St. Ext. (S.C. Hwy. 763), 100 yds. E. of its intersection with Alice Dr. (S.C. Hwy. 120), Sumter

Site of First Methodist Church in vicinity of Sumter. Influenced by Bishop Francis Asbury, Richard Bradford gave land and with others built a wooden chapel in 1787, first called Bradford's Meeting House. Here Santee circuit riders preached until 1827 when church was closed and services held for convenience of the members in growing village of Sumter. *Erected by Sumter County Historical Commission, 1950*
GPS Coordinates: 33° 55.261' N, 80° 22.38' W

43–3 High Hills Baptist Church

S.C. Sec. Rd. 43–488, (Meeting House Rd.), ½ mi. E of S.C. Hwy. 261, Stateburg vicinity

(FRONT) Organized by Rev. Joseph Reese, this church was established Jan. 4, 1772. First located on land given by Dr. Joseph Howard (later moved to present site purchased from Gen. Thomas Sumter), it ordained, 1774, young Richard Furman, whose patriotic oratory caused Lord Cornwallis to put a price on his head, and who became one of the outstanding ministers of the gospel of his day.

(REVERSE) This church was a leader in the early struggle for liberty, religious and political, and was the mother of many churches. Inspired by Dr. Furman, Rev. John M. Roberts, Pastor here by 1799, opened Roberts Academy, First Baptist Educational institution in this state. Furman Institute followed in 1826, and later, the Southern Baptist Seminary. *Erected by Sumter County Historical Commission, 1950*
GPS Coordinates: 33° 59.144' N, 80° 32.037' W

43–4 Salem (Black River) Presbyterian Church

N. Brick Church Rd. (S.C. Hwy. 527), about 2 mi. N of U.S. Hwy. 378 and 4 mi. SE of Mayesville

(FRONT) This house of worship, commonly called Brick Church, was founded by Scotch-Irish settlers in 1759 on land given by Capt. David Anderson. Original log meeting-house

was replaced by frame building and named Salem Presbyterian Church (1768). The first brick church was built in 1802 and used until 1846 when the present church was built of brick made on the grounds.
(REVERSE) Old session house (1846) in the rear contains large library given by James Mc-Bride in 1862. Land for cemetery, dating from 1794, was deeded by Robert Witherspoon in 1830. Among the notable ministers to serve this church was Dr. Thomas Reese, scholar, teacher, and preacher before the Revolution. In 1867 Negro members withdrew to form Goodwill Presbyterian Church. *Erected by Sumter County Historical Commission, 1950*
GPS Coordinates: 33° 55.958' N, 80° 9.629' W

4.3–5 Early Charleston Road

N. King's Hwy (S.C. Hwy. 261) at its intersection with U.S. Hwy. 378/76, Stateburg vicinity

This road largely followed the Catawba Path (1696). Widened by Public Act, 1753, and called "The Great Charleston Road," it joined that city with Camden and "The Back Country." Over it came Indians, pack-animals laden with hides, drovers, rolled hogsheads of produce, wagoners, and stagecoaches. The armies of two wars passed over it. Like other main roads, it has often been called "The King's Highway." *Erected by Sumter County Historical Commission, 1952*
GPS Coordinates: 33° 56.738' N, 80° 31.437' W

4.3–6 St. Mark's Episcopal Church

Millcreek Rd., just SE of its intersection with Camp Mac Boykin Rd. (S.C. Sec. Rd. 43-51), Fulton Crossroads vicinity

(FRONT) By Act of Assembly St. Mark's Parish was established in 1757. The first Church stood at Halfway Swamp. Others were built near Williamsburg-Sumter Line, near Rimini, and near this site. These four churches were abandoned or burned. Soldiers and Patriots of the Revolution were members of St. Mark's Parish.
(REVERSE) The present church, designed by Edward C. Jones and Francis D. Lee, of Charleston, was built of brick made of local clay, on land given by R. C. Richardson and R. I.

Manning. The cornerstone was laid by Bishop Thos. F. Davis, Feb., 1854, and the church consecrated March, 1855. Six Governors and many noted citizens worshipped here. *Erected by Sumter County Historical Commission, 1952*
GPS Coordinates: 33° 44.844' N, 80° 30.721' W

4.3–7 Col. David DuBose Gaillard Engineer of the Panama Canal

Millcreek Rd., 3 mi. S of S.C. Hwy. 261, at intersection of Milford Plantation Rd. (S.C. Sec. Rd. 43-808) and Camp Mac Boykin Rd. (S.C. Sec. Rd. 43-51), Fulton Crossroads

(FRONT) Born at Fulton Crossroads, Sept. 4, 1859, David DuBose Gaillard spent his boyhood in this section. He was graduated from West Point in 1884, rising to rank of Lieutenant-Colonel of Engineers. During the Spanish American War he organized and commanded the 3rd U. S. Volunteer Engineers. He served on the general staff of the army and on major engineering projects, including the Panama Canal.
(REVERSE) Gaillard Cut of the Panama Canal was named for Col. Gaillard as a tribute to his distinguished work there. He planned and supervised the digging through the backbone of the continent at Culebra, acclaimed as a feat of engineering genius. He succeeded in this where others had failed, but gave his life to the effort, dying from the result of overwork, Dec. 5, 1913. *Erected by the Sumter County Historical Commission, 1979, replacing a marker erected by the same organization in 1953*
GPS Coordinates: 33° 43.653' N, 80° 30.708' W

4.3–8 Sumter's Court Houses

Sumter County Courthouse, corner of N. Main St. and Law Range, Sumter

(FRONT) By Act of 1798, Commissioners were named "To ascertain and fix upon the most central place for the erection of a court house in the District of Sumter," and meanwhile "to fix upon a proper place for the sitting of the court." During 1800–01, court was held in the John Gayle home (N.E. corner Main and Canal Streets) until a suitable court house was ready for use, Jan. 1802, though not completed until 1806.

(REVERSE) The second court house, designed by Robert Mills, was built of brick and stucco. It was authorized in 1820, completed in 1821, enlarged in 1848, and in use until 1907, serving also as a place of public gatherings for 86 years. This building remodeled is now occupied by the National Bank of S.C. The present court house, authorized in 1906, was dedicated in 1907. *Erected by Sumter County Historical Commission, 1953*
GPS Coordinates: 33° 55.343' N, 80° 20.483' W

43-9 General Thomas Sumter

Near intersection of Acton and Meeting House Rds., Dalzell vicinity

(FRONT) Monument to General Sumter stands 500 yards south. Born August 14, 1734, in Hanover County, Virginia, he was a frontiersman and Indian fighter. Coming to South Carolina by 1764, he became a planter. As Partisan leader and later brigadier general of state troops, he harried the British in the Revolution. He served in U. S. House and Senate and died at South Mount, June 1, 1832.
(REVERSE) Monument to General Sumter was erected by General Assembly of S.C. and unveiled Aug. 14, 1907, at ceremonies attended by Sumter Guards of Charleston, 300 U. S. Regulars, First Artillery Band and Sumter Light Infantry, with address by Hon. Henry A. Middleton Smith. Chairman of commission and moving spirit in erection of this monument was Col. John J. Dargan of Stateburg. *Erected by Sumter County Historical Commission, 1953*
GPS Coordinates: 33° 59.451' N, 80° 30.975' W

43-10 Battle of Dingle's Mill/Battle of Dingle's Mill April 9, 1865

S.C. Hwy. 521, 100 yds. from Turkey Creek Bridge, 1.5 mi. S of Sumter

Battle of Dingle's Mill (FRONT)
Here on Apr. 9, 1865, the day of Gen. Lee's surrender, was fought one of the last battles of the War between the States. 158 Confederates rallied by Col. Geo. W. Lee stopped, for several hours, the advance of 2700 Union troops under Gen. Edward E. Potter. Casualties: Confederate 12; Union 26.

Battle of Dingle's Mill April 9, 1865 (REVERSE)
A Confederate homeguard of old men, boys, and convalescents here made a gallant stand in an effort to halt Potter's Raid, an expedition which left Georgetown on April 5, laid waste the country, and by April 21 had accomplished its chief objective—the destruction of the railroads between the Pedee and Wateree. *Erected by Sumter County Historical Commission, 1956*
GPS Coordinates: 33° 52.556' N, 80° 20.143' W

43-12 Church of the Holy Cross, Stateburg (Episcopal)/Holy Cross Churchyard

[Marker number 43-11 was never assigned.]

N. King's Hwy. (S.C. Hwy. 261), Stateburg

Church of the Holy Cross, Stateburg (Episcopal) (FRONT)
This church is the successor to the nearby Chapel of Ease of 1770. Present building is on the site of the old Claremont Church of 1788, built on land given by General Thomas Sumter. Holy Cross is constructed of pise de terre, which is rammed earth. The cornerstone was laid on September 11, 1850.
Holy Cross Churchyard (REVERSE)
In the surrounding churchyard are the graves of many distinguished South Carolinians. Veterans of three wars rest here. The Parish House was built in 1956, designed in general to conform to the architecture of the present church structure. *Erected by the Sumter County Historical Commission, 1958*
GPS Coordinates: 33° 57.195' N, 80° 31.954' W

43-13 The Sumter Institute 1867-1901

Near the corner of Washington & Calhoun Sts., Sumter

(FRONT) A boarding school for girls located on the northeast corner of Washington and Calhoun Sts. Founded by Laura Fraser Browne and Eliza E. Cooper in 1867. Incorporated in 1888. H. Frank Wilson, president, 1892–96. This marker sponsored by Sumter Institute Association
(REVERSE) Sponsored by Sumter Institute Alumnae Association, 1958. This school

inspired Sumter's revival from war's desolation. Beginning as a one-room day school, it became a girls' boarding academy, ranking high among South Carolina educational institutions, a center of the social, spiritual, and cultural life of the community during Reconstruction days. *Erected by Sumter County Historical Commission, 1958*
GPS Coordinates: 33° 55.538' N, 80° 20.645' W

4.3–14 General Sumter Memorial Academy 1905–1911/General Sumter Memorial Academy

Near intersection of Acton Rd. and Meeting House Rds., Dalzell vicinity

General Sumter Memorial Academy 1905–1911 (FRONT)
This forerunner of the modern consolidated rural high school with Colonel John Julius Dargan, noted educator, as founder and principal, offered classes in agriculture, home economics, and music. Day students from four districts were transported by mule-drawn covered wagons. *Erected by Sumter County Historical Commission, 1963*
General Sumter Memorial Academy (REVERSE)
Acton, built in 1803 on this site by the Kinloch family, housed the Academy from 1905 until 1911 when the building burned. In 1908 the U. S. Department of Agriculture established one of the earliest school demonstration farms here. J. Frank Williams, agriculture teacher, later became the first Sumter County Farm agent. *Sponsored by Academy Faculty and Alumni, 1963*
GPS Coordinates: 33° 59.463' N, 80° 30.941' W

4.3–15 Richard Richardson

Millcreek Rd., 1.5 mi. S of S.C. Hwy. 261, Fulton Crossroads vicinity

An early plantation owner in this area, he was a Commissioner of St. Mark's Church who donated land for its construction. He was Magistrate and Delegate to the First and Second Provincial Congresses. In the Revolution he was Colonel in the Snow Campaign and later Brigadier General. Six Governors of South Carolina are among his descendants.

Erected by Sumter County Historical Society, 1969
GPS Coordinates: 33° 44.866' N, 80° 30.726' W

4.3–16 Birthplace of Mary McLeod Bethune

Intersection of S.C. Hwy. 154 & U.S. Hwy. 76, Mayesville

(FRONT) This noted humanitarian and educator was born five miles north of Mayesville, S.C., on July 10, 1875. She was one of the first pupils of the Mayesville Mission School, located fifty yards west of this marker, where she later served as a teacher. She died on May 18, 1955, and is buried at Bethune-Cookman College.
(REVERSE) Mrs. Bethune devoted her life to the advancement of her race. As the founder of Bethune-Cookman College, Daytona Beach, Florida, she directed its policy for thirty years. She founded the National Council of Negro Women in 1935. Honored by four presidents, she was a consultant in the drafting of the United Nations Charter. *Erected by Sumter County Historical Commission, 1975*
GPS Coordinates: 33° 58.885' N, 80° 12.557' W

4.3–17 Bethel Baptist Church

Bethel Church Rd., 2 mi. S of U.S. Hwy. 15 S, SW of Sumter

(FRONT) Bethel (Black River) Baptist Church was organized in 1780 and admitted to the Charleston Baptist Association in 1782. Its mother church was High Hills Baptist Church. Bethel was incorporated in December 1823. The Reverend Solomon Thomson served as its first pastor. John China, Revolutionary War veteran, is buried in the cemetery.
(REVERSE) The land for this church was donated by Hezekiah and Jesse Nettles. The present sanctuary, third on this site, was erected in 1849, of dense-grained Rosemary pine; all material cut and sawed by hand, the joints mortised and pegged. In 1967 a remodeling preserved the original dimensions, roof line, framing timbers, flooring, ceiling, and gallery. *Erected by Sumter County Historical Association, 1974*
GPS Coordinates: 33° 49.591' N, 80° 23.717' W

43–18 Lenoir Store

Horatio Hagood Rd. (S.C. Sec. Rd. 43-37), 2 mi. W
of N. King's Hwy (S.C. Hwy. 261), Horatio

Since before 1808, the Lenoir family have op-
erated a general store at the site of Horatio,
S.C. Lenoir's Store is mentioned in the 1808
will of Isaac Lenoir, and later appears on
Mills's 1825 map and McLaurin's 1878 map of
Sumter County. The present structure was
erected prior to 1878 and is maintained by
Lenoir descendants as a traditional country
store. *Erected by Sumter County Historical
Commission, 1976*
GPS Coordinates: 34° 1.312' N, 80° 34.081' W

43–19 William Tennent

Intersection of U.S. Hwy. 378/76 & N. King's Hwy
(S.C. Hwy. 261), Stateburg vicinity

Third Presbyterian preacher of this name,
Tennent died several miles south in 1777.
He was born in 1740 of a renowned family
of ministers and educators. From 1772 he
served as pastor of the Independent Church
of Charlestown. As a patriot, he prepared the
up country for the Revolution and advocated
the dissenters' appeal for equality in religious
rights. *Erected by The Presbyterian Synod of
the Southeast, 1977*
GPS Coordinates: 33° 56.667' N, 80° 31.398' W

43–20 Clara Louise Kellogg

Corner of S. Main & Dugan Sts., Sumter

(FRONT) Clara Louise Kellogg, said to be the
first American-trained prima donna, was born
near here in 1842. Her family later moved to
New York, where, at age 14, she began to study
voice, making her debut four years later. Miss
Kellogg soon became world famous. A leading
operatic soprano in America and abroad, she
sang in such cities as London, Vienna, and
Saint Petersburg.
(REVERSE) In 1873, Clara Louise Kellogg,
world-famous American prima donna, helped
organize the English Opera Company, one
of the earliest attempts in this country to
produce opera in English. At the height of
her career, Miss Kellogg included her native

Sumter on a concert tour. In 1887, she married
her manager, Carl Strakosch, and withdrew
from public life. She died in New Hartford,
Connecticut, in 1916. *Erected by Sumter
County Historical Commission, 1980*
GPS Coordinates: 33° 55.142' N, 80° 20.514' W

43–21 First Baptist Church

107 East Liberty St., Sumter

(FRONT) Organized in 1813 with 13 members,
this branch of Stateburg's High Hills of Santee
Baptist Church (founded before 1772) became
an independent congregation on September
24, 1820. It became known as Sumterville Baptist Church, and among early ministers who
preached there were Dr. John Roberts and Dr.
Richard Furman, noted pastor, patriot, and
educator.
(REVERSE) By 1820 this congregation had built
Sumter's first church. Subsequent buildings
date from 1854, 1902 (now Brown Chapel),
and 1973. Named First Baptist in 1901, the
church has been active in Southern Baptist
associations and conventions, as well as in
missions. It has sponsored four churches and
ordained a number of ministers. *Erected by
Sumter County Historical Commission,
1983*
GPS Coordinates: 33° 55.219' N, 80° 20.366' W

43–22 Furman Academy and Theological Institute

At the end of Dodgen Hill Rd. at Benenhaley Rd.,
.7 mi. S of S.C. Hwy. 441, Dalzell

(FRONT) Established by the S.C. Baptist Convention in 1825, Furman opened in Edgefield
in 1826. Later sites were here at High Hills
(1829–1834), Winnsboro (1837–1850), and
Greenville in 1851 (now Furman University).
In 1859 the theological department became
the Southern Baptist Theological Seminary,
which moved to Louisville, Ky. in 1877.
(REVERSE) The Rev. Jesse Hartwell was director
of this school at High Hills, which took its
name from Dr. Richard Furman (1755–1825),
noted patriot, theologian, and educator. A
native of New York state, Furman moved
to High Hills with his parents in 1770. The

property here was given to Sumter County Historical Commission by Furman University in 1978. *Erected by Sumter County Historical Commission, 1984*
GPS Coordinates: 34° 1.318' N, 80° 28.567' W

43–23 The Tuomey Hospital

129 N. Washington St., near the corner of Washington and Calhoun Sts., Sumter

Sumter Hospital was begun 1904 by Drs. S. C. Baker, Walter Cheyne, Archie China, H. M. Stuckey, and was built shortly thereafter nearby. Renamed Tuomey following purchase in 1913 with funds from will of T. J. Tuomey (1842–1897) which specified that a community hospital be established. Gifts were added by Mrs. Tuomey (Ella Bogin), & Neill O'Donnell, a relative. Generous citizens give their continuing support. *Erected by Sumter County Historical Commission, 1987*
GPS Coordinates: 33° 55.444' N, 80° 20.656' W

43–24 Sumterville Academy

N Washington St., near its intersection with Liberty St., Sumter

This site of one acre was given in 1837 for use for a public school by COL. JOHN BLOUNT MILLER (1782–1851), Lieutenant-Colonel in War of 1812, a public-spirited citizen and advocate of education; attorney at law, orator, writer, founder of Sumterville Library Society and Baptist Church; first notary public (1805) and commissioner in equity (1817–51) for Sumter District. *Erected by Sumter County Historical Commission, 1950*
GPS Coordinates: 33° 55.278' N, 80° 20.687' W

43–25 Military Post/Potter's Raid

Corner of W. Calhoun St. and Church St., Sumter

Military Post (FRONT)
After the Civil War ended in 1865, a Federal military occupation garrison was located for sometime in this area of Sumter. Known locally as "Yankee Camp," the post contained officers' quarters, barracks, and a guard house. Here sentinels could be seen guarding their posts while prisoners and soldiers performed various camp chores.

Potter's Raid (REVERSE)
On April 9, 1865, the day that Robert E. Lee surrendered at Appomattox Court House, Federal troops under Gen. Edward E. Potter occupied Sumter. They destroyed railroad property (locomotives, cars, shops, store houses, the freight depot), burned cotton and the jail, ransacked businesses and looted homes. Potter, whose headquarters was at the present courthouse site on Main Street, left Sumter on April 11th. *Erected by Sumter County Historical Commission, 1993*
GPS Coordinates: 33° 55.476' N, 80° 20.8' W

43–26 Henry L. Scarborough House

425 North Main St., Sumter

The Henry Lee Scarborough House was built 1908–09 by Scarborough (1866–1929), a leading Sumter County farmer, businessman, and public servant serving as county treasurer (1894–1902), commissioner of public works for six years and clerk of court (1912–1929). This house, an excellent example of the Neo-Classical Revival style, was listed in the National Register of Historic Places in 1995. *Erected by the Sumter County Historical Society, 1996*
GPS Coordinates: 33° 55.715' N, 80° 20.492' W

43–27 Elizabeth White House

421 North Main St., Sumter

The Elizabeth White House, built about 1854, was for many years the home of Miss White (1893–1976), a Sumter native who was an internationally-acclaimed artist and lifelong patron of the arts. White, who studied at the Pennsylvania Academy of Fine Arts, is best known for her etchings of South Carolina scenes. This Greek Revival cottage was listed in the National Register of Historic Places in 1978. *Erected by the Sumter County Historical Society, 1996*
GPS Coordinates: 33° 55.715' N, 80° 20.492' W

43–28 Bethel Methodist Church

Martinville Church Rd. (S.C. Sec. Rd. 43-12) & Lodebar Rd. (S.C. Sec. Rd. 43-100), Oswego

(FRONT) Established in 1856 by French

Huguenot families with the consolidation of Lodebar, Rembert, Clark, and Sardis Methodist Churches, all dating from the early settlement of Sumter District. The first minister was Rev. Bond English; trustees were James W. Rembert, W. F. Deschamps, Leonard Brown, Dr. Henry I. Abbott, Alex M. Watts, D. A. Foxworth, M. T. McLeod, N. S. Punch, and Rev. Henry D. Green.
(REVERSE) Members donated materials and both free and slave labor to construct the sanctuary, completed in 1858 under the supervision of James W. Rembert. Galleries were removed and ceilings lowered in 1887, and Sunday School rooms were added in 1951. This community was first named Lodebar for the nearby camp ground founded in 1787, but was renamed Bethel for this church in 1856. It has been known as Oswego since 1890. *Erected by the Sumter County Historical Commission, 1996*
GPS Coordinates: 34° 2.078' N, 80° 17.277' W

4.3–29   St. Paul African Methodist Episcopal Church

835 Plowden Mill Rd., SE of Sumter

(FRONT) This congregation was organized before the Civil War and held its services in a brush arbor until 1875 when its trustees bought land near this site from B. W. Brogdon and built a sanctuary there. First church officers were trustees Cuff Brogden, Robert Brogden, and James Witherspoon. By 1880 the church was affiliated with the South Carolina Conference of the African Methodist Episcopal Church.
(REVERSE) St. Paul A.M.E. Church bought this property in 1886 in conjunction with Pinehill Church, and the parcel was divided between the two churches in 1913. Initially part of a three-church circuit, St. Paul received its first full-time minister in the 1950s. The present sanctuary was completed in 1975 and an education annex was added in 1990. *Erected by the Sumter County Historical Commission, 1997*
GPS Coordinates: 33° 53.936' N, 80° 15.077' W

4.3–30   Battle of Beech Creek/The Civil War Ends in S.C.

North of Beech Creek on (N. King's Hwy.) S.C. Hwy. 261, Stateburg vicinity

Battle of Beech Creek (FRONT)
In April 1865 Confederates formed a defensive line along the high ground above Beech Creek to oppose Brig. Gen. Edward Potter's Federals advancing through Stateburg toward Camden. S.C. militia, the 9th Ky. Mounted Infantry, and the 1st Ky. "Orphan" Brigade fought off repeated Federal attacks in almost daily fighting between April 11th and 15th.
The Civil War Ends in S.C. (REVERSE)
A full Federal assault on April 15th pushed the Confederates back but the line held, forcing Potter to bypass the position. He briefly occupied Camden, but returned on April 19th. The 25th Ohio Infantry, 157th N.Y. Infantry, and 4th Mass. Cavalry charged across Beech Creek and drove the 53rd Ala. Partisan Rangers and 11th Ga. Cavalry from the line in the last action of the war in S.C. *Erected by the Beech Creek Historical Association and Sumter County Historical Commission, 1997*
GPS Coordinates: 33° 58.328' N, 80° 32.4' W

4.3–31   Enon Baptist Church

3805 Starks Ferry Rd. near Bethel Church Rd., Sumter

This church was organized in 1872 by Rev. Benjamin Lawson and held early services in a brush arbor. The first sanctuary, a log building, was built about 1883, during the ministry of Rev. S. B. Taylor; its timbers were reused to build a frame sanctuary in 1905. The present sanctuary here, dedicated in 1972, was built during the ministry of Rev. T. O. Everette, who served Enon from 1958 to 1980. *Erected by the Sumter County Historical Association, 2000*
GPS Coordinates: 33° 50.081' N, 80° 26.324' W

4.3–32   Potter's Headquarters/ Federal Order of Battle

At the Sumter County Courthouse, 141 N. Main St., Sumter

Potter's Headquarters (FRONT)
Federal troops commanded by Brig. Gen.

Edward E. Potter, on a raid through this area in the last days of the Civil War, advanced to Sumter after defeating a small Confederate force at Dingle's Mill on April 9, 1865. The Augustus Solomon House, which stood on this site, was Potter's headquarters April 9–11. His troops left Sumter April 11 to carry out the destruction of Confederate trains at Manchester. Federal Order of Battle (REVERSE) Potter's Provisional Division, Military District of the South: First Brigade (Infantry): 25th Ohio, 107th Ohio, 157th N.Y., 56th N.Y. (2 companies)/Second Brigade (Infantry): 54th Mass. (Colored), 32nd and 102nd U.S. Colored Troops/Other Units: 4th Mass. Cavalry (2 companies), 3rd N.Y. Light Artillery (Battery F), 1st N.Y. Engineers. *Erected by the Sumter County Historical Commission, 2002*
GPS Coordinates: 33° 55.349' N, 80° 20.485' W

43–33 Skirmish at Dinkins' Mill

N. King's Hwy. (S.C. Hwy. 261) at Dinkins' Millpond, N of Stateburg

(FRONT) Following the battle of Boykin's Mill on April 18, 1865, Federal troops commanded by Brig. Gen. Edward E. Potter advanced south to Middleton's Depot, on the Wilmington & Manchester R.R. below Stateburg. Here, on April 19, they attacked and attempted to flank a Confederate force commanded by Maj. Gen. P. M. B. Young which defended this crossing.
(REVERSE) The 25th Ohio Inf. and 157th N.Y. Inf., supported by the 102nd U.S. Colored Troops, skirmished with the 1st Ky. Brigade (Cav.), 53rd Ala. Partisan Rangers, 11th Ga. Cav., Hamilton's Arty., and S.C. militia. After slight losses on both sides most of the Confederate force withdrew towards Beech Creek. *Erected by the Sumter County Historical Commission, 2002*
GPS Coordinates: 34° 2.524' N, 80° 32.132' W

43–34 Oakland Plantation

N. King's Hwy. (S.C. Hwy. 261) above Rafting Creek, N of Stateburg

(FRONT) This plantation was established in 1735 with a royal grant to William Sanders, who built a house and tavern, or "publick house,"

here. That house was either extensively remodeled into or replaced by the present house featuring a central hall, built ca. 1816 by William Sanders IV and further enlarged by his son William Sanders V shortly before the Civil War.
(REVERSE) On April 18, 1865, in the last days of the Civil War, this house was the headquarters of Confederate Maj. Gen. P. M. B. Young and was struck by an artillery shell in a brief skirmish. The next day it was the headquarters of Federal Brig. Gen. Edward E. Potter and a field hospital. Renamed "Dixie Hall" in the 1950s, it remained in the hands of the Sanders family until 1981. *Erected by the Sumter County Historical Commission, 2002*
GPS Coordinates: 34° 3.91' N, 80° 33.212' W

43–35 Wedgefield Presbyterian Church

Presbyterian Dr., Wedgefield

(FRONT) This church was founded in 1881 with assistance from Harmony Presbytery. It had 12 charter members, with elders Cornelius McLaurin and James Caldwell and deacons Dr. Henry J. McLaurin and Edward H. McCutchen. Rev. H. B. Garris, Wedgefield's first minister, preached two Sundays a month in an old school nearby.
(REVERSE) The church sanctuary, often called "the church in the pines," was completed in 1882 on land donated for the church and cemetery by James H. Aycock. Rev. Garris, the first permanent minister, was installed by Harmony Presbytery in 1885. Rev. Perry H. Biddle had the longest pastorate, serving 1947–1968. *Erected by the Congregation, 2006*
GPS Coordinates: 33° 53.496' N, 80° 30.983' W

43–36 Battle of Stateburg

N. King's Hwy. (S.C. Hwy. 261), Stateburg

(FRONT) In April 1865 2,700 Federal troops commanded by Brig. Gen. Edward E. Potter left Georgetown in a raid against the railroad lines between Sumter and Camden. After briefly occupying Sumter Potter advanced to Manchester and remained there for a few days. On April 14 he ordered the 25th Ohio

Infantry and 107th Ohio Infantry to advance toward Stateburg in a reconnaissance in force. (REVERSE) The Confederate force here was the 9th Kentucky Mounted Infantry, a section of an artillery battery, and a few S.C. militia. After it drove back the first Federal attack Potter brought up the rest of his division on April 15 and fought "quite a Sharp skirmish" which forced some Confederates back but did not break their lines. On April 16 he bypassed Stateburg and proceeded to Camden. *Erected by the Sumter County Historical Commission, 2006*
GPS Coordinates: 33° 56.911' N, 80° 31.63' W

4.3–37 St. James Lutheran Church

1137 Alice Dr., Sumter

(FRONT) This church, the first Lutheran congregation in Sumter County, was organized in 1890 as a Home Mission, with six charter members and with Rev. F. W. E. Peschau as its first pastor. The congregation met in area churches, public buildings, or homes for several years. Its first church, built 1894–96, was a frame building at the corner of Washington Street and Hampton Avenue.
(REVERSE) The longest-serving pastors of St. James were Revs. J. Emmet Roof, who served 1947–1963, and Alvin H. Haigler, Sr., who served 1972–1992; the present brick sanctuary was built 1977–78 and consecrated during Rev. Haigler's pastorate. Six members of St. James entered the ministry between 1956 and 2002, and three members became missionaries to Africa in 1968 and 2002. *Erected by the Sumter County Historical Commission, 2006*
GPS Coordinates: 33° 56.683' N, 80° 23.115' W

4.3–38 Kendall Institute

Watkins St. between Manning Ave. (U.S. Hwy. 521) & S. Lafayette Dr. (U.S. Hwy. 15), Sumter

(FRONT) Kendall Institute, founded on this site in 1891, was one of the first black schools in Sumter. It was funded by the Board of Missions for Freedmen of the Presbyterian Church in the U.S.A. The institute was named for Mrs. Julia B. Kendall, late wife of Rev. Henry Kendall, secretary of the Board of Missions 1870–1892. It emphasized academics for

primary and secondary grades; some students boarded here in a girls' dormitory or a boys' cottage.
(REVERSE) The pastors of the Second Presbyterian Church of Sumter were also principals of Kendall Institute: Revs. J. C. Watkins (1891–1903); A. U. Frierson (1903–1916); J. P. Foster (1916–1928); and J. P. Pogue (1928–1932). Under Foster's tenure the institute boasted 272 students in 1918 and added agricultural and industrial classes and athletics. It closed in 1932 after the Presbyterian Church in the U.S.A. stopped funding its Southern parochial schools during the Depression. *Erected by the Sumter County Historical Commission, 2006*
GPS Coordinates: 33° 54.751' N, 80° 20.382' W

4.3–39 Mt. Zion Methodist Church

130 Loring Mill Rd., Sumter

(FRONT) This church, with its origin in a brush arbor where services were held during the Civil War, was formally organized in 1873 with a Rev. B. James as its first pastor. Col. James D. Blanding sold the trustees a small parcel to build their first permanent church, a frame building; church trustees bought additional acreage in 1883. The first Mt. Zion Methodist Church burned in 1913.
(REVERSE) The present church, also a frame building, replaced the first church. The cornerstone was laid in 1914; later renovations included the application of brick veneer in the 1980s. Rev. Isaiah DeQuincey Newman (1911–1985), who was pastor of Mt. Zion 1975–1982, was a civil rights activist and state senator 1983–85 and the first African American in the S.C. State Senate since 1886. *Erected by the Sumter County Historical Commission, 2008*
GPS Coordinates: 33° 55.145' N, 80° 23.591' W

4.3–40 Henry J. Maxwell Farm

Intersection of Pocalla Rd. (U.S. Hwy. 15) & Maxwell Ave., Sumter vicinity

(FRONT) Henry Johnson Maxwell (1837–1906), Union soldier, U.S. postmaster, state senator, and lawyer, lived here from 1874 until his death in 1906. Maxwell, the son of Stephen J. and Thurston Johnson Maxwell, was born free on Edisto Island. After serving as a sergeant in the 2nd U.S. Colored Artillery, he returned to S.C. to teach and work for the Freedmen's Bureau in Bennettsville.

(REVERSE) Maxwell, postmaster of Bennettsville 1869–70, was said to be "the first colored postmaster in the United States." He was admitted to the S.C. Bar in 1871 and represented Marlboro County in the S.C. Senate 1868–1877. Maxwell and his second wife Martha Louisa Dibble Maxwell bought this 44-acre farm in 1874, raising eight children. He was a longtime member of Sumter 2nd Presbyterian Church. *Erected by the Naudin-Dibble Heritage Foundation, 2008*
GPS Coordinates: 33° 53.612' N, 80° 20.482' W

4.3–4.1 Beulah School

3175 Florence Hwy., Sumter vicinity

This two-room African-American school was likely built between 1922 and 1930 for students in grades 1–7. It had 50–100 students and an academic year of four to five months until 1939 and six to eight months afterwards. Janie Colclough and Brantley Singletary taught here from 1932 through 1946. Beulah School closed in 1952 and was merged into Mayesville Elementary School. *Erected by Beulah A.M.E. Church, 2008*
GPS Coordinates: 33° 57.729' N, 80° 14.941' W

4.3–4.2 Temple Sinai

11 Church St., Sumter

(FRONT) Sumter's Jewish community, dating to 1815, has long been one of the largest and most influential in inland S.C. Mark Solomons, Franklin J. Moses, and Montgomery Moses brought their families to Sumter District from the old and well-established Jewish community in Charleston. Other families, from Spain, Germany, Poland, Russia, and other European nations, followed. Two organizations founded shortly after the Civil War would later join to form a congregation.

(REVERSE) The Hebrew Cemetery Society was founded in 1874, the Sumter Hebrew Benevolent Society was founded before 1881, and the two societies agreed to merge that year. A formal merger in 1895 created the Sumter

Society of Israelites, the official name of Congregation Sinai. The first synagogue, a frame building constructed by 1900, burned. It was replaced in 1913 by this Moorish Revival brick synagogue, listed in the National Register of Historic Places in 1999. *Erected by the Jewish Historical Society of South Carolina, 2009*
GPS Coordinates: 33° 55.305' N, 80° 20.797' W

4.3–4.3 Cane Savannah Plantation

Intersection of Wedgefield Rd. (S.C. Hwy. 763) and St. Paul's Church Rd. (S.C. Sec. Rd. 43–40), Cane Savannah

(FRONT) Cane Savannah Plantation was established in 1784 by a 4000-acre grant to Lt. Col. Matthew Singleton (1730–1787), state representative and officer who had served under Francis Marion during the American Revolution. The plantation is named for Cane Savannah Creek, a branch of the Black River. Singleton had moved from Va. to S.C. with his wife Mary James Singleton in 1753.

(REVERSE) Singleton built a house nearby, where he died in 1787.Cane Savannah then passed to his daughter Nancy and her husband Isham Moore (1750–1803), state representative and judge. Their son John Isham Moore (1792–1852) was a militia officer and state senator. The main house burned about 1920, cotton production soon declined, and Cane Savannah was eventually divided into tracts. *Erected by the Sumter County Historical Commission, 2010*
GPS Coordinates: 33° 54.087' N, 80° 26.999' W

4.3–4.4 Concord Presbyterian Church

3350 E. Brewington Rd., Sumter

(FRONT) This church, organized in 1808 by Rev. George G. McWhorter of the Salem Black River Presbyterian Church, held its first services in a brush arbor near Concord Springs. The next year Gen. Thomas Sumter donated two acres to the Concord Society to build a "Meeting House," which was built soon afterwards.

(REVERSE) Concord is the mother church of First Presbyterian Church of Sumter (1823). In 1832 noted college president and theologian

James Henley Thornwell (1812–1862) professed his faith during a service here, while he was teaching at an academy in Sumter. The present Greek Revival sanctuary was built in 1841. *Erected by the Congregation, 2010*
GPS Coordinates: 33° 54.572' N, 80° 13.381' W

43–45 Millford Plantation

Intersection of Camp Mac Boykin Rd. & St. Mark's Church Rd.,, Pinewood vicinity

(FRONT) Millford, 1 mile west, is the finest Greek Revival house in S.C. and one of the finest in America. It was built from 1839 to 1841 for John Laurence Manning (1816–1889), a planter, state legislator, and governor 1852–54, and his wife Susan Hampton Manning, a daughter of Gen. Wade Hampton I. Some contemporaries who thought it extravagant called the mansion "Manning's Folly."
(REVERSE) The three-story, stucco-over-brick house features a massive portico with six fluted Corinthian columns. Notable interior features include a dome and oculus over a circular stair, and double parlors. Many elaborate interior finishes are designs from Minard Lefever's Beauties of Modern Architecture (1835). Millford was designated a National Historic Landmark in 1973. *Sponsored by the Classical American Homes Preservation Trust, 2012*
GPS Coordinates: 33° 44.883' N, 80° 30.731' W

43–46 The Britton Community /Britton Siding

S.C. Hwy. 521, Just North of intersection with Britton Rd., Sumter vicinity

The Britton Community (FRONT)
Following his discharge from the Confederate Army, John James Britton began buying farm property on the Pocotaligo Swamp in 1864. His grandfather, Henry Britton, came to the Sumter area from Britton's Neck (Marion County) in 1806. By the late 1800s J. J. Britton had built a large home on this road just north of this location. Farming continued as the main business until the early 1900s.
Britton Siding (REVERSE)
Beginning as a large-scale farming operation, John Bossard Britton, grandson of J. J. Britton,

expanded the business to encompass other ventures, including a general store, cotton gin, planing mill, and fertilizer plant. Located along the Atlantic Coastline Railroad, which ran one mile east of here, Britton Siding's growth had made it a regular flag station by 1915. *Sponsored by the Sumter County Historical Society, 2014*
GPS Coordinates: 33° 50.5651' N, 80° 18.008' W

43–47 Lincoln High School

20–26 Council St., Sumter

(FRONT) Lincoln High School can trace its origins to the establishment of "Lincoln School," which was built as the first public school in Sumter, S.C., for African American students in 1874. Lincoln High School, which opened in 1937, occupies the same site and operated as an African American high school until 1969. Lincoln was highly regarded for its academic programs, with an award-winning student newspaper called "The Echo" one of many accomplishments.
(REVERSE) Funding from the Works Progress Administration offset labor costs of the large-scale construction. In 1952 funds from S.C.'s public school equalization program were used to add two large wings to the original building. In 1970 Lincoln H.S. consolidated with the formerly all-white Edmunds H.S. to form Sumter H.S. This building remained in use as the Council St. Campus of Sumter H.S. until 1983. It was listed in the National Register of Historic Places in 2015. *Sponsored by the Lincoln High School Preservation Alumni Association, 2015*
GPS Coordinates: 33° 50.563' N, 80° 17.943' W

43–48 55th Fighter Squadron

Shaw Drive, Building 1605, Shaw Air Force Base, Sumter vic.

(FRONT) Established as the 55th Aero Construction Squadron in 1917, the 55th was assigned to Shaw AFB from 1946–1951 and returned in 1994. During their 100 year history, the squadron participated in combat operations in the European Theater for both WWI and WWII, and provided nuclear deterrence during the Cold War. The squadron also participated

in the Gulf War, Operations Northern and
Southern Watch, and Iraqi Freedom.
(REVERSE) The 55th Squadron earned WWI
and WWII service streamers, as well as WWII:
Air Offensive Europe; Normandy; Northern
France; Rhineland; Ardennes-Alsace; Central
Europe; Air Combat, European-African-Mid
Eastern Campaign streamers. Since 1991 they
earned SW Asia: Defense of Saudi Arabia;
SW Asia Ceasefire; Iraqi Surge, Iraqi Sover-
eignty; New Dawn Campaign streamers, and
the Global War on Terrorism expeditionary
streamer. *Sponsored by Shaw AFB, United
States Air Force, 2017*
GPS Coordinates: 33° 58.818' N, 80° 28.384' W

4.3–49 *Randall v. Sumter School District*

Shaw Drive, Building 1505, Shaw Air Force Base,
Sumter

(FRONT) Though the U.S. Supreme Court had
declared racially segregated school unconsti-
tutional in the landmark decision *Brown v.
Board* (1954), school boards in much of the
South maintained segregated school systems
well into the 1960s. This included Sumter
School District No. 2, which served families
stationed at Shaw AFB. In 1963, 14 African
American airmen from Shaw challenged the
legality of the segregated system.
(REVERSE) The lead plaintiff was Col. James E.
Randall, who had been a Tuskegee Airmen
and flew missions in Korea and Vietnam, and
renowned civil rights attorneys Matthew J.
Perry and Ernest Finney Jr. argued the case.
In Aug. 1964 the U.S. District Court ruled that
Sumter County's segregated school system vio-
lated the rights of the plaintiffs and ordered
Sumter Co. to begin district-wide desegre-
gation in the fall of 1965. *Sponsored by Shaw
AFB, United States Air Force, 2018*
GPS Coordinates: 33° 58.818' N, 80° 28.384' W

4.3–50 *Pinewood Cemetery/African American Cemetery*

625 Gordin St., Pinewood

(FRONT) Pinewood Cemetery, also known as
Weeks Cemetery, began as a family burial

ground associated with the plantation owned
by James Dickson Weeks (1804–87). Both
Weeks and his wife, Elizabeth Ardis Weeks
(1815–93), have prominent headstones in the
cemetery. By the mid-1950s the Weeks Cemetery was filled and the cemetery was expanded,
with new burial plots added to the east.
(REVERSE) The Weeks plantation household
included both white and enslaved African
American members. Local tradition holds
that enslaved people were buried just to the
east of the original Weeks Cemetery. A 1956
plat, drawn when the cemetery was expanded,
denotes a "Colored Cemetery" between the
Weeks plot and the modern portion of Pinewood Cemetery. All of the African American burials are unmarked. *Sponsored by the
Friends of Wesley and Hattie Brown, 2018*
GPS Coordinates: 33° 45.246' N, 80° 27.602' W

4.3–51 **77th Fighter Squadron**

Shaw AFB, N. of Rhodes Ave., Sumter vic.

(FRONT) Established as the 77th Aero Squadron on 20 Feb 1918, the unit trained WWI
aviators. It was assigned to Shaw AFB from
1946–1951, returning in 1994. During its
100-year history, the squadron was part of
combat operations in the European Theater in
WWII, performed nuclear deterrence during
the Cold War, and participated in many
contingency operations from the Gulf War to
Operations Iraqi and Enduring Freedom.
(REVERSE) The squadron earned a WWII service streamer, as well as WWII: Air Offensive Europe; Normandy; Northern France;
Rhineland; Ardennes-Alsace; Central Europe;
Air Combat, European-African-Mid Eastern
Campaign streamers. Since 1991 they earned
SW Asia: Defense of Saudi Arabia; SW Asia
Ceasefire; Iraqi Liberation; Liberation and
Defense of Kuwait Campaign streamers, and
a Global War on Terrorism expeditionary
streamer. *Sponsored by Shaw AFB, United
States Air Force, 2018*
GPS Coordinates: 33° 58.732' N, 80° 29.167' W

43–52 79th Fighter Squadron

Shaw AFB, No. of Rhodes Ave., Sumter vic.

(FRONT) Established as the 79th Aero Squadron on 22 Feb 1918. The unit trained WWI aviators. It was assigned to Shaw AFB from 1946–1951, returning in 1994. During its 100-year history, the squadron was part of combat operations in the European Theater during WWII, performed nuclear deterrence during the Cold War, and were part of many contingency operations from the Gulf War to Operations Iraqi and Enduring Freedom. (REVERSE) The squadron earned a WWII service streamer, as well as WWII: Air Offensive Europe; Normandy; Northern France; Rhineland; Ardennes-Alsace; Central Europe; Air Combat, European-African-Mid Eastern Campaign streamers. Since 1991 they earned SW Asia: Defense of Saudi Arabi; SW Asia Ceasefire; Liberation and Defense of Kuwait; Iraqi New Dawn Campaign streamers, and Global War on Terrorism expeditionary streamer. *Sponsored by Shaw AFB, United States Air Force, 2018*
GPS Coordinates: 33° 58.732' N, 80° 29.167' W

43–53 WWII Prisoner of War Camp

Shaw Air Force Base, Sumter

(FRONT) From 1942 to 1945 more than 400,000 Axis-power prisoners of war were shipped to the United States from Europe and North Africa. Nearly 500 prisoner-of-war camps were built to house them, predominately in the South and Southwest. More than twenty camps were built in S.C., including one at this site on Shaw Field. Opened in March 1945, it operated only briefly and housed several hundred German prisoners.
(REVERSE) Many of the prisoners worked as laborers on local farms that were experiencing steep labor shortages with so many military-age men fighting in the war. Farmers paid both the laborers and the U.S. Government for their work. Later, many of the POWs were sent back to Europe to help rebuild cities devastated by war. Most were repatriated to Germany by 1947. Some POWs would later return and obtain U.S. citizenship. *Sponsored by Shaw AFB, United States Air Force, 2019*
GPS Coordinates: 33° 57.477' N, 80° 29.475' W

43–54 Goodwill School

221 N. Brick Church Rd., Mayesville

(FRONT) Goodwill School was established by missionaries from the Northern Presbyterian Church shortly after the Civil War. The school served freed people and their children. In an 1872 report, the Committee on Freedmen of the Presbyterian Church reported that Goodwill School served 350 students and was one of the most active Presbyterian parochial schools in South Carolina.
(REVERSE) The building that stands today was built about 1890. The Presbyterian Church continued to sponsor the school until 1933. Goodwill Presbyterian Church continued to operate the school until it was consolidated with Sumter Co. Public School District 2 in 1960. Throughout its history Goodwill School provided education to African American students from Sumter Co. and beyond. *Sponsored by Sumter County Historical Commission, 2019*
GPS Coordinates: 33° 54.731' N, 80° 8.949' W

Union County

44–1 Otterson's Fort

Whitmire Hwy. (U.S. Hwy. 176), just N of Beattys Bridge Rd. near the Tyger River, 9 mi. S of Union

One mile east of this point, built by the pioneers of Union County, was one of several stockades used as refuges during the Cherokee War, 1759–1761. It was probably named for James Otterson, an early settler on Tyger River. *Erected by Fair Forest Chapter, D. A. R., 1957* [First word ("one") printed on marker in lowercase.]
GPS Coordinates: 34° 35.353' N, 81° 35.277' W

44–2 Rose Hill Mansion

Rose Hill Plantation State Historic Site, 2677 Sardis Rd. (S.C. Sec. Rd. 44-16), E of Sedalia, 8 mi S. of Union

Erected in 1828–32 by William Henry Gist (1807–1874), lawyer, planter, legislator, and Secessionist Governor of South Carolina, Rose Hill was named for its landscaped rose garden. Its fanlights, carved doors and spiral staircase are noteworthy. The porches were added in 1860. In 1960 it became a State Park. *Erected by the S.C. State Commission of Forestry, Division of State Parks, 1963*
GPS Coordinates: 34° 36.317' N, 81° 39.933' W

44–3 Cross Keys House

Intersection of Cross Keys Hwy. (S.C. Hwy. 49) & Jones Ford Rd. (S.C. Sec. Rd. 44-22), Cross Keys

(FRONT) A post office was established in 1809 at Cross Keys, S.C. In 1812–14, Barrum Bobo erected this house at the intersection of the Piedmont Stage Road and the Old Buncombe Road. During the antebellum period, it was the center of a prosperous plantation. The gables of the building contain the cross keys insignia and the dates of construction. (REVERSE) On April 30, 1865, during the retreat from Richmond, Virginia, Jefferson Davis passed through Cross Keys, S.C.,

accompanied by the Confederate cabinet and his military escort of five brigades. Mrs. Mary Whitmire Davis, who owned the Cross Keys House at that time, afterwards related to her descendants the story of President Davis's luncheon at the house. *Erected by Cherokee District, United Daughters of the Confederacy, 1970*
GPS Coordinates: 34° 37.95' N, 81° 46.41' W

44–4 Fairforest Meeting

Cross Keys Hwy. (S.C. Hwy. 49) between Lower Fairforest Church Rd. (S.C. Sec. Rd. 44-77) and Boatman Springs Rd. (S.C. Sec. Rd. 44-78), 8 mi. SW of Union

1.5 miles SW stood the original Fairforest Baptist Church. The members, led by the Reverend Philip Mulkey, came from North Carolina to Broad River about 1759. In 1762, the church moved to Fairforest where, as the first Baptist church in the up country, it established other churches. During the American Revolution, it was in a Tory controlled area. *Erected by S.C. Baptist Historical Society, 1975*
GPS Coordinates: 34° 41.01' N, 81° 42.546' W

44–5 Union County Jail

W. Main St. at N. Enterprise St.,Union

(FRONT) The S.C. Board of Public Works had at least fourteen public buildings under contract in 1822–23, when Robert Mills, Acting Commissioner of the board, rejected a partially built jail of inferior brick before proceeding with this one. Experiences like this fitted him for his later career as Federal Architect and designer of the Washington Monument. (REVERSE) This building was completed in 1823 under the supervision of Robert Mills. Campbell Humphries was the contractor. The stone is said to have come from nearby Humphries Quarry. The north and west wings were added in 1954 and 1960 respectively with Robert Gibbes Fant as architect. The jail was placed

on the National Register of Historic Places in 1974. *Erected by Union County, 1976*
GPS Coordinates: 34° 42.913' N, 81° 37.568' W

44–6 Fairforest Church

Jonesville Hwy. (S.C. Hwy. 18), Bonham vicinity, 4 mi. N of Union

Led by Philip Mulkey, 13 converts of the Great Awakening movement traveled from N.C. to S.C. in 1759, settled on the Broad River, and organized a Baptist congregation, the oldest in the upcountry. Three years later, they moved to what is now Union County and took the name Fairforest. The present site succeeds several earlier ones in Union County. *Erected by the Congregation and S.C. Baptist Historical Society, 1984*
GPS Coordinates: 34° 46.05' N, 81° 38.417' W

44–7 Battle of Blackstock's

Intersection of Cross Keys Hwy. (S.C. Hwy. 49) & Monument Rd. (S.C. Sec. Rd. 44–51), Cross Keys vicinity

This battle of the Revolution took place on William Blackstock's plantation, 3 miles N. on the south side of the Tyger River, November 20, 1780. Gen. Thomas Sumter commanded the American patriots who repulsed Lt. Col. Banastre Tarleton's British forces. Sumter was wounded here, and this prevented his taking an active part in the war for several months. *Erected by Union County Historical Foundation and Daniel Morgan Chapter, Sons of the American Revolution, 1986*
GPS Coordinates: 34° 38.715' N, 81° 49.059' W

44–8 Sims High School

Union Blvd. (S.C. Hwy. 496), Union

Sims High School stood here from 1927 until the early 1970s and was the first black high school in Union County. It was named for its founder, Rev. A. A. Sims (1872–1965), who was its principal 1927–1951. It included grades 6–11 until 1949 and 6–12 afterwards, and educated blacks from Union and surrounding counties. In 1956 it moved to a new building on Sims Drive. The high school closed in 1970, but that building now houses the present Sims Jr.

High. *Erected by the Historical Marker Committee, Sims High School Alumni, 2004*
GPS Coordinates: 34° 42.43' N, 81° 37.077' W

44–9 Padgett's Creek Baptist Church

843 Old Buncombe Rd., (S.C. Hwy. 18), Union vicinity

(FRONT) This church was founded in 1784 by Revs. John Webb and John Cole, with Barnet Putman and William Wilbanks, Sr. as its first deacons. It was first called "the Church of Christ on Tyger River" and renamed Padgett Creek Baptist Church by 1800. The first sanctuary, a log building, stood about a mile south. (REVERSE) The second sanctuary, a frame building, was completed nearby about 1810. This sanctuary, described as "elegant and commodious" by an early church historian, was built 1844–48. It was enlarged by the addition of a portico and steeple in 1958. The church was listed in the National Register of Historic Places in 1971. *Erected by the Congregation, 2004*
GPS Coordinates: 34° 37.433' N, 81° 44.667' W

44–10 Union Community Hospital /Dr. L. W. Long

213 W. Main St., Union

Union Community Hospital (FRONT)
Union Community Hospital served the black community of Union County and nearby areas from 1932 to 1975. Built as a house ca. 1915, it was converted into a hospital by Dr. L. W. Long in 1932 with the support of several local churches. The building was covered in brick veneer in the 1930s, and a rear addition was built in 1949. The hospital was listed in the National Register of Historic Places in 1996.
Dr. L. W. Long (REVERSE)
Dr. Lawrence W. Long (1906–1985), a native of Union County, was educated at Howard University and Meharry Medical College before returning to Union and founding this hospital. Long also hosted annual clinics attended by doctors from S.C. and the Southeast 1934–1975. A lifelong leader in medicine and public health who was also active in civic affairs in Union, Long was named S.C. Doctor

of the Year in 1957 and National Doctor of the Year in 1958. *Erected by the L. W. Long Resource Center, 2004*
GPS Coordinates: 34° 42.877' N, 81° 37.539' W

44–11 Episcopal Church of the Nativity

320 S. Church St., Union

(FRONT) This parish was established in 1855 with the Rev. John DeWitt McCollough (1822–1902) as its first rector. This Gothic Revival church, consecrated in 1859 and called "probably the most exquisite gem of a Church in our whole Diocese" the next year, was designed by McCollough. He adapted a plan by architect Frank Wills, whose St. Anne's Chapel, Fredericton, in New Brunswick, Canada, is virtually identical.
(REVERSE) The inspiration for this church came from Mary Poulton Dawkins (1820–1906) of London, England, wife of Judge Thomas N. Dawkins, and her sister Jane Poulton McLure, wife of Maj. John W. McLure; their families founded this church. The fine marble baptismal font is by the noted American sculptor Hiram Powers (1805–1873). The Church of the Nativity was listed in the National Register of Historic Places in 1974. *Erected by the Congregation, 2009*
GPS Coordinates: 34° 42.598' N, 81° 37.177' W

44–12 Culp-Beaty Hall

300 N. Mountain St., Union

(FRONT) This Greek Revival house was built ca. 1857 for Benjamin Dudley Culp (1821–1885) and his wife Cornelia Meng Culp (1830–1888). Culp, a Union merchant, owned stores on Main Street with partners J. T. Hill and H. L. Goss from the 1850s through the 1870s. In early 1861 the "Johnson Rifles," a volunteer company soon to become a Confederate company in the 5th S.C. Infantry, received its silk flag in a ceremony here. The flag is now (2006) in the Union County Museum.
(REVERSE) In 1876 Gen. Wade Hampton, running for governor, made a campaign speech from the second-story portico. The house passed to the Beaty family through B. D. Culp's daughter Cornelia C. Beaty (1864–1892), wife

of William T. Beaty (1864–1944). This house, which features massive fluted Doric columns and a full-width two-story portico with large brackets and a pierced balustrade, was listed in the National Register of Historic Places in 1975. *Erected by the Union County Historical Society, 2006*
GPS Coordinates: 34° 43.158' N, 81° 37.308' W

44–13 Presbyterian Cemetery

Corner of N. Pinckney St. & Wedgewood Ct., Union

(FRONT) This cemetery, the oldest in Union, was established ca. 1817 and sometimes called the "village cemetery." In 1818 a Presbyterian "union" church used by other denominations as well moved here from a 1783 site about 2 mi. E. Alexander Macbeth then deeded the cemetery to the elders for use as a "burying ground of a Presbyterian Meeting House."
(REVERSE) This cemetery includes the graves of many prominent citizens of Union, both Presbyterians and members of other denominations. Governors David Johnson (1782–1855) and Thomas B. Jeter (1827–1883) are buried here. This is also the site of the first Union Presbyterian Church, a frame church built ca. 1819 and which was sold to the Union City School District in 1883. *Erected by the Union County Historical Society, 2006*
GPS Coordinates: 34° 43.15' N, 81° 37.45' W

44–14 Site of Union Church 1783–1819

Lockhart Hwy. (S.C. Hwy. 49), Monarch

(FRONT) A "union" church, one founded as a Presbyterian congregation but also used by other denominations, stood here from ca. 1783 to ca. 1819. The church was founded ca. 1765 at Brown's Creek, 2 or 3 mi. NE. It met there in successive log churches, but suspended services at times during the American Revolution. The congregation moved here and built a hewn-log church on this site not long after the war, probably ca. 1783.
(REVERSE) The church, with entrances on the west and south, featured a high boxed pulpit and was used by Baptists, Quakers, and others. Both Union County, founded as a judicial district in 1785, and its county seat Unionville

(now Union) were named for this "union" church. Several veterans of the American Revolution are buried here. The congregation moved to Unionville and built a church there ca. 1819. *Erected by the Union County Council, 2006*
GPS Coordinates: 34° 43.254' N, 81° 35.346' W

44-15 Fair Forest Plantation /Emslie Nicholson House

2403 Cross Keys Hwy., Union vicinity

Fair Forest Plantation (FRONT)
Fair Forest, named for nearby Fairforest Creek, was the plantation of Col. Thomas Fletchall (d. 1789), prominent militia officer before the Revolution and Loyalist during it. Captured in 1775 and briefly jailed, Fletchall moved to Charleston in 1780, then to Jamaica when the war ended; he died there in 1789. After the Revolution his plantation was confiscated and sold at auction.
Emslie Nicholson House (REVERSE)
Col. Thomas Brandon (1741–1802), who bought Fair Forest about 1785, had been a Patriot militia officer and was a longtime state representative and state senator. The Tudor Revival house built in 1923 near the site of the plantation house was designed by Robert & Co. of Atlanta. It was built for Emslie Nicholson (1863–1939), president of textile mills in Union, Lockhart, and Monarch. *Erected by the Union County Historical Society, 2008*
GPS Coordinates: 34° 40.883' N, 81° 41.317' W

44-16 Balloon Landing 1861

In front of Mt. Joy Baptist Church Recreational Building, 657 Pea Ridge Hwy. (S.C. Sec. Rd. 44-13), Kelton vicinity

(FRONT) On April 20, 1861, only days after the Civil War began at Fort Sumter, scientist and aeronaut T. S. C. Lowe (1832–1913) landed the Enterprise, a large gas balloon, on a nearby farm. Lowe was on a test flight in preparation for a trans-Atlantic attempt. Southeasterly currents had carried him 800–900 miles by air from Cincinnati to Union District in less than nine hours.
(REVERSE) Many locals assumed that Lowe was a Yankee spy, and it was difficult for him

to convince them that he was not. He was taken to Union and spent the night there under guard. Taken to Columbia, he was allowed to return north by train after several gentlemen vouched for his reputation as a scientist. Lowe later founded and directed a balloon corps in the U.S. Army in Virginia 1861–1863. *Erected by the Union County Historical Society, 2009*
GPS Coordinates: 34° 50.025' N, 81° 34.776' W

44-17 Sims High School

200 Sims Dr., Union

(FRONT) Sims High School, located here from 1956 to 1970, replaced a 1927 school on Union Boulevard, which in 1929 had become the first state-accredited high school for African-American students in the upstate. It was named for Rev. A. A. Sims, founder and first principal 1927–1951. James F. Moorer, principal 1951–1969, also coached the football team to 93 consecutive conference wins 1946–1954. C. A. Powell, who was white, was the school's last principal, 1969–1970.
(REVERSE) A new school was built here in 1956. Notable alumni include the first black head coach in NCAA Division I-A football, the first coach of a black college basketball team in the National Invitational Tournament, and the first black Chief of Chaplains of the United States Army. Sims High School closed in 1970 with the desegregation of Union County schools. This building housed Sims Junior High School 1970–2009. Sims Middle School opened on Whitmire Highway in 2009. *Erected by the Sims High School Reunion Committee, 2011*
GPS Coordinates: 34° 42.036' N, 81° 36.573' W

44-18 Thomas N. Dawkins House

Dawkins Ct., one block N of E. Main St., Union

(FRONT) This was the home of Thomas N. Dawkins (1807–1870) and his second wife Mary Poulton Dawkins (1820–1906). Dawkins, a lawyer, state representative, and judge, married Poulton, a native of London, in 1845. They named this house "The Shrubs" after her grandfather's home in England; Mrs. Dawkins designed her garden to feature shrubs.

Dawkins served in the S.C. House in the 1830s and again during the Civil War.

(REVERSE) Gov. Andrew G. Magrath, the last Confederate governor of S.C., left Columbia on Feb. 16, 1865, a day before it surrendered. Forced to move the state government to temporary headquarters, Magrath arrived in Union on Feb. 21. Dawkins invited him to stay here, and Magrath used the library as his office for several days in late February and early March. The house was listed in the National Register of Historic Places in 1973. *Sponsored by the Union County Historical Society, 2013*
GPS Coordinates: 34° 43.030' N, 81° 37.215' W

44–19 Poplar Grove School

Near 109 Tinkler Creek Rd., Union

(FRONT) Poplar Grove School opened in 1927 as a four-classroom school for African American students in Union Co. An extra classroom was added in 1941. In the mid-1960s the original four classrooms were removed and the remaining large classroom was made into a private residence. As of 2018, the remaining portion of the building is the last of the Rosenwald-era African American Schools in Union Co.

(REVERSE) Local tradition holds that Poplar Grove School was a Rosenwald Schol and it offered educational opportunity to African American students at a time when S.C. schools were racially segregated. Of the rural African American schools in Union Co., Poplar Grove produced the largest number of college graduates. *Sponsored by the South Carolina Humanities Council and Poplar Grove Alumni, 2018*
GPS Coordinates: 34° 36.294' N, 81° 35.007' W

Williamsburg County

45–1 Indiantown Presbyterian Church

4865 Hemingway Hwy. (S.C. Hwy. 512/S.C. Hwy. 261), about ½ mi. W of Indiantown

Organized in 1757 with John James and Robert Wilson as founding elders. Burned by the British in 1780 as "a sedition shop." Rebuilt after the Revolution. Present building begun in 1890, remodelled in 1919. Maj. John James, Revolutionary hero, is buried in the churchyard. *Sponsored by the Margaret Gregg Gordon Chapter, D. A. R., and erected by Williamsburg County, 1967*
GPS Coordinates: 33° 43.5' N, 79° 33.683' W

45–2 Battle of Lower Bridge

S.C. Hwy. 377 between U.S. Hwy. 521 and the Black River, Salters vicinity

Gen. Francis Marion and his men defeated the British at this place in March 1781. Advancing from the west and finding the bridge on fire, the enemy rushed the nearby ford, but here they were repulsed by troops led by John James, Thomas Potts, and William McCottry and forced to abandon their plan to invade Williamsburg. *Sponsored by the Margaret Gregg Gordon Chapter, D. A. R., and erected by Williamsburg County, 1958*
GPS Coordinates: 33° 43.5' N, 79° 33.683' W

45–3 Battle of Kingstree

S.C. Hwy. 527, W of Kingstree

Somewhere northwest of Kingstree on the night of Aug. 27, 1780, while scouting for Gen. Marion, a South Carolina militia company led by Maj. John James attacked a British force sent to ravage Williamsburg District, capturing prisoners and gaining information that persuaded Gen. Marion not to risk a general engagement. *Sponsored by the Margaret Gregg Gordon Chapter, D. A. R., and erected by Williamsburg County, 1958*
GPS Coordinates: 33° 40.359' N, 79° 50.406' W

45–4 Old Muster Ground and Courthouse

Williamsburg County Courthouse, 125 W. Main St., Kingstree

This lot was designated the parade ground in the original survey of the town in 1737. It served as the muster ground for the local militia during colonial and Revolutionary times. The present courthouse, designed by Robert Mills, was built in 1823. The second story burned in 1883 and was repaired. The courthouse was enlarged in 1901 and remodelled again in 1954. *Sponsored by the Margaret Gregg Gordon Chapter, D. A. R., and erected by Williamsburg County, 1964*
GPS Coordinates: 33° 39.809' N, 79° 49.869' W

45-5 Ebenezer United Methodist Church

Intersection of S.C. Sec. Rd. 45-34 & 45-40, Crooks' Crossroads, about 3 mi. NE of Hemingway

This church is said to be the oldest Methodist congregation in present Williamsburg County. It was established prior to 1822 when Samuel Heaselden, in his will, reserved two acres of land for the congregation; in 1837, his heirs deeded this land to the trustees of the church, "which will bear the name of Ebenezer." *Erected by Three Rivers Historical Society, 1978*
GPS Coordinates: 33° 46.629' N, 79° 24.637' W

45-6 Black Mingo-Willtown/Black Mingo Baptist Church

County Line Rd. (S.C. Hwy. 41/51), about 1 mi. N of Rhems

Black Mingo-Willtown (FRONT)
By 1760, Charles Woodmason had established a store near here, following a 1745 Act of the General Assembly that provided for clearing of the watercourses at the head of Black Mingo Creek. Soon thereafter, schooners carried local products to Charlestown; by the early 1760s Black Mingo settlement, later known as Willtown, had developed on the creek.
Black Mingo Baptist Church (REVERSE)
By 1804 Black Mingo stage stop had a tavern and about twelve wooden houses. About 1843, local merchant Cleland Belin built on his own land the Black Mingo Baptist Church. Now listed in the National Register of Historic Places, this church is all that remains of the early inland settlement. *Erected by Three Rivers Historical Society, 1981*
GPS Coordinates: 33° 37.017' N, 79° 26.117' W

45-7 Black Mingo Presbyterian Meeting House

Intersection of County Line Rd. (S.C. Hwy. 41/51) & Brown's Ferry Rd. (S.C. Sec. Rd. 45-24), Rhems

(FRONT) One of the earliest Dissenter congregations in South Carolina north of the Santee River was located about two miles south of here. Its church building had been completed by 1727 when the Rev. Thomas Morritt, Episcopal minister of Charleston, visited the area. (REVERSE) In 1742, this Dissenter congregation of the "Presbyterian Persuasion . . . of Scotland" received 100 pounds currency from Wm. Swinton for a new building. Also in 1742, William Thompson, Jr., willed the Dissenters 100 pounds and 4 acres, and their brick meeting house was soon built. By 1824, the church had dissolved. *Erected by Three Rivers Historical Society, 1982*
GPS Coordinates: 33° 36.137' N, 79° 26.427' W

45-8 Benjamin Britton Chandler 1854-1925

Henry Rd. (S.C. Hwy. 512), Henry vicinity, about 2 mi. NW of Rome Crossroads

Active in the Red Shirt campaign which resulted in Gen. Wade Hampton's election as S.C. governor, 1876, Chandler later served as supervisor of Williamsburg County. He was twice elected to the S.C. House and was known as "an honest and manly Representative" of his people. His home, which burned in 1985, was located here. *Erected by Three Rivers Historical Society, 1987*
GPS Coordinates: 33° 40.583' N, 79° 28.967' W

45-9 Early Settlers/Potatoe Ferry

Intersection of Thurgood Marshall Hwy. (S.C. Hwy. 527) and County Line Rd. (S.C. Hwy. 41), just NE of Black River, Warsaw vicinity, near Williamsburg County-Georgetown County line

Early Settlers (FRONT)

Among the first settlers of Williamsburg County, members of the Witherspoon family sailed from Belfast to Charleston in 1734, arriving about December 1. With a year's provisions, they embarked on an open-boat voyage. Traveling up the Black River, the settlers came ashore near here and lived in Samuel Commander's barn while constructing their "dirt houses."

Potatoe Ferry (REVERSE)
By 1775, Potatoe Ferry was operating on the Black River about ¼ mile downstream from here. During the Revolution, Brigadier General Francis Marion employed the ferry to transport troops on a planned expedition against British forces in Georgetown. In 1810, Bishop Francis Asbury, pioneer of American Methodism, crossed the river here during his travels. *Erected by Three Rivers Historical Society, 1989*
GPS Coordinates: 33° 29.685' N, 79° 32.447' W

45–10 Williamsburg Church
411 North Academy St., Kingstree
This Presbyterian church was established 1736 by John Witherspoon and other early Scotch-Irish settlers. Originally located about 1 mile east at Williamsburg Cemetery, the congregation moved here to Academy Street in 1890; the present sanctuary was completed in 1913. A number of congregations have come from this church, which is the oldest continuing ecclesiastical group in Williamsburg County. *Erected by the Congregation, 1993*
GPS Coordinates: 33° 40.127' N, 79° 49.915' W

45–11 Captain William Henry Mouzon
Sumter Hwy. (S.C. Hwy. 527), NW of Kingstree
(FRONT) This was the plantation of Capt. William Henry Mouzon (1741–1807), prominent militia officer in the American Revolution. Mouzon, of Huguenot descent, was educated in France as an engineer. He was a lieutenant in the 3rd S.C. Regiment, then raised the King's Tree Company and became its captain. This militia company numbered about 75 men when it was disbanded after Charleston fell to the British in May 1780.

(REVERSE) Capt. Mouzon's company reformed in July 1780, then joined Col. Francis Marion. British troops under Col. Banastre Tarleton burned Mouzon's plantation house and outbuildings in August. Shortly thereafter, on September 28, 1780, Capt. Mouzon was severely wounded in Marion's victory at Black Mingo Creek and forced to retire from further active service. He died in 1807 and is buried in the Mouzon family cemetery nearby. *Erected by the Williamsburgh Historical Society, 1996*
GPS Coordinates: 33° 43.98' N, 79° 55.993' W

45–12 Stephen A. Swails House
Corner of Main St. (S.C. Hwy. 261) and E. Brooks St., across from the Williamsburg Funeral Home, Kingstree
(FRONT) Stephen Atkins Swails (1832–1900), U.S. Army officer and state senator, lived in a house on this site 1868–79. Swails, a free black from Pennsylvania, came to S.C. in 1863 as a 1st sgt. in the 54th Massachusetts Volunteers (Colored), the first black regiment organized in the North during the Civil War. He was wounded twice and was commissioned 2nd lt. by Massachusetts Governor John Andrew in early 1864.

(REVERSE) Swails, one of only about 100 black officers during the Civil War, was promoted to 1st lt. in 1865. Afterwards he was an agent for the Freedmen's Bureau and practiced law in Kingstree. He was a state senator 1868–78 and served three terms as president pro tem. Swails was also intendant of Kingstree 1873–77 and edited the Williamsburg Republican. He is buried in the Friendly Society Cemetery in Charleston. *Erected by Williamsburg Co. Historical Society, 1998*
GPS Coordinates: 33° 39.921' N, 79° 49.446' W

45–13 Burrows's Service Station/ Cooper's Country Store
U.S. Hwy. 521 and Martin Luther King Ave. (S.C. Hwy. 377), Salters vicinity
Burrows's Service Station (FRONT)
This significant cultural and architectural example of a 20th-century country store was built in 1937 by Theron Burrows (1910–1973) when U.S. Hwy. 521 was finished from

Georgetown to Manning. A combination grocery and gas station with family living quarters on the second floor, it was affiliated with Esso (now Exxon) and had the motto "we serve the needs of the neighborhood." Cooper's Country Store (REVERSE) Burrows's Service Station sold not only staple goods, fresh meat, and produce, but also clothing, farm supplies, hardware, feed and seed, and automotive products and parts. After Burrows died in 1973 his son-in-law George Cooper bought the business, renaming it "Cooper's Country Store;" it now boasts several second- and third-generation employees and customers. *Erected by the Williamsburgh Historical Society, 2001*
GPS Coordinates: 33° 34.885' N, 79° 49.351' W

45–14 Mt. Zion A.M.E. Church

S.C. Hwy. 521, 4.5 mi. W of S.C. Hwy. 41, Andrews vicinity

(FRONT) This church was founded in 1867 on land donated by Moses and Matilda Watson. It was the first African American church in the Bloomingvale community and was organized by trustees Orange Bruorton, Augusta Dicker, Sr., Fred Grant, Esau Green, Fortune Session, Moses Watson, and Richmond White. It was also mother church to Bruorton Chapel A.M.E. Church, active until the 1950s.
(REVERSE) Mt. Zion also sponsored Mt. Zion School, which closed in 1958. The first sanctuary here, a wood frame church, was replaced in the early 1920s by a second wood frame church built by carpenter Rev. W. C. Ervin, Sr. The present church, the third serving Mt. Zion, was built 1948–1954 by carpenter Rev. W. C. Ervin, Jr. It was covered in brick veneer in the late 1950s. *Erected by the United Bruorton/Brewington Family Reunion and the Congregation, 2003*
GPS Coordinates: 33° 32.334' N, 79° 35.819' W

45–15 Cooper's Academy/Bethesda Methodist Church

2000 Cades Rd. (S.C. Hwy. 512), Cades

Cooper's Academy (FRONT)
Cooper's Academy, built in 1905–06, was a private boarding school for the black children

of this community until 1927, and a public school 1927–1958. Founded by Moses Cooper, H. J. Cooper, and Ada E. Martin, it was first called Cooper's Academy, Normal and Industrial Institute for Colored Youth. The school closed in 1958 when black schools at Battery Park and Cades were consolidated.
Bethesda Methodist Church (REVERSE)
Bethesda Methodist Church, founded in 1879, was organized in a brush arbor. Its first permanent church, a one-room sanctuary built about 1884, stood ¼ mi. W. The congregation bought a two-acre site here in 1893, and soon built a one-room frame church. The church was rebuilt in 1971, during the pastorate of Rev. J. B. Bowen. *Erected by the Cooper Academy/Bethesda Methodist Church History Committee, 2009*
GPS Coordinates: 33° 45.72' N, 79° 40.379' W

45–16 Suttons Methodist Church

3168 Santee Rd., Suttons

(FRONT) This church, founded in 1825, is the second oldest Methodist congregation in Williamsburg County. That year Robert Sutton gave the "Methodist Society" of this community a parcel 100 yds. square. Its first church, a frame building, was sometimes known as "Suttons Meeting House." It appears in Robert Mills' Atlas of South Carolina, published in 1825, as "Suttons M.H."
(REVERSE) Suttons Methodist Church also hosted several annual camp meetings between 1825 and 1860. The second church, a frame building, was completed in 1884. The present brick sanctuary was built in 1953. The cemetery, established in the first half of the nineteenth century, includes the plots of many early church families. *Erected by the Congregation, 2005*
GPS Coordinates: 33° 24.327' N, 79° 46.261' W

45–17 McCollum-Murray House

72 C.E. Murray Blvd., Greeleyville

(FRONT) This house, with Classical Revival architectural influences, was built ca. 1906 for Edward J. McCollum (1867–1942), African-American businessman and machinist with the Mallard Lumber Company. In 1922,

when twelve-year-old Charles E. Murray's
father William died, McCollum and his wife
Margaret (1886–1949) took him in. They considered him their foster son and encouraged
him to pursue his education.
(REVERSE) Charles E. Murray (1910–1999),
prominent African-American educator, lived
here from 1922 until he died. A graduate of
what is now S.C. State University, he taught
at Tomlinson High in Kingstree 1929–41 and
1945–60. He was principal of the Williamsburg County Training School (after 1972 C. E.
Murray Elementary and High School) 1960–
83. This house was listed in the National Register of Historic Places in 2006. *Erected by the
Dr. Charles E. Murray Historical Foundation
of Greeleyville, 2007*
GPS Coordinates: 33° 34.899' N, 79° 59.528' W

45–18 St. Alban's Episcopal Church

113 E. Church St., Kingstree

(FRONT) St. Alban's Episcopal Church has
long been the only continuously active Episcopal congregation in Williamsburg County.
It was founded in 1879 by Carrie Simons
(1849–1938), who persuaded Bishop W. W.
Howe to help her organize a mission church
with a few communicants. In 1887 Simons
moved to Kingstree and married Michael F.
Heller. She continued to support St. Alban's
until her death.
(REVERSE) This sanctuary, a fine example
of the Carpenter Gothic style, was built between 1889 and 1895 and was completed
during the tenure of the Rev. Herbert Jarvis.
Jarvis, priest here 1894–98, named the church
St. Alban's. The Revs. William Guerry and
William Moore, supply priests here 1891–94
and 1940–44, later became bishops. White
and black families have worshipped together
at St. Alban's since the 1890s. *Erected by the
Congregation, 2008*
GPS Coordinates: 33° 40.021' N, 79° 49.782' W

46–19 McClary Cemetery

Sims Reach Rd. (S.C. Sec. Rd. 45-285), .75 mi. S
of its junction with S.C. Hwy. 527, Kingstree vicinity

(FRONT) John McClary (1760–1833) established
this cemetery about 1789, locating it on high

ground near Boggy Swamp. McClary's
will, dated 1831, provided for headstones for
himself and his three wives: Mary Raphield
(1757–1792), Margaret Blackwell (1769–1789),
and Sarah Raphield (1760–1815). Many of John
McClary's descendants and other members of
the community are buried here.
(REVERSE) McClary, born in Northern Ireland,
came to S.C. by 1780. He and his brothers
served under Gen. Francis Marion during the
Revolution. In 1791 he was one of the commissioners who surveyed and laid out the town
of Kingstree. A Presbyterian elder, he helped
reunite the Williamsburg and Bethel churches
in 1828. He was perhaps the wealthiest planter
in Williamsburgh District at his death. *Erected
by the Williamsburgh Historical Society,
2009*
GPS Coordinates: 33° 37.874' N, 79° 46.509' W

45–20 Union Presbyterian Church

4501 S.C. Hwy. 377, Salters

(FRONT) This church was organized in 1857
by members of Williamsburg Presbyterian
Church who lived south of Black River and
wanted to worship closer than Kingstree,
8 mi. north. William Lifrage conveyed this
tract, on what was then Broomstraw Rd., to
trustees for the new congregation. The frame
church here was built between 1857 and the
time the congregation was more formally
established in 1863.
(REVERSE) In December 1863 thirty members
of Williamsburg Presbyterian Church received letters of dismissal to join this church,
with Rev. E. O. Frierson as their first pastor.
This church, built by that time, has served its
congregation for 150 years. A frame building,
its interior was remodeled about 1905 and a
portico was added in 1947. The cemetery here
dates from 1876. *Sponsored by the Congregation, 2013*
GPS Coordinates: 33° 34.042' N, 79° 49.988' W

45–21 Williamsburg High School

Earle Rd., opposite Earle United Methodist Church,
Andrews vicinity

(FRONT) The brick school built here in 1935
consolidated ten rural districts between the

Santee and Black Rivers into a single district. The school was dedicated in 1936 by Gov. Olin D. Johnston and state superintendent James H. Hope, with J. H. Felder as county superintendent. Williamsburg High School, built on ten acres, featured fifteen classrooms, a 500-seat auditorium, and a gymnasium. (REVERSE) The school's enrollment of 500 in grades 1–11 was said to be the largest of any consolidated school in S.C. when it opened. Its first graduating class, the Class of 1936, numbered only six graduates. Grade 12 was added in 1948. A new high school was built next to the 1935 school in 1956, and a new gymnasium replaced the 1935 one in 1964. Both schools closed in 1983. *Sponsored by Williamsburg High School Alumni, 2013*
GPS Coordinates: 33° 27.897' N, 79° 38.193' W

45–22 "Let Us March On Ballot Boxes"

Tomlinson St., between Lexington Ave and Eastland Ave, Kingstree

(FRONT) On May 8, 1966, Dr. Martin Luther King Jr. visited Kingstree. King's speech, which came after passage of the Voting Rights Act of 1965, urged an audience of 5,000 who had gathered on the grounds of Tomlinson High School to "march on ballot boxes" and use the vote as a means to pursue social and economic justice. King also called for grassroots mobilization and challenged each attendee to help register new voters.
(REVERSE) King referred to the current moment as a "second Reconstruction" and reminded the audience that during the first Reconstruction S.C. had elected African American representatives to serve in the State House and U.S. Congress. If they had done so before, then they could do so again. His message ranged beyond political and civil rights, to a vision of a day when all would enjoy adequate jobs, food, and security. *Sponsored by Williamsburg County Development Corporation, Tomlinson Alumni, Inc., and the citizens of Williamsburg County, 2016*
GPS Coordinates: 33° 40.174' N, 79° 49.134' W

York County

46–1 King's Mountain Battleground

Intersection of W. Alexander Love Hwy. (S.C. Hwy. 161) and N. King's Mountain St. (U.S. Hwy. 321), just N of York

Twelve miles northwest the Battle of King's Mountain was fought October 7, 1780. The 900 Whigs were under Colonels Campbell, Shelby, Sevier, Hill, Lacey, Williams, Cleveland; Lieutenant Colonels Hawthorn, Hambright; Majors McDowell, Chronicle, Winston, Chandler. The 1100 Tories were under Col. Patrick Ferguson, Capt. DePeyster, Lieut. Allaire. This brilliant victory was the turning point of the American Revolution. *Erected by King's Mountain Chapter, D. A. R. York, 1937*
GPS Coordinates: 35° 2.334' N, 81° 15.432' W

46–2 Bullock Creek Presbyterian Church

Intersection of Lockhart Rd. (S.C. Hwy. 49) & W. McConnells Hwy. (S.C. Hwy. 322), Bullock Creek

Under leadership of Dr. Joseph Alexander, pastor 1774–1801, this church, organized in 1769, was a Whig stronghold during the Revolution. Three hundred yards west is the site of one of the earliest academies in upper South Carolina, established in 1787 by Dr. Alexander. One and one half miles southwest is the site of Dr. Alexander's home, used as a hospital during the American Revolution. *Erected by Mrs. S. M. McNeel, of King's Mountain Chapter D. A. R., York, S. C., 1937*
GPS Coordinates: 34° 51.414' N, 81° 24.66' W

46–3 Trinity M.E. Church, South

22 E. Liberty St. (S.C. Hwy. 5/161), York

Organized 1824 by the Reverends Wm. Gassaway and Jos. Holmes with former as pastor, Trinity is the oldest M.E. Church, South in York County. The original building was erected on College Street, 1826. The first Sunday School in York County was organized at Trinity, March 3, 1829, by James Jefferys. *Erected by the members of Trinity M.E. Church, South, York, S.C., 1938*

GPS Coordinates: 34° 59.586' N, 81° 14.444' W

46–4 Jefferson Davis's Flight South, April 26–27, 1865/Last Confederate Cabinet Meeting, April 27, 1865

N. White St. (S.C. Hwy. 160), near W city limits, Fort Mill

Jefferson Davis's Flight South, April 26–27, 1865 (FRONT)

Confederate President Jefferson Davis and his Cabinet, making their way south from Richmond, Va. with a cavalry escort, stopped at Fort Mill on April 26, 1865. Davis spent the night at Springfield, the home of Col. Andrew Baxter Springs, about 3.5 mi. N; others stayed here at the home of Col. William Elliott White.

Last Confederate Cabinet Meeting, April 27, 1865 (REVERSE)

On the morning of April 27, 1865, Davis's Cabinet met here on the lawn to discuss the resignation of Secretary of the Treasury George A. Trenholm, appointing Postmaster General John H. Reagan to succeed him. The group, hoping to join the few Confederates still in the field, left for Yorkville later that day. *Erected by the White Homestead, 2005, replacing a marker erected by Elliott White Springs in 1940*

GPS Coordinates: 35° 0.963' N, 80° 57.072' W

46–5 Jefferson Davis' Flight

Corner of Eden Terrace and Myrtle Dr., Rock Hill

Having crossed the Catawba at Nation Ford, April 27, 1865, the President of the Confederacy fled south along this road following the fall of Richmond. He was accompanied by the remaining members of his cabinet and a detachment of cavalry under Gen. John C. Breckinridge. *Erected by Ann White Chapter, U. D. C.*

GPS Coordinates: 34° 56.766' N, 81° 1.236' W

46–6 Nation Ford

[No longer extant.]

Cherry Rd. (U.S. Hwy. 21) at the Catawba River, about 2 mi. N of Rock Hill

Two miles downstream, prehistoric crossing of Catawba Indians, site of legendary battle between Catawbas and Cherokees. Used by Virginia traders in 1652. Sumter with 500 men had a fortified camp here in July, 1780. Federal cavalry burned the railroad bridge in April, 1865.

46–7 Columbia Seminary Chapel

1043 Founders Ln., Winthrop University Campus, Rock Hill

This building was designed by Robert Mills and erected in Columbia, S.C., as the stable and carriage house of the mansion of Ainsley Hall; Chapel of Columbia Theological Seminary (Presbyterian), 1830–1927; first home of Winthrop College, 1886–1887. Woodrow Wilson accepted and confessed Christ here in 1873. The chapel was moved to Rock Hill, 1936. Site is 350 yards SW. *Erected by the Presbyterians of Rock Hill, South Carolina, 1967*

GPS Coordinates: 34° 56.498' N, 81° 1.821' W

46–8 First Presbyterian Church/ Church Leaders

234 E. Main St., Rock Hill

First Presbyterian Church (FRONT)

This church was begun in 1834 as Antioch Chapel of Ebenezer Church under the leadership of Rev. John O. Richards on land of the Steales and Workmans, 3 mi. south of Rock Hill. Mission moved in 1858 to this site, obtained from A. T. Black and later paid for by Mrs. Ann Hutchinson White and J. Spratt White. The church was organized on Nov. 13, 1869, with forty-six charter members led by Rev. R. E. Cooper, pastor.

Church Leaders (REVERSE)
First ruling elders: J. F. Workman, H. H.
Hart, R. D. L. McLeod. First deacons: Wm.
Whyte, A. H. White, J. N. Steele, R. W. Workman, David Gordon. Three pastors have been
moderators of the General Assembly, Presbyterian Church in the U. S.: Rev. W. T. Hall,
Rev. W. L. Lingle, Rev. Alexander Sprunt. The
longest pastorate has been that of Rev. Francis W. Gregg, 1910–1947. *Erected by the Congregation on the Occasion of the Centenary of
the Church, AD 1969*
GPS Coordinates: 34° 55.457' N, 81° 1.498' W

46–9 Sims Home Site

E. White St., between Stonewall St. and Jones Ave.,
Rock Hill

Near this spot stood the Rock Hill residence
of Robert Moorman Sims, Captain, C.S.A.,
who on April 9, 1865, carried the flag of truce,
which led to the surrender of Lee's forces at
Appomattox. He later was S.C. senator for
Lancaster County, 1868–70, and S.C. secretary of state, 1876–80. He began the beautification of the S.C. State House grounds. He
was born in Fairfield County in 1836 and died
at Columbia in 1898. *Erected by the Beulah
Meredith Chapter, United Daughters of the
Confederacy, 1970*
GPS Coordinates: 34° 55.316' N, 81° 0.866' W

46–10 White Home

Corner of E White St. & Elizabeth Ln., Rock Hill

About 1839, this former plantation house was
built by George Pendleton White (1801–1849)
and his wife, Ann Hutchison White (1805–
1880). It has since sheltered five generations
of a pioneer Rock Hill family. During the War
of 1861–1865 needy Confederate soldiers were
cared for here. The house contains a Prophet's
Chamber, reserved for the exclusive use of
visiting ministers. The east wing was erected
about 1878. Two renowned sons of this house
were the Reverend James Spratt White (1841–
1891) moderator of the Presbyterian Synod
of S.C. and founder of the Rock Hill Public
Library and of the Rock Hill public schools,
and Andrew Hutchison White (1843–1903),
intendant of Rock Hill, grand master of the

Grand Lodge of Ancient Free Masons of
South Carolina, and president of the State
Agricultural and Mechanical Society. *Erected
by the Ann White Chapter, United Daughters
of the Confederacy, 1972*
GPS Coordinates: 34° 55.542' N, 81° 1.344' W

46–11 Bratton House Site/Jefferson Davis' Flight

8 N. Congress St. (U.S. Hwy. 321), York

Bratton House Site (FRONT)
Robert Clendinen, Yorkville lawyer and
South Carolina senator from York District
(1816–30), purchased this land in 1813. The
house, which he built here before his death in
1830, was acquired in 1847 by Dr. James Rufus
Bratton, a surgeon in the Confederate Army.
It was razed in 1956.
Jefferson Davis' Flight (REVERSE)
Jefferson Davis, president of the Confederacy,
spent the night of April 27, 1865, in the home
of Dr. James Rufus Bratton, which was located
on this site. Davis, in danger of capture and
arrest by Federal troops, was attempting to
reach some remnant of the Confederate Army
in the South or West with which he could find
protection and continue the war. *Erected by
York County Historical Commission, 1977*
GPS Coordinates: 34° 59.607' N, 81° 14.541' W

46–12 Town of Sharon

York St. (S.C. Hwy. 49), Sharon

(FRONT) John L. Rainey, owner of large tracts
of land on which Sharon was established,
conveyed land to the Presbyterian church in
1889 and 1898, the Methodists in 1897, and the
Methodist Episcopal Zion church in 1904. The
First National Bank, established here in 1909,
was the only bank in western York County to
survive the depression. The Hill Banking and
Mercantile Company was founded prior to
1915.
(REVERSE) The town of Sharon grew up around
and took its name from Sharon Associate Reformed Presbyterian Church, which existed
here in 1800. When the Charleston, Cincinnati, and Chicago Railroad came through in
the 1880s, John L. Rainey donated land for
the station. The town was incorporated by

the S.C. General Assembly in 1889. *Erected by York County Historical Commission, 1979*
GPS Coordinates: 34° 57.11' N, 81° 20.286' W

46–13 McConnells

Intersection of Chester Hwy. (U.S. Hwy. 321) & McConnells Hwy. (S.C. Hwy. 322), McConnells

After the Kings Mountain Railroad was completed in 1852, the McConnellsville Post Office was established here in 1854. The town, named for the McConnell family, was incorporated in 1906. The first intendant was J. T. Crawford; wardens were J. F. Ashe, S. H. Love, J. O. Moore, and J. M. Williams. The post office was renamed McConnells in 1951. *Erected by York County Historical Commission, 1979*
GPS Coordinates: 34° 52.167' N, 81° 13.605' W

46–14 Village of Rock Hill/City of Rock Hill

E. Main St. and Hampton St., Rock Hill

Village of Rock Hill (FRONT)
Main Street was laid out on Alexander Templeton Black's land by Squire John Roddey in 1851. The post office was established in 1852. The village was incorporated by the General Assembly in 1870 with an area of one mile square; its center was Gordon's Hotel, which stood just west of here. John R. Allen was first intendant and wardens were J. M. Ivy, Dr. Thos. L. Johnston, John Ratterree, and M. W. Russell.
City of Rock Hill (REVERSE)
Rock Hill was incorporated as a city by act of the General Assembly on December 24, 1892, with an area of two miles square. Center of this square was a point in the middle of Main Street, opposite the Methodist Church. This marker stands near that point. The first mayor was Dr. John William Fewell and first aldermen were E. R. Avery, W. N. Irby, W. S. Morgan, E. E. Poag, J. J. Waters, W. H. Wylie. *Erected by York County Historical Commission, 1979*
GPS Coordinates: 34° 55.518' N, 81° 1.597' W

46–15 Ebenezer

Intersection of Ebenezer Rd. (S.C. Hwy. 274) and Herlong Ave., Rock Hill

The town of Ebenezer was incorporated in 1893. Dr. W. B. Fewell was the first intendant, and the first wardens were J. W. Avery, A. A. Barron, S. A. Fewell, and J. B. Neely. The post office here from 1890–1911 was called Old Point. Earlier post offices were Ebenezer Academy (1822–1837) and Ebenezerville (1837–1866). The town was annexed to Rock Hill in 1961. *Erected by the York County Culture and Heritage Museums, 2005, replacing a marker erected by the York County Historical Commission in 1980*
GPS Coordinates: 34° 57.426' N, 81° 2.778' W

46–16 Hickory Grove

Wylie St. (S.C. Hwy. 97), Hickory Grove

(FRONT) The land on which the town of Hickory Grove developed was granted to John McKenney in 1771 by George III of England. The Hickory Grove Post Office was in operation as early as 1831, and a free public school was located here by 1851. In 1888 the Charleston, Cincinnati, and Chicago Railroad completed its line through Hickory Grove, connecting this area to coastal S.C.
(REVERSE) At the time of its incorporation in 1888, Hickory Grove was one square mile in size, its center being the intersection of York Street and Wylie Avenue. J. N. McDill was the first intendant and Dr. J. W. Allison, J. W. Castles, T. M. Whisonant, and J. H. Wylie were wardens. The Associate Reformed Presbyterian Church maintained its orphanage here from 1897 until 1905. *Erected by York County Historical Commission, 1981*
GPS Coordinates: 34° 58.71' N, 81° 24.906' W

46–17 King's Mountain Military Academy Site/Micah Jenkins

234 King's Mountain St., York Place Episcopal Church Home for Children, York

King's Mountain Military Academy Site (FRONT)
Micah Jenkins and Asbury Coward, graduates of The Citadel in Charleston, founded this

Yorkville school in 1855. Closed during the Civil War, it was re-opened in 1866 by Coward, who later became head of S.C. Military Academy. The school closed permanently shortly before 1909, when the property was sold to the Episcopal Church Home.
Micah Jenkins (REVERSE)
Micah Jenkins, born 1835 at Edisto Island, graduated from The Citadel with first honors in 1854. Leaving King's Mountain Military School to enter the Confederate Army, he became known as a brave and daring leader, fighting through many significant battles and becoming brigadier general in 1862. He was killed at the Battle of the Wilderness, Virginia, in 1864. *Erected by York County Historical Commission, 1981*
GPS Coordinates: 35° 0.247' N, 81° 14.438' W

46–18 Town of Clover

Bethel St. (S.C. Hwy. 55), Clover
In 1887 the town of Clover was granted a charter by the General Assembly, its city limits to extend "one-half mile in every direction from the railroad depot." Clover Post Office had been established in 1874 with Zimri Carroll as postmaster. Six years later the Chester and Lenoir Railroad had completed its line here. The town's first textile mill, organized by Captain W. Beatty Smith, was chartered in 1890. *Erected by York County Historical Commission, 1981*
GPS Coordinates: 35° 6.678' N, 81° 13.596' W

46–19 McCorkle-Fewell-Long House/Oakland

Corner of College Ave. and Sumter Ave., Rock Hill
McCorkle-Fewell-Long House (FRONT)
This two-story frame house with central hall was a typical piedmont farmhouse when built, probably by Stephen McCorkle prior to 1821. Samuel M. Fewell significantly altered the house during his ownership 1867–1890. In 1906 the house was purchased and renovated by Alexander Long. In 1893 some of the land here was given to the state for the development of Winthrop College.
Oakland (REVERSE)
Rock Hill Land and Town Site Company,

incorporated in 1890, bought and sold land here. Developing the area known as Oakland were company founders William L. Roddy, James M. Cherry, Richard T. Fewell, W. Blackburn Wilson, Jr., and subsequent associates. The location of Winthrop in Oakland was assured when the company conveyed 30.5 acres to the state in 1893 for the sum of $5. The college opened in 1894. *Erected by York County Historical Commission, 1981*
GPS Coordinates: 34° 56.328' N, 81° 1.624' W

46–20 Town of Yorkville/Town of York

York County Courthouse, corner of W. Liberty & S. Congress Sts., York
Town of Yorkville (FRONT)
Formerly known as Fergus's Cross Roads, later Yorkville, this county seat was established in 1785 on land originally granted to John Miller in 1767. According to Robert Mills, the town in 1826 had eight stores, five taverns, a male and female academy, post office, printing office, and about eighty houses. The coming of the railroad in 1852 brought prosperity, which was reflected in fine homes, public buildings, and educational institutions.
Town of York (REVERSE)
During the Reconstruction period, turmoil in this area resulted in the sending of Federal troops under Col. Lewis Merrill to Yorkville and the declaration of martial law in 1871. Merrill was stationed at nearby Rose's Hotel. During this time the agricultural economy of the area suffered greatly, but Reconstruction ended in 1876 and recovery gradually took place. In 1896 textiles came to the town, whose name was changed to York in 1915. *Erected by York County Historical Commission, 1981*
GPS Coordinates: 34° 59.679' N, 81° 14.404' W

46–21 Fort Mill

Corner of Main & White Sts., Fort Mill
(FRONT) Fort Mill was established on land received in 1787 by Thomas Spratt, one of the first settlers in this area. According to local tradition, the 4,535-acre tract in Catawba Indian territory was given Spratt by the

Catawbas who were grateful for his assistance in routing the Shawnees from their lands. (REVERSE) Fort Mill is said to have taken its name from Webb's Grist Mill and a Catawba Indian fort near here. The post office was established in 1811 and named Fort Mill in 1833. Fort Mill Mfg. Co. (now Springs Mills) began here in 1887. Area native Leroy Springs later became its president. By the time of his death in 1931, Springs was a nationally-known textile magnate. Erected by York County Historical Commission, 1982
GPS Coordinates: 35° 0.432' N, 80° 56.718' W

46–22 Site of White's Mill

Intersection of Saluda Rd. (S.C. Hwy. 72) and Strait Rd. (S.C. Sec. Rd. 46–739), Ogden vicinity, about 3.7 mi. SW of Rock Hill

About 1½ miles south of here on Fishing Creek were a house and mill mentioned on a 1766 royal landgrant to Hugh White. British Colonel Banastre Tarleton and his Legion were encamped at White's Mill for several days in September 1780, during which time Tarleton lay "dangerously ill of a fever." *Erected by York County Historical Commission, 1983*
GPS Coordinates: 34° 51.54' N, 81° 4.344' W

46–23 Rock Hill Buggy Company /Anderson Motor Co.

Corner of W. White St. & N. Wilson St., Rock Hill

Rock Hill Buggy Company (FRONT)
In 1886 A. D. Holler, who had long owned a wagon and buggy shop in Rock Hill, founded Holler and Anderson Buggy Company with his son-in-law John Gary Anderson (1861–1937). Anderson built a factory here in 1892, with separate blacksmith, woodwork, trim, and paint shops. Renamed Rock Hill Buggy Company, it was known for quality materials and craftsmanship. By 1900 it was an industry leader and sold 6,000 buggies a year.
Anderson Motor Co. (REVERSE)
The firm became Anderson Motor Company and began building automobiles in 1916. Its first cars were the Anderson Six, a 6-passenger touring car, and the Roadster, a 3-passenger convertible. By 1923 there were 8 brightly-colored luxury cars with innovations such as

the first floor dimmer switch. At its peak in 1923 the factory made 35 cars a day. It built the last Anderson in 1924 and closed in 1926. Fewer than a dozen Anderson automobiles still survive. *Erected by the Culture & Heritage Museums of York County and the City of Rock Hill, 2009*
GPS Coordinates: 34° 55.772' N, 81° 1.731' W

46–24 William Hill 1741–1816 /Hill's Ironworks

Hands Mill Rd. (S.C. Hwy. 274), about 4 mi. N of Newport near Nanny's Mountain

William Hill 1741–1816 (FRONT)
William Hill, who served in the American Revolution and was present at many battles, built an ironworks near here on Allison Creek about 1776. Hill and his partner, Isaac Hayne, manufactured swivel guns, kitchen utensils, cannon, ammunition, and various farm tools. His ironworks was burned by British Capt. Christian Huck in June 1780.
Hill's Ironworks (REVERSE)
Rebuilt 1787–1788 near here on Allison Creek, Hill's Ironworks consisted of two furnaces, four gristmills, two sawmills, and about fifteen thousand acres of land by 1795. Around eighty blacks were employed here as forgemen, blacksmiths, founders, miners, and in other occupations. A nail factory with three cutting machines was operating here by 1802. *Erected by the York County Historical Commission, 1988*
GPS Coordinates: 35° 2.874' N, 81° 5.94' W

46–25 Town of Smyrna

Intersection of Rock Cut Rd. (S.C. Hwy. 97) and Main St. (S.C. Sec. Rd. 46–11/46–233), Smyrna

This town was named for Smyrna Associate Reformed Presbyterian Church, organized ca. 1842. An academy was established here by 1870, and in 1888 the Charleston, Cincinnati, and Chicago Railroad completed its line here. Four years later the post office was established. The town was incorporated in 1895, its limits extending one-half mile in every direction from the railroad depot. *Erected by the York County Historical Commission, 1981*
GPS Coordinates: 35° 2.554' N, 81° 24.456' W

46–26 First Associate Reformed Presbyterian Church/Dr. Arthur Small Rogers 1869–1964

201 E. White St., corner of E. White St. and S. Oakland Ave., Rock Hill

First Associate Reformed Presbyterian Church (FRONT)
This church was organized in 1895 with 26 charter members. The sanctuary, completed in 1898 and enlarged in 1911, was designed by Charlotte architect C. C. Hook and is listed in the National Register of Historic Places. Four pastors have served the church: Dr. A. S. Rogers (1895–1948); Rev. W. P. Grier (1948–1963); Rev. H. L. Smith (1963–1966), and Dr. R. J. Robinson (since 1967).
Dr. Arthur Small Rogers 1869–1964 (REVERSE)
Dr. Arthur Small Rogers (1869–1964), a native of Newberry, was educated at Erskine College, Erskine Theological Seminary, and Muskingum College. He came to Rock Hill in 1895 as a seminary student and became the first pastor of this church; his pastorate here was one of the longest in the history of the A.R.P. denomination. Dr. Rogers retired in 1948 and died in Rock Hill in 1964 at the age of 95. *Erected by the Congregation, 1996*
GPS Coordinates: 34° 55.583' N, 81° 1.445' W

46–27 Emmett Scott School

Emmett Scott Recreation Center, 801 Crawford Rd., Rock Hill

(FRONT) This school, founded in 1920, was the first public school for blacks in Rock Hill. Named for Emmett J. Scott (1873–1957), a prominent educator who was then secretary of Howard University, Emmett Scott School included all twelve grades until 1956 and was a junior high and high school from 1956 until South Carolina schools were desegregated in 1970. The original two-story frame school, built in 1920, was demolished in 1952.
(REVERSE) This property is owned by the City of Rock Hill and has been a neighborhood recreation center since the school closed in 1970. Seven principals served the Emmett Scott School during its fifty-year existence: Frank H. Neal 1920–1924; L. B. Moore 1924–1938; Ralph W. McGirt 1938–1959; W. H. Witherspoon 1959–1967; George Land 1967; Richard Boulware 1968; Samuel Foster 1969–1970. *Erected by Emmett Scott Alumni and Affiliates, 1996*
GPS Coordinates: 34° 55.038' N, 81° 2.298' W

46–28 Huck's Defeat

S.C. Sec. Rd. 46–165 (Brattonsville Rd.), ½ mi. from the intersection of Brattonsville Rd. and S.C. Hwy. 322, Brattonsville vicinity

On July 12, 1780, at Williamson's Plantation about one-fifth of a mile east from here, Loyalist forces under Capt. Christian Huck were defeated by American forces led by Cols. William Bratton, William Hill, Edward Lacey, Richard Winn, as well as Captain John Moffett. Six months after this battle, known as "Huck's Defeat," came the pivotal American victories at Kings Mtn. in Oct. 1780 and Cowpens in Jan. 1781. *Erected by the Catawba Chapter, Daughters of the American Revolution*
GPS Coordinates: 34° 52.422' N, 81° 10.878' W

46–29 David E. Finley Birthplace

Corner of N. Congress and Blackburn Sts., York

(FRONT) David Edward Finley, Jr. (1890–1977), first director of the National Gallery of Art, was born in this house. Finley moved to Washington, D.C. as a child when his father was elected to Congress and was educated at the University of S.C. and George Washington University Law School. He practiced law, served in World War I, then worked for Secretary of the Treasury Andrew W. Mellon.
(REVERSE) Finley and Andrew W. Mellon worked for years to establish a national art gallery with Mellon's collection as its nucleus, but Mellon died in 1937 just as the project began. Finley directed the construction of the National Art Gallery and was its director 1938–1956, building it into "a treasure trove of art." He was also chairman of the National Trust for Historic Preservation 1950–1962. *Erected by the Yorkville Historical Society, 2000*
GPS Coordinates: 34° 59.94' N, 81° 14.302' W

46–30 Episcopal Church of Our Savior

144 Caldwell St., Rock Hill

(FRONT) The first services were in private homes and at Rock Hill Academy 1857–1861. The church was organized Easter 1870 with the Rev. Roberts P. Johnson as its first rector. Founders included the families of Col. Cadwallader Jones, Halcott Pride Green, Maj. John R. London, Col. J. M. Ivy, and Samuel G. Keesler. This structure, completed in 1872 with alterations since, is the oldest church building in the city.

(REVERSE) The first parish house, built in 1922, contained one of the first gymnasiums in Rock Hill. Under the leadership of the Rev. W. Preston Peyton, it was a center for community activities. It was replaced by the present parish house, built in 1991, which contains a hall dedicated to the memory of the Rev. William W. Lumpkin (1910–1969), rector 1951–1969. *Erected by the Congregation and Friends in Memory of Walter Thomas Jenkins, Jr., 2000*

GPS Coordinates: 34° 55.563' N, 81° 1.487' W

46–31 Lacey's Fort

Intersection of W. McConnells Hwy. (S.C. Hwy. 322) and Blanton Rd., between Bullock Creek and McConnells

(FRONT) Col. Edward Lacey (1742–1813), prominent officer in the American Revolution in the S.C. backcountry, occupied this hill west of Turkey Creek in the late summer of 1780. Lacey, who commanded S.C. militiamen in the battles of Rocky Mount, Cary's Fort, Hanging Rock, and Fishing Creek in July and August, built a 15-ft. log stockade near this site.

(REVERSE) The fort here was sometimes called "Liberty Hill" by patriots but "Patriot's Folly" by Loyalists. It was occupied by S.C. militiamen under Cols. Edward Lacey and William Hill after they participated in the American victory at Kings Mountain 7 October 1780. Gen. Charles Cornwallis, commanding British forces in the South, later camped here briefly in January 1781. *Erected by the Historical Commission of York County, 2001*

GPS Coordinates: 34° 51.42' N, 81° 20.88' W

46–32 First National Bank of Sharon

4028 Woodlawn St., Sharon

(FRONT) This bank, built in 1909–10 by W. W. Blair, was the first bank in the town of Sharon, incorporated in 1889. Its first officers were J. H. Saye, president; J. L. Rainey, vice president; and A. M. Haddon, cashier. From 1910 to 1929 the U.S. Bureau of Engraving and Printing produced national bank notes for this bank. It was the only bank in western York County to survive the Depression.

(REVERSE) At the time of its merger with First Citizens Bank in 1986 the First National Bank of Sharon was the oldest continuously operating national bank in York County. The bank, with its distinctive arched corner entrance, is part of the Sharon Downtown Historic District, listed in the National Register of Historic Places in 2001. *Erected by the Culture & Heritage Museums of York County, First Citizens Bank, and the Rainey Foundation, 2008*

GPS Coordinates: 34° 57.072' N, 81° 20.412' W

46–33 Dickey-Sherer House

Wilson Chapel Rd., Sharon vicinity

(FRONT) A two-story log house built ca. 1771 for John Dickey (1703–1789) stood about 100 yds. NE until 1988, when it was moved to Kings Mountain State Park. Dickey, a native of Ireland, emigrated to Virginia with his wife Martha McNeely Dickey in 1737. They moved to this area after 1770, when Dickey received a grant of about 175 acres. He was an elder at nearby Bullock Creek Presbyterian Church.

(REVERSE) In 1844 Richard Sherer (1796–1888) bought the house and 76 acres from the descendants of Martha McNeely Dickey. Members of the Sherer family lived in the house until ca. 1918. In 1988 Ruth Duncan Latham donated the house to the S.C. Department of Parks, Recreation, and Tourism. It has been restored and now serves as the park headquarters for Kings Mountain State Park. *Erected by the Broad River Basin Historical Society, 2004*

GPS Coordinates: 34° 54.744' N, 81° 22.176' W

46–34 Clinton Junior College

1029 Crawford Rd., Rock Hill

Clinton Junior College, affiliated with the A.M.E. Zion Church, was founded in 1894 by Revs. Nero Crockett and W. M. Robinson as Clinton Institute. Named for Bishop Isom C. Clinton, it featured primary and secondary courses as well as a two-year college program. It became Clinton Junior College in 1965. Dr. Sallie V. Moreland (ca. 1898–2000) served 48 years as president of the college from 1946 to 1994. *Erected by Clinton Junior College, 2005*
GPS Coordinates: 34° 54.828' N, 81° 2.682' W

46–35 The CCC in York County /Tom Johnston Camp (S.C. #10), CCC

Piedmont Medical Center, 222 S. Herlong Ave., Rock Hill

The CCC in York County (FRONT)
One of the most successful of Franklin D. Roosevelt's New Deal programs was the Civilian Conservation Corps (CCC), created in 1933. It gave many young men and World War veterans jobs planting trees, fighting forest fires and soil erosion, and building state and national parks. Almost 50,000 men served in S.C. between 1933 and 1942. York County included three CCC camps: Kings Mountain, York, and here at Ebenezer.
Tom Johnston Camp (S.C. #10), CCC (REVERSE)
Young men, most of them between 17 and 25, lived in camps commanded by U.S. Army officers. The CCC camp here, described as "a busy little city," was named for Thomas L. Johnston, Rock Hill banker and farmer. It opened on August 19, 1935 and specialized in soil conservation. Its 250 men also participated in many educational, vocational, and recreational activities as well. The camp closed on July 27, 1942. *Erected by the Rock Hill Citizens Club and the York County Culture and Heritage Museums, 2005*
GPS Coordinates: 34° 57.372' N, 81° 3.12' W

46–36 Andrew Jackson Hotel /Vernon Grant

223 E. Main St., Rock Hill

Andrew Jackson Hotel (FRONT)
The Andrew Jackson Hotel, built in 1926, was funded with more than $250,000 raised by citizens of Rock Hill. Designed by Charles Coker Wilson, it is a fine example of the Beaux Arts style and has been called one of the city's "greatest triumphs." In 1938–39 many stars of early country and gospel music, such as the Monroe Boys, Delmore Bros., and S.C. native Arthur Smith, recorded hit songs for RCA in sessions here.
Vernon Grant (REVERSE)
The building also included the Rock Hill Chamber of Commerce before it closed as a hotel in 1970. Vernon Grant, director 1957–65, was a leading American illustrator from the 1930s to the 50s. Best known as the creator of Kellogg's "Snap! Crackle! Pop!" and Rock Hill's Glen the Frog, he illustrated thousands of ads and magazine covers. He married Elizabeth Fewell of Rock Hill in 1936. In 1947 Grant moved his family to York County, where he lived until his death in 1990. *Erected by the Culture and Heritage Museums of York County, 2006*
GPS Coordinates: 34° 55.518' N, 81° 1.597' W

46–37 McCrory's Civil Rights Sit-Ins/"Friendship Nine"

137 E. Main St., Rock Hill

McCrory's Civil Rights Sit-Ins (FRONT)
This building, built in 1901, was occupied by McCrory's Five & Dime from 1937 to 1997. On February 12, 1960, black students from Friendship Jr. College in Rock Hill were denied service at the McCrory's lunch counter but refused to leave. Their "sit-in" was one of the first of many calling attention to segregated public places in downtown Rock Hill. These protests lasted for more than a year.
"Friendship Nine" (REVERSE)
Many Rock Hill protesters were arrested, convicted, and fined. On January 31, 1961, ten students from Friendship Jr. College were arrested when they refused to leave McCrory's. Nine would not pay their fines and became

the first Civil Rights sit-in protesters in the nation to serve jail time. This new "Jail No Bail" strategy by "the Friendship Nine" was soon adopted as the model strategy for the Freedom Rides of 1961. *Erected by the Culture and Heritage Museums of York County and the City of Rock Hill, 2007*
GPS Coordinates: 34° 55.531' N, 81° 1.607' W

46–38 Rock Hill Cotton Factory
Corner of White and Chatham Sts., Rock Hill

(FRONT) This textile mill, built in 1881, was the first in Rock Hill and the first in S.C. to use steam power. A. E. Hutchison, J. M. Ivy, W. L. Roddey, and A. H. White founded the Rock Hill Cotton Factory to boost the city's status as a cotton market and to spur further industrial and economic growth. This two-story mill was designed and built by A. D. Holler and modeled after the Camperdown Mill in Greenville.
(REVERSE) This was the first of seven textile mills built here from 1881 to 1907. Rock Hill soon became the model of a "New South" city, its population grew from 800 to more than 6,000, and White Street became its "Textile Corridor" and industrial center. This mill, sold and renamed several times before it closed in 1967, was listed in the National Register of Historic Places in 1992 and renovated into offices in 2007. *Erected by the Culture & Heritage Museums of York County and the City of Rock Hill, 2007*
GPS Coordinates: 34° 55.681' N, 81° 1.628' W

46–39 St. Anne's Parochial School
648 S. Jones Ave., Rock Hill

(FRONT) St. Anne's Church, the first Catholic church in York County, was founded in 1919 by the Rev. William A. Tobin of Columbia. The first building, erected on Saluda Street in 1920, closed in 1961. St. Anne's opened its first parochial school in the church rectory in 1951, with 17 pupils in the kindergarten and first grade. A second grade was added in 1952. A new St. Anne's School opened here in 1956.
(REVERSE) In 1954 St. Anne's became the first school in S.C. to integrate, when it enrolled 5

students from St. Mary's, the predominantly African-American Catholic Church in Rock Hill. The school included grades 1–8 by 1957, and by 1961 had 15 black students enrolled. Worship services for St. Anne's Church were held in the school auditorium 1982–1994. In 1998, St. Anne School moved to a new facility on Bird Street. *Erected by the Culture & Heritage Museums of York County, St. Anne School, and The Hands of Mercy, Inc., 2009*
GPS Coordinates: 34° 54.822' N, 81° 1.11' W

46–40 Standard Cotton Mill/Highland Park Manufacturing Co.
369 Standard St., Rock Hill

Standard Cotton Mill (FRONT)
The Standard Cotton Mill, built in 1888–89, was the second textile mill in Rock Hill. It was promoted by John R. London and financed entirely by local citizens, including schoolchildren, who bought stock for 50¢ a week. Built by contractor A. D. Holler with 200 looms, it expanded to almost 500 looms by 1893, producing gingham cloth, shirting, and towels. The mill was a major factor in the growth and development of Rock Hill for the next 30 years.
Highland Park Manufacturing Co. (REVERSE)
The Standard Cotton Mill was sold to a Charlotte firm and renamed Highland Park Manufacturing Company # 2 in 1898. A significant expansion of the mill in 1907 resulted in the corresponding expansion of this mill village as an important community in Rock Hill. The mill, which closed in 1968, was listed in the National Register of Historic Places in 1992. It was renovated in 2005 as housing for seniors. *Erected by the City of Rock Hill, 2008*
GPS Coordinates: 34° 55.218' N, 81° 0.648' W

46–41 Rock Hill High School
At the site of the school, E White St., Rock Hill

(FRONT) Rock Hill High School has its origins in the Rock Hill Graded School, opened in 1888 for grades 1–9. The name Rock Hill High was first used in 1907–08 for a boys' school housed in the former Presbyterian High

School. A property dispute closed the school after a year; its students returned to Rock Hill Graded School. In 1914 a new coeducational Rock Hill High School was built here with students in grades 8–10.

(REVERSE) Grade 11 was added in 1917 and grade 12 was added in 1948. Additions or new buildings were constructed 1923–1952. Agriculture and commercial courses were added to standard courses, as were music, art, sports, and other activities. Rock Hill High and Sullivan Jr. High on Eden Terrace traded buildings in 1965. A new Rock Hill High was built on Springdale Rd. in 1977; the 1914 school was torn down in 1978. *Erected by the Rock Hill High School Class of 1961, 2007*
GPS Coordinates: 34° 55.408' N, 81° 1.151' W

46–42 U.S. Post Office and Courthouse/Citizens' Building

Corner of E. Main and Caldwell Sts., Rock Hill

U.S. Post Office and Courthouse (FRONT)
This building was described as "handsome in every respect" when it opened in 1932. It replaced a 1906 post office and housed a new district court and federal offices. It served as a post office until 1986 and provided offices and headquarters for several U.S. Congressmen, including Thomas S. Gettys 1965–75. Listed in the National Register of Historic Places in 1988, it was renamed in honor of Gettys in 1997.
Citizens' Building (REVERSE)
This six-story structure was Rock Hill's first high-rise office building. Built in 1924–25, it opened in 1926 with Citizens Bank & Trust on the 1st floor. The bank closed in 1927. Rock Hill National Bank opened on the 1st floor in 1941 and remained here until 1976. WRHI Radio, one of S.C.'s earliest stations, signed-on with studios on the 2nd floor in 1944 and broadcast from here until 1977. Civil Defense used an observation deck on the roof during World War II. *Erected by the Culture & Heritage Museums of York County and the City of Rock Hill, 2007*
GPS Coordinates: 34° 55.501' N, 81° 1.555' W

46–43 Black Plantation/Hampton Campaign

Corner of Black and Hampton Sts., Rock Hill

Black Plantation (FRONT)
This area was once part of the 448.5-acre plantation of Alexander Templeton Black (1798–1875), for whom Church Street was renamed Black Street. In 1851 Black deeded land for a right-of-way and depot to the Charlotte & S.C. Railroad. He also created and sold 23 town lots along a new Main Street, fulfilling his dream to establish a town here. The post office that opened nearby on April 17, 1852 was named "Rock Hill" after the hill the railroad tracks cut through.
Hampton Campaign (REVERSE)
The 1876 S.C. gubernatorial election was bitterly contested by Republican Gov. Daniel H. Chamberlain (1835–1907) and Democrat and ex-Confederate general Wade Hampton (1818–1902). On Oct. 12, 1876, citizens welcomed Hampton to Rock Hill near this site; this street was later renamed for him. Mounted Democratic clubs led him to Chatham Ave., where he spoke to a crowd of 3,000. The vote in York County and the upcountry was critical to Hampton's eventual victory. *Erected by the Culture & Heritage Museums of York County and the City of Rock Hill, 2008*
GPS Coordinates: 34° 55.47' N, 81° 1.628' W

46–44 Hickory Grove Schools

W side of Wylie Ave. between Wilkerson St. & Oxford Ave., Hickory Grove

(FRONT) Hickory Grove School, a two-story brick building constructed in 1916 on Peachtree St., was built for grades 1–11. In 1928 Hickory Grove High School, a one-story brick building, was constructed at the corner of Wylie Ave. and Wilkerson St. as a separate high school. The Works Progress Administration built a teacherage, bus shed, vocational building, and lunchroom in 1939.
(REVERSE) The high school and elementary school closed in 1975 and 1988, respectively. The 1916 elementary school was demolished in 1998; the 1928 high school was demolished

in 1990. The 1939 vocational building, lunchroom, and bus shed are still standing. In 2010 the vocational building houses a magistrate's office, and the lunchroom houses a senior citizens' community center. *Erected by Comporium and the Culture & Heritage Museums of York County, 2010*
GPS Coordinates: 34° 58.697' N, 81° 24.883' W

46–45 Springfield Plantation

U.S. Hwy. 21, 3 mi. N of Fort Mill

(FRONT) This house was built ca. 1806 for planter John Springs III (1782–1853), who served in the S.C. House 1828–34 and was a partner in several banks, railroads, and textile mills before the Civil War. His son Andrew Baxter Springs (1819–1886) enlarged and remodeled this house in the 1850s. He served in the S.C. House 1852–56 and was also a delegate to the Secession Convention.
(REVERSE) On April 26, 1865, Confederate President Jefferson Davis and his Cabinet, making their way south from Richmond, Va., stopped here. Davis and part of his party spent the night here at the insistence of young ladies who greeted them with flowers. Springfield, listed in the National Register of Historic Places in 1985, has been headquarters of Leroy Springs & Company since 1987. *Erected by Leroy Springs and Company, Inc., 2010*
GPS Coordinates: 35° 2.879' N, 80° 55.624' W

46–46 Rock Hill Depots/Rock Hill Street Railway

Trade St., Rock Hill

Rock Hill Depots (FRONT)
The first of six railroad depots was built here in 1851 on the Charlotte & S.C.R.R., after the citizens of Ebenezer objected to a new railroad yard proposed there. The town that grew up here was named Rock Hill after the flint hill found when the railroad bed was excavated. The six depots built here between 1851 and 1912 served passengers and freight for a combined 122 years. The two-story brick depot built nearby in 1912 was a local landmark until it was torn down in 1973.
Rock Hill Street Railway (REVERSE)
From 1891 to 1918 a street railway connected

Railroad Ave., the depots, Main St., and Winthrop College. Nicknamed "Rock Hill Electric Railway," it was pulled by mules named "Lec" and "Tric" for 21 years, then ran on battery power. Its rails were salvaged during World War II. Railroad Ave. was renamed Trade St. by 1920, as the largest retail center in the area. Trade St. was all but eliminated by urban renewal in 1973. *Erected by the Culture & Heritage Museums of York County and the City of Rock Hill, 2008*
GPS Coordinates: 34° 55.647' N, 81° 1.601' W

46–47 James Milton Cherry House

200 Oakland Ave., Rock Hill

(FRONT) The home of James Milton Cherry (1856–1920) stood here until 1974. Cherry was a businessman, public servant, agriculturalist, and real estate developer in Rock Hill for 50 years. He helped found the Young Men's Loan & Trust Co., one of the first banks here and later the Savings Bank of Rock Hill. Cherry was also a founder of the Rock Hill Light & Power Co., the Land & Town Site Co., and the Rock Hill Telephone Co.
(REVERSE) Cherry was intendant, or mayor, of Rock Hill 1890–91 and later a longtime city councilman. A partner in the Rock Hill Buggy Co., he founded the Carolina Traction Co. to power an electric street railway. He was known as "The Alfalfa King" for advocating hay as a cash crop and a national spokesman for diversifying crops. Cherry Road, named for him, was paved in 1920 and was one of the first concrete roads in S.C. *Erected by the City of Rock Hill and the Culture & Heritage Museums of York County, 2008*
GPS Coordinates: 34° 55.896' N, 81° 1.488' W

46–48 Bethesda Presbyterian Church

4858 McConnells Hwy. (S.C. Hwy. 322), McConnells vicinity

(FRONT) This church, which held services as early as 1760 about 1 mi. E, gave its name to a Scots-Irish community in this area before the Revolution. It was formally organized in 1769 by Rev. William Richardson. In 1771 John Fondren donated land here for a second frame church, built ca. 1780 after the church 1 mi. E burned.

(REVERSE) Rev. Robert B. Walker (1766–1852), the first permanent minister, served here 1794–1834. Bethesda hosted many revivals during the Second Great Awakening. The cemetery dates to 1777, and this brick church was built in 1820. The church and cemetery were listed in the National Register of Historic Places in 1977. *Erected by the Congregation for its 250th Anniversary, 2010*

GPS Coordinates: 34° 53.88' N, 81° 10.642' W

46–49 Unity Presbyterian Church

303 Tom Hall St., Fort Mill

(FRONT) This church, founded in 1788, predates the present town of Fort Mill and has occupied four sites in the vicinity. The first church, a log building, stood about 2 mi. NE in a community known as "Little York." It burned in 1804. A log church was built 5 blocks N, where the first church cemetery was laid out. That church burned in 1838, and the congregation moved to a site just E of the current location. (REVERSE) The second church cemetery, laid out nearby, became a municipal cemetery in the 1920s. The third sanctuary, a frame building, burned in 1880. A Romanesque Revival church built here in 1881, featuring a central bell tower, was constructed with bricks made from local clay. It and the historic cemeteries nearby were listed in the National Register of Historic Places in 1992. A new sanctuary was built here in 2010. *Erected by the Congregation, 2010*

GPS Coordinates: 35° 0.44' N, 80° 56.304' W

46–50 Hermon Presbyterian Church

446 Dave Lyle Blvd., Rock Hill

(FRONT) This church was organized in 1869 with Rev. J. A. Rainey as its first pastor and is one of the oldest black institutions in Rock Hill. With support from Northern Presbyterians, it ran a private school as early as the 1880s and was a mission church until 1912. This Gothic Revival sanctuary, built by church members who were also brickmasons and carpenters, was built between 1897 and 1903.

(REVERSE) This church features a three-story tower and pointed-arch and quatrefoil stained-glass windows. The congregation was a center of the local Civil Rights Movement of the 1950s and 1960s. Hermon Presbyterian Church was listed in the National Register of Historic Places in 1992. After the congregation moved to a new church 1 mi. SW on Heckle Blvd. in 1999, this historic church became a community center. *Erected by Historic Rock Hill, 2011*

GPS Coordinates: 34° 55.777' N, 81° 1.338' W

46–51 Barnett Brothers Circus 1929–1945/Bennett Brothers Circus 1929–1938

Near the intersection of E. Jefferson St. & Roosevelt St., York

Barnett Brothers Circus 1929–1945 (FRONT) This site was the winter quarters of the Barnett Brothers Circus, briefly known as the Wallace Brothers Circus, from 1929 through 1945. Founded by Ray W. Rogers (1889–1946), the circus was one of the first to travel by truck instead of by train. That freedom helped it succeed during the Depression and World War II. It began its tour each March or April with a performance in York, then returned in November.

Bennett Brothers Circus 1929–1938 (REVERSE) A highlight of the York Christmas parade was Santa Claus riding an elephant. In 1929 five sons of C. P. and Olive Bennett, living nearby, started their own circus with encouragement from Ray Rogers, who loaned them his big top and a few animals. All six Bennett sons and two daughters participated, along with other local children. Their circus performed in York, Rock Hill, Clover, and Sharon through 1938. *Sponsored by the Yorkville Historical Society, 2012*

GPS Coordinates: 34° 59.496' N, 81° 14.526' W

46–52 Yorkville Female Institute/ York Graded School

212 E. Jefferson St., York

Yorkville Female Institute (FRONT) Yorkville Female Institute or Yorkville Female College was the first school here, where private schools and then public schools operated 1854–1987. The institute, founded in 1852, opened in 1854 and built a three-story brick school. During the Civil War it housed refugees for a few years as classes were held on and off site. Yorkville High School, a private boys' and girls' school, operated here 1882–1888.

York Graded School (REVERSE)
Yorkville Graded School, a public school, occupied the old institution 1889–1900. It burned, and a new brick school was built in 1902, with an east wing and theater added in 1922. This became an elementary school after a new high school was built in 1951. In 1973 it was renamed to honor George C. McCelvey (1888–1973), principal 1912–1948. Since the school closed in 1987, McCelvey Center has been used by the community and the Culture & Heritage Museums of York County. *Sponsored by the Yorkville Historical Society and the Culture & Heritage Museums of York County, 2012*
GPS Coordinates: 34° 59.417' N, 81° 14.394' W

46–53 Bethel Presbyterian Church

2445 S.C. Hwy. 557, Clover vicinity

(FRONT) This church was founded in 1764 by Rev. William Richardson, who organized Scots-Irish settlers in this area, from both S.C. and N.C., into a congregation. Incorporated in 1786 as "The Presbyterian Church of Bethel Congregation," it grew steadily and built its third church building here in 1809. Bethel later became the mother church for eight area Presbyterian churches.

(REVERSE) The present church was described as "large and tasteful" when it was dedicated in 1873. It was listed in the National Register of Historic Places in 1980. The earliest marked grave in the cemetery is from 1774. The cemetery contains graves of veterans of all of America's wars, including several Patriots who fought at the nearby battle of Kings Mountain on October 7, 1780. *Sponsored by the Congregation, 2013*
GPS Coordinates: 35° 6.709' N, 81° 9.190' W

46–54 Oakland Avenue Presbyterian Church

421 Oakland Ave., Rock Hill

(FRONT) This church, which grew out of First Presbyterian Church, was discussed as early as 1901, with the first definite plans made in 1909. The leaders of First Presbyterian required that a new church be built before any members left the old church. This church was intended to serve the faculty and students at nearby Winthrop College (now Winthrop University).

(REVERSE) This Gothic Revival church, built in 1912, was designed by Charlotte architect C. C. Hook and held its first services in December 1912. The church was formally organized in September 1913, then dedicated that November. Rev. Alexander Martin, who served both First and this church 1912–14, became the first full-time pastor here in 1914, serving until 1931. *Sponsored by the Congregation, 2013*
GPS Coordinates: 34° 56.158' N, 81° 1.645' W

46–55 Laurelwood Cemetery

Laurel St. & W. White St., Rock Hill

(FRONT) This cemetery, the first municipal cemetery in Rock Hill, was established in 1872 when the city acquired a six-acre tract from Anne Hutchinson White. Her son Rev. James Spratt White and Mayor Iredell Jones laid out the cemetery, and Rev. White named it Laurelwood. Two additional tracts were acquired from the White family in 1894 and 1914 to enlarge the cemetery to its present size of almost twenty-five acres.

(REVERSE) Noted landscape designer Earle S. Draper was hired by the City of Rock Hill to design a plan for the 1914 tract, featuring winding drives and streets and selected plantings. This cemetery, with more than 11,000 graves, includes individuals and families significant in the history and development of Rock Hill from 1872 to the present. It was listed in the National Register of Historic Places in 2008. *Sponsored by the City of Rock Hill, 2014*
GPS Coordinates: 34° 55.847' N, 81° 1.822' W

46–56 Allison Creek Presbyterian Church/Clay Hill Graveyard

5780 Allison Creek Rd., York

Allison Creek Presbyterian Church (FRONT)
This church was founded in 1854 by residents
of the Clay Hill community on Allison Creek,
who were members of Bethel (1769) and Ebenezer (ca. 1785) Presbyterian churches. They
built this church soon afterwards, on land
donated by J. D. Currence. Rev. J. R. Baird,
the first pastor here, served until 1866.
Clay Hill Graveyard (REVERSE)
A graveyard just E of the church cemetery
was begun in the 1850s for both slave and free
black members of the church. Used until ca.
1896, it contains about 300 graves, 14 with
engraved stones and the rest marked by field
stones or unmarked. After 1865 black members of Allison Creek left to form Union Baptist (1892), Liberty Hill A.M.E. Zion (1896),
and New Home A.M.E. Zion (1897). *Sponsored by the Culture & Heritage Museums of
York County, 2014*
GPS Coordinates: 35° 2.401' N, 81° 6.153' W

46–57 Afro-American Insurance Company

538 S. Dave Lyle Blvd., Rock Hill

This building, constructed ca. 1909, was
built for the Afro-American Insurance Co.,
a black-owned firm with offices throughout
the South. It was designed by William W.
Smith (1862–1937) of Charlotte, an African-
American builder and designer. Smith, though
not a registered architect, was well-known
for his designs in N.C. and S.C. The building
was listed in the National Register of Historic
Places in 1992. *Sponsored by the African-
American Cultural Resources Commitee of
Rock Hill, 2014*
GPS Coordinates: 34° 55.313' N, 81° 2.125' W

46–58 Friendship School/ Friendship Junior College

445 Allen St., Rock Hill

Friendship School (FRONT)
Friendship College, on this site from 1910 to
1981, was founded in 1891 by Rev. M. P. Hall

and sponsored by the Sunday Schools of the
black Baptist churches of York and Chester
counties. It first met in nearby Mt. Prospect
Baptist Church before acquiring 9 acres here
in 1910. Also called Friendship Normal and
Industrial Institute, it was chartered in 1906
and combined an elementary and secondary
school curriculum with an industrial education for much of its history.
Friendship Junior College (REVERSE)
Dr. James H. Goudlock was president here 42
years, 1931–1973. The college dropped grades
1–7 in 1938, then dropped grades 8–12 in 1950
and became Friendship Junior College. In
1960–61, students who protested segregation
at "sit-ins" at McCrory's on Main St. became
pioneers of the Civil Rights Movement. The
struggling junior college closed in 1981, and
the buildings on this site were demolished
in 1992. *Sponsored by the African-American
Cultural Resources Commitee of Rock Hill,
2014*
GPS Coordinates: 34° 55.767' N, 81° 2.274' W

46–59 Mount Prospect Baptist Church

339 W. Black St., Rock Hill

(FRONT) This church, founded in 1883, first
held services in private homes in Rock Hill.
Formally organized as First Baptist Church,
Colored, in 1885, it was later renamed Mt.
Prospect Baptist Church. Its first pastor, Rev.
Thomas S. Gilmore (1855–1938), served here
55 years, until his death in 1938. The first
permanent church, a frame building, burned
and was replaced by a second frame church
about 1900.
(REVERSE) In 1891 Mount Prospect hosted
the first classes of Friendship College,
founded by Rev. M. P. Hall to offer an education to Rock Hill blacks before there was
a public school for them. The school held
classes here until 1910. The second church
burned in 1914, and this brick church, with
Romanesque Revival elements, was built in
1915. It was listed in the National Register of
Historic Places in 1992. *Sponsored by the
African-American Cultural Resources
Committee of Rock Hill, 2014*
GPS Coordinates: 34° 55.760' N, 81° 2.096' W

46–60 New Mount Olivet A.M.E. Zion Church

527 S. Dave Lyle Blvd., Rock Hill

(FRONT) This church, organized in 1873, held its first services in private homes and then under a brush arbor on Pond St., near the railroad tracks. First called Mt. Olivet Methodist Zion Church, it bought this tract in 1896 and built its first permanent church, a frame building, in 1898. Renamed Mt. Olivet A.M.E. Zion Church ca. 1900, it built this brick church 1923–27, under Revs. J. D. Virgil and C. L. Flowers.
(REVERSE) The church was renamed New Mount Olivet A.M.E. Zion Church in 1937. In May 1961, when an interracial group sponsored by the Congress of Racial Equality (CORE) launched the first Freedom Rides from Washington to New Orleans, the first violent opposition in the South occurred in the bus station in Rock Hill. That night this church held a mass meeting to honor and support the Freedom Riders. *Sponsored by the African-American Cultural Resources Committee of Rock Hill, 2014*
GPS Coordinates: 34° 55.307' N, 81° 2.113' W

46–61 William Bratton Plantation/ Battle of Huck's Defeat

1444 Brattonsville Rd., McConnells

William Bratton Plantation (FRONT)
In 1766 William Bratton and his wife Martha Robertson purchased 200 acres on the South Fork of Fishing Creek and built a single-pen log house here at the junction of several important colonial roads. The Bratton home was the first in what would become the community of Brattonsville. Bratton was an important civil leader, serving also as an officer in the patriot militia during the Revolution.
Battle of Huck's Defeat (REVERSE)
James Williamson also settled on Fishing Creek in 1766 and built a log house 400 yards SE of here. On July 12, 1780, 120 British and loyalist troops, led by Capt. Christian Huck, camped at the Williamson home. They were attacked and defeated by 140 local patriot militiamen led by Col. William Bratton and other officers in the Battle of Williamson's

Plantation, or "Huck's Defeat." *Sponsored by Culture & Heritage Museums of York County, 2015*
GPS Coordinates: 34° 51.906' N, 81° 10.531' W

46–62 Celanese Celriver Plant

1 Dunkins Ferry Rd., Rock Hill, off Cherry Road at the site of the old Celanese Celriver plant

(FRONT) This plant, once called "a miracle of modern technology," produced synthetic yarn and fibers for clothing, synthetic flakes for making plastic household and industrial goods, and other synthetics from 1948 to 2005. The Celanese Corporation of America chose this 1,100-acre site on the Catawba River for its capacity of 100 million gallons of water a day. The plant began operations in 1948.
(REVERSE) The plant had its own power plant, water purification and treatment plants, and chemical recycling. It was long among the largest employers in York Co., with an average of 1,600 and a peak of 2,300. Its work force was unionized, unlike most S.C. industries. At one time this plant was one of the largest producers of synthetic yarn in the U.S. As global demand for its products slowed, Celanese Celriver closed in 2005. *Sponsored by Culture & Heritage Museums of York County, 2015.*
GPS Coordinates: 34° 58.753' N, 80° 58.725' W

46–63 Battle of Stallings' Plantation

S.C. Hwy. 5 at entrance to Derby Downs subdivision, approximately four miles east of York

(FRONT) In 1768 John Stallings purchased 470 acres on Millican's Branch on Fishing Creek. During the American Revolution, Stallings (known locally as "Stallions") remained loyal to the British, but his wife, Sarah Love Stallings, was a Patriot. Such family divisions were common during the Revolution.
(REVERSE) In the late summer of 1780, Patriots and Loyalists met in a brief battle at Stallings' Plantation. Stallings' brother-in-law, Cpt. Andrew Love, and Col. Thomas Brandon led 50 Patriot militiamen against 35 Loyalists camped at Stallings' home. Although the Loyalists were defeated, Sarah Stallings was

accidentally killed. *Sponsored by the Catawba Chapter, Daughters of the American Revolution and the Culture & Heritage Museums of York County, 2016*
GPS Coordinates: 34° 58.391' N, 81° 10.136' W

46–64 York County Courthouses

Corner of S. Congress St. and E. Liberty St., York

(FRONT) There have been four York County courthouses on this site. The first courthouse was constructed of squared logs in 1786. In 1799 it was replaced by a small brick building. Noted S.C. architect Robert Mills designed a third courthouse, completed in 1825. This building was constructed of local granite and red brick, with a large portico and Doric columns. The second story was badly damaged by an accidental fire in 1892.
(REVERSE) The 1825 courthouse was remodeled following the 1892 fire. It was replaced by a Classical style courthouse completed in 1915. Designed by William Augustus Edwards, the courthouse was one of nine Edwards designed county courthouses in S.C. The monumental two-story yellow brick building features a colossal Ionic tetrastyle portico. It was listed in the National Register of Historic Places in 1981 and renovated in 2016. *Sponsored by the Yorkville Historical Society and the Culture & Heritage Museums of York County, 2016*
GPS Coordinates: 34° 59.641' N, 81° 14.533' W

46–65 Elias Hill Homeplace /Liberian Migration

5780 Allison Creek Rd., Rock Hill vicinity

Elias Hill Homeplace (FRONT)
Elias Hill (1819–1872) was born enslaved at Hill's Ironworks on Allison Creek. He and his parents were emancipated prior to 1860. Although physically paralyzed at an early age, Elias was well educated and became a Baptist minister, a school teacher, and a Union League leader. In 1869 he purchased 40 acres from J. M. Ross on Allison Creek ¼ mi. E of here.
Liberian Migration (REVERSE)
During Reconstruction (1865–1877), the Ku Klux Klan persecuted Rev. Hill and other freedmen in York County. In October 1871, 166 free blacks from Clay Hill emigrated to Liberia, West Africa, led by Elias Hill, Solomon Hill, June Moore, and Madison, Harriet, and George Simril. Arriving in Liberia in December, they began new lives at Arthington as planters and political leaders. *Sponsored by Culture & Heritage Museums and Allison Creek Presbyterian Church, 2017*
GPS Coordinates: 35° 2.401' N, 81° 6.160' W

46–66 Wright Funeral Home

8 Hunter St., York

(FRONT) Isaac "Bub" Wright Jr. was a master craftsman who began making caskets in the early 1900s. In 1914 he began Wright Funeral Home at this location. The two-story building here served as a funeral parlor and chapel, with an embalming room in the rear. Later, a pressing club (dry cleaners) also operated at the rear of the building. The second floor served as a casket making shop. Isaac Wright died in 1918, but his widow, Fannie C. Wright, continued to operate the business.
(REVERSE) Wright Funeral Home was among the earliest black-owned businesses in York and remains family-owned after 100 years. It played an important role serving the African American community during the era of racial segregation. The Wright family also operated a grocery store, which was replaced by a modern brick funeral home in 1985. In 1998, the original funeral home building was repurposed as the Alice Wright Smith Historical Museum. *Sponsored by the Yorkville Historical Society, 2018*
GPS Coordinates: 34° 59.481' N, 81° 14.105' W

46–67 Brick House/Lynching of Jim Williams

Brick House (FRONT)
In 1841, Dr. John S. Bratton began construction of a new, all-brick two-story house at Brattonsville. Completed ca. 1843, the Greek Revival building housed the Brattonsville Store and Post Office. A two-story rear frame section was added ca. 1855 to house the Brattonsville School. Napoleon Bratton took over the store by 1870 and constructed a new store building ca. 1885. It closed in 1915.
Lynching of Jim Williams (REVERSE)

In March 1871, York Co. Ku Klux Klan members, led by Dr. J. Rufus Bratton, lynched black militia Capt. James Williams, hanging him from a tree near his home 1.5 miles away. His body was carried to the Brick House the next day where a coroner's inquest was held. The murder was part of a wave of Reconstruction-era Klan violence that led to a declaration of martial law in nine S.C. counties. *Sponsored by Culture and Heritage Museums of York County, 2019*
GPS Coordinates: 34° 51.841' N, 81° 10.526' W

46–68 George Fish School

401 Steele St., Fort Mill

(FRONT) This was the site of Fort Mill's longest operating school dedicated to African Americans. Built on a 4-acre parcel acquired in 1925, the brick school opened in 1926 and cost $12,200, a portion of which was paid by the Julius Rosenwald Fund. The school was named for George Fish (1868–1933), a white mill manager who supported its construction. African Americans were previously taught at the old Fort Mill Academy building 1 mi. SW. (REVERSE) The design of the George Fish School followed the Rosenwald Fund's six-teacher floor plan and included six classrooms, an auditorium, stage, and library. By the 1930s, the school enrolled grades 1–8 before adding a ninth grade and, by 1941, a high school. It remained a segregated school for African Americans until 1968, when it integrated and became Fort Mill Jr. High. The school was sold in 1986 and later demolished. *Sponsored by Fort Mill School District, 2019*
GPS Coordinates: 35° 0.654' N, 80° 55.995' W

Index

This subject index organizes historical markers by a variety of subject areas. Some subject areas cover longer time periods, such as the Colonial Era; others encompass shorter time periods of large consequence, such as the American Civil War; and additionally, a number address the history and contributions of groups of people or broader themes. Under each heading, markers are grouped by county and are organized by the date the text was approved. Users are invited to explore a given county, region, or even the entire state of South Carolina, to discover people and places whose contributions fall under these headings. Ambitious users might "complete" the index by visiting each marker listed under a given heading or even each marker in the index itself! Additional headings could be added to this list; however, users are invited to create their own "tours" as they explore the state's history and its historical markers.

American Revolution

Civil War

Reconstruction Era

World Wars I and II

African Americans